D1265461

End and Beginning

European Perspectives
A Series of the Columbia University Press

End and Beginning

On the Generations of Cultures and the Origins of the West

Franz Borkenau

Edited with an Introduction by Richard Lowenthal

New York   Columbia University Press   1981

Library of Congress Cataloging in Publication Data

Borkenau, Franz, 1900–1957.
End and beginning:

(European perspectives)
Bibliography: p.
Includes index.
1. Civilization, Occidental. I. Lowenthal,
Richard, 1908–   . . II. Title.   III. Series
CB245.B66   909'.09821   81-1789
ISBN 0-231-05066-6   AACR2

Columbia University Press
New York   Guildford, Surrey

Contents

Preface

I

This book presents the published and unpublished contributions of my
late friend Franz Borkenau to the comparative theory of civilizations or
"high cultures," and to the history of our Western civilization. I believe
that they will not only constitute an important stimulus for the scholarly
discussion of those vital problems, but also a help to all those who look
for an orientation about the historic role of the West in past, present,
and future.

The opening chapters on the nature of culture cycles and culture generations, the concluding reflections on present and future, and also a few
chapters in the central part dealing with the origins of the West are based
on essays that were published long ago in various countries but have
hitherto remained scattered. The bulk of the central part, however, consists of unpublished manuscripts for a major work on the origin of
Western civilization. The fact that this central part constitutes a book by
itself, though incomplete, is the reason why the chapters have been
numbered separately from the other parts. After Borkenau's early death—
he died in May 1957, only 56 years old—his widow entrusted them to me,
because we had been friends for 30 years. But while we had many
interests and not a few experiences in common, and while I was and am
convinced of the importance of what he had to say in those manuscripts,
I am not myself an expert in the early history of the West. That is why
I have hesitated so long to undertake this edition. To overcome my
hesitation, an initiative from outside was needed.

That impulse came when, almost two years ago, Professor Daniel Bell
of Harvard, in an article in the *Times Literary Supplement*, described
Borkenau as an unjustly neglected important author and also mentioned
the existence of an unpublished manuscript. Promptly, John D. Moore
of the Columbia University Press inquired from Bell where that man-

uscript could be got hold of, and was steered on to me. I felt that I could no longer make excuses to myself and others—and the result is this book.

Details about the sources and their handling are given in Appendix I. Here I wish to mention only three points. The first is that part of both the published essays and the unpublished manuscripts were written in English and part in German; as editor I have also carried out the translation of the German texts (Appendix I indicates which texts were in Borkenau's German), and I have in one case (Part I, chapter 3) made an English condensation of one English essay and one posthumously published German manuscript dealing with the same subject. In another case (Part II, chapter 1) I have inserted a long passage, translated from an essay published in a German book, into an English manuscript, because the German version was from a later time and clearly expressed a further development of the author's thought since writing the English manuscript.

The second point is that while as far as I know all the unpublished manuscripts were written during the postwar period, between 1945 and 1957, I have received no indication of the dates of individual manuscripts, nor in most cases of their sequence in time; in ordering them, I therefore had to rely on the inner logic of the contents only. In a few cases, apparent contradictions between different texts suggest that the author tried out different explanations of the same phenomenon at different times; I have generally refrained from eliminating such contradictions, except in the above-mentioned case where exactly the same point was treated twice in obvious succession. But I have mentioned them in the Introduction where they offer possible clues to the development of the author's thought.

My third point concerns the footnotes. As a number of Borkenau's manuscripts had not been finally prepared for publication, they did not always contain footnotes indicating the literature to which he referred in general terms in the text. I have tried to fill this gap where I could, but was bound to fail here and there; the footnotes have therefore had to remain incomplete. As my added footnotes contain only references to sources, I have not specially marked them: all footnotes containing comments on the text or supplementing it in any way are the author's own.

II

The list of those to whom I owe gratitude begins, of course, with Franz Borkenau himself. The reader will find more about his life and work in the Introduction. Here I wish to say what he meant for me.

I met him first in 1926, when I was an 18-year-old freshman at Berlin University and had just entered the German Communist party. He was then national leader of the German Communist students and worked at the same time in an international research section of Comintern, which gave him an unusually wide international horizon. I became his political pupil and later his successor as student leader; but by the end of 1929 we, together with several friends, broke with the Communist party, refusing to accept a policy which treated the Social Democrats as the "main enemy" while the Nazi danger was rising.

In later years our ways often separated both geographically and politically: I eventually became an active Social Democrat; he never joined a party again. But we remained friends, in wartime England and again in postwar Germany, and his immensely creative and original mind always remained a vital source of inspiration for me, whether I agreed with him or not. In the last decade of his life, he often spoke to me about the problems treated in this book—problems that were then in the center of his interest; and gradually, thinking in terms of a plurality of cultures became for me, too, a key to the understanding of history.

My thanks are due also to the late Frau Hilde Borkenau, who gave me the manuscripts—she has since died in an accident—and to his two sons, Peter and Felix, who made it easy for me to come to an arrangement with them about the rights for this publication. The same goes for the editors of *Commentary* (New York) and *Der Monat* (Berlin) and the publisher of *Psyche* (Heidelberg), who granted me the rights for reprinting essays first published by them. Special thanks are due to the publishers of Borkenau's 1947 book *Drei Abhandlungen zur deutschen Geschichte*, the Vittorio Klostermann Verlag in Frankfurt, who kindly permitted me to incorporate a long quotation from the first essay in that book in Part II, chapter 1 of the present one.

Finally, I want to thank Daniel Bell for the impulse and John D. Moore of Columbia University Press for his active interest in the publication—and, last but not least, the late and lamented Charles Frankel and his successor Dr. William Bennett for inviting me to the National Humanities Center in North Carolina for the period of working leisure needed to edit the book—and thus repay an old debt to a friend.

December 1979   Richard Lowenthal

End and Beginning

Editor's Introduction

The Theme

This book contains the elements of a philosophy of history, as well as a major contribution to the history of our Western culture. Its author, the late Franz Borkenau, had been an active Communist and even an official of the Communist International in his youth. The experience of Stalin's policies and Stalin's crimes had caused him to break first with the Communist party, and later also with the materialist utopianism of Marx. But he remained unwilling to abandon the Hegelian belief that the history of mankind is meaningful in the sense that, through all the sufferings and crimes of men, through all the failures and catastrophes of human empires and enterprises, its road leads ultimately to ever higher self-knowledge, ever deeper understanding of the human condition.

In Borkenau's mind, this affirmative view of the meaning of history met with an acceptance of what he regarded as the irrefutable evidence of the decline of our own Western civilization. He had become familiar with the ideas of Oswald Spengler as a student in Germany after World War I, and with those of Arnold J. Toynbee as an exile in Britain in the middle thirties; and to the ex-Marxist, who was also a trained historian, the view that a plurality of high cultures or civilizations—two terms which, in conscious contrast to a certain German tradition, he always used as synonymous—constitute the basic units of human history, and that each of them lives through an inescapable cycle of rise and decline, had come to appear self-evident.

Living through the age of Stalin, of Hitler, and of the first atomic bomb, he had no difficulty in convincing himself that the decline of Western civilization was far advanced. Yet he firmly rejected the fundamental cultural pessimism—he called it nihilism—implied in Spengler's view that there is no substantial relationship between one high culture and another, so that the spiritual heritage of a perished civilization—as distinct from isolated technical elements—is lost forever. By contrast, he saw in Toynbee's concept of the "apparentation" and "affiliation" of successive civilizations a vital clue for the development of a meaningful view of human history as a whole, but a clue of which, in his opinion, Toynbee had made quite inadequate use.

It was this critique of Spengler and Toynbee that Borkenau's work on the theory and history of civilizations took as its starting point. His central concern in that work was the question of how new civilizations had risen out of the decay of old ones, and how they could rise again. That was the main theme of his theoretical essays which are presented in the first part of this book under the title "Culture Cycles and Culture Generations." That was also the reason why he undertook to write a major work on the origins of our Western civilization, the incomplete manuscripts for which make up the second part. That question also inspired his thoughts on the fundamental problems of his time, as shown in a few samples in the third part. And that is finally the meaning of the title the editor has given to this book: "End and Beginning."

The present Introduction has a double purpose. First, it wishes to offer a brief outline of the personal and intellectual development of the author which led him, during the last quarter of his short life, to concentrate on the problems treated in this book. Second, it is intended to facilitate the understanding of a work consisting of scattered essays and unpublished manuscripts by offering the reader a first, condensed presentation of its guiding ideas.

The Author

Franz Borkenau was born in Vienna in December 1900. He came from a family belonging to the "enlightened" bureaucracy and judiciary of the Austrian monarchy; one uncle was the famous Hofrat Pollak, chief of the political police under successive regimes. A half-Jew by origin, Borkenau got a severely Catholic education at the Schottengymnasium, an elite school run by the Jesuits. He grew up in passionate rebellion against parents and school, monarchy and church, and became at the end of World War I one of the youngest members of Vienna's most radical youth movement, the "Jugendkultur," founded and led by Siegfried Bernfeld. A number of prominent psychoanalysts, including Bernfeld

himself, and a number of leading German Communist intellectuals, including Ruth Fischer and her brother Gerhard Eisler, have come from
that movement.

To study history and philosophy, Borkenau soon left the confining
climate of small postwar Austria to throw himself into the upheavals of
Germany. At Leipzig University, he became active in the socialist students' movement, and by 1921 joined the German Communist party.
In the course of his studies, he first became familiar with Spengler's
Decline of the West, thoroughly rejecting it at the time; he used to recall
with amusement that an interdisciplinary research seminar on the book
was stopped after the first three contributors had each stated that the
book seemed to be highly significant in general, but was factually all
wrong in their respective fields. Yet the rejected book was later to become
an influential stimulus for his own work—as was the rejected Catholic
influence of his early education.

Having taken his Dr. phil., Borkenau in 1924 joined the staff of the
Communist International: he became a member of a research section that
worked secretly in the building of the Soviet Embassy in Berlin under
the direction of the exiled Hungarian economist Eugene Varga. The
section had the task of studying international developments in politics,
economy, and the labor movement, and of writing confidential reports
on them for headquarters in Moscow; at the time, it may have been the
only institution of the Comintern required to form independent opinions
on such developments before there was an official international "line"
on them. Borkenau's personal task was to study the social democratic
parties of diverse European countries on the basis of their own publications—in the process, he acquired the ability to read ten languages. At
the same time, he continued—under an alias—his political activity as
national leader of the Communist students of Germany. I first met him,
more than 50 years ago, in that role, and as he became my first political
teacher, I profited much from the unusual width of his international
horizon.

Conflict with "the party" came in 1928, when Stalin's internal "left
turn" to forced collectivization of the peasants was accompanied by a
corresponding international "left turn" proclaiming the approach of a
revolutionary situation in the capitalist world, declaring the social democrats to be the "main enemy," and soon attacking them as "social
fascists," at the very time when the Nazi movement in Germany was
rising fast under the impact of the economic crisis beginning in 1929.
Borkenau was among those who opposed this disastrous course, fully
realizing its connection with Stalin's domestic struggle against Bukharin;

when, in 1928, the "section Varga" was transferred to Moscow, Borkenau foresaw the end of its intellectual independence and preferred to stay in Berlin. For one more year, he served the West European Bureau of the Comintern, which was then also in Berlin and directed by Manuilsky; as its reporting officer, he travelled to Britain, Belgium, Spain, and Norway to report on the situation in those countries and in their Communist parties. But by the end of 1929, the open expression of his opposition to the policy of the German C.P. led to his expulsion.

Instead of continuing a fruitless political activity in one of the leftwing splinter groups then mushrooming in Germany, Borkenau decided to engage in historical research. With the help of a grant from the Frankfurt "Institut für Sozialforschung," home of the later widely known "Frankfurt school," he undertook an ambitious book on the emergence of modern, "bourgeois" categories of thought in the West after the end of the Middle Ages, seeking to demonstrate the structural parallelism between the new ideas in rationalist and mechanistic philosophy, mathematical physics, the new theories of law and the state and certain aspects of reformation theology, and their links with the emerging new structures in society and the state. The highly original questions Borkenau raised were clearly inspired by Marxist sociology, for he tried to show that the structure of society was influencing the categories of thought and thus the directions in which knowledge could advance at a given period; but the book was not Marxist in an "orthodox" sense, since it did not seriously try to derive those categories from the "relations of production," and the references to the "period of manufacture" in its subtitle and opening chapter were superficial and only conceived as an afterthought under "orthodox" criticism from within the Institute, to whose inner circle Borkenau never belonged. Accordingly, the Institute was not pleased with the book they published in 1934[1] in Paris after Hitler's seizure of power, and published a bitterly doctrinaire critique at the same time.

Borkenau also had to leave Germany after the Nazi victory, and after a short period in his native Vienna he went on to Paris. The need to make a living led him to accept for a year a professorship in Panama; a short book on the ideas of Pareto, published after his return, is a byproduct of his teaching. In 1936 he settled in London, where all his books appeared from then to the end of the war.

1. *Der Übergang vom feudalen zum bürgerlichen Weltbild: Studien zur Geschichte der Manufakturperiode* (Paris: Alcan, 1934). Reprinted Darmstadt: Wissenschaftliche Buchgemeinschaft, 1971.

The Spanish civil war called him back not to political activity, but to a passionate concern with political analysis. He decided to write a book based on observation on the spot. Though refused admission to Franco's part of Spain, he could pay lengthy visits to the Republican territory, the diaries of which together with his analytical conclusion constitute *The Spanish Cockpit*.[2] The combination of intense human sympathy for the (non-Communist) revolutionary Left and the knowledge and analytical methods of a historian and political sociologist assured the book an international success. The experience of the Communists' terror against their political allies, behind the Republican lines, which ruthlessly transplanted the methods of Stalin's domestic blood purge of the same years, made Borkenau's break with Soviet-style communism much more profound than it had initially been. At the same time, the heroic failure of the concepts of the utopian Trotskyite or anarchist Left led him to a fundamental critique of the utopian element in Marxism, first formulated in an essay on the myth of the Paris Commune.[3] He had now achieved the necessary detachment from the revolutionary hopes of his youth to write, at the age of 38, a history of the Communist International;[4] written without any reference to his personal experiences as a Communist—"this is not a book of disclosure," he said in the Preface—it has become a classic, indispensable for understanding both the self-sacrificing enthusiasm the Communist idea inspired in its believers and the persistent failure of the Moscow-centered organization founded by Lenin and taken over by Stalin (up to the time when, later on, some Communist parties were able to fight their way to power in independence from international directives).

Borkenau's next major venture in political analysis had no such lasting success. Written in the early months of World War II under the impression of the Hitler-Stalin pact, *The Totalitarian Enemy*[5] was one of the early books on "totalitarianism" stressing the common features of fascist and communist single-party rule. But while it is true that important common features between both types of party dictatorship exist, there exist also important differences—whether the common features

---

2. *The Spanish Cockpit: An Eye-witness Account of the Political and Social Conflicts of the Spanish Civil War* (London: Faber & Faber, 1937). Reprinted Ann Arbor: University of Michigan Press, 1963.

3. "State and Revolution in the Paris Commune, the Russian Revolution and the Spanish Civil War," *Sociological Review* 29, no. 41 (1937), pp. 41–75.

4. *The Communist International* (London: Faber & Faber, 1938). Reprinted with an introduction by Raymond Aron, *World Communism: A History of the Communist International* (Ann Arbor: University of Michigan Press, 1962).

5. *The Totalitarian Enemy* (London: Faber & Faber, 1940).

or the differences matter more, depends on the specific question the analyst has in mind. Despite some superficial similarities, foreign policy is *not* one of the fields where the common features are decisive: otherwise, we should all have perished in an atomic war by now. By regarding the Hitler-Stalin Pact as the direct expression of a common "essence" of both regimes and not foreseeing their ultimate deadly conflict, Borkenau condemned his book, including many true insights, to inevitable political oblivion when that conflict broke out.

Among the overlooked insights contained in the book was the idea that the totalitarian ideologies of our time are not products of some alien devilry suddenly threatening the West from outside, but have sprung from an inner crisis of our own Western civilization. National Socialism was a "revolt against the West" from within, and while the sickness that produced it first seized Germany alone, it has produced other manifestations throughout the West after Borkenau's lifetime. Bolshevism cannot be understood historically except as the outcome of the spread of the Western heresy called Marxism on the non-Western soil of Russia. The threat of the "totalitatian enemy" thus appeared to Borkenau as evidence of how far the inner forces of cultural decay had advanced in the West; and while at the time of writing the book, he was convinced that the immediate danger could be overcome by a Western victory, he became deeply pessimistic about the outcome of the war after the fall of France in 1940, and was again rather pessimistic soon after victory about the prospects of avoiding another world war without a wholesale capitulation of the West to Stalin's Russia.

Though Borkenau lived to survive both those immediate fears, the roots of his pessimism for the future of Western civilization were more profound, as stated in the beginning of this Introduction. His concern to balance that "cultural pessimism" by an optimistic belief in a higher civilization beyond the West—a civilization that might rise on the ruins of the West as the West had risen on the ruins of classical antiquity—and his corresponding interest in working both on the theory of the culture cycle and on the origin of the West, had become urgent by the end of the war. He had spent a large part of the intervening time in British internment as an "enemy alien," most of it in Australia. When he came back to Europe, he was eager to leave Britain and used the first postwar opportunity to return, with an American press service, to occupied Germany.

To his surprise, Borkenau found that his 1934 historical work, published in Paris in the German language, was much appreciated in German scholarly circles; he was soon called to a chair of history at Marburg University. In 1947 he published a volume of three essays on German history[6]—one of which, on Lutheranism, dealing with the impact of non-Western elements in German history, had first been published in English during the war. But he found the atmosphere of the Marburg faculty not congenial and soon left it. What remained from that episode was a marriage—his third—to a postwar student at the university, who gave him his two only sons.

During the last decade of his life, he divided his time between the study of current developments in the Soviet Union and the Communist world movement, and his work on the theory and history of civilizations. It may fairly be said that he lived *on* the first but largely *for* the second. The reputation established by his prewar book on the Communist International and the keenness of his observation and analysis of new developments in this field assured him a living—for two years as editor on the American-sponsored, specialized German journal "Ost-Probleme," later as an international freelance and as author of a new book on "European Communism."[7] This book, dealing in the main with Communist history from the prewar Popular Front period through the war years and the crisis of liberation to the practice of the new "Communist Information Bureau" (Cominform), founded in 1947, was written with less detachment and in parts also with less care than his 1938 book: critics complained about inaccuracies of detail and above all about excessive speculation. But this speculation on the background of Soviet and Communist policy during the late Stalinist period sprang from what was, on the other hand, a real merit of the book: an early attempt to interpret the policy of a totalitarian regime, in this case the late period of Stalin's rule, not as "monolithic" but as characterized by persistent personal and political rivalries behind the scenes, which could be inferred from the interpretation of what later came to be called "esoteric communications" in official Communist statements.

But during the same period, Borkenau was steadily working on the subjects treated in the present book, publishing a number of relevant essays and accumulating manuscripts for sections of the work on the origins of the West. It was for the purpose of this work, too, that he repeatedly changed his country of residence in the last years of his life, staying successively in Paris, Rome, and Zurich, with an interlude in his native Vienna. It was in a Zurich hotel room, where he lived all alone,

6. *Drei Abhandlungen zur deutschen Geschichte* (Frankfurt/Main: Klostermann, 1947).
7. *European Communism* (London: Faber & Faber, 1953).

that he succumbed to a heart attack on May 18, 1957, at the age of 56 years. It was the end of a lonely and restless life, restless not only in the frequent changes of location and occupation, but also in the inner tensions of his intellect and character. Those tensions had existed not only between the political and intellectual positions he had taken at different periods of his life—as between revolutionary utopianism and a sense of history, centered on spiritual changes and encompassing millennia—but also between the methods used for his work, which combined the bold, heuristic use of a sometimes visionary intuition with the disciplined hard work of critical historical research: he was as averse to the narrowness of the mere specialist as to the abuse of intuition as a defense against rational and factual criticism. If those inner tensions were the source of much suffering—Borkenau's thorough knowledge of Freudian psychoanalysis and his intense preoccupation with the problem of death clearly had their background of personal suffering—they also were a vital source of his productivity, in which alone he found peace.

It was hardly an accident that this man came to see the historic clash of cultural attitudes constituting opposite poles as the constellation typical for the origin of great civilizations; that he saw the creative achievement of the new civilizations in the crystallization of a synthesis from such opposite elements; and that he regarded the exclusion of alternative, equally legitimate ways of human existence as the necessary price of such achievement. But in this driven and restless life, there was one abiding passion: the thirst for truth, for learning, for a never-ending approach to knowledge.

"Barbaric Ages" and "Culture Generations"

We said at the outset that this book contains the elements of a philosophy of history. As we come to review the theoretical essays presented in Part I of the book, we must add at once that it does *not* contain a philosophical system. Rather, in starting from the approach to history developed in different ways by Spengler and Toynbee, Borkenau criticized *their* systems, raised new philosophical questions on that basis, and produced original answers of a tentative nature. The value of those answers lies in their fruitfulness as clues to a new understanding of historic problems, not in any pretence at doctrinaire finality: to the end of his life Borkenau remained a seeker after truth, trying out different and sometimes contradictory ideas within a general direction determined by this method. His work remained open-ended, not only because of his early death, but because he was conscious of the inevitably fragmentary character of his insights.

We have seen that Borkenau's search for a meaning in history started from his acceptance of the thesis, common to Spengler and Toynbee, that the evolution of civilization is not a unilinear process, but that world history consists of the rise and fall of a plurality of distinctive civilizations or high cultures, each characterized by the specific fundamental attitudes of its members to the problems of life and death. Among the authors, there are some disagreements of detail about the list of these high cultures in the history of mankind, but it is clear that they include the following: the early river valley civilizations of Egypt, Mesopotamia, the Indus valley, and China, some of them succeeded by new civilizations in the same area after a major crisis, as well as the Minoan civilization of ancient Crete; the broadly contemporaneous Hellenic and Judaic civilizations and a later, multifaceted Middle Eastern civilization which produced both Christianity and eventually Islam; the Eastern Christian civilization centered on Byzantium and later on Moscow, and the Western Christian civilization issuing into the modern West; the later East Asian civilizations of China and Japan, and the pre-Columbian civilizations of America. In the views of both Spengler and Toynbee, and also of Borkenau, each of those civilizations, with all its specific spiritual values and all its material achievements, is living through an inevitable cycle of rise and decline.

But we have also seen that Borkenau rejected as "nihilistic" Spengler's view that those high cultures are "monads without windows," unable to communicate their basic spiritual attitudes to one another or to leave a substantive cultural inheritance to their successors, "following their way from nothingness to nothingness in sublime absence of purpose." By contrast, he agreed with Toynbee that relations of "apparentation" and "affiliation" may exist between older and younger civilizations, but considered that those relations are both richer and more complicated than Toynbee assumed. First, he argued that a new, emerging civilization may be affiliated to more than one parent: rejecting, for instance, Toynbee's classification of Christianity as the "universal church" constituting the final stage of classical antiquity, which had enabled him to view the Western and Eastern Christian civilization as affiliated to antiquity only, Borkenau saw Christianity essentially as a product of Judaic and Middle Eastern civilization and the two Christian civilizations as affiliated both to classical antiquity and to that Middle Eastern root. But more important, Borkenau also saw a substantive and not merely accidental role of "barbaric" interludes in the rise of new civilizations.

   Borkenau's original contribution to his theme starts from here. Stimulated by the interest that Spengler had taken in the significance of "barbaric ages" in his later, posthumously published writings, Borkenau
developed the thesis that there exist two basic types of affiliation of a
younger civilization to one or two older ones: affiliation may proceed
directly, as the Eastern Christian civilization of Byzantium grew out of
classical antiquity and oriental Christianity, or it may be mediated by
a barbaric interlude following the collapse of an older civilization, as
happened in the West after the collapse of Rome. A barbaric age in that
sense, however, is not a primitive age: undisturbed primitive cultures
are ahistorical and noncreative. It is the clash between primitive, tribal
culture and a declining high civilization which transforms the former
primitives into barbarians: the contact with the decaying old civilization
disrupts the balance of the unchanging primitive traditions and pulls the
tribes into the stream of history, but has no longer the strength to integrate them. Thus barbaric societies are characterized by terrible internal
conflicts resulting from the disintegration of the former primitive order,
while at the same time they may enter part of the domains of the old
civilization as conquerors. Both inner conflicts and outward conquests
mark the beginning of their historical experience; both are typically reflected in the formation of myths, which are at the same time the fore-
runners of the new high culture in the making, the first expression of
some of its formative attitudes and values.
   It is this appreciation of the creative contribution of the barbarians to
the emergence of a new civilization out of the decay of the old which
is Borkenau's first major discovery; indeed he proclaims that new civilizations affiliated to their predecessors through the intermediary of a
barbaric interlude, like the Hellenic and our own Western civilization,
are likely to be more creative than directly affiliated ones like that of
Byzantium. But, of course, he does not deny the contribution of the
older civilization either, which would amount to denying the idea of
affiliation itself. Rather, he sees the process of the creation of the New
as beginning simultaneously in two geographically and culturally opposite regions, the barbarian element predominant in one of them and
the heirs of the older civilization in the other, and the new synthesis
finally emerging in an intermediate zone where mutual disruption of the
two opposite elements, but also their interpenetration and their competition for influence, have been greatest.
   The myth produced by the barbarians is thus not yet an expression
of the new cultural synthesis, but of one of the elements to be synthesized—
but its study is of vital importance for an understanding of the process,

for it gives voice to that element which had never been formulated before. Borkenau has therefore given great attention to the study both of Hellenic and of Germanic mythology. It is his contention that such a study must always proceed on two different levels: the unearthing of the events of crucial importance in the history of the barbaric peoples which their myths reflect in more or less distorted form, and the analysis of the psychological conflicts and mechanisms underlying the distortion, which in turn reflect the moral crisis typical of the "Dark Ages." Borkenau's highly original method of mythological interpretation is strongly influenced by the psychoanalytical theories and techniques of Sigmund Freud and his school; so is his emphasis on the fact that the dissolution of the moral order in the Dark Ages, in the interval between the decay of an old order and the emergence of a new one, leads to the massive appearance of "primal crime"—family murder and incest—which, because it is generally felt as intolerable, becomes one of the forces pressing towards a new cultural synthesis. But while deeply influenced by the Freudian approach, Borkenau is by no means inclined to accept uncritically Freudian hypotheses on social and historical development, as his surprising interpretation of the Oedipus myth (in chapter 4 of Part I) and his critique of the hypothesis of an aboriginal patricide at the beginning of human history (in chapter 10 of Part II) will show to the reader.

A second major innovation of Borkenau's concerns the importance of successive "culture generations," in the sense that cultures of a later generation are marked by certain common changes compared with the earlier ones. Toynbee, who had originally proclaimed the "philosophical contemporaneity" of all high civilizations, had hinted in his later volumes at the existence of this phenomenon, but had not developed the hint. For Borkenau, the phenomenon has become central in the context of his thesis that successive generations of cultures are characterized by their opposed attitudes to "the antinomy of death." It is here that Borkenau goes furthest in integrating his theory of history with a philosophy of the human condition.

Borkenau sees one of the central problems of human existence in the insuperable antinomy between the external experience of the mortality of all men and the inner impossibility for man to imagine his own death, formulated by Freud in the famous dictum that "the unconscious is immortal." While evidence suggests that many primitives sought to evade the dilemma by denying the need for all human beings to die, deriving from that "death-denying" attitude a belief that each individual death was the result of black magic, which necessarily led to a state of universal mutual suspicion and deadly hostility within the tribe, it is Borkenau's thesis that successive generations of high cultures have alternated between more or less "death-transcending" attitudes, postulating an individual life beyond death, on the one hand, and more or less "death-accepting" attitudes deemphasizing the belief in immortality, on the other. On that basis, he distinguishes between a first generation of high cultures, consisting of the ancient river civilizations of Egypt, Mesopotamia, and the Indus Valley, in which the belief in a life after death took a variety of forms ranging from the rise of the dead Pharaoh to the sun symbolized in the pyramids to the more modest chthonic burial cults of the common people; a second generation embracing both the Hellenic and Judaic cultures, in which the afterlife was reduced to a shadowy existence in Hades or Sheol, while the longing for eternity was concentrated on lasting individual glory in this world in the Greek and on the ultimate triumph of the community in the early Jewish case; and a third generation of the Christian and Islamic civilizations, in which death transcendence of the individual again became central but became largely separated from attempts to preserve the dead body, concentrating instead on the immortality of the soul. Moreover, Borkenau seeks to show that within the lifespan of any one culture, its evolution starts with one of the polar attitudes, which is then gradually eroded to the point of approaching its opposite, thus preparing the next culture's start from the other pole: thus he sees Ekhnaton's struggle against the chthonic cults as preparing the transition to a death-accepting attitude, and the late developments in Judaism and Hellenism as leading toward the death-transcendence of Christiantiy.

In the two long, overlapping essays devoted to these ideas (which the editor has integrated into one, appearing here as chapter 3 of Part I), Borkenau came close to outlining a view of an ultimate, developmental meaning of history as a whole. Observing the far advanced turn towards "enlightened," post-Christian death-acceptance in our own civilization as well as in the Russian domain of Eastern Christianity under Communist rule, he seemed to foresee two alternatives for the next stage: either a "death-embracing" attitude insisting on the destruction not only of the body but of the soul, or a breakthrough of scientific research into the realm of transcendence, replacing mere belief in immortality by knowledge of a world beyond space, time, and causality. Borkenau saw the developments both in twentieth-century physics and in the access to the human unconscious as portents of such a breakthrough into a world of timeless being beyond the world of our human existence. While I believe that the value of most of his contributions to the understanding of history is independent of those literally meta-physical views, I have included an essay outlining them (Part I, chapter 5) because of its obvious relevance for his ultimate perspective: a breakthrough to transcendent knowledge of a world of timeless being would clearly overcome the antinomy of death, the dilemma of mortality in the world of outward existence versus immortality of the unconscious—and might open the road to a history of mankind beyond the culture cycle and its generations.

Borkenau was aware that, while all civilizations had a specific attitude to the problem of death, not all of them fitted into his generation scheme developed for the Middle Eastern and European civilizations in our own line of descent. He knew, and wrote, that for successive civilizations of India awareness of a kind of immortality in the form of a belief in metempsychosis was conceived as awareness of a curse, with the eventual overcoming of the individual soul by its return into the All, or into nothingness, seen as the ultimate bliss. He also believed that the pre-Columbian American cultures had "death-embracing" features, and that such features existed also in the Japanese cultural tradition. What was universal, in his view, was that each culture had to work out its specific attitude to the antinomy of death; in addition, the principle of polar changes of those attitudes in successive culture generations applied wherever clearly marked culture generations existed.

Borkenau seems to have developed his theory of the antinomy of death as a factor in the sequence of culture generations only in the last years of his life: there is hardly a trace of it in his manuscripts on the origin of the West. That even in those last years he was not committed to the polarity of attitudes to death as the "single cause" of the process of cultural generation change, but was still trying out how far this idea would take him, is suggested by a very late two-part study on the transition from Minoan to Hellenic culture as reflected in mythology, in which that factor plays no role. On the contrary, that study (printed here as chapter 4 of Part I) is remarkable for its demonstration of another type of polarity in the sequence of two successive cultures: that of matricentric versus patricentric, or even fully patriarchal, religions and institutions.

The Minoan civilization of Crete belonged in time to the same culture generation as the neighboring river valley civilizations of the Middle East; and Borkenau offers good reasons for the assumption that it shared with them the fertility cult of the Magna Mater, and that in connection with that cult priestly and royal power in Crete were inherited in the female line. On the other hand, in a surprising but highly ingenious analysis of the Hellenic Oedipus myth, Borkenau argues that the historic events underlying that myth originally had nothing to do with either patricide or mother incest, but with the usurpation of power in a still matricentric Thebes of the Helladic period by patricentric barbarian invaders from the Northwest. He suggests that the leader of those invaders, having killed the native king, had to marry his widow, the queen-priestess, in order to acquire a matrilinear right of succession in the eyes of his new subjects—but that he also had to claim descendence from the slain king in order to preserve patrilinear legitimacy among his own original followers. As he was later overthrown, the tradition of the native establishment came to accuse him of having brought a curse on the city by forcing the hand of the queen-priestess—an extreme outrage in the matriarchal context which came to be reinterpreted as mother-incest by later, patriarchal generations.

The reader will find the detailed arguments for that interpretation of the myth in the text. What matters in the context of Borkenau's general theories is that his interpretation suggests that the transition from matricentric beliefs and institutions in the Minoan and Helladic cultures to patricentric and patriarchal beliefs and institutions, introduced into the Mycenean and Hellenic ages by successive waves of barbarian invaders, was a crucial element in this particular case of the sequence of culture generations. By bringing the horrors of the myth of the Atrides, culminating in the Oresteia, into the same context of a transitional period between matrilinear and patrilinear legitimacy of rule, Borkenau indicates that the frequency of "primal crime," of family murder and incest, which he had seen as a typical consequence of the breakdown of the traditional tribal order in barbaric dark ages, may have a more specific explanation where the breakdown of the tribal order is linked with a transformation of the family structure.

The Rise of the West

Working on his vast subject in the free time left to him after the current political writing by which he made his living, Borkenau was not able to complete his projected book on the origins of Western civilization: all we have are a number of manuscript drafts for chapters and a few published essays dealing with aspects of the same theme. Yet what we have is sufficient to indicate not only his approach and a number of partial results, but his broad view of the factors that came together to produce the new culture.

That broad view is sharply different from the conventional idea that Western civilization arose from the confluence of the heritage of classical antiquity with the new inspiration of Christianity. Borkenau accepts that idea for the origin of the *Eastern* Christian civilization of Byzantium. But he insists that the influence of Christianity in the Western Roman empire remained superficial throughout the centuries of that empire's decay, striking serious roots at first only in non-Latin North Africa. Only when Christianity reached the barbarians of the North—the Western Germanic tribes and before them the Irish—did their meeting produce the creative spark that enabled a new culture to emerge and eventually integrate the heritage of Latin antiquity as well. Thus, while Eastern Christianity developed in a more or less straight line by the Christianization, and indeed the partial orientalization, of the Greek-speaking Eastern part of the empire, a distinctive Western Christianity was, according to Borkenau, a considerably later creation in which the contribution of the Northern barbarians played an essential part from the beginning. That view is most clearly stated in chapter 6 of Part II, dealing with the role and impact of Pelagius, and above all in chapter 11, summing up the stages on the road to Western civilization; but it is implied in the entire structure of the manuscript.

As a prelude to his study, Borkenau starts with the analysis of some striking changes that occurred in Western languages since the Voelkerwanderung, since language is bound to express the deepest underlying attitudes of the people who speak it. He shows that in Old Norse a new use of the personal pronoun, beginning with the I for the first person, in conjunction with names, appears from the fifth century A.D. first in a few cases and gradually becomes more and more general; and that soon after its first usage the personal pronoun appears also as a suffix to the verb, later to be shifted into its modern position ahead of the verb. Following the spread of this "I-saying habit" from Scandinavia into Germany, Britain, and France, Borkenau argues that the time and place of its emergence cannot be explained by mere linguistic convenience— distinctive personal endings of verbal forms were still available at the time—but only as the first cry of a new individualism born among the Northern barbarians. Borkenau sees in this not an innate, racial tendency of the Germanic tribes—he points to the absence of such use of the personal pronoun in the Gothic documents of an earlier period, above all the Gothic bible—but a result of the great migrations, particularly the overseas migration of the Northern Germanic tribes, which decisively loosened their collective clan structure and strengthened the individualist institution of the "following" of a leader. Moreover, he shows that the personal pronoun in Irish is of a different type, suggesting an origin independent of the Norse model, and raises the question of a possible similar development also in other Celtic languages as a result of the earlier Celtic migration, though this cannot be documented. Conversely, he sees in the fact that the use of the personal pronoun with the verb has not become general in Italy and Spain an indication that these Mediterranean countries have been less profoundly affected by the new impulse.

It is Borkenau's thesis that this new, Western type of individualism is inevitably coupled with a sense of ultimate loneliness and distance between individuals; and he finds its delayed linguistic effect in the later development by the West, alone among all civilizations, of the "you-habit"—the plural of the second person pronoun as a universal form of address among adults, stressing distance and respect. The fact that in the English language the "you" has completely replaced the singular "thou" is regarded by him as evidence that Britain has developed the most thoroughly "Western" attitude of all European nations.

At the same time, Borkenau stresses that Western individualism is not of a contemplative nature, but linked with an active attitude of the personality to the world—and he finds this reflected in the emphasis on active verb forms and sentences in most Western languages, and again above all in English, in contrast to the frequency of impersonal and reflexive constructions in the Slavic languages. He does not fail to notice, though, that in this respect, German is a less outspokenly "Western" language than the others.

Borkenau had indicated that he wished his book to begin with that linguistic chapter. The bulk of his other manuscripts clearly fall into two main parts, devoted to two converging, and in part overlapping, main lines of development. One deals with Germanic mythology as a source for the contribution of the Germanic barbarians; the other seeks to trace the emergence of a meaningful Western Christianity on the soil of the Western part of the Roman empire, but largely due to Irish and oriental impulses.

The discussion of Germanic mythology begins, after a statement of Borkenau's view about the historic function of the myth among barbaric tribes, with a preview of the characteristic traits and role of the Germanic mythical hero. Borkenau stresses that, more than other mythical heroes, the Germanic hero is from an early stage both doomed and lonely in his death. As the dissolution of the tribal order advances with the Voelkerwanderung, he is also typically entangled in insoluble moral conflict:

bound to a strict code of warrior's honor, including the duty of revenge for his kin, he gets precisely by following that code involved in acts of crime, including murder in the family, the guilt for which he recognizes and must finally pay for with his own death. This special form of the acceptance of total individual responsibility and inevitable tragic guilt accounts for the peculiar gloom of most of the Germanic myths; it is also seen by Borkenau as part of the background for the ultimate readiness of the Germanic tribes for Christianization.

Borkenau naturally concentrated his concrete analysis of Germanic mythology on the Siegfried saga or Siegfried myth in its various versions, down to the final medieval texts of the *Nibelungenlied*. On one side, he seeks to uncover which historic events have entered into the saga, and how they have been transformed in its successive layers. He finds an early core in the fate of Arminius, hero of the Teutoburg victory over the Romans in the first century A.D. He shows that both the clan of Cheruscan nobles, from which Arminius came, and that of related Chattian leaders, from which he took his wife, carried names beginning with the syllable Seg- or Sig-; that Arminius after his victory aimed at a new type of supertribal, personal power on the model of the Roman principate, and was involved in fierce conflict inside the clan as a result; and that he was in all probability murdered by his own kin in collusion with Rome. He finds a second root, after several centuries, in the takeover of the kingdom of the Ripuarian Franks (who included part of the former Chattians) by Clovis, the founder of the Merovingian dynasty of the Salic Franks, who first instigated and then exploited the murder of the Ripuarian king by his own son (both again carrying Signames), as reported both by Gregory of Tours and in the Finnsburg fragment of the Beowulf. He shows how the story came to be distorted, first by the Ripuarian Franks in order to eliminate the guilt of the son of their last king and turn him into a shining hero, and then by the Salic Franks, who later took over the saga from their conquered neighbors, and now wished to suppress their guilt both in destroying the independence of the Ripuarian Franks and soon afterwards that of the Burgundians, where Clovis had operated by instigating fratricide among their rulers. He suggests that in the course of this distortion, the originally unrelated event of the earlier expulsion of the Burgundians from their former seats near Worms by the Huns was drawn in. He thus sees the myth as developing through an ever-repeated denial of murderous guilt—first the guilt of Arminius in trying to overthrow the tribal order, then that of the Ripuarian prince, then that of Clovis against the Ripuarian Franks which was shifted onto the Burgundians, and finally the fictitious guilt of the Burgundians which appears to have been eliminated when queen Brunechildis, ruling the Burgundians as part of the Frankish realm, sought to effect a reconciliation. But while the underlying historic events were transformed beyond recognition by those successive denials, the central mythical theme of the shining hero who perishes through treason by his own kin remained.

On the other hand, Borkenau sees in the figure of the murdered hero also an "archetype," rooted in a myth about gods: the figure of Balder, originally a sun and fertility god of the ancient Wanic religion, long dominant among the Northern and part of the Eastern Germanic tribes and penetrating in its late manifestations as far as Lower Saxony. Borkenau stresses that this ancient religion was originally closely similar to the even more ancient fertility cults of the Near East, and shows from older versions of the myth that, like the Near Eastern sons of the *Magna Mater*, Balder originally died annually with the coming of winter, to be reborn like all nature in the spring. Yet at some time early in the Christian era, coinciding with the decline of the Wanic religion in general, the Balder myth was changed to make the death of the god irrevocable: now he would never return, or—in a still later version—return only after the end of the world with the other gods.

This myth of a dead god, unique in the pagan world, seems to reflect the parallel processes of the beginning dissolution of the traditional tribal order and of the decay of the Wanic religion with the onset of the great migrations, and it has become one more important element in the characteristic gloom of Germanic mythology. Borkenau produces many parallels between the archetypal elements in the Siegfried saga and the Balder myth; and he quotes material from other Germanic myths of the period that underlines the growing preoccupation with the problem of the finality of death.

In speaking of the decline of the Wanic faith, we have already anticipated Borkenau's chapter about the Germanic gods. It is his thesis, advanced with thorough scholarly discussion of the sources, that the widespread assumption of a major overlap in time of the Wanic and the Ase gods, and in particular of a very early cult of the Ase gods, is entirely wrong, and that no Ase cult can be demonstrated anywhere before the seventh century A.D.; he offers strong arguments against the view that Tacitus' report about a cult of Hercules, Mars, and Mercury in the Germania of his time refers in "Romanized" form to a cult of the Ase triad of Wotan, Ziu, and Thor in the first century A.D., and that the later correspondence between the Latin and Germanic names of the days of the week confirms that.

Rather, Borkenau sees the cult of Wotan in particular as a later development of the legend of the furious host of the spirits of the dead, and that legend only arose after the battle on the Catalaunian plains between Troyes and Chalons-sur-Marne—the greatest battle of the age of the Voelkerwanderung, at which the Roman commander Aetius and his Germanic allies stopped the Huns in 451 A.D. Then it proved impossible to bury the dead, so that their spirits were believed to fight on in the air: only later, Borkenau argues, Wotan became the personified leader of that furious host.

The importance of this thesis is that it suggests that throughout the Voelkerwanderung the Germanic tribes worshipped only impersonal *numina*, like the points of their swords in war, or certain beams of their houses and certain sacred trees, hills, or sources in peacetime, but had no personal gods with whom they could have communicated as believers— yet another aspect of loneliness and despair. The later development of the Ase gods, Borkenau states, was already partly conceived as a defense against alien Christianity; the later Eddic songs about Wotan and the "twilight of the gods" show distinct "theological" intent. The high point of the cult of Thor, on the other hand, coincides with the high point of the Vikings—an optimistic interval of unbroken heroic morality in a less disrupted milieu than that of the Western Germanic peoples. But this period did not outlast the transition of the Norsemen to statehood and its disciplines.

Borkenau's account of the emergence of a meaningful Western Christianity starts from Ireland; and here he faces the double difficulty that almost nothing is known of Irish history before the early Christianization, apparently sometime in the fourth century, and that what is known hardly fits his general concept of barbarism: an "undramatic" Christianization appears as the only culture shock the Irish clan society experienced at the time, its structure remained largely intact, and no myth in Borkenau's sense, as distinct from harmless fairy tales, arose. Yet it is from this Far Western outpost that the first specifically Western impact on the development of Christianity emerged in the form of Pelagianism.

Pelagius, possibly himself an Irishman and at any rate a Celt, has been shown by modern research to have exercised a dominant influence on most of the Irish church—an influence which seems to have been responsible for its long maintenance of an organizational schism with Rome. But his peculiar doctrine, which penetrated that Church, was the idea that moral perfection was attainable for human beings by a mere effort of their free will, independent of any act of divine grace. That doctrine,

which to the historian indeed appears not only as heretical but as essentially non-Christian, but which in the case of Pelagius and his followers
was coupled not only with a sincere belief in Christ but with an ascetic
moral effort of heroic dimensions, provoked the passionate opposition
of St. Augustine with his insistence on original sin and predestination
as foundations of the irreplaceable role of divine grace: and it ultimately
led to the condemnation of Pelagius' teaching by a Council.

However, though Pelagius failed to get his views accepted by the
Western church, by provoking that discussion he succeeded in putting
the problems of moral conduct, of sin, and of grace permanently into
the center of theological debate and religious development in the West,
in contrast to the Eastern church which remained primarily concerned
with debates about the nature of the trinity and of Christ. The conflict
between Pelagius and Augustine has thus become the starting point for
an original development of Christianity in the West.

As Borkenau sees Pelagianism as an outgrowth of the heroic moral
optimism typical of the fresh cultural development of a no longer purely
traditional, yet essentially undisrupted Irish society, so he sees Augustine's achievement, for all the individual features of a towering personality, as possible only on the background of the African church, then the
most vital part of the churches closely linked with Rome.

It was the church in the Roman province of "Africa," comprising
today's Tunisia with its Carthaginian background and neighboring Eastern Algeria, that had taken the decisive initiatives for what was to become
Roman church discipline. From there Tertullian, the first great theologian
in the West, had proposed a formula on the nature of Christ which came
to be accepted as the basis of future orthodoxy by the East, but which
to him had above all been a prescription for assuring the unity of the
church by ending sterile controversies. From there the proposal had come
to establish the central authority of the see of Rome. There, the church
had reacted to a number of bitter splits, over the admission to its membership or even to the priesthood of men who had once denied their faith
under persecution, by finally establishing the principle that the church
was not meant merely for an elite of athletes of the faith, but for all who
wished to believe and to obey the hierarchy, however weak they might
prove otherwise. The church had to be "catholic," all-embracing, not
only geographically, but in being a church for sinners—under strict authority. Here was the opposite pole to the heroic moralism, the ascetic
perfectionism of Pelagius; but here was also, from another angle, the
basis for a permanent need for the church to busy itself with problems
of moral discipline.

Yet a church that was primarily concerned with keeping its doors open to the flock, and that was at the same time increasingly used for secular administrative functions by the Christianized Roman empire, was unlikely to give a new spiritual content to a decaying society; Augustine's intense sense of sin was not typical for the church of his time. In the East, those really concerned with asceticism and meditation went away from the sinful cities and their lax Christian hierarchy to live as hermits in the desert. Borkenau, in his chapter on the beginnings of monasticism, describes the first successful attempt, undertaken by Pachomius in Upper Egypt, to avoid by a disciplined collective organization of monks both the temptations and the worst miseries of isolated living and the danger of a clash with the bishops in the towns: he achieved a large measure of autonomy for his order in return for a pledge of loyalty to his metropolitan in all matters of doctrine and church politics.

But while Pachomius' style of limited asceticism, however successful, continued to be too mild for numbers of Eastern ascetic extremists, the attempt of Athanasias, the Metropolitan of Alexandria, to transfer the new monastic institution to the West at first failed to strike roots, because the ascetic urge was apparently lacking there in his time: the first Italian monasteries were almost without exception founded from above, by bishops or their close relatives, and soon withered, and the more promising attempt of Benedict of Nursia was interrupted before it could spread by the destruction of his foundation, Monte Cassino, in the course of the Langobard invasion.

The next serious attempt at Western monasticism, undertaken in France by St. Martin of Tours, suffered from a limitation opposite to that of the early Italian enterprises: St. Martin owed his immense popularity not only to his profound piety, but to his passionate partisanship for the poor and downtrodden in the social conflicts of the time, and this led him to feel bitter hostility toward the episcopal hierarchy whose members normally came from the upper classes—a hostility which continued even after he himself, in an exceptional event, had been elected bishop of Tours. Thus he became a legend in his lifetime, but his plebeian following relapsed into passivity after his death—and his foundation, too, remained withouth sequel.

A monastic order of a more conformist character was then founded, also in Gaul, by St. Honorat of Lerins. Its abbots and most of its monks seem to have come from the nobility; they also included an outstanding scholar of Eastern origin in the person of Cassian. Borkenau's manuscript on the origins of Western monasticism breaks off at this point before the decisive developments have been reached. But we learn from his sub-

sequent chapters that the monasteries of Gaul were repeatedly infected
with the general corruption of the Gallic church in the Merovingian age,
and were unable to play the role of a spiritual counterforce. For centuries,
the only serious efforts at a religious revival came from outside—from
missionaries from Ireland and later from Anglo-Saxons from Northumbria and the English Southwest, whose monasteries had been founded
under Iro-Scottish and Welsh influence before the synod of Whitby
achieved the unity of the English church under Rome.

The Irish church had from the first been organized not around bishoprics, but around monasteries. This seems to have been due to the
predominantly rural nature of Ireland, but it had the consequence that
Irish monks were far less exclusively concentrated on prayer and contemplation and far more concerned with mission among the laity than
the Eastern monks, apart from their remarkable Greek scholarship. The
heroic moralism bequeathed by Pelagius thus took the form of missionary
zeal, and by the sixth century, Irish missionaries undertook to spread
their spirit in France. The greatest of them, Columbanus, founded new
monasteries with an extremely stern discipline; he also attempted a moral
conversion of the dissolute Merovingian court. But the rulers, who had
at first been intimidated by his supposed magic prowess, finally expelled
him, and soon the monasteries he had founded relapsed into their earlier
laxity.

Merovingian France, in which a barbarian Frankish rule had been
superimposed on the remnants of the decaying Roman civilization, thus
proved repeatedly to be stubbornly opposed to the beginning of a new
spirit. The next generation of missionaries, the Northumbrians, concentrated their effort on the Eastern, purely Germanic regions of the
Frankish realm, which had been less thoroughly disrupted by contact
with Roman decay; and they were more lastingly successful in their
German foundations. In an essay devoted to the latest and greatest of
that group, St. Boniface, Borkenau describes how he organized the German church on a principle based on a compromise between the Roman
system of bishoprics in the great urban centers and the Irish system of
a church built around monasteries, by creating bishoprics in the countryside that were to become urban centers. It was his astounding organizational success that caused the new rising dynasty of the Carlovingians
finally to call him into France and to entrust him once again with the
task of reforming the Gallic church and its monasteries—in the spirit of
the Anglo-Irish missionary tradition and with the backing of the new
German church he had built up.

Meanwhile another cultural development had begun in post-Roman

Italy: the emphasis on the suffering Christ in religious art. The recurrent denial of the human nature of Christ, or at least of the human will in him, by oriental theological schools, though never finally accepted by the Byzantine church, had found its visual expression in the fact that Byzantine art always depicted either a mere symbol of Christ or the triumphant Christ ruling the world, the Pantokrator, but never the suffering Christ on the cross. Now Roman art, which had long been completely dominated by Byzantine and Ravennese models, begins in the eighth century to show the crucifixion with increasing realism, as well as dramatic images of the agony in the garden, the scene regarded as classic biblical evidence for the existence of a conflict between a human and a divine will in Christ. This coincides in time with the immediate aftermath of the Monotheletic dispute on precisely that latter question in the Christian East, and with the outbreak of the iconoclastic controversy which led the Popes of Rome to break with the Byzantine empire and to appeal to the Franks for help.

The new kind of religious painting turns out, on closer inspection, to be partly based on another type of oriental model, hailing from Syria, but it goes beyond it. Moreover, by the ninth century, Roman paintings show another striking new development—a far greater emphasis on dynamism and individual human emotion than was ever known in Byzantine art. Here, too, Borkenau mentions a kind of oriental, in this case Armenian, model for the most striking example of the new style, the fresco in San Clemente in Rome depicting the rise of the Virgin to heaven; but here, too, the Roman painting shows a dramatic upward movement not to be found in the model. Borkenau concludes that the break with Byzantium, combining the insistence on an independent, "Western" interpretation of Christianity with a political option for a Western alliance, had led in Rome to new cultural expressions ahead of the simultaneous development of art in France.

We have followed Borkenau along two converging lines of development—Germanic mythology as an expression of the contribution of the Germanic barbarians in preparing the ground for a new civilization on the one hand, and the emergence of elements of a specifically Western outlook in the Christian church on the other. But we still have two very striking manuscripts summing up the process as a whole, the confluence of the new creative contributions from different sources, which I have placed at the end of this part—leaving only Borkenau's remarkable essay on the *Chanson de Roland* as a postscript.

Both of these manuscripts are concentrated on France, the battleground, the center of the cultural cyclone, where disruption was deepest and the Dark Ages darkest, but where the final synthesis first emerged, in Borkenau's view. The first deals with the alternatives with which the barbarians were faced by the reemergence of primal crime, of family murder and incest, from the disruption of the traditional order in the Dark Ages: they had, in Borkenau's view, the choice either to face this terrible reality and accept its tragic guilt, or to deny the guilt by projecting it on outside enemies. The first alternative was chosen by the Goths, as shown by the oldest part of the Eddic songs: they faced the primal crime and accepted its guilt—and they perished. The second alternative was chosen by the Western Germanic tribes, in particular the Franks, who had been less totally uprooted by their gradual advance into Gaul than the Goths by their far-flung migrations: as shown in Borkenau's analysis of the Siegfried saga, they denied the guilt and projected it outside, with the result that primal crime and mutual distrust became endemic and produced the aggression-dominated society of the Merovingian age—but they survived. In Borkenau's formulation, it was a "paranoiac" society, not of course in the sense of universal clinical madness, but in the sense of producing widespread character structures marked by the inability for trust and love and the pervasive hostility which in its extreme form is typical of paranoia. Such a society pays for its survival with a state of cultural regression in which "man to man is wolf"—a regression which, in the Merovingian age, is characterized by its inability to make any use of the newly adopted Christianity except as a device of protective magic. It constitutes the nadir of the decay of civilization.

The desperate longing for a credible new order among the people experiencing such decay is not enough to produce a creative solution. A new spark from outside must stimulate the spiritual renewal, and Borkenau sketches the stages of the process in the second of these manuscripts. He describes first the Irish mission of Columbanus and its failure, and then the more successful work of St. Boniface in the 8th century, backed in his work of church reform in France by his remarkable achievement in Germany and by the support of the rising Carlovingians. This second, more broadly based religious revival, coupled with the growing ties between the Frankish realm and papal Rome leading to Charlemagne's new Roman empire, issued into the moral and cultural optimism of the Carlovingian renaissance; it also brought the rebirth of the Benedictine order under the leadership of Benedict of Aniane. But Borkenau insists that the optimism of this attempt at a solution was still too shallow, too little based on a conscious acceptance of guilt, for a lasting renewal, and that also the effort to reintegrate the classical heritage remained superficial at that time. He shows that already the generation following Charlemagne saw not only a dramatic decline in the outward cohesion and internal order of the newborn empire, threatening a return to the Merovingian state of affairs, but also a corresponding religious crisis. But that crisis, he states, brought not only the first inner-Frankish theological debate, but also for the first time a solution from within this core society, which proved lasting.

While the theological debate brought forth such wide-ranging extremes for treating the moral dilemma of man's salvation as the semi-Pelagianism of Johannes Scotus Erigena and the despairing passive surrender to a strict predestination of the individual to grace or damnation advocated by the monk Gottschalk, Borkenau attributes the solution to Paschasius Radbertus, later abbot of Corbie, who in 831 first put forward the doctrine of transsubstantiation, or the physical presence of Jesus Christ in the Eucharist. The idea of the physical incorporation of the Savior, he argues, suggests that he will help the believer from within in his everlasting struggle against sin. Instead of the Pelagian optimism of the avoidance of sin by man's unaided effort, and the morally inacceptable idea of a predestination independent of man's effort, it symbolizes the idea of a moral effort aided by the sacrament, and thus makes the acceptance of guilt possible without despair. It is in this that Borkenau sees the final emergence of the specific Western Christian attitude to the human condition—and the basis for the growth of a spiritually vigorous civilization, in which the experience of guilt is no longer denied but moral struggle is encouraged at the same time: the moral problems raised by the Northern individualism of total responsibility find a solution in a transformed version of Eastern Christianity.

Following this climax of Borkenau's central argument on the origin of the West, I have added as a postscript an essay of his dealing with a development of the eleventh century: the Chanson de Roland and its function in the evolution of the army and state of William the Conqueror. Borkenau offers detailed arguments for the hypothesis that the final version of the Chanson was created in Normandy not long before the battle of Hastings, and was recited in William's camp on the eve of the Channel crossing. He then shows from the text that one central theme was to demonstrate, by the consequences of Roland's refusal to blow his horn and call for succor in time, the irrationality of the Viking tradition of lone-wolf heroism if applied to the conduct of the emerging knightly armies. By sympathetically showing Roland's heroic motives but demonstrating the disastrous consequences of his conduct not just for himself, but for the cause of his master, Charlemagne, the Chanson argues that the duty and honor of fealty should be regarded in the new age of the Normannic states as superior to the honor of the Nordic hero's lonely death. In Borkenau's view, it thus marks a crucial stage in the development of rational military and political discipline in the West, a stage which could not have been reached without the preceding development of a new Christian discipline which he ascribes to the Cluniac movement. It may not be irrelevant to this argument that abbot Lanfranc of Bec, close friend of William before the conquest and later his archbishop of Canterbury, is historically known for his elaboration and defense of the very doctrine of transsubstantiation which Borkenau has traced to its origin with Paschasius two centuries before.

Visions of the Future

This book contains none of the numerous articles which Borkenau devoted to current political developments, mostly in the Communist world. But I have thought it important to include three major essays dealing with future perspectives, because they are based on Borkenau's concept of the history of civilizations, and because they exhibit his ultimate personal concerns.

The first of those essays, entitled by him "After the Atom" and first published in the British monthly *Horizon* in 1947, may shock many readers by its very subject: it raises the question of a possible future alternative between an atomic world war leading, even in the case of Western "victory," to a collapse of Western civilization, and a surrender of the West to Soviet domination. Writing in the bitter initial phase of the Cold War and at a time when the West still had an atomic monopoly, Borkenau felt sure that no Western power would engage in "preventive" atomic war on the Soviets under those conditions: the problem that concerned him might arise later, after the expected catching up of the Soviets in atomic armament. Even for that later period, Borkenau did not see his alternative as inevitable. But he took seriously the possibility that it *might* arise; and he considered it important enough to discuss this future, potential alternative in advance.

Writing more than 30 years later in a world of a rough nuclear balance of power, I still think it unlikely that Borkenau's desperate alternative will arise. I have included this essay here not because I think the question topical, but because the arguments used by Borkenau in his answer throw a light on his world view. Borkenau starts from the thesis that civilizations may have two kinds of final phases: an ossification without either further growth or death, as Byzantium eventually ossified, or a dramatic collapse leading through the horrors of a barbaric age to the rise of a new, creative civilization. He suggests that our world is strewn with the inert bodies of ossified civilizations that can neither live nor die, but have nothing more to offer to mankind—whereas the rise of our own, Western civilization out of the barbaric age that followed the collapse of Rome illustrates the other alternative. He concludes that, seen from the angle of the evolution of humanity as a whole, a collapse of Western civilization after an atomic war, with all the horrors of the war and of the following barbaric period, would open a perspective preferable in its long-term creativity to ossification after submission to Soviet rule. I shall not attempt here further to anticipate this passionate plea for a post-Western future for mankind.

The second essay, published in the United States in 1951, bears the title "Will Technology Destroy Civilization?" If offers two important sidelights on Borkenau's general philosophy of history. First, it shows that his emphasis on the spiritual essence of each high culture and on the primacy of spiritual driving forces in history does *not* go, as it does with Spengler and Toynbee, with a low opinion of the material aspect of civilization: Borkenau rejects the "dualistic" separation of the spiritual from the material and believes in their interdependence. In particular, he sees the technological achievements of our Western civilization—according to him, the first major breakthrough since the neolithic advances that created the preconditions of the great river civilizations—as inseparably linked with the achievements of modern science, including its promise for a future breakthrough to meta-physical relevance, as outlined in chapter 5 of Part I. Second, this essay argues for an element of continuity transcending the histories of each particular high culture. It contains the only passage in which the author uses, without polemics, a particular version of the German distinction between culture and civilization, to wit Alfred Weber's distinction between the pluralistic "cultural process," characterized by essential discontinuity, and the basically unilinear "process of civilization" in the technological and organizational sense; the results of the latter may be inherited, with a fundamental continuity despite major interruptions, from one high culture to the other. Borkenau, in rejecting the pessimistic view of the ultimate cultural irrelevance of technology and of the probable—and desirable?—disappearance of our technology and science with the end of Western civilization, is conscious that he is at bottom defending a concept of progress, not in the sense of a material automatism, but of the possibility of cumulative advances in human knowledge and self-knowledge that alone, to him, makes history meaningful.

The third and final essay deals with the future of the Jews. Written in 1955 on the occasion of the publication of the final volumes of Toynbee's *Study of History*, which in one notorious passage put the Jewish treatment of the Palestinian Arabs in founding the state of Israel on the same moral level as the Nazi genocide of the European Jews, it marks Borkenau's adoption of a highly positive view of the cultural function of the Jews in present and future, and even to some extent of a Jewish cultural identity. In his 1947 essay on the choices before Western civilization, he had described the history of the Jewish community since the founding of the religious university at Yabne on the eve of the destruction of the second temple as an example of an ossified civilization which could neither grow nor decline, and the appearance of modernizing, "assimilated" Jews, as well as the adoption of a Western type of nationalism by the Zionists, as forms of leaving that ossified community in favor of an alien civilization. Now, Toynbee's not too dissimilar thesis, that the Jews had preserved for many centuries a "fossilized" existence as an oriental *"millet"*—a nonterritorial community with an identity defined exclusively by religion—but were losing their true cultural identity by creating a territorial national state on the Western pattern, caused him to reexamine the whole question.

While agreeing with Toynbee that the Jews had long survived in the form of a *millet*, Borkenau made the point that they differed from such other oriental *millets* as the Armenians, Assyrians, Copts, etc., in fact all except the Parsees, by having *chosen* the *millet* existence in order to preserve a religious culture that had existed *before* their territorial independence was destroyed. This meant that their *millet* existence looked back to a culturally identical pre-*millet* past of the greatest historical importance—a civilization that had "mothered" the two universal religions of Christianity and Islam—and that the Zionist effort to link up with that past was not artificial, but promising, particularly in the context of the—for Toynbee surprising—return to the land and the prophetic elements in Israeli cooperative socialism. On the other hand, Borkenau now ascribed to the modernized Jews a unique ability to preserve a core of identity underneath even the most successful outward assimilation, as evidenced in the remarkable clinging of prominent modernized Jews to a belief in the prophetic social ethics transformed into modern political and social ideas, as well as to a belief in a rationally comprehensible (divine) order. Rejecting the idea that Jews could have a future only either in the *Galut* (diaspora) or in the *Yishuv* of Israel, Borkenau concluded that both had a mission in the contemporary world: the *Yishuv* as a revived Jewish community, in which the significant experiment of a merger of Western and oriental Jews could be made, the *Galut* as a cultural leavening within our declining Western civilization; and he did not exclude the possibility that in the case of a new totalitarian barbarization of the West, the intellectual elite of Westernized Jews might, in transmitting Western cultural achievements to a happier future, have a function comparable to the scholars of the church in the Dark Ages following the collapse of classical antiquity.

In making this emphatic profession of his faith in the future mission of Jewry, Borkenau made it clear that he was neither a nationalist nor a religious Jew, "though very much a Jew in the sense of the Nuremberg laws." Clearly, he saw himself as one of those modern Jews who could play a role in preserving the continuity of the Western cultural inheritance.

PART ONE

Culture Cycles and Culture Generations

CHAPTER ONE

Thinking Beyond Spengler

Discussion about Spengler has hitherto been conducted with the purpose of assigning his work its proper psychological and sociological place. That is the appropriate approach to something that is over and done with. In my view, however, Spengler is by no means "done with." True, Arnold J. Toynbee has taken over, explicitly or implicitly, many important ideas from Spengler, and has also corrected some of his major errors. But Toynbee, who is not the subject of this essay,[1] has also failed to understand and rejected so many basically important and fertile contributions of Spengler that he cannot be accepted as having really promoted the solution of the group of problems first treated by Spengler. Spengler's work still stands like an unhewn, wildly fissured rock in a flat desert—a hitherto never accepted challenge to researchers to take hold of the pieces of that cyclopean structure and use them for productive work of their own. Here, only the simplest and most direct approach can help. Instead of writing treatises on Spengler's place in the sociology of our time, we should ask ourselves: what is the nature of his achievement, which are his errors, in what direction must he be continued? In other words: instead of discussing Spengler as a person, it is better to take a stand on the questions he was the first to raise.

Spengler did not know it, but his critics have pointed out to him that the philosophy of Time as a nonmeasurable form of existence which underlies his construction of history derives from Bergson. But Bergson is more or less the source of all modern existentialist interpretations of Time. Here, Spengler simply follows the trend of the general contemporary evolution of philosophy, and inasmuch as Bergson's interpreta-

---

1. See Part I, ch. 2 below.

tion of Time as a form of existence is justified, Spengler is justified as well.

A second main point in Spengler's philosophy is his symbolism. His doctrine consists precisely in regarding all aspects of a given culture as particular symbols derived from a single primal symbol. Here, too, Spengler is by no means original. Symbolism was the slogan of his time and dominated its art. Spengler's primal symbols can hardly be distinguished from the archetypes of C. G. Jung, so that any polemics against the basic views of Jung would automatically apply to Spengler as well.

The most valuable part of a recent critique by Adorno[2] seems to me his pointing out the inherent contradiction of this point of view. In dealing with a purely rationalist approach it was justified to point to the ever-present role of symbols in the human consciousness. Yet a pan-symbolism claiming to interpret symbolically the whole of human existence is nonsense, in history even more than in psychology. Any symbol must symbolize something that is itself not a symbol—otherwise we are dealing, as Adorno states rightly, with "a soul playing with itself." Such plays do occur, but it would be absurd to claim that life consists of them—and just this would follow stringently from Spengler's basic assumption. It is, of course, quite another question whether it is sufficient to oppose to such pan-symbolism "human reproduction" as the basic content of culture, as Adorno, following Engels, has done. But this thesis does not belong into out present context, as it is only artificially linked with the questions raised by Spengler.

Taking all in all, Spengler is a very poor philosopher, neglecting the developed techniques of philosophical thought and trying in vain to express the currents of ideas popular in his generation in a philosophical language of his own. If one accepts his own hierarchy of thought which places philosophy at the top, his "system" deserves not so much to be rejected but to be cast aside as irrelevant. But the question remains whether we are entitled to take this easy option.

The value attached by important men to particular aspects of their work need in no way correspond to the real importance of those parts. We do not see Goethe's principal achievement in his theory of colors, as he did, nor do we share Adam Smith's estimate of himself as primarily a moral philosopher. For the value of great scientific discoveries hardly anything is less important than the particular road that led to them. Copernicus based a wrong calculation of the paths followed by the planets

---

2. Theodor W. Adorno, "Spengler nach dem Untergang" (Spengler after the Decline), *Der Monat* no. 20 (May 1950).

on a wrong philosophy of the metaphysical uniqueness of the circle, but that did not prevent him from bringing about the greatest and most fertile transformation in human ideas of the universe; others, Kepler and Galileo, corrected his calculations, thus proving that his philosophical assumptions were superfluous and, appearance notwithstanding, alien to the subject. In dealing with Spengler, we are faced with an analogous task. His philosophy is wrong; so are many details of his work. Nevertheless, the basic idea is revolutionary and merely requires technical correction and further development.

Spengler's substantial doctrine—as distinct from the philosophical claims with which he has surrounded it—rests on a dual thesis. The first part of that basic thesis states that those processes of historical rise and decline, which long before him were investigated by Aristotle, Machiavelli, Gibbon, and Montesquieu, have as their substratum not the nation, but the culture or civilization, where "culture" has to be understood as a spatiotemporal unit stretching over some thirty generations and comprising a plurality of peoples and other communities. This thesis, which provoked tremendous excitement among many, ought really to be (as Spengler expected) one of those statements that have only to be once pronounced to be regarded as self-evident. For nobody will dare to deny that rise and decline are basic phenomena of history. To maintain that there could be any case in which something that had historically arisen would not also experience its decline and fall amounts to claiming that man could create social structures that last eternally. The fury directed against the "prophets of doom" thus proves to spring from a mixture of self-deification and a fear of death transposed to society.

Earlier thinkers chose as substratum for those processes of rise and decline—processes which we shall henceforth call "cyclical"—the unit that was in each case underlying the social structures of their time: in classical antiquity it was the city-state, and, with the approach of the modern bourgeois age, with increasing clarity the national state. Inasmuch as it is Spengler's crucial achievement to have put "culture" and its cycle in the place of those units, his work is one of the phenomena accompanying the decay of nationalism and the national state—certainly not a position that would deserve condemnation. Spengler has to be given all the more credit for it as he openly mocked the racism popular in Germany as a substitute for the nation in the interwar years, and did so even after the victory of National Socialism. At any rate, this change in the substratum of the cyclical process must be regarded as the only part of the "thesis of decline" that deserves a scholarly discussion.

Of course, the moral merit of an author's sentiments proves nothing for the truth of his theory. Other substrata of the cycle are conceivable, for instance the classes according to Marx and Engels or the changing political systems according to Aristotle; indeed it is obvious that these, too, undergo a cyclical evolution as do the nations. But the mere comparison of the cyclical process in the evolution of nations, political orders, and classes is sufficient to show that none of the theories based on each of those structures (or any others) alone can uphold its claim to exclusive validity, and that proves that none of those structures can be the ultimate substratum of the historical process. The problem cannot be solved by attempting to assign the character of substratum to just one in the long list of subordinate cyclical processes. The question can be formulated only in this way: is history, like a storm at sea, the result of an incalculable and definitely nonrepetitive interference of innumerable wave movements, or does there exist a cyclical process superior to those chaotic undulations which is repetitive and thus "lawful" in the meaning of everyday language, which comprises all the subordinate cyclical processes and explains them as elements of a whole? That is the true Spenglerian question, which in my view has not been appreciated at all in discussion to date. But a critical discussion that does not start from the central thesis of the opponent is without purpose and substance.

At this point, the other part of Spengler's basic thesis comes in. He tried to prove the role of "culture" as the ultimate substratum of history by arguing that cultures had the character of Leibnitz's "monads without windows"—arising out of absolute nothingness and issuing into nothingness. If that were true, Spengler's entire system would have been stringently proved. But it is not true, and by asserting it Spengler has only rendered a disservice to his basic concept.

In fact, Spengler has not built up his doctrine of the "monadism" of cultures merely to support his thesis of culture as the ultimate substratum of history. Rather, this monadic doctrine is in itself one of his basic concerns, closely linked with his doctrine of the primal symbol and of the symbolic character of all culture—views that in turn are inseparably connected with Spengler's assertion that the individual cultures follow their path from nothingness to nothingness "in sublime absense of purpose." Who indeed could doubt that here Spengler is a spokesman of despair, of a malicious hatred against all ultimate creative success, of the rejection of all transcendent values and obligations—in short of the evil side of German thought in the interwar period? Only, if his critics introduce psychology and sociology into the discussion of the substantial problems, one is entitled to demand that they should be complete. As mentioned before, Spengler's doctrine fitted in no way into the concept of the Nazis, both because of its implicit condemnation of human self-deification and because it far transcended the ideas of nation and race. Spengler's work reflects one of the most magnificent struggles between construction and destruction ever fought out in the soul of a student of the destiny of man. This profound ambivalence has undoubtedly made possible the far-reaching momentum of his discoveries, but has forced Spengler at the same time to strike at the root of his finest insights.

The theory of the monadism of cultures is wrong. It is usually contested by pointing to the "influences" flowing from one culture to another; but this objection ignores Spengler's argument that such foreign models would be misunderstood without exception, because a culture could in the last resort only integrate what was already its own. This argument cannot be refuted by any cumulation of individual facts. However, the monadic doctrine proves to be untenable in the light of Spengler's own basic assumptions. He himself speaks of a bundle of high cultures as little distinct from each other in their fundamental structures (i.e., in their articulation in such social forms as family, people, state, economy, estates and classes, religions and churches, the arts, science and philosophy, etc.) as in their span of life and the type of their cyclical course. Spengler has never noticed that even the most profound differences in the "symbolism" of individual cultures are secondary compared to those structural uniformities. The high cultures form a *genus* defined by many common characteristics, for which genetic unity must be assumed as with every generic phenomenon.

But the idea of a clearly defined beginning and end of each culture seems to stand and fall with the "monadism." If the clear temporal outline of the typical culture cycle falls, can the doctrine of the culture as ultimate substratum of history be maintained? Is it possible to demonstrate the existence of the culture cycle without making use of the monadic concept? The reply to this question must decide whether Spengler's construction must be put aside as a failure, or must be seen as an important insight requiring further work for its development.

If monadism is wrong, then the periods between the high cultures, which Spengler contemptuously shoved aside in the first volume of his *Decline of the West,* but of which he took notice in the second volume as "Merowingian" and "Fellahin" periods, are gaining a significance of their own. Spengler himself recognized this, even though not explicitly, in the inspired fragment on the second pre-Christian millennium, to be found in the volume of his writings published after his death.[3] He died

3. Oswald Spengler, *Frühzeit der Weltgeschichte: Fragmente aus dem Nachlass* (Munich: Beck, 1966).

too early, in the midst of a profound transformation of his system. We are attempting to continue his thought on the lines of his late period.

It is a typical sequence that each high culture is preceded by a "barbaric" age and followed by another, though the depth of the downfall is not the same in all cases. It could probably be shown that the more profound the barbaric downfall, the more creative the subsequent culture. (This is stated in conscious stark contrast to the total lack of understanding which Toynbee has shown for the barbaric epochs and therefore, as I shall try to show presently, for the inner mechanism of the rise of a culture). Those barbaric epochs are something utterly different from the more or less timeless cultures of primitive tribes, with which they are often confounded: they are distinct from the latter above all by a clear rhythm in time. As Spengler quite rightly gave the individual high cultures about a thousand years (he suggested downward adjustments for the dates of origin of the first great river civilizations at a time when the specialists were still working with fantastic figures that are now wholly discredited), it is possible to attribute to the fully developed barbaric periods about half a millennium. It is true, however, that both for the barbaric phases and for the high cultures, there exist cases of only rudimentary development with a corresponding shortening of their duration.

Barbaric periods are the result of three completely distinct, but regularly combined processes. The first is the self-dissociation (decline and fall) of a high culture. This opens the gates to the surrounding primitives who thus come into contact with the high culture in process of dissociation. By that contact, the primitive cultures are also disrupted. Where the dying high culture mixes culturally and ethnically more and more with its primitive environment in process of disruption, there develops a region of all-sided cultural disintegration. Not that the elements of culture would disappear: in the past generation, Alfons Dopsch has devoted much paper to the completely superfluous proof that the cultural elements live on[4]—he overlooked the fact that both the elements of the high and of the primitive culture live on, and that in both cases the unifying bond between the elements is dissolved. To take the example closest to us, in the succession of classical antiquity and in the immediate prehistory of our Western civilization, a world of floating cultural wreckage arose in that way. The same is true for every transition from one high culture to another.

---

4. Alfons Dopsch, *Wirtschaftliche und soziale Grundlagen der europäischen Kulturentwicklung: Aus der Zeit von Cäsar bis auf Karl den Grossen*, 2 vols. (Vienna: Seidl, 1923.-24).

But as the functionalist school of cultural anthropology has shown, each society is all the time striving to integrate its cultural elements: it must do so in order to function. To state that may be a banality, but it is also the most telling objection to Spengler's theory of symbols. Not a symbolic function permeating all aspects of life, but the need of human beings for a society satisfying their requirements compels cultural creation. It is deplorable, however, if a philosopher like Adorno seriously advocates the view that these requirements could be in the last resort adequately defined as "reproduction"—as if man's confrontation with death, i.e., religion, were less fundamental than his confrontation with life!

In a decaying high culture and in a barbaric phase, the same forces making for the disruption or preservation of a culture are active as in times of cultural rise and flowering: only their respective chances of success are different. To "will" a culture, to look for it longingly, to assemble all existing cultural wreckage in order to create it are typical signs of decline and barbarism. For wishing for a culture and creating a culture are two different things. While the parts of the wreckage are disparate, such efforts often only serve further desintegration. An illustration of what that means may be found, for instance, in Paul Frankl's profound work on early medieval architecture.[5] The author has insightfully described how Northern and Central Europe were for centuries looking for "models." Each of the innumerable theories about the origin of Romanesque and Gothic architecture, each pointing to foreign influences from Rome to the Arctic circle, is in the right—but equally in the wrong. For Romanesque architecture, like any other cultural form of the West, arose neither from one particular among those "influences" nor from their eclectic mixture, but—after very long efforts—from the working out of a principle that did not exist in any of the "influencing" areas: the depth of the longitudinal nave and its association with a contrasting transverse nave. This type arose once for all time with the building of the second church of Cluny and spread from there—as later the Gothic type spread from St. Denis, as Sedlmayr has shown.[6] It was the grain which, thrown into a salty solution, started the process of crystallization.

Accidentally? That would be incomprehensible, and the regularity of the time rhythm denies that possibility. Rather, the process of the origin of cultures has its inclusive and its exclusive aspects. Not all that happens to flow in is used productively, but some elements *must* be used under

5. Paul Frankl, *Die frühmittelalterliche und romanische Baukunst* (Wildpark-Potsdam: Atlantis, 1926).
6. Hans Sedlmayr, *Die Entstehung der Kathedrale* (Zurich: Atlantis: 1950).

the laws governing the process. Again, the origin of the West may serve as example. Western civilization, like all "affiliated" high cultures dependent on earlier cultures, appears in the first place as the integration of two elements which continue their lives in it with the maximum completeness that can be achieved: the culture of late antiquity on one side, Germanic-Celtic culture on the other, hence one high culture and one primitive culture. If we have just illustrated the act of birth of a new high culture by the image of the grain thrown into a saturated solution, we cannot find a similarly apt image from crystallography for the process of gestation preceding birth. Rather one may think of the biological image of the formation of a chrysalis, which is known to consist in a considerable reduction of the specific organization of matter, creating a largely formless kind of living substance within which a mysterious process of reshaping may take place precisely thanks to its reduced level of integration. The image becomes complete if we keep in mind that the formation of the chrysalis was preceded, at some distance in time, by an act of generation. In that act, two fully integrated units merged—but the final product of that merger can appear only after a process of temporary and partial disintegration: otherwise, the caterpillar that emerged from the egg would never become a butterfly.

Our description of the barbaric phase as a chrysalis stage makes it possible to draw more exact conclusions both about its own character and its distance from a high culture. Barbaric periods are not to be measured by their products. What they add has largely originated in their own primitive past, without which, however, the contents of the subsequent, affiliated high culture could never be explained. (Such institutions as the Celto-Germanic "following," which became the basis for Western feudalism, are proven to hail from a time preceding the great migrations, just as do stringed instruments, stave rhymes, the belief in fate, etc.) The only field in which the age of the migrations was productive was poetry, as Toynbee observes so brightly—as if chrysalis stages could be productive of "achievements"—and in fact, it is not even wholly true for poetry. The true productivity of such phases lies entirely in the soundless integration of at first wholly incompatible elements.

Yet as far as the West is concerned, one main point is still missing in what has been said here. The preceding high culture contributing to the rising Western civilization, though reasonably unified in language and space—we are talking of a "Latin" culture—is not unified in spirit: it is an amalgam of elements from antiquity and of Christian elements from the East, and in the Latin realm as distinct from the Byzantine it is an amalgam that has not yet been fully integrated. On closer inspection, it thus appears that the culture of the West has originated from the integration of not one but two primitive culture groups (the Germanic and Celtic ones) with not one, but two high cultures (those of antiquity and early Christianity). The case is not unique. And just as we stated above that the "height" of the new cultural phase was conditioned by the "depth" of the preceding barbaric phase, we may now add that the richness of a high culture is to an essential degree conditioned by the number of the earlier high cultures integrated in it. At one end of the scale we may think of the third Chinese culture beginning with the Han, following the Shang and Chou cultures, which arose exclusively from the contact of the declining Chou culture alone with a single group of primitive cultures of neighboring populations; at the other end, we have the outcomes of magnificent cultural cross-fertilizations like the Hellenic and Western cultures.

From the recognition of the variety of basic elements of a newly arising high culture follows the insight into its inner structure: "integration" would indeed be an empty phrase if it did not imply the articulation of a whole into parts linked by their functions. The structure results from the nature of the basic elements. Starting once again with the West, we find that the new culture bears distinctive traces of its growing together out of one zone of primitive and one of high culture—the former traces preserved in the North, the latter in the South. But the separation survived only in the framework of integration. Antiquity and Christianity have deeply penetrated also the "Saxon" area on both sides of the North Sea that is central for the European North, and conversely even Spain and Italy cannot be imagined without their Germanic cultural elements. These main divisions and lines of separation between the Germanic and the Celtic, the antique and the Eastern Christian cross each other in manifold geographical "faults" which cannot be discussed here. But above all the old frontier between the realm of high culture and that of the primitives has become thoroughly blurred. Between those antique and Nordic core areas that can still be clearly identified there stretches a broad intermediate zone—Northern France, Southern Germany with Burgundy, Southern England, Lombardy—in which the two basic elements have interpenetrated each other to the point of becoming indistinguishable. This intermediate zone, present in every highly integrated culture, is the real birthplace and homeland of the new high culture.

Understanding of this dual process of *systole* and *diastole*, of integration linked with articulation, now permits an insight into the course of a culture's development. The so-called "Merowingian phase" (which in the West comprises also a good deal of Carlovingian history) is essentially an era of the penetration of the opposite elements into the previously strictly separated zones of high culture and barbarism. It is not by accident that so few germs of Western culture have arisen in the intermediate zone, so many in the marginal regions of the East and North on one side and of the West and South on the other. But the act of birth takes place when those influences burst from all sides into the hitherto passive intermediate zone and there achieve the breakthrough of a new cultural system. From now on, an unending struggle begins between the marginal regions, meaning primarily the old zone of high culture and the old zone of barbarism, for the central zone. In the course of that confrontation, integration is deepened, because the wooing of the central zone requires adaptation to it. The central zone thus becomes the connecting link permitting an ever more intense exchange between South and North—a process that never ends during the lifetime of the culture concerned.

But there is an opposite process as well, starting from the very origin of each culture. *Omnis determinatio est negatio* (each definition is also an exclusion)—this dictum of Spinoza's should be the motto for any philosophy of culture. The new principle which makes possible the basic integration of a new culture implies choices between different potentialities of human nature. Each principle of valuation is exclusive, one-sided, incomplete. In the course of its development, each culture is struggling to comprise the largest possible realms of existence without abandoning its own principles. But this effort meets inherent limits, due not at first to the potential infiniteness of human nature in general (this becomes directly effective only in the acute disruption of the final stage) but, much more immediately, to the limits of the capacity for integrating the disparate elements out of which each high culture is constituted. The tendency towards increasing integration of those disparate elements is thus balanced by a tendency towards their disintegration. The latter begins to get the upper hand once the first third of a culture's lifespan has passed. To take again the example of the West: the growing unity of the Romanesque period, culminating in the early Gothic, is followed by a growing confrontation between North and South, which in the fifteenth century finds its fullest expression in the contrast between the already fully developed Renaissance in the South and the late Gothic Flamboyant style developing rapidly in a Northern direction. Thus the West moves, like every highly integrated culture, towards its great midway crisis (in the West the Reformation, in the Middle East Islam etc.), the essence of which is a renewed sharp divergence between the two constituent zones of the high culture concerned. After that, unity is reconstituted once more, but no longer completely. Indeed, the precariousness of the restored unity is shown by the fact that, while previously the struggle was conducted mainly between spiritual currents, now open fighting between the two principal regions and the corresponding belief systems plays the main role. Their contacts assume the character of a mutual blunting and disruption of the basic cultural principles, until an "age of enlightenment" raises doubt about the whole of the axioms that originally made possible the creation of the culture, and thus initiates the process of dissolution.

Yet such periods of dissolution have their own historical function. They are neither, as modern liberalism would have it, the times in which light is at last dissolving the terrible "darkness' of culturally positive epochs, nor, as modern reaction claims, times of total negativity and moral decay. They simply mark the point when a particular cultural creation has exhausted its potentialities of development and is therefore succumbing to the assault of the tendencies which it originally excluded and rejected.

Wherever the philosopher of history may choose his starting point, he will ultimately be brought to recognition of the contradiction between the potential infinity and the actual finiteness of human existence—a recognition taught by all great religions and indeed in a sense identical with the essence of religion itself. The processes of dissolution which constitute the final phase of high cultures do not simply express human wickedness and insufficiency, not simply a "failure of strength," but precisely that contradiction. Periods of dissolution are often even times of an unheard-of unfolding of strength, as we can observe in our own period and may understand today also in the case of earlier, analogous periods. What they cannot produce is only this: a coherent culture developing according to immanent laws. While the cycles of the great high cultures are characterized by a singular evolution of style that might almost be described as logical, this is lacking in all fields in the periods of dissolution: this lack is their innermost essence. For style, whether one speaks of the style of clothing or of art, in a metaphorical sense of the "style" of government and economic life or—almost blasphemously—of the style of religion, is necessarily formed by acts of positing, defining, limiting, and excluding. By laying down a style, high cultures gain the possibility of complete fulfillment of their immanent potential through many generations; but at the same time they offend against primal realities by positing a limited way of life as if it were the only and absolute one. Periods of dissolution correct this offense and are therefore closer to the inexhaustible nature of reality; yet it is a negative closeness—an avoidance of limitations which is paid for by the failure of long-lasting creation. Such is the human condition.

What is created in such epochs is bound to disappear again from the surface of historical events, because it cannot become generally recognized law and hence a basis for continuous evolution. The deep-rooted principles which characterize the opening phase of any new culture presuppose not merely a longing for faith, but the inner capacity for unquestioning faith in society as a whole. This capacity is specific to times that are directly accessible to the myth, hence to the primitive. Every cultural cycle may therefore be described as a road from the mythical, on which culture may be founded, to the nonmythical which disrupts it. This law, too, Spengler has been the first to pronounce distinctly. Again we are facing one of the basic contradictions constituting the human condition which articulate themselves in the historical process! Again an approach to an understanding of the function of barbaric ages: they are the epochs that lead back from criticism to myth, and thus to the rejuvenation of culture.

Yet it is not true, as Spengler would have it, that the creations of the final periods of dissolution disappear into nothingness. As Toynbee has shown in the later volumes of his main work (in an unstated continuation of Spengler's last writings), there do exist generations of cultures. With regard to the part of human history enacted in the Near and Middle East and Europe, he distinguishes three of them: the generation of the great river civilizations, the ancient Hellenic and the Hebraic culture, and finally the group of Christian and Islamic cultures. But Toynbee has not attempted to make a sharp conceptual distinction between those three generations. The meaning of those genealogical tables will only become apparent, in my view, once it is recognized that each cultural generation relates to the previous one as its negation—a thesis that cannot be fully explained in the present essay. But this much may be said: the following culture generation always links up with the final products of the dissolution of its predecessor—in other words, it takes over the products of its process of dissolution across the barbaric interregnum, and gives them a positive sign. Thus Echnaton's struggle against the Egyptian death cults was turned into the Hellenic-Hebraic weakening of the belief in a life after death; thus the victory of that latter belief in the Hellenic-Hebraic late phase became the basis of Christianity.[7] Thus the link between suc-

7. See Part I, ch. 3 below.

cessive cultures may be demonstrated, not by an arbitrary collection of proofs for "influences," but as deeply anchored in their basic structures.

It is time to return to the question we developed in the beginning. Can the culture cycle be defined as a clearly limited unit without making use of the evidently false doctrine of "monadism"? In other words, can Spengler's concrete insights be given a rational, nonnihilistic interpretation; can they be further developed without abandoning that great scientific progress implied in the formulation of the concept of "culture cycle"?

We feel that we have shown this to be possible. We found the driving force of cultural creation not in Spengler's "primal symbol," at once mystical and empty, but in the necessity for a coherent society. We defined the coherence needed for the functioning of a society in agreement with Spengler as unity of style. We tried to demonstrate its dialectics as springing from the alternation between limitation and expansion which forms part of the innermost core of human existence. We showed the character of the process of limitation as the integration of elements from high cultures and primitive societies on the background of a barbaric epoch, and we explained how this process of integration—and the counterprocess of disintegration—dominates the course of the culture cycle quite as much as the original rise of a culture. The history of the high cultures thus came to appear naturally as consisting of phases of style-bound high cultures on the one hand and not style-bound intervals on the other. We hinted that the most profound link between successive culture generations consists in their opposing attitudes persisting across the intervening barbaric ages, and not in any positive heritage, however big the role of the latter may be.

It follows that inasmuch as the border between periods that are or are not style-bound is clearly recognizable—for the beginning of the growth of a unified style can be sharply marked, and its end is usually also quite distinctive—it is indeed possible to speak in each case of a sharply circumscribed culture cycle as defined by Spengler. But this clearly definable cycle is, contrary to Spengler's opinion, compatible with the unity of the history of high cultures as a whole: that is the main correction that must be applied to Spengler's ideas.

But every problem that is solved raises a new one. Throughout the present discussion, the phenomenon "high culture" itself was assumed as given, as it is by Spengler. We did not discuss, let alone solve, the question of how it came about that the bundle of short-lived and high-curved high cultures arose out of the flat-curved prehistoric cultures with their enormous timespan. Yet it is clear that no full understanding of the "high-culture-phase" of history is possible so long as only its individual elements have been explained and not the phase as a whole. The demand for such an understanding of the whole is all the more justified as what has been explained really amounts only to a "wheel of rebirth" for the high cultures—hardly less desperate than is the Indian wheel of rebirth for the human individual. Yet the mere sequence of the culture generations suggests the idea that something more is involved here than a purely repetitive process—even though this could not be proven so far. Perhaps because we ourselves have not yet outgrown the process of culture cycles? If that is the reason, it may be that we have not to wait very long, by the yardstick of world history, for a more comprehensive insight into the cultural process. For the immense breakthrough to the control of nature that we are experiencing hints at the possibility that man may find a road to a metaphysical knowledge without the need for mythical garbs, and may thus overcome the main factor underlying the cultural cycle.

Perhaps the day is no longer distant when Spengler's insights in the culture cycle will be completely subordinated to a—today still unattainable—understanding of the essence of the high-culture-phase of humanity as a finished epoch of human existence. Only what is finished may be fully comprehended. But is not then the dawning of an understanding of history as a whole the clearest indication that we are today approaching not only the cyclical end of a single culture, our Western civilization, but the end of a far larger historical cycle? A presentiment of that process—that may well be the true way of "positively" transcending Spengler.

CHAPTER TWO

Toynbee and the Culture Cycle

According to his own account, Toynbee conceived his theory of history at about the same time that Oswald Spengler was formulating his own somewhat similar ideas. It would therefore be wrong to accuse Toynbee of an unacknowledged dependence on Spengler's work. However, since Spengler's *Decline of the West* appeared much earlier than the first volumes of *A Study of History*, one regrets that Toynbee has paid so little explicit attention to it; all the more so as his relation to Spengler constitutes the starting point for any serious assessment of his contribution.

Spengler's real originality did not consist in his ideas about historical rise and decline as such. Those had been a theme of European historical speculation since Machiavelli. Where Spengler went beyond such thinkers as Machiavelli, Montesquieu, Gibbon, and Burckhardt was in applying the concept of rise and decline to whole civilizations or cultures, rather than just to nations and countries. The notion of a frame of historical development larger than the political-linguistic unit formed by the nation-state had always been latent in Western Christian thought, and by the early 19th century the German historian Leopold von Ranke had made it explicit in his attempt to write a collective history of the "Romanic and Germanic" nations.[1] Ranke, however, was wilfully blind to the larger processes of cultural change, and did not visualize Romanic-Germanic (i.e. Western) history in terms of rise and decline. Spengler's achievement was to combine the idea of a supranational civilization or culture with that of a cyclical development in history. The theory of culture cycles that he created now dominates our historical thinking—at

---

1. Leopold v. Ranke, *Geschichte der germanischen und romanischen Völker,* in *Sämtliche Werke,* vol. 33 (Leipzig, 1874).

least our thinking about such grandiose historical phenomena as civilizations and cultures. We see evidence of this in the universal employment of the term "the West"; and "rise and decline" are words which we often employ to express our present anxiety about the future of our way of life. Here Toynbee has to be regarded as Spengler's epigone; his claim to have made his discoveries independently cannot take away from Spengler's achievement and precedence in opening our eyes to this whole new constellation of ideas.

Spengler next tried to extend his view of the culture as a historical unit from the West to the other groups generally accepted as "higher civilizations." In doing this he found it necessary to establish a strict definition of the central experience peculiar to each culture. That is, he wanted to identify and isolate a unique heart and core whence the whole development of any civilization flowed. It was in this attempt, praiseworthy in itself, to define just what differentiated and separated higher civilizations from all the others that Spengler made his basic errors. Following a current of thought popular before 1914, but now half forgotten, he treated all the outward expressions of a civilization as "symbols." Symbols of what? Spengler's implied answer was: symbols of the inexpressible inner core, the "soul," of the particular civilization, which is supposed to be its highest contribution to the domain of values. But these are empty words, empty German words, serving only to conceal the total denial—implicit throughout Spengler—that a civilization is built for human survival and human needs and a total denial that what happens to human beings in history matters; that the fruits of human experience can be accumulated over the long run and passed on from one civilization to another.

Nor was that "symbolism" improved by the Kantian element Spengler infused into it. Kant argues that space and time are *a priori* patterns which we impose on the chaotic raw material we receive from our sense impressions; these patterns, however, have no intrinsic relation to ultimate objective reality, the *"Ding an sich."* Spengler historicized this philosophical idea by maintaining that each and every civilization had its own unique conception of space, which was reflected in all its expressions and works. This notion in itself is hardly worth serious discussion—especially when we see how Spengler derived from it the entirely untenable theory that the mathematics developed in the various civilizations were basically dissimilar, that a mathematical truth for one culture was not one for another.

But where Spengler sinned through extravagance, Toynbee sins through triviality. If his dictum that "all civilizations are fundamentally contemporaneous" means anything, it means that there are no radical differences between them. What significance, then, does human variety itself possess? Toynbee's view—that differences don't matter—betrays an ultimate pessimism about the meaning of human development equal to Spengler's, if not as conscious or consistent.

Moreover, the "philosophical" contemporaneity he claims for all civilizations opens the door to many forced and far-fetched comparisons and the perception of similarities where none exist. A major instance of this is his assertion that the decline of every civilization is marked by the period of a "universal state"; yet a universal state marks the beginning, not the end, of Ancient Egypt's history. Another example is his claim that all higher civilizations end with the establishment of "universal churches"; yet there have been only four or five such churches, and Toynbee himself lists twenty-one higher civilizations. Conversely, he holds that a "universal church" is always coterminous with a single civilization. This point may appear rather technical, but it is responsible, as I will try to show later, for Toynbee's faulty analysis of his most important and—for him—most specialized subject, the history of the Near and Middle East.

In his later volumes Toynbee does try to make amends for his original contention that all civilizations are philosophically contemporaneous by distinguishing three different "generations" of cultures: the "primary," river valley civilizations, then the pre-Christian and pre-Buddhist ones, and finally the Christian and Buddhist civilizations with their offshoots. But since he continues to cling somehow to "philosophical contemporaneity," and to insist on strained and artificial analogies between cultures moving on altogether different levels, this modification in terms of "generations" creates confusion rather than clarity, and remains unreconciled with the rest of his position. In any case, Toynbee's unrestrained penchant for finding parallels wherever he looks in history frustrates any serious attempt on his part to discuss the specific characteristics of the various civilizations. Spengler at least correctly posed a great problem— what distinguishes one culture from another?—even if he failed to solve it, but Toynbee loses sight of the problem entirely, and thus falls short of his predecessor.

At another and more important point, however, it is Spengler who comes off worse. His belief in a particular spatial "*Ursymbol*" (primordial symbol) for every civilization allows him to postulate the absolute uniqueness of all cultures. For him, civilizations are—to use Leibniz's term—"windowless monads," unable to understand or communicate with or profoundly influence one another. Each comes out of nowhere and, though leaving behind material ruins, bequeaths no genuine spiritual remains to humanity. Here Spengler (though he was himself a brave and outspoken anti-Nazi) reflects most clearly the destructive mood, the cultural nihilism, of pre- and proto-Nazi Germany. Toynbee is obviously right in opposing to this cruel nonsense about civilizations being hermetically sealed off from one another his notion of cultural "affiliation."

Historians have long been aware that civilizations, whether contemporaneous or separated in time, exert influence upon one another. It is also normal for younger civilizations to spring from older ones; the larger part of Toynbee's last four volumes is devoted to the discussion of such cases of culture contact and "affiliation." But though undoubtedly superior to Spengler in this aspect of his thinking, Toynbee, for all his learned parallels, falls considerably below the standards of historical research obtaining today. No serious historian would question the fact that many extraneous influences go into the making of a young civilization, but Toynbee simplified the matter unduly by maintaining that each younger civilization is affiliated with some older one in the relation of child to parent. Must such children be limited to only one parent?

The most relevant case in point is Western civilization. According to Toynbee, it is affiliated in its origins with "Hellenic" civilization, that is, the civilization of classical, Greco-Roman antiquity. So far so good— but what about Christianity, which is surely a force largely unexplained by Hellenic culture? Toynbee's answer is that Christianity is the universal church that developed out of Hellenism in decline. But where, then, do Jewry and Judaism come in? Toynbee assumes they played no part at all in the emergence of Christianity.

I am forced to rehearse the obvious: Christianity was a product, originally, of the eastern shores of the Mediterranean, of what Toynbee calls the "Syriac" civilization, but in its mature form it represents a merging of the "Hellenic" and the "Syriac" spirits. Hence Eastern Christianity was "affiliated" to two civilizations, not just one. Western civilization is likewise "affiliated" to two civilizations, the Hellenic and the Syriac— and even in this reckoning Northern barbarian influences on the West are left out, as are Transjordanian (neither Hellenic nor Syriac) influences on Christianity. A generalization that, like Toynbee's, does not provide for the possibility of a nascent civilization's having multiple affiliations is clearly unsuited to serve as the starting point for a philosophy of history and of civilizations.

Spengler, whose nihilistic mood was typical of the old Imperial Germany (Toynbee is quite wrong in seeing the *Decline of the West*, which was published at the height of the German victories in the spring of 1918, as reflecting Wilhelmian Germany's defeat in World War I), was completely amoral—as rigidly so as Marx, with the sole difference that for Marx morality reflected class, whereas for Spengler it reflected *"Ursymbol."* Toynbee, by contrast, abounds in moral sentiment. But this is no reason for giving him a plus mark. In my recent review of Toynbee's attitude towards modern Jewry,[2] I gave some examples of how he applied his moral principles in discussing history and politics—thus, he found the Israelis' treatment of the Arabs of Palestine morally equivalent to the Nazi treatment of the Jews of Europe. It would be altogether mistaken to think that this kind of moralizing is restricted to his section on the modern Jews and is attributable solely to the indubitable hostility he feels toward them. Quotations to illustrate his "moral" attitude can be gleaned in plenty from any part of his work.

The effect of a moralizing approach to history can best be seen in Toynbee's treatment of the problem of "decline." Decline, it turns out, sets in whenever a civilization is unable to cope with the "challenges" that face it. In substance, however, this is as obvious as saying that men die when their bodies prove unable to fulfill their organic functions. The real questions as regards both men and civilizations are: *which* functions break down, and *why* do they at one moment rather than another? Toynbee offers no explicit or rational answer to these rather elementary questions. Throughout his work, he seems to explain every case of decline by the wickedness of the particular civilization at the stage when decline ensues, by some "sin" that it has committed. But in view of the terrible atrocities and crimes that have characterized the early, "rising" stages of every high civilization, our own Western one not excepted (see the early medieval *Penitentials*, which make one blush for the gross and wicked conduct they imply on the part of the ordinary man), how can it be said that periods of decline are intrinsically more "sinful" than others?

The decline of a civilization may indeed have something to do with sinfulness, but if so, it is with special *types* of "sin." The question to ask is why certain types of sin are connected with decline; put thus, the question might provide the starting point for a serious inquiry. Every time Toynbee comes across such an opportunity, however, he escapes into the doctrine of free will, which in this case is a veritable *asylum ignorantiae.* He contents himself with saying in effect that men sin because they sin, just as civilizations break down because they break down. This will do for a sermon, but not for a philosophy of history.

2. See Part III, ch. 3 below.

Toynbee's underlying assumption that in every situation there is but one good choice, which man has only to see and make, will cause modern economists (who stress the subjectivity of all economic choice) as well as modern theologians of all faiths (who stress the ambiguity and paradoxicality of all human action) to shudder. Of course, Toynbee may retort that both the economics and the theology of our day are wrong, but in that case let him *show* that they are wrong and really defend his own views.

I happen to think that the apparent "skepticism" and "subjectivism" of modern thought about man and his behavior contain new and important elements of truth. It turns out that the choice facing a human being who exercises free will is never between *one* good and *one* evil. In the first place, anything a man does not only affects his own moral character, but has consequences for many different sides of life: the family, the community, economics, politics, aesthetics, religion, etc.,etc., all at one and the same time. In the second place, the real difficulty of making a choice stems from the fact that every good involves its own evil, so that a choice is generally among different goods each of which entails some evil.

Towards the end of his work Toynbee addresses himself to the two great modern problems of war and unemployment. He abounds in good advice—e.g., unless we avoid war we shall all perish—but nothing more pertinent or concrete than that. What, again, he does not seem to realize is that the solution of major problems, now as in the past, requires us to make compromises; that we cannot choose between absolute good and absolute evil; that any effective steps we can possibly take against either war or unemployment must at best strike the perfectionist as half-measures. There is no help for it. A predominantly moralizing approach like Toynbee's to the difficulties of human existence means only to evade and dissemble the humiliating experience of one's ordinary human inadequacy—and to do this by riding the high horse of moral superiority to, and contempt for, one's fellow human beings.

The inescapable subjectivity, the ineluctable ambiguity of all human choice and action have a direct relevance to the problem of the rise and decline of civilizations—but a relevance that Toynbee's sermonizing obscures. A civilization is essentially a bundle of closely correlated beliefs and rules of conduct on the basis of which various communities act and interact. Now these beliefs and rules at bottom constitute social choices, and hence always lead to the adoption of one style of life to the exclusion of others. They may imply the rejection of whole areas of human possibility that in themselves are as justified or even more attractive than those actually adopted. But debate about this must be halted at some point or other in order to make the accepted rules valid and binding. To invest them with such validity, they are legitimized on a basis supposedly, but never really, unchallengeable.

The acceptance of conventions on the ground of a legitimization that is treated as unchallengeable is called traditionalism. All civilizations are traditional to some degree in their early stages: questionable rules of conduct are handed down unquestioningly from one generation to another. A civilization *emerges* precisely as such traditions are established; it rises as they are elaborated and as society is permeated by them. The traditions themselves arise under the pressure of disorder and disarray, for the emergence of most higher civilizations is presaged by the collapse of traditions left over from anterior high cultures and from the primitive tribal units in contact with them. Almost every civilization is born out of a "dark age" of chaos in which no rules of behavior are accepted as unquestionably valid.

The choosing of tradition rather than nontradition, of cut-and-dried rules rather than chaos, carries its own evil with it. All rules are ambiguous, all rules are inadequate, all rules exclude essential and valuable parts of human experience. Though, formally, tradition is rooted in some principle of legitimacy, in actuality it derives from the need to avoid chaos. That need decreases, however, in proportion to the success with which civilization fulfills its primary purpose of stabilizing a social order; and with the decrease of this need, greater and greater scope in questioning the social order is permitted. The very increase of social adjustment, by making the social processes and the "tissues" of society more complex, undermines that simplicity of basic conventions which alone gives social processes and tissues their firmness. A stage is reached at which the elements of disintegration get the upper hand, and a gradual loosening of tradition and of established rules sets in.

These forces of disintegration, far from being in the service of unbridled drives and urges, operate in obedience to a fuller truth and for the sake of a more exact social adjustment. They are indeed the very forces that, after a certain point, keep society and civilization moving. Without them there would be no human development, no history at all, but only changeless social stability and/or that passive surrender to new and hostile forces which we see in the case of some primitive, ossified societies upon whom more dynamic cultures impinge. Only at a very late stage in the development of a civilization, when tradition has been deeply and irreversibly undermined, do the drives formerly suppressed by rules of conduct break out into the open again; and it is in this phase that "moral" decline becomes a major factor in cultural change.

I think we can see now how the basic ambiguities of human existence, stressed in closely related terms by the social sciences on the one hand and by theology on the other, open a direct avenue to an understanding of the culture cycle. What appear in social science and theology as the innate limitations and ambiguities of the human condition, figure in history as the repetitive alternation of opposed attitudes. Toynbee himself has occasionally pointed out the occurrence of such an alternation—as, for instance, between an immanent and a transcendent God. Any number of similar alternations could be adduced. (It might even be argued—there isn't the space to go into this here—that on some fundamental questions, like the belief in survival after death, cultures seem to take views antithetical to those of the civilizations with which they are "affiliated," and under whose tutelage they are supposed to be.) The culture cycle as a whole might be described as an alternation between rigid traditionalism and tendencies to disruption and chaos. And history knows of no resting point in this up-and-down pattern.

Yet not all processes in history are repetitive, and attitudes that have been discarded tend to return, not unchanged, but on a "higher level"—enriched and deepened by new elements acquired during their period of discard.

Toynbee is right in calling our present age one of moral disintegration, but he never identifies the roots or specifies the future implications of our crisis. He does not seem to realize that disintegration is just as creative, if less pleasant, a process as integration, and that new civilizations can never arise without the disintegration of old ones—in other words, he fails to treat the matter historically. And he also fails to understand that the framework of a stable civilization cannot accommodate *all* human ends, and that some of the most important of human objectives cannot be attained without an intervening period of deep crisis. It is precisely to accommodate these realities that a theory of cultural affiliation has to be framed, and precisely in this respect that the culture cycle has universal meaning. But here as elsewhere Toynbee fails to show a firm grasp of his own theories. Cultural affiliation or no, he regards the disintegration of culture or civilization, wherever he finds it, as an entirely negative process, and here he agrees wholly with Spengler.

This comes out most conspicuously in Toynbee's angry rejection of modern technology. I myself heard him say, at an Anglo-American historical conference in 1935, that the ancient Greeks had already achieved all that could profitably be done in the line of material civilization, and that our own modern technology was one big mistake from first to last. His argument was, of course, nothing but a play upon the ambiguous sense of the word "material," which means two entirely different things when applied to ancient Hellas and to modern Western civilization.

All civilizations have striven for greater knowledge about nature and man. But the West alone has to its credit truly gigantic achievements in the department of rational, useful knowledge. These achievements, how-ever, have been paid for by an unprecedented cultural crisis that may threaten the very existence of mankind. The West's accomplishments in scientific knowledge came almost entirely in the later stages of its his-torical development, when skepticism, rationalism, and antitradition-alism abounded, and when there was a decline in positive religion and inherited moral standards. Does it follow, then, that the first, tradition-bound phase of our own or any other civilization is to be judged as better than our intensely modern and advanced one? This is what Toynbee seems to imply, but the implication has only to be stated to be rejected.

Higher civilizations, I noted a short while back, almost always arise out of barbaric ages whose chaotic disintegration and paranoiac savagery make the reshaping and reestablishment of tradition an overwhelming necessity. According to Toynbee, barbaric or "heroic" ages are good for nothing except the production of epic poetry. Nevertheless, where there is a relatively weak infusion of barbaric influence into a newborn civi-lization, the result is usually insufficient cultural vitality. Obviously, close contact with barbaric peoples can prove invaluable to a civilization in its first stages.

Eastern Orthodox Christianity offers the classic example of a civili-zation that suffered because insulated too soon from contact with non-civilized peoples. Nothing could have been a more potent agent of re-juvenation for a moribund civilization than the newly fledged Christianity of the Middle East. Yet Byzantium, the heir of Rome, was incapable of exploiting this historical chance to the full. Once barbarian influences from beyond the Jordan and other border areas had been warded off and suppressed, the Eastern Roman Empire stiffened into a rigidity out of which it never stirred. And Islam, the illegitimate child of Byzantium, soon followed the same course.

The "second generations" of both the original Chinese and Indian civilizations experienced a similar premature ossification. True, as the centers of these civilizations moved steadily southward they moved into barbarian territory; but at the same time they moved away from the more vigorous barbarian pressure on their northern confines. Meeting relatively little barbarian resistance in their southward migration, both "affiliated" civilizations soon fell into a stagnation like the Byzantine. On the other hand, where there were large-scale, vigorous barbarian invasions, like that of Greece by the Dorian tribes, or where the center of a culture was transplanted to the homeland of the invading barbarians, as happened with both the ancient Hebrew and the modern Western societies, the ultimate result was a civilization more creative than most others.

Barbarian peoples, whose primitive cultures are almost always in a process of disintegration by the time they appear within the ken of history, cannot but be deeply affected by the higher civilizations with which they come in contact. And history shows that the permanence of barbarism is not the real threat to civilization—barbarism being almost everywhere a passing phase—but the paralysis and stagnation of civilization itself. Such stagnation is not effectively dispelled where the heirs of an old and high civilization can achieve quick and overwhelming cultural ascendancy over barbarian neighbors and "converts"; when that happens, the old, exhausted forms of faith and life are able to reassert themselves before experiencing an access of vitality from the younger peoples on which they are imposed. It would seem that the emergence of a strong new civilization in the "second generation" or later depends on the intrusion of energetic barbarian peoples, secure in their own homelands, who in the course of many centuries imbibe the spirit and transform the ways of the older civilization or civilizations to which their culture affiliates.

If it can be said that the Western is probably the most vigorous of all civilizations since the river valley ones of the "first generation" in Egypt, Mesopotamia, and China, this is certainly due to the great part played in its development by barbarian peoples who stayed put in their homelands in Northwestern Europe. Western Christianity could not have become the powerful, vital religion it did without drinking at that source. (To avoid common misunderstandings, let me say that when I speak of "Northern barbarians" I have in mind such figures as Charlemagne and William the Conqueror, not agitators from the slums of modern big cities, like Hitler—who exploited a new-fangled and entirely mythical barbarian "Past" to justify his gangsterism.)

The part played by barbarians in the affiliating of new civilizations with old ones is as repetitive a phenomenon as the culture cycle itself. One can sum it up by saying that "affiliations are the more successful the greater the extent to which they take place in a barbarian milieu."

Toynbee's rejection of this view has involved him from the start in a number of astonishingly oblique interpretations. The oddest was his attempt to extract Sparta (and with it, by implication, the Doric core of the Hellenic world) from the context of Hellenic civilization and treat it as a separate, "arrested civilization"; yet Sparta was obviously a residual survival of the earliest, most decisive age of Hellas, and retained the vitality to play a crucial role throughout its climactic phase.

Toynbee hardly does much better when he treats the early medieval civilizations of Ireland and Scandinavia as "abortive" but independent cultural units. Admittedly, the different historical elements that go to make up any civilization are at first more or less independent of one another. The ultimate relation of these elements to the new culture arising from their fusion must depend in the first place on their individual share in creating it. Now it seems plain that much of what makes up Western as opposed to Eastern Christianity is of Irish origin; nothing but a stubborn blindness to the importance of barbarian influences in the emergence of new civilizations could have led to neglect of this essential fact. As for Scandinavia, it is not the Old Norse literature and religion, so beloved of the Nazis, that form its essential contribution to emergent Western civilization; these features of Old Norse culture must be considered rather as survivals of a pre-Western Germanic stage of development that was preserved in Scandinavia longer than in Germany and was able to reach fuller maturity there because of Scandinavia's greater distance from the Christianized parts of Europe. What was crucial to Scandinavia's relations with the rest of Western Europe was the unmatched role the Vikings played in the creation of the modern Western state: first through the centralized government of Normandy, then through the establishment of the Kingdom of Scotland and the conquest of England, and finally through the conquest of Sicily, where a momentous merger of Eastern and Northern systems of government took place. To shut the Vikings out of the political history of Europe is tantamount to eliminating its intelligible frame of reference. Needless to say, once Western civilization had broken out of the chrysalis state, it reacted upon the Irish and Scandinavian elements that had helped bring it to life, and eventually drew them into its own orbit.

These examples raise the more general problem of the role of geographical areas in the emergence and later history of a high civilization. Though a full discussion of this would exceed the limits of the present article, it can be stated as a general law that areas destined to become altogether marginal in the later stages of a civilization usually play a dominant part during its creative phase—the period when it does not yet possess a cultural center of gravity. Thus such border regions as Thessaly and Crete were of focal importance to prehistorical Hellas.

Geographically, the genesis of a civilization usually consists in the invasion of forces from outside that finally converge and become concentrated in one or more centrally located areas. These areas, generally, start out as border regions, lying between the domains of an older civilization and those inhabited by the barbarian peoples who now infuse the civilization with their vital energy. Thus all three cradle areas of Western civilization—Normandy, Lorraine, and Burgundy—were places where Latinized influences met and cross-bred with Germanic ethnic and cultural elements. The same cross-breeding defines the relation between the Indus and the Ganges valley cultures in the "second" Indian civilization; between lowlands and plateau cultures in both the pre-Columbian civilizations; between North and South in Mesopotamian civilization; and so on.

If adequate weight is given to this recurrent fact, a clear pattern for the culture cycle begins to define itself. During the prenatal phase of a "second generation," or affiliated, civilization, two important but separate areas are involved, one the homeland of the anterior, parent civilization, the other the homeland of the barbarians who threaten it. When the civilization is finally born, a new cultural center usually materializes in the borderland between the two, and the further history of the civilization tends to be marked by an alternation of cultural and political dominance between the two areas.

Thus the constant struggle for preponderance between North and South is an obtrusive feature of the history of the West. In the beginning the regions fairly close to the northern limits of our civilization predominated; gradually the center of gravity moved southwards until it came to rest, in the 15th and 16th centuries, in Southern Europe. The original trend in the West, therefore, would appear to have been away from the homeland of the former barbarians to that of the old, parent civilization. Then, however, a fierce reaction set in—the Reformation, which led to a large-scale breaking away of the old barbarian countries from their cultural servitude to the South. Once this partial cultural schism had been achieved, the old barbarian domains reasserted their political leadership and the center of political power again moved northward—to turn westward across the Atlantic in our day.

The swing back toward the old barbarian lands has usually coincided with a great crisis such as seems to have marked the middle of every culture cycle, and in which the shifting of the center is as a rule compelled by a religious upheaval—e.g., the Reformation or Islam. In such an upheaval, the different cultural and spiritual inclinations of the recently civilized barbarians reassert themselves against the traditions of the older cultures to which the barbarians had submitted during the early development of the particular civilization. In the Islamic "movement," a genuinely Oriental attitude took the field against the half-Hellenized Orientalism of Byzantium; during the Reformation, a Germanic belief in destiny, clothed in the doctrine of predestination, asserted itself against Roman Catholic Hellenism.

These geographical shifts are, of course, tied up with the rise and decline of a civilization, but even more intimately and decisively with the profound, pivotal crisis that seems to overtake every civilization around the middle of its life-span—a crisis arising precisely from the fact that a "second generation" civilization tends to be a symbiosis of two vastly different elements. In connection with this point, the story of the Renaissance and the Reformation in the West throws much light on the history of Byzantium and Islam. Though these last constitute the field most congenial to Toynbee and the one wherein he lays claim to being an expert in his own right, it is the field in which he fails most signally. Whatever else one may say about his relation to Spengler, his debacle here must be laid to his neglect of the findings of his predecessor.

With some justification, Toynbee advances the idea of a "Syriac" civilization that arose between Sinai and the upper Tigris in the second half of the second millennium B.C., finding its main political expression in Assyria and its "universal state" in the Persian Empire of the Achaemenians. One might conclude that Alexander's conquests and the ensuing Hellenization of the Middle East marked the death of this civilization and the emergence of a new affiliated civilization from the fusion of the East and Hellas. But this would introduce the notion of a double parentage, which we have seen that Toynbee implicitly repudiates. He prefers a different conclusion: that, with Alexander, the Syriac civilization, far from dying, went into a deep slumber that lasted for a thousand years and reawakened when the 'Abassid Caliphs defeated the Omayyads and moved the capital of the Caliphate from Damascus to Baghdad in 740 A.D. The Syriac civilization's new lease on life lasted until 1922, when the rump of the Ottoman Empire was secularized—and not even this late date marks its conclusive end.

Why, however, should the Syriac provide the only known example of a civilization's capacity to hibernate? If this is hibernation, then one can discover similar cases elsewhere: how the Indus civilization slept until it reemerged as the "Indic" or classical Indian civilization, only to doze off again and reemerge a second time as the Hindu civilization; how Hellenism slept until it awoke transformed into Western Christianity; how Mayan culture fell into a slumber before reawakening as the Toltec-Aztec culture; and so on and so on. In other words, the Syriac civilization offers a typical example of the process Toynbee describes as "affiliation," but for the sake of a romantic whim, he makes it an exceptional case.

Yet Spengler, too, sensed something untypical in the history of the Middle East. In his view, the Middle Eastern civilization that he calls "Arabic," and Toynbee "Syriac," never fell asleep, but for centuries wore the mask of Hellenism. To cover this situation, Spengler devised the term "pseudomorphosis." This was meant to express the fact that the overwhelming formal strength of Hellenic tradition, which survived the death of Hellenic civilization itself, prevented the Arabic world from realizing itself naturally and natively; instead, it was compelled to cast its utterly un-Hellenic thoughts and feelings in Hellenic molds. This, according to Spengler, explains the fierce reaction when at long last the Arabic world found its own indigenous expression in the form of Islam.

The concurrence of two minds as different as those of Spengler and Toynbee in finding an exceptional character in Middle Eastern history suggests the existence of truly exceptional objective circumstances in Arabic-Syriac society. These circumstances—they are not really unique but only rather infrequent—are revealed by a comparison of the Middle Eastern culture cycle with that of Western civilization. Normandy, Lorraine, Burgundy, and Saxony—only a short time out of barbarism or else newly barbarized—were the dominant areas of the West in the earliest phase of its culture cycle. By contrast, the Middle East, in the earlier phases of its culture cycle, was dominated not by such half-barbarian areas as Iraq, let alone Arabia proper, but by Antioch, Alexandria, and Byzantium—its most Hellenized centers. But the preponderance of the barbaric element in the early evolution of Western civilization, and the contrasting preponderance of Hellenism in the early stages of Middle Eastern civilization, confront us with a relative, not an absolute, difference.

What is present in both situations is the merging of two old civilizations in a barbarian setting. If in the Middle East the old culture area predominated, and in the West the old barbarian one, the reason for the difference is not far to seek. The barbarian setting in which the Middle Eastern civilization arose was the same disadvantageous one that Byzantium, the civilization of Eastern Christianity, had to cope with; and when, with Mohammed, its original Arabic elements erupted to the surface of Middle Eastern civilization and took control of it, it was at a late stage in its development. Spengler's term "pseudomorphosis" is not adequate for the analysis of this historical process, and Toynbee's theory of "hibernation" is even less so.

But Spengler, unaware of Toynbee's "sleeping beauty" theory, at least kept a firm grasp on the essential unity of the whole historical phase that began with the Roman Empire and ended in a new barbarization following the fall of the 'Abassid Caliphate in the 12th century. Lacking Toynbee's compulsion to insist on the notion of a final "universal church," Spengler—to my mind, correctly—identified Islam as, at bottom, a Christian heresy.

We did not know in Spengler's time, as we do today, that Mohammed gleaned his basic ideas neither from Orthodox Christianity nor Orthodox Judaism, but from the Ebionites, a residual Judeo-Christian sect. Nonetheless, in the Christian heresy of Monophysitism there lay a clear connecting link between Orthodox Christianity and Islam; with this evidence in hand, Spengler was able to discern in the rise of Islam a fairly exact parallel with the rise of Protestantism in the Western world. And he also saw a similar analogy between the rise of Assyria in the 9th century B.C. and the pivotal change in Hellenic civilization at the end of the 6th century B.C.—a parallel he also drew with pivotal moments halfway in the evolution of other civilizations.

Finally, if the geographical plan of the Arabic civilization was untypical in the beginning, it was not so later on—the emergence of Islam in its second phase made it conform to the standard pattern by shifting the cultural center to an area that had previously been the homeland of barbarians. Yet insofar as the post-Alexandrian civilization of the Middle East attained its "natural" geographical plan only with the triumph of Islam, its previous geographical structure must be considered an aberration, and Spengler's coinage of the term "pseudomorphosis" to describe it has some justification.

In the final stages of their respective interpretations of Middle Eastern civilization, Spengler and Toynbee again converge, only quickly to separate once more, and in the most dramatic way. Spengler, owing perhaps to his systematic effort to isolate and define the individual identity of each civilization, was generally ahead of Toynbee in analyzing the political structures of civilizations in their own terms. Such obvious features as the role of the *polis* in Hellas and of the nation-state in the West assumed for him the status of major symbols setting off the respective civilization from all others. Within this context, Spengler discovered that, for the post-Alexandrian civilization of the Middle East, the religious community, usually in the form of a church, played the political role assigned to the *polis* in Hellas and to the nation-state in the West. Here he concurred in the main with Toynbee, who insisted on the basic importance of the *millet* system of communal organization in the Near and Middle East.

Yet once again at this juncture Toynbee, having barely announced his own formulation, proceeds to disregard it. If the *millet* is the counterpart of the "parochial" political units of other civilizations—and what else can it be?—it should follow that the sum total of the *millets* of the Middle East formed the body and political substance of the post-Alexandrian civilization of the region. This view was consistently adhered to by Spengler, who regarded Orthodox Christianity, Monophysitism, Nestorianism, Talmudic Jewry, Sunnitic and Shi'itic Islam, etc., as the "nations" of the post-Alexandrian culture area and culture cycle. (This idea, incidentally, seems to me to be Spengler's most relevant contribution to the study of history, far surpassing in value the more general notions of his system.)

Toynbee, on the other hand, in one of those illogical reversals which characterize his whole work, suddenly, after having asserted that the *millet* system defines the political order of Syriac civilization, turns around and proceeds to treat each *millet* community as a separate civilization. Thus we are presented with Orthodox Christian, Nestorian Monophysite, Judaic, Sunnite, and Shi'ite *civilizations* (why Toynbee does not extend the classification to the Druzes, Maronites, and numberless other sects scattered through Syria and the Lebanon, I do not know). Spengler's signal insight, that this whole welter of religious communities expressed various aspects of one and the same cultural current, is discarded by Toynbee, who thus creates the greatest confusion in the field where he is supposed to be most expert. . . .

In sum, however, the basic objection to Toynbee's treatment of the culture cycle—his main subject—is that he does not sufficiently investigate the factors which, taken together, constitute its actual dynamics. The formula of "challange and response," however unobjectionable in itself, is far too abstract and general to cover even the most elementary problems of cultural development. Fundamentally a biological notion, it cannot furnish the key to any of the special problems of the subject in hand. Rather, it permits Toynbee to evade them all by easy references to "free will,"

My own observations in this article do not pretend to any finality. I shall be satisfied if they have given the reader some sense of the vastness of the problems implicit in any study of the culture cycle and of the general forms under which civilizations arise and develop. And I shall be satisfied if my remarks have conveyed a notion of the great gaps that remain in both Spengler's and Toynbee's elucidation of even the more elementary aspects of the subject.

CHAPTER THREE

The Antinomy of Death and the Culture Generations

The thesis tentatively outlined in this paper is that the self-contradictory experience of death is a basic element in shaping the course of human history; that the conflicting attitudes towards death traceable in the individual are equally at work within every human culture, and in the relationships between historic civilizations; that changes in the popular attitudes towards death mark great epochs of historical evolution; and that their study can serve as a guide to some problems of the philosophy of history.

The Antinomy in the Individual

Much has been altered, or at least ought to have been altered, in our thinking about death by Freud's terse dictum: *the unconscious is immortal.* In all previous philosophy, perhaps excepting only Spinoza, the idea of immortality had appeared as something secondary: a result of revelation to the believer, of metaphysical speculation for the dualist, of imagination misled by the impulse to self-preservation to the skeptic. Awareness of the inevitability of death was thought to be deeply embedded in the human mind, and the belief in immortality seemed a facile and illusory attempt to veil it. Freud himself, forgetful of his own more profound insights, was in later years to dismiss such beliefs as "nursery tales." Yet

This chapter is the editor's condensation of an essay in English and a posthumously published manuscript in German, dealing in a different way with the same ideas. See Appendix I, "The Sources and their Handling."

his basic statement on the subject stands and has been strengthened by later psychoanalytical investigations: according to those, apparent fear of death is viewed as a phobia based on unconscious fears that are not really directed to death and have only been "shifted" to it as an external object of consciousness. Like any phobia it should be curable, whereas the sense of immortality cannot be eradicated, either by rational argument or by experience of the death of others. Though we know empirically that all others must die, we can apply that insight to ourselves only intellectually, since man cannot have an inner awareness of a world of which he himself would not be the central point of reference. In the light of this reversal of the generally accepted view, immortality appears, psychologically speaking, more certain than death itself; its idea becomes— in Freud's treatment—something primary, preceding all experience and all thought, hence—as we may continue his argument—something inborn and phylogenetically acquired, an archetype. Its conflict with the knowledge of death is thus inescapable, a deep antinomy given with the existence of man which he cannot avoid, as atheists were inclined to believe, by simply "rejecting" the faith in immortality.

It is all the more remarkable that Freud himself decisively clung to his rejection of that faith, without realizing the self-contradiction in which he involved himself by calling it a nursery tale. This blindness becomes even more striking in view of the close link between the statement about the immortality of the unconscious and other elements of the Freudian doctrine. In a closely related context, I have pointed to Freud's theory of the "timelessness" of the unconscious.[1] Just like immortality, this timelessness is by no means part of the content of the unconscious, but of its given phylogenetic structure. But it is obvious that timelessness and immortality are linked almost to the point of being identical, for mortality is finiteness in time and impossible without the category of time. In the paper just mentioned, I also undertook a critical examination of Freud's thesis of the "strict determinacy" of the unconscious, seeking to show that he had mistakenly transposed this latter concept from mechanics into psychology and that in pyschic processes, both conscious and unconscious, we are never dealing with causality but only with finality, as is confirmed by the very principles underlying psychoanalytic procedure.

But timelessness, noncausality, and immortality together amount to "substantiality"—a form of "being" resting in itself outside the conditions of spatio-temporal "existence." As such a being the soul experiences

1. See Part I, ch. 5 below.

itself in its innermost essence. Those are qualities which, in Kantian language, belong to the *Ding an Sich* and not to the phenomenon; and the full weight of Freud's discoveries becomes obvious from the insight that there exists, after all, no such absolute barrier between the "thing in itself" and empirical experience as earlier philosophy stipulated. To characterize such "substantiality" as an illusion appears even more questionable than the rejection of the belief in immortality alone. Still, an attempt at defending that position might yet be made unless its last bastion, the belief in the validity of the system of spatio-temporal and causal categories in the field of external phenomena, had collapsed—but just this is known to have happened during the last two generations. In my above-cited paper, I tried to show that subatomic physics is moving towards precisely the same nonspatial, nontemporal, noncausal system of categories as is depth psychology. The correspondence of the new systems of categories sprung from totally different fields guarantees their objective reality. Thus the collapse of the mechanistic view of the world brings us in contact with a layer of being which the metaphysicians of all times have striven to know, and the mystics of all times have experienced in brief moments of ecstasy. Correspondingly, the conflict between the experience of death and the certainty of immortality is not a conflict between an empirically known sad truth and a deceptively beautiful illusion of the unconscious—it is a conflict between two realities.

But why a conflict? If death is a necessary element of finite existence, while immortality belongs in the realm of transcendent being, why should they clash? But the painful experience of the clash of both types of experience cannot be circumvented by an abstract separation of the two underlying layers of reality. To understand that, a critique of Freud's teaching about the idea of death is necessary. It is obviously wrong that the fear of death is merely a phobia like any other. Not all human beings are phobics and not all phobics suffer from the same phobia—but all men know the fear of death. Here, too, Freud's blindness is striking—a blindness which he rarely showed in the purely psychological field, but each time he came into the remotest contact with the transcendent. After all, he himself had been the first to describe the "complex" which directly leads to a critique of his view, but has failed to utilize it for the problem of death. We are speaking of something as closely linked to death as birth, of the "birth trauma." This trauma consists in the danger and fear of suffocation which every embryo experiences during birth. That experience remains anchored in the unconscious: it has given the impulse to normal breathing and perpetuates itself in the lifelong effort of breathing.

Death, then, again typically consists in a failure of heart and lungs, thus once more in suffocation. All human beings experience the fear of death as a fear of suffocation (heart throb, shortness of breath). The fear of death thus does not represent other fears that have been "shifted" to death by an illusion, but a completely realistic if unconscious linking up between the anxiety lived through at birth and that to be expected in death. To use psychoanalytic terminology, the fear of death, while it may in some circumstances be pathologically increased to a phobia, is basically a completely "real fear." It is a type of experience *sui generis*, which is hardly surprising since only birth and death are not, properly speaking, experiences in life but events comprising life.

The birth trauma is an experience of the individual—his first. The anxiety acquired through this trauma thus, in contrast to the certainty of immortality, is not one of the collective archetypes, but the deepest layer of the acquired part of the unconscious. Yet this description is incomplete. Birth anxiety could not be transformed as early and insistently into fear of death unless that transformation was preformed phylogenetically, i.e., archetypically. The knowledge of death is thus located on the border between the phylogenetically and the ontogenetically acquired parts of the unconscious.

Freud knew, however, that the fear of death is not death's only representative in the human psyche. Having in the course of his therapeutic work encountered a mute aversion to recovery, which could not be explained as an individually acquired neurotic trait, and finding this congenital resistance in some manner remotely linked to masochism, aggression, and the destructive impulse generally, he advanced the hypothesis of an ever present, yet ever silent "death instinct" with roots going deeper than the experience of the individual—a self-destructive impulse ultimately governing the individual's lifelong approach to death. But since this supposed death instinct could not be traced directly as an unconscious wish, it was described as "metapsychological"—a point of view soon to be sharply questioned among Freud's followers. At present it seems to be generally admitted that the term "death wish" or "death instinct" is at any rate a misnomer, since wishes plainly do belong to the realm of psychology. In fact, however, Freud seems to have hinted at something more clearly, because less psychologically, stated by certain modern philosophers: the presence of death as a motive force behind all forms of human activity and as an inherent goal of all human striving.

This is as profound an insight as Freud's statement concerning the immortality of the unconscious. Each reflects a basic aspect of the human situation, though they are mutually exclusive. It is then scarcely surprising that their proponents seem at a loss to synthesize the contradictions arising from their respective discoveries.

To turn to a discussion of our *knowledge* of death, we must move from the unconscious to consciousness. We saw that the unconscious knows only the *fear* of death. Its transformation to a certainty of death belongs—in sharpest contrast to the certainty of immortality—to consciousness, even though the latter links up also in this regard with the archetypically preformed experience of the species. All the same: certainty of death is only acquired gradually by teaching and external experience, in the course of aging probably also by the internal experience of one's own organic wear and tear. With regard to the certainty of death, as distinct from the fear and anticipating expectation of death, Freud was undoubtedly right. He was right also on another point: the emotions due to fear of death which "sabotage" the recognition of the certainty of death are supported by the fact that death is unimaginable to man not only for emotional reasons—though the Ego may be thought away, it may not be eliminated in imagination (it is still I who thinks it away). Nor can it in imagination be removed from the spatio-temporal context in which it exists and experiences itself. This nonimaginability of the absence of the Ego, fundamental for human self-knowledge, quite naturally serves the death-denying emotion, and the understanding of this link led Freud to the conclusion (that suited him anyhow) that belief in immortality was a "nursery-tale." Yet he himself had proved that this belief was by no means a mere product of emotions but an element of the unconscious given before all self-consciousness! Hence man's attitude to death moves in a circle of insoluble antinomies: death is and also is not.

The foundations of the certainty of immortality are of a quite different kind from those of the certainty of death, but the result is rather similar in both cases. The certainty of immortality is neither individually acquired nor can it be confirmed by experience; it thus appears at first sight as a pure archetype, similar to the "primal symbols." But this is not really true. Those primal symbols filling so large a part of our dream-world and poetry are products partly of the evolution of the human species and partly even of the evolution of man's animal ancestors. Nothing of the kind applies to the certainty of immortality. Though animals know the fear of death, they surely have no trace of a certainty of immortality, hence the latter cannot be derived "genealogically." Rather, the contrast points to that certainty as to a direct representative of transcendence, of eternal being, in the human soul. Psychologically, one would therefore have to describe it as "pre-archetypal" in contrast to the "post-archetypal" knowledge of death.

It would be facile to assume that this pre-archetypal certainty of immortality and the post-archetypal knowledge of death are in insoluble conflict from the beginning. But things are not so simple. The unconscious knows no negation, let alone the exclusion of contradictions: there, each idea stands alone in absolute validity. Before the certainty of immortality and the knowledge of death can clash, *both* must have entered consciousness. How this occurs with regard to death we have discussed. What about the certainty of immortality? At this point, the greatest surprise awaits the questioner. The depth psychologist is accustomed to encounter the products of the unconscious in consciousness only in a shape distorted by conflict and repression in their main contents. But the certainty of immortality seems directly to enter consciousness—similar to the certainty of death, but more intact and free from conflict than the latter.

On closer examination, the matter proves to be far less miraculous than it seems at first sight. It simply is misleading to use the same term "the unconscious" both for the individually acquired unconscious and for the collective archetypes. The individually acquired contents of the unconscious remain unconscious because they are associated with displeasing sentiments and have therefore been repressed. The archetypes can in their nature have no such displeasing associations nor underlie the typical mechanism of repression—hence they are not unconscious in the same sense and suffer no distortion when entering consciousness. (It was this fact that made them so attractive for the school of Jung in its effort to deny the *repressed* unconscious!) The same primal symbols which flood the manifest content of dreams are also encountered in poetry: only where they hint at repressed experiences of the individual, that context is also repressed. Otherwise, their function is to unveil rather than to veil. And what is true of the primal symbols is a thousand times true of the pre-archetypal unconscious certainty of immortality: it is based on no experience of the individual or the species, is not linked with painful ideas, is rather a blissful conception giving meaning to life. Why should it be repressed? Thus it sees the light of consciousness as the same conviction, which it bases in the profound archetypes of the collective unconscious. It thus appears as the least changeable part of the soul.

And yet this certainty of immortality is not free from inner contradictions. Though it is not, like the knowledge of death, linked to negative emotions from the beginning—quite the contrary—it is similar to death knowledge in its existential nature. The latter, we saw, led into contradictions because one's own death is both certain and unimaginable. On a different foundation, exactly the same applies to the certainty of immortality: as with death, we may *think* immortality and may think it correctly, as a form of being outside time. But we cannot *imagine* anything outside time; even immortality we can only imagine as an existence of infinite duration *within* time. Out of this magic circle no way leads back to the true infinity of being. Empty time may be thought, but not imagined, just like absence of time. The idea of an infinite existence in this-worldly time is therefore filled with other, not conceptually necessary features of a this-worldly life that is merely infinitely extended and thus is immersed in all the rational and emotional relations of this life, unitl immortality appears as a poor duplicate of this world in which merely some arbitrarily chosen features of the latter, such as corporality, are absent. Rationally, immortality thus becomes absurd, emotionally it becomes a defense against death fear and death certainty and thus gets involved in all the deeply emotion-laden contradictions which confound the magic circle of death knowledge. It is part of the human condition that this confusion, just like that surrounding death, can be overcome in thought but not be eliminated in imagination and experience: it is the very shape that being assumes inescapably once it is immersed in human existence.

Ultimately we are thus dealing with a triple antinomy. Death, to the reality of which our innermost certainty testifies, is also unimaginable and thus appears as unreal; immortality, also affirmed by our innermost certainty, is equally unimaginable and also appears as unreal; and whichever of the two sides our intellect chooses in the conflict of each of these two contradictions, death and immortality remain incompatible for the imagination, because in its realm there always apply the conditions of existence, above all temporality, so that here death *can* only mean finite duration, immortality infinite duration of the soul *in time*. And yet, although we cannot simultaneously imagine death and immortality, we have an inner certainty of both.

The coexistence of incompatible inner experiences concerning the limitations of human life thus seems both inevitable and intolerable: one of the inherent antinomies of human existence, perhaps the most basic of all, which in denying tranquillity to man compels him to move restlessly from one halting-place to the next. The tension gives rise to an urge to eliminate one of the incompatibles; yet whichever one chooses, its opposite must reassert itself in the never-ending debate, since it is no less deeply rooted. From time to time the endless struggle gives rise to an attempted synthesis—always incomplete, since the underlying inner experiences can never be fully harmonized. Each synthesis, therefore, dissolves into the contradictions noted above, yet this state of affairs prepares the way for another attempted solution at a higher level, since the compulsion to overcome the basic antinomy is as real and powerful as the antinomy itself. It is one of the dominant powers in the existence and evolution of the individual as of humankind.

"Death Denial" in Primitive Cultures

We start our examination of the cultural effects of the antinomy with some remarks about prehistory. Here the fear that our understanding of religious origins may be impaired by the chance disappearance of material witness to spiritual processes is, I think, validly countered by the statement that purely spiritual developments do not occur. Whatever is basic in human existence has left some trace in tools or implements. Man is a toolmaker, and there cannot have been any human activity which left no material trace. If the remnants of the early Paleolithic do not include any evidence of cult or worship, we seem entitled to conclude that man was then actively concerned only with the satisfaction of his bodily needs.

Yet Oswald Menghin has taught us to rely on the observation of primitive cultures surviving in modern times where prehistoric materials are silent. The primitives of the present, hence—as we may conclude *a fortiori*—the people of prehistoric epochs, all reject more or less clearly the necessity of dying. Their fear of death is more intense than that of people in high cultures, for they are exposed to a thousand real dangers which we have surmounted and to a thousand other imaginary ones springing from their magical ideas. They also see that all old people die sooner or later. Objectively, the certainty of death ought to impress them therefore much more strongly than us. Nevertheless, they deny it and stay arrested at the stage of mere fear of death.

Even the late nineteenth century regarded that attitude merely as a symptom of intellectual backwardness, like Lévy-Bruhl in his study, *The Primitive Mind*. In the light of depth psychology, that view becomes untenable. Rather, such death denial is based on the close connection between fear of death and certainty of death and acts as a defense against the latter. Primitive man knows death much better than modern man, but in contrast to the latter knows nothing about the *necessity* of dying, because he does not *want* to know it. (Compare the similar circumstance that many primitive cultures deny the facts of human generation and conception, though they are well known to them in the context of the raising of livestock.)

The mechanism of such death denial consists in the sharp separation between the attitude to the death of others and to one's own death, as Freud has shown from the study of modern cases. That others must die seems to cause little worry—only oneself is, of course, immortal. If such mechanisms can still be found working in the unconscious of modern man, how much more sharply pronounced must they have been among the earliest primitives! Their death denial is shown, for instance, in their total indifference towards corpses. Throughout the early phase of the paleolithic, which probably lasted several hundreds of thousands of years, there are—despite a considerable evolution of tools—no traces of burial. The dead were left to decomposition and to the wild animals— they did not concern the living.

But by the middle paleolithic, beginning with the Moustérien, the first signs of a new attitude appear: graves. The first burials prove that the principle of material provision has now been extended to the dead. They, too, must now be covered and fed, later their livingness must be protected by painting them in the colors of life—in order that there be no death. Until that happened we may assume that man's mind floated vaguely between a dim awareness of death and the hope to escape it. The emergence of burial rites clearly suggests a sharpened consciousness of mortality: for burial rites are techniques designed to satisfy the sense of immortality by securing some form of post-mortem survival. It is a decisive historical step, presumably identical with the awakening of religious consciousness. Up to then, what corresponded to the death denial of the individual was only indifference towards the death of others. Now, the jolting of that denial produces a reaction that is important for world history—the first deliberate, socially sanctioned attempt to overcome death after it has taken place by preserving life in the tomb—to overcome the antinomy of death by assuring the victory of immortality over death!

But growing provision against death increases the conflict between the ever greater importance attached to death and the means of defense against it, and the obstinate denial of its more and more intensely experienced inevitability. Though the means employed in the most primitive types of burial are very ample compared with the poverty of the material goods available, they are ridiculous and entirely unconvincing compared to the reality of death, and the excessive expense announces what it is meant to hide—a nagging doubt about the effectiveness of all the efforts. The knowledge of death must have reached a high degree of inescapable terror before, say, a hunter used to keen observation can persuade himself that the corpse in the grave continues to be physically alive. Yet there was no choice: as long as the denial of death had not been finally abandoned, the dead had to be provided with all the attributes of continued physical life, and immortality had to be imagined as continued life in this world. The idea of a "beyond" remains deeply immersed in the categories of this world and linked to usages of patent absurdity. That way holds no relief from the antinomy: instead of denying only the one insight of the certainty of death, society now must deny also the second one that the buried body is finally dead. While the emotional content of death denial previously only concerned one's own death, it now comprises in the context of burial rites also that of the others. A decisive step forward, the breakthrough into consciousness of the certainty of immortality, is paid for with the severe step backward of the conscious generalization of death denial. Moreover, the entry into consciousness of the certainty of immortality also means its immersion into all the limitations of existence, hence confusion and the shaking of that certainty itself: what will happen to the dead if they are not fed and cared for?

Again, burial rites in primitive society, and to some extent in higher types of culture too, are directed towards a twofold goal: to keep the dead alive, and to keep them away. These incompatible aims also reflect the basic contradiction in the human attitude towards mortality: the rites intended to put the dead "to rest," to console them, to propitiate them, to avert their wrath, the numerous stringent taboos regarding contact with them and their graves, all presuppose that the dead are really alive— and dangerous. On the other hand, such ceremonial actions as the applications of paint to the bodies of the deceased, the provision of nourishment and tools for enclosure in the tomb, preservation of the bodies by certain techniques culminating in mummification, all suggest an effort to preserve life in the dead, on the assumption that otherwise the spark would die. There is no strict dividing line between these two aims, and there are rites, such as sacrifices performed at the tomb, which being propitiatory and preservatory combine both functions.

This shifting character of the attitude behind the rite of burial reflects a continuing uncertainty about the relation of death to life, a carryover from the old paleolithic mentality though qualified by clearer insights. One may ask: is the practice of ochre-painting the dead—characteristic of certain burial rites—intended to *symbolize* the continued biological existence of the departed? Or is it a *means* of depriving death of his victory over life? There certainly is no clear answer in the minds of those performing the ritual. In primitive tribal society we seem to be confronted with an infinite variety of burial rites, but also with an infinity of shades of meaning, not merely as between one culture and another but also as between individuals, and even as between individual occurrences of death and burial. Much of the late paleolithic ritual appears to reflect a somewhat firmer grasp of the inevitability of death, and consequently a growing elaboration of ideas of another life beyond the grave. But side by side with customs expressive of such ideas one frequently encounters what amounts to an assertion that man need not die. While on one side ever more scope is given to the reality principle in the control of external reality, people react to the pressure of advancing knowledge of death by getting further and further away from truth with regard to inner reality.

Where this happens, it tends to convert tribal society into a madhouse. Already the simple, subjective denial of death in the earliest times contained an element of delusion. That enhancement of the knowledge of death which is massively expressed in the invention of burial compels at the same time an enhancement of the delusion, an expansion of the psychotic core to a fully developed system of madness. The custom of burial itself leads to the systematization of the delusion by extending the death denial from each particular individual to all. It thus turns back on each particular individual: if burial pretends to assure an element of this-worldly immortality to all, the particular subject included, it demonstrates at the same time to all that every one must die one day. Only a generalized denial of the necessity of dying may now be opposed to an experience that can no longer be repressed. There arises the absurd conclusion: nobody needs die—death is exclusively the consequence of black magic.

The life of the tribe now centers not so much on the procurement of the necessities of existence as upon the search for witches who appear to threaten life much more than famine and disease. Whole tribes surrender to a general persecutory paranoia and the witch-hunt becomes their chief occupation. The dangers arising from such paranoia produce, as the price for sticking to death denial, a greatly increased risk of a drastic shortening of real life. We know today that the earliest man was a very harmless creature, living on berries and small animals. No doubt it was hunting that first moved him out of that "paradisiac" state of innocence. But the hunt was still a continuation of animal behavior with human tools. Later man is, however, the only living being that fights against its own species, outside the struggle for the females. The explanation of this primary trait of man as a social being by shortage of food is an artificially introduced materialist nonsense: the most primitive peoples stoically accept starvation and famine. Rather, it is almost compellingly plausible that the outbreak of murderous passions is closely connected with the breakthrough of the "death paranoia" which we just characterized as *opposing man to man as enemies.*

This applies with unmistakable certainty to cannibalism, so characteristic for the early phase of the murderous rage, and the analogous custom of head-hunting, which are both known to serve exclusively the purpose of appropriating the life-threatening magical qualities of the enemy, with the additional advantage that devouring is a method—and within the realm of those ideas really the only method—to assure that the enemy is really stone dead. Compared with those simple forms of "working out" the death paranoia, the more refined means used by neolithic cultures for "witch-smelling" appear as highly civilized. But the denial of death invariably goes with a socially organized persecutory paranoia, and while it rarely occurs in a pure form it is hardly ever completely absent from primitive cultures, since it corresponds best to the unconscious sense of immortality.

Five Theses on the Sequence of High Cultures

1. Each high culture starts with a myth stressing one side of the antinomy of death, and ends with a rationalization seeking to assert the opposite side. (Ancient Egypt began with the most magnificent unfolding of the belief in immortality—Ekhnaton ended with its total denial).

2. All high cultures of one "culture generation" are passing through the same cycle (Mesopotamia, Crete, and the Indus Culture show the same cycle as ancient Egypt, though in a much weakened form). The phases of the unfolding of the antinomy are thus tied not to individual cultures but precisely to those bundles of cultures, the culture generations.

3. Each successor culture ("affiliated civilization") begins with a primal myth corresponding in content to the rationalizations of the late phase of the preceding culture generation, and logically ends with a rationalization corresponding in content to the primal myth of the preceding culture.

4. Between successive cultures or culture generations, there frequently lie barbaric phases, characterized by a partial relapse into the death paranoia of the late stone age. But the inversion between the preceding and succeeding cultures described in thesis 3 with regard to the content of the antinomy of death takes place as if no such barbaric interlude had intervened.

5. Within the history of high cultures, the death antinomy runs through a cycle comprising two culture generations, starting from "death transcendence" and passing through "death acceptance" back to death transcendence.

The Rise of Death Transcendence in the Great River Civilizations

On the threshold of the high cultures, the analogy with primitive tribes surviving in the present can no longer help us: there is no present culture that would correspond to the state of primitive cultures at the moment of their transition into the first high Cultures, the great river civilizations of Egypt, Mesopotamia, and the Indus Valley. We have to rely on historical sources—but those are still quite inadequate for the critical transitional stage, the "predynastic" and early dynastic phase of those river cultures. Only the Pyramid texts and analogous Sumerian sources yield information of the kind needed in our context—but in them, we encounter no longer the beginnings of the high culture but its first climax.

We thus know next to nothing about the end of the persecutory paranoia of the last primitive stage. We merely know that in the course of the decisive millennium of transition, the fourth before Christ, paranoia radically lost its central role in the spiritual life, even though it did not disappear completely. The emergent first type of higher civilizations does not mark the end of death denial, but it corresponds to significant changes in the underlying assumptions. The burial rites disclosed in the Pyramid texts still imply Pharaoh's direct ascent to heaven without passage through death; but Pharaoh, although human, is also a god, and genuine immortality is now vouchsafed only to demigods, such as rulers and heroes. The paranoiac witch-hunt of the death-denying tribe has thus become superfluous, for Pharaoh is certain of direct immortality (and so are, though somewhat less explicitly, his Sumerian royal opposites) while all his subjects are equally certain of extinction. Mortality is socially stratified—perhaps the only point where religion and society are wholly merged. In part this stratification relates to the more powerful "mana" of the ruler, in part to his greater material means for obtaining adequate burial. The aristocracy, too, although excluded from direct immortality, can through mummification achieve a species of immortality after death. Only the fellah, unable to arrange for adequate burial and unknown to the gods, is denied all hope of an afterlife.

On this basis we see a new, no longer paranoiac culture, comprising in urban agglomerations and a centralized bureaucratic state incomparably larger communities than ever before and spurring them to achievements never before envisaged. We understand that this comparatively sudden jump from small tribe to great state, from agriculture and livestock raising to the planning of magnificent projects would not have been possible unless the universal, self-destructive persecutory mania separating man from man had been overcome. We also understand, despite the absence of historical documents, the main factor in the process of the overcoming of that mania. The young high cultures are distinguished from even the highest primitive cultures by the fact that they accept the certainty of death, thus uprooting the delusion that every death was due to black magic and at the same time liberating an incalculable amount of psychic energy that had hitherto been used up by the struggle against the realization of the certainty of death. That energy is now flooding into the great effort of building the high culture: a great sacrifice, probably the greatest ever made by man in his history, was not made in vain. Recognition of the necessity of dying shows to man, in a degree not hitherto imaginable, the way to an improvement of this world, and within this effort specifically to the perfection of substitute satisfactions for the finally abandoned belief in an eternity down here. It is no accident that the rise of great art dates from that decision, and that art is linked so closely with the hitherto unknown striving for posthumous fame. In turn, provision for material existence becomes the basic principle of the newly created hydraulic bureaucracies and attains a scale never before imagined.

The revolution in the conditions of existence linked to the acceptance of the certainty of death affects ideas about life after death rather less than most other realms. The basic principle of preserving the dead body in the grave as if he were alive is taken over from the late primitive stages and merely perfected, like other fields of activity, by the rapid increase in technical competence: absurd procedures like ochre-painting are replaced by scientific methods of preservation culminating in mummification. A share of total social labor that is still incredibly large by modern standards is devoted to tomb building and tomb cults—a symptom of the still felt pain of the only recent renunciation of the faith in immediate, this-worldly immortality.

Yet, the consequences of that effort are quite unexpected. The preservative effect of primitive burial rites might have been credible up to a point, as long as nothing else was known or feasible. But the early stage of the high cultures invents deliberately organized material progress, striving from summit to summit of technical perfection. As it devalues the primitive in general, it also devalues the ancient methods for keeping the dead body alive; how could an expert on mummification feel anything but contempt for a practitioner of ochre-painting? But the very devaluation of the primitive substitutes for aliveness raises the question of what kind of substitutes would really be sufficient: is the mummy really more alive than decayed bones? The tremendous breakthrough of the reality principle, expressed in the new control over nature and society, cannot arbitrarily be stopped at any point—not even at the edge of the grave.

The problem is immensely sharpened by the new structure of society. Primitive societies know only rudimentary class differences (apart from a mild form of slavery). The early river civilizations are based on the extreme exacerbation of those differences. Mummification is a privilege of a thin upper stratum, big tomb buildings that of a tiny group of kings and territorial lords. But if doubt begins to arise even with regard to those highest techniques of preservation, it is completely obvious that all those who cannot afford those techniques are damned to eternal death. Ever since mankind began to make this-worldly and other-wordly provisions against death, absolute death was never accepted (except for the enemies devoured by cannibals). Now immortality becomes a class privilege, and the struggle for the right to a life after death the first demand of the lower strata.

In fact, as Breasted has shown, democratic insurgence against the class privileges of immortality occurs a good deal earlier than any corresponding movement for social levelling in the material sphere; the class struggle manifests itself first on the plane of religion. The popular deities who gradually encroach upon the royal house gods derive their credit from their power to provide immortality for all. In the course of a gradual transition the belief in *direct* immortality dies out—and with it the solar tombs of the Pyramid type. In its place arises a more and more elaborate image of a better world *beyond* the grave. Ritual remains the precondition of survival in the beyond—man can still die an absolute death where due ritual has been neglected. But with the growing democratization of belief, insistence on right moral conduct in this world becomes a requirement for "positive" immortality, while the concept of a "negative" immortality—hell—appears for the first time.

By the time that stage was reached, the belief in immortality could maintain itself only if separated from the material preservation of the corpse. That separation is, again according to Breasted, the core of the spiritually and socially revolutionary cult of Osiris which is victoriously advancing in the declining phase of the Egyptian "Old Empire." It teaches that not mummification, but just conduct during life assures a blessed immortality; and from the introduction of the moral point of view, it follows inescapably that the main contrast to this blessed immortality is no longer, as in the faith of the Pyramid builders, absolute death as punishment for nonritual burial, but hell, the immortality of the damned. The belief in immortality is thus freed from its class character; it relies directly on the soul's inner certainty of its immortality and expresses it consciously in a completely new way while devaluing the continued physical existence of the corpse. In its most developed form, the Osiris religion gets very close to the idea of a purely spiritual soul whose fate in the beyond depends on its conduct in this world.

The new prayers for the dead in the Osiris religion are based on the solemn assertion of immortality like the old Pharaonic rituals of the Pyramid texts, but now take account of the fact of death, Side by side with a qualified death denial there arises a qualified acceptance of physical death—anterior to the choice between heaven and hell. Those later Egyptian rituals thus represent the first pronounced attempt at a synthesis between the two basic contradictory attitudes towards mortality: out of the mutual limitation and qualification of death denial and death acceptance, there arises a new concept which accepts death but also aims at transcending it.

Yet the synthesis proves unstable. The moral requirements treated as prerequisites of "positive" immortality are really quite extraneous to the basic idea. The myths concerning the afterlife and the rituals attached to them consequently degenerate into scurrilous attempts to deceive the gods as to the deceased's moral conduct on this earth. The burial cult does not vanish either—only its heroic forms embodied in Pyramid-building disappear and are replaced by more modest, generally accessible forms: it is thus illogically preserved side by side with the belief in a judgment of the dead. The ritual itself loses prestige with the growth of rationalism; the religion and the arts bound up with it grow shallow.

Those contradictions seem to reflect two factors: the gradual weakening of the mythopoeic, creative force (which takes place in every culture cycle) on one side, and the effect of the social descent of certain religious ideas on the other. The first of those two factors refers to the insight, first formulated by Schelling, later reformulated by Spengler on the basis of a more comprehensive knowledge of the variety of cultures, that the beginning of each culture cycle consists in the formation of some basic communities—peoples, states, churches, the culture as a whole— whose emergence rests on the simultaneous rise of certain myths indissolubly linked to them. Conversely, it follows that the basic myth of a culture can only arise at its beginning and gets weaker in the course of its development, until finally a "phase of enlightenment" almost completely suffocates it. (The term "myth" is, of course, not intended here to deny the objective truth content of the ideas concerned, which may vary from one case to the other.)

In the case of Egypt, the cult of the sun and the belief in the God-Pharaoh's rise to it, objectified in the building of Pyramids, were such archetypes dominating the Egyptian culture cycle from its mythopoeic beginnings to its "enlightened" end in the sun' cult of Ekhnaton. The Osiris cult represents a middle phase of that course that follows the first profound shock to the basic myth. In such a phase, the new myth (the judgment in the nether world) no longer has the strength to replace the old one (cult of tombs and rise to the sun)—rather the old continues to exist side by side with the new and their contamination leads to a progressive devaluation of both. The void thus opened *must* then be filled by pragmatic and rationalist ideas. For the myths which constituted the original social hierarchies lose their power to convince, with the double consequence that on one side the social hierarchies themselves are shaken (as happened drastically at the end of the old Empire), and on the other the arising new social orders are no longer legitimated mythically, but practically and morally. The resulting merger between a weakened myth and a morality which is sanctioned by it but is practical and egalitarian can be found in some form in the middle stage of every culture—on this point, the Western Reformation may be said to correspond to the Osiris-cult.

As disbelief in the effectiveness of the burial cults deepens, the moment comes for an at once spiritual and social revolution that is lacking in no culture: the short-lived but portentous attempt by Pharaoh Ekhnaton to abolish all the death cults and destroy their priesthood, and to replace them by the worship of the sun—not the actual sun which rises and sets, but a fantastic, ever-shining sun which destroys all chthonic gods of the dead. Its exclusive worship would have meant nothing less than the radical denial of life after death. The revolution failed, like all such revolutions, due to its incapacity to overcome the mythological legacy, half-dead as it already was, and the hierarchies linked to it through their vested interests. The end was a mechanical return to the old myths and cults, and ossification.

This cycle is not by any means limited to Egypt, or even to Egypt and Mesopotamia. It appears to be generally true of civilizations that they terminate with a concept of death opposite to that with which they started. This is hardly surprising. Every culture attempts some synthesis between the two extremes sketched earlier, but no synthesis lasts forever, because no solution can do away with the simultaneous presence of two incompatible inner experiences. But when a particular synthesis breaks down, the pendulum, having in the meantime swung from one extreme (e.g., death denial) to a compromise with the other (death acceptance), does not return to its starting point: in our above example such a return would have involved a revival of the old Pharaonic death cults which had in the meantime become wholly incompatible with the new forms of social life. The tendency is rather for the pendulum to swing wholly to the opposite extreme—in this case to the abortive experiment of founding a new religion exclusively upon acceptance of death as final.

The Partial Regression of Barbaric "Dark Ages"

There seem to be two different types of end phases of a high culture, characterized by a choice between ossification and disruption. The first need not further concern us here, since it involves merely the "ghost," as it were, of an archaic religion which has lost its original meaning. Disruption, i.e., the advent of a "dark age," is more relevant. Egyptian civilization may be said to have ossified—its "archaistic" period brought back the gods and the rituals of the Pyramid age, now both emptied of content and misunderstood into the bargain. By contrast, the civilizations of Mesopotamia and the string of smaller cultures forming a hemicycle from Crete to the Persian gulf were disrupted, and a "dark age" ensued over that wide area. In this latter process, there decayed (along with other higher cultural elements built on writing, systematic thought, and state organization) the high cultural systems of dealing with the antinomy of death. Though such decay does not proceed down to zero level—as little as with any other elements of culture—it proceeds deeply enough to bring, in any barbaric interval, the death denial—which the high culture had rejected and repressed into the unconscious—back to the surface.

It may be remarked that, in contrast to higher civilizations which offer a wide variety of responses to the problem of mortality, the various dark ages resemble one another in the prevalent attitude to death. This need not surprise us. When the higher forms disintegrate, the archetypes reemerge and rise to the surface. But not unchanged! The basic tendency of barbaric ages consists in a regression to the primitive, but that tendency finds a limit in the insight into reality that has been acquired in the preceding high culture and never completely lost again. A "relapse into barbarism" is something different from a reversion to the primitive level. The first is a regular occurrence in the story of mankind, the second an idle hope or an idle fear. But though the basic conflict of barbaric ages is not identical with that of late primitive ages—the conflict between death denial and the *dawning* knowledge of the necessity of death—it is closely related to it: it is the conflict between the already *acquired* knowledge of the necessity of death and the death denial welling up anew from the unconscious.

The situation created by that conflict offers both close analogies with the late primitive period and limited differences from it. The barbaric interludes show no explicit, conscious denial of the necessity of dying, hence no quasi-official death paranoia, no "theory" that each death must be due to black magic. But in fact, the death denial has broken through far enough to create a practically analogous state of affairs. In fact, black magic and the defense against it take the place of any developed belief in deities. In fact, any death is viewed as caused by a physical or magical murder, and this leads to the conviction that everybody is a murderer. As a result of that conviction, everybody does *become* a murderer, and the paranoiac idea of *homo homini lupus* becomes a horrible reality. Fear and fear-born hatred displace all love. Hence the primal crimes (the murder of siblings, of the father, son, or husband), which in high cultures are held down not just by coercion but by manifold ties of love, are breaking through any inhibitions, become everyday occurrences (particularly the murder of siblings) and main subjects of the saga. That is an untenable state of affairs which, just like the late primitive death paranoia, by itself forces man back on the road to a greater recognition of reality, hence of a higher culture.

But rational insight into the necessity of such a turning back to high culture as a condition for avoiding the ruin of all could never by itself achieve a collective cure from the collective madness that has broken through again. That requires the establishment of firm new hierarchies and religious rules, which only the myth-creating power can bring about. But the essence of barbaric ages (which excludes a purely negative judgment about them) is precisely that regression to deep strata of the unconscious, which manifests itself *simultaneously* in the recurrence of primal delusions and in the revival of the myth-creating force. The dismantling of the barriers which in a high culture separate the rational from the unconscious sets free both the germs of the disease and the remedy. And if at the early stage of barbarization the madness manifests itself more strikingly than the curative myth, the reverse is the case in the late phase of barbaric ages: then, the new myth helps, as throughout history, to promote the rational needs of social reconstruction.

But the "new" myth is not new in its core content: there, it coincides with the rationalist formulations of the end phase of the preceding culture generations. Moses and Homer will continue Ekhnaton's struggle against the cult of the dead, and early Christianity will link up with the spiritual insights of Plato and the Stoa. What is new is in each case not the thought, but its form of insertion in the psychic structure of the collective and the individual: the replacement of rationalism by a myth which couples the originally rational thought to the archetypes of the unconscious. The potential for this kind of coupling can never be absent, since those archetypes—including above all the two sides of the antinomy of death—are incessantly active as psychic representatives of transcendent realities. The world of the archetypes is that Mother Earth of Antaeus the contact with which renews the creative force of the giant Humanity. In that renewal, the rationalist opposition of the late Egyptian revolution against the cults and gods of the dead turns into the pure, this-worldly beauty of the Olympians; the platonic idea transforms itself into the incarnated Logos. Such a transformation, to be worked only in the depth of the unconscious, constitutes the greatness of the barbaric interludes—regardless of all the atavistic horrors that dominate their surface.

"Death Acceptance" in the Hellenic and Hebraic Cultures

At the moment when—to return to recorded history—the Hellenic civilization emerges from the dark age following the collapse of the great river civilizations, its culture is primarily distinguished by a revolutionary change in the ritual of burial: the physical preservation of the body (by mummification) is replaced by its destruction through fire. Concurrently, the elaborate imagery of survival characteristic of the old river-valley religions is superseded by the concept of Hades: the shadowy notion of a realm of shadows, symbolizing not a fuller but an infinitely less complete existence than the life of the living. Here, we have no more than a grudging concession to the inner certitude of immortality. Again, the gods, which in the river civilizations were of inhuman shape and led a transtellurian existence, are now closely identified with human life on the planet, their immortality as questionable as that of the shadows in Hades. It is not without significance that the other seminal culture to emerge from the preceding dark age—that of Israel—though in other respects sharply distinguished from the Hellenic, shares those essential attitudes. There is no substantial difference between Hades and Sheol, unless it be the attribution of markedly negative magical properties to the latter, which have no counterpart in Greek religion. Immortality is in both cases reserved for a few heroes (the concept of death opposed to the official one is never *completely* absent), although the Jews did not adopt cremation.

In contrast to the *death transcendence* of the first culture generation, we call this attitude *"death acceptance."* If Hellas is more closely associated in our minds with the acceptance of death as final, the reason is that classical antiquity has vanished, while Jewry has survived into an entirely different epoch, and, though hesitantly, adopted its basic beliefs, including that in immortality. The real creed of ancient, and to a large extent of medieval Jewry, of course, was not immortality but the future glory and worldly dominance of Israel: the particular Jewish solution of the problem, that is to say, was the transference of immortality from the individual to the community. The parallel Hellenic solution was the extolling of the individual's undying glory, the hero surviving death through his own fame. The underlying attitude is basically identical, as the contrasting one was basically common to Egypt and Mesopotamia. The deep-rooted "generational" unity of the apparently so different Hellenic and Hebraic cultures, the natural and necessary character of their fusion at the end of their course is shown in this near-identity of their ideas of death.

The increasingly hectic effort in both cultures to give a quality of eternity to life in this world—in the Hellenic in the form of posthumous glory and "eternal" beauty, in the Hebraic in the form of eschatological prophesies—is, of course, also the chief symptom of the silent continued effectiveness of the belief in immortality in both cultures and its rebellion against their death-accepting solution. The conflict between those semi-rationalist attempts at a solution and the basic myths, and their mutual undermining and enfeeblement, end in the fusion of the two cultural currents in a new faith in immortality that marks the decisive line of separation of Christianity not only from the Hellenic world but also from ancient Judaism.

It thus appears to be confirmed that a particular attitude towards the problem of mortality is not peculiar to individual civilizations, but rather to a group of them. Civilizations forming a group of this kind may be regarded as being, in a very rough sense, contemporaneous, but what really matters is the identity of their respective positions in the *sequence* of cultural epochs. (The terms "culture" and "civilization" are here, as throughout, used interchangeably.)

Thus the death-transcending group of river-valley civilizations and their minor kindred represents the first layer of "higher" cultures emerging directly from the neolithic. The subsequent Judaeo-Hellenic group is characterized by its position as heir to the death-transcending civilizations. The cycle of cultural units definable in terms of their attitude to death is thus wider than the culture cycle of individual civilizations identified by Spengler and Toynbee.

Secondly, the swing of the pendulum from one attitude towards death to the other, which takes place between the rise and fall of one and the same civilization, also applies to the relation between one group and the next. The river-valley cultures were "death-transcending," while the Judaeo-Hellenic group was characterized by "death acceptance," just like the Ekhnaton religion, as though no dark age (more pronounced in the case of the Hellenes than that of the Hebrews) had intervened. The second group starts where the earlier one left off, and thus begins its march with a set of beliefs the exact opposite of those of its predecessor in the corresponding early period. In consequence, its own life-cycle proceeds, so to speak, in the reverse direction.

Thus Greek and, albeit in a different manner, Hebrew society tried to encompass all the glory and fullness of life within the limits of an existence confined to what is discernible to direct human experience. But the search for perfection within those limits suggests that a gnawing sense of imperfection and a yearning for something unattainable within mortal life was never absent. And thus one can see Hebrew and Hellenic civilization running the full course from the elaboration of a crude belief in earthly perfection—though they held different notions as to what that perfection implied—through a gradual loss of faith in this solution, and in the end to its precise opposite: a firm belief in immortality; at which point the division between the Jewish and Hellenic world is obliterated by the rise of Christianity.

Christianity and the Rise of a New Death Transcendence

What appears striking about the rise of Christianity is the transition from death-acceptance to a new phase of death-transcendance without the intermediary of a fully developed dark age. This at any rate seems true of the Eastern Mediterranean, where the fundamental transition occurred. But a full-blown collapse *did* take place at the Western and Northern end of the geographical area in question. Both circumstances must be considered separately.

If the phenomenon we have called a "dark age" arises from the collapse of a death-transcending culture into death-denying and paranoiac barbarism, it would seem logical that the reverse process gives rise to a different conclusion. Loss of faith in survival leaves a void which must be filled; on the contrary, where such a faith asserts itself, there is no void and no room seems left for a paranoiac retrogression. Yet the emergence of a genuine dark age in the Roman world, similar to that of the second millennium B.C., suggests that our formula is still inadequate. It would appear that typically, two distinct forces are at work: loss of faith on the one hand, and a barbarian invasion of the higher culture on the other. There is no need to labor the point that such an invasion occurred both in the case of the pre-Hellenic world of the second millennium B.C., and in that of the Roman world in the first centuries of our era.

I should like to venture the suggestion that the second of those invasions was facilitated because the Christian response to disintegration failed to take full effect in the Western half of the Mediterranean world: here the precondition of Christianity's full impact—the fusion of the Hebrew and Hellenic traditions—was lacking, and the new metaphysical message came through, as it were, only very faintly. Thus, instead of transforming itself into transcendence of death, the old attitude of accepting human life as finite disintegrated into something very like the barbarism described earlier. The spiritual energy which enabled the Christianized East to ward off the German invaders (and the Mazdaan Persians into the bargain) was absent in the Western half of the old Roman empire. Here, therefore, the barbarians infiltrated without encountering much resistance, destroying in the process both the civilization of their victims and their own tradition-bound way of life, and thus establishing the necessary conditions for a genuine "dark age."

What follows is written on the assumption that the group of Christian civilizations (plus their Islamic counterpart and appendix) have by now completed so much of their course that their development can be viewed as a whole.

It is hardly necessary to emphasize that transcendence of death is at the core of the Christian message. The Gospels and St. Paul are at one on the subject. "Oh death, where is thy sting!" One catches an echo here of the old river-valley religions, separated from Christianity, as it were, by the Hellenic interlude. Western scholarship since the Renaissance and the fashionable neoclassicism of the eighteenth and nineteenth centuries have done less than justice to this theme, but a good many obscurities have recently begun to vanish, and the gaps in our understanding are being filled: the abyss separating Christianity from the Hellenic mind is becoming clearer. In essence, we now see, the Christian attitude towards death harks back to the ancient Near East. This suggests a qualification of Toynbee's well-known views concerning the relationship between a new culture and its predecessor: in addition to "affiliation" among cultures contiguous in space and time, there seems to be something like a return to more ancient models, separated from the present by a whole interval, in which the most ancient stratum was temporarily buried and lost from sight.

But the phrase "return," too, needs qualification, for the intermediate phase—in this case the seemingly harmonious, actually tragic death acceptance—has left profound traces. There could be no simple return to the almost light-hearted treatment of mortality in the religions of the ancient Near East, where death seemed to be reduced to the status of a disagreeable *contretemps*. The deepening awareness of finality had indeed, as we have seen, produced a gradual insistence upon making the afterlife available to all, but it was left to Christianity to place transcendence of death at the center of its perception of the human situation.

St. Paul, as we know, still believed in the integral Assumption of the faithful—their rise to heaven straight from life—after the impending end of the world. It was the decisive achievement of the second generation of Christians that faith in victory over death was preserved, although belief in the imminence of the "kingdom" had waned. Thus the doctrine of the Fall, which was far from being the core of Judaism, became the core of the new faith: death being the "wages of sin," salvation was conditional upon a thorough experience of, and victory over, death. There is no need to dwell upon the decisive importance of this concept in relating death transcendence to moral effort, and in promoting a theology based upon the substitute sacrifice of the Lamb of God. Death, in this context, is no longer an incident, hence no longer a stumbling block to faith. On the contrary, it is firmly integrated into the belief in Salvation and ultimate triumph. A partial relapse into a simpler, quasi-Egyptian form of death transcendence is not excluded—we have the example of Islam—but once the step was taken, there could be no complete going back.

Yet the swing of the pendulum has been felt even in the history of Christianity. By integrating morality more profoundly into metaphysics than any previous creed, the new religion went farther than any other in establishing a genuine synthesis instead of an alternation of extremes;

but it can hardly be said to have solved the problem altogether. The swing of the pendulum in our own age is all too clear, and it is a mistake to date it only from the nineteenth century. Leaving aside the question whether a complete synthesis is conceivable at all, the fact remains that the new faith had scarcely triumphed when its foundations were coming under attack.

At this point of our historical analysis, there arises the basic problem for a philosophy of history to which this entire essay is pointing: if the double cycles of death transcendence and death acceptance repeat themselves, if the new myth repeats in its core-content the old philosophy, if the Christian belief in immortality is in its core "only" a return to the Egyptian belief in immortality—is then our double cycle of the antinomy of death not truly a kind of Hinduist "wheel of rebirth," only transposed from the individual to the culture cycle? And is this not confirmed as our own, death-transcending culture is dissolving before our eyes in a rationalist final phase and showing unmistakable symptoms of a return to death acceptance, to the rejection of the idea of immortality?

The answer to this ought to be sought in the actual course of history. We have already seen that the Christian belief in immortality, though closely linked to the Egyptian in content and evolutionary history, in no way repeats the latter. The Egyptian belief had never really overcome the idea of a material afterlife in the beyond, had never really completed the separation of the sphere of earthly existence from that of transcendent being, and therefore never really separated the certainty of immortality from the certainty of death, but mixed them up. The best it could achieve was a linkup between the faith in immortality and the moral sphere; but that remains, even in its highest versions (never reached in Egyptian thought), a this-worldly principle. In truth, ideas of the beyond so closely tied to this world still contain a massive element of death denial, and it was the clash between this death denial and the reality principle which caused the Egyptian faith to fail in its rationalistic late phase.

That failure of the first culture generation justifies the existence of the second. This second culture generation did not only deny individual immortality—it also, by its harsh rejection of the death cults, prepared the ground for a truly spiritual conception of the problem of death: in fact, it has itself, in its own rationalist phase, newly formulated the problem on a higher level as a spiritualist theory of ideas, and has built the moral imperatives hailing from the Osiris religion on the idea of the Good instead of on the promise of a this-worldly Beyond. In this spiritualized form, they became the basis of Christian morality; from demands imposed on the individual by gods or men, they became an expression of the spiritual share in human nature, appearing in the daily conduct of the individual in his existence.

Christianity in turn began its intellectual development with the concept of *pneuma* and thus with the radical proclamation of a purely spiritual principle. Here for the first time this world and the other, existence and being, appearance and substance, death and immortality were kept apart clearly in the concrete form of belief. Thus the "return" of Christianity to the death transcendence of the first culture generation is not the return of a circle in itself—it is the return to the same conception on a higher level and shows a completely unmistakable spiral of development.

Accordingly, the problem of Christianity is different from the Egyptian one, even its contrary: ancient Egypt with its faith in immortality still definitely clung to the material. In Christianity, the fact that the tendency to confuse transcendent being and earthly existence has still not been finally overcome, and perhaps can never be overcome within the human condition, appears not so much as a tendency to treat being like a piece of existence, but to treat existence like a part of being—to tear away the soul from earthly existence even while it is still on earth. In the ancient Orient, the relation to the beyond was problematic; the problem of Christianity was always, and in the West much more than in the East, the relation to the world. Thus it is the rebellion of the mere "down here" against the beyond that has become the driving force of the processes of disruption in our rationlist period.

Post-Christian Prospects:
A "Death-Embracing" Culture . . .

If there is an alternation of death-transcending and death-accepting cultures, the disintegration of the Christian faith in immortality should give rise to a revival of the attitude prevalent in classical antiquity. In fact this has, since the Renaissance, been the solution favored by free-thinking humanists. But we have seen that simple revivals of the past do not occur. Just as Christianity, in returning to the death-transcending concepts of the ancient Near East, was compelled to synthesize them with the death acceptance of Hebrew and Hellenic religion, so our modern post-Christian attitude has somehow had to come to terms with the ingrained Christian belief that life without immortality is nothing. This conviction, once the concomitant belief in an afterlife is abandoned, results in despair, which indeed has increasingly colored the more recent phase of Western—and latterly of Eastern—Christian history. There is an obvious tendency for the Christian concept of personality, with its moral responsibility, to follow the Christian belief in immortality into limbo. In consequence, modern secularism is patently about to end in nihilism, i.e., in denying the relevance, almost the existence, of personality.

The denial of personality finds its original expression in the quest for some higher unit, to which mortality would be less relevant. The individual is advised to find satisfaction by merging himself in some group—social, national, or racial—endowed with semidivine attributes: absolute value and virtual eternity. But this solution remains largely verbal until tested by the final proof of self-abandonment: death for the sake of the community. And, since personality is a stubborn thing, even death does not nullify it, as long as it has the character of deliberate martyrdom, freely accepted or even consciously sought. Only where physical extinction is preceded by the total crushing and abandonment of personality has real proof been achieved that the individual is null, mortal, and the community the only real (and undying) entity. Thus the phase in which individuals yearn to be consumed by the fire of their collective belief is succeeded by one in which the community feels the urge to sacrifice to its absolute claims the largest possible number of its own members, against their personal inclination.

Koestler, in *Darkness at Noon*, has described the first of these two phases; he was mistaken, however, in treating it as the "highest" one, in believing that the "real" Communist, in contrast to the unwilling victims of the regime, is the man who by his own free will chooses not only death but also self-abandonment in the service of the party. This is still an echo of the Christian point of view. Orwell—in *1984*—saw that there is no "real" totalitarian in this sense, for to be a "real" Communist or other believer one must first be a full and real human being, which is precisely the thing the system described by him as "death worship" abhors. In this final stage, all are equally deprived of freedom and no one is allowed even to retain the right to choose suffering willingly for the sake of the larger whole. Indeed, as Orwell has demonstrated, such free acceptance of martyrdom becomes the ultimate heresy! Self-inflicted suffering in the service of the cause is in effect still an echo of an earlier attitude. The genuine, full-fledged totalitarian system is bound to dispense with it. This culture, as it were, embraces death, and thus stands at the extreme remove from the naiveté which denies it.

In searching for early historical examples of a death-embracing attitude incorporating itself in a full-fledged civilization, one can hardly fail to be struck by the evidence offered by some great Asian and the pre-Columbian American cultures. Indeed, in the latter case, one is able to discern two different and yet interrelated models on the same plane. Inca civilization was based on the complete merging of the individual with the community, and may thus be described as an early forerunner of our modern totalitarian experiments. Aztec culture seems to have worshipped death more directly. Both were, however, shot through with what appears to have been a remnant of faith in immortality, rather reminiscent of Egyptian religion.

A different form of death-embracing is shown by the civilizations that have issued from India, but they, too, are not based on a denial of immortality: in striking refutation of those who regard belief in immortality as an ordinary wish-fulfillment, every form of Indian belief since the Upanishads has treated metempsychosis, hence immortality, as both a certainty and a curse! Indian thought and its Buddhist derivatives in China, and even more so in Japan, are occupied with the problem of liberation from this curse, be it by dissolving the individual in the absolute, or by vouchsafing him eternal death on condition of the faithful performance of certain ascetic techniques. Among certain Japanese sects the final outcome has been a veritable religion of suicide, an active search for death. Thus death worship, without its modern materialist hue, appeared clearly as a kind of faith.

Yet the modern form of death-embracing is far less apt to create a viable civilization, because it is based on a post-Christian denial of immortality. The gulf separating death transcendance from death acceptance has become much more profound owing to the teaching of Christianity. Its thesis was that the eternal belongs to a spiritual world which is sharply separated from the world of existence whose true ruler is death. It was just this sharp separation of the spheres which called forth a passionate protest in the name of the devalued this-worldly values—a protest that constitutes the basic content of the attack on Christianity. But that protest finds a very different opponent from the one encountered by Ekhnaton and Moses: it no longer has to uproot the belief, and the superstition, in a this-worldly beyond and its goods, but rather the faith in a purely spiritual realm and the human soul as its representative in this world. The Christian way of treating the question can no longer be circumvented, and this ultimately drives its Communist opponents to be not content with denying the soul in theory, but to seek to destroy it in practice. This obsessional effort to stamp out even the last spark of the soul is indeed the secret driving force of all totalitarian systems of belief: in them, the destruction of the soul is transformed from an act of rebellion against the spirit into the central cult of a "positive" religion.

This modern form of the worship of death therefore tends to call forth phenomena analogous to those produced in past ages by the denial of death. Just as the denial of death could only be maintained by "uncovering" a magic murderer for each case of actual death, so the modern worship of death can only be maintained by seeking to destroy each soul that gives a sign of life. In either case, the result is murder without end, as the soul can as little be abolished as death, so that the ever-new confirmation of the reality of either provokes ever renewed persecution. Nothing confirms the reality of the antinomy of death as decisively as the obvious similarity of the phenomena brought about by the denial of either of its two basic elements: the denial of death and the denial of immortality equally end in madness.

The modern totalitarian regimes, however, lack consistency. This is because genuine belief proves impossible where no freedom is left to anyone, and the priestly caste itself loses the distinctive status required for the functioning of a religious system. The upshot is an abrupt transition from the total self-sacrifice demanded from everyone to the total hypocrisy actually practiced by those living under the system, where on pretense of saving the community each individual in fact tries to save his own skin and to demolish someone else. But that, too, may result in a social paranoia not differing materially from the witch-hunt of the tribe.

. . . or an End to the Cycles?

The analogy we have drawn between the social paranoia of the death-denying tribe and that of a soul-denying and death-embracing totalitarian system does *not* apply to their historical context. The late primitive death denial was based on as yet very incomplete advances of the reality principle, and could therefore be overcome gradually, even if with acute crises—just as the individual's fear of death only gradually turns into certainty of death; once that stage has been reached, only comparatively short relapses remain possible. But the certainty of immortality knows no such stages: relating to being, not to existence, it is in its core indivisible. That is why all earlier death acceptance only took the form of a devaluation, never of total denial of immortality. The modern attempt at its total denial—the first in human history but for isolated precursors—creates a total, irreducible conflict with the reality of the human soul.

No way can be envisaged of how this conflict could be mitigated by a compromise. The belief in Hades can be revived as little as the belief in Zeus, and failing a belief in Hades the alternative between death worship and death transcendence pointed out here remains inescapable. The historic hour permits only decisions which surpass the alternatives of previous history by their definiteness of principle. In essence, the choice today is either the psychical and probably also physical perdition of humanity, since mankind now possesses the means to achieve the total self-destruction implied in some creeds, or a—by historical standards—quick triumph of a determined death transcendence. In other words: it is probable that the present phase of death acceptance, nay death embracing, will no longer develop into a full culture cycle: more likely the second half of our present double cycle, the beginning of which we are living through, will not get beyond that early stage. Thus the hypothesis arises that we may well stand at the end of the cyclical movement of the high cultures, and that something entirely new may be beginning—as new as the first high cultures were when compared with the primitive tribal cultures, but analogous to the latter rather than the former because like the primitive cultures and unlike the high cultures so far, the new evolution will not have a cyclical character.

Here we seem to have reached the limit where speculation ceases to be valuable. Yet one further factor must be discussed which suggests that we are caught up in a process that may usher in a world vastly different from any we have known in the past. In this discussion we have only considered the antinomy of death, and have left aside the factor of our growing control of reality for the time being. If we stopped there, this would in my opinion be a wholly unjustified concession to the "spirit of the times," which in the midst of the most grandiose successes of science insists on the nihilistic abuse of its effects. For modern science means immense power, which indeed in a nihilistic overall context can only have nihilistic effects.

But does science itself really have no implications for the shaping of that context? What if science is today confronted in all directions, contrary to its conscious self-confinement to this world, with experiences reaching beyond this world of our existence and bearing characteristics of eternal being? What if it is forced, contrary to the assumptions of a doctrine ruling for centuries and contrary to its own method, to pierce the wall between this world and the beyond, between existence and being, and to show in practice not only that a world beyond this world exists but that it touches this world everywhere? Would not this break-through from existence to being fit exactly the situation in which man-kind once more would *like*, in a cyclical turning away from the knowl-edge of being, to immerse itself in the captivity of pure existence, but can no longer do so? Would it not fit the above developed alternative between perdition and a recognition of being no longer subject to a cyclical dialectic? How different would a world be in which empirical research, carried out according to the strictest methodic rules, would by itself converge with metaphysics guided by the reality of the spirit!

There have been philosophers who claimed absolute validity for the senses, and others who denied all validity to them; similarly with regard to reason. Now we have progressed much further in understanding nature, and the testing of our capacities is much more of a practical than of a metaphysical kind. What has been the result? In our physics we have drifted away from the direct witness of the senses. We know for certain that not a single piece of objective reality is "similar" to the witness of our senses, which, in consequence, might appear to be thoroughly dis-credited. Actually, of course, the contrary is the case, and modern science is one long and glorious vindication of the empirico-mathematical method, the only method capable of providing the knowledge we have gained—and, incidentally, leading us, through the senses, to cognition of a cosmos no longer material in the old meaning of that term.

I do not see why something similar should not in principle apply, in its own sphere, to the witness of the unconscious. Yet for all the recent advances of depth psychology in our culture, there is still a stuborn refusal to accept the evidence of the unconscious concerning death, to which reference has been made in the first section of this paper. The great stumbling block in this matter appears to be the absence—in contrast to the physical sciences—of all means of empirical verification. But this may be a parochial attitude. There is evidence that Eastern psychology has evolved stringent and critically tested techniques which allow direct access to the disembodied mind and even to a metapersonal sphere of experience. Those techniques have doubtless been impaired by their close connection with a death-embracing culture, and in any case have ossified together with the civilization that gave rise to them. Like every *caput mortuum* of a defunct society, they need the kindling spark of contact with a living culture to come to life again. One need not believe that they allow absolute cognition of anything, but they do seem to hold the key to hitherto unknown spheres of inner experience. They will not provide "evidence" for immortality, but they may make it more intelligible. Will Western thought prove capable of utilizing them and bringing them up to date?

Once it is recognized that belief in immortality is part of the innermost core of personality, it is arbitrary to opt, like Freud, in favor of mortality. For the last three centuries it has been generally admitted that a testing of the validity of sensual and rational cognition must precede metaphysics. Recently, a new dimension of cognition has been opened up by the science of the unconscious. Needless to say, that new dimension has no reference to our knowledge of the external world, and in this respect its contents must indeed be regarded, unless otherwise verified, as dreams and fantasies. But does that also apply to what the innermost core of personality knows about itself? Such an attitude was quite appropriate to a materialistic age which treated as foolery everything that could not be tested in the outside world; but after all, psychoanalysis won its triumphs in criticizing these assumptions.

As experimental techniques had to be evolved before it was possible to discuss the real nature of the physical universe, so all our talk about the nonmaterial world is presumptuous until an adequate technique for testing it has been established. We are merely on the threshold. Descartes, concerned to justify the validity of human knowledge of the external world, held that "surely God cannot deceive us" by giving us faculties leading inevitably into error. Such an argument, of course, is technically valid only for those who accept his particular interpretation of the divine. But may it not be adapted to our predicament? Surely mankind could not survive if any of its basic intuitions were radically misleading—and the despair which goes with the intellectual denial of our inner certainty of immortality is a case in point. If we believe that our deepest feelings are in harmony with the nature of the universe, we may gladly bear our ignorance, gladly enjoy a sense of curiosity about the beyond, borne up by the faith of Spinoza, who was not given to superstition: *scimus et sentimus nos immortales esse* (We know and feel that we are immortal).

CHAPTER FOUR

From Minoan to Greek Mythology

I. The Cretan "Flower Prince" and Minoan Civilization

It can hardly be an accident that by far the most impressive pictorial representation of an entire culture known to us remains enigmatic as to its subject. Who is that "flower prince," unforgettable to every visitor of Crete, whose painting—found as a fresco in the palace of Knossos—Evans[1] has reconstructed so beautifully, though with regard to the face with unavoidable arbitrariness? He is called a flower prince because his head has on it a crown of flowers. He appears as a prince because his image, contrary to usage, is of more than human size (2.10 metres), and because his proud, challenging gesture seems to be fitting only for a person of the highest standing. On the other hand his youth and his lone appearance in an attitude fitting no ceremonial make it impossible to see him as a king. Hence the "prince."

Since the reconstruction of the face had to be arbitrary, it is impossible to decide whether the original artist wanted to give him individuality or treat him purely as a type. But here an analogy may help us. In Cretan art, more or less portraitlike representations of low-born people are not lacking. But no portrait of a high-born person is known to us. Friedrich Matz stresses in his fine comprehensive work "the strangest fact that no image of a Minoan king could so far be identified with certainty, although the whole array of monumental architecture and of craftsmen's art obviously revolves around such a center."[2] What is stated here about royal

---

1. See Sir Arthur Evans, *The Palace of Minos: A Comparative Account of the Successive Stages of Cretan Civilization*, 4 vols. (London: Macmillan, 1921–36).
2. Friedrich Matz, *Kreta, Mykene, Troja: Die minoische und die homerische Welt* (Stuttgart: Klipper, 1956), p. 65.

images applies also to royal names: we know of no definitely pre-Indo-Germanic king's name and no unmistakably pre-Indo-Germanic King's saga from Crete, though Herodotus and others have preserved so many of those from Egypt and Babylon.

More than that: the deciphering of the Cretan so-called "Linear B" script has shown that the word king occurred in Crete even in early Achaean times only in the plural (basilées [βασιληες])—thus in that Homeric meaning which knows no sharp dividing line between nobles and kings.[3] But if the Achaeans in Crete eliminated the royal power which they had well developed on the Greek mainland, we must assume all the more that pre-Indo-Germanic Crete knew no royal power in the proper meaning of the term! Yet that deepens the enigma of the flower prince: a king's son in the absence of kings is unthinkable—but so is the representation of a young nobleman in superhuman size in contrast to all usage.

We shall have to resign ourselves to the fact that all analogies, be it to Indo-Germanic or to oriental kingship, fail in the case of Crete. We may suppose that the riddle of the flower prince is only a special case of the more general riddle formulated by Matz in the sentence quoted above. But perhaps this special case can contribute to the solution of the general problem.

If no advance is possible in a particular case, the solution may often result by looking at another case that is no less enigmatic in isolation. We shall try to solve the problem of the flower prince by bringing in a work of Cretan small-scale art, a signet ring known by the name of the "mountain mother," the significance of which is also sharply disputed.[4] Undoubtedly, it represents a goddess, which immediately calls up the analogy in the treatment of gods and kings in Minoan Crete. In Cretan large-scale art, there are no representations of gods either—the female figures carrying serpents, which were once regarded as representing the Magna Mater, have been proved to represent priestesses bearing the attributes of the great goddess. But small-scale art leads further with the gods than with the rulers, even though representations of gods in signet rings are not frequent either. The mountain mother here discussed bears its name because it stands on the top of a mountain, a figure of impressive stature: straight upright, almost a little backward bent, the left arm horizontally stretched forward, holding a staff vertically in her left hand; behind her a temple full of the Cretan state symbol, the double axe, labrys, from which the labyrinth bears its name; at her feet

---

3. Ibid., p. 135.
4. M. P. Nilsson, *Geschichte der griechischen Religion* I (München: Beck, 1935) contains a picture: Table XVIII, 1.

two lions in the attitude well known from the lion's gate at Mycenae, showing the goddess as *potnia theron* πότνια θηρῶν. And at the right edge of the signet she is faced by a youthful male figure standing in the plain, even more outsize in relation to the goddess than is the flower prince in relation to the average size of human images at Knossos. The young man's aristocratic, rather feminine-looking wasp waist, his attitude with the loosely planted legs and the backward-bent upper part of the body, correspond perfectly to that of the flower prince. Obviously, he also was wearing a head adornment, but this piece is not recognizable because the right edge of the signet is damaged. Only the gesture is completely different: while the flower prince stretches backward in a swinging movement, touching his breast in proud affirmation with the right hand, we see on the ring with the mountain mother only the left hand of the youth, raised to his brow half in adoration and half as if to protect his eyes.

Now there is no doubt about the person of the mountain mother: she is the Magna Mater or Magna Dea, in her particular version as goddess of mountains and beasts. The character of the youth, however, is disputed. Evans, who discovered the signet ring, and Glotz, the leading French expert on Minoan culture, have both explained him as the goddess's "*paredros.*" That expression refers to the idea, dominant all over the Near East and prominent in all its ancient religions, of a divine couple in which the female partner is the Magna Dea (Isis, Inanna, Ishtar, Cybele), the male partner a rather effeminate youth (Dumuzi, Tammuz, Adonis, Attis). The goddess is immortal, embodying the eternal fertility of the earth, and the dominant role; the youth, however, who is "sitting with" her, dies annually with the arival of the drought and his death has a violent, tragic character, but the goddess succeeds in reviving him: a symbol of the annual revival of the fertility of nature, a pledge of the rebirth of the dead, which reflects a society ruled by an extreme type of matriarchate.

But if the youth on the signet ring is the *paredros* of the Magna Dea, then the flower prince is the same *paredros*, only with the difference that on the signet ring he is presented in the presence of his mistress, on the fresco in the palace alone. The different gesture of the hand corresponds exactly to this different situation: in the palace, the *paredros* is among men, and with every fiber of his being he insists on his divine character—while at the foot of the mountain of his goddess, he expresses his devotion to her while protecting himself against being blinded by her unbearable splendor.

True, Nilsson, the greatest authority in this field, has denied that the youth facing the mountain mother must be her *paredros*, suggesting the signet ring was simply showing the vision of a believer to whom the goddess is appearing in her splendor.[5] Now it is not obvious why this interpretation should be more plausible than the one suggesting a *paredros*— for while we have no documentary evidence of a *paredros*, this is only because we have no documentary evidence of the pre-Indo-Germanic religion of Crete at all; the idea itself fits in faultlessly with the religious concepts of that cultural region. Yet I should not like simply to reject Nilsson's objection: it may lead to a further stage of understanding. For on one point, Nilsson is undoubtedly right: both the youth facing the mountain mother and the flower prince are not figures who at once strike the observer as gods. The youth looking at the mountain mother is too humble, the flower prince, for want of a better word, too arrogant, not sufficiently unconcerned in his posture—Hellenes might have talked of "hubris" in such a figure. Thus far, Nilsson is right in doubting the divinity of the youth on the signet ring. But he is as certainly wrong in regarding him as merely human, making by implication the flower prince merely human too: that assumption is refuted by the bodily size of both figures alone, which in pre-Hellenic cultures is only granted to gods or to the royal god-man. Only an understanding of these double aspects and double meanings of both figures permits in my view an approach to the whole problem.

The solution is offered by a closer investigation of the relation between the *paredros* and his goddess. Their act of love is a sacred wedding, a *hieros gamos* (ἱερός γαμός) the consummation of which is needed to give nature its fertility. But this kind of fertility magic is older than the personal gods, as we have known since Mannhardt; it is practiced all over the world by the peasant and his wife uniting in the field during spring festivals. Only with the development of the high gods was such magic transferred to their heaven. But the believers demand for a ritual, on which their existence wholly depends, better guarantees than are offered by an all too modest peasant custom on one side or an all too remote divine wedding on the other. Between the tiller of the soil and the god of fertility there arises a human "divine couple," the (ritual) king and his high priestess who now consummate the *hieros gamos* at the annual festival of the great goddess—in later times probably only ritually and symbolically, but in the early periods of the high cultures physically. And even that is not the end. The ancient legends are known to be full

---

5. Ibid., p. 298ff.

of tales about loving unions between divine and human partners, and where such legends have not simply sprung from the heraldic needs of noble families, they can without exception be interpreted as referring to a *hieros gamos*. But a profound and revealing change can be observed in their evolution. Hellenic sagas report almost always the relationship between a God and a mortal woman, as for instance the countless love affairs of Zeus; this corresponds to a patriarchal outlook. But there are cases of the opposite kind that are obviously more archaic, like those referring to the surrender of Aphrodite to mortal men; here we are faced with the reflection of a matriarchal phase.

A particularly interesting story of this kind refers directly to Crete. In the fifth book of the Odyssey Homer tells of the Cretan king Jasion, with whom the earth goddess Demeter united on a thrice ploughed field; for this sacrilege, Zeus slew the king by his lightning. The transition from the matriarchal to the patriarchal phase can be clearly followed in this tale. The name of Jasion, his kingly office, and the judgment of the rite as a sacrilege belong to the early Hellenic period. But originally there stood here another pre-Indogermanic name. Its bearer was not a secular king, and his deed was not a sacrilege, but on the contrary the consummation of the most important rite of the year—with the goddess herself. The Jasion legend contains unmistakable traces of a human *paredros* whom the goddess raised to her side—traces which are especially interesting because goddess and *paredros* here still behave like the peasant wife and her husband (which indeed is most fitting for Demeter, as the goddess of agriculture), and because the story refers just to Crete. Otherwise, it is by no means unique.

Besides the three forms of the *hieros gamos* enumerated above, we must thus assume a fourth one, the union of the Great Goddess with a human *paredros* whom she raises up to herself. It hardly needs a moment's thought to understand that this form of the sacred wedding must have been ritualized and that means institutionalized, a regularly celebrated rite. It clearly could only be carried out in a state of mysterious, possibly drug-induced ritual delusion. In its primitive form, as a direct transfer of the peasant custom to the Goddess and her human lover, it could not be maintained when the idea of a divine wedding took root. Now, Crete's highest summits proved to be fit places for the mystery. There, perhaps in a ritually guarded mountain cave, the human *paredros* united with his goddess, and no image or word reported the sacred act. What our signet ring reproduces is merely a prelude to the real mystery, the appearance of the goddess before her human lover. Thus in my view, Nilsson is both right and wrong: right, inasmuch as that youth is indeed a man offering his adoration to the goddess; wrong, inasmuch as that is completely compatible with his character as her *paredros*, and as his entire behavior and outward appearance are only comprehensible in that context.

But in understanding the youth before the mountain mother, we also understand the flower prince. We understand his manner of preening himself: there *is* hubris in that manner, even in the literal meaning of the word which originally denotes the conduct of a man who put himself on a level with the gods, thus preparing his terrible destruction. Also, the cause of that hubris is now suddenly clear. We are dealing here with an exact correspondence between two forms of the same ritual mystery, the *hieros gamos*. In these two forms, the person of the goddess is always the same, and so is her relation to her paredros: only *his* person is different— once he is a god, say Adonis, and once a man, like the flower prince. But by becoming the *paredros* of the goddess, he enters the role of Adonis— as such identification of the different forms of the *hieros gamos* is the very core of the religion of the Near and Middle East: he must die annually, to be mourned and revived by the goddess. Only a short stay is granted to him; soon the song preserved for us in a story from late antiquity under the equivalent name of Tammûz—*thammous, thammous pammegas tetheke* (θαμμούς, θαμμούς, παμμέγας τέθηκε)—will be sung about him. (This text, it will be recalled, was once mistranslated as "The great Pan is dead!") But the song of mourning for the early death of the god of spring sounded for millennia, both for the god and his human sub-stitutes—with the difference that the god dies only ritually, but the human substitute really.

By a detour, we have arrived at something well known. Frazer, in *The Golden Bough*, has assembled an immense body of material in order to prove that human, mortal gods have occurred all over the earth, and that all of them after a short spell of glory die a sacrificial death. As is generally known, he took as a prototype of this rite and myth the priest-god of Nemi, who had to murder his predecessor in order to obtain his succession, and whom everybody was free to murder who longed for his succession in turn. No doubt a sacrificial death also awaited the Cretan *paredros* at the end of his role, as with every other member of this group. Small wonder, then, that he preens himself in his short-lived divine glory, so as to silence his fear of the not distant end. At one stroke, thus, the mythographic analysis of the great Knossos fresco reveals its psy-chological content. May we assume that the *hieros gamos* with the goddess was indeed the climax of his career and the immediate prelude of his sacrificial death? In that case, the hubris of his manner on the fresco as well as the ecstatic undertone of his conduct on the signet ring would find a natural explanation not only from a theological, but also from a psychological viewpoint.

It remains uncertain at what intervals of time and in what manner the *paredros* was sacrificed. Originally, it must have happened annually; one must assume as self-evident that at such a feast, not only the *paredros* but all the following of this "god for a time" perished—but the Theseus legend reports an *annual* blood sacrifice of Athenian young men and girls to "Minotaurus." Whether the intervals for the sacrifice of the *paredros* were later extended, whether the annual character stuck only to the other human sacrifices we cannot state with finality at present, nor the manner of the sacrifice, which however proves to have been extremely cruel in all cases for which we have anthropological or mythological material. One more contribution to the hectic-ecstatic conduct of the *paredros* in our pictorial representations!

Much may be gained from all this, however, toward an understanding of the structure of the Cretan state, which was almost unique of its kind. There is no reason to expect—only the deciphering of the pre-Indogermanic Linear A script can bring ultimate clarity—that we shall still find genuine Cretan kings from the pre-Indogermanic period, nor genuine images of high gods from it. The sequence of rulers was obviously purely matrilinear: the daughter (the youngest of the nubile daughters?) inherited from the mother the only ritual power to rule, and that means the only ruling power that was legitimate according to early oriental concepts. The female ruler took, we do not know whether by free choice or according to some conventions, successively various *paredroi*, from whom she, as embodiment of the goddess, conceived children. At the end of his ritual career the *paredros* consummated, on mountain summits or in a mountain cave, a mystical *hieros gamos* with the goddess herself— as a prelude to his equally ritual sacrifice. It was the main function of the *paredros* to share the queen's bed; besides, he carried out certain ceremonial acts—only those that could take place in the tiny ruler's hall of Knossos. War, political administration, and the management of the enormous royal estates, which largely coincided with the administration, were practically carried on by the *basilees* without any ritual distinction, including certainly the male relatives of the queen. Thus Crete in its apogee—not necessarily in its early period—lacked an effective royal power. The student will not hesitate to link this evolution of a very archaic, matriarchal political order—which is rather extreme for a high culture— with the Cretan "Thalassocracy"—the unique reign of peace on an island preserved for centuries from external and internal enemies. It will then be understood that such an order could not maintain itself with the approach of the great migrations of sea-going peoples, and that the native nobility, even if the structure of state and religion was still completely intact, had to concede precedence to foreign warriors and thus pave the way for disruption.

What has been said so far depends by no means on depth psychology. But it will be shown that without an understanding of the assumptions outlined here concerning Minoan civilization, a correct viewpoint cannot be found for a psychological analysis of later, Hellenic myths.

II. The Oedipus Myth and the Transition from Matriarchal to Patrilinear Culture

As a paradigm for the Hellenic transformation of Minoan religious ideas after the collapse of Minoan culture, we choose, out of the large number of Hellenic myths, that of king Oedipus, because it permits us to describe the transition from the mythology of a matriarchal to that of a patriarchal society with unusual clarity. The choice has the additional advantage of permitting at the same time a critical discussion of Freud's interpretation of the myth.

Let us state at the outset that Freud in his interpretation of the Oedipus myth followed methods which he would undoubtedly have rejected for the analysis of his patients, and which are also untenable in the light of a historical criticism of sources. For Freud relies exclusively on a single source, the Sophoclean tragedy, and even there only on fragments of it. The many versions of the myth that derive from other sources and lead to quite different interpretations remain unexamined. That is due to the fascination which the theme of incest, which is manifest in the Sophoclean treatment, exerted on Freud. But if, as Freud assumes throughout, a myth has to be interpreted according to the same methods as a dream—"myths are the secular dreams of humanity"—then what is fair for the dream must also be valid for the myth: the manifest content of the myth cannot coincide with its unconscious meaning any more than that of the dream, however much the manifest text of the myth may impress the student as directly derived from the unconscious.

That something has really gone wrong here is shown by any attempt to apply Freudian principles to the motives which start off the entire action in the Oedipus myth: the finding of the exposed child Oedipus in the mountains, his growing up with foster parents in Corinth whom he takes for his real parents, and his resulting misunderstanding of the oracle warning him against patricide and incest. Of course, this motivation contains, among other elements, an exoneration of Oedipus from guilt, because he had committed his crimes unwittingly. But this exoneration would only be relevant by modern standards and is quite misplaced in interpreting a myth of antiquity: according to Hellenic sentiment, no such exoneration was conceivable in case of severe crimes, hence it could not be the motive for presenting Oedipus as a foundling. On the contrary, just Freud and Reik have taught us that this foundling version of "the birth of the hero" has a self-contained meaning of its own in the context of the "family novel." This meaning we must now study.

In his book on Moses, Freud started from his knowledge that in foundling stories, just as in the underlying "family novel" of the small child that has become unconscious, normally the pretended high-born parents are not the real parents, whereas the alleged foster parents are. His completely convincing argument in the case of Moses is based on the reversal of that statement for that particular case: *since* in the Moses myth the daughter of Pharoah appears as foster mother, she, the high-born, is in this case the real mother, while the man's modest Israelite descent turns out to be mythical. But what is fair for Moses is fair for Oedipus. If the legend treats Oedipus as the son of a Theban king, reared first by shepherds in Cithaeron, later at the Corinthian court, his real origin remains ambiguous (and for very good reasons, as we shall see); what is plain, however, is that he was not really a Theban King's son at all but merely usurped that position. Countless completely historical events in which usurpers constructed a false genealogy to prove themselves heirs of the native ruling family converge to confirm the conclusion which stringently follows from all Freudian assumptions: Laios is not Oedipus' father at all, nor Jocasta his mother—and thus the whole, apparently so convincing interpretation of the myth falls down at one stroke. Instead, we are faced with an enigma.

But the solution of that enigma cannot be found by trying to advance directly along the paths of dynamic psychology. Rather, our most urgent concern at this point must be first of all to find out the real origin of Oedipus—for only if we know that shall we be able to understand the conduct of Oedipus towards the other figures in the myth.

The surest, though hardly the most important factor in this investigation concerns Oedipus' foster parents in Corinth. Contrary to the novel, the myth does not invent localizations: if it does not know where an event took place, say the migrations of Oedipus after his flight from Corinth, it confesses that, for example by stating in this case that he wandered for years "around the world." All the more certainly, the naming of Corinth as the place where he grew up describes the place where he really stayed until reaching maturity. Oedipus thus was a Corinthian king's son who left his parental home and usurped power in Thebes. That in doing so he was driven by fear of incest the myth reports explicitly, and we must accept it, but in no other sense than we could for any other young man "fleeing" his parental home. Here we gain a first insight into the mechanisms that guided the formation of that myth. The incest motive towards the real Corinthian parents, that has been projected onto the oracle, is activated in relation to the fictitious Theban parents who belong only in the family novel. At once, we have reached the viewpoint required for the dynamic interpretation of psychic prod-ucts: the repressed emotion remains unconscious in relation to its real object, but can be consciously discharged toward a substitute object.

But we are as yet far from the end. Between Oedipus' exodus from Corinth and his arrival at Thebes, the myth knows only *one* other lo-calization: the Schiste Hodos, a well-known crossing of roads in three directions, at which Oedipus slew Laios, the king of Thebes. Pausanias, the "Baedeker" of Hellas under the Roman empire, has exactly described the place.[6] That localization is particularly interesting because obviously no place of worship was found there; that excludes the usual interpre-tation of such localizations as mythically rationalized explanations for a local cult, as a so-called "*aition*." That leaves only one alternative: at the Schiste Hodos, there must really have taken place a murder important in Theban history.

The legend seeks to insert this erratic block of historic reality among its mythical transpositions by letting Oedipus arrive from Delphi, where he is supposed just to have received the oracle warning him against parricide. But while this version is geographically possible, it contradicts the story of Oedipus' "years of wandering," supposed to have been due to the oracle and hence to have followed it in time. Thus while the Schiste Hodos is a historically important location, the oracle is an *aition*, a rationalizing invention of the legend, intended to link Oedipus' flight from Corinth with the event at the Schiste Hodos, but again containing the fear of incest with its crucial importance for depth psychology.

The two events linked both causally and unconsciously by the incest oracle—the flight from Corinth and the murder at the Schiste Hodos, both

Three roads

6. Pausanias' *Description of Greece*, X, 5, 2 (Harmondsworth: Penguin Books, 1973).

true historical facts—thus do not belong together in reality. Evidently Oedipus arrived at the Schiste Hodos not from Delphi, but—geographically and historically far more plausibly—from *Northern* Phocis: the Schiste is, after all, a triple fork. He was a conqueror coming from Phocis who slew the Theban king in battle—the legend speaks, after all, explicitly of Laios' following. In short: in the figure of Oedipus, *two* historic personalities, one conqueror from Corinth and one from Phocis have been merged. One wonders how it would be possible to interpret a legend based on the merging of two heroes in one person, without taking note of this dual historical root.

In the whole story, the name of the slain king is highly suspect: Laios. The underlying root is *laos*, a people. The fitting adjective is *laikos*, belonging to the people. A noun derived from *laos* is missing—if one existed, it would have to be *laios*. Thus Laios is he who belongs to the people, and since we are here dealing with a king, the people's king. Only the later, semirationalist transformation of the legend could interpret this word as a proper name: actually, the name only describes the native king in contrast to the foreign usurper. But the concept of the people's king also clarifies as its opposite the conceptual element that made possible the merging of the Corinthian king's son with the invading conqueror from Phocis: both of them were not Thebans but foreign intruders. A new aspect of the real history underlying the legend becomes visible: its subject is the loss of Theban independence, a trauma of a collective rather than individual kind.

Indeed, our investigation leads at this point definitely into the realm of real history. There can be no doubt that we are dealing here with traces of one or, more plausibly, both of the Northwestern Greek migrations, the first of which started about 1700 B.C. and the second about 1200 B.C. The name of "Laios" for the last representative of the last native royal house gains a specially emphatic meaning in that context: he is not just Theban, in contrast, say, to a Corinthian, but a civilized man in contrast to the Northwestern barbarians. The people that he represents are not just the citizens of one polis among many, but distinguished themselves from the foreign conquerors as later Hellenes from barbarians. We shall see presently how the difference manifests itself concretely, and as we see it, the core of the myth will become comprehensible step by step. Only this should be anticipated here: this contrast does not include the relation between the old Theban royal house ("Laios") and the Corinthian prince—the Corinthian was no barbarian. The memory of his milder conquest has later covered that of the horrors of the barbarian invasion.

But neither the Corinthian, nor the Northwestern Greek can have been called "Oedipus" with his real name—as little as "Laios" was called Laios. Nobody, least of all a Greek, calls his son "swollen foot." The legend removes this offense in the typical Hellenic form of an *aition* by explaining the name as a nickname referring to the piercing of Oedipus' ankles when he was exposed. But this only pushes the contradiction one step further: there is no need to paralyze a newborn child, as it cannot walk anyhow. The piercing of the ankles, in itself deserving to be recognized as a historical fact just because of its absurdity, must belong to another context.

To discover that context, a detour is needed. There exists in the Oedipus myth itself a parallel to the absurdity of the exposure story: the story of the end of Laios. In the case of the "son," Oedipus, we are dealing with the circumstances surrounding his birth, in that of the "father," Laios, with those of his death. Between those two events that were later linked by the patricidal motive, the myth has even earlier established another link: the feet play an equally fatal role before the death of Laios as after the birth of Oedipus. For Laios is not literally slain by his unrecognized son, as the legend is often inexactly repeated (by Freud among others): Oedipus slays not Laios, but the driver of his chariot; Laios he only pushes down, with the result that the king is entangled in the reins of his horses and dragged to death. How one can, just by a fall, get entangled in the reins in such a way that they do not loosen themselves again at the first violent jolt; how the horses can suddenly tear themselves clear of the shafts and run away with the dragged king—this cumulation of improbabilities remains unexplained, as is typical for the rationalizing *aitia* of Greek legend. It remains strange, however, that the lack of credibility of this event has struck modern commentators as little as that of the piercing of the ankles in the case of Oedipus. Since they did not clearly recognize the rationalizing-aitiological character of both narratives, they have also in neither case asked the question of what the *aition* was to rationalize, or to rationalize away.

Yet closer inspection shows that the paralyzing of Oedipus and the dragging to death of Laios really refer to the same procedure. To drag somebody to death, the reins used to tie his ankles must be specially fastened with knots; and even this remains uncertain, since the storm chase of the horses over hedge and ditch may loosen the reins all the same. Only the piercing of the ankles can offer certainty for this purpose; only in the context of such a deliberate dragging to death both elements, the piercing of the ankles and the entangling of the reins, make real sense. They are indeed both found in the famous account of the *Iliad* about the dragging of the dead Hector. But there, too, the original meaning is distorted to the extent that the deed is a senseless barbaric brutality, the desecration of a corpse. The action would indeed be meaningful, not towards a corpse, but only as an act of ritual execution. But precisely that most profound meaning is avoided by the Hellenic myth at any price.

And nothing is more understandable. We already know the underlying procedure: the immemorial sacrifice of the divine-royal *paredros*, particularly central for the Minoan culture; for dragging to death was one of the many rituals for that sacrifice. The denial, the repression of the memory of those ritual human sacrifices (which, however, were still quite usual in Arcadia as fertility rites even in Hellenic times, though no longer clearly linked with the political system) thus proves to be a basic moving force behind the formation of Hellenic myths. Behind the concrete historical events which took place in Boeotia at the time of the invasion of the Northwestern Greek barbarians, the repressed and distorted memory of even earlier occurrences thus appears—not of unique specific events, but of the permanent usages of a destroyed culture, whose customs and basic religious ideas were detested by the Hellenes.

What matters at this point for the Oedipus myth is not primarily the Minoan-Helladic (i.e., pre-Mycenean) culture of Boeotia, but that of Southern Thessaly, the country of Oedipus' origin. This again is proved by a hitherto not discussed detail of the legend of the paralyzing of the hero—a detail apparently given the least attention of all, though it is most revealing. For one story that appears at first sight completely meaningless is that of the *swelling* of Oedipus' feet. True, a piercing of the ankles may naturally cause an inflammation and thus a passing swelling, but those fast and very violent swellings which make a profound impact on memory only arise from poisonous stings. The explanation of the swelling by the piercing is thus also a typically Hellenic *aition*. In truth, killing by a poisonous thorn or arrow also belongs to the realm of the sacrifice of the *paredros*—not, of course, as an element of killing by dragging, but as its alternative. But it is not remarkable that, after the waning of clear historical memory, the two procedures contaminated each other, since both concerned a type of action very strange by Hellenic standards—an execution "by the feet." If the dragging of the dead Hector offers a slightly distorted model for the sacrificial rite of dragging, the killing of Achilles by Paris's poisonous shot into his heel offers a slightly distorted imitation of the Helladic poison-thorn ritual. Again and again, the reference to Achilles, who apparently belongs to quite a different realm. Again and again therefore the allusion to his home, Thessalic Magnesia.

The key for understanding that surprising link was offered to us by the hint of Graves that Pholus and Chiron, the other two South Thessalian mythical heroes, also die from poisoned arrows—and they alone.[7] We are dealing with a specifically (though not for that reason exclusively) Thessalian variant of the sacrifice of the king. And that closes the ring of the arguments which have gradually led us to regard Oedipus—or rather the most important among the various historic figures merged in the mythical figure of Oedipus—as a Southern Thessalian conqueror of Thebes.

But we may still penetrate somewhat more deeply into the historic context. The motive of the swollen foot and poisoned thorn refers to a purely sacrificial rite—to see it one only has to escape from the biblical exclusiveness of sacrifice by burning. The dragging motif also reflects the ritual of the replacement of one *paredros* by another—but here we are no longer dealing with a mere sacrifice. In mythology, this motif of an allegedly accidental, in fact ritually prescribed dragging to death occurs regularly in the context of a chariot race—as classically in the legend of how Pelops overcame Oenomaus and won his daughter Hippodameia. The stake is regularly a crown or, what is the same in a matriarchal order, a royal daughter, and just as regularly the race ends with the death of the vanquished contender. With this rite, we find ourselves in a historical phase where changes of the throne no longer take place according to ritual rules and at times fixed by the calendar, but where within given rules of the game an element of personal prowess plays a role. That corresponds to a state of affairs where the royal power no longer has a purely religious character, but also a military and political one—a state more adjusted to the permanently war-threatened Helladic mainland culture than the peaceful customs of Minoan Crete, perhaps even a later state already adapted to the dangers of the great migrations. Thus in the accounts of the paralyzing of Oedipus and the dragging to death of Laios, *two* rituals corresponding to different times and places and different sociopolitical structures are reflected.

Indeed, even a third stratum may be discerned, and it is the most important one. From it originates the change of throne after a ritual armed duel, in which the aging king has to defend himself against younger pretenders until he succumbs to one of them. That is the phase best embodied in the ritual of the priest king of Nemi which persisted into imperial Roman times, and which Frazer made the starting point of his entire investigation of this field. It hardly needs to be stated that

7. Robert Graves, *The Greek Myths* (Harmondsworth: Penguin Books, 1955), vol. 2, p. 115.

this is the youngest phase and that its ritual corresponds to a time of savage wars between peoples, hence originally to the great migrations themselves. Here we find the matriarchal order in full disruption; though the ritual still takes over some fragments of it, the real decision about the throne neither depends on ritual nor calendar nor female choice, but on the strong arm of the hero in war. And while the older rites for the transfer of the throne are just alluded to in the Oedipus myth, this latest rite which includes the violent death of the old ruler seems to be *completely* contained in the story of the slaying of Laios by Oedipus.

The myth of king Oedipus has arisen from the historical event of the slaying of the last Theban people's king by a barbarian from Magnesia; it arose because this was the end of the native dynasty, and the corresponding ritual order, hence an event marking a profound break. The origin of the myth thus falls into one of the great periods of migration; the earlier elements, such as the poison and dragging rituals of the change of throne, have been fitted into the frame given by this great political and collective trauma. But now we are faced with a second surprise, analogous to our interpretation of the foundling motif: in the original myth, or in the first account that was still very close to historic reality, not only the theme of patricide and incest was absent but *any* theme of guilt. We find at first nothing but a heroic deed in war, which may well have been accomplished in the ritually prescribed forms of the duel for the crown.

Where, then, did the guilt theme, which so obviously forms the core of the myth in its later form, come in? This we must now take up, pursuing the development to the point where the guilt is finally formulated as concerning incest and patricide.

The first step in the unfolding of the sense of guilt is linked to the circumstances of the killing of Laios. We have just seen that such a killing corresponded to a valid ritual, and may not have deviated from it at all in the actual event. But in the final form of the myth known to us, the circumstances of the slaying of the people's king are nonritual, nay repulsive in their barbarism. Whoever usurped the throne in such a manner was always a stranger; once more a surfeit of proof that Oedipus was not a Theban king's son, that he committed neither patricide nor incest. (It would be entirely wrong to identify even symbolically the killing of the king with that of the father; whenever would the slaying of an enemy ruler and the conquest of his realm have appeared as sacrilege to a people of migrant warriors?)

Not only does the legend report explicitly that Oedipus committed the deed in a senseless fury (about the hampering of his movement on a narrow road), but this intepretation is also confirmed by the absence of any hint at those rituals which would have had to accompany a formal duel for the crown. For instance, a stranger who wanted to slay the priest king of Nemi had first to get hold of a branch of the holy oak growing in front of the Nemi temple: by this he joined the immemorial cult of the trees which formed one aspect of the great fertility cults, and announced at the same time his legal intent to win the throne. Nothing of the kind in the case of Oedipus. The later dragging to death of Laios, which anyhow belonged in no way to a ritual duel, appears all the more as a deed of crude violence and ultimately as a barbaric desecration of a corpse just like the almost identical outrage done by Achilles to the body of Hector. The observance of residual elements of the ritual has here turned into its savage travesty.

The possibility cannot be excluded that several reports have been merged even at that point. Perhaps there once existed a third account about a ritual duel, besides the poison and dragging rituals, for a change on the throne. Such a report could at the same time quite well refer to one specific ritual duel. It would then correspond to a stage when the barbarians were still moving completely within the framework of the Helladic or Minoan order, as shown by the deciphering of the late Minoan Cretic script. In a later phase, another barbarian may have brutally ignored the ritual and thus have brought about the catastrophe of the matriarchal order in Thebes. Such assumptions do not represent an impermissible *multiplicatio causarum*: there is no myth in which not at least half a dozen superimposed layers could be identified. But in this case, such separate phases cannot be proven—nor does it matter much. For from the viewpoint of the barbarians, not even such a savage act of brutality could cause much dishonor. Thus the Iliad lets the hero Menestheus report succinctly and coolly that he had seen the funeral of Oedipus in Thebes, "who had been overthrown; he had there defeated all the Cadmaeans."[8] It is this oldest of all source texts, not sufficiently weighed by any of the interpreters of the myth, which clearly shows to us the absence of any sense of guilt in the early stage of the myth.

But the source tells us more. Once again, that Oedipus was a foreign conqueror, not a "Cadmaean"; and beyond our findings up to now, that he was defeated and killed in a civil war (for in a war between states, one may fall but not be overthrown). The latter harmonizes with the account of Sophocles, according to which after the death of Oedipus,

8. *Iliad*, book XXIII, verse 679 ff.

Creon, the brother of the queen, retook power according to purely matriarchal law. Thus the old-established dynasty had gained the upper hand once more after a terrible crisis.

That turn has become decisive for the further evolution of the Oedipus myth. The viewpoint of the defeated won a hearing in the legend besides that of the victors, because the temporarily defeated old establishment also gained control once more in political reality. To them, the doings of the barbaric intruders appeared as a mockery of any divine and human order: Oedipus had brought a curse on the city by his conduct.

The party of the native establishment used that curse to explain all the terrible calamities which befell Boeotia, as the most advanced North-western outpost of Minoan culture at the time of the Northwest Greek migrations. It reorganized those events as a family history of Oedipus: the brothers' quarrel; the expedition of the "Seven" against Thebes; even the raging of Creon, the restored representative of the matriarchal order, against the descendants of Oedipus. All this was ascribed to the great evildoer; so was even the destruction of the city by the epigones—a historic fact, proven by the absence of Thebes from the catalogue of ships in the Ilias, where only a market town, Hypothebai, at the foot of the castle is found instead.

But in the version of the myth known to us, which dates from a time not only after the destruction, but after the rebuilding of the city, this point of view has been merged in a contradictory synthesis with the opposite one put forward by the conqueror's party. The latter replied to the reproaches of the native establishment by claiming that Oedipus, far from bringing a curse on the city, had liberated it from a terrible curse: that of the Sphinx. According to this party, Oedipus owed his power to having overcome and eliminated that daemon, not to crude violence and a series of grave outrages. But the proofs adduced for that version are far-fetched indeed. The Sphinx—the original name is sphix, meaning "she who ruins"—has originally nothing to do with Oedipus at all. She is a daemon of sickness, not specifically Theban by origin, though this nightmare figure may well have been linked with a local plague legend and later again with the riddle of the three ages of man, hailing from still other sources. As presented in Sophocles' version of the myth, she must have been inserted centuries before for plainly propagandist reasons. Thus the myth known to us is a product of extreme contrasts.

But what, in the view of the native establishment, had been the terrible sacrilege of Oedipus that brought the curse on the city? Even from their point of view, it could not have been the nonritual form of the killing of Laios—for they lived under matriarchal law, and under that law the Erinyes only punish violence against the mother; what one man did to another could not be a crime against the divine order under that system. And still the consequences, if only the *indirect* consequences, of the killing of Laios are here of decisive importance. In pre-Hellenic law, such a deed established a claim to the crown through the hand of the queen, i.e., it established the right to marry the heiress to the throne, as all the Hellenic legends about duels for a woman's hand presuppose—but on condition that the victor had defeated his opponent by legitimate methods. That Oedipus was charged with not having done, and thus he had no legitimate claim to Jocasta's hand. Yet he had to gain that hand at all costs: without it, he remained an illegitimate intruder with no claim to recognition by his subjects. Thus political necessity compelled him to get hold of Jocasta in one way or another. The story of the Sphinx serves, from the viewpoint of the conquerors, the purpose of giving Oedipus a legitimate claim to the marriage with Jocasta, without criminal violence. Here we reach the core of the matter: the fate of Jocasta.

In the Odyssey she is called Epicaste, a name suggesting no further explanation, hence obviously the true historic name of the wife of that people's king whom Oedipus killed. The name of Jocasta given her in Sophocles and all other sources is of later origin but points to a more ancient context: it arose by an identification between Epicaste and Jo (or Io). The latter was, according to the classic Hellenic version of her legend, a high priestess of the Argivian Hera, hence of the same goddess, ultimately identical with the Magna Mater, who was venerated as Hera also in Thebes. Zeus was after her, and although she turned herself into a cow to escape him, the God found her and raped her; according to one of the versions of the legend she died, after long erring around, from grief and shame. In an older version, obviously still closer to Minoan religion, she was herself the goddess of the moon—hence herself the Magna Mater. But Epicaste, as priestess of Hera, was at the same time a goddess in the strictest sense—just like Jo.

But that meant, of course, that she was taboo. As Wilamowitz has stated, the raping of a goddess appeared still in Hellenic times as the most terrible sacrilege. We have no reason to try to "correct" this well-documented idea and to look underneath such rape for incest as the really "more profound" outrage. What is a sacrilege in any culture is determined by the view of that culture, and even to the Hellenes, whose incest taboo was certainly strict, that other taboo appeared even more grave. Only: in the context of Greek religion, where the gods are living unapproachably on Mount Olympus, this is an unrealizable, almost absurd idea, explicable only as a remnant of the earlier, Helladic-Minoan culture. There, where Gods and men lived in a real-mythical communion, as shown in the first part of this study, the raping of a goddess could indeed occur and did occur whenever the sacred rites of the *hieros gamos* or the sacred right to sexual self-determination of the queen-priestess were violated. As the *hieros gamos* was guarded by strict rules, physical violence was not required for the offense: any kind of duress inflicted on the priestess-goddess constituted sacrilegious rape.

In the sight of the conquered—not, of course, of the conquerors— Oedipus committed exactly that crime by pressing Jocasta to marry him. *That is the primal crime of Oedipus*; the killing of Laios originally created only the legal premise for the offense. But that alone would be sufficient to call up the vengeance of the Erinyes, who protect the matriarchal order. Jocasta, as priestess and queen the guardian of the entire legal order in the vanquished culture, adds the utmost compulsion for the Erinyes by killing herself and thus making Oedipus her murderer—a murderer, by the way, not only of the wife, the priestess, the queen, but also of the mother: for the Magna Mater, appearing as Hera and embodied in the priestess-goddess Jocasta, is the mother of *all* men. In that sense Oedipus commits, in the context of the Minoan-Helladic system of identifications, the same horror as Orestes does by murdering Clytemnestra—a matricide, and that without being able, like Orestes, to call up another, patriarchal law as his justification.

It is true that, inasmuch as the Magna Mater and therefore her priestess is in a religious sense also *his* mother, he also commits incest. But among the many aspects of his relation to Jocasta just the incestuous one is in itself not criminal, odd as it may sound. For inasmuch as the priestess-goddess is a kind of incarnation of the Magna Mater, every sexual act with her is an incest—and such incest, if only consummated in ritual forms, is as uncriminal as, say, in Christianity (or for that matter in the Judaic or Hellenic culture) the sexual act within a correctly concluded marriage is fornication. The misunderstanding which sees Oedipus' primal crime in incest thus has its basis in applying the ideas of *our* culture to one that is older by more than three thousand years.

But this does not mean that the fact of incest—even of an originally by no means criminal incest—had no influence on the evolution of the Oedipus myth. For later, after the catastrophe of Helladic Thebes, woman was subjected to man in the course of the Mycenean cultural period. The promiscuous and orgiastic aspects of the fertility cults as well as the human sacrifices were proscribed, and incest became the object of a strict taboo. Then, to a backward-looking view on Oedipus' conduct, the use of pressure for marrying a woman appeared as something rather harmless, the tragic character of which was no longer understood, the incest however appeared as dreadful—an attitude that corresponds to a patriarchal order as naturally as the reverse to a matriarchal one. It follows that the theme of incest came into the Oedipus myth in two distinct phases. Originally, the crime of Oedipus consisted of exerting duress on the queen, and it existed only from the viewpoint of the old, defeated Helladic culture. Much later, in late Mycenean times at the earliest, the patriarchal conquerors from northwestern Greece turned this crime against the matriarchate, which they could no longer understand, into a typically patriarchal crime, by stressing in the complex "criminal" conduct of Oedipus to Jocasta just that element which had originally been quite unimportant: the incest (in the sense of the religious identity of priestess and mother-goddess). But since they could no longer understand that identity either, they interpreted the act no longer in a religious, but in a material sense—no longer as "incest" with the priestess of the mother-goddess but as incest with the physical mother. The psychoanalytic contribution to an understanding of this context consists in the insight that what has happened is not a mere rational "misunderstanding": the new age inserted its new main taboo into a legend built on quite different premises precisely because incest had meanwhile become the most profound taboo.

Once again the question arises here of the number of layers out of which finally the versions of the myth found in the Odyssey and in Sophocles grew together. As argued before, it would be absurd to shrink back from the assumption of a large number of such layers. At least the "swollen foot" aspect of the legend goes back to the third millennium B.C.; but the self-punishment theme of the Sophoclean version arose in the eighth century at the earliest. How much may have happened in the intervening millennium and a half! While any hypothesis is difficult to prove, it seems probable that the narrative of the evil king Oedipus who overthrew all law and thus brought the curse on the city grew up between the seventeenth century and the middle Mycenean period, while the replacement of the theme of inflicting duress on the priestess-queen by the theme of incest took place in the course of the second northwestern Greek migration; for while the first wave of barbaric conquerors largely adapted itself to the culture of the conquered peoples, the second wave clung to the patriarchal order it had brought along from the Northwest. That would fit well with the insight, evident in itself, that the incest taboo did not arise from the myth, but the myth in its Hellenic shape arose out of the incest taboo, so that its real evolution can only be explained from that of the latter. But the history of the incest taboo in its turn may, in the absence of direct historical testimony, be best inferred from the myth reflecting that development.

We are faced here with a massive factum, a theme dominating the whole world of Greek legend, of which the Oedipus myth only constitutes a particular case. It may be defined as the direct inversion of the matriarchal relationship between mother and son, and we must here recall one main feature of the Middle Eastern and Minoan religions we had so far left to one side. Adonis, after all, is the son of Astarte, Attis the son of Cybele—all the *paredroi* were in mythology, and at first obviously also in reality, sons of the goddess whose lovers they became. Thus here we meet for the first time not a fictitious, but a real incest theme—but not in the shape of an incest taboo, but of an incest duty as the highest religious rite. To look behind that incest duty for an even more archaic incest taboo would be arbitrary for two reasons: first, because in anthropology numerous highly archaic usages can be documented in which precisely incest with the mother is by no means forbidden or, almost more significant, only quite lightly disapproved of; second, because the transformation of the *hieros gamos* from the chief ritual of Minoan culture into a sacrilege in Hellenic culture, which we discussed above, can undoubtedly be understood as the inversion of the original constellation into the opposite, and the assumption of an even earlier and more profound taboo appears here as completely superfluous.

But the inversion concerns not only the moral valuation of the divine wedding, as expressed for example in the myth of Jasion and Demeter, but above all the view of the relation between mother and son, and further between man and woman generally. In all the matriarchal myths, it is the mother who chooses the son for incest, and thus for an early and cruel sacrificial death. Jo is such a mother goddess, and "Swollenfoot" originally such a sacrificed son. At the end of the evolution, the inverse is without exception the case: it is no longer the strong goddess who forces a weak *paredros* to share her bed, but conversely a strong god who does violence to a weak goddess ("priestess," "nymph," "demigoddess"). It is not by accident that the Hellenic legend shows Zeus, the son-god *par excellence*, as raping the Magna Mater in innumerable incarnations. Nor is it by accident that an obvious original identity links the raping of Jo by Zeus and the raping of Jocasta by Oedipus. Only the incest theme has now frequently disappeared from the surface—for what in the earlier real myth was conscious, and in certain conditions fully legitimate, is now subject to a severe taboo and almost intolerable to consciousness; here the Oedipus myth is a rare exception.

Freud has based his entire interpretation of religion and mythology, but above all of this myth, on the thesis of the rebellion of the son against the father. The general inversion of the original relation between goddess and *paredros*, found in almost every Greek legend, proves that this thesis is wrong—not absolutely wrong, inasmuch as the son's rebellion stands really in the center of the Sophoclean version of the myth, but wrong as an answer to the question of what constitutes the truly archaic, primordial theme. That now appears to be not the rebellion of the son against the father, but the rebellion of the son against the mother. That is the insight, relevant not only for mythology but also for psychology, which results from an interpretation that considers all the versions and phases of the Oedipus myth.

We are faced with the typical, not to say natural basic conflict of a matriarchal society in which the mother prevents the son from maturing to masculine independence and finally kills him. No proof is needed any more that this conflict, seen from the son's angle, takes place on an oral basis, corresponding to the ambivalent concept of the feeding and the killing mother. From the mother's angle it looks entirely different: here an order exists which sanctions the highest unfolding of female genitality at the expense of artificially holding back the full development of the male one. That is clearly enough reflected in the predominantly feminine character of Minoan culture: that flower prince with whom our investigation started can certainly not be seen as a model of fully developed masculinity, as the Hellenic gods are seen later.

The sexes are thus fighting here for the right to fully developed genitality, and that struggle of the sexes, primarily rooted in the relation between mother and son, is historically and genetically more archaic than the conflict of generations between father and son. Matricide is a more archaic crime than patricide, while mother incest still in historical times was no crime at all if only certain rules were observed. How, then, did it become a crime?

Here at last our study issues into those considerations which Freud wrongly applied to an entirely fictitious primal period, but which were really decisive during the transition from a matriarchal to a strictly patriarchal order. The incest taboo became a compelling necessity for the ruler during that transitional period in order to protect his wife from the grasp of his sons. The case of Oedipus does not yet show that necessity in fully developed form but in a preliminary stage: Oedipus must slay Laios in order to take Jocasta as wife—he must take her as wife in order to be recognized as legitimate ruler by his subjects still living under a matriarchal order—but he fails in that. If he had kept to all the rules of the matriarchate, there would be no problem—the crown is conquered in a duel which also decides the hand of the queen. But Oedipus cannot act according to matriarchal law: as a member of a northwestern Greek people, he lives himself in a patrilinear order where rule is inherited from father to son (which is by far not yet the same as the fully developed patriarchate with its terrible taboos). Thus in order to achieve recognition for himself and above all for his sons from his own tribe, he has to claim a patriarchal Theban descent. To bring the patriarchal law of the conquerors into harmony with the matriarchal law of the conquered, he falsifies his genealogy—and thus commits a fictitious incest; at his time, certainly not yet the worst of the offenses, not even from the viewpoint of his own following.

That is the situation at the time of the migrations, when the new dynasties had not yet struck firm local roots, when at the same place one conqueror followed another, when in fact the sword, in the best case with respect for some rituals, decided at once about the crown and the hand of the queen. A tragic situation arises only in the fully developed Mycenean period, when the dynasties have become sedentary without the conquerors and the conquered yet having truly merged. For now the victors' crown is effectively inherited, according to the conquerors' law, from father to son—and in speaking of a "crown," we are referring not only to the king in the modern meaning of the term, but to the late Minoan and Mycenean concept of the *basilees* comprising the entire nobility. But those generations of rulers following each other in patrilinear succession must legitimate themselves before their subjects matriarchally, which is only possible through the hand of a female heiress, normally of the first degree, hence only through the hand of a mother, a sister or even—as with Thyestes in the legend of the Atrides—a daughter. The entire Atride myth turns almost exclusively on this struggle between the heirs for the women matriarchally entitled to inheritance, and reveals at the same time that permanent tragedy of incest the reaction against which then produced the Hellenic (and also the Jewish) legal order. What Freud projected back into primeval times was in fact a typical phenomenon of the postmigration period of the second pre-Christian millenium.

But the whole depth of the crisis can only be understood if one envisages once again that during late Helladic times, the crown tended to pass from one king to the next by the law of the sword. As any marriage reported in the legends shows, the wives of the new ruling dynasties mostly came from the nobility of the subject people; that applies to the marriage of Pelops and Hippodameia just as much as to that of Oedipus and Jocasta. Why, then, should the sons orient themselves in accordance with the paternal rather than the maternal ethos, if the former implied waiting for the distant death of the father, the latter a quick seizure of the throne? What had been customary in the later matriarchal system, the murder of the king by a stranger, now broke into a patrilinear system where murdering the king meant murdering the father or brother.

Incidentally, the content of the legends in no way confirms Freud's assumption of a primacy of incest with the mother in such cases: a sister or even a daughter had a much better chance to live long, thus assuring a long possession of the crown to her master. It is no accident that in the legends, incests among siblings far outnumber the mother incests, some of which can moreover be reduced to fictitious, "genealogical incests," intended to prove that the conqueror-husband of the queen was at the same time the son of the murdered king. It must be admitted, though, that at this point, the factor of historical reality diverges from the factor of unconscious motivation. While the strongest realistic considerations tended to make sibling incest appear more desirable than mother incest, the primordial struggle between mother and son, rooted in the early Minoan phase, pulled back towards a violent, aggressive mother incest—at least as an orally conditioned instinct. In the former case fratricide, in the latter patricide were inescapable corollaries, and both might be combined when, in the absence of legal primogeniture, the father favored one of the sons so that another son could rise to the throne only over the dead bodies of father and brother, which required the hand of the sister all the more. An illustration of those conflicts is supplied by the Atride myth, with its countless family murders and incests. A contrasting example is offered by the Egyptian usage of ritually prescribed sibling marriage (which not infrequently also occurs elsewhere), which once and for all combined the inheritance of the *Sacra* by the female hand with that of the *Regalia* by the male line, thus preventing any kind of Atride horrors.

Incest thus arises as a regular occurrence, laden with profound real conflicts, from the clash between patrilinear and matriarchal forms of life. From precisely the same situation, however, arises the incest taboo, which causes the patrilinear order to evolve into that kind of radical patriarchalism, that total subordination of the woman which we meet in the Jewish and the Hellenic ethos. Here we have no longer to conclude from legends on their underlying historic content: history itself is talking here. Not the Myceneans, but the last wave from northwestern Greece, the Dorians, have evolved this complete patriarchalism and transferred it to the other Greeks, thus laying the foundation for Hellenic culture. There is no occasion to assume that during their pastoral period, they would have lived more patriarchally than their predecessors coming from the same area, the Achaeans. Only the new wave of conquerors achieves that which the long-settled Myceneans could no longer bring about: it overcomes the self-destructive chaos of Mycenean inheritance and family law, it resolves all conflict by a far-reaching enslavement of the old matriarchal strata and a correspondingly radical rejection of their culture.

It is self-evident how this ultimate phase of development is reflected in the Oedipus myth: in the light of the Mycenean atrocities, the genealogical incest of Oedipus appeared as real incest, and his murder of a pretended father as real patricide. The myth as we know it is, like the Atride myth, a Hellenic reaction no longer to the problems of the late Helladic and early Mycenean, but to the horrors of the high and above all the late Mycenean period.

As to Freud's backward projection of those matters into primeval times, it has its own historic roots—not, of course, in the Hellenic but in the strictly analogous Jewish development. The claim that the patriarchate had been instituted together with the creation of man, that there had never been another legitimate order, was an effort to veil its real prehistory in order to make its validity seem absolute—in the Hellenic as in the Jewish case. Freud was just unable to free himself from that pretended absoluteness—as from many views about the nature and psychology of woman and some others linked with that "ideology." For all the psychic depths into which he penetrated, his image of the real world remained tied to two convergent factors—the Victorian ethos and the Jewish tradition. That is why he could not uncover the roots of the Oedipus myth and was at this point driven to a "direct interpretation" equally mistaken in method as in substance. That today it is already possible to see so much more clearly into those matters is only a consequence of the decay of that patriarchalism which was still a matter of course in Freud's youth and in his environment.

CHAPTER FIVE

The Philosophical Background: Beyond Space and Time

I. The Collapse of the Mechanistic Model in Physics

Among the commonplaces of the history of science with which we have all been made familiar, there is the legend that the growth of true scientific understanding has been characterized by the triumph of empirical enquiry over metaphysical speculation. Empiricism presumably means reliance upon the evidence of the senses, which raises the interesting question just what Aristotle was doing when he relied upon his senses to inform him that the sun revolves round the earth, or that all bodies tend to fall towards a center; as against, e.g., Copernicus and Galileo who refused to take experience on trust. The fact is, of course, that distrust of immediate sensory reality is fundamental to science. The primitive treats all phenomena as real, whereas cultural progress has always manifested itself in the acceptance of a distinction between immediate appearance and an underlying reality transformed by the human mind and connected with the phenomena of experience by increasingly tenuous links.

One can see the beginning of this process in the ancient Near East, whose learned priest-astronomers believed the stars to have more "reality" than the sublunary world. Pythagoras, Plato, and Euclid regarded the realm of mathematical symbols as more "real" than sensory experience, without, incidentally, being able to reduce the latter to the former. It is common knowledge that, in postmedieval times, Descartes undertook a similar unsuccessful attempt to derive sensory appearance from mathematical reality. That a genuine advance was made towards the solution of the problem we owe to his contemporary, Galileo, who inaugurated a compromise between Aristotle's naive sensualism and Descartes' mathematical intellectualism. The next development came with Newton, who managed to secure his concept against metaphysical criticism ("Hypotheses non fingo"). But his empiricism was only apparent. In reality he was convinced—as Locke was to state explicitly—that the universe of mechanical categories is the "real" world, to which in the last resort all sensory impressions can be reduced. Thus mechanics became *the* basic scientific discipline, a conceptual framework which was not to disappear finally until our own days.

Yet the late eighteenth century had already witnessed the first harbingers of subsequent trouble. Originally this was not due to the further progress of science, which on the contrary seemed to confirm the mechanicist world picture and its presuppositions: Euclidean space and an analogous time sequence. The first serious doubts were raised by Kant on epistemological grounds. Then came the discovery that it was possible to operate with non-Euclidean terms, though not to obtain a sensory representation of the new kind of spatial concept. Finally, at the beginning of the present century, there occurred, as we all know, the great dethronement of mechanism: its categories were shown to be inadequate both in the field of astrophysics and in that of atomic physics. Science was compelled to postulate non-Euclidean space, a spatially and temporally limited universe, and elementary particles which had no mass (and consequently could not be described as "matter"). These atoms, moreover, seemed to alter their position in (non-Euclidean) space in such a way as to skip the intervals between them. Some of this could be blamed on the inadequacy of macroscopic instruments for the study of microscopic processes, but other phenomena—e.g., the dissolution of the atom—suggested a fundamental indeterminacy of the process as such: that is to say, neither more nor less than the absence of causality.

Now all this would not have been fatal for the traditional epistemology if it had resulted in the development of a new system of categories, however remote from the senses. The real trouble is that there is no such system, and that physical science has consequently been compelled to operate in the newly conquered fields with a variety of different, and frequently incompatible, hypotheses. This state of affairs in turn was bound to deepen the scepticism concerning the ontological significance of physical research which Kant had been the first to proclaim and which Helmholtz had explicitly introduced into natural science. Such scepticism had in fact preceded the new discoveries—a phenomenon familiar from other phases of the history of science. Even before the emergence of the new atomic physics, thinkers like Ernst Mach, Henri Poincaré, and William James had proclaimed the ontological meaninglessness of natural science and stressed its strictly practical orientation. So far from buttressing the philosophical self-confidence of the physicists, the grandiose discoveries of subsequent years could only serve to deepen this attitude. Today it has on the whole become common form among natural scientists to refrain from metaphysical interpretation of scientific research. Where this self-denying ordinance is not observed one either encounters attempts to save the validity of the classical spatiotemporal categories, or else a plain expression of scepticism (in the traditional meaning of the term).

Yet neither attitude is really satisfactory. The classical system derived its strength from the fact that, while it reduced the validity of sensory experience to an often extreme degree, it never really conflicted with it or went beyond it in principle. Space, time, mass, measurability, predictableness—these are all categories which conform to sensory experience, so that the classical mechanicist system can almost be defined as an attempt to construct, with the aid of a minimum of sensible experience, a world picture which in principle is capable of indefinite expansion and development. Such a system was just barely defensible as long as the non-Euclidean geometrical forms introduced since 1819 could be treated as an affair of "pure" mathematics. The moment one began to construct a physical universe on this basis, the link between science and the sensory realm had, as a matter of principle, been broken. Even were it possible (which is far from likely) to bring the various hypotheses of the new physics into conformity with each other (e.g., the strict causality of Relativity physics with the evident noncausality of essential aspects of atomic physics), the incompatibility of the sensory world with the universe of science would still constitute an insurmountable obstacle to the emergence of a unified system of categories.

The proper course clearly is to drop all sceptical doubt concerning the "reality" of this whole realm, and to accept it as it presents itself, for all the methodological confusion this entails. That, however, involves an alteration of the epistemological starting-point. It is fortunate from our point of view that the collapse of mechanism makes this possible. The leading role played by mechanics in the classical tradition was due to the fact that, apart from mathematics, it provided the only existing system which clearly was derived from first principles. With the dissolution of this system, mechanics can no longer aspire to the place it once occupied. It has indeed become apparent enough that what the eighteenth and nineteenth centuries regarded as the "natural" edifice of science—i.e., an edifice founded on a pervasive mechanicism—was in fact the most unnatural construction imaginable: nothing surely is farther removed from the immediate sensory experience than a concept of external nature from which all the qualities of concreteness have been totally abstracted. If scientific development has done nothing else, it has restored the right to place immediate experience (and notably human self-awareness) alongside those mechanist principles whose hegemony in all methodological and epistemological fields was still accepted, by Kant, for example, as the most natural thing in the world.

II. The Timelessness and Noncausality of the Unconscious

Now the point to be noted is that, side by side with the new science of what might be called "depth physics", the modern period has witnessed the emergence of what is commonly called "depth psychology." The parallelism is not fortuitous, and if it has not hitherto been seriously investigated, the cause presumably lies in the mutual antipathy which has characterized the relationship of physics and psychology since time immemorial. It must, of course, be conceded that the experiential methods applied in their respective domains are radically different. While physics concentrates exclusively on the external world, the psychologist, though he views the objects of his study "from outside," in the last resort reflects upon his own inner experience. It is therefore advisable to set aside, for the time being, what we have learned about the significance of unconscious processes, and to fix our attention upon the formal structure of the unconscious, as it reveals itself in dreams, hallucinations, and similar phenomena. In doing so one cannot help being struck by the curious resemblance between certain features of unconscious psychology and the structure of the subatomic world, as reflected in modern physical theory. To guard against possible misunderstanding, let me say at once that this suggestion is not intended to revive the absurdities perpetrated by early representatives of the psychoanalytic school, who tried to explain physical theories in terms of unconscious processes. The point at issue is a more modest one, namely the existence of structural resemblances, and their possible significance.

What these resemblances are has already been indicated by reference to the partial dissolution of the category of causality in modern physics.

Now lack of causality is a familiar element of dreams and other unconscious processes. In dreams we skip over space and time, and the "absurd" appears entirely possible. Yet space, time, and causality are not
entirely absent from dreams, any more than from modern physics. Apart
from the fact that the dreamer is embedded in a spatiotemporal reality,
the latter makes its appearance in the "manifest" content of his dream.
The dream cannot do without the spatiotemporal continuum: its pictures
are spatial, its actions evolve in time, and incoherent fragments of causality are carried over from waking. Yet these elements of the dream are
all constituents of waking life, comparable to the physical instruments
which operate within the framework of spatiotemporal causality. The
dream process as such seems indifferent to the causal nexus, whence it
used to be concluded that dreams, like hallucinations, are explicable only
in terms of a physiological disorder of the brain. To us it appears that
the welter of incompatibilities present in dreaming is no worse than that
which we encounter in microphysics, and if it is objected that atomic
physics, unlike dreaming, yields coherent results, the answer is not far
to seek: dreams, too, can be translated (by the analyst) into logically
coherent structures. Doubtless the atom and the dream belong to different
worlds; they are incommensurable—as uncommensurable as thought and
matter! Yet the philosophical axiom that thought and matter stand apart
has always been accompanied by the reminder that the categories of
thought have the peculiarity of being able to render external reality
comprehensible, predictable, and governable. When one comes to think
of it, this curious coincidence of thinking and being—identity in the midst
of total discontinuity—is *the* basic problem of classical and, for the most
part, of European philosophy. Is it really so surprising to encounter an
analogous relationship at the level of modern science?

The point can be defined more narrowly. Of the two dimensions of
the spatiotemporal continuum, space ranks first in physics, time in psychology. True, the dream dispenses with spatial limitations, but then the
unconscious—like all inner awareness—is anyhow not concerned with
space. What appears striking is the loss of the time dimension. Time,
if we are to believe Kant, is the basic category of internal apperception;
that the unconscious ignores it appears not merely in the phenomena of
dream and hallucination, but in what Freud calls the "timelessness" of
unconscious reactions where they impinge upon consciousness. Thus,
however urgent an action or a decision is from the conscious viewpoint,
the unconscious may and does react as though it had an eternity at its
disposal, as though neither time nor death existed. This absence of the

time dimension is the obverse of noncausal relationships: what cannot be measured in temporal terms is not predictable, and predictability is a basic constituent of causality.

Yet we find Freud asserting that the unconscious is "strictly determined"; he even goes so far as to suggest that his own discoveries were made possible by a bias in favor of thoroughgoing determinism. How can this hiatus be bridged? One is driven reluctantly to conclude that a gap is bound to remain. This is one of those instances where Freud's attachment to crude nineteenth-century determinism stands in the way of a correct formulation of his own insights. Yet his formula reflects a fundamental datum of analytical work which merely requires a different expression. In the mechanicist terminology on which Freud was brought up and to which he adhered throughout his life, there is always one and the same causality which either determines or—conceivably, but not actually—fails to determine the processes of the material world. This frame of reference is entirely adequate for inanimate nature, though physics has in the meantime taught us that there are noncausal processes. But once we enter the realm of life, of consciousness, and *a fortiori* of the human mind, the contrast between timelessness and indeterminacy, which raises so many puzzles in atomic physics, vanishes. Here the absence of the time dimension is no longer incompatible with determination of a sort. Trivial though it is, one is compelled to stress the distinction between external and internal determination, between the physical push or pull and the psychological process. In the light of this distinction, let us take a glance at Freud's development as a scientist, as it has been disclosed to us by some recent publications.

III. Determinism and Freedom in Depth Psychology

Freud was originally a pupil of Bruecke, himself a disciple of Helmholtz; as a theorist therefore he derives from Helmholtz, Herbarth, and Fechner. His starting-point was in fact mechanicist in the extreme: every psychological event must have an *external* cause. On this assumption, causation in the realm of psychology is due to physiological lesion of some nervous function. In later years Freud was to comment humorously on his early attempts to trace the secrets of the soul (or the psyche, as he rather prudishly preferred to call it) in the medulla oblongata. He had, however, broken away from this extreme attitude long before he made his first psychoanalytic discoveries. In his paper on aphasia, which was considerably in advance of his time, he showed that while there was a general connection between disorders of speech and lesions of the vocal organs, no precise link was traceable between a specific lesion and the functional disorder arising from it. The latter appeared rather to be determined in the main by the sequence in which the patient had obtained his command of language. This suggestion represented a definite departure from the notion of external causation—an innovation whose significance seems to have escaped Freud.

The first step away from mechanism had been purely empirical; the next was virtually unconscious. When Freud turned to hypnosis and, to his surprise, found that his patients flooded him with a mass of sexual recollections released in this state, it was natural for him to conclude that psychical disorders were primarily due to disturbances of sexual development. This notion could without difficulty be given its place in a general doctrine pivoting, if not on mechanics, at any rate on biology—a doctrine, moreover, which in the last resort suggested a physicochemical basis for the whole process. Not long after Freud's first discoveries in his chosen field, this line of approach was in fact taken up quite independently by others, and eventually gave rise to the present-day doctrine of secretion, hormone disturbances, and hormone therapy.

The really remarkable thing is that Freud did not pursue this line of thought, which was so closely in accordance with his mental training; instead, as we know, he radically renounced all thought of biochemical causation and founded his therapy exclusively upon the unconscious mental processes of his patients—processes which indeed turned out to be largely founded in sexual experience. And the reason was that his first halting hypnotic-cathartic cures had given him an insight into the 'determination' of psychic events by repressed memories to the elucidation of which he was to devote the remainder of his life. Sexuality remained the core of psychoanalytic theory and practice, but a complete breach was effected with physiology, its place being taken by a unique soul-therapy in which sexuality as a physiological factor represented only the general background. Inevitably the concept of sexuality tended in time to become more elastic, and psychoanalysis gradually was transformed into a general theory and therapy of personal development.

What then is the inner psychic determination of events in the human soul whose discovery we owe to Freud? The answer is contained in the therapeutic method: the patient suffers from symptoms which he cannot overcome as long as they remain incomprehensible, and analysis exercises its healing function by helping him to understand them. It does not do this by acquainting him with sexual-biological theories; instead it illuminates the repressed psychic process from which the symptom arose, discloses the unconscious function of the latter, and thus helps to make it meaningful. *What this therapy brings to light are not causal connections but teleological ones*: repressed desires, conflicting urges, and unstable compromises between instinctual drives and ethically or socially motivated prohibitions. The picture which unfolds in this way (though Freud of course would not have admitted this) is best described in Aristotelian and scholastic language: *causae efficientes* and *causae finales* and the relevant distinction between external occasion and inner volition. The genuine novelty of Freud's approach lay precisely in the fact that, without denying the sphere of external causation (biologically founded instinctual urges) he made therapy entirely dependent upon the disclosure of the repressed *telos*.

In the light of this innovation, the conflict between determinacy and indeterminacy in the realm of unconscious processes appears capable of solution. The point to bear in mind is that teleological behavior is not peculiar to the unconscious, but is even more characteristic of the conscious personality. What Freud really did—in clear contrast to his original starting-point—was to found a science which serves to subject the unconscious to the teleology of reason. As long as the unconscious had not been understood it appeared senseless, and its products, such as dream and hallucination, were regarded as absurd and capable only of explanation in terms of physiological causality. Freud's innovation, whose significance was veiled from him, consisted in showing that this semblance of pseudocausality vanishes when the neurotic symptom has been understood, i.e., assigned its place in a finalistic order. This leads to the further conclusion that what Freud described as the determined character of mental life had better be defined as its freedom. Needless to say, this freedom is not absolute. The human being is confronted with a mighty external world, of which his own body forms part and parcel. This "given" situation is the substratum of human volition and action; but in dealing with this set of circumstances we do not mechanically obey their impulses: we rearrange the conditions of life in accordance with the principles governing the mental process.

It is, of course, possible to suggest that this apparent freedom is really nothing but another form of causality—to be precise: the determination of each individual action by inherited and acquired characteristics of the personality. Here, too, there is no sharp distinction between conscious and unconscious processes, and once more the way out of the difficulty is suggested by what we have learned about the unconscious. In this case the relevant phenomenon is the so-called "choice between neuroses": a stumbling-block for psychoanalytical theory, but a source of illumination for the philosopher. Its significance for the subject of human volition has repeatedly been stressed by philosophically minded psychoanalysts. Briefly, the problem is this: if both conscious and unconscious processes are subject to a thoroughgoing "inner" determinism, then it must be possible to coordinate at least the major types of pathological mental aberration with clearly definable disturbances in the hereditary constitution or in the development of individuals.

To this end, Freud's doctrine of sexual phases appears to offer a favorable starting-point. As is generally known, Freud postulates a number of partial instinctual urges linked in each case with a particular bodily zone, and an interconnection between these drives; neuroses and perversions are then related to constitutional handicaps or, more important, to traumatic disturbances in the development of the respective phases of sexual development, and their peculiarities are determined by the particular character of the phase to which they are linked.

Unfortunately, this theory is not wholly borne out by practical experience. The weak point appears to be the doctrine of chronological development in the evolution of the particular instinctual urges, which in their totality come together to form what is regarded as normal sexuality. It is becoming increasingly evident that all the various partial urges are already demonstrable in the first years of life, from which it follows that the connection between specific neuroses and specific phases of development is beginning to look dubious. What emerges in practice is the concept of a syndrome of various neurotic and psychotic traits, between which no causally determined selection can be demonstrated. Incidentally, Freud himself on one occasion formulated this kind of insight when he remarked that it is possible to comprehend a neurosis from its various "determinants," but not to predict their result, and that a different combination of the same determinants (i.e., the same unconscious wishes and aims) in the form of a different neurosis or psychosis would be equally plausible. This is as much as to say that, while analysis discloses the unconscious significance of a particular neurosis, the same meaning might have been fulfilled in a variety of ways freely chosen by the individual.

Doubtless Freud was unaware that two decades earlier, in 1888, Bergson had said the same of the operation of consciousness, and at the same time established a close connection between conscious and unconscious processes by his concept of the *décision profonde*. Bergson held that while we can always obtain some sort of hindsight understanding of the peculiarly personal (i.e., not conventionally routine) decisions of an individual, we can never, as a matter of principle, predict them with an adequate degree of reliability—a statement which happens to correspond both with the experience of daily life and with the unpredictableness of historical development familiar to the politician and the historian. It is surely no accident that this doctrine of the unpredictability of the *décision profonde* is linked in Bergson's thought with a belief in the "timelessness" of human activity at the deeper levels. Bergson's *durée*, which he counterposes to the chronologically ordered time sequence of physics, resembles Freud's unconscious in eluding measurement and prediction.

It may be suggested that we have here the key to the paradox of those unconscious operations which are described as being both timeless and strictly determined. The determination in question is not one belonging to the spatiotemporal continuum with its causal relations; it is teleological, self-determined, and thus identical with freedom. What Freud did, quite without knowing it, was to dethrone the mechanicist principles of psychology and to reconstitute the ancient concept of freedom common to philosophers from the Stoics to Descartes; and he did so by demonstrating that freedom is not arbitrariness, but rather the highest degree of self-determination in accordance with the necessities of one's own being. Presumably he would not have been too pleased to be told that this concept of liberty is substantially that of the scholastics, of Thomas Aquinas, of Descartes and Spinoza, and lastly of Hegel. Perhaps the only doctrine with which it is wholly incompatible is the existentialist one, which declares man to be "absolutely" free, i.e., radically independent, and, in the last resort, godlike: an aberration as pregnant with latent consequences as the causal universe of mechanism which now lies behind us.

PART TWO

Contributions to the Origin of the West

Linguistic Prelude

CHAPTER ONE

The Rise of the I-Form of Speech

"I, Hlegestr from Holt made this Horn." Thus runs a runic inscription, found on a golden horn, an object of some value, at Gallehus in Denmark. Experts put its date at a little after 400 A.D. It does, therefore, belong not by any means to the oldest runic inscriptions we possess, yet to the oldest phase of runic script and of the Old Norse language known to us. Is there any specific significance in it?

The content, to be sure, is trivial enough. The craftsman who made the horn found it beautiful enough to give praise to his own craftsmanship. Similar inscriptions more often refer not to the maker but to the owner of some object. There is nothing remarkable in either. There is to be found, however, in the inscription quoted above, a linguistic peculiarity so striking that it is a little surprising that, as far as I am aware, due emphasis has never been laid upon it. The peculiar feature is the use of the personal pronoun "I" (old Norse "ek") in this context. The "I" stands before the name of the person who is "I." Our inscription is not an isolated case of such use of the personal pronoun in runic inscriptions. There are many inscriptions of an exactly identical type, though the one quoted is among the earliest. The use of the personal pronoun was, however, not obligatory in contexts of this kind. There abound inscriptions with texts such as "Toeler owns this bracelet," inscriptions in which the author, owner, maker of something speaks of himself in the third person.

Every student of Latin and old Greek knows that the use of the personal pronoun as found on the golden horn of Gallehus would be inconceivable in any inscription dating from any period of classical antiquity. Ancient Greek and Roman inscriptions invariably conform to the type of our second quotation, that of the owner of a bracelet speaking of himself in the third person. A Roman craftsman might have said: Gn. Manlius faber hoc cornu fecit—The craftsman Gn. Manlius made this horn. The use of the first person in such a case would be in glaring opposition to the spirit of the Latin language.

The use of "I" together with a proper name is not only different from any kind of expression known in the classical languages, it also sets off old Norse from the most important contemporary language of Northern Europe. We have a considerable number of inscriptions in "Ogham," the archaic script of old Irish. They are possibly somewhat later in date than the oldest runic inscriptions—the matter is controversial—and, in contrast to the latter, all belong to Christian times. Most of them are inscriptions on burial stones. But never once appears the pronoun "I" on any of these Irish inscriptions, whether in connection with the maker of the stone, the man buried beneath it, or the person who set it.

The use of the word "I" in old Norse might also have been a common Germanic habit. But this is not the case. There is known to us at least one Germanic document older than the oldest runic texts: the Gothic translation of the bible. This work, dating from about 350 A.D., and preserving a teutonic language spoken between the Danube and the Don, shows no trace of any such use of "I," though the many emphatic speeches of the gospels would give ample opportunity for it. The use of "I" as revealed in the runic inscriptions from Scandinavia is thus unique, in respect to the habits of classical antiquity, of Northern Europe during the period in question, and of older Germanic idioms.

Such an isolated habit is a striking fact. It is conceivable that it should be nothing more than a freak. But it is as likely that it reveals an important change in outlook, far-reaching in both its causes and its effects. The whole course of our subsequent investigation is intended to prove the latter.

Let us first follow the fate of the pronoun "I" in old Norse. It has an interesting history, which we are summing up in a few words, without unnecessary quotations. Those who wish to study the details will best consult Noreen's grammar of Old Icelandic,[1] which gives all the facts, without, however, emphasizing their uniqueness. In the oldest phase of Norse known to us, we can only trace the use of "I," of the first person

1. Adolf Noreen, *Altislandische und altnorwegische Grammatik* (Halle/S.: Niemeyer, 1923).

pronoun. Later the second and third person also appear. And at the same time the pronoun starts being connected not only with names but also with the verb. "Jarl Ufr heitek," runs an inscription of the sixth century from Jaersberg in Sweden. "Heite" has no full counterpart in English; it is the German "heisse," "I am named." The letter k at the end is the shortened form of Norse "ek," "I." Thus the word "I" is suffixed to the verb. "Jarl Ufr *I* call myself", runs the inscription. The contrast with old Greek and Latin is, again, absolute. In both these languages the personal pronoun is not used with the verb, except in order to avoid ambiguity or emphasize some contrast. The Roman says "facio"; the verbal ending makes it clear that this means, not, e.g., "he does," but "I do." We moderns say "I do." So did, for the first time in the history of Indo-European speech, the old Norsemen, only that they started by putting the pronoun behind the verb, shortening it to a single consonant, and not before it, in proud isolation, as we moderns do. Very soon the third person of the pronoun is also suffixed to the verb, though not regularly. And some time later the pronoun creeps from the end of the verb forward to its beginning. In the bars of the poetic Edda, dating from the ninth century, this process is completed. In the prose Edda, which dates from much later, but whose material is probably, in part at least, not more than two hundred years younger than that of the poetic Edda, the use of the pronoun with the verb has become obligatory, exactly as in modern English, French, and German.

Be it added that no trace of such a connection of pronoun and verb could be discovered in Gothic, any more than a connection between pronoun and proper names. No trace of it can be discovered in Church Slavonic, the oldest form of Slavonic known to us and dating back to the ninth century. The prominence of the personal pronoun marks off old Norse from contemporary languages in all directions; though not without qualifications to be mentioned later.

As said already, this uniqueness in its own period of the use of the personal pronoun in old Norse has not been noticed by anybody. The contrast, however, between the ample use of this pronoun in the modern languages of Northern Europe and its scanty use in classical antiquity could not pass unnoticed. Linguists, naturally, have sought for an explanation of this contrast. But all their attempts in this direction have been misdirected by their neglect of the problem where the new type of speech first emerged. Had they taken old Norse into account, instead of comparing classical and modern languages directly, they would have seen that the new use of the personal pronoun does not start in connection with the verb but with names. And this is of the greatest importance for the sake of discovering the real and profound meaning of the habit. Several arguments can be brought up to prove that the use of the pronoun before the verb is convenient for speech, and this use can be explained as a matter of mere expediency; whereas no expediency can be invoked to explain the use of "I" before names. "I Harald did it" is, as an inscription, not in the least more useful than "Harald did it." The latter, Latin way of expression is shorter, simpler, and more elegant.

But though this disregard of the Norse use of pronoun plus name vitiates all theories brought forward about the use of "I" in modern languages, we shall nevertheless have to begin by considering these theories, which have their own merits. We may bring them in the main under two headings. The most exclusively linguistic theory maintains that the use of the pronoun arose because the verb endings became indistinguishable. The verb in je fais, tu fais, il fait sounds exactly alike. It is impossible to distinguish between them but by prefixing the pronoun. Conversely, almost all current grammars of modern languages seem to accept it as a sufficient explanation of the absence of such use of the pronoun that the verbal endings are sufficiently clear in themselves without it. According to these commonsense grammarians, the absence of the pronoun before the verb in such languages as Italian and Spanish, Czech and Polish, is sufficiently explained by the fact that the verbal endings in these languages differ sufficiently from one another to leave no doubt about the person which is meant.

This explanation, though the one accepted by almost all grammarians, is yet totally unsatisfactory. It may, in some cases, explain why at a certain moment, in certain languages, the use of the pronoun became obligatory. But it does not explain how it started centuries before the endings of the verb became indistinct. Thus there is no possibility of using this explanation in the case of old Norse, the oldest case known to us, because in old Norse the endings were perfectly clear. And they were clear in other Germanic languages which adopted the same use, as we shall soon see. Verbal endings were quite clear in themselves in Medieval French and Provençal, which also both used the pronoun amply. It must be added that, where the avoidance of ambiguity is really the motive force behind the change, the new forms remain limited to those cases where ambiguity would otherwise arise. Thus, in modern Bulgarian, the personal pronoun is used in those tenses where there are no verbal endings, but remains unused where they exist.

Finally, it must be maintained that the explanation of the use of the pronoun through the disuse of verbal endings is arbitrary. Why not conversely explain the disuse of the verbal endings through the use of the pronoun? There is, as far as I am aware, not a single case where it can be proved that the verbal endings disappeared *before* the use of the pronoun became obligatory. Nor is such a development easily conceivable. But then it can be just as true that the growing use of the pronoun made the endings more and more useless. Prefixed pronouns and verbal endings seem to be mutually interdependent, and there is no reason to suppose that loss of endings has brought about the use of the pronoun where the theory of interaction between the two processes is so much more satisfactory.

We must therefore conclude that the presence of full verbal endings should never be used as an explanation for the absence of the personal pronoun before the verb, which is obviously due to much deeper reasons, and that by contradistinction the use of the personal pronoun before the verb can be regarded, in many cases, as an adequate explanation for the loss of verbal endings. Occasionally, and in particular in French, where the spirit of the language insists so strongly upon complete clarity, the gradual slurring of verbal endings may have been a contributory factor not in the emergence of the use of the pronoun with the verb, but in its becoming obligatory.

The second view here to be considered is not to be found explicitly in any grammar, but is implied in a widely accepted theory about the evolution of language. The use of the pronoun with the verb might be regarded as one element in a general development of language from the "synthetic" towards the "analytical." The meaning of these terms is simple. Language has the task of expressing representations in words. There are languages tending to express in one word as many representations as possible. They are the "synthetic" languages.[2] Other languages prefer neatly to divide speech into the constituent elements of the underlying representation. These are analytical. The Latin said "feci," expressing in one and the same word the idea of doing, the fact that something was done in the past, and the third idea that it was "I" who did it. We say "I have done," assigning one word to each of these three notions. It is maintained that the general trend of development goes from the synthetic towards the analytical, that the ancient languages are synthetic, the modern languages analytical. The wider prominence of the personal pronoun might be regarded as simply a part of that change.

2. The term "synthetic" is taken over from French, and we are using it henceforth in the meaning given to it in French linguistic theory, despite the slightly different connotations of the term in English.

With this theory we feel as if, suddenly, we emerged from a narrow estuary into the open sea. Here is a doctrine which does not treat language as something isolated in itself and obeying what specialists so fondly call "its own laws." The inadequacy of explaining major changes of speech in terms of speech expediency only, without taking full account of the role of speech as an expression of changing ideas and conceptions, is obvious. Now the transition from synthesis to analysis is not a linguistic fact only, but a general trend of evolution finding expression in all aspects of life, speech being one of them. Analytical speech is not more expedient than synthetic speech, much the contrary. Nothing could be simpler than the Latin expression "feci," which needs three words to translate it into any modern language of North-Western Europe. Nothing also could be more precise. Students of classical languages know how many of their shades and refinements have been lost in our modern languages without economy of words. Translations into Latin from any modern language, with the one significant exception of English, are invariably shorter than the original. The transition from the synthetic to the analytical mode of speech cannot therefore be the result of expediency and simplification. It is due to a fundamental change in psychology. This change of psychology is connected with the deepest changes in the structure of civilization.

Into this problem of the fundamental changes of civilization our investigation is now leading, after having started from the apparently modest fact of a new use of the personal pronoun. What is revealed in the change of language must be reflected in other aspects of civilization in general. If, out of these many aspects, we select language as a starting point, it is merely for the sake of convenience. Any other aspect might have been chosen, and our further investigation will carry us through many of them. If we use language as a starting point it is because more than any other aspect of civilization, it is emphatically a means and not an end. Any other starting point is bound to raise the endless query about fundamentals and superstructures in social life. Whether you choose economics or religion, or any other factor of social life, you are sure to raise the controversy as to whether you have selected something essential, or something superficial. This query can hardly be raised in respect of language. Language is obviously there to express something other than itself. But at the same time it is a generalized form of expression for everything, a fluid, epitomizing instinctively all attitudes and modes of behavior to be found in a society. *Language*, in one word, *is the most direct reflection of the instinctive underlying attitudes of a civilization.* The study of language, if used in this sense, seems to me the most direct and the most penetrating access to the core of any given civilization. Therefore problems such as the causes of the transition from a synthetic to an analytical mode of speech go right to the essence of the distinctive features of various civilizations.

So far, the study of language has not been sufficiently used for this task. This is largely due, I believe, to the special shape linguistics assumed after the beginning of the last century, when the unity of the Indo-European languages dawned upon linguists. Since then languages have been arranged into "natural" groups, groups into subgroups, subgroups into individual languages, and those languages into dialects and groups of dialects. The tracing of the connection between the most remote village dialect and the aboriginal language of the Indo-Europeans became the ideal determining method down to its details. But the unity of Indo-European languages is of small importance in the history of the higher civilizations. On the one hand our Western civilization is no nearer to that of India than to that of China, though Indo-European languages are spoken in the greater part of India. On the other hand one of its strongest roots leads back to the semitic civilizations, though Babylonian, Hebrew, and Arabic have hardly any linguistic connection with the languages of the West. The existence of a hypothetical Indo-European language, which was probably spoken somewhere about 5000 years ago, must have reflected a unity of civilization of the tribes that spoke it, at the time when they spoke it. It has for more than three thousand years at least ceased to reflect anything, except the power of conservatism in language habits.

What is so obvious in the case of the Indo-European family of languages is less obvious, though no less true, in the case of the major subgroups of this family. The close interrelation, in terms of linguistic proximity, of all the Latin, all the Teutonic, all the Slavonic languages respectively, does not necessarily reflect any particularly close relation between the civilizations of the peoples who speak them. These subgroups, to be sure, have remained united much longer than the whole trunk of Indo-European languages; most of them, even today, live in geographical proximity, and therefore in many cases cultural and psychological similarities correspond to the similarity of language. But one has only to think of France and Romania, of England and Austria or, in terms of non-Indo-European languages, of Finland and Turkey, to realize that the conclusion from the existence of language ties to ties of civilization is inadmissible. Comparative linguistics, as long as they dealt with their subject from the viewpoint of the common origin of languages, dealt with something which, if not irrelevant, is at any rate of only limited importance for the study of civilizations.

Let us take it for granted that, as a child acquires all the main elements of speech which, in later life, it is going to use for purposes essentially different from those of children, so the languages of the higher civilizations go back, in all essentials, to a remote primitive past which has little in common with the present. Only the more reason for linguistics to insist upon those acquisitions which have been made in a later age, along lines different from those along which language originally developed. In other words, if we want to study languages in their relation to higher civilizations we must group them along lines in accordance with the boundary lines of those civilizations, and not along the boundaries of the linguistic groups. "Natural" language groups, i.e., groups of common linguistic descent, may be essential in abstract linguistics, but should be disregarded, as much as possible, by the student of history in his use of language as an approach to the "soul" of a civilization. Thus, as we shall see in a moment, Sandfeldt-Jensen, a Dane, has produced almost a revolution in linguistics through his "Linguistique balkanique," a work bringing out the profound similarity of all Balkan languages, though they belong to no less than four different language groups (Latin, Greek, Slavonic, Illyrian), and tracing these profound similarities to the underlying community of the Byzantine civilization.[3]

The problem of the transition from the synthetic to the analytical type of language is a case in point. It is a process affecting, to different degrees, all modern European languages, in close connection with their affiliation to various modern civilizations, but with little reference to the natural language groups. Take the case of the declension of the noun. Most Balkan languages have lost the Dative, and have thus maintained three cases, the Nominative, Genitive, and Accusative. But Serbo-Croat has kept seven cases, while neighboring and closely related Bulgarian has lost all but one. The Western Latin languages have lost the case endings completely, but not so Romanian, which conforms to the Balkan pattern. English has kept the Saxon genitive, while German has preserved, in a much reduced stage, a declension of four cases. It should be obvious that the tendency of eliminating cases and replacing them by the nominative with a preposition is a common European trend, and that languages can be grouped according to the degree of their participation in it. The

---

3. Kristian Sandfeldt-Jensen, *Linguistique Balkanique: Problèmes et résultats* (Paris: Champion, 1930).

measure of that participation, to say it again, is closely related to their cultural affiliations, and very little to their "natural" language affiliation.

Now let us try to find out how far the emergence of the pronoun with the verb in all modern languages of Northern Europe can be traced to the trend away from "synthetic" and towards "analytical" speech.

The synthetic stage of language, as classically (and almost exclusively) represented by the older Indo-European languages such as Sanskrit, Old Greek, Latin, Gothic, Church Slavonic, old Lithuanian, and several others, may look like a "primitive" form of speech. It is nothing of the kind. Linguists are agreed that it must have been preceded by an "isolating" stage, a stage where neither declension of the noun nor inflection of the verb existed, where there were only roots which were mechanically put together. Many primitive languages have maintained this type to this day. In this period, in order to express tense, an adjective of time would have to be put next to the verb; in order to express person, a personal pronoun. The flexible Indo-European languages evolved, through various intermediate stages, from isolating languages, as the various pronouns, adverbs, and other particles regularly prefixed and suffixed to verb and subject, merged with the latter, being completely transformed in the process. It is, in particular, a generally accepted hypothesis that the personal endings of the Indo-European verb were originally independent personal pronouns. Thus our present use of the pronoun is nothing but a resumption of the habits of our linguistic ancestors of more than five thousand years ago, with the one difference that they, apparently, put the pronoun behind the verb, where we put it before it. But we have already remarked that in old Norse, and we shall see that also in a number of other languages, the pronoun in its reemergence passed through a stage when it was suffixed to the verb, before being prefixed to it.

The intellectual effort involved in the development of inflected languages out of isolating languages must have been great indeed. Inflection arises out of the slurring of short particles. But in order to make such slurring possible and the slurred endings still intelligible, it is necessary to treat the various cases of the noun, the various tenses, modes, persons, etc., of the verb as no more than modifications and, as it were, functions of one and the same basic idea, represented in the root of the verb and of the noun. Isolating languages want as many roots as they can have, because their basic ideas must be simple, elemental.

The flexible Indo-European languages tried to reduce the number of roots. In order to bring about that process of reduction, vast numbers of expressions (such as the hundred or more forms of one Greek or

Sanskrit verb) were reduced to functions of one root only. It has already been mentioned that this involved treating a compound of notions as a unity. If we analyze so simple an expression as "feci," "I have done," we find that it is a verb corresponding to the concept of doing, in the past tense, perfective aspect, indicative mood, in the active, singular, first person. The logical content of such a linguistic synthesis is enormous. Most of this achievement has been lost again in the development away from the early Indo-European languages towards our modern languages, which are, again, much more isolating in type.

Henri Bergson, the great French philosopher, has insisted upon the importance of synthesis of this kind. Wherever, he maintains, life and its expressions are concerned, there are two modes of understanding them. One is by intellectual analysis, which dissolves the smallest piece of life into an infinite number of elements, which again dissolve into an infinite number of similar elements. But there is also an approach to life, as it were, from inside, the instinctive approach which we have towards our own life if we experience it without any reference to its position in the external world, and this approach shows every action as a unity, merging into the wider unity of the individual as a whole, which in turn is merged into the wider unity of life as a whole, which is the same as the universe as a whole. Bergson treats intellect and analysis, instinct and synthesis, as opposites. But what we said above about language shows that, in our context at least, the contrast is a relative one, and that synthesis is not a product of an original instinct but of long development and great intellectual effort. Bergson discusses the case of an arm trying to raise a load; which, investigated by science, dissolves into an infinity of muscular, mechanical, chemical, atomic processes, but is felt and executed as a single, indivisible act by the person who does raise the load. True! Yet one must not conclude that this instinctive effort is not therefore intellectual, or that it is primitive in any way. The man who would use atomic theory for raising his arm would be mad. But the new-born cannot raise its arm to good effect. Everybody knows that it is possible to acquire instinctive control of highly complex actions such as are needed, e.g., in fencing or piano playing, but that this is the result of long effort, part of it keenly intellectual. Exactly the same applies to the acquisition of synthetic speech, first by the group, and later by the young individual.

It is the beauty, the lure, the tragedy of the early Indo-European civilizations to have brought this synthesis to what, probably, is the highest possible degree within reach of mankind. What we call the "harmony" of Greece, a thing for which we shall ever long and which we shall never achieve again, is essentially this synthetic capacity. A wholly synthetic language such as ancient Greek is a clear revelation of this harmony. Yet we should never forget that, for such harmony, a price must be paid which we, the civilization of the "I"-sayers, would never be prepared to pay. However great the effort, however great the artistic gift (and the artistic gift is altogether, in essence, the gift of synthetic or "harmonious" expression), the limits to every synthesis are very narrow. A first-rate skier may instinctively coordinate several dozen muscular actions, with their infinite shades. He could not coordinate several thousand muscular actions. But a modern plane consists of several thousand elements which are coordinated mechanically, whereas every care is taken that the number of levers the pilot has to control should be reduced to the unavoidable minimum. Similarly, a highly complex ancient Greek verb may express, synthetically, a dozen different connotations. But any attempt to go beyond that charmed circle of linguistic synthesis is no longer "good Greek," is a move in the direction of analytical speech, away from the spirit of classical antiquity. One of the reasons why the classics get linguistically so "difficult," to the despair of school-boys, as soon as they try to deal with the abstract, is the highly synthetic character of the classical languages which obliges them to condense where we moderns would expand.

We are not dealing here with the classical civilizations, and we are using the classical languages only as a foil against which to mark off the problems of modern speech. This much, however, must be said: the effort to achieve a harmonious, limited synthesis is characteristic of classical antiquity as a whole. Here we are on the ground covered by Spengler, ground which, however rightly contested in many directions, is firm, I believe, where his interpretation of the classical world is concerned. He has made it clear that narrowness in space and time is fundamental to the ancients' conception of the world. He takes this as a fact rooted in the Greek incapacity to understand empty, infinite space. I do not believe in any such incapacity and believe, on the contrary, that it was rooted in the Greek struggle for a synthesis. Spengler's interpretation leaves an abyss open between the civilization of classical antiquity and our own, and that is his intention, in accordance with his doctrine that there exists no bridge between one civilization and another, and no common history of mankind. I believe on the contrary that we must try to discover the common human problem behind the specific solution given to it by the Greeks. Accordingly Spengler, who has had so much that is profound to say about Greek science and philosophy, poetry and politics, has failed to note the synthetic character of the Greek and Latin languages, and its meaning in terms of classical civilization.

Viewed as an attempt at cultural instinctive synthesis, all the characteristics of Greek civilization mentioned by Spengler fall into their place. Thus the Greeks could not conceive of a state which would have reality only in terms of the work of a central bureaucracy, and of its records and statistics. The modern state is precisely such a unit. The Greeks, however, wanted to see the state with their eyes as a unit. No more pathetic expression of this could be imagined than Aristotle's view that it should be 'possible to overlook the territory of a state from its Acropolis. It is implicit in all Greek constitutions that it should be possible to assemble the body of the citizens on the market place, where a common will emerges as an instinctive unity, a common urge towards a common goal, needing, in fact, very little by way of any elaborate procedure, not much more than a conversation at a symposium. But it is also obvious why a state of this kind must collapse when faced with more than local tasks, such as inevitably emerge with the growth of communications. And the same limitations apply, *mutatis mutandis*, to the visual-spatial geometry of Euclid, to the physical-spatial unity of Greek statuary art, to the problems of Greek philosophy and, last but not least, of Greek language.

One more word will be necessary to set classical antiquity off against other contemporary civilizations. We said that the synthetic trend was common to all the older Indo-European languages. But the same could not be said of all the civilizations which used these languages. It could not be said, in particular, about the civilizations of India, which proceeded on entirely different lines, very far from the Greek conceptions of measure, harmony, and narrow limitation of outlook. The explanation of this does not seem far to seek. Before the recent excavations in the Indus valley the Indian civilization seemed essentially "Aryan," a product of the conquerors speaking an Indo-European language. But since, between the two wars, the ruins of Mohenjo-Daro and of Harappa have been uncovered, we know that this is not at all so, and that the Aryan conquerors, in India, were only heirs to a fully developed previous civilization. Language being infinitely more conservative than beliefs and institutions, it is no wonder that the conquerors should have kept their speech while merging themselves into their subject's civilization. Now it is true that the originality of Greek civilization can also be overrated. We know, since Evans's excavations in Crete, that not only were the early Hellenes subject to all sorts of Asiatic influences, but the very homeland of their civilization had been ploughed deeply by the Minoan, pre-"Aryan" island civilization of the Aegean. Yet it is probably only right to say that, whereas the Aryan conquerors in India became thoroughly Asiatic, the kindred Hellenes, after centuries of struggle, asserted their individuality very thoroughly against their Asiatic surroundings.

After this inevitable digression—back to language! We explained that the limits of language synthesis are narrow, and that its higher degrees suppose an extraordinary intellectual effort. It needs training of the highest kind to make complex reactions instinctive, as every sportsman knows. It needs a great subtlety of mind to make the correct use of, let us say, the conjunctive and optative modes of the Greek verb instinctively. Yet, if we read any of the great Greek orators, we cannot avoid the conclusion that the citizens' assembly of Athens was perfectly able to appreciate all these shades. (It is a mistaken idea to imagine that only the "upper classes" were citizens; thousands of citizens did not earn enough to afford an armor, whereas thousands of the aliens and many even of the slaves were educated and wealthy.) It is clear that when, for general reasons already alluded to but not to be discussed here in detail, the strength of the instinctive synthesis, the quality of the training of mind and body to instinctive adequacy, declined, the effects upon language must have been profound. The finer shades would become more and more unintelligible. This is what actually happened, not as a process of language transformation following its own laws, but as a reflex of a general decline of civilization. This disintegration of the old synthetic forms of speech and their replacement, to varying degrees, by newly developed analytical forms can be observed in every European language, and in every part of speech. It must, however, be noted that various languages and various cultural zones differ greatly in the extent to which they have shed the old and developed new types of expression. We shall here concentrate upon those changes which are most relevant for the emergence of our own Western group of modern languages, and shall deal in particular with the verb, as the part of speech most closely related to our original problem, the new use of the personal pronoun.

From Greece to Iceland, all modern languages have evolved composite tenses, a thing unknown to all of them in an earlier stage of their development. Everywhere that process had gone far by, let us say, the eleventh century A.D. The appearance of composite tenses all over Europe is perhaps the most impressive symptom of that decay of the synthetic approach to life which had been brought to the highest perfection in the Mediterranean, but which was common to all European nations at a certain period. Yet that process has not gone to the same lengths everywhere. Some languages have lost most simple tenses, using composite tenses as their substitutes. They are, in the first place, the Germanic languages. Here, as in every respect, the North has moved further from the models of classical antiquity than the South. Other languages, while developing composite tenses, have kept all their old simple tenses. They are, roughly speaking, the Slavonic languages (with the exception of Russian and Bulgarian) and the Celtic languages. A third group effects a compromise between these two extremes. This group consists of Greek, Southern Albanian, Romanian, and all Western Latin languages. In other words the Slavonic and Celtic languages have kept as near as possible to a synthetic stage, the Germanic languages have moved away from it as far as possible, whereas the present languages of Southern Europe (with the exception of the Slavonic Balkan languages and Northern Albanian, which have remained primitive in this respect) stand in the middle between the two.

In order to understand the character of that compromise between the old and the new in most Southern European languages we must once more come back to the synthetic character of old Greek and Latin, and discuss characteristics of these two languages not yet mentioned. Synthesis, we said, trends to create an instinctive integration of a number of elements to the exclusion of others. Now which are the elements conspicuously excluded in ancient classical speech? The answer lies in a statement of what this type of speech emphasizes. When I say "feci," all the many sides logically implicit in that simple statement are integrated into a simple realization of one act. The word "feci" is the ideal expression of pure, instinctively integrated action without any reference to any other aspect of experience. When, in modern English, I say "I did," there is automatically implicit the reference that it was "I" who did it. A great many other things refer to "I," which is a focus of many experiences. "I" not only did, I also do, and shall do in the future. But I not only do, I also perform thousands of other actions, have thousands of other experiences, all referred to this nodal point of experience, "I." Such separation of the individual from its acts is rarely expressed in Greek and Latin, and only for the sake of special emphasis. Where all modern languages are essentially psychological, classical antiquity is entirely and unreservedly given to the expression of the outward event in its purity. No wonder therefore that Spengler, with a wealth of material, describes "living in the moment" as one of the main features of that civilization, though perhaps he somewhat overstresses the absolute lack of planning and foresight in classical antiquity. Yet in the main the contrast he draws between modernity and antiquity is real. Nothing can be more telling in this respect than the Greek perfect tense expressing repetition of an act, and its final achievement, by reduplication of the first syllable of the verb. The modern says "I have finished sleeping" (English is particularly strong in expressing actions lasting a long time and leading up to a definite conclusion). The Greek could not express such a thing. He originally said something like "slept-slept," later slurred into "sle-slept." Classical synthesis tends to reduce every event to a momentary pure action, with no extension in time or relation to anything else.

Now it is obvious where the weak points of such a synthesis must be sought. It is easy to visualize in this way action in the present, and action performed and finished in the past. It is difficult to visualize as a pure momentary act repeated action in the past, as well as action in the future. No wonder then that the Greek perfect and future tenses are the two tenses where disintegration of the simple synthetic verbal forms sets in. It appears therefore that the muddle cropping up, towards the end of the pre-Christian era, in the use of Aorist and perfect tenses is not due only to the subtlety of the distinction between the two. It is also due to the distintegration of that very complex synthesis which, by means of reduplication, expressed in one single verbal form action over a long time with a result still valid. It can be seen how the composite past arises partly as an attempt, and a successful one, to get out of the dilemma between Aorist and perfect tenses.

Thus throughout the crises of the classical languages at the time of the collapse of Greek-Latin civilization, the main meaning of the tenses remains more or less the same. The complex synthesis of the Greek perfect is broken up, but the Greek Aorist, expressing momentary action in the past, remains much what it was before, and the composite past becomes more or less of a substitute for the lost perfect, so that, in the end, the distinction between permanent and momentary past action is maintained, though superficially the form of expressing it has changed. Latin had no such distinction between perfect and Aorist. The Latin simple past also disintegrated, and a composite past was formed in "vulgar" Latin. But as the Greek Aorist so the Latin simple past continued to exist. Thus the Latin languages in the end had one more perfect tense than Latin had, the composite past, which is now used to express much the same thing as the composite past in modern Greek, in other words much the same thing as the classical Greek perfect. In that way, the modern Latin languages have acquired one of the basic distinctions of classical Greek, though they express it in an analytical, not a synthetic fashion, through a composite, not through a simple tense.

But in practically all languages which have acquired composite tenses, even in so primitive a language as Serb, a struggle between the simple and the composite past, between synthetic and analytical speech, is going on. It must have happened in the Germanic languages also but there it led to a reduction of the number of the simple tenses at a very early date. In the South, however, the simple past, the Greek Aorist and its counterparts in Serbian, Italian, Spanish, and Provencal, have so far well maintained themselves. The struggle is more bitter where the two conceptions, the Northern and the Southern one, meet: in French, in Rhaetian (the Latin dialect spoken in the Grisons) and on the borderline of German and Italian speech. "The Rhaetian dialects in particular," says Meyer-Luebke's standard work on the comparative grammar of Latin languages,[4] "have dropped the perfect (the tense corresponding to the French *passé défini*) almost completely. The same applies to Venetia, Lombardy, Piémont, Savoy, the Dauphiné, the "Suisse romande," Southern Lorraine, and part of Belgium, also to the Picardie, and last but not least to conversational French as spoken in Paris." He quotes a passage from J. Lemaitre, a novelist. "M. Fabre, being a Southerner, makes abundant use of the *passé défini*, even in familiar conversation. He abuses this tense which, in Paris and all central France, is exclusively employed for literary purposes." Indeed! The struggle between two ways of life can be observed in this struggle between two types of speech, the one emphasizing, in the Southern way, "living in the moment" and the graceful succinctness of speech going with it, the other one heavy with circumlocution and psychological analysis. In this special case, the influence of Germanic settlements seems undeniable. The Rhaetian lands and the above-mentioned districts of Northern Italy were the centers of Longobard settlement; Dauphiné and the Suisse romande, centres of the Burgundians; Southern Lorraine was probably the most advanced outpost in the colonization of the Alamans; while Belgium and the Picardie were settled by masses of Frankish colonists, the Somme being the Southern boundary of Germanic mass colonization there.

But the inclusion of Paris in the list shows that we are not here confronted with a simple remnant of Germanic civilization which disintegrated in a more highly developed Latin milieu. At no time has Paris been anything but a center of Latin speech and civilization. Also, having been for many centuries a magnet attracting Frenchmen from every part of France, the Southern strain in its population must be, and in fact is, much greater than the same strain in the surrounding provinces. If never-

4. Wilhelm Meyer-Luebke, *Grammatik der romanischen Sprachen* (Leipzig: Tues, 1890–1902), vol. 3, section 107.

theless Paris speech tends to be closer, not to the Southern but to the Northern dialects, than that of the surrounding districts, it is because the Northern, anticlassical speech is more "modern" in type, is closer to the substance of the modern soul; and because great cities tend to be more progressive. In a border-zone between the Northern and the Southern way of life, such as is Northern France, the countryside may cling to the more ancient ways, which are the Southern ways, whereas the metropolis inevitably tends in the opposite direction. It is too early, at this stage of our investigation, to say much about the relation of the struggle between national groups to the history of civilization. But instances such as this sharply point to the fact that the differences between one nation and another do not explain everything in that story. The presence of Germanic farmers in regions otherwise quite Southern in background certainly contributed to those regions adopting certain elements of analytical speech. But in the case of a metropolis the same result could be achieved without outside pressure, merely by immanent factors. The process of civilization, and in particular of urbanization, would seem largely to consist in precisely such bringing to the surface of implicit features of a civilization.

Now let us turn to the history of the future tense, which is even more interesting. For action in the future is never entirely an external event. It is always something at least foreseen, if not actually willed and intended. The main emphasis of the future tense falls inevitably upon the inner, not upon the external experience, for in this case only the inner experience is real, the outward event still only imagined. Inner experience at present, corresponding to probable future action in the external world, is about the most difficult synthesis of representation to be performed. Its breakdown at an early stage of language transformation is therefore no more than natural.

A study of the transformation of the future tense may thus be expected to be rich in results. In approaching the subject we are at once struck by a great anomaly. In other respects, not to be discussed here, the Balkan languages have kept more closely to the classical pattern than the Western Latin languages. But with the future tense the opposite is the case. It is the Balkan languages which, on the whole, have lost the simple future tense altogether, and the Western Latin languages which, while evolving an only half literary composite future have also evolved a simple future tense. (*Je ferai*, side by side with *je vais faire*.) And, more remarkable even, the simple future tense of all modern Latin languages (with the exception of Romanian, which like other Balkan languages has no simple future) does not derive directly from the future tense of classical Latin, in other words is not simply a remnant of a past phase of speech, but, on the contrary, an innovation. During the period of "vulgar" Latinity, of the decay of the Latin literate tradition, a composite future evolved, consisting of the infinitive of the verb with the conjugated forms of *habere*, "to have," added to it. *Facere habeo*, I have to do, took the place of *faciam*, the simple Latin future tense. The synthetic expression of the future tense had broken down. And nothing could be more significant than the use of *habere* as an auxiliary verb in the new composite future, as in the new composite past. For in classical Latin, *habere* is very little used, and expressions denoting ownership are constructed, in an impersonal way, with *esse*, "to be," and the Dative. From the fourth century A.D. onwards, however, *habere* with the nominative becomes prominent, a sure sign that even in Southern Europe ownership is no longer conceived as an impersonal relation, but as a personal domination over objects. And not only is *habere* now used richly, in all sorts of secondary meanings besides the primary one, but it is also the first auxiliary verb used for the formation of composite tenses.

But lo and behold! With time the synthetic expression of the future tense reasserted itself. There took place a development exactly parallel to that which had led to the formation of the tenses of classical Latin. Then, tenses had been formed by making independent suffixed words part of the verb itself. The same now happened to the forms of *habere*, added to the infinitive as an expression of the future. They were slurred, until they became part of the verb, which was conjugated, again, with the personal endings. The synthesis of root and endings thus happened twice in Latin, once in remote antiquity (in all tenses), the second time in the earliest middle ages (for the future tenses only). But the second time it happened only in the West. It is obvious that no phonetic reasons could possibly explain the absence, in Romanian and modern Greek, of a development which had taken place in old Greek and was again taking place in all Western Latin languages. The only conceivable reason for the difference is the striving of Italians, Frenchmen, Spaniards towards a new synthetic expression of future action, a striving which was conspicuously absent in the East. In other words, the "living in the moment", the experiencing of life as a series of momentary actions and events, was to a large extent abandoned in the East, but passionately clung to in the Western part of the Mediterranean world.

But it is one thing to cling to a way of life and quite another thing to have it, unquestioningly. The emergence of the new simple future tense had already been a reaction against a process of spontaneous disintegration of that type of expression. A parallel disintegration had taken place in the Germanic languages, where also the simple future, never very strong there, disappeared, in this case for good. And the reaction towards a simple future tense in French, Italian, etc. proved not to be final. Towards the end of the middle ages those languages, in respect to the future tense, started to conform to the Germanic languages, developing a composite future, which became more and more popular. For in the use of the future as in the use of the past, the history of the modern Western Latin languages reveals a constant alternation between ancient classical and modern Northern ways of speech, echoing a constant conflict between ways of feeling. A great deal of the history of Italy, Spain, and also France is reflected in this conflict.

It is impossible therefore to deal with the composite future tense in the West without discussing some details of the Germanic languages. The important thing about the composite future is the choice of the auxiliary verb for forming it. No language has available any verb expressing the future directly. In dealing with this difficulty, English and Scandinavian use the verbs "shall" and "will," expressions of obligation and decision, which have nothing to do with action as such. They belong, by contradistinction, to the sphere of inner experience, and within that sphere more particularly to the realm of firm determination. No auxiliary verb could be more closely connected with that forethought which all Latin languages avoid expressing, and none could be more closely related to the sphere of the "I." In fact, it would hardly be imaginable to think of "will" and "shall" without, at the same time, emphasizing the person who wills and who shall. The use of these two auxiliary verbs also gives an indication of the special direction in which the sphere of the "I" is emphasized in these languages. It is not the sphere of searching of the soul, so much emphasized in the Hindu and Russian civilizations, but the sphere of concentrated planning of a subject aiming to *control* outward life.

French and Italian, by contrast, use "to go" parallel to the English circumlocution "I am going to do," which is, in English, used as it were to soften the harshness implicit in the future tense proper. Going is a notion very near acting, but with the element of intention and decision taken away, so that only pure action remains. The Western Latin languages try to express the future by a form as near the original meaning of the Latin concept of pure action as possible. German, most characteristically, uses "becoming," an expression where the "I" is completely eliminated, where no synthetic realization of momentary action is involved, but where future events appear as a sort of impersonal process.

The Russian composite future is expressed in the same way. It is a first indication that, perhaps, German is not quite as much a "Western" language as some of its characteristics may make one think.

Some special mention of the composite tenses of all the languages of the Iberian peninsula may be useful. In the past tenses, the Iberian languages use *haber*, to have, sharply distinguishing this auxiliary verb from *tener*, which means "to own." Late Latin *habere*, as said above, had precisely this meaning. Spanish however takes pains to make it clear that the auxiliary verb has no such meaning, thus tending to return to the classical use of *habere*. The future is formed from "*ser*," to be, which is sharply distinguished from "*estar*," to be momentarily. Linguists know that this sharp distinction carries into Spanish an element which in Slavonic languages is known as "aspect." But here we are concerned with something else. The distinction between the momentary, which dominates the type of speech of classical antiquity, and the lasting and permanent, which is so much more in the foreground of modern life and speech, has become conscious in Spanish which, as it were, uses one expression for each of the two modes of being. The clash between them, which, as said above, is the underlying *leitmotif* of all modern South-Western history, has here become explicit. The same applies to the other Iberian languages, Portuguese and Catalan, and the various subdialects of all three of them. S. de Madariaga has drawn an argument, from this duplication of the verb "to be" in all Iberian languages, for the unity of Iberian civilization, and he is, I believe, (culturally) in the right against those scholars who treat Catalan as a dialect of Provençal, on strong grounds of phonetics and vocabulary. Yet, if the view maintained in this study is the correct one, syntax is more important in establishing affinities of civilization than phonetics and basic vocabulary.

Now we turn to the East. Here the first remarkable fact is that the development of the future tense (and of the infinitive) has proceeded on identical lines in Greek, Romanian, Bulgarian, and Southern Albanian (the so-called "toskan" dialect), but not in Serbo-Croat and Northern-Albanian ("guegan"). Here, as in certain other features of language, an abyss is revealed between the Byzantine civilization of Bulgaria and the primitive civilization of Serbia, which has hardly been influenced by Greek speech and civilization. As to Albanian, the language reflects what every student of Balkan affairs knows: the deep penetration of Greek influence in the South, and the absence of that influence, as well as the existence of a certain amount of Croat influence, in the Catholic North. Important features of language, of syntax in particular, are a sure indication of cultural affinity or lack of affinity between nations. There is also no doubt, as Sandfeldt-Jensen has proved, that the common features of modern Greek, Bulgarian, Romanian, and Southern Albanian are due to the influence of Greek upon the latter three.

The simple future starts weakening in ancient Greek at about the time of Christ, and it seems that, in common speech, the process had gone far in the sixth century A.D., at the same period which also saw the complete disintegration of the simple future tense in vulgar Latin. Medieval Greek at first evolved a composite future tense, formed by combining the auxiliary verb "will" with the infinitive of the verb, exactly as in English. Bulgarian, Romanian, and Southern Albanian followed suit. "To will" is certainly the most logical auxiliary to be used for the formation of the future, but where it does not correspond to a deep urge emphasizing willpower, it is also the most irritating one. Any colorless particle would naturally be preferable to an Eastern race. Thus, in fact, abandoning the typically classical tendency to preserve logical clarity in speech, medieval Greek soon reduced the auxiliary verb *thelo*, "I will", and its six persons of singular and plural, to the one meaningless particle *the*, thus eliminating any deeper meaning of the tense. There could hardly be more economy of speech, but also hardly a greater impoverishment of language than the reduction of a rich future tense to the infinitive used with an invariable prefix. Again Romanian and Southern Albanian follow suit, but no longer Bulgarian. However deep the influence of Greek upon Bulgarian, the Slavonic method of expressing the future through an aspect is too simple not to be preferable to the infinitive with a meaningless prefix. Bulgarian drops its one attempt to form a composite tense and returns to the old ways.

It would have been natural for the three other languages to remain in the stage of forming the future tense thus attained. Yet at this point another factor, another process of disintegration of synthetic speech interfered. Greek, and in consequence Romanian, Southern Albanian, and also Bulgarian, lost the infinitive of the verb, in varying degrees of completeness. This process in Bulgarian deeply influenced the formation of dependent sentences, but could no longer influence the formation of the future tense. In Greek, Romanian, and Southern Albanian, it influenced it profoundly. For in the absence of the infinitive, the future tense had to be expressed through a dependent sentence. Instead of saying "I will sleep" it was now necessary to say "I will, so that I should sleep." Intention, in Greek, was expressed by the "final" conjunction "hina," shortened, in medieval and modern Greek, to "na." Thus the future, in Greek, after the loss of the infinitive, had to be expressed by the particles "the na," followed no longer by the infinitive, but by a verb in the present tense. This change seems to have occurred, in common speech, at about the seventh century A.D., and again Romanian and Albanian followed suit.

At a much later stage, probably after the fall of Byzance in the fifteenth century, "the na" was slurred into "tha" which at present is the particle used in Greek before a verb in the present tense to express the future. "The" had already become a prefix without intrinsic meaning. "Na" still had the meaning "in order to." The slurring of the two into one made the resulting word meaningless, except as a prefix indicating the future tense. Also, the formation of dependent sentences expressing intention was affected in the same direction by the loss of the infinitive. Where we say "I intend to sleep," the modern Greek, Romanian, Albanian, and Bulgarian says "I intend so that I should sleep." The parallelism with the development of the future is obvious, and affords proof that it is really the loss of the infinitive which has brought about the whole transformation described above.

Sandfeldt-Jensen has taken considerable pains to emphasize the uniqueness of this development, and also to disprove the idea that it might be due to the influence of a hypothetical common Balkan language, spoken perhaps before the first millenium B.C., whose remnant would be Albanian. The normal use of the infinitive in Northern Albanian is sufficient proof of the inadequacy of such a view, Northern Albanian being more archaic than Southern Albanian. If Southern Albanian has lost the infinitive, it is due to Greek influence, and it is in Greek that the whole development started. Nothing can indeed be more convincing. Yet is it sufficient? It is easy to explain the loss of the infinitive in languages so weak as Romanian, Bulgarian, and Southern Albanian by the overwhelming influence of the highly civilized Greek speech of their political masters. But how explain the loss of the infinitive in Greek? It is quite literally a unique fact in all the Indo-European languages. It is contrary to their whole structure, for the infinitive is one of the great Indo-European inventions. Its loss brings about complexity and clumsiness of expression. It is certainly not mentally easier to say "I intend so that I should sleep" rather than saying "I intend to sleep." Therefore mere language decay does not afford an explanation. It is true, of course, that the infinitive of the verb, expressing an action in the abstract, without reference to tense, person, etc., is a synthetic mode of speech. But "transition from the synthetic to the analytical" is only a general formula, and must not be accepted instead of a concrete explanation of changes of speech habits from case to case. The preservation of the infinitive in all other Indo-European languages shows sufficiently that normally there does not exist any tendency to discard it. Its lapse in modern Balkan languages is strange indeed, and it is still stranger that a linguist of the standard of Sandfeldt-Jensen should not have attempted to find the reason for it.

I am well aware that the explanation I am now going to propose, and which is apt to throw light on certain aspects of the history of Near Eastern civilization, is bound to stir up reminiscences of a once passionate controversy not yet complelely settled. I maintain that Sandfeldt-Jensen, who is the greatest master of the "geographical" school of linguistics and who taught us to disregard "natural" language groups where cultural units provide a better approach, has yet failed to go sufficiently far with his own method. Sandfeldt-Jensen in his "Linguistique Balkanique" confined himself to the study of Indo-European Balkan languages belonging to various language groups. I suggest that the riddle of the loss of the Greek Infinitive is to be solved by reference to other languages of the Levantine area, not belonging to the Indo-European language group and not spoken in the Balkans. If the method of Sandfeldt-Jensen is valid, as I believe it indeed is, then the geographical unit to be considered as the basis of common features of speech must be coterminous with the boundaries of one common civilization. Today the Balkans, in certain respects, can in fact be regarded as a self-contained unit; there is such a thing as a common Balkan way of life, contrasted with both the Western and the Moslem way of life. But this was not so during the first millenium A.D., when all the changes under consideration occurred. The basic unit, then, was the Byzantine empire and its immediate neighbors as far as they were under the sway of its civilization. This Empire extended, apart from the Balkans, Sicily, and parts of Southern Italy, over Anatolia, Syria, and Egypt. Here, I believe, lies the fallacy to which Sandfeldt-Jensen has succumbed: in speaking of "Balkan linguistics" he has chosen too narrow a unit. If nevertheless his approach has been very fruitful in results, it is because Greek was so much stronger a language than all the other Balkan languages (with the exception of ruggedly primitive Serb). But his method breaks down where the problems involved in the transformation of Greek itself are concerned.

The controversy about the forces behind the evolution of modern Greek is extensive, and turns mainly about the characteristics of that common Greek speech of late antiquity, the "Koiné," which is the basis of modern Greek, but about which we know less than we would like to know. It is generally accepted that its main features derived from the dialect of Athens, with a certain admixture of "Ionian," the dialect of the Greeks on the Western shores of Anatolia. The complete conquest of the whole of ancient Greece by the Athenian dialect is what one would expect to have happened, in view of the shining supremacy of Athens in all matters of culture. There is therefore no problem in admitting that the phonetics, the main features of noun and verb inflection, and many other characteristics of the Koiné must be traced back to "Attic," the dialect of Athens. But does the story end there? I should think not. The preponderance of Athens was a fact in the fourth and even in the third century B.C., when the Koiné first emerged. In a sense, but only in a sense, it also continued during the second and first century B.C. But can it be assumed that this situation, and its results in speech, afford an adequate explanation of the peculiarities of modern Greek syntax, all of which developed much later?

Let us leave aside language altogether for a moment. Let us remember the main historical facts. Alexander the Great had carried the Greek language into Asia. There, for a long time, it subsisted. The Greek colonies were at first fairly sharply distinct, in their way of life, from the surrounding Asiatic countryside. But at a fairly early date a process of merging Greek and Asiatic civilizations set in. It did not go far in Western Anatolia, where the basis was essentially Greek. It did not go far in Eastern Anatolia, which remained emphatically Asiatic in character. It was no very great success in Egypt, where Greeks, Jews, and Egyptians (later Copts) never merged, despite all efforts. But it did go very far in the Seleucian Empire, in Syria.

Now during the last two decades there has happened a sort of revolt among specialists against the underrating of the transformations which took place there. It is true that research is inevitably biased by the fact that the Egyptian papyri are so much better preserved than most sources from Syria, but A. J. Toynbee has entered a well-justified protest against concentrating upon the comparatively trivial, though quantitatively important evidence of the papyri, instead of the most searching investigation of every scrap of evidence from Syria. Spengler, as usual, moves in the same direction, but goes further, emphasizing that, in the whole history of the Levant from the time of Christ onwards, there is hardly a single feature which cannot ultimately be traced back to Syria.

The process of culture change in Syria must be understood as flow and counterflow. In the early period, before the Maccabean wars, Greek civilization was very much in the ascendancy, and was imposed upon Asiatics much more ruthlessly than in any other part of the Alexandrine world. Then followed the counterblow. Asiatic ways were reasserting themselves, mainly in the form of the most powerful religious revival in human history, one of whose products was Christianity. The historical position of this movement was only recently understood. Until not so long ago, Harnack could describe the many Gnostic sects of Syria in the first, second, and third centuries A.D. as standard-bearers of a process of acute Hellenization of that part of the world, and a host of pupils worked out his idea. Today nobody believes that the new religion in the Middle East had more than a few verbal expressions in common with classical Greek thought. It was all thoroughly oriental in character. This has been finally demonstrated in Hans Jonas's researches on Gnosticism.[5] And as with religion, so with other aspects of civilization. It is clear that the Roman Empire as reorganized by Diocletian at the end of the third century A.D. was an oriental sultanate. It is clear, in particular, that its court ceremonial was mainly borrowed from Persia. Spengler has drawn attention to the fact that nearly all the great jurists who, in the third century, developed the bases on which later the codification of Justinian was based, were Syrians, and that the Roman law of that period differs totally in spirit from Republican Roman law. Riegl has demonstrated that late "Roman" sculpture is not simply a product of decay but is based on principles entirely different from classical Greek principles, namely, oriental principles.

It is time to round off the picture by extending it to linguistics. In every other respect it has been proved that the impact of Hellenic civilization upon the middle East was short-lived, and that the main result of the conquests of Alexander the Great was not so much, in the end, to hellenize nearer Asia but to orientalize Southeastern Europe. Only in linguistics the opposite view still prevails. This is largely due to the concentration of research upon one unhappily chosen subject, the language of the New Testament. Perhaps nine-tenths of the existing research about the Koiné and the later development of Greek turn about this one problem. That is only natural. For, in the first place, it is certainly important for a correct understanding of the gospels to know whether they were conceived by their authors in the spirit of the Greek language, or whether the evangelists thought in Aramean, and painfully translated their ideas into Greek. Linguistically also the gospels are of great interest insofar as, presumably, their authors were not highly educated and their language therefore is probably nearer to popular speech than that of most literary documents of the time. Thus a heated controversy has developed about the presence or absence of semitic elements in the language of the

5. Hans Jonas, *Gnosis und spätantiker Geist* (Göttingen: Vandenhoeck & Rupprecht, 1954). See Jonas, *The Gnostic Religion* (Boston: Beacon Press, 1958).

gospels. For a time the "semitic" school was very much in the ascendancy, but of late the "Hellenic" school has got the upper hand again, and as a consequence the belief in a strong semitic strain in the formation of medieval Greek has fallen into discredit.

Most unjustly, in my view. For its seems to me that the whole controversy about the New Testament has only a limited bearing upon the main problems of the formation of medieval and modern Greek. It would, naturally, be interesting to find in the gospels indications of later developments, but even the most "Aramaic" interpretation of the text cannot establish any such development. Modern Balkan languages differ from ancient Greek through lack of the Dative, the future tense, and the infinitive. Neither of the three is lacking in the gospels, though there are perhaps faint indications of a dislike for the use of the future. All those Aramaic features which have been discovered, rightly or wrongly, in the text of the New Testament, have therefore little relevance to the problem of how the main syntactic features of modern Greek and other Balkan languages arose. This applies with particular emphasis to the most singular of them all, the loss of the infinitive. Thus even if a very great deal of Aramaic influence upon the gospels were proved, we should still be little advanced in our search for the causes of the emergence of modern Greek syntax. Conversely all that the most "Hellenic" interpretation of the gospel texts can prove is that the authors of the gospels (apart from the author of the Book of Revelations, who unquestioningly was very feeble in Greek) knew more Greek than was suspected, hence were better educated than was assumed before. This is interesting as a contribution to the sociology of the early Christian communities in Syria and Palestine, but hardly revealing as to the history of language.

It would be inconceivable that anybody should not have cared to speak correct Greek in the first century A.D. But probably few people did care in the fifth century. The importance of old Hellas, and of Athens, its center, had vanished at about the time of Christ. True, the prestige of Greek as a language lasted longer than the prestige of Greece. But more and more the East asserted itself—witness the increasing number of authors writing on religious matters in Syriac (late Aramaic) instead of Greek. The transfer of the capital of the Empire to Constantinople changed little in the process, for it never became the dominant center of intellectual life. Thus the center of Greek speech shifted towards the non-Greeks of the East, and only when this process had gone far can we expect to find it reflected in profound changes of language.

We have found that the disappearance of the infinitive in Greek stands in contrast to the whole structure of the Indo-European languages, is equally foreign to their earlier as well as to their modern stage of development, and creates almost unconquerable problems of speech. Now this loss of the infinitive, so inexplicable in terms of a self-contained development of Greek, becomes easily intelligible once the Semitic languages are taken into consideration. For Hebrew, Aramaic, and Arabic do not have the infinitive (in our sense). It would not be quite exact to say that those languages have no infinitive at all, as it is not quite exact to say that modern Greek and the other Balkan languages lack it completely. They all have it in the same way, as an independent substantive, and if we speak about the loss of the infinitive we mean that both the Balkan and Semitic languages cannot use it with the verb.

The absence of the infinitive in the Semitic languages stands not isolated in its Semitic context, as it does in an Indo-European language. For it also is very doubtful whether the Semitic languages have tenses of the verb in the Indo-European sense. They have an "imperfect," to be sure, but no past, present, or future tense, only one general tense, usually called an Aorist, but used for expressing present and future. When, in the Gospels, Aorist and present are frequently used to express the future, we are confronted with evidence of Aramaic influence. Only at that period, that influence was superficial. Later on the Greek future tense did not disappear to be supplanted by the Aorist, but to be supplanted by a composite tense, an auxiliary verb with the infinitive. Still later, the final "Aramaization" of the Greek future tense did not proceed from a mixing up of the tenses but, as we saw, from the destruction of the infinitive.

There is little doubt that in the Semitic languages the absence of both the infinitive and the tenses corresponds to a conception of the world where both time and action plays a very small part, an attitude to reality of which we Westerners have no real conception. It is this conception of the world which from about 500 A.D. onwards gets ascendancy over the remnants of the ancient Greeks. But not fully so. There is a limit to the decay of the forms of the Greek verb. They decay, and Greek comes to lean upon an entirely alien, oriental type of speech. But it clings stubbornly to many other elements of its native speech, as Byzantine civilization, that half-breed of decaying antiquity and half-amalgamated Asiatic elements, clings to its Greek background.

It is of some importance to note that not only has Greek assimilated oriental elements, but that from a certain moment onwards, Balkan and Semitic languages, though never merging into one, yet move in the same direction. The formation of the future tense is one of several cases in point. Aramaic, as said above, has no means of forming a specific future

tense at all. Arabic, however, has acquired means for doing so. The "sa"
is prefixed in Arabic to the Aorist in order to express the future. "Sa"
originally derives from the Arabic substantive meaning "end," "finish,"
but has become exactly as meaningless, outside its function as a future-
specifying prefix, as the Greek prefix "the," "tha." Though the future-
specifying prefix in Greek and in the other Balkan languages was originally a verb, and in Arabic a substantive, the final result is the same in
both cases. The future is formed from the present with a prefix, a result
as far outside the scope of the structure of Semitic languages as the loss
of the infinitive is outside the scope of the Indo-European ones. Here
we can observe how, by degrees, an oriental and a Hellenic civilization,
originally totally distinct, grow into one. We have here linguistic proof
of Spengler's view that the entire Near and Middle Eastern civilization
from the time of Christ onwards must be regarded as one coherent
whole, none of whose parts can be understood without taking account
of all the others. This civilization, as every great civilization, is, in the
main, a self-contained unit. It is impossible to understand the history of
the Balkan languages—but it is also impossible to understand the younger
developments in Semitic speech—without reference to late Greek. It would
be completely pointless, however, to draw into the debate, on the one
hand, the history of Western Latin, and, on the other hand, the history
of Pali or some other Indian language. In both cases their influence, if
any, can only have been marginal, not touching any essentials.

One additional observation in connection with the infinitive obtrudes
itself concerning the extent of the Near Eastern zone of civilization.
Arabic influence, I believe, is traceable in the formation of the infinitive
in Portuguese. Portuguese is certainly the only Indo-European language
to have two infinitives: one to be declined as a noun, in the ordinary
Indo-European manner, and the other one to be conjugated, as if it were
a tense with a singular and plural and three persons. This has always
been regarded as very puzzling, and at the same time as a particularly
strong development of the infinitive. I am inclined to take the opposite
view. The infinitive as a noun is used, in Portuguese, where the infinitive
is also used in modern Greek and Arabic. The infinitive as a verbal tense
is used together with verbal expressions. In English, not even an idea
can be given of that usage, which is easier to counterfeit in French. It
is as if a Frenchman, instead of saying "je veux dormir," said "je veux
dormirais," or something like it. Now it is obvious that this usage steps
in exactly where a dependent sentence is used instead of the infinitive
in modern Balkan languages and where the infinitive could not be used
in Semitic languages. It is also clear that a conjugated infinitive is no

longer an infinitive, but a kind of duplicated conjugated tense. In other words, the use of the infinitive in Portuguese is exactly parallel to that in the Balkans and the Middle East; except that where in those parts a dependent sentence is used instead of the lost infinitive, a conjugated form deriving from the original infinitive steps in in Portuguese.

The case is extremely interesting, because it reveals a type of language change not easily recognized by linguists of the old school. It would be wrong to say that the Portuguese infinitive has been copied from Arabic. What has been copied is the general attitude toward the infinitive, the reluctance to use it in the normal Indo-European way. This is not a linguistic detail, but a piece of social psychology. From this reluctance Portuguese has developed a solution very different from the Arabic solution, yet leading up to the same result.

It might be asked why, if the Portuguese infinitive is really a result of an oriental mentality, it does not appear in neighboring Spanish. It is, perhaps, difficult to give a final answer. One thing is certain, however, that the conjugated infinitive in Portuguese derives from Gallego, the speech of the northwestern corner of Spain. And perhaps the fact that this type of speech is consequently to be found all along the western shores of the peninsula can be attributed to the weaker roots of Latin civilization in that region as compared with the thoroughly latinized rest of the peninsula.

We are now in a position to gather the fruits of that lengthly disquisition about the transformation of the verb. We started upon it in the hope of finding in the transition from the synthetic to the analytical mode of speech an explanation for the emergence of the new use of the pronoun with the verb. This hope has not been fulfilled directly. But in surveying our results, and summarizing them into a short statement, it becomes apparent that indirectly we have approached very close to a solution of our problem. For the sum total of our results amounts to this:

There does exist such a thing as a merely negative disintegration of synthetic types of speech, a loss of grasp of the meaning of its finer shades. That disintegration, which transforms classical Latin into "vulgar" Latin and classical Greek into middle Greek, is embodied in such features as the loss of the Greek perfect and the Greek and Latin simple future, as well as in the loss of the case endings of the noun and other changes not to be dealt with in these pages. But it is also clear that this merely negative disintegration of language is a very fleeting and unstable phase, exactly as the merely negative disintegration of the civilization of classical antiquity. Something new is eagerly substituted for the old disintegrated forms. And whereas the decay of synthetic speech as such does not afford a contribution to the solution of our problem concerning the pronoun, these new developments do contain, though only by implication, the trends leading up to the new use of the pronoun.

There are three such developments. Firstly Greek, in the process of losing its synthetic character, comes to lean upon Aramaic and Arabic, amalgamating several important though most uncongenial features of those languages. Bulgarian, Romanian, and Southern Albanian follow suit, though Bulgarian to a slightly lesser extent than the others. The result of all this is that the modern Balkan languages, though fully Indo-European in phonetics and vocabulary, are nevertheless partly Semitic in syntax. At the same time a parallel transformation of Semitic speech takes place, and certain Indo-European elements are adopted into Arabic.

Secondly, "vulgar" Latin does not at all take part in these developments, with the exception of proto-Romanian, the Latin dialect of the Northern Balkan peninsula. As a result, a broad gap opens between modern Greek and the modern Latin languages, a gap much broader than existed between ancient Latin and Greek. The civilization of the Mediterranean which, in Hellenistic and early Roman Imperial days, was a unity, sharply divides into a Western Mediterranean and Eastern Mediterranean civilization. The Latin speeches of the Western Mediterranean, after a few centuries of chaos, return to the tendencies of ancient Latin, evolving new synthetic forms of speech, thus keeping as closely as possible to the civilization of classical antiquity. But this return is not fully successful. To varying degrees, the modern languages of the Western Mediterranean have amalgamated distinctly Northern speech habits. But the fact remains that this zone has not shared fully in either the development of the Southeast or of the Northwest.

Finally, certain Northern French dialects, Rhaetian, and certain dialects of the Po valley, in common with all the Germanic languages, have gone very far in shedding all characteristics of synthetic speech. Besides the total decay of noun declension which most, though not all, of these languages share with Italian, Provençal and the Iberian languages, the main features of this new development are the decay of the simple past and the simple future tense, as well as of verbal endings in general. And together with all these, this Western group of languages is characterized by the new use of the pronoun.

It appears clearly that this new use of the pronoun is by no means a *result* of the emergence of analytical speech. On the contrary, in the Southeast and in the Southwest this type of speech, despite the profound decay of the opposite, synthetic type of speech, was arrested in its development owing to the lack of instruments able to bring it to comple-tion. Greek became Semitized, and Italian and other Latin languages returned to synthesis, because they were unable to put anything new in the place of the decaying old types of language. This, of course, must not be understood in the crude sense that they would have been unable to invent the technical instruments for a new type of language. They have all, on the contrary, been very ingenious in evolving a new psy-chology which would have been compatible with a completely analytical type of speech.

But not only cannot the verbal endings be scrapped completely as long as the regular use of the pronoun with the verb is unknown—even the emergence of composite tenses must remain something unstable without it. Spanish, Provençal, Italian tend ever again to return to the use of simple tenses because the use of composite tenses without the pronoun is a halfway house, neither succinct and synthetically visual, nor logically complete and analytically satisfactory. The tendency is obviously either towards fully analytical speech as spoken in the Northwest, or towards a return to synthetic speech as traceable in the emergence of a new simple future in the Latin languages. Of this return to synthesis we shall hear more later. The fact is that not without the regular use of the personal pronoun is a fully analytical use of the verb conceivable.

But this regular usage of the pronoun, in its turn, is not merely a linguistic fact. As the return of Italian towards synthesis is an expression of the Italian tendency to live in the way not of the moderns but of the ancients, as the loss of future and infinitive in Greek are expressions of the orientalization of Byzantine civilization, so the new use of "I" reveals the emergence of a new soul, the soul of our own Western civilization: Thus *the test of language provides an insight into the distinctive basic attitudes of various civilizations, and into their geographical boundaries.*

Our further disquisition will therefore aim at discovering in what this new basic attitude of life, expressed in the new usage of the pronoun, consists. But though we hope to have proved that linguistics do not provide a self-contained explanation of the new habit, which must be understood in a much wider context, yet language shall still remain our guide. So far we have only set off the new habit as it appears, for the first time, in old Norse, against earlier forms of speech to which it is unknown. Let us now try and find out what is the history of this new habit, and how much we can learn from it for an understanding of its meaning.

We mentioned in the beginning that the use of the pronoun both before names and before the verb was unknown to Gothic, and it is therefore reasonable to infer that it was generally unknown to all Germanic languages before the Voelkerwanderung, though the case of Scandinavian is somewhat complex. Here no evidence for this use goes back beyond the end of the fourth century A.D., but earlier evidence is much too fragmentary to state with assurance that before that period it was unknown. The use of the pronoun before the verb is found frequently both in the oldest Anglo-Saxon and in the oldest German documents, but has nowhere (including old Norse) become obligatory before the eleventh century. It is therefore impossible to state with any precision at which period that use emerged in these two languages, except that the absence of it in Gothic makes it unlikely that it should have been used before the Voelkerwanderung.

A solemn oath sworn by the army of King Louis II is regarded as probably the oldest document in old French, dating as it does from 842 A.D. In this document, the use of the personal pronoun before the verb is quite normal, though again not found invariably. This document may be later than the language of the oldest German document, the *Hildebrand-Lied*, but again it is impossible to state the age relation with any exactitude, as this song, despite its archaic language, has come down to us in a relatively late manuscript. All we can say, therefore, is this: Old Norse had the use of the pronoun at a time when the other Germanic languages, and, of course, Latin, did not have it. As soon, however, as any German, French, and English literature emerges, they all have the use of it. When, in the eleventh century, a Provençal literature emerges in Southern France, it uses the pronoun amply, and it is again impossible to make out whether the use of the pronoun has percolated through Northern France into Provence, or whether it developed there independently, at an unknown period. It might be useful to make a detailed study of contemporary Latin documents.

Here, inevitably, the question of Scandinavian influence, first upon early Anglo-Saxon and old high German, later upon French and Provençal, comes up. But at any rate, as far as the latter two are concerned, an independent source must first be taken into consideration. That source is old Irish.

Far be it from me to pretend to any understanding of the labyrinthine difficulties of that language. Some facts, however, seem to be clear enough and mark out the case of old Irish as a peculiar one. We have a considerable number of old Irish inscriptions in "Ogham," an archaic type of script, almost all of them on burial stones. The dates are disputed, but it is probable that many of them are not much younger than runic burial inscriptions from Scandinavia though, naturally, the Irish inscriptions are Christian. Now not a single of these Irish inscriptions uses the "I" with the name of the buried or burying person in the Scandinavian manner. One thing is therefore certain: the characteristic old Norse use of the I with names was unknown in Ireland. How about the usage of the pronoun with the verb? This is a more complex problem. On the whole, the early Irish MSS have this use, though it is as little obligatory in old Irish as in old Norse, Anglo-Saxon, old French, and German. But by far the greater number of these MSS do not go back beyond the 8th century A.D., a period when all the above-mentioned languages had adopted the use of the pronoun. There exists one fairly sizable linguistic document whose language is probably more archaic, the so-called Cambrai homily. But precisely in this one document no ample use of the personal pronoun can be traced. Clearly, it seems, Irish has only shared with other European languages in the spread of a new language habit coming from Scandinavia.

But another set of facts must also be taken into account. The Irish personal pronoun, as we make its acquaintance from the eighth century A.D. onwards, differs totally in structure from the old Norse, Anglo-Saxon, and old German pronoun, so much so that the conclusion obtrudes itself that we are here confronted with an independent development. Norse, like Greek and Latin, knows only one type of personal pronoun, Greek and Latin because they use the pronoun only when it is emphasized, Norse because here the pronoun, where used, is invariably emphasized. Old Irish, however, knows no less than four different types of personal pronouns: an independent pronoun, corresponding in use to the Latin "ego"; this pronoun emphasized by a suffix, corresponding in use to the most emphatic use of "ek" in old Norse; a shortened form, suffixed to the verb, but only in the oblique cases (not in the nominative), parallel to the Greek *mou, moi, me,* shortened from *emou, emoi, eme;* and finally a suffix syllable, in all cases including the nominative, normally added to the verb in order to state the person. The wealth of this development is as remarkable as its total divergence from the simplicity of things in old Norse.

We must briefly analyze the various forms. The third one, the suffixed pronoun in the oblique cases, is most easily disposed of. There is nothing psychologically interesting in the use of the personal pronoun in oblique cases. The personal pronoun, in these cases, is a simple attribute or object, as every other noun. There is no profound difference between saying "This belongs to Tom," and "This belongs to me." All languages having a personal pronoun use it in such contexts, those of classical antiquity as much as those of the modern West. As pronouns are used much more than any other nouns, it is natural enough that they were slurred in ancient Greek as much as in Irish, where the strong interaction of neighboring words provides an additional reason for slurring. In one word, it is, for once, a matter determined, in fact, not by psychology but by linguistic convenience.

The second form is, in the main, no more than a compound of the first and the fourth. The independent pronoun for "I" is old Irish "me." The suffixed form is "-se." The emphatic form is "messe." The only thing remarkable is that Irish was not content with simple "me," but felt the need of developing a still more emphatic form; a symptom of a burning urge to provide for every shade in the emphasis of personality.

Our investigation therefore comes down to a discussion of the "independent" and of the "suffixed" form, of "me" and "-se." These forms cannot be brought under one common denominator, and their coexistence must be regarded as a characteristic feature of Irish, or, more exactly, of the Gaelic group of languages. Obviously, Irish shares this characteristic with French, which also uses, side by side, the independent pronoun, and the dependent pronoun joined to the verb. True, in modern French the pronoun is normally prefixed, not suffixed (j'ai, not ai=je). But the second form is still used in question and exclamation, and was commonly used with the indicative, down to and after the time of Rabelais.

That the French "je" derives from Latin "ego" is subject to no doubt. But the origin of the French independent pronoun "moi" is more debatable. It has, of course, the same root as the oblique cases of Latin *ego*, viz. *mei, mihi, me*, and in the chaos of cases characteristic of late vulgar Latin every interchange between an accusative and a nominative is conceivable. But "moi" has also the same root as Irish "me," to which it corresponds completely in use; and the dipthong in French is almost certainly due to Gaelic influence. The only conceivable explanation of the parallel use of an independent and dependent pronoun leads back not to Latin usage, nor to Germanic influences, but only to the Celtic tradition. We must assume that, in the decline of Roman civilization, especially in Western France (the Frankish Neustria where French originally emerged), which had always been a backwater of Roman colonization, Celtic influences asserted themselves again. After all, to this day a Celtic language is still spoken in large parts of Britanny. The usage of two pronouns seems to go back to this influence, and both Latin and Celtic were used in building up the distinction between the two forms—Latin for the dependent, Celtic for the independent pronoun.

Be it added that the same obtains, not in the literary, but in the popular speech of other Latin-speaking regions, which at an earlier date had been invaded by Celts—in Raethian (in the Grisons) and in some Northern Italian dialects, in particular those of Lombardy. Here also we find shortened suffixed pronouns side by side with fully developed prefixed personal pronouns. In one word, the use of the pronoun is traceable to two distinct sources, one Germanic, leading to the obligatory use of one and the same pronoun for all purposes, the other Celtic, distinguishing between independent and dependent use of the pronoun.

The influence of old Irish, or more exactly old Celtic, upon French and some dialects of other continental languages also provides us with a clue to the degree of antiquity of the Celtic form of the pronoun. It is a fact, established through the completely undamaged state of Irish MSS preserved on the continent, that Irish was understood in no continental country at the date when these MSS were first brought there by Irish monks. It is therefore out of the question that the popular speech of France could have been influenced by the Irish monks in the least. The Celtic elements of syntax existing in modern French must have got into the speech of Gaul in the process of the transformation of classical Latin into vulgar Latin, in the late Roman period. But in order to affect Latin in its decay, they must have been fully developed at least in the earliest centuries of our era, and probably earlier, before the Roman conquest of Gaul. For this rich variety of pronominal forms cannot be due to Latin influence, and it is unlikely that, under Latin domination, the Celtic dialects in France underwent a rich independent development or borrowed strongly from developments across the channel.

If this is so, then we can clearly distinguish between two phases of Celtic speech development in respect of the personal pronoun. At a very early phase, perhaps much earlier than the frequent usage of the pronoun in old Norse, the Celts must have been extremely sensitive to all shades of expressing the ego. Yet in spite of this, the normal usage of the pronoun with the verb does not seem to antedate the eighth century, and as this is the period of the beginning of Norse raids, can probably be traced to their influence. The rapid and complete borrowing of the Norse habit is easily explained, for the instruments for adopting it were already present as a result of the rich development of the pronoun in old Irish.

The detailed study of the mutual interference of these various trends with one another is of considerable interest, and sometimes provides a more direct approach to an understanding of the civilization of certain nations than a study of their literatures. In fact, not only two but three influences are at work, for to the Germanic and Celtic influences there must be added the permanent influence of Latin, as an expression of the still existing classical way of life. Here are a few remarks about this struggle between various civilizations, meant not as an adequate treatment of the subject, but as an incitement to further research.

As to French, the struggle is mainly between the Celtic and the Germanic conception, and it is a distinct victory for the latter when, with the approach of the classical age of French literature, the suffixed use of the dependent pronoun becomes impossible in the seventeenth century and the pronoun, in the indicative at least, is prefixed to the verb. At about the same time, the use of the pronoun with the verb becomes obligatory, a process achieved in German as early as the eleventh century. Here we have one more indication that this obligatory use of the pronoun is connected with profound changes in the French outlook, and not simply with phonetic developments. The age which finally made the prefixed pronoun obligatory was not by chance the "grand siècle." There is no period of history when the development of France and England was more parallel, that of France and Italy more distinct.

But the story of the pronoun in Provençal is even more exciting, and throws back light upon the history of the pronoun in French. For a study of the use of the pronoun in Provençal we are favored with the work of specialists, a rare exception in problems of this kind. We can, in particular, rely upon V. Brusewitz's "Etude historique sur la syntaxe des pronoms personnels dans la langue des Félibres." After stating (on page 3 of his study) that the use of the personal pronoun in the Provençal of the troubadours was much more frequent than in the revived modern literary Provençal of the "Félibrige," Brusewitz compares French and Provençal usage in this respect. "It seems," he says, "that in old Provençal the use of the pronoun as subject was more or less arbitrary. . . . One finds more or less the same in old French. As to modern French, one knows how the use of the pronoun as subject has become more and more common during the fifteenth and sixteenth century, and became general in the seventeenth century." Then follows the well-known theory of the need of using the personal pronoun owing to the decay of verbal endings. But the same, our author maintains, does not apply to Provençal. Here the climax of the use of the personal pronoun comes in the fifteenth and lasts throughout the sixteenth century, probably as a result of French political preponderance. This usage declines again from the seventeenth century onwards (until, at present, the pronoun in Provençal is reduced to the place it held in Latin)—probably, the author believes, because by then the distance between French and Provençal had become too big.

The perplexity of the author in the face of an apparently inexplicable reversal of a well-marked trend shines through this poor attempt at a hypothesis. If the Greek koiné was influenced by Semitic syntactic forms, and if Bulgarian copies essential linguistic features from Greek, it is difficult to accept the view that Provençal, in the seventeenth century, had become so different from French as to make it incapable to bring to final conclusion the amalgamation of French speech habits already largely received into Provençal. Since Sandfeldt-Jensen we know how easy it is for synthetic forms of speech to cross the highest language barriers. Again, the political influence of France in Provence became overwhelming in the very beginning of the thirteenth century, and continued unchanged from then onwards, hence is not a very convincing explanation of a change of language during the fifteenth century. But it should be invoked in dealing with language developments in the ninteenth century, for whereas the regime in that region was more or less the same from the thirteenth to the eighteenth century, the French revolution marked an enormous step forward in centralization and did, in particular, abolish the use of Provençal in self-government and local administration. Thus the whole theory of Brusewitz falls to the ground.

It is obvious that in the fifteenth century Northern and Southern France share in one and the same shedding of many remnants of a Southern, Latin, ancient mentality, and that Spain and Italy share in that trend to some extent. Whereas in the North this move leads to the surge which, in the "grand siècle," makes France the leading nation of Europe, the South of Europe falls behind in the seventeenth century. Of this, the loss of the personal pronoun in Provençal is only one minor symptom. The collapse of Italian civilization at the end of the Renaissance, and the victory of France over Spain on the field of international politics, are major aspects of the same development. The forward and backward move of the usage of the personal pronoun is one of the symptoms of this process.

We observe on the one hand how France sheds the fetters of ancient classical tradition. We observe it in this use of the pronoun. But we also observe it, to take only one of an endless number of facts, when, in the "battle of the books," the validity of the classical models for modern literature is challenged directly for the first time. If, on the other hand, Provençal dropped its pronouns, it was not because Provençal speech could not catch up with French speech, but because Provençal souls could not catch up with the vertiginous *tours de force* of the Normans Pascal and Corneille, the Breton Descartes, and the whole change of the soul of Northern France which took place in that century. Thus the idea of a spread of the use of the pronoun from a center to its periphery merely by geographical contact falls to the ground, and it is revealed even more clearly how the use of the pronoun is one of the main characteristics of our Western (or more exactly Northwestern) civilization, and how its ups and downs give an almost measurable indication of the strength of this civilization in various regions at various times.

At the same time, in the area where our civilization has achieved its most complete fulfilment, speech habits become more and more clearly marked and coherent. The use of the personal pronoun started from two divergent sources, Norse and Celtic. In the course of time, as the final completion of Western civilization approaches, the more extreme and consistent of the two types of usage, the Norse one, asserted itself more and more over the Celtic one, though never completely. The personal pronoun is now no longer suffixed but prefixed to the verb even in French and Rhaetian, thus acquiring a much more emphatic strength, though the distinction between a dependent and an independent pronoun is maintained in these languages. At the same time the use of the pronoun becomes more and more obligatory. In old Norse, Anglo-Saxon, old German, old Irish, and old French, it was not obligatory, however frequent. It becomes obligatory in German as soon as middle German arises out of old German, during the eleventh century. It is obligatory in English from the beginning. It is obligatory in the prose Edda. But in French it becomes obligatory only in the seventeenth century. That summary of the usage of the pronoun should alone be sufficient to remove every merely linguistic interpretation of the facts concerned, and to establish the parallelism between the forward move of Western civilization and the use of the personal pronoun.

Again there emerges the question: if the use of the pronoun is so immensely characteristic of our civilization, what, then, does it express? Of the many theories of the origin of Western civilization there is one which, at first sight, would seem to agree completely with our results, though arriving at its own conclusions from a different starting point. This theory is contained in H. de Tourville's work.

The author belongs to the Le Play school of sociology, which insists, on the one hand, upon the structure of the family as the essential basis of every civilization, and on the other hand, upon the formation of the social type of a group through the road it took in its wanderings. According to Tourville, in the early centuries of our era a fundamental change took place, when Scandinavian settlers started to occupy empty Norway, which was to transform the whole history of mankind: the "particularist" family arose there instead of the patriarchal family. The latter, the family type hitherto characteristic of all higher civilizations, was an "extended family" of parents, children, grandchildren etc., all of them under the direct control of the patriarch. The former is a small unit of parents and immature children only, based upon freedom of all adults from parental power, and on freedom of choice of a partner in marriage. It is this family which, according to Tourville, has brought into the world that attitude which the English describe by the term "individualism." He traces its spread first into Northern Germany, then France and England, by way of expansion of the Norse civilization. But before tracing its spread, he traces its origin, relating it, in the main, to the geographical features of the Norwegian fjords, where no large patriarchal family could have lived and where a man was entirely dependent upon himself alone. Thus the whole of Western civilization, down to the emphatic individualism of the Yankees, would be directly traceable to that one event, the migration of Germanic tribes, first into Eastern Scandinavia, then into Norway.

It is a most attractive theory, and attractive, in particular, in relation to the results of our previous investigation. It would explain to complete satisfaction why the use of the personal pronoun (which there is no difficulty to regard as an expression of "individualism" or "particularism") was unknown, in the specific modern sense, to Gothic; how it developed in Scandinavia, and how and to what extent it spread from there. It is therefore with great regret that one refuses to take advantage of a hypothesis which would make many difficult problems easy.

The following are my reasons for this rejection. First of all, if the emergence of the new type of life took place in Norway, then its characteristic linguistic features must also have evolved there. But this is not the case. Few things are more certain than that the new use of the personal pronoun originated in what today is Denmark and Sweden, more so than in Norway. This is clear from the places where the relevant runic inscriptions have been discovered. It is true that Tourville regards the occupation of Denmark and Southern Sweden by certain Germanic tribes as a necessary prelude to the emergence of the "particularist" society through the occupation of Norway. But this "prelude" is not distinct enough a fact to explain revolutionary changes of speech. Norway's geographical structure does indeed make impossible the living together of large patriarchal units. But there are few places in the world where the existence of such units would be more favored by nature than in Denmark. The only geographical factor Tourville can bring up to make us accept his view that the particularist society was prepared in Southern

Scandinavia is that there the sea lay between the immigrants and their old seats, thus cutting them off from any continuous influx of patriarchal traditions. But even this is doubtful. In order to strengthen his thesis Tourville then develops the hypothesis of the conquest of the whole area by a second, "Odinic" immigration, coming from the foothills of the Caucasus. But the interpretation of Icelandic myths on which this view is based is so naive as not to deserve serious consideration. It speaks for the historical genius of Tourville that he should have divined that something basic for the creation of modern civilization happened early in our era in Southern Scandinavia. But his attempts to find some farfetched explanation for it are only vain efforts to back up an instinctive insight by misdirected hypotheses. It remains a fact that the geographical conditions of Norway (which, indeed, would favor the emergence of individualism) cannot be made to explain a historical event which took place in Denmark and Southern Sweden.

Besides this basic objection, there are many subsidiary ones. It is perhaps correct to say that classical antiquity never conceived of our modern "particularist" family, as we know it in its maturity. But it is also undoubtedly a fact that late Roman law and custom diverged from classical Greek law and custom and went far in the direction of our modern conception of the family. On the other hand, it is a hopeless attempt to claim Norse descent for lower Saxon institutions. The idea that in a not clearly explained manner Norse institutions percolated into Lower Saxony before the Saxon conquest of England and also reached the Franks before the conquest of France, is entirely arbitrary. It is, on the contrary, certain that Norse influence, or more precisely old Norwegian influence (for only in Norway, according to Tourville, was the particularist family born) came to bear upon the continent only in the second half of the eighth century, and not in any strength before the ninth. And had Tourville used our language tests, he would have seen that the peculiarities of old Irish and of old French preclude any Norse influence upon the original conception of personality in the oldest Gaelic civilization.

But if Tourville's attempts at an explanation of his facts are beside the point, his find is no less of the greatest importance. He argues, roughly speaking, that a new type of "individualism" is the basis of Western civilization and that it can be distinguished, first in Scandinavia, then in England and Germany, and finally in France. That is exactly what our language test, centered round the personal pronoun, reveals, with the one addition that a second independent source of the same development can be discovered in Ireland. And his views complete ours and vice versa, for they give a clue to the meaning of the new use of the personal pronoun, which taken in isolation might, after all, mean many different things.

Yet if we survey our problem as it appears at this stage, we must admit that it has become only more puzzling. The new individualism is not due to inherited racial characteristics, for Gothic and presumably other pre-Voelkerwanderung Germanic languages did not have it, and it would be absurd to assume a basic racial difference between, e.g., ancient Goths in South Russia and ancient Goths in Southern Sweden. It is not due to surroundings, for it would be difficult to point to any fundamental difference between various parts of the great European plains, important enough to explain so important a development. It is not due to any influence of Roman-Greek civilization, to an "affiliation" of Norse civilization to that of classical antiquity, for the simple reason that neither Greek nor Latin has this use of the pronoun. Also, were any such influence involved, the new development must start near the confines of that civilization, and not at the opposite end of Europe.

There is only one fact which is traceably connected with the new developments in language, an element already invoked by J. Grimm, the father of Germanic linguistics, in order to explain the various stages of the evolution of Germanic speech. This fact is the great migration. The only premigration Germanic language known to us, Gothic, did not have the use of the pronoun. All postmigration languages have it. It is true that our assumption only holds good if the Norsemen actually did migrate from the Russian or Turkistan plains to Scandinavia, an assumption we make in common with Tourville and most authors on the subject. For if Scandinavia were the cradle of the Germanic nations, migration could not be invoked as an explanation of any language change in Southern Scandinavia. Our own evidence however is additional proof of the opposite view.

But how can this explanation (as far as explanation it is) be brought to agree with the assumption of a second independent source of the new individualism, a source of Celtic origin? After all, the Celts did not take part in the Voelkerwanderung! They certainly did not take part in the *Germanic* Voelkerwanderung which started in the third century A.D. But we saw that the main pecularities of the Celtic pronoun must go back to a much earlier date, must have existed even before the Roman conquest of Gaul. And the period preceding that conquest was precisely the period of the *Celtic* Voelkerwanderung, which we can well trace in prehistoric finds and historic records. About the fifth century B.C., or even earlier, the Celts conquered France, then passed into Britain and Ireland, conquering aborigines probably related to the modern Basques. In the fourth century B.C. they conquered Northern Italy, early in the third century they appeared in the Balkans and in Asia Minor. This wave of migrations, as lasting and as powerful as the later Germanic wave, might well account for changes parallel to those undergone by the Germanic tribes.

[At this point, Borkenau's manuscript raises the question why similar language changes were not caused by other great migrations, from those of the ancient Italic peoples to those of the Mongols, and proceeds to speculate that "in the original makeup of the Indo-European group there was something lacking in the makeup of other groups, something making them capable of such a development." However, in a German essay written *after* this manuscript and published in his book *Drei Abhandlungen zur deutschen Geschichte*[6] he developed a more concrete hypothesis, linking the rise of the new individualism with the special effect of *overseas* migration on the loosening of clan ties and the strengthening of the individualistic institution of the "following" (Latin *trustis*). The editor has therefore preferred to replace the older, more speculative passage by a translation of the corresponding passage from the later German text as representing the author's more mature thought, with kind permission of the German publishers.]

> The rise of Western individualism is clearly reflected in language; this applies no less clearly to the connection between individualism and voluntarism. But no compelling proof can be adduced for the connection between this new attitude of man toward the world and concrete historical events. Still, I should like, tentatively and for purposes of discussion, to raise the question whether the new individualism is not closely linked with the gradual dissolution of clan ties.
>
> Our language development indicating an early individualism goes back as far into pre-Christian times. That it has something to do with the great migrations is highly probable. Yet it is certain that migrations in themselves need not lead to a weakening of clan ties, and that the rigid clan ties of the earliest Germanic and Celtic periods were incompatible with a sharply marked strengthening of individualism. Where is the solution for those contradictions? Does there perhaps exist a special type of migration which dissolves clan ties while other types of migration may strengthen them? We must consider the historic material.

6. Franz Borkenau, *Drei Abhandlungen zur deutschen Geschichte* (Frankfurt: Klostermann, 1947).

True, that material offers no categorical reply, but it yields certain indications. Let us first look at the situation in Ireland, one of the core areas of the clan organization. Nowhere was the power of the clan greater than in Ireland: even the Irish monasteries, the Irish Church were based on the clan. Nevertheless, the power of the clan over the individual had its limit at one point—the mission. The overseas mission (besides the emigration to Iceland) offered to the individual a chance to break away from the clan organization. Individuals and groups that were not clan-bound went to Scotland, to Northern England, or to the continent to live there as hermits or in their not clan-bound monasteries.[7] The group, for instance, which St. Columbanus rallied around himself at Luxeuil was the spiritual counterpart of the following of a secular leader.[8]

Now we must ask: are we here simply dealing with a result of Christianization, or have Christian and pre-Christian elements merged here? It has rightly been pointed out that the far-flung missionary activity of the Irish opened a field of fulfilment to the boundless Irish migratory instinct. But whence that migratory instinct? Modern Bretons or Welshmen show little of it. If one takes France as a whole as the most important representative of Celtic characteristics, the Celts as such would have to be regarded as the most sedentary element of the modern world. But that again does not fit the immense migratory treks of early Celtic history, nor the *Wanderlust* of the modern Irish and Scots. Obviously, the *Wanderlust* or its absence had nothing to do with the Celtic character as such.

By contrast, the guess might be risked with all due caution that the tremendous Irish missionary activity had something to do with the earlier tremendous Celtic migrations—that the *Wanderlust* of the individual appeared perhaps when the migrations of the clan had stopped. In that case, the missionary activity in its secular aspect would appear as a transformation of migration from a collective to an individual form. There remains the question why such transformation is found to so high a degree among the island Celts, again excepting those of the Welsh highlands, but not at all among the continental Celts.

---

7. Compare e.g. Albert Hauck, *Kirchengeschichte Deutschlands*, Part I (Leipzig: Hinrichs, 1911). Unfortunately, a modern comprehensive study by specialists in Celtic research is lacking.

8. Compare *Vita Columbani* in J. P. Migne, *Patrologia Latina*.

All this may appear highly problematic. Yet it may contain a useful hint. For the transformation from tribal migration into individual migration does constitute a typical phenomenon. . . . Indeed such a transformation of the collective into the individual is missing only in exceptional cases—only where the tribal organization excludes any breaking out by the individual, as with the Mongol peoples. It seems that such extreme clan collectivism is particularly developed among nomadic horsemen, at least while they enjoy boundless space for their movements: any enforced settlement changes the picture at once. The final stage of the great migrations is always formed by the migrations of individuals or freely formed groups of the type of the Italic *ver sacrum*.

That appears simple and may indeed offer a clue for an understanding of the Irish missionary movement—yet it is still not satisfactory: for it does not yet explain the different attitude of the continental Celts and the island Celts toward migration. It only proves that the halting of the great migrations and their petering out into individual enterprises has everywhere an individualizing effect. Some phenomena of the final period of the Germanic Voelkerwanderung may be explained that way; above all, a light may be thrown on the early individualist tendencies in the culture of antiquity. Let us look further.

The ancient Germanic clan organization has been completely preserved for the longest time in Iceland. That is explained without difficulty by the fact that ancient Nordic customs were preserved there for the longest time, free from influences of the Christian West. That simple and conclusive answer is apparently made more convincing by a comparison with the Irish situation. In both cases we are dealing with islands whose colonists arrived at the extreme end of great migrations. In both cases, the traditional clan organization hardened in isolation. In neither case did the adoption of Christianity produce a profound change in the social structure. Yet if, as we just saw, the old fire of the migratory impulse went on burning in Irish culture as if under the blanket of the clan organization, only to turn against the clan structure under changed conditions, then we ought to be somewhat suspicious also about the integrity of the Icelandic clan organization. After all, a not negligible percentage of the settlers in Iceland were Irish. The toughness of the outer shell of a social order does not always indicate its inner solidity.

In fact, we must ask whether a proper clan organization had

been really possible in Iceland in the beginning. For in most cases not entire clans migrated to settle there—only splinters of clans and often individual clan chiefs with friends, retainers, and servants. No doubt that presupposed a loosening compared to the tight and strict cohesion of the clan in Norway and Ireland.[9] On the other hand, it must not be forgotten that the clan determined the rank of the man, and that Iceland had been primarily settled by noblemen.

It is always useful to compare the evolution of parallel situations in far distant times and at different places. Why do modern Americans in the South or New England so often stress a century-old kinship with English families with whom they no longer have any real ties? Why do they stress it so much more than the average Yankee? First because the average American lives in a society without distinctions of rank, where origin does not matter, while in the Southern states and New England it counts. Origin is there so much underlined just because it is not a fact obvious in daily life. The apparently far-fetched American parallel has not been introduced here arbitrarily; for it seems to me that all cases of North European colonial settlements are closely related events of a single type, as will soon be shown. For now, I only wish to raise the question: do the Icelanders perhaps emphasize their clan ties so strongly just because they used to live in fact in primitive conditions in a society of almost equals, because the claims of the individual here did not flow automatically from his clan membership as in the home country? Does the Icelandic sense of clan membership have a primarily heraldic character? Or more exactly, did it have such a character in the first generations after the taking of the land, before genuine clans rooted in the soil could arise?

Under the circumstances, this must have been the case. For few phenomena evolve according to so compelling a pattern as colonial cultures. Colonial cultures always combine extremes, without exception. The reality of colonial existence is inevitably primitive, the selection among colonists favors the self-made man, the conditions impose independence on the individual, produce a cool, sceptical realism and a ruthless individualism. But at the same time, the colonists are largely cut off from the normal in many ways intersecting influences of the developing culture of the home

9. The entire Icelandic tradition would have to be referred to as proof. The clearest survey of the colonization is given in the *Landnamabok*, particularly enlightening because it attempts no systematic presentation but describes hundreds of individual cases.

country. In their primitive conditions they must cling to those cultural elements they have carried along with them. Hence each colonial culture contains major archaic features. The present culture, nay the present language of French Canada reflects the French culture of the *ancien regime* almost unchanged. The culture of Spanish America is the Spanish culture of the eighteenth century. The United States, in particular New England and the Southern states, have preserved essential features of the puritanism of the seventeenth century on one side and of its "cavalier" culture on the other. And all that side by side with traits of an uninhibited individualism, of a freedom from ties that is breathtaking compared with the slower development of Europe! Should that not apply to Iceland just as well? Of course it does. Icelandic culture is the longest and best preserved branch of the ancient Nordic culture. But cool realism and scepticism, a stormy desire for freedom combined with a keen legal sense are generally, and rightly, regarded as its characteristics. Now those are both highly modern and also individualistic features; together they constitute a typical colonial culture. But again we must ask: why does the personal realism free from traditions, why does the unbending impulse towards freedom just here go so far? In the case of Iceland, the answer seems to be obvious. But let us first consider a third case.

With the Anglo-Saxons, even in the oldest literary documents accessible to us, the "following" plays a particularly significant role besides the clan. But clan and following are competing structures. Even though clan loyalty is reserved in the obligations of a follower to his leader, the main weight of day-to-day duties has shifted from the clan to the following. But the following, in contrast to the clan, is a thoroughly voluntarist, individualistic structure. One joins it by a free act of will; one is also free to leave it. The follower chooses his lord, not the lord the follower—he only accepts him. And within the following, there operates, besides the loyalty towards the lord, the tie of friendship movingly described as a decisive motive force just in Anglo-Saxon poetry.[10]

There can thus be no doubt about the weakening of clan ties by the institution of the following and about the voluntarist-individualistic character of the latter. But the question arises: do Anglo-Saxon conditions really offer something special regarding

10. The chief document here is the Beowulf. (See for a recent English version *Beowulf and the Fight at Finnsburg* (Boston: Heath, 1950). The significance of the institution of the following is also otherwise expressed in Anglo-Saxon literature as nowhere else.

the unfolding of the following? Almost the entire relevant literature treats the following as something common to the Germanic tribes. One fact of particular historic significance is mostly emphasized: the Frankish following, the *trustis*, as precursor of the institution of vassalage so important for world history.[11] Similarly, according to recognized teaching, the Langobard institution of the gastalds, the king's men, has developed from the king's following. Other examples for the role of the following are by no means lacking. They are found everywhere—from Tacitus to the sagas, from the Ostrogoths to the Saxons.

But have we not still oversimplified? Is the institution of the following common only to the Germanic peoples? Was it unknown to the Celts, the Italic peoples, the Achaeans and Dorians, the Aryans? Is there even any proof that it was limited to the circle of peoples of Indogermanic speech? Does not rather everything indicate that the free following of a war leader is necessarily found wherever peoples or tribes permit their members to engage in war without declaring their every campaign as a tribal war? Voluminous ethnographic material may be quoted in support of that thesis. Thus the statement that the following is common to all Germanic peoples loses all specific content. Followings arise wherever there are "private wars"; they disappear where the tribe, or the state, enforces a monopoly of warmaking.

Thus, for instance, the matter presents itself without any ambiguity in Jordanes' history of the Goths.[12] The young Theodoric undertakes a short campaign with a following of volunteers and returns victorious. But once he has become king, he moves into Italy with the Gothic people. The difference between the campaign of the following and the tribal war is perfectly clear to the historian despite some awkwardness of expression. He also knows that in the latter case it is irrelevent that a fraction of the people stays behind in its old lands. Jordanes, when talking about the Goths, knows no other forms of war but the short campaign of a following and the tribal war. Now it is obvious that in those conditions, the campaign of a following may often have given the young men an opportunity to move outside the bonds of tribal and clan discipline, but otherwise did not change the social order.

11. For the prevalent scholarly view see among others Heinrich Brunner, *Deutsche Rechtsgeschichte* (last edition Berlin: Ducker & Humblot, 1958).
12. Jordanes, *De Getarum sive Gothorum origine et rebus gestis* (Freiburg & Tübigen: Mohn, 1882).

One may imagine that the situation was quite similar among some far-migrating tribes, such as the Vandals and the Burgundians, but also with the more sedentary Alemanns. In all those cases, I should suppose that one may conclude from the absence of a clearly distinctive, permanent and structural role of the *"trustis"* that the alternative between tribal war and the campaign of a following described by Jordanes was practiced.

A different situation arises once the following acquires a decisive significance *within* the people's war, and beyond it in time of peace. Perhaps the state of affairs with the Langobards showed a transitional form—for there the *trustis* became definitely a permanent institution, and its members became the "king's men." Still, Langobard history shows that in the last resort, the tribal nobles in their own right were more important than the royal *gastalds*.

If in the light of this state of affairs among the continental Germanic tribes we look at the situation among the Anglo-Saxons, characterized by the prevalence of the "following" relationship in daily life, the difference, nay contrast, at once strikes the eye. Why is this decisive prevalence of the following met nowhere else in this form, why this reduction of the role of the clan just among the Anglo-Saxons? Is it not obvious that it must be linked somehow with the process of colonization?

We know very little about the Anglo-Saxon settlement of England. But this much is clear, that neither the Saxons nor the Jutes, nor in all probability the Angles emigrated as a people. It was individual groups consisting of leaders with their following which moved to England. Thus the following as an institution became the basis of settlement in England. It is also unlikely that women and children were taken along at first on those overseas expeditions. The bulk must have been unmarried young men, somewhat similar to the followers who joined the campaigns of the young Theodoric—only with the essential difference that those overland expeditions were passing adventures, while with the Anglo-Saxons the crossing of the sea by the young crew became the basis of their settlement.

Proof is hardly needed that such customs, once developed in the early times of a people, strike deep roots and cling firmly. To this very day all Anglo-Saxon migration, including the entire gigantic process of the settlement of America and Australia, has developed from the enterprise of young men; events like the family emigration on the "Mayflower" are definitely exceptions. Virginia was first settled by men only.[13] The women were brought over only after the land had been taken and the new settlement been secured. As is known, there is to this day a shortage of women in outlying regions of America: the peculiar form of Anglo-Saxon migration thus shows its effects even today.

In England, an emphatic harking back to the clan organization of the homeland, such as took place in Iceland, was superfluous. Iceland was settled by individual chieftains, England by large bands that had no need to cling to a form of organization inadequate to their new situation. The clan ties were thus weakened in England from the beginning. This may explain the striking "modernity" of Anglo-Saxon conditions, compared with those of the mainland Germanic tribes, throughout the early period.

What a contrast indeed between the Gothic and Vandalic peoples in arms, who moved over land clanwise, with women and children, cattle and mobile goods, and the bold bands associated for the crossing of the sea who looked for a new home and a new scene of activity on the other shore, without the ballast of family and possessions! Recognition of that difference is an important key to the understanding of Western history.

And now we shall no longer be astonished to have found the first evidence for an independent use of the "I," completely separate from the verb, appositive and proud, in that very bay of the North Sea from which the Anglo-Saxon migration started, and at that very time when it began. Let us add that the separation of the Saxons from the North Germanic tribes constitutes a problem: how far can those Northerners in that period be distinguished from the Saxons? At any rate the Northern Germanic overseas migration of the Vikings appears as a natural expansion and continuation of the Saxon one. After all, the Beowulf thoroughly identifies the Saxon and Nordic customs of seafaring and of the following! Hence the winning out of the I-form of speech in the entire Northern Germanic area requires no further explanation either. However, the linguistic development taken as a whole shows that the breakthrough of individualism took place not only after arrival in the colonial country, but already at the continental coast—as soon as the great overseas migration began.

At last, then, Irish, Anglo-Saxon, and Nordic material is joining

---

13. An excellent description of all phases of the process of American settlement is found in Henry Underwood Faulkner, *American Economic History* (New York: Harper, 1949).

in a transparent if still undeniably hypothetical unity. The development of the personal pronoun in Irish takes place earlier than in the Germanic languages: the overseas settlement of Ireland took place centuries before the Germanic overseas migrations. The new individualistic type of language has not reached the same coherence in Ireland as in the Northwest Germanic languages: but then, the Irish migration came to a halt and had to transform itself into individual migration, while inside Ireland the clan society ossified once more. Conversely, England shows us the highest type, the freest unfolding of a society built around the institution of the following: just so, the clearest linguistic announcement of the new individualism is found among those Jutes just about to sail for Kent.

Here, it seems to me, the basic law governing this entire process becomes visible. It has no mysterious connection with Indogermanic, Nordic, or Germanic roots. The Irish, the Saxons, and the Vikings are its carriers, because they are the three peoples who in the course of the Voelkerwanderung make the transition from land migration to overseas migration. In doing so, they use the age-old institution of the following, by itself of quite subordinate importance in tribal life, but acquiring decisive significance at the point where the ocean tears up the ties of tribe, clan, and family. The veiled, misty line which separates land and sea all over the North has proved to be the frontier between the slavish collective bondage of the individual and the freedom of the person. Up to this line, semi-nomadic migrant tribes prevailed. But he who crossed it sailed into a new, proud I-consciousness—into a new freedom from which the new Western culture was to arise.

The sea is the great source of freedom. That sentence finds an echo in the blood of the Englishman as of the Dane, the Norwegian, and the Irishman, and also the Hanseates of the German coast feel it in their bones, but the true landlubber fails to understand it. Why should that be so? Hardly one Anglo-Saxon could give a convincing reply to that question; what is offered are mostly poor rationalizations. What I put forward here is in part an attempt to make comprehensible this instinctive feeling for the link between seafaring and freedom: without the sea, I maintain, there could never have been a Western civilization, based on the freedom and will, indeed the "free will," of the individual person and fundamentally different from that of Eastern Europe. This implies the opinion that in the presentation of the early Middle Ages, Anglo-Saxon and Irish history has never received its full due as compared to Frankish history, however, much the experts are conscious of the importance of Anglo-Saxon and Irish influences. After all, the Frankish realm received in the seventh and eighth centuries the most important elements of its culture from England and Ireland. That can be understood only in our context.

But here arises something still more important. Among no mainland Germanic people is the institution of the following as strongly developed as among the Franks. As is known, vasallage exists only in embryonic stages with other mainland Germanic tribes; with the Franks it has developed fully—from the *trustis*. How was that possible? Perhaps here, too, we cannot go beyond guesses. But it seems to be established that the role of the *trustis* with the Franks did not arise only with the conquest of Gaul but goes back to earlier times. It is also certain that it was the Salic Franks, coming from a coastal region, who founded the realm, and that they had been pirates and seafarers for centuries before they turned towards expansion on land. And it is certain finally that those Frankish seaborne expeditions preceding the time of the Voelkerwanderung were in no way distinct from the Saxon ones. Here it may be useful to remember that the Frankish and Saxon confederations only gradually developed from a tangle of coastal and inland tribes: for an early phase of that development, there is no occasion to draw a firm line of separation between groups of peoples anywhere between Jutland and the Scheldt. Is it, then, far-fetched to explain the strength of the *trustis* among the Franks by their seafaring phase, and to see in the role of the institution of the following in the Frankish realm, in the final rise of vassalage and medieval feudalism, an indication of the important fact that here creations of the seagoing peoples were transferred to a land people?

Perhaps it was in that way that a process of decisive importance for the whole of Western history began: the reverse action of the individualism of the seafaring peoples on the continent from which they had started. Suppose the seafarer's culture—for basically one may, despite the undeniable profound differences between those peoples, speak of an Irish-Anglosaxon-Viking cultural zone—had remained limited to the islands and the continental shores directly facing them, or suppose it had expanded from there across the oceans only, the result would have been a separation between island culture and mainland culture, and the latter,

even in Western Europe, might have ended as a mere outpost of
the culture of the East European steppe. Indeed, a firm frontier
cannot be drawn between the East and West of Europe either
geographically or culturally. . . .

As for the island cultures, they have never felt completely at
one with the culture of the continent. The tendency resolutely to
turn one's back on the European mainland and to look exclusively
to the West is inherent to the Anglo-American, the Irish, the
Viking-Western-Scandinavian culture. If in the last resort that
tendency has not prevailed decisively, it is because the coastal
region of Northwestern Europe formed a strong link between the
island realm and the mainland. That applies to Norway, Denmark, the German North Sea regions, the Low Countries, and—
far more important than all of them—to France, the feudal nation
formed by Salic Franks which, after receiving the seeds of a higher
culture from Ireland and England, in turn under Norman com-
pulse extended its grip to England. In the form of vassalage the
institution of the following, highly developed by the seafaring
peoples, came to a synthesis with the family-bound rural lordship
of late antiquity, and the West sprang from it. Here the interpenetration of Northern-maritime original creation and ancient
cultural tradition took place, which alone made possible the rise
of a Western culture. Without that interpenetration, the island
culture would not only have broken away from the mainland
culture, it would also have got stuck in old Nordic heroic morality, as happened in Iceland, and would thus have ossified and
withered early as an "abortive civilization" in the sense of A. J.
Toynbee's term.

Toynbee is perhaps the first to have insisted sufficiently upon the
independence of both the Scandinavian and the Irish development. Struck
by this independence, but also by the early withering of the civilizations
of these two countries, he listed these developments under the heading
of "abortive civilizations." Our linguistic analysis again brings out the
significance of these two countries but also that there is no question here
of any "abortive civilization." On the contrary, the basic attitudes to life
of both the Irish and the Scandinavian civilizations have become the
foundation of our own Western civilization, so that these two developments must be simply regarded as embryonic forms of the latter.

What happened was simply that the foundations were laid in Scandinavia and Ireland, but the full development took place, under inspi-

rations from the Mediterranean area, much farther South. We are therefore confronted, in the case of the decline of Scandinavia and Ireland,
with no more than a shifting of the geographical center of a civilization,
a shifting which, in the history of every civilization, takes place more
than once. If Toynbee did not recognize this, it is apparently due to his
firm assumption that the roots of our Western civilization must be sought
in the South. Looking at it from that angle, the civilizations of the North
must indeed appear as entirely independent of our civilization, but at the
same time as "abortive," as their blossoming ended when the rise of
Western civilization in France just began. In fact those older civilizations
have been amalgamated into the maturing civilization of the West, of
which they make up an integral part.

Having thus concluded our survey of the context in which the new
type of speech arose, we are brought back to our fundamental question:
what is the meaning of this new type of speech? We can now give a more
precise sense to our query. Knowing that it will be impossible to discover
any utilitarian or "psychological" "explanation" of it, we must simply
ask: what does the new "I"-saying mode of speech express?

The answer to this cannot be given in a few words. So far we have
only collected a certain amount of evidence to show that the habit is
indeed characteristic of an entirely new development, and that its alter-
ations somehow coincide with important changes of civilization in other
respects. This gives a strong presumption in favor of regarding it as the
expression of something essential, but not more, of course, than a presumption. Final proof can only be found in the whole subsequent analysis
of the origins of our civilization. For in itself the use of "I" can mean
a great many things, and the full extent of what it means can only be
brought out by a survey of all the most important aspects of our civilization. The few things to be said now are therefore largely stated in
anticipation.

That the habit expresses a new forcible emphasis upon the individual,
a reluctance to treat it as a simple element in a chain of events, there is
no doubt. It is also clear that this emphasis starts from the "I," not from
the "he," that it reflects a view of life where the "I" is, more than before,
felt to be the center of the world, and at the same time something
permanent and identical to itself. But it is important to remove a possible
misunderstanding. Our Western civilization is not more "egotistic" than
any previous civilization, if by "egotism" we mean the ruthless pursuit
of private interests. On the contrary. If only owing to the Christian
elements which entered into that civilization at an early date, we subject

ourselves to many inhibitions quite unknown to earlier civilizations. Nothing could surpass, in particular, the ruthless pursuit of money and pleasure by the Greeks, to whom pity was almost unknown. The "egotism" which is reflected in "I"-saying speech is of a different kind.

It is, again, an "egotism" which, as Spengler emphasized, no longer regards individual life as a series of outward and, as it were, unconnected events. It reflects an attitude for which the "soul," as a permanent substratum of inner experience, is the center of the world. In this respect it agrees with the new civilization of the Southeast which also, in its own way, puts the soul into the center of the world, and it is perhaps this common attitude of the Southeastern and the Northwestern civilizations which has made Christianity acceptable as a common basis for both; though the civilization of the Near East is timeless, and our own civilization keenly time-conscious. In both cases the reaction from the Greek life, which was centered in actuality and in the physical world, is obvious. In the case of the new Oriental civilization from which Christianity arose, the term "reaction" is perhaps an adequate description of what actually happened. For the Near East actually reacted against the worldliness of Greek civilization. But no such direct reaction can be involved in the case of the Norsemen. Here the new inwardness is an independent birth, and if, though in different forms, it happened at about the same time in two areas so widely different in every respect, this is powerful proof that there is something like one common "drift" in the whole history of mankind.

Yet, of course, the term "inwardness" is not sufficient as an analysis of I-saying speech. On the contrary, the mere inwardness of the East precisely did *not* lead to the emergence of the I-saying habit. Semitic languages, for reasons different from those obtaining in Indo-European languages, have always used the pronoun, but despite the force of the Semitic impact upon the Balkans modern Greek has not adopted this use.

Here it occurs that the new inwardness leads to entirely different attitudes towards one's neighbor in East and West respectively. In the East, the new inwardness led to a crushing of the proud, worldly self-assertion of the Greek individual, and to the wiping out of the individual in the face of the eternal. In the West, the opposite obtained. Here inwardness meant, from the beginning, the opening of an unbridgeable chasm between one individual and all others, the emergence of strangeness between man and man. This is, as will become more and more apparent in the course of our study, the most distinctive feature of our civilization. It is also the one most closely connected with the I-saying habit.

At the present stage of our investigation, only hints can be given of the meaning of this. One must read only one good modern tragedy to understand that all modern tragedy is a tragedy that involves a failure of communication. Othello kills Desdemona because there is no basis any longer on which their souls can speak to one another. Macbeth is finished at the moment when it appears that their common crime has opened a chasm between himself and his wife, and all the rest of mankind in the bargain. Hamlet cannot speak to the soul of any being round him, and that is his tragedy. Romeo and Juliet perish through the sudden feeling of isolation which hopelessly breaks upon them. The list could be endlessly extended.

By contrast Oedipus, Tiresias, and Jocasta can speak to one another with perfect clarity, directly touching the innermost springs of their lives. It is an error about facts which destroys Oedipus. Creon and Antigone perfectly understood one another; they only clash about their respective conceptions of duty. Odysseus and Philoctetes do not move on different planes; only Odysseus tries to cheat Philoctetes. The Furies chase Orestes; but Clytemnestra, had she had time to explain, would not have tried to make him see that he misunderstood her motives in murdering Agamemnon.

The position in the East is different, and can be mentioned only in anticipation of later remarks. Yet this much should be clear: whereas the great novels and the great tragedies of the West invariably lead up to catastrophe through estrangement, Russian art, and in particular Dostoevski, invariably concludes with the overcoming of it. The strangeness between man and man is here denounced as something specifically Western, and the task of life is to overcome it; an achievement possible through Christian love. But Christian love, in this view, can only become real against the background of the Russian folk-spirit.

Individualism in the West, I maintain, means in the first place the estrangement of man from man. This estrangement is the root problem, the root tragedy, and the root of the greatness of our own civilization. It is revealed in every aspect of its shape. It is, among other things, closely connected with that physical sense for wide distances which Spengler emphasized. But we do not share Spengler's view that the predominant conception of space can be the fundamental distinctive mark of any civilization. One must look for something nearer direct inner experience. We shall find it, I believe, in what Nietzsche called *Das Pathos der Distanz*, a phrase so difficult to translate, because so dense in meaning, that I prefer to put it here, in the first place, in the original. It is something entirely unknown to antiquity, fiercely fought in the East. The phrase points to a feeling of profound reserve, of "distance" of one human being from another, a feeling which is a glory and a tragedy at one and the same time.

In the present chapter, we are directly concerned with linguistics. It would not be admissible to interpret the I-saying habit as an expression of the *Pathos der Distanz* if there were no further linguistic evidence to corroborate the connection. But such evidence exists. The *Pathos der Distanz* is more directly expressed in another speech habit, the use of the plural of the second person pronoun, the "you," in polite speech.

The point of using the plural is, of course, that you treat your partner as if he were more than one ordinary human being. The form was amplified, in Spanish, into "Vd.," "vuesa merced," "your grace," used with the third person of the singular. Spanish manners being the model of most European manners from the sixteenth century onwards, but with a slight mollifying of their strictness, the "grace" was dropped in other languages, while the third person singular was maintained, instead of the older second person plural. Hence the Italian "lei," the German "er," later combined with French "vous" into "Sie," the third person plural. Danish also followed in the wake of German tradition.

But the literal meaning of this florid form of speech has little to do with its actual significance. This has been blurred in modern literary English through the disappearance of the "thou," leaving again only one form of address, as in Greek and Latin. In all other European languages there exists the distinction between polite and familiar address. "Thou" is used between relatives, friends, colleagues, lovers and, in primitive social conditions, by superiors towards their subordinates, as always towards children. In all other cases "you" is used. The boundary line between the two types of speech is instinctively understood by everybody to coincide with the boundary line between intimacy and "reserve." As the use of the "I" so the use of the "you" reflects, in its ups and downs, the forward and backward leaps of Western civilization.

I have always been astonished that something so singular and so significant should be so much taken for granted by historians. But my surprise is probably due to the circumstance that I myself witnessed and shared in one dramatic development in this sphere, the breaking down of the obligatory "you" between the sexes in the defeated countries after World War I, which was a major symptom of the revolt against the "Western" spirit in those countries. Having lived through that change, I naturally could no longer take the "you"-habit for granted. In fact, it is unique in the whole history of the manners of mankind. Other civilizations are in some respects much more ceremonial than our own, but (except where copying the habit now from the West) have no such way of expressing "distance." In particular, neither Byzance nor the polite society of the Khalifs knew it. It has sprung up within the confines of our own civilization, but not in the same area as the "I"—rather at the opposite end of the lands of the West, in "Provence," that is to say in Southern France.

There might be some doubt whether Provence is really the country of origin of this kind of speech, or whether it was, from the beginning, common to all France. For it appears in very early, though not in the earliest French. What points to the South of France as its place of origin is, however, one circumstance which is of interest in other respects also. Strangely enough, in prose documents, especially those of a legal type, the "thou" is maintained until far into the twelfth century, even where persons of very high rank are addressed. This is the more remarkable because these Provençal legal documents make a very ample use of the "I" before names of persons, reminding one of runic inscriptions. One reason for the absence of the "you" is perhaps that most of these documents are written in a queer mixture of Latin and Provençal, and in Latin "tu" is of course the only form available. It is certain, at any rate, that the "you" habit originated together with the poetry of the Troubadours, and for at least a century is found only in that poetry, as the obligatory form of address both for the Troubadour's lady and his male superiors in rank. And as there is no doubt that this poetry originated in Southern France and was only later adopted into France proper, it is, I believe, safe to surmise that the "you"-habit originated in Provençal feudal courts. It originated there together with the other basic forms of chivalry.

It is, in contrast to the rise of the "I" habit, a type of behavior not sprung from everyday life, but from the solemn romanticism of Provençal poetry. Refined manners, of which it is an essential part, originally belonged to dreamland and from there gradually crept into practical life. To this reversal of the role of the ideal and of the commonplace corresponds a dramatic shift of the geographical center of the change of behavior. The I-habit originated in the extreme North, the you-habit in the extreme South of the lands of Western civilization. The term "extreme South" must be taken quite literally, for Catalonia was part of Provence and a great many Troubadours were Catalans. South of Catalonia there lay the lands of Islam.

Now here is an opportunity to study, in some detail, what cultural "affiliation" really is. It is, in our case, emphatically not the borrowing of habits from a foreign civilization, the sort of "culture-contact" most often studied by sociologists. The you-habit is not borrowed from anywhere; it was *invented* in Provence. But why was it invented? Obviously because the "Thou" in contact with one's mistress was felt to be rude. And if the you-habit could not be borrowed from abroad, the concept of rudeness could. It is not distinctive of any one civilization, but a common inheritance of all of them, with a difference, however. The rise of a higher civilization out of more primitive customs is always, among other things, marked by a new strong emphasis upon manners. In that sense the Germanic conquerors were rude, and must have realized it in prolonged contact with their subjects. Then, at an early stage of the development of feudal society and of feudal court manners, precepts hitherto neglected were borrowed from more polite neighbours. One of these precepts of politeness, already expressed in the manner book of Ptahotep in the old Egyptian Empire, and common to all higher civilizations, is that one should carefully emphasize one's inferiority towards superiors. It is rude to behave to a superior as if he were an equal. It is this notion which the Provençals apparently borrowed when they started to develop refined manners. They could not, incidentally, have borrowed it from classical antiquity. All things rather point to Arabic influence percolating through Spain. For how, otherwise, could it be explained that it is not Italy where the habit originated?

But in Latin and Arabic the second person singular was not felt to be unduly familiar, because neither "thou" nor "I" was generally used and because the whole idea of familiarity being offensive could not have arisen in those civilizations. But the Provençal of that period, as we know from the documents, used "I" and "thou" a great deal. And it started to be felt that this constant emphasis of "I" was presumptuous self-assertion, which indeed it was if our interpretation of the whole use of the personal pronoun is right. As long as the individual was not emphasized at all, no special hesitations, doubts, and possibilities of taking offense could attach to the use of the personal pronoun. But with the new, emphatic use of the pronoun it was different. Now it was elementary politeness to express in speech something like "I am I, of course, but you are as big as myself several times." The you-habit is a polite denial of the self-assertion implicit in the I-habit.

In this simple story a whole crisis of behavior is contained in a nutshell. The first stage of the development we study was violently to assert the otherness of one individual from all others: a sharp, ruthless challenge. "I made this piece of craftsmanship, not you," the runic inscriptions seem to say. The idea of politeness does not fit with the idea of a Viking.

That attitude travels South, fairly rapidly, with the various conquerors, first Celtic, then Germanic, and nothing happens to it except that it loses a little of its strength. In the ninth and tenth centuries, in the vernacular documents from all parts of France, the "I" is very much in evidence. The habit has now finally established itself on the Southern confines of what is to become the area of Western civilization. But on these confines it is exposed to the impact of older, more refined civilizations. At first this impact is disregarded, but no longer when a social hierarchy of a new type has arisen and feudal courts set out to become centers of refinement in their turn. Now the original impulse is curbed in outward expression. But as is the case with most forms of politeness, and with inhibitions in general, the original aim is yet achieved, indirectly, but perhaps even more thoroughly. For whereas the original fierce self-assertion is now mitigated by exaggerated expressions of veneration for others, these new types of expression turn at once into forms to express distance and reserve, and to exclude the idea of intimacy. But "distance" is a notion no Greek, no Roman, and no Moslem would have understood.

There is much interest in following the spread of the you-habit. It travels in the opposite direction from the I-habit. The I-habit travels slowly from Iceland to Provence. The you-habit travels back from Provence to Iceland. Only it is not easy to trace the journey in all its details, for chivalrous poetry in Northern France, England, Spain, and Southern Italy is almost indistinguishable over a long period from Provençal Troubadour literature (even Dante hesitated to write in his native tongue rather than in Provençal) so that the poetry of these countries need not reflect any local habits. Popular literature and the language of the prose documents, on the other hand, though certainly of genuine local color, is bound to be considerably behind the development of refined manners at the feudal courts. It is therefore good luck to have a text such as the "chanson de Roland" which, composed in Northern France in the eleventh century, shows the you-habit in full development, while an almost literal German adaptation in the late twelfth century invariably puts "Du" where the French original has "vous." At this late stage the knights of Southern Germany were apparently still ignorant of the finer forms of politeness and of any conscious emphasis on reserve. Even Emperor Henry VI, in his love poems, used invariably the "thou," and it is not before the thirteenth century that the "you" creeps up in German texts with any frequency. But at the same time, in Iceland, the Prose Edda is still completely unaware of this type of expression, which was apparently adopted in Scandinavia only about the time of the reformation.

The gradual spread of the you-habit from some social relations to others would be an extremely instructive subject to study. At which time, e.g., was the "you" no longer used exclusively by subordinates in speaking with real or pretended superiors, but also by superiors in speaking with subordinates? Certainly nowhere before the seventeenth century, and in most places probably much later. Another, geographical, consideration is also of interest. The I-habit spreads from North to South, the you-habit from South to North. But there is a qualification in the second case. The Eastern part of the area of Western civilization was very reluctant to accept the "you." There is infinitely more "Du" in Germany than "toi" in France where, after all, over centuries children even said "vous" to their parents. Here we strike one of the meanings of the term "Western" civilization which, as we saw before, is not always adequate as a pointer to the geographical center of our own civilization. But in this case it is. When refined manners are concerned, it is indeed the West which has fully developed all the devices of the politeness of distance and reserve, which Central and Northern Europe never fully adopted.

The fiercest struggle about the "you" was fought in England. In that country there exist large remnants of an unbroken primitive thou-habit, as evidenced in the popular speech of Northern England. On the other hand, English is the only language to have driven out "thou" completely in refined speech. This is due, as so many other things in the English national character, to the crisis of the Puritan movement, which shunned all intimacy as "creature-worship" and almost in itself sinful. One group, the Quakers, reacted desperately against that tendency, attempting to reintroduce the general use of "thou," but failed dismally outside their own circle. The country as a whole, including the most un-Puritan sections of the community, was won over to the Puritan habit. The reason is obvious. Even the most Tory groups of society shared with the Puritans, at bottom, the idea that extreme reserve is the only decent form of human attitude towards your neighbor. The general you-habit in English speech is a direct reflection of all those forceful English conventions which exclude what on the continent is regarded as normal intimacy. The country which only uses "you" is also the country where "never show your feelings" is an essential educational precept, a precept unintelligible to all continentals. England has gone much farther than any other part of the Western world in developing the sense of distance and reserve.

It is remarkable that, at the same time, English is the only language to give special emphasis in writing to the "I," by using a capital letter. This is apparently due, originally, to peculiarities of English medieval script, but script and spelling are not very stable things. If the habit, now no longer understood, nevertheless stands, it is difficult to deny its symbolic value. Both the I-habit and the you-habit have been carried to the last extreme in that country.

Thus, gradually, a geographical stratification of our civilization emerges. In Northern Europe the basic impulses of that civilization have been developed most fully, its refined expressions least fully. In the Latin-speaking parts of our world the weakness of the basic impulses of modern life contrasts, often enough, strangely with the elaborateness of the outward expressions and forms found for these impulses. But England has shared fully both in the root development of the new individualism and in the development of the more refined forms of social intercourse. The English are the Western race par excellence. When they speak of Western civilization they invariably think, in the first place, of their own civilization.

Our discussion of the you-habit has brought out part of the meaning of the I-habit, but not by any means the whole. In this discussion of the linguistic aspects of the problem at least one more feature must be mentioned. We have already observed, in connection with the use of the auxiliary verb "will" and "shall" for the formation of the future tense, that the "inwardness" of the Western soul is not in the first place the inwardness of mystical contemplation. The "I" which Western speech emphasizes is in the first place a center of action. It lives nearly as much in the outward world as man in classical antiquity. Only the outward world in the classical age is primarily a world of objective events of a momentary character, whereas in our civilization it is a world which is given to the individual as a substratum of will and duty, of planning and doing and fitting actions into a coherent whole.

This is not directly expressed in the use of the pronoun, but is implicit in it. For the separation of the ego from its various actions, as expressed in the ever-recurring separate use of the pronoun, makes the "I" a center of the most varied types of actions and experiences. There is, apart from the personal pronoun and the auxiliary verb of the future tense, other direct evidence of that "active" interpretation of the "I" in Western civilization. The question of the active and passive use of the verb must be studied.

The synthetic passive mode of the verb is one of the forms completely lost with the disintegration of classical Latin, and the cumbrous circumlocutions evolved instead have always been shunned as much as possible in speech. There are, however, two entirely different ways of avoiding the passive forms of the verb. The one is to express as many passive forms as possible by reflexive and impersonal idioms. This question of impersonal expressions has been made the subject of a special study by Miklosich, and we have only to quote his main results: "The Germanic and Slavonic languages," he says, "have developed turns of phrase without a subject more richly than any other [Indo-European languages], and as far as the Slavonic languages are concerned it can be said that they have a greater wealth of impersonal expressions the more they are removed from the influence of European languages developed under classical influence."[14] In one word, German is more impersonal than English, Polish more impersonal than German, Russian the most impersonal of all. On the other end of the ladder, English is characterized by quite an extraordinary amount of active, personal turns of speech.

Miklosich is, however, not quite correct in saying that the influence of the classical languages, or its absence, is the governing factor. Latin (not so much Greek) is certainly poorer in impersonal expressions than Russian, but many things which Latin expresses in an impersonal way or through "*Deponentia*," verbs which exist only in the passive mode though to us they seem to have an active meaning, are expressed as actions in English, which is an extreme case in this respect as in so many other aspects of speech. Just to make quite clear what is meant, I will give a few instances. To express pleasure the Englishman says "I enjoy" where the German says "es freut mich" and the Frenchman "cela me plait," or "je m'amuse." Expressions for dislike in the three languages show parallel differences. English words like "to deal" are really untranslatable, and the word "manage," so essential in English, is so foreign to all continental speech that it is, in many languages, directly borrowed from English. There are hundreds of instances of the same kind. Life, to the Englishman, to judge from his language, appears in the first place as an incessant flow of directed activities.

It would be quite wrong to imagine that these extremes, which so sharply differentiate English civilization from classical civilization, are simply part of the Nordic heritage. "Old Norse," says Dietrich, "in dealing with situations and events not or not exclusively dependent upon man's actions, prefers the impersonal turn of speech in a degree which we cannot achieve, which is perhaps not shared by any of the older languages."[15] And Miklosich makes the same remark about old Irish.[16] This may seem strange, but I think the explanation is fairly obvious.

14. Franz Miklosich, *Subjektlose Sätze* (Vienna: Braumüller, 1883).
15. *Zeitschrift für deutsches Altertum* 8 (1871?), p. 23.
16. Miklosich, p. 62.

Both old Irish and old Norse developed an increasing number of turns of speech where the personal pronoun was used with verbs expressing activity. But this use has something challenging, almost dangerous about it, as we saw in discussing the reasons for the invention of the polite "you." Latin verbal expressions without the pronoun became stale and colorless as soon as the I-habit became general. No wonder therefore that both these languages should develop two extreme types of speech side by side: on the one hand the emphatic use of the personal pronoun with active transitive verbs, and on the other hand impersonal expressions which exclude every thought of the use of "I." Therefore, in both Norse and Irish, two potentialities are present. The one, the active, personal one, is developed to the highest degree in English. The other, impersonal one, is strongly developed in German, and much more strongly in Russian, which, as we shall see in a moment, has grown up under strong Norse influence.

Again, we strike upon a crossroads of civilizations. The new consciousness of the I could be evolved to the extreme, which is reflected in English, but it could also emerge only to produce a very strong countercurrent leading up to a conscious and intentional negation of individualism, as was the case in Russia long before the revolution. Therefore in order to round off our linguistic picture of the Western civilization and its neighbors, a few short remarks about Russian will perhaps not be amiss.

There exists in old Bulgarian—or, what amounts more or less to the same thing, in Church Slavonic—a bundle of trends which differ rather widely from the basic trends of most other groups of European languages. It is interesting to note that, from a merely phonetic point of view, Balto-Slavonic is the only European group of Indo-European languages of the "satem" type. It is not important in our context to explain what that term means. It is enough to know that it is a type of sound formation common to the Indo-Aryan, Iranian, Armenian, and other Indo-European languages in Asia. Thus even in matters of sound Slavonic is nearer to Asia than to Europe.

But other features are much more significant. Slavonic shares with the non-Aryan languages of the middle East the lack of a genuine future tense, which, very much as in Aramaic—though without the remotest possibility of Aramaic influence—is expressed by certain forms of the present. Still more significantly, the very notion of tenses is weakly developed in Slavonic, whereas another notion, that of "aspects," is predominant in the formation of the verb. Aspect, in contrast to tense, does not emphasize the relation of an action to time, but its relation to permanence. It expresses the permanent, passing, repeated, etc., character of an action or event. Aspect is not a specific characteristic of Slavonic alone. It is discoverable in other Indo-European languages, such as Irish, and apparently at a very early stage was common to all of them, prior even to the development of tenses. But Slavonic has not only kept aspects fully alive. In some branches of the Slavonic family of languages, aspect tends to drive out tense, thus creating a type of speech close to the "timelessness" of the Semitic languages.

It is of interest to watch these developments in the various Slavonic languages. In order to get however superficial a picture of the process, it is important to realize that no Slavonic language has proceeded very far on the road from the synthetic to the analytical type of speech. The Balto-Slavonic group is, at present, the only Indo-European language group in Europe still strongly synthetic. Here we have a clear revelation of the fact that the Slavs are still, basically, virgin soil in all matters of civilization, that they are now starting on a cycle of development which passed away in ancient Greece two thousand years ago. This implies that they are the great hope of the next centuries.

The synthetic character of the Balto-Slavonic languages (with the exception of modern Bulgarian, which has fallen completely under the spell of Greek) is most clearly marked in the declension of the noun, with normally seven fully developed cases, three more than the Germanic languages could boast when they first were fixed in writing. The same features appear in the conjugation of the verb, though mostly not in the formation of the tenses. If we consider only tenses, the differences between the Slavonic and other European groups do not seem to be very great. Old Slavonic had three tenses, present, imperfect, and Aorist, of which the latter is everywhere in decay. Instead, in all languages except Bulgarian and the Russian group, composite past tenses of the European type have evolved. But this Europeanization of the Slavonic verb is quite superficial, because not tense but aspect is the dominating feature of the Slavonic verb. And aspects, in all Slavonic languages, are invariably formed by a rich and almost inexhaustible variety of prefixes and suffixes, in an entirely synthetic and, at the same time, extremely flexible way. Even some of the most Westernized Slavonic languages such as Polish have had a richer development of synthetically formed aspects than other, less Europeanized groups such as Serbo-Croat.

Thus the Western group of Balto-Slavonic languages (Czech, Polish, Slovak, Letto-Lithuanian) and the Southwestern group of Slavonic languages (Serbo-Croat, Slovene) have developed, side by side, typically

Western composite tenses, and typically Slavonic simple aspects. Here it can be seen how, in the Western and Southern Slavonic world, a veneer of Westernization clashes sharply with profound underlying tendencies of an entirely contrary character. But farther East there is no such clash. In Bulgarian no composite tenses have been developed, and in the Russian group (Muscovite, Ukrainian, Byelo-Russian) aspect has driven out tense, making these languages entirely synthetic and timeless at one and the same time. This Eastern Slavonic group is not based on phonetic characteristics (Bulgarian belongs to the Southern, not to the Eastern group of Slavonic languages phonetically) but on highly significant syntactic peculiarities. This group of syntactic peculiarities is found among those Slavonic nations belonging to the Greek Orthodox church (with the exception of the Serbs, who speak the same language as the Catholic Croats).

In modern Bulgarian, and to an infinitely more marked degree in Russian, the substitution of aspect for tense is accompanied by another most remarkable development, the decay of the auxiliary verb. The two trends seem to be interconnected, as can be seen in the case of the imperfect. Originally, a composite imperfect, formed by a past participle with "to be," crops up. But then the "be" drops out, leaving only a participle with sex and plural endings, no longer a true verbal tense at all. What happens to "be" happens to "have." It is impossible, in Russian, to say either "I am" or "I have." As to the latter, impersonal turns of expression must be used to indicate possession as in Latin. There could be no more extreme contrast than that between those European languages which, following late Latin, use "have" as one basic element in the formation of composite tenses, and Russian, which avoids even the use of "have" as an independent verb, shrinking from any direct indication of personal ownership.

While this process makes Russian probably the most synthetic language that ever existed, it makes it at the same time almost completely "timeless," and almost seems intentionally to avoid representing the individual as the center of things. Yet this development is demonstrably spontaneous. Step by step, as Church Slavonic transforms itself into Russian, the decay of tenses and the disappearance of the auxiliary verb can be followed. Russian, in that process of depersonalization and detemporalization, is working out an implicit destiny, exactly as much as English is working out the opposite trend of becoming more and more I-conscious and action-conscious. No later influences can be invoked to explain the earlier and basic phase of that development. It is all implicit, from the beginning, in the prevalence of aspect over tense in the Slavonic language group, which I am inclined to interpret as a reflection of the close Asiatic associations of the Slavonic peoples. Nobody will doubt the latter after Strzygowski's demonstration of the overwhelmingly strong Caucasian and Armeno-Iranian influence upon the early civilization of Southern Russia.[17] Only whereas the Western Slavs were hampered by the overwhelming impact of the West upon their life at a later stage, the Eastern Slavs could work out their original destiny in full.

But that is not the whole story. However much Russian might be the embodiment of what is to become the Slavonic civilization, and however much it, like English, has evolved to the last consequences the basic assumptions of a way of life, nevertheless it differs from English in that there is a basic contradiction in its makeup, of which there is no parallel in English. We have above quoted Miklosich to describe the rise of the impersonal type of speech. We saw how, in Old Norse, a conflict between extreme personal and extreme impersonal tendencies exists; how German takes up many of the impersonal tendencies of old Norse, thus partly moving out of the orbit of Western speech; how, in the Slavonic languages, these impersonal tendencies are carried one step further, on the basis of a primarily less time-conscious and less personal approach to life; and how this impersonal approach to life becomes intentionally antipersonal in Russian. Yet there exists a crosscurrent running in the opposite direction. In general, no Slavonic language has the use of the personal pronoun before the verb and that, of course, is a very strong factor in the building up of an impersonal type of speech. But to this general rule, which applies to the Slavonic and the Southern European languages, there is one exception: Russian has the use of the pronoun.

The history of the Russian language is a field quite insufficiently known, and I believe Slavists would find themselves richly repaid for detailed research in the history both of the decay of the auxiliary verb and of the rise of the personal pronoun. The problem is a difficult one, because the older Russian documents are, on the one hand, interwoven with Church Slavonic literary elements, and, on the other hand, invariably handed down to us in relatively late versions. It is therefore very difficult to decide what forms of speech belong tᴏ the various periods reflected in these documents. Then the Tartar yoke brought with it a long and almost complete break in literacy over which the history of the language cannot be followed very well. Yet it is certain that both the decay of the auxiliary verb and the rise of the pronoun occurred in the

---

17. Josef Strzygowski, *Die altslawische Kunst: Ein Versuch ihres Nachweises* (Augsburg: Filser, 1929).

older, pre-Tartar period of Russian history. That also excludes any hypothesis of the use of the pronoun being borrowed from German.

But in contrast to what we said above about aspects in the Russian verb, there can, in the case of the pronoun, be no question of a spontaneous development. In order to be regarded as spontaneous, this type of speech would have to be found, in embryonic form at least, in old Slavonic, and its development to full maturity would have to be traced by degree. But no such germ of a personal type of speech can be detected in old Slavonic. Also the absence of the pronoun in all Western Slavonic languages, with their otherwise much more personal structure, is a sufficient argument against such an assumption. The crisis of the migrations, which stood us in good stead in the case of Norse and Irish, cannot be invoked in the case of Russian. For if the Czechs, who demonstrably migrated from the Russian plains into their present sites, where they Westernized themselves, do not use the pronoun with the verb, it is quite impossible to credit any imaginary migrations of the old Russians with such an effect. Again, the conversion to Christianity was certainly an incisive event in Russian history. But all other Slavonic groups were subjected to the same crisis, yet do not use the pronoun with the verb. Also, if Christianity were the cause of the rise of personalism in the Slavonic world, its effects would have to be seen in the later phases of church Slavonic, which is not the case. Again the Eastern version of Christianity is not personalist at all, and it could not have effected in Russia what it did not effect in Syria and in Greece.

I think it can be regarded as fairly certain that the use of "I" in Russian is borrowed from its original source, the Vikings. The Viking invasion is a fact sharply setting off Russian history from all other Slavonic history. The center of the Viking power was Kiev, and it is therefore not surprising that documents such as the Kiev annals should first show the use of the pronoun in the Norse way. The Vikings were Slavized very quickly, but their descendants remained the ruling group. No wonder then that, whereas their language disappeared in Russia, their proud personalism should have left deep traces in the language they adopted.

It is also, I believe, possible to trace the struggle between the personal Viking and the impersonal Slavonic conception in the early phases of the use of the pronoun, at least in the third person. For the old documents do not use the present form of the third person "on," but the reflexive form "sya," himself. This, in Russian, is not an emphatic way of expressing personality. On the contrary, the reflexive pronoun is all the time used with the verb in order to cut off the sharp edges of expressions denoting activity. If Russian so richly uses reflexive forms, it is because they are nearer the passive than the active mood. Only very gradually, the more active form "on" emerges.

It is a matter for speculation, and perhaps a tempting surmise, that the dropping of the auxiliary verb "to have" is a reaction against the personalism brought by the Vikings. In its own way the disappearance of the auxiliary verbs is no less incompatible with the spirit of the Indo-European languages than the loss of the infinitive in modern Greek, to which it affords a parallel. Both developments are reactions in an "oriental" direction against the activism and personalism of the West. Whereas the decay of "to be" is foreshadowed in Church Slavonic, the dropping of "to have" is not by any means explicit in the trends of that language. It is a novel development, starting about the same time as the adoption of the use of the personal pronoun. Thus Russian seems to embody the extreme forms of personalism and of impersonalism side by side.

Let us sum up this last stage of our linguistic disquisition. At a certain moment in the West, or more exactly in the Northwest, a creative effort springs up, not to be paralleled by any event known in written records of history, but probably similar in kind to the creative effort which had brought synthetic language into being. The new creation is the emergence of personalism or individualism of an activist type. It is originally not based upon the disintegration of the Greek synthesis. But when it comes into contact with the decaying world of classical antiquity, it fits in ideally with its needs, providing a new principle of life, no longer synthetic, but on the contrary inward-tending, reflective, reserved, making the isolated individual the pivot of the world. There is no longer any question here of harmony. On the contrary, this new way of life is based upon the sharpest contradistinction between I and you, between me and the world. Therefore, at its very origin, it calls forth a reaction of antipersonalism, reflected in the prevalence of impersonal turns of speech in old Norse. From this dilemma there are two ways out.

In the West, the impersonal strands of the new attitude are cut out, individualism is carried to the last extreme, thus providing, by its very one-sidedness, a substitute for the lost synthesis of classical life. This new pseudosynthesis is held together by the development of a rigid code of conventions of reserve and distance, unknown to any previous civilization. East of Norway, the opposite process takes place. The impersonal elements of the Janus-face of the new civilization are more and more emphasized, until they culminate, in an almost oriental way, in the Eastern Slavonic civilization. But this latter, by the accident of Viking conquest at the moment of its birth, also acquires a strong element of individualism. The contrast between personalism and impersonalism was already very strongly marked in the Russian civilization. For in the latter, the impersonal element appears in the form of a language which was not only synthetic from the beginning (old Norse and old Irish were too) but becomes more and more synthetic as it evolves, becoming at the same time more and more impersonal and "oriental" in its basic syntactic characteristics. Into this passive, timeless conception of life breaks the Viking assertion of "I," provoking by reaction a development of the impersonal forms of speech unknown in any other Indo-European language.

Compared with the "harmony" of classical speech, the tension between incompatible elements reflected in modern speech seems enormous. But that tension, in its turn, is child's play compared with the discordant elements contained in Russian. A weaker language, and a weaker civilization, would long ago have disintegrated, as Bulgarian did, under such pressure. Russian, on the contrary, achieved a new synthesis of it all. The Russian civilization in its incipient stage appears almost as an integration of the basic elements of Near Eastern, classical, and Western civilization. There is more than one hint that it promises to become more fiercely tragical than even our own Western civilization.

But this, for our purposes, only serves to put our own Western civilization into its geographical and historical context. Linguistic analysis cannot provide more than hints about the direction in which we must conduct further research. Features such as "I" and "you," the loss of case endings, the growth of composite and the loss of simple tenses, the ever more important role of transitive verbs and active expressions, indicate clearly enough the general character of our Western civilization. The structure of language provides some general clues pointing to the salient features of a civilization. But only the direct study of its ideas and institutions can give us certainty about how to interpret the clues.

CHAPTER TWO

The Mythical Starting Point [fragment]

All elements of Western civilization were shown in the previous chapter to have been taken over from other cultures and transformed—excepting only the contributions from the North of Europe made by the Germanic and Celtic peoples. Those contributions are new, because the peoples of the North, the Germanic ones in particular, had never before been able to make a lasting historic impact in the domain of a high culture. We are therefore turning first to that new element.

As far as its spirit manifests itself in words, this happens in the early times only in metrical language—in those alliterative verses which had quite naturally resulted from a phonetic development, the transition from the floating Indo-European accent to the Germanic accent tied to the first syllable of the root. The small forms of this poetic art, like proverbs or riddles, are not specific to any people or social stratum nor can they be definitely attributed to the stage of the primitive or the higher cultures— they are the common heritage of the larger part of mankind. That applies also to the fairy tale. The fact that we know the Germanic fairy tales only in very late, mostly prosaic versions does not invalidate that statement, since comparative studies have proven the spread of a fairly unitary type of such tales over large parts of our planet.

Yet the fairy tale is akin to a higher form of art, the myth or saga (both words meaning the same, to wit a narrative). Fairy tale themes of worldwide popularity are found distributed over Germanic as much as

over Hellenic, Indic, and other myths; but the myths and sagas themselves by no means wander boundlessly like the fairy tales—they each have
their limited, even if extended location in a particular region, with a
particular people or group of peoples, in a particular historic period, but
always with a socially elevated stratum of warriors. The fairy tale lives
and does its work in the loose world of the unconscious, entering consciousness as something miraculous. The myth, by contrast, stands at
the threshold of history and is therefore itself subject to historic change.
The fairy tale is no concern of the historian—the myth must be his starting
point.

I

Wherever the myth is found, it presents a much tangled skein in which
everything is linked with everything else. Not without effort may different layers be distinguished. Its beginnings are blurred in the darkness
of prehistory, its offshoots stretch far into the age of rational thought.
Here we are not concerned with its later layers, but with its first beginnings and early high points—above all in the West. But these can only be
understood if we also look beyond the West. For there are historic con-
stellations which, wherever they may arise, produce the myth with necessary regularity.

In order to grasp the nature of that process, we must first of all define
the concept of myth—and defining is formally an arbitrary act, since the
selection of some particular characteristics out of their large number is
an arbitrary decision. Such a decision justifies itself by the insights it
opens up. We select, as the defining quality separating the myth from
a fairy tale, the element of historic reality in the former. According to
our definition, a historic event is hidden in every myth or saga: dramatic
turns in the life of peoples or individuals in the case of a purely human
saga, epochal events in faith and ritual in the case of a myth about gods,
often a mixture of both historic elements where the myth speaks of both
gods and humans. That historic element is lacking in the fairy tale, which
consists of timeless archetypes. Not that the saga rejects the archetypes—
it even shows a distinct tendency to reinterpret historic reality under the
influence of the archetypes. But it does not succeed completely in that,
and indeed does not wholly intend it.

The fairy tale dreams what is desired, history reports what is real. The
myth stands midway between both. The people who create it have not
yet overcome the sweet habit of taking dreams for reality, poetry for

history. But in contrast to the fairy tale, the myth must also fulfill precisely circumscribed social functions: it describes the downfall of a dynasty, of a political community, a legal order or a cult, and the rise of new powers in their place; and by describing them with distortions which are often—consciously or unconsciously—highly expedient, it legitimates them at the same time. Where myth has become a spiritual power, the political and social order can no longer subsist without it. By often translating dire political necessity into the archetypal language of the fairy tale, it at the same time harnesses the vigorously surviving archetypes for practical purposes. Its roots are growing in a stratum that knows no conscious purpose—its farthest branches often reach into the realm of a political propaganda which consciously knows no truth, a fact frequently overlooked by romantic students of the sagas interested only in the "poetic" element.

With that, we have also pointed to the historic situation in which the myth originates. It can arise only where the fairy tale has not yet declined into a mere childish plaything—hence, one might think, among primitives. But that is wrong: the primitives do not create a myth as defined here, because they do not need one. Their way of life appears to them as unconditionally valid and subject to no change—regardless of whether that is in fact the case.

Because the tradition of the primitive community is regarded as fixed once and for all, as eternal and unchangeable, such communities may well know a kind of individuality, but never an individual claim that could be raised against that tradition. Nor can a certain logic be denied to that attitude. For while the traditions and customs in question must have arisen at some time, they evidently have in fact changed very little over very long periods. Therefore, the world of the primitives not only *appears* to them as ahistoric, it also *is* that, apart from destructive irruptions of the high cultures into their domains. For that reason also, the dialogue between the experience of outward reality and the claims of the unconscious as embodied in cult, magic, and fairy tale has come to a standstill with them—for all time, as it were: the two spheres are mutually adjusted, and neither of them has to submit to ever new painful tests in profoundly changed conditions, such as only the historic process grants and imposes. Equally, for those communities there exists no "higher" world in contrast to that of the daily round—*both* worlds form part of the same daily round.

What kind of "historic" happening is possible in such a world, which unique event can rise above the timelessness of eternal repetition? The myth presupposes a break with tradition, a profound shock to an order, a violent intervention with irreversible, long-term consequences. All truly archaic myths without exception deal with such events. The myth arises, then, where primitives are pushed out of their timelessness, where they are forcibly dragged along by the wheel of historic change. It arises among primitives who find themselves in revolutionizing contact with one of the great high cultures.

In such conditions, it arises inescapably, regularly—with *one* qualification: it does not arise where the primitive communities become mere passive objects of integration in the high culture. The intrusion of the white man into the South Seas has not produced any great historic myths there—only the ruin of so many South Sea peoples. Enslaved and half-enslaved Negroes have not brought forth a Homer—they merely assimilated to the whites as a lower stratum. For the myth is always political without exception—and where contact with the high cultures merely dissolved or depressed the primitive communities, the myth found nothing to say. Only where, in a political *decline* of the high culture, the political communities of the neighboring primitives *rise*, while their internal order is disrupted at the same time—only there the myth has its historical place.

But particular conditions are needed for the primitives neither to die out nor to assimilate quickly and completely to the intruding high culture, for a kind of cultural chaos to develop in which the unifying bonds between the cultural elements are destroyed and the floating cultural wreckage becomes free for new creative use. The prospects for such a development are favorable only when a high culture that is no longer intact clashes with primitives who stand only *one* stage below it. Seminomadic herdsmen can awaken to historic life in clashing with a highly developed agricultural village culture, and so can the latter in turn when clashing with a fully developed urban culture—and perhaps the time will come when long ossified urban cultures with a strong peasant foundation will be newly inspired at the touch of an ultramodern atomic culture. Never, on the other hand, could a hunters' culture, be it as refined as that of the Australian aborigines, be reawakened from its sleep at the touch of a modern urban culture. Only where a high culture is already sufficiently weakened to offer to certain primitives of a not to remote cultural level a chance to move from the passive to the active role, from the role of a colonial to that of a dominant people, only there can those historical figures develop who, as precursors of a new high culture, characterize a "barbaric" age: the charismatic hero who tears up the ties of the tribal order, reverses the roles and conquers the domain of the old culture, and his followers who have also broken with the traditional tribal order. Thus arises historically effective individuality, both on the level of the creative leader in war and politics and on the more modest one of the young men who attach their cause to his by a free, purely personal decision. The war they fight is therefore a quite different one from the traditional fighting of the primitives over the abduction of cattle or women, with the themes of which the Irish saga, for instance, has remained stuck. It is consciously experienced as unique—more indeed than it really is. With that kind of war, historicity is born, the consciousness of the total changeability of any human order, the extreme contrary of primitive consciousness. From this reality of a barbaric-heroic age springs the heroic myth, and it is its primary subject—prior to any archetypal unconscious forces.

The myth thus appears in its first phase, without exception, among primitives who are invading a decaying high culture as conquerors. The revolutionary shocks to the internal and external existence of the primitives which this clash brings about form its proper subject, however much its specific treatment—half fairy tale, half history—may obscure that.

For that reason, the myth is full of evidence on the succession of one high culture by another—on the process, in other words, which Toynbee has called the "affiliation" of cultures, though without presenting a differentiated typology of such transitions. Precisely the myth shows that two basic types exist. There are cases where two high cultures follow each other almost without a gap, nay overlap each other in time and space, as was the case with the orientalization of antiquity; there are, on the other hand, cases where a "dark age" intervenes between the older and the younger culture, as between the Minoan and the Hellenic culture and between that of antiquity and that of the West. The myth belongs to the second type, that of "indirect affiliation," not to the first one of "direct affiliation"; for it presupposes a deep intrusion of primitive peoples and of their way of thinking.[1] An absolute contrast, however, exists here as little as elsewhere in history. Even with mainly direct affiliation, somewhere a role of primitive elements is found in most cases and with it the rudiments of a myth; conversely, there is hardly any case where the contact between two successive high cultures would be mediated *only* by a "barbaric" interlude passing on to the younger culture what it has taken over from the older one. Rather, the geographic domain of an

---

1. The whole foolishness of the thesis of Alfons Dopsch, claiming that the Middle Ages in all their aspects arose gradually and organically from classical antiquity, becomes obvious at this point. Could one maintain, for instance, that the Nibelungen saga or the Atli song developed gradually and organically from the rhetorical use of the Hellenic gods in late antiquity? Or do those products of a completely nonantique world deserve no notice?

indirectly affiliated younger culture consists usually, as the analysis presented in the preceding chapter makes clear, of one zone identical with a marginal area of the older high culture that was never entirely destroyed there, another zone which forms completely virgin soil for the high cultures, and a zone intermediate between those two.

The myth, being a product of the contact of the two contrasting forms of life, has its true homeland neither among the primitives nor in the domain of the old culture, but precisely in the border zone—in the case of the West along the Danube and the Rhine. In the old Germanic areas that were but little touched by the Roman impact it was borrowed only at a late stage from further South—for here the psychic and social shocks produced by culture contact, which would offer a fertile soil for it, were lacking at first. In the land of the Brythonic and Hibernian Celts, whose inhabitants remained, in spite of all Christian influences, shielded by the sea from the most massive forms of contact with the high culture of antiquity, the myth never rose entirely above the level of the fairy tale. In Southern Europe, opposite causes led to the same result: there no myth arose because the Christian urban culture absorbed the Germanic element, leaving no room for an intermediate culture. Only Lombardy and Friaul (in the large geographical meaning attributed to both terms in the early middle ages) make an exception: as we saw already in the first chapter, they were turned by intensive Germanization into "barbaric territory" and thus into a main focus of myth formation. For myth is the primary spiritual form in which a barbaric society expresses itself.

The term "barbaric" is used in historic and anthropological literature with widely differing meanings that are never clearly defined. Here I want to reserve it, leaving its original meaning among the Hellenes on one side, for the forms of existence evolving among primitives whose traditional forms of life are disrupted in the course of their conquering intrusion into a world of high culture. In the domain of the old civilizations the rule of such barbarians, who are themselves in a stage of moral and social decay, is felt as a terrible plight, and such it is. Yet it is undeniable that this very horror contains an irreplaceable potential for renewal.[2] Directly affiliated cultures are sickly. Even so worldshaking an event as the foundation of Christianity could not preserve its immediate heir, Byzantium, from the fate of early ossification and stereotypization; only in the West, whose culture, in contrast to Byzantium, was affiliated to the civilization of antiquity only indirectly, mediated

2. I am speaking here of real barbarians, as they arise directly from nonurban, primitive cultures—not of modern "city plants" who have acquired a would-be barbarism by reading. Not Atli and Hagen, but rather Caligula and Nero offer a true historical parallel to Hitler.

by a barbaric age, could Christianity develop the truly revolutionary potential that was to transform the face of the earth. The later civilizations of India and China, that originated after the beginning of the Christian era and are closely attached to their predecessors in time and space, show features analogous to Byzantine culture, while cultures that grew out of dramatic barbaric upheavals, like the first Aryan culture of India, the ancient Judaic and the Hellenic civilization, unfolded a no less untrammeled creativity than later appeared in the West. In each of those latter cases, the intermediate zone and the virgin soil (the Ganges valley, Palestine, European Hellas, Northern Europe) showed the longer breath and the more far-reaching elan compared to the territory of the older culture (the Indus valley, Northern Syria, the Ionic coast, Southwestern Europe).

That is the myth's doing. Viewed soberly, after the manner of the rationalist people of the high cultures, the victory of the barbarians must result in despair. Yet the myth is sober only in one of its aspects. It frankly describes the reality of a barbaric age in all its horror—but then it translates it into the language of fairy tale, of magic, of wish-fulfilling dreams, of the archetypes that arrive unshakably in the deepest layer of the soul. That language dates from an ahistoric period, when the reality principle had not yet proscribed the dream, when the individual was integrated in apparently unshakable institutions that took care of him like a mother of its infant. That period is close enough—chronologically it still seems tangible—for the barbarian to take refuge in its consoling ideas. Thus the myth draws from the primal source of the ahistoric the strength with which the barbarians confront and overcome the unleashed demonic forces and create a new culture out of that which they have overcome. The still tangibly close prehistoric time is the elixir from which the most powerful of the high cultures drank during their barbaric prelude—it is the mother earth whose contact enables the declining old civilization to be reborn, like Antaeus, to youthful giant strength. It was the source from which the four streams of the first oriental high cultures— Egypt, Mesopotomia, India, China—must have sprung in a manner which still remains thoroughly mysterious for us in the main. It also offers creative power to the later cultures if only they drink from it in their beginnings. But the "directly affiliated" cultures, which link up with an older culture without a barbaric interlude, lack this miraculous draught. They cannot confront the demonic forces whose destructive power is also a power of procreation, let alone tame them and turn them into their servants. They take shelter from the contact with the demonic— which rises as a product of decay also in the direct transition from an older to a younger culture—behind the values inherited from the older culture, thus completing the process of ossification of those values, whereas the intervention of the barbarians may revive them. If the culture arising out of barbarism is archaic, the directly affiliated culture is archaistic from the beginning. But what may be the destiny of mankind if the primal source of ahistoric existence should ever dry up completely?

II

In this mythical world the harmony between outer and inner reality, which primitive man often achieves at the cost of largely renouncing a purposeful adjustment to the outside world, is broken. Of course, the unconscious continues to be active; but while earlier it supported the "eternal" order, it now rebels against the disorder of awakening historicity. As a rigid conscience, it continues to insist on obedience to the old moral commandments as it did at the time when the tribal order was still unshaken. Then it directed its admonitions only against individual misdeeds which could not hurt the tribal order itself; but now such misdeeds are everyday occurrences, for they are partly the cause, partly already the consequence of the dissolution of the entire tribal order. Conscience may indeed be more vocal even than before, but the fixed rules that it presupposes no longer exist—hence it can offer ever more cruel reproaches and self-reproaches but no counsel on how to behave in the new, no longer primitive but barbaric conditions. For the unfettered conflict with external foes has struck back into the inner life of the tribal society and made it a theater of terrible atrocities. Once, the inviolable peace inside the clan was the mother's womb that protected against all dangers; now the clan itself has become a snakepit where everybody is daily threatened with death from everybody's hand. The horrors of the murders within the clan make the need for a firm order evident to the most savage. But no order is created just by wishing it, and for a long time no way out is discernible. Just from this hopelessness, in which even the most noble cannot act without committing terrible deeds, and cannot commit them without finally paying for it, the idea of the tragic receives its classic form of fateful entanglement. It already finds dramatic expression in the dialogues of the oldest Eddic songs.

Some of the Eddic songs are our earliest written sources for the Germanic myth. (The statements by Roman authors on the subject can only be used as stop-gap aid on particular points.) But we must assume that the sources available to us were preceded by a period of epic poetry from which nothing is preserved. We may reconstruct its outlines by starting from the earliest documents we have. Then, by linking the reconstructed primeval time with the preserved documents of an early period, we may be able to form a clearer picture of the original and motivating forces of the Germanic myth; that in turn would open the way to a comparison with the myth of other cultures.[3]

The song of the Hunnish battle, a very archaic fragment of the Hervara saga, accidentally preserved (and printed in the *Eddica Minora*), offers a useful starting point. The story is very simple in the archaic manner. Two brothers are fighting for the inheritance of their father, one a pure Goth, the other from a Hunnish mother. The Goth, Angantyr, denies to the Hun, Hloedr, the right to a share. He slays him in battle. But he does not rejoice—instead he mourns the grim fate that has driven him to fratricide. (A female figure has been introduced into the story only by a late addition.)

The persons are "legendary," not to be identified with any known historical figure. The story, however, is based on full historic truth in its general content. It refers to a state of affairs that existed between 375 and 454 A.D., when Huns and Goths lived closely together, first in Southern Russia, then in Hungary. It may even refer to the particular year 454 A.D., when the Hunnish power collapsed after the death of Attila, broken up chiefly by the Ostrogoths. We know that an inheritance dispute between one Hunnish and one half-Gothic son of Attila played a major role in those events. Mixed marriages were extremely frequent, above all in the upper stratum. Struggles like the one described in the saga must have formed part of the big conflict in which the Hunnish empire was broken up.

The poem unfolds, as it were, in two dimensions. On one side it is a straightforward description of a battle, on the other it deals with a conflict between brothers originating from a mixed marriage. Such a conflict, typical after 375, would have been in Gothic territory atypical before 375 and almost unthinkable before 250. What does a type of song like that of the "Hunnish battle" become if the theme of the conflict between brothers is eliminated? A simple description of a fight between two men. Here we get one of the primal forms of Germanic epic poetry— and, to judge by Homer, not only of the Germanic one.

3. Properly, one ought to speak of the myth of a culture only in the singular. As the individual, according to Freud, does not have many neuroses but always only one neurosis, in which all unconscious factors are merged into a whole, thus also the unconscious roots of the conflicts in a culture form a whole which can only by abstraction be analyzed into partial "myths." The myth itself exerts a synthetic function in striving in the course of its evolution clearly towards a comprehensive epos merging all "cycles of sagas" into a unity.

The treatment of the struggle keeps very close to historic reality. In songs sung during the lifetime or immediately after the death of the victor, it must have kept to it even more closely. In that case, we are no longer dealing with a "saga," but with the well-known "song of praise." There, the singer might poetically embellish and exaggerate the actual event, but a basic transformation, as it occurs in each "saga," was *not* required and was indeed impossible. The mythical element, the recourse to the miraculous and archetypal, was thus, surprisingly, in the earliest stage of Germanic epic poetry not more highly developed than in later stages, but was on the contrary entirely or almost entirely absent. We can see that such recourse does not occur "spontaneously"—only a later, critical situation will compel it, in agreement with our statement that the myth does not belong to an ahistoric, but to a barbaric period. The result we just reached is ultimately no more than a direct consequence of that earlier insight.

Thus in that germinal form of the later Eddic song, the singer described battles and praised heroes; as Heusler has stated,[4] the epical and the lyrical were mixed. The myth was absent. But was the tragic element absent as well? In the Hervara song it was not: it was contained in the final speech of Angantyr, his lament about the fratricide imposed on him by fate—this, too, like the praise of the hero, a report transformed into lyrical expression. Yet the fratricide forms part of the intrusion of barbarism— does not the tragic coda as well?

That is not the case. We know the subject of only a single song of praise from the period preceding the great migrations: Tacitus reports that the "barbarians" were still singing the praise of Arminius in his time. No doubt that song, too, ended with a lament for the dead. Then the song of praise is lost from our sight, until we encounter it again in the highly complicated late form of the Norse Skalds—and there again we meet the closest link between the praise for the hero and the mourning for his death! In contrast to the fratricidal outrages that may be specifically attributed to the period of the Voelkerwanderung and hence to the earliest layer of Eddic poetry, that tragic conception of the hero's death thus appears to be common to all Germanic periods, including, presumably, the primeval Germanic period. Long before the great migrations, it may have been the germ, encapsulated in ahistoric existence, which, having later received in the storms of the Voelkerwanderung the stimulus of psychic conflicts, grew to bring forth the great tragic songs of the Edda.

The link between heroism and the hero's death was deeply rooted in

---

4. Andreas Heusler, *Lied und Epos in germanischer Sagendichtung* (Darmstadt; Wissenschaftliche Buchgemeinschaft, 1960).

Germanic feeling. We know from Tacitus that the Germanic warrior despised the "straw death," and praised the fighting death. That the epic hero must always meet his doom at the end of his deeds is thus not simply the result of literary conventions followed by the Edda and the sagas, but of a moral principle underlying those poems. The hero must fight all his life and finally fall when his hour has come. The poet only lets survive evil magicians like Wieland or king Joermunrek, who stand outside the code of the warrior's honor. Otherwise, the greater the glory, the more certain the doom; the nobler the clan, the more complete its annihilation. On that point, Germanic epic poetry remains true to itself, from the archaic Eddic *Hamdismal* to the high medieval German *Nibelungenlied* and beyond it. (Exceptions during the Carlovingian age will be discussed later.)

This idea of the death-doomed hero does, however, undergo a development, as the tragic and suicidal psychic conflicts presented in the Edda make their impact on its archaic core. As the pre-Eddic idea of heroic death as a *duty* merges with the Eddic idea of the hero's involuntary *entanglement* in his doom, there is evolved an at once aesthetic, moral, and religious *concept of fate*, whose representative, the *Urt*, is supposed to tie the knot of the hero's life without his knowledge from his birth with a view to his death. The hero might indeed escape that fate by evasion, but that would be shameful and *morally* impossible. In submitting to his warrior's duty, above all the duty of revenge, he gets caught in the nets of fate. At the approach of death, he becomes conscious of his entanglement. Only now, in his awareness of the inescapable nature of the *Urt*, the hero's heroism becomes visible in its full greatness—the moral principle becomes transformed into an *aesthetico-moral* one. Where this principle itself, beyond any individual fate, is explicitly grasped by the hero (or the poet), it is presented as a justification of the *Urt*: she alone can bring true heroism, that supreme value, to its highest self-expression and visibility. The *Urt*—that is the harmony of the world order with the basic moral principle of heroism. It is therefore a *religious* principle: it includes not indeed a cult of the dead, but a cult of death—death worship in the meaning of that term coined by George Orwell for the Japanese.

This attitude continues until deep into the Christian Middle Ages, until the eleventh century, when finally the Anglo-Normannic *Chanson de Roland* opposed to the idea that the doom of death equals beauty, duty, and religious consecration, the rationalist criterion of foolishness and the political one of irresponsibility.[5] The final, almost doctrinaire

5. See Part II, ch. 12 below.

expressions of this kind of lone hero's honor, to which the author of the *Chanson de Roland* unambiguously refers, naturally belong only to the latest pagan period. But the core of the idea exists, as already stated, even before the Voelkerwanderung.

We have described the idea as "primeval Germanic." But that statement slams a door. Just how primeval, how old is the world of those ideas, for which—as distinct from battle description and praise of the hero—few parallels can be found among other peoples? There is no direct road to answering that question. But we may find it by looking at another aspect that becomes visible once we follow the unfolding of the great, basic Eddic themes into a somewhat later phase: the loneliness of the hero.

Angantyr and Hloedr are not alone—they are leading their armies into battle. In the later saga, that is never again found in that form. Even where historic tradition makes a battle between armies the starting point, as in the Dietrich saga and the epic of the Nibelungs, myth and poetry take care to make the heroes fight their tragic struggles in growing loneliness; the central hero meets his death completely alone. There is even a clear, almost arithemetic line of development: Angantyr has an army; in the oldest of the Eddic songs, the *Hamdismal*, two brothers wage their struggle against the evil king Joermunrek in great and self-caused loneliness, as the poet emphasizes (and are slain at two different places); in the *Atlikvida*, the high point of the early Eddic phase, king Gunnar, having rejected the demand to dishonor himself, dies in magnificent loneliness in king Atli's snake-tower. From the Atlisong a road (the twists and turns of which do not concern us here) leads to the Icelandic Aekhter sagas, whose heroes hold their own for years all alone against a world until the *Urt* catches up with them: here loneliness has become the central theme. Roland, too, dies alone, because he refused to call for help.

Thus the loneliness of the hero first appears in the epos in the context of the great psychic conflicts of the barbaric phase and appears to arise from them. Where the clan was the only human tie, the tearing of that tie must leave the individual lonely. Yet if we follow the gradual unfolding of the theme of loneliness from modest beginnings to the grand climax of the *Atlikvida* backwards, it leads, just as in the case of the psychic conflicts, to a hypothetical zero level at the beginning, where the loneliness of the hero existed as little as the conflicts in his soul—where he fought in the ranks of the community just as he lived within its order.

But this parallel, which at first glance seems to fit so well into the schema we have so far developed, becomes questionable as we note that the link between conflict and loneliness is not as close as such a theory would require. In the *Atlikvida*, that *locus classicus* of the loneliness of the Eddic hero, king Gunnar experiences no psychic conflict—it is his sister Gudrun who perishes from the destructive contradiction between her duty of revenge and her duty as wife. Gunnar, on the other hand, walks open-eyed into the trap set for him by the gold-greedy Atli—for no other reason but that it would be cowardly to evade it; just as half a millennium later, Roland falls victim to the traitor Gamelan for no other reason but that it would be cowardly to call for help from Charlemagne against superior numbers of the pagans. It would be even more cowardly if Gunnar were to buy his life from Atli by handing over to him the Nibelungen treasure—so he chooses the end in the snake-tower and, to make sure that nobody can betray the treasure's hiding place *after* his death, takes care that Hoegni should be killed before him. One sees that the whole tangle of motives introduced by the poet to bring about Gunnar's loneliness in death is only there to give the hero the opportunity to prove his heroism in self-chosen isolation in the snake-tower—just as the isolation of the great Aekhters in the Icelandic saga has only been brought about by a tangle of obligations of law, marriage, and revenge in order to give them the opportunity to show not only physical courage in a hopeless struggle of one man alone against an entire clan, but also boundless psychic courage in withstanding years of utter loneliness. The true hero is here as essentially lonely as he is essentially doomed—both aspects belong together in history and in substance, even if the breakup of the clan structure in the period of the migrations was particularly apt to increase both the real and the poetic isolation of the hero.

Thus we must regard both the loneliness and the doomedness of the hero as "primeval Germanic." But ultimately, such a "primeval" character is only relative; and without establishing the actual age of those twin ideas about the hero, we cannot grasp the context of motivations from which they have arisen. But for that, we must go very far back into the past.

[Here follows a reference to the invasion of the Northern European plain by the "Corded Ware People" in the seventeenth century B.C., which however breaks off at once, before the intended connection with the previous argument has been established. ED.]

CHAPTER THREE

Historic Layers in the
Siegfried Saga

In the evolution of the great heroic saga, policy needs have stood god-father to a much greater extent than either depth psychologists or literary historians have realized. In place of the tribes, states arise in the barbaric age as the products of war and political action. They are, at first, rootless creations, whose masters, never sure of the next day, cling anxiously to the remnants of the Germanic tribal order on one side and of the Roman state on the other, destroying both even more thoroughly in the process. They all rely at first on physical force, and most of them do so during the whole modest duration of those entities. No state, of course, without force! But neither can any state subsist by force alone. From necessity of state, from the needs of political reality it becomes urgent to let those new political structures arising on the ruins of the old society take root in the hearts at least of the strata supposed to be the state's main support. Is it not one of the main tasks of all political art to anchor what is objectively necessary in the depth of the unconscious of the people?

Sagas are not the products of a fantastic anonymous *Volksgeist*, which could be assumed in no period with less likelihood than in the middle of the total disruption of all traditions in a heroic age. It is policy which in such a period gets hold of the incoherent remnants of archaic thought in order to justify its arbitrary new creations with their help. Often that effort fails, sometimes it succeeds—and where it succeeds, the new creation has lost the character of something arbitrary or even sacrilegious, and confronts us as a new organic whole, looking as if it had never been an inorganic amalgam. We owe to Schelling the insight that without the myth, the growth of a people in a heroic age is unthinkable, that the new peoples are legitimate children of policy *and* the myth. From the union of those parents the nations of the West have arisen just as have the Hellenic polities.

Of course, the myth distorts the political-historic reality which it encounters; otherwise it could never fulfill the task of giving to each people *its* myth. But it is not the same if that happens in heroic ages, or if modern lying political propaganda attempts to imitate it. One of the most striking consequences of the sudden transition from a profoundly ahistoric existence to radical exposure to total change is an extreme maladjustment of the ruling forms of thought and experience to the new reality. Even the lawless leading personalities still live in a magic world, though with evil magic increasingly displacing the healing kind. All the more the ordinary people feel compelled to explain to themselves the monstrous and incomprehensible events, which are happening all around them and in which they themselves are involved, by means of the images of the fairy tale. Policy, itself entangled in all that, may at the same time get hold of it to further its own aims. Though the border between dream and reality is more marked in the topmost social stratum than further below, it has even at the top not the knife-edge sharpness as in modern conditions. Further down, the monstrous, incomprehensible character of heroic events actually produces a new dream world. Hence the distortions of historic reality which make up the saga reflect on one side the typical, basic moral and social conflicts of the time, on the other their transformation into a kind of dream under the impact of typical unconscious forces. Behind those "archetypes" which keep modifying the historic account until it corresponds to them there stand ultimately half-forgotten gods or godlike figures—and those in their turn not in their shaken godliness, but cut down to human size, involved in human transgressions and human fatality.

Thus the evolution of the myth is subject to two dynamic forces—one political, one mythopoeic. The memory of the peoples preserves nothing that belongs only to day-to-day politics. But just because the evolving myth eliminates again and again what already belongs completely to the past, crevices arise again and again in the mythical structure granting admission to new topical political material corresponding to the actual situation. At the same time, the assimilation of the content of politico-historical reality to the archetypes continues, precisely because the political role of the myth diminishes with the growing distance from the ahistoric past and also with the political stabilization after the end of the Voelkerwanderung. Step by step, policy as it were "releases" the myth, hands it over to the archetypes and thus really to "pure" poetry. And while we have only indirect evidence of the archaic shape of the Germanic myth, now the number of texts handed on to us multiplies, so that the disproportions in the handing down of the materials of the history of the saga distort our image of its course.

Arminius

Cantaturque adhuc barbaras apud gentes: the barbarian tribes still sing of him today. Those are the known concluding words of Tacitus' account of Arminius' life and death.[1] It is the first specific mention of a Germanic hero's song, and certainly not an accidental one. Individual deeds in battle may even earlier have enjoyed a shortlived glory and found a quickly forgotten echo in metric verse. But the fate of Arminius is the first to possess a truly historic quality, and only to that corresponds the lasting quality of the songs which reported his heroic life. Here the beginnings of great history and great poetry belong together. Arminius embodies for the first time a coherent destiny of the Germanic type; in his career the specific Germanic entanglement of heroism, guilt, fate, and death can be grasped for the first time. Here is, if not the ultimate foundation, at any rate the first distinctive unfolding of that germ from which arose the Nordic share of the Western way of life.

True, with regard to sources we face a very unsatisfactory situation. Of the heroic songs mentioned by Tacitus, not a line has come down to us; we must make do with Latin and Greek sources. Tacitus is ponderous and offers little answer to precise questions. Dio Cassius and Strabo only give a skeleton. Velleius Paterculus, a highly gifted and excellently informed staff officer of Germanicus, sober and yet on a level with the impact of the events, confines himself to the Teutoburg battle and its immediate context. With regard to the internal conditions among the Germans that interest us most, they all confound and contradict each other.

But a historian is not worthy of the name if he capitulates in the face of the poverty of his sources: not the convenience of the available material, but the historic importance of the events themselves must determine the scale of his efforts. A history of the Germanic idea of the human person would be easier to document if one started with the period of the Voelkerwanderung, or even with the sixth century. But it would then not only become incomplete but wrong, because it would present ideas looking back to a long evolution as if they had been new at that time.

1. Tacitus, *Annals*, II, 88.

Without an understanding of those beginnings from the period of the first lasting contact between the Germanic tribes and the Romans, any presentation of Germanic culture must remain fictitious. It is thus indispensable to squeeze from the sources the utmost they can yield.

We must start with the name of Arminius. It soon attracted attention, because it is not a genuine Western Germanic personal name. The latter kind is known to consist always of two elements; here, once we remove the Latin ending, we have only one. Yet a plausible Latin or Celtic derivation has not been found either.[2] However, we find the Germanic root *ermin* given in Arminius' name also in the name of the Suebian tribal league of the (H)erminones, of the shrine of the Saxon Irminsul, of the Ostrogothic despot Ermanarich. We are faced with an appellative term meaning approximately sublime, exalted, or august; as proved by the Irminsul—pillar of the exalted—it may be used for a god as well as a ruler. We are thus dealing not with a name but with a surname—one certainly bestowed on its bearer only after his unique victory over Varus, but presumably immediately after it. His real name we do not know, as Much has already stated.[3]

Yet in searching for Arminius' real name, one has paid too little attention to the no less real surname. Arminius was a Roman citizen and knight and had served as an officer in the Roman army. One should have started from the assumption that such a surname must have a political meaning, and that a man like Arminius would not have chosen it without reference to Roman titles, his hatred of the Romans notwithstanding; this all the more as the name has been "gallified," by changing the opening "e" to "a," hence was meant also for effect in the Roman province. So let us retranslate it into Latin, and we get—Augustus.

Unthinkable that Armin and his following should not have been conscious of this context! With regard to the political fact, it indeed hardly adds anything new to the Tacitean report—that Arminius had striven for monarchic power, but failed in that effort; an enterprise that must naturally have been directed not only towards ruling his own Cheruscan tribe, but the whole, great Western Germanic confederation, which he intended still to extend to Bohemia and Bavaria by war against Marbod. Still, the fact that he exploited his victory over the Romans to assume

---

2. Undeniable is the statement by Kosinna that the opening A of the name is of Celtic origin; the Germanic form of the name would be *Ermin*. Quite misguided, on the other hand, is Kosinna's attempt to look underneath the Latin form Arminius for a Germanic Armino-merus, merely in order thus to construct a normal, two-part Germanic name; the sounds contained in Arminius provide no justification for that.

3. R. Much, "Die Sippe des Arminius," *Zeitschrift für das deutsche Altertum* (1891).

the title of Augustus, implying a claim to rule of the type of the Roman principate, remains characteristic for his dreams and thus for his personal type: it marks a conscious attempt at totally shaking off the traditional ties of the tribal order. It discloses a limitless hubris.

It will still have to be discussed to what extent this hubris of a great personality can be explained by the autochthonous conditions of development of Germanic tribal society. But the immediate occasion of its outbreak was without doubt the disruptive impact on the tribal order of contact with the Romans. In the innumerable reports on the history of the free Germanic tribes in the first two centuries of our era, it becomes tangible how the old tribal orders, tribal leagues and tribal conflicts came to be replaced by the struggle between two political parties comprising the entire Western Germanic world—one Roman and one anti-Roman. As is known, Tacitus equates the contrast between those two parties with that between nobles and free commoners, and although he surely simplifies here and applies a Roman coloring to Germanic conditions, we may believe without hesitation that the systematic Roman favoritism towards the noble families drove the commoners into the ranks of the opponents of assimilation—exactly as later among the Saxons in the age of Charlemagne. Thus tribal and clan feuds became subordinate elements of a great political struggle for national and social goals, the size of which was in itself sufficient to incite the hubris of a victorious party leader—and Arminius was first of all that—to an extreme degree.

But though this hubris becomes comprehensible only in the context of those great political upheavals, it affects its subject primarily in the context of the old, shaken clan ties. We know that Arminius' own clan became fatal to him; he was murdered by his "nearest," as Tacitus reports with characteristic rhetorical vagueness. But who formed that clan?

His father, so we learn from Dio and Valleius, was called Segimer—not to be confused with his namesake, the brother-in-law of Arminius, son of Segestes, the dux of the Chattic tribe neighboring the Cheruscans. Segestes had another son called Segimund. As one sees, the syllable "seg" or "sig," equalling today's German *Sieg*, was very widespread in the Chattic and Cheruscan princely families as an opening part of names. But with the old Germanic nobility, the opening syllable of the name frequently has the role of the modern family name; it is often inherited from generation to generation, in contrast to the second syllable. The frequent occurrence of the "sig" syllable in both the Cheruscan and Chattic ruling families thus indicates that both belonged to one and the same clan, though we ignore the exact family relationships. But what a clan! In a society in which marriage is already regarded as a peaceful legal transaction between two clans, Arminius has abducted Segestes' daughter Thusnelda, thus acquiring his lifelong hatred—so much so, that Segestes used one of the numerous turns of the destiny of the Roman war to get hold again of his runaway daughter and take her as a kind of booty with himself into the Roman camp. Tacitus reports that this deed and the birth of a son in Roman captivity had brought Arminius to the verge of madness—one more trait of the new individualism: for the popular legal tradition shows clearly that among the Germanic tribes living within inherited custom, their wives were simply regarded as possessions whose loss would have been felt as damage rather than as dishonor and psychic suffering.

Thus daughter stands here against father, son-in-law against father-in-law. But Segestes' son Segimer shares the feelings of his sister, turns—what monstrosity!—against his own father and moves into the camp of his sisters' abductor, of Arminius. Conversely, Arminius' brother drops his Germanic name in order to serve, under the name of Flavus, in the Roman army—in the most bitter hatred of his brother. This Flavus married another daughter of the Chattic ruling house, and according to Tacitus it was his father-in-law Gandarius, probably identical with the Chattian prince Catumerus, who wrote a letter to the Roman senate offering to poison Arminius. But Much has—with an intuition that was more astonishing 70 years ago than it would be today—pointed to the absurdity of such a letter and uttered the hypothesis that the alleged proud rejection of that offer by the Roman senate was a Roman propaganda trick, intended to divert attention from the real murder plot which, he assumes, Segestes, Flavus, and Gandarius carried out with Roman consent and support, and to which Arminius succumbed—in a manner we do not know.

We have dealt with this state of affairs in some detail, because with the ancient Germans, as with all societies based on a tribal order, the clan was the only social unit within which peace was an absolute commandment and the use of force was therefore viewed in all circumstances as a crime deserving death. Yet in those decades of struggle between peoples and parties, it happened that almost the entire Chattic branch of the Sig-clan went over to the Cheruscan Arminius, while the major part of the Cheruscan branch—in the end also Arminius' father's uncle Inguiomerus—came over to the Chattic ruling house. The party struggle thus tears up the basic institution of the clan and intensifies the hubris to the most profound guilt, only to be avenged by death.

The roots of a tragic view of life, of an implicit philosophy turning around fate, guilt, and death and of a poetry expressing it are here so obvious that we may assume without hesitation that the songs about the hero Arminius mentioned by Tacitus were not simple songs of praise of the later Skaldic type, but tragic heroic songs of the later Eddic type. For how could the bard who recounted the deeds of his hero long after his death have bypassed that tragic death itself, or if he mentioned it, left out the terrible moral situation that led to it? And how, we may go on asking, could such songs, touching both the inmost nature of the dissolution of all psychic ties and the utmost drama of warlike and political struggle, have vanished without leaving the faintest trace?

Here the question once more arises: what, after all, was the "real" name of the hero? The answer must be incomplete, but it can be clear. The first half of Arminius' name was almost certainly the syllable "sig." On the basis of that assumption, Delbrück, Much, and Ludwig Schmidt have postulated a second syllable, "fried," or more correctly in accordance with the state of sound development at the time, "bert" or "ferdh," or "fredh."[4] Arminius would thus have been the true, historical Siegfried. It is one of those hypotheses which in the course of time have not so much been refuted as shunted aside.

Now the weakest piece of that hypothesis, which has made it easier to "forget" it, is that relating to the second syllable, "fried." For as is yet to be shown, the names Siegebert and Siegefred occur in late Frankish history in contests directly linking their persons to the Nibelungen saga. So there is no way to decide whether those rulers of the Salic and Ripuarian Franks respectively adopted their names in memory of an already existing Siegfried figure, or whether their names were ex post transferred to the figure of the great Cheruscan who had such a very similar "sig" name. But that question of the *name* is also irrelevant if it can be shown that important elements of the *figure* of Arminius have been integrated into the Siegfried figure of the Nibelungen saga. And that, I believe, can be shown.

In the first place, we have here the total image of Arminius the man— "a youth of noble origin, great physical force, quick understanding, a more than barbaric intelligence"—in one word the ideal image of the Germanic hero in appearance and action, in counsel and deed, which the myth has taken over, omitting only the political ability as irrelevant in its context. And besides the figure the destiny: the doom after a glorious life, the death from the hand of the wife's family, the fatal role of the

---

4. Hans Delbrück, *Geschichte der Kriegskunst im Rahmen der politischen Geschichte*, vol. 2, *Die Germanen* (Berlin: de Gruyter, 1921; reprinted 1966).

R. Much, see note 3 above.

Ludwig Schmidt, *Geschichte der deutschen Stämme bis zum Ausgang der Völkerwanderung*, vol. 2, *Die Westgermanen* (München: Beck, 1970).

violently taken woman in causing the enmity of the clans, the evil counsel of an uncle of the in-laws. And the geographical framework: though the deeds of Arminius were done neither at Xanten nor at Worms, which in his time were both in Roman hands, the territories of the Chattic and Cheruscan tribes are close enough to the theaters of the first part of the Nibelungen saga to facilitate a transfer to the point of self-evidence. Together with the "Sieg" name, this should be sufficient to make Arminius plausible as *one* prototype of the Siegfried figure—though not, as Delbrück would have it, as the only one. Moreover, there is evidence that part of the Chattian tribe migrated to the Xanten neighborhood on the Lower Rhine later in the first century, and that it was in their new territory that the Germanic cult of the Hercules Magusanus subsequently sprang up.

Hercules Magusanus

"The Germanic tribes assert that Hercules, too, had been among them, and at the beginning of a battle they sing of him as the first among the heroes" (*primum virorum fortium*), writes Tacitus. Eduard Norden, in his late work about Tacitus' Germania, has linked up this note of Tacitus with the cult of Hercules Magusanus on the lower Rhine, and has identified that Rhenish Hercules with Siegfried.[5]

The Germanic Hercules reported by Tacitus is well attested also by archaeological finds in the Roman-occupied Germania on the left bank of the Rhine. In the inscriptions found there, he appears with different epithets, of which the most important is Magusanus. Identical with that Magusanus is one Hercules Deusoniensis, whose name, however, later fades behind that of the Magusanus. This last was apparently venerated already in the second century all along the Roman Lower Rhine, in the third century by all Germanic tribes in Roman territory, also those along the Upper Rhine. Even late in the third century, the Germanic legions carried his name in their ensigns. With the Christianization of the imperial house under Constantin, the name of the Magusanus disappeared, but his heraldic animals remained as emblems of the Germanic cohorts, perhaps to the end of the Western Roman empire.

So great a Numen, almost to be interpreted as an all-Germanic godhead, at least among the legions, could in no case simply represent the

---

5. Eduard Norden, *Tacitus' Germania: Die germanische Urgeschichte in Tacitus' Germania* (Leipzig: Teubner, 1923).

Graeco-Roman Hercules. Cults of Hercules existed indeed throughout the territories of antiquity, and that long before the Roman empire. Norden has shown that already in the time of Herodotus some such cults, including the very important Egyptian, were sharply distinguished from that of the Greek heros. In fact, all those nonclassic cults of Hercules concern autochthonous local gods, with the name Hercules only playing the role of a translation. Such cults must be clearly distinguished from cases of an actual merging of local cults in those of the Graeco-Roman gods and heroes. The Magusanus, in other words the Germanic Hercules, was and remained a Germanic Numen.

According to the Tacitus statement quoted in the beginning he was *primus virorum fortium*, hence, as Norden comments convincingly, not a god, but the most noble, brave and vigorous of all heroes. A "heros" he would also be in Greek, but this Germanic Hercules is not a demigod either—they did not exist for the Germanic tribes—but a man. Still he receives a cult, even if only in the *Roman* Germania. A contradiction?

Before that can be clarified, the question arises: *who* is that greatest of all heroes, seeing that he is human? Norden replies: Siegfried, and the whole of Germanic saga confirms him. Also the origin of the cult of the Germanic Hercules on the Lower Rhine fits that assumption, since Siegfried came from Xanten, a Roman armed camp in just that region. Yet we remain unsatisfied—first, because we still have only an assumption, however plausible it may be, and second, because this only shifts the problem one stage further instead of solving it. It now runs: who was Siegfried? Only when that question has been answered can we say who was the Magusanus—only then can we form a concrete idea of the origin of his cult.

Norden has evaded giving an answer to this second, crucial question—for the sake of a prejudice. He, the classical philologist, did not wish to "transgress" into the field of ancient Germanic history; he repeatedly stressed that—proof enough that he knew that much pertinent matter for his theme was to be found there. For Norden knew, of course, that Ludwig Schmidt, Delbrück, and lastly Much had identified Siegfried with Arminius,[6] and that was clearly the thesis which he would have liked to invoke in support of his own, but did not dare to touch out of a pious respect for the borderlines of disciplines. We have reported their convincing arguments above. Here we shall pursue one lead which follows from correlating their thesis to Nordens: it turns out that the Magusanus cult arose in part of the same tribe in which much of Arminius'

6. See note 4 above.

activity took place, and not long after his death—to wit, with the (later Frankish) Chattians, whose main part became the ancestors of today's Hessians.

Arminius himself was, of course, not a Chattian, but a Cheruscan. His tribe became later, in the third century, absorbed by the Saxon confederation of tribes, whereas the Chattians became Franks. But in the first century the tribes were by no means yet separated along those lines—rather the ruling clans of both were closely akin as we have seen. However, both tribes and both clans were divided into two bitterly hostile parties, one pro-Roman, the other anti-Roman, with Arminius as leader of the latter. Later, when the Chattians had become Franks and the Cheruscans Saxons, this had the consequence that the saga based on Armin's fate took root in both major confederations, but particularly in their common border area—naturally in the form of songs of praise and mourning on the fallen hero.

But Chattians were also the first who venerated the Magusanus. More exactly, they were Batavians, also known as Chamavians. Betuwe is to this day the name of the Dutch region between the rivers Wal and Lek. The Batavians had, in the course of the conflict within the tribe, separated from the main part of the Chattians and had moved from the middle to the lower Rhine. Exactly when this took place is not clear; the duality of the name—Batavians and Chamavians—suggests that it happened in several waves. By the middle of the first century, when Plinius the Elder wrote his lost work on the Germanic wars amply used by Tacitus, this movement was obviously already concluded. It is impossible not to think, in the context of so rare an event in the Germanic world as the splitting of a tribe, of the terrible conflicts that had shaken the Chattians in the context of Arminius' policy.

That the Germanic Hercules was first venerated in the Batavian land is shown by Norden from the origin of the names of Deusoniensis and Magusanus. The first he relates—leaving aside Duisburg, where no altar of the Deusoniensis ever existed—to present-day Doesburgh at the confluence of the Yssel and the Rhine, then the greatest harbor of the Rhine estuary with wide contacts across the Western seas and into rivers flowing to the West, later a Franco-Saxon frontier town. The Magusanus he links with the medieval locality of Maguseham near Arnhem—quite convincingly, although the full placename was Fregimaguseham (today Vreeswijk). But what Roman could have pronounced such a monster of a name! Moreover, the initial Fregi seems to refer to a cult of Freyr attested also elsewhere in the Netherlands, and it was clearly impossible to include the elder god in the name of the new Magusanus. Besides,

Freyr was a god of the peasants, Magusanus an outspoken protector of the soldiers. Close to Maguseham, there was a camp of the Batavian cohorts, bearing the name *castra Herculis*.

The further political history of the Batavians also argues for an identification of the cult of Hercules with a cult of Arminius-Siegfried. True, the Batavians in no way avoided Roman service, after the storm of the Arminian movement had calmed down; once cast out into the Roman frontier area, they had hardly another choice as professional warriors. But through centuries, they jealously garded the right to complete Batavian units with their own officers. To judge by the ensigns, the Magusanus cult seems to have been intimately linked with that institution. Nor were those cohorts particularly pro-Roman. In 70 A.D., they formed the core unit in the Gallo-Germanic uprising of Civilis, who once attempted to separate Gallia from Rome—under Batavian leadership and with the incitement of Batavian prophetesses. Two hundred years later, they played exactly the same role in the armies of the Gallo-Germanic secessionist emperor Postumus, who wanted to separate the West from Rome. Again hardly a century later, it is the Batavians who raise the pagan emperor Julian on the shield in Paris (the first use of that Germanic custom for the proclamation of an emperor) and follow him as his elite unit to the East. One generation later the Frank Arbegast, evidently from the same area, leads as *major domus* of Eugenius the last desperate military struggle of paganism against Eastern Rome—again with the support of the Germanic elite forces on the Rhine, who are still formed and welded together by the same politico-religious ideas.

The above may be sufficient for placing the Magusanus cult into its sociological context. Yet it does not solve the riddle of the cultic veneration of a mere human. The fact that Arminius himself claimed godlike strength and adopted a divine surname no doubt offered a bridge from the admiration of the living man to his worship after his death—without that bridge, the phenomenon would be unthinkable. But it is not sufficient for a full explanation. It is, after all, one of the differences between Germanic and Hellenic religion that the former in contrast to the latter does not know any "divinization" of human beings. Arminius appears there as the only exception, and a doubtful one at that: his enterprise failed, his hubris led to his doom. How could his cult last for centuries?

Here we must look more closely at the Siegfried figure in the saga. In the songs, and still in late prose, it appears as the image of a radiant hero without flaw. Already the earliest songs of praise and mourning must have expressed that very convincingly; for one gains the impression that such unilateral glorification of the hero even largely influenced the picture drawn of him by his Roman opponents. Reality shows a more complex, less unmistakably flawless picture. What indeed could have been more horrible, from the viewpoint of Germanic custom, than a feud inside the clan, of which the guilt had to be borne by him who had broken the tribal rules, thus forcing the tribal leadership to rise in their defense? That, clearly, had not been Segestes who had clung to the aristocratic and federalist tribal constitution and to the autonomy of the tribe within it, but Arminius who strove for an emperor's crown to which all continental Germanic tribes were to submit. The outrage could only be justified by a special, quasidivine charisma—and it was just that which he arrogated to himself and which his followers ascribed to him after his death. Into that context belongs the image of the flawless, radiant hero, behind which boundless ambition, brutal persecution of opponents, woman's abduction within his own clan, expropriation of clansmen and presumably much else could be made to disappear. The raising of the hero above human measure is here a condition for his acceptance—if not free from moral norms due to his charismatic gift, he would be a common criminal against the tribal order. Surely, the bards of both parties engaged in a war of songs, where the one side's verses of invective balanced the other's songs of praise—an opposition the important role of which in the formation of any heroic saga, not only the Germanic one, is regularly ignored.

In this war of songs, the decision was clearly brought about by Arminius' death. The victorious party had certainly little cause to return too often to the whole bitter story now that it appeared to have remained episodic. The vanquished, after all, had moved far away—and they alone preserved the memory of the fallen hero in their songs. But the crucial element was the manner of his death: as we saw, Arminius was foully murdered by his opponents, most probably in collusion with imperial secret agents. Only *this* rounded his image and gave to the saga the basic form it was to preserve as long as it was sung and told: the radiant hero falls victim to foul assassination by his relatives by marriage. That assassination extinguishes all stains in his image; it divides the world as seen from the hero's angle into one realm of the good and exalted and another realm of baseness and perfidy. By taking the grave guilt of the final act upon themselves, the opponents of Arminius have enabled his followers to deny any guilt for their hero. Guilt, above all political guilt, is easily forgotten and repressed once it impairs the glory of one's own community. Yet guilt has, as depth psychology knows, an incomparable capacity for reemerging again and again from the unconscious. We shall have to trace the continued effect of that guilt in the later versions of the myth.

An Ahistoric Interval?

Those later stages are linked with later historic events and their out-standing figures, as will be seen. But besides them, an archetypal figure, representing that element of the myth that is directly linked with ideas about the gods, makes an important thematic contribution to the Siegfried saga which we shall discuss in the next chapter. And finally, there are topics involved which refer to a lower sphere than the heaven of the gods, and which could best be described as fairy tale themes: the miraculous birth of the hero, his growing up in anonymity, the smith's craft regarded as magic, the miraculous sword, the exodus into the wide world, the slaying of the dragon and winning of the treasure, invulnerability, magic hood and belt, understanding of the birds' language, overcoming of a treacherous dwarf, blazing flames and marvellous maid—without exception themes from the story of the hero's youth. They are, of course, much older than the historic elements of the myth. They belong, as it were, to a timeless realm, which is also shown in the fact that they are tied to no particular place: similar themes are found, in countless transformations, all around the earth. But they form by no means the prime substance of the myth to which the historical content would form a later addition, as so many psychologists think. Rather, the myth has obviously grown out of the historical report which it transformed—on one side, as already shown in the example of Arminius and still to be shown further, by adjustment to the *political* feelings of narrator, bard, and audience, on the other by adjustment to the universal human unconscious which shifts the concrete, historical content in the direction of the archetypal. We are now asking: *when* did those numerous fairy-tale themes get into the Arminius songs and transform them?

There are no sources for an answer, and there cannot be in view of the worldwide and archetypal character of the added material. We can only hazard some guesses. The fairy tale itself has a historic place—it belongs to the "ahistoric" times which are completely embedded in a traditional order and, while they know conflict and struggle, know no conscious revolt against that order, hence no great individual living in a state of tension with the community. The great saga or myth, as distinct from the fairy tale, arises only where tradition has been profoundly shaken, and that in turn happens only as the primitives come into contact

with high cultures. Arminius is the product of the first great clash between the Germanic and Roman societies, and there could be no great
saga before him. But it is just the paradoxical result of Arminius' own
deed, of the Teutoburg battle, that the Roman-Germanic relations were
once more largely disentangled and that the free Germania once more
sank back into an ahistoric existence. I believe that we can ascribe the
overgrowing of Arminius' figure with fairy tale tendrils, its reinterpre-
tation as a fairy tale hero to this period, that is mainly to the second
century A.D. in the free Germania.

The End of the Ripuarian Franks

Only the period of the great migrations lifted the saga, which had
sunk back to fairy tale level, again to the height of relevance for tribal
history. To be more precise, out of the Chattians and some other tribes,
the two peoples of the Ripuarian and Salic Franks had developed in the
meantime; the conflict between those two now gives the myth a second
starting point, originally independent from the first.

Gregory of Tours reports[7] that Sigibert, king of the Ripuarian Franks,
had been old and infirm. Then Clovis had sent envoys to his son, charged
to tell him: "your father is old and lame on one foot; if he died, you
would be the right heir and be sure of our friendship." The son thereupon
has his father killed on a journey to the beech mountains (*buconica silva*)
and reports to Clovis: "My father is dead and his realm and treasure are
in my power. Come and I shall gladly hand over to you whatever in
that treasure pleases you." But instead of Clovis himself, only his envoys
arrive and assure the murderer that Clovis wanted no part of his treasure—
they would only like to see it. He leads them to the chest "where my
father piled up his golden pieces" and opens it. But as he bends down
deeply, the axe of one of the envoys hits him. "Thus his outrage against
his father was paid back in his own body." Then the Ripuarian Franks
chose Clovis as their king. Thus Gregory.

That account, presumably based on written sources, is still historic
almost without a change. It seems at first to furnish a basis for a great
saga only in its very historicity, inasmuch as it is concerned with a major
historic event: the union of all Franks in a single kingdom, with the loss
of the political independence of one of their branches, that of the Ripuarian Franks. Only here and there, legendary themes have already at-

---

7. Gregorius Turoniensis, *Historia Francorum*, II, 27, 28.

tached themselves to the story (incidentally, a refutation of the fashionable view that would like to treat legend and song as completely identical, whereas in fact the formation of the legend must have progressed to a certain point before the first song could be heard). Such a theme is undoubtedly the treasure chest which becomes a trap to the victim—a theme taken over with slight variation from the Wieland saga. The *buconica silva*, which might well be identical with the Spessart or Odenwald hills, may also be such a theme: how would the old, lame king Sigibert get there from the Lower Rhine? Both the locality and the king's "death in the forest" have been taken over into the Siegfried myth. Anyhow, there is much reason to assume that in Gregory's time, Frankish legendary songs much farther removed from historical reality were already current.

The name of Sigibert fits into the Siegfried myth first of all as a "Sig" name (could the dynasty of the Ripuarian Franks have been akin to the old Cheruscan and Chattian ducal houses?), and further inasmuch as "Sigibert" may have emerged by sound shift from an earlier Sigifreth, whom we find in the Anglo-Saxon Finnsburg fragment dating from the seventh century; but Sigifreth is naturally identical with Siegfried, and the sound shift may simply be due to Gregory's Latin. True, in the Finnsburg fragment Sigifreth, while also a Frankish leader, appears as a young fighter. But this change may have taken place in the meantime— above all if we assume that the king of the Ripuarian Franks, anyhow genealogically linked with Arminius, had in the course of the transformation of history into myth assumed some features of Arminius, whose real name obviously also contained the syllable Sig. All that would be highly plausible in itself, but not compelling.

What is indisputable, however, is that behind the murderous Hagen of the Siegfried saga Clovis is hidden. For Widukind calls Clovis Hugo, the Quedlinburg Chronicle calls the Franks Hugones, and that meaning of the name is also otherwise attested. Hagen's predicate "von Tronje"— acknowledged to have been originally "from Troja"—leads to the same conclusion: only Clovis and his dynasty did, under the stimulus of Vergil, claim Trojan descent. Now the proof of the identity of Hagen with Clovis also lends certainty to the identity of Sigebert with Sigefreth-Siegfried; and identity of the two rulers in the myth with the two rulers in Gregory proves that the myth has emerged from the accounts of the end of the kingdom of the Ripuarian Franks. That this has been ignored constitutes the most grievous gap in research on the Nibelungen saga.

To Hagen, the characteristic features of Clovis—low cunning, greed for gold, thirst for blood—have clung unchanged. Conversely, the pitiful figure of Sigibert has been transformed into the radiant hero Arminius, behind whom even more transfiguring fairy tale themes are recognizable—proof enough that the myth originated with the Ripuarian Franks whom it consoled about the loss of their political independence. The oldest form of the song must have trembled with hatred of Clovis. The complicity of Sigibert's son, shameful for the Ripuarian Franks, was covered by benevolent oblivion—one more denial of guilt, this time without any plunging back into fairy lore.

The treasure theme, though preformed archetypically, had a completely realistic meaning in the context of the narrative. It was the time of the collapse of the monetary economy. Taxes no longer came in, yet the king could only hold together his following by gifts of gold. In such conditions, the policy of the rulers was for a considerable part concerned with the hunt for golden treasure; if Gregory's narrative conveys the impression that Clovis was more eager to get the royal treasure than the royal territory of Sigibert, that certainly corresponded to the real situation. The looting of the treasure is thus sufficient both as a motive for Clovis's outrage and as a motive for saddling him with sole guilt. This corresponds exactly to a feature of the later saga which the interpreters could never explain properly: obviously there must have existed a very old version according to which the treasure, and the treasure alone, was the root of all horrors—particularly of the murder of its owner Siegfried. Here, in the story of the end of the realm of the Ripuarian Franks, we are faced with that version.

During the time of the Voelkerwanderung, there was no more return to ahistorical existence and therefore none to thinking in fairy tales. Nevertheless, no other element of the underlying historical events has in the later myth fallen back so deeply to the fairy tale level as the treasury theme. Undoubtedly we are facing here a revival of older fairy tale elements—but only followers of C. G. Jung can evade this puzzle: in what special conditions could such a fabulous distortion of historic horrors take place at a time when the distinction between fable and grim reality was already quite clearly made. The Ripuarian Franks had no interest in forgetting the real historical role of the royal treasure in the destruction of their independence. But the immediate successors of Clovis as rulers of the Salic Franks, the Merovingians, had such an interest. As Ripuarian Franks and Salic Franks quickly merged into a single people, the new rulers of that entire people also took over spiritual leadership: it was in the Merovingian realm and from a Merovingian need to throw off the burden of guilt that the treasure theme was shifted back into a past distant and legendary even in the perception of the time, and linked with the slaying of dragons and the like. A third denial of guilt on the road of the myth!

The Doom of the Burgundians

The same tendency of the Merovingians to get away from the atrocious origins of their power has accompanied the further evolution of the myth. Yet in historic reality, it encountered at first opposing tendencies aggravating their guilt.

Already Clovis attempted by treacherous means to obtain possession of the Burgundian realm, the seat of whose ruler was Autun. Gregory reports[8] that two brothers, Gundobad and Godegisil, had wrestled for the rule over the Burgundians, and that Godegisil had appealed for aid to Clovis. Clovis attacked Gundobad, Godegisil apparently rushed to help the brother, but went over to Clovis in the midst of the battle, took Gundobad prisoner, and had him beheaded and his wife drowned. That the story is analogous to that of the Ripuarian Franks is obvious: in the latter case Clovis had exploited the hatred of the son against the father, with the Burgundians a quarrel between brothers. We recognize a recurrent theme, inherited from Arminius' time: feuding within the clan, the worst of all crimes in Germanic eyes. But how much of that story has actually entered the late Nibelungen saga?

Directly, it seems, only the name of Godegisil, and even that only in a form merged with a much older Burgundian king, Gislahari (Giselher), who was killed fighting against Attila's Huns; he however is known to have once been a far more important figure in the saga than in the later verions that have fully come down to us. He may be one of the connecting links that brought the Huns into the saga. But before that could happen, several other changes had to take place.

First of all—and that was easy indeed—the *plot* of Clovis against the Burgundian realm was condensed with the later *destruction* of that realm by one of his sons; an outrage within one and the same people was thus turned into an outrage against another people—in the place of the Ripuarian Franks, the Burgundians became the victims. In the Finnsburg fragment, we no longer find Siegfried and Hagen, Ripuarian Franks and Salic Franks, fighting—but Sigefreth and Gundere (Gunther), Franks and Burgundians. (Hagen is missing in the preserved fragment of the Finnsburg song.) Second, since the Burgundians were made to appear as the de-

8. Ibid., II, 19, 21.

stroyers of the Ripuarian Franks (it is clear that the Finnsburg fragment reported the downfall of Sigefreth in fighting Gundere) they were made, according to ancient Germanic ideas, legitimate objects for the vengeance of the conquered. It would fit into such a version that first Gunther slew Siegfried, then Hagen slew Gunther—thus transforming Clovis' vile outrage against the king of the Ripuarian Franks into legitimate Merovingian vengeance executed on his murderer. Possibly part of the action in the Finnsburg song took place along those lines. After all, even with Gregory, Clovis' treacherous murder of the son of Sigibert appears as just punishment for the latter's patricide, so that the blood-soiled Clovis-Hagen becomes the executant of the law. Still, with Gregory, Clovis is still known to have himself incited the plot against Sigibert for which he later takes revenge on the patricide. The insertion of the Burgundians eliminates the guilt! Not, indeed, without an inconsistency—inasmuch as Hagen is no clansman of Sigefreth: the Germanic rule according to which the immediate clan of the murdered man is alone entitled to avenge his blood in blood is no longer observed. Though Hagen's outrage is for the first time presented as revenge for an earlier outrage, the revenge no longer fits the outrage exactly.

But in a political struggle, one uses what arguments are available. After the insertion of the Burgundians, the saga is no longer well constructed. It compensates for this weakness by its achievement—by eliminating not only the Merovingian guilt against the Ripuarian Franks, but also their analogous guilt against the Burgundians. True, according to strict Germanic law, the annihilation of the Burgundian dynasty remains an outrage. But we are no longer dealing with a world of strict Germanic law, but with a world of the full dissolution of all legal concepts in the early Merovingian realm. Here it is still useful enough if the murdered man appears as an infamous fellow.

We are thus postulating a phase of the saga in which the Merovingians were still held responsible, in accordance with historic truth, for the doom of the Burgundians, but sought to justify it by the alleged Burgundian outrage against the Ripuarian Franks. Presumably, the treachery of one Burgundian brother against the other also played a role in that phase. At first sight, such a phase appears not to be documented by the sources. Yet it is—by the very fact that the Burgundians have been inserted into the saga at all.

Attempts have been made to explain that insertion by the events of the year 437 A.D., when a Hunnish host destroyed the Burgundian realm around Worms and forced the remnants to move, through the *porta*

Burgundica, into latter-day Burgundy. Those events constituted a first downfall of the Burgundians, analogous to the second of 534 A.D. They have indeed left traces in the saga: the Burgundian kings in 437 were Gundahari (Gunther) and Gislahari (Giselher). But scholars have never been quite happy with that explanation: they were conscious that those events were, by the standards of the migration period, of little significance, and hence hardly apt to be remembered for a long time. They thus talked of an accidental insertion into the saga. Of course, the matter would not be so accidental if we were dealing with a Burgundian saga; there, those events might very well be remembered, and the first downfall of the Burgundians could well be later condensed with the second. But nobody has ever maintained that we are dealing with a Burgundian saga. How, then, should such recondite events have got into a Frankish saga in the absence of closer relations to its main content?

We may, on the contrary, consider it an axiom that anything in the great myths which is not of religious or archetypical origin must be linked with historical events of essential importance for the community transmitting the saga. To ignore that is to misunderstand a basic aspect of saga formation. The saga is not, as an aestheticizing view would have us believe, a purely literary product; it becomes that only in the period of its decline. In the time of its growth it is an account of the decisive factors in the evolution and shaping of the political community carrying it, and with it the justification of that community's right to existence. As Schelling has correctly seen, the community concerned would not be there without it: the saga is the spiritual side of the revolutionary growth of tribe and state. (Just for that reason, ahistoric communities need no sagas and indeed cannot have them; anything justified by the saga is always a later stage compared to an already given one.)

Clovis' plots against Ripuarian Franks and Burgundians both belong to the same late phase of his rule. They are basically distinct both from the conflicts with the Visigoths and Alemanns, that can only be considered as border adjustments, and from the liquidation of the Gallic remnants of the Roman empire. In contrast to the latter, the Ripuarian and Burgundian enterprises amount to the creation of a tribe-transcending territorial dominion. How could the saga take one of them, the Ripuarian one, as its starting point and completely bypass the other, Burgundian one, seeing that both are completely analogous in their meaning and their course? And how could it instead recur to Worms and to the early fifth century? Apart from Arminius, the historic aspects of the Nibelungen saga are centered around Clovis, and those two alone are worthy to be the central figures of a myth. Not by accident, the Burgundians remain in the saga ultimately in the passive role which history had assigned to them: to their end they move like puppets manipulated by Hagen's fingers, however much their relations to him may shift in the course of repeated transformations of the saga.

But how, then, has the first downfall of the Burgundians, for which the Huns were responsible, come to take the place of the second one, to be accounted for by Clovis (and one of his sons)? Quite simply as a further exoneration of the Merovingian house from the burden of guilt. But it would be all too easy to see here only continuing effect of an unconscious sense of guilt and its denial. Rather, a certain historic context may be discovered here, too. This cannot be looked for in purely Frankish motivations: consciences were not that tender in the sixth century. But there existed a point where the Franks had an intense interest in sparing Burgundian feelings.

The Burgundians did not merge with the Franks, as the Ripuarian Franks had merged with the Salic Franks. Rather, the repeated divisions of the Merovingian inheritance assured the continued existence of Burgundy as a Merovingian partial state, and the decisive personality at the Merovingian-Burgundian court in Autun became the Visigoth princess Brunichildis, equally remarkable for her classical culture, her interest in sagas, her political discernment, and her murderous hand. Involved in conflicts with the other partial states, Brunichildis could not do without the support of her own. Nothing was more inadmissible from that viewpoint than to treat "her" Burgundians as scapegoats for the outrage of Clovis. No doubt this great ruling personality, to whose influence on the evolution of Germanic spiritual life we shall have to come back repeatedly, had literary knowledge of the catastrophe of 437, perhaps even knowledge of Burgundian songs lamenting it. Nor could she be short of bards doing her bidding. I should not hesitate to derive that phase of the saga's evolution which had the Franks replaced by the Huns as enemies of the Burgundians from literary reminiscences consciously exploited by Brunichildis so as to promote a reconciliation of Franks and Burgundians. A sixth denial of guilt!

But as it often happened with that tragic and much misunderstood figure, there was, hidden behind the political propaganda—why shy away from the word in that context—a more profound change of the inspiring viewpoint. Hitherto, each transformation of the saga had served the demands of a new hatred or the justification of a new crime; here, for the first time, the saga was to serve pacification and reconciliation. It finally exonerated the Franks, but not for the purpose of oppressing the Burgundians; nor did it serve the revival of a warlike Burgundian tribal feeling directed against the Franks. Rather, it served to decontaminate the entire subject by projecting the guilt onto another, already perished people, the Huns, onto another time and other geographical areas.

It is true, however, that this operation also cut the sinews that had held the myth together: between that which king Gunther did to Siegfried, and that which king Atli-Etzel did to Gunther, there was no longer a context of just retaliation in the Germanic sense. As a way out, the idea of female vengeance carried out through Gudrun-Kriemhild's marriage with Etzel has been inserted in a context yet to be discussed. But that is known to be a much later addition; the old Atli song knows nothing about it yet—there Gudrun appears as avenger of her Burgundian brothers, and Atli's only motive is the looting of the treasure, now also shifted away from the Franks to Hunnish account. Finally, even Hagen is turned into a Burgundian and subordinated to Gunther. But here the persistence with which the true roots of the saga survive and remain effective despite all distortions becomes visible. On one side, no plausible Burgundian origin can be constructed for Hagen—the range of variants reaches from a son of Albs to an uncle of Gunther. On the other, the formal subordinate takes leadership again and again. Clovis was too powerful and terrible a figure to be pushed into the second rank—even as hero of a saga.

But the gravest change was that the social function of the saga was thus radically altered. It was still a Frankish saga—but one in which the Franks, at least the Salic Franks, had apparently ceased to appear! A saga diligently covering up those great historic events from which it had sprung and which continued as before to shape and determine the existence of the Merovingian state! True, the saga is now decontaminated, and that corresponds to a basic tendency at the end of the sixth century, that of drawing a line under all the hatred and feuds of the time of the Voelkerwanderung. But by its decontamination it has also become depoliticized and thus unfit to represent further the "soul" of the Merovingian realm. In that sense, the transformation of the Frankish state myth into a saga of conflict between Burgundians and Huns is the direct prelude to the spiritual death of the Merovingian realm as such, already almost consummated at the death of Brunichildis; the prelude also to a new spiritual-political order no longer based on myth, the Carlovingian. The saga, alienated from the major political concerns, now really begins to decline into a purely literary phenomenon. Those scholars who, like

Heusler, begin their research only with the song of the doom of the
Burgundians take up the thread only where it is already thinned out to
the tearing point.

The Women's Quarrel

To complete our outline of the saga, only the women's quarrel is now
missing. Its origin and the manner of its insertion into the overall context
can only be understood if we keep in mind the depoliticization of the
saga begun by Brunichildis. Not that political references were absent
from the theme of the women's quarrel; but they are less specific and
more covered up by archetypal elements than anything that was added
to the saga in the three quarters of a century between the death of Sigibert
of Cologne and the rise of Brunichildis of Autun.

A female archetype, more precisely a dual female archetype to which
we shall return, was at hand. The political theme indispensable for saga
formation was brought in by the Visigothian Brunichildis herself, undoubtedly the most powerful figure in Merovingian history next to
Clovis. (Her name may well have sprung from an earlier fairy story of
the virgin and the flaming blaze.) Her husband was another Sigibert, a
fact mostly overlooked; he died by murder. Author of the murder was
her rival Frede-gundis, whose name could so easily be linked with the
root syllable Gund- of the names of the Burgundian ruling house; from
that arose the figure of Gudrun. In order for Fredegundis to be exonerated
and Brunichildis charged with the murder of Sigibert, only raging hatred
of the latter was needed. That was found in plenty among the Austrasian
nobility, whose members rebelled against the royal absolutism of Brunichildis and finally, after decades of struggle and long after the peaceful
death of Fredegundis, had Brunichildis murdered in a horrible manner.
In historic reality the early death of Sigibert had been a terrible blow to
Brunichildis, but indeed also the starting point for her personal reign in
the name of her still minor children; in the distortion by the hostile party,
she herself was supposed to have incited the murder. Who indeed would
not, in those years, have thought Brunichildis capable of that kind of
deed? Seventh shift of guilt in the saga! But again, as always in such
cases, the historic reality shines through the veil of distortion: the saga
has never come to a clear decision on whether Brunichildis was Siegfried's
wife or not—originally she had to be, first because she really was, and also
because otherwise she could not be called a murderess of her husband.

But though the figure and the events are of political origin, the motives of Brunichildis and of her antagonist 'Gudrun are no longer. True, the sudden tremendous rise of womanly power, before which men are like so much chaff, is the historic basis of the saga of the two queens. But Brynhild in the saga acts not as ruler, but as an offended woman. As repeatedly in the development of the saga, one is inclined to see here the effect of two opposite points of view on the interpretation of one and the same figure. Originally, Brynhild was probably accused of having arranged the death of Siegfried-Sigbert exclusively out of her passion to rule—hardly in the song, probably just in the clamor of contemporary political propaganda.

That first version seems to have gained firm belief outside of her direct area of rule even in her lifetime—at any rate, the death of Brynhild in the saga is totally different from her historic death. Later, presumably after the queen's death, an opposite view claimed a hearing which sought to mitigate her guilt, though without doubting her responsibility for Siegfried's death, and to make her conduct understandable, by letting the woman's treachery be preceded by treachery of the man towards her. The first of those two versions obviously originated from Austrasia. The second shows its opposite tendency already in its total indifference toward the honor of the Austrasian Siegfried, whose memory is for the first time defiled in the ugly story of the fraud practiced on Brynhild. We could follow the dispute between the two views in greater detail, but it is no longer of interest in our context: it belongs to the history of literature.

What matters is only that we are suddenly confronted with a new archetype which is worlds away from the early Merovingian period: the conflict between the sexes, the revenge of a woman offended in her dignity—offended, we may add, not in the only manner understandable to classical antiquity, by sexual abuse, but conversely by disrespect for her longing for union with the man she loves. That belongs indeed in the group of basic occidental archetypes. But before we can discuss it, the male side of the myth must first be examined for its archetypal elements.

CHAPTER FOUR

The Archetypes in the Siegfried Myth

We have followed the Nibelungen saga through some of the turns of its evolution, conditioned by the turns of Frankish political history. The history of this saga has a prelude at the time of the emperors Augustus and Tiberius, preceding its main development by almost half a millennium. One important element, the Burgundian catastrophe of 437 A.D., was only later included in the saga's material. Its proper history begins with the catastrophe of the Ripuarian Franks, presumably around the turn of the fifth to the sixth century, and ends not long after the death of Brunichildis which took place in 613 A.D. In the course of this span of scarcely a century, no part of the saga remained in its original place, hardly one escaped being turned into its opposite—with one single exception: from its prehistory in the first century through the main developmental phase of the saga in the sixth century to its last poetic rearrangements in the high and late Middle Ages, in Southern and Northern Germanic territories, the figure of Siegfried (and of his Nordic variant Sigurd) has remained unchanged, both in its basic character traits and in its function in the myth (except only for the late story of the fraud practiced on Brynhild). Such constancy in the midst of universal changes of context is the mark of the archetype. Once we concentrate our attention on the latter, the complicated evolution of the saga appears only as a changing framework within which this most profound core is preserved unchanged. Without it, the myth would not be there—though, of course, it would not be there either without the impact of the shocks of the period of the migration on the entire pattern of Germanic social life. It arises precisely from the interplay and opposition of one historically changeable and one archetypal factor.

Once we define this fate of Siegfried, remaining constant through all the phases of the saga's evolution, as the archetypal element in the Nibelungen saga, it is not difficult to outline its content. Here is a young, radiant hero without flaw, guided from birth by superhuman powers, granted all the joys of victory in war and love—and lo! his flower is broken all too early by black treachery and he finds an early grave. Looking back we can see how this image, ever present to the spirit of those who shaped the saga, has deeply transformed already the idea of the fate of Arminius, but even more that of the fate of Siegebert of Cologne and of all that followed later. To that extent, the archetype is given in advance and dominates the experience of real history through many centuries. Yet somewhere, this supremacy of the archetype over experience finds its limit in time and space: the validity of the archetype began at some point in history and ends at some point. And what has been said for the "when" applies equally to the "where": in both respects, the archetype we speak of is something "relative," requiring and permitting historical derivation. It is obviously close to Spengler's concept of the "primeval symbol" of a culture, but distinct from it precisely by its derivability. From the Jungian concept of the archetype it is moreover distinct by our rejection of the fiction of its primordial nature.

Any archetype has for those who are under its spell the force of inescapable necessity. The Germanic view of fate, of which there will be much further discussion, is only a particular variant of this common character of the archetype as such. But not every saga is archetypal in its core. To Siegfried's fate, characterized by its strict inevitability, we may oppose the story of Dietrich von Bern, which may be regarded as a prototype of an extremely nonarchetypal saga. While the life of Siegfried, from the time he learns the craft of a smith from Mime, leads in every particular feature towards highest splendor with the compelling consequence of deepest fall, the adventures of Dietrich are loosely added one to another and could be exchanged at will; his death, above all, has no inherent connection with his life. Such a story shows a profound, if entirely nonexplicit aftereffect of the concept of *Tyche* from Hellenistic late antiquity, which embodies the philosophical idea of the absence of any archetypal order in human happenings. The Rhenish saga (with its Gothic offshoots) on one side, the Langobardic-Bajuvarian saga on the other thus embody two major, incompatible types belonging to wholly different zones and tendencies: one reflects South European thought, leading from the saga of mere adventures through the romance of chivalry to the enlightened doctrine of the omnipotence of coincidence, which has found its classical expression in Voltaire's "Candide." The other type, coming from the North, insists on the strictly directed character of human events, to which Shakespeare has given the highest expression. We are not here concerned to derive the Southern type—that is a task for classical studies. Our subject is the Nordic type of the saga as a first embodiment of the Western idea of human existence.

But how are we to approach our subject? However we may twist and turn the saga around, it helps us only to define, not to derive the archetype. To derive a phenomenon means always to place it into a causal context, and that means in any case a *metabasis eis allo genos* (transfer into another class). Here it means that in a double sense. First of all, the archetype precedes in time the unfolding of the myth—and, since the myth is the oldest form of manifestation of culture, it precedes the emergence of the culture concerned. *The archetypes underlying a culture are transformed sediments of cultural elements which the culture concerned has inherited from an earlier one.* But the inherited cultural elements are, as a rule, integrated by the younger culture into a different sphere from their place in the older one; in our case, as will be shown, they come to the sphere of Western heroic saga out of the sphere of pre-Western religion.

Balder

We get the core of the Siegfried archetype almost without admixtures in the myth of the god Balder, as handed down to us chiefly by Snorri, who evidently retold a lost Eddic song of the god. The kinship is so close that one is entitled to say that in Siegfried, a god was hidden or humanized, condensed with such historical figures as Arminius and Siegebert. Neckel in his basic study has put together the most important elements of comparison.[1] Balder, too, is a magnificent war hero, radiant with strength, beauty, and noble goodness. He, too, dies young, in his flowering. He, too, dies by treachery. He, too, falls victim to the ill-conceived care of a woman (his mother Frijja, as with Siegfried and his wife Kriemhild). He, too, possessed magic invulnerability and could be killed only in one single way (by the throw of the mistletoe, as Siegfried by the shot into his shoulder). His death, too, is the prelude to a total catastrophe (here Ragnarök, there the doom of the Nibelungen). Compared to such massive identities, the differences hardly count. Some simply correspond to the difference between the human and the divine world, others amount to minor variants of a saga. Siegfried and Balder

1. Gustav Neckel, *Die Überlieferung vom Gotte Balder* (Dortmund: Ruhfus, 1920).

thus are one and the same person, once in human, once in divine shape. Did the death by treachery now come into the Siegfried saga out of the myth of the God, or out of history? Strange correspondence!

At first sight, Balder seems by no means to stand alone in religious history. According to Neckel's description, he is a God of vegetation and the sun, of peace and the harvest, and in all that he has most in common with Freyr and other Wanic Gods. On the other hand, he, and the other Wanic gods like him, have very close relations to the cults of the ancient Near and Middle East, also directed to fertility and the sun. No serious scholar doubts today that direct influences from Asia Minor are involved and not a mere parallelism of development; the special feature of the Wanic religion, compared to its oriental models, lies only in the fact that Frey and Balder are gods of vegetation *and* the sun in one person, while the Asian gods of vegetation are dominated by the chthonic element exclusively—quite naturally, since in the deep South, the sun is an enemy rather than a promoter of the growth of vegetation. Correspondingly, sun gods and vegetation gods are separated in the South, but united in one person in the North; in the South the death of vegetation is mourned in late spring and its resurrection celebrated in the fall, in the North, mourning belongs to the fall and jubilation to spring—March or May, according to the climate. But that difference touches in no way the common core of the Wanic and the Near Eastern religious ideas.

Those ideas agree to an astonishing extent. There is always a divine couple; she, the Great Mother (Inanna, Ishtar, Cybele, Freya) has a young lover (Dumuzi, Tammuz, Attis, Adonis, Freyr, Balder) who loses his life by an outrage or accident. Desperately the goddess searches for him, follows him into the underworld, liberates him under difficult conditions. Meanwhile on earth, a feast of mourning accompanies the annual death of the beloved, a feast of jubilation his annual resurrection. We may well say that all the myths of the dying god, to which the Balder myth unmistakably belongs, go back to those Near Eastern fertility cults. So far there is thus hardly a problem. The countless, ever-changing couples of the Wanic gods are basically always one and the same couple of vegetation gods; originally, Balder with Nanna belonged to them as well.

Yet with Balder there is an essential departure from the pattern. Once for him, too, the same lament was sounded as for the Babylonian Tammuz: "Tammuz the all powerful is dead," which the emperor Tiberius misunderstood as "The great Pan is dead." But the mourners then knew that their Tammuz would return in the fall. *Balder, however, does not return.* It cannot have been like that in Wanic times: the Balder myth agrees with the Adonis myth down to the god's death too clearly for us to accept that it had completely deviated from it following that event. Yet no myth of Balder's return has come down to us.

I hear objections: does not the Völuspa proclaim explicitly that Balder will return when, after the Ragnarök, the end of the world, the destroyed world is resurrected? But just here is the decisive point: Adonis returns *annually*, and his return is a precondition for the cycle of the seasons and of vegetation, it is anchored in the main ritual of the Near Eastern cultures. It will yet have to be shown how much this comprises of exactly defined religious ideas. Balder, by contrast, will return *after the end of the world*, when not only all living men, but also all the gods have died—an idea no longer connected in any way with human existence as it is lived and to which no immediate hopes are tied, a purely poetic idea, possibly with a touch of theological polemic against Christianity. How could one equate a return in the next year with a return in the next aeon, how treat the latter as a mere "variant" of the former, without realizing that an idea of the twilight of the Gods and an end of the world must have been fully developed before the idea of another aeon could be added as a postscript? Precisely by this announcement of his eventual "return," Balder is proven to be a *dead God*.

That this was not always the case, that Balder once returned annually just like Adonis, can only be proved by the detour of his identity with Freyr. Other proofs have also been looked for, but none of them is conclusive, because all are based on the agreement of the Balder myth with that part of the Adonis myth that deals not with the return, but with the death of the god. By contrast, it can be shown that the Germanic tribes actually celebrated the annual return of Freyr,[2] and the original identity of Balder and Freyr can be proved point by point in its turn.[3] The differentiation of the two cults obviously took place only when the myth split into two myths, one of which had as its subject the return of the god of vegetation, the other the failure of the effort to bring him back.

This identity of Balder and Freyr in a phase before the myth of the

2. Neckel, (p. 105) speaks correctly of a god worshipped annually. Most enlightening in this respect is the myth and ritual of the legendary Swedish king Froði, whose identity with Freyr is generally recognized. The death of Froði was the theme of annual processions. See A. Olik, *Denmarks Heltediktningen*.

3. See Neckel, pp. 103ff. Balder is, like Freyr, a god of the sun and vegetation, of harvest and peace. In the Völuspa, it says: "Freyr er betstr allra Ballriða" (Freyr is the best of all gods). Not only does this epithet "the best" recur again and again with Balder (as with Siegfried), Neckel also points out that the verse does not "stave" properly—it must once have run: Balder is betstr allra Ballriða".

dead god existed also solves the riddle of the Balder cult. Local names with Balder are rare, hints at a Balder-cult highly vague. But this is not the crucial point. We do not hesitate to claim that the idea of a Balder-cult in the sense of a cult of the dead god is absurd. In contrast to Odin, Balder is not a God of the dead—he does not rule Hel, known to be a female domain. He only sits in Hel but without any function. One would underestimate the utilitarian character of pagan cults if one took the view that a god who is dead and has nothing more to give could be appealed to. (Adonis is not appealed to either during the period of his stay in the underworld!) What traces of a Balder cult there are evidently refer to the phase when he was not yet a dead god and his name was a mere epithet of Freyr: whether one interprets the name of Balder as equivalent with the noun of the same sound meaning "Lord," or whether one connects it with the Indogermanic root *bal* for "to shine," we are dealing with a name that would fit Freyr just as well. Out of this epithet, the separate god characterized by Snorri developed when the separate idea of the dead god split off from the general myth of the vegetation gods.

To say that it "split off" is, by the way, a rather mild expression for what happened. An examination of the elements of the myth as reported by Snorri, hence in the Eddic song available to him, shows a conscious break, a determined rejection of the belief in the god's return which presupposes a religious revolution. Since we are here concerned with the starting point of our entire view of the origin of the West we must inevitably deal more closely with some of the details.

The first change concerns the role of the mother goddess. In the myths of Asia Minor, the Magna Mater is the savior of the fertility god who has perished by some mishap—a wild animal, a misdirected arrow; it is she who brings him back from the underworld. In the Balder myth, this saving mother is completely missing. Instead of the Magna Mater, who was mother and mistress to the young god, we now find two figures—Frijja as mother, Nanna as wife. Nanna—who in the Sumerian version of the myth, as Inanna, has the part of female savior—now shares Balder's fate of eternal death and is burnt with him on the ship of the dead; Frijja *tries* to play the saving role, *but that role of hers is turned into its contrary*: she herself becomes guilty of Balder's death by avoiding, out of misplaced cleverness, getting the mistletoe to swear the oath on Balder's life and safety which all other creatures must perform. We see that not only has the poet of the younger Balder myth consciously turned the original function of the mother goddess into its contrary, but also a general change in the view taken of woman has come about. In the cults of Asia Minor, as in the Wanic cult, she was the all-giving and all-protective, from whose never-tired breasts all creatures could draw the eternal force of life; now she becomes, in her split existence in two figures, part helpless victim and part cause of evil. The change is so radical that we surely cannot attribute it to the poetic needs of the narrator but only to profound structural transformations in the thinking and existence of the Germanic tribes.

With Siegfried, the two women are found again, and one of them, Kriemhild, will cause his death in exactly the same manner as Frijja that of Balder. Only now it is not as with Balder the mother, but the wife who causes Siegfried's ruin by her deadly betrayal of the secret of his vulnerable spot. A further blackening of woman's role has taken place. The pure, suffering-loving victim, Nanna, is missing. In her place the wife, Gudrun-Kriemhild has entered the role of the loving-ruining mother of the Balder myth. But that older, less soft female figure who in the Balder myth caused the god's ruin by neglect, in the Siegfried saga consciously causes his doom in raging vengeance. We understand that just as behind the historical Siegfried an archetype was found, thus behind the two quarreling queens of the saga two archetypes exist: the woman counselling the hero's death unintentionally, and the other one causing it intentionally. In one word: the archetype of life-giving woman has been replaced by that of death-giving woman. Is a more striking inversion into the contrary conceivable?

Second, the tool of death, the mistletoe, owes its role to a similar inversion to the contrary. Not only is it much more harmless than other weapons, such as the miraculous sword whose victim Balderus becomes according to Saxo,[4] it is indeed so harmless that it is absurd to regard it as a cause of death—and the saga makes no attempt to explain that. Modern commentators have quite rightly stated that behind that harmless mistletoe of Snorri's, the dangerous sword of Saxo's must be seen; we add that the sword belonged to the older, truly Near Eastern form of the saga (probably in an even earlier layer a spear or battleaxe stood here), while the mistletoe belongs specifically to the myth of the dead god. For it has, as has also been stated quite correctly, an eminent symbolic force—as a symbol of fertility. It has this role perhaps because it is a parasite, but chiefly because it is an evergreen occurring in the farthest Northern regions. It therefore has an exquisite meaning in fertility rites: the man who catches a girl under the mistletoe at Jultime wins power over her maidenhead (a custom widespread in the North to this day, but now reduced to the playful right to a kiss). Now what could be more

4. *Saxo Grammaticus*, III, 69–73.

striking than the transformation of that branch, which as an evergreen maintains the hope for a return of fertility during the eight months of the Northern winter, into a deadly weapon thrown at the god of fertility and the sun? It is as if with that story the whole religion of fertility should be stabbed to death—not a mere parable, for to the ancient Germans listening to it, the symbolism of the mistletoe was as familiar as the meaning of Balder as a god of fertility. In Saxo's older version, Balder fell in a struggle of two brothers for Nanna—a version quite compatible with his return; in Snorri's later version, on the contrary, he perishes from his own strongest magic weapon, the mistletoe—as if to say that the god of fertility kills himself.

Third, the same tendency is visible in Snorri's account of the joint burning of Balder and Nanna on a blazing ship pushed out into the sea. The rite belongs specifically to the Vikings—it is also found in the joint funeral of Sigurd and Brynhild, and archaeological evidence is not lacking. All the more striking that according to Snorri, Balder's death-ship at first cannot be moved, that a witch is needed to push it into the sea, that Thor in his rage about that wants to kill the witch and is barely held back by the other Ases. (We note in passing that here Balder has been wholly transferred from the Wanic into the Asic world.) This can hardly be understood in any other way than that such pushing of the burning ships out to the sea is aimed at the simultaneous destruction of the bodies by fire and water, hence their most complete imaginable, total destruction; it is evidently that which arouses Thor's terrible wrath and requires the cooperation of a witch. The Ases, Snorri reports, are still foolishly waiting for Balder's return—which evidently seems incompatible with funeral by ship.

Now the point is not that *any* funeral by cremation would be incompatible with a belief in the rebirth of the dead. Rather, cremation has prevailed in the North just in the Bronze age, thus in the very period for which the Scandinavian rock drawings bear most certain witness to the taking over of the great Asian vegetation cults. But there may well be a difference between pure cremation, supposed to facilitate the etherean soul's way to heaven by liberating it from the body, and the funeral by fire *and* water which seems to prevent that; and inasmuch as the latter opens to the heroes the road to Walhalla—that does not arise for Balder, who has died just *in* Walhalla. However that may be, at any rate Thor wanted to preserve his body—and failed. In this context it is significant that just with the beginning of the Voelkerwanderung, funeral by burial is becoming accepted again. It is, for instance, underlying the Helgi saga, the significance of which for the Balder myth will be discussed later—

246

evidently burial has become a compensation for the lost belief in the return of the dead. We now find both types of funeral—burial and cremation—side by side, and just the mention of Balder's death may teach us that this was by no means a peaceful coexistence. For the meaning of the narrative is obviously that the Ases are passionately resisting the destruction of Balder's body, because they regard it as final and only a witch, an evil being, can accomplish such a deed.

As a fourth and last main element the story of Hermod's journey to Hel finally offers itself. Like the analogous saga of Orpheus and Eurydice, it contains strong rationalist elements and reads like a parable aimed at proving that nobody who has once died ever returns, not even a god. Once more we note in the margin the intense worsening of the woman's role: it is the man who attempts Balder's rescue, while a woman, Hel, makes it as difficult as possible and another woman, the witch þökk (behind whom Snorri looks for Loki) finally prevents it. Hermod is provided in the narrative with supernatural means for solving his task: on Odin's horse Sleipnir (originally there can have been as little reference to Odin here as to Thor in the story of the burning ship) he jumps across the bridge of the dead which otherwise no living being can cross. He forces Hel to agree to give back Balder if all nature cries for him—"as do all beings when coming from the cold into the warm"—which is nothing else but the picture of the annual melting of the snow. But in an approach coming close to the Christian outlook, but not for that reason necessarily taken over from Christianity, nature has lost its healing power. Once more, as in the burning scene, recourse is had to the evil world of primeval nature, to the giants and witches: one witch—one ice giant—refuses to join in crying, and Balder remains forever a prisoner of Hel.

So much for Snorri and our interpretation of his account. We abstain from the analysis of those variants that claim knowledge of an avenger of Balder's or of a vain attempt to awaken a successor for him—they all reflect only the same range of problems. It must be explicitly stated, however, that the four closely linked main episodes of the narrative of Balder's death discussed above cannot have arisen more or less simultaneously with that of his return after the Ragnarök. At the time when Balder's final death first became a theme of poetry, it had to be presented in conflict with a living faith in return and rebirth—that is the evident meaning of all those stories. In such a situation, the story of Balder's eventual return would have revoked the meaning of the new myth, the radical negation of the traditional nature cults. Centuries had to pass between this new departure and that later turn which already presupposes an absolute faith that everything individual is bound to end with death, and permits the consoling pointer to a new aeon to follow that confession of faith. On the other hand, at least the story of the mistletoe must have belonged to the phase of the break with the nature cults. We are thus inferring three phases of the Balder myth: First, nature cult in identification with Freyr, then the dead god, finally a god who will return in another aeon. For the origin of each of these concepts, a separate date must be found.

The dating attempts of Neckel and Much[5] are beside the point, because they are based on the unspoken assumption that the origin of the Balder song and that of the Balder myth were one and the same thing, and thus hopelessly confuse the different phases. Much even puts both into the Wanic age. Still, we agree with his assumption that this age—and with it the Freyr myth—goes back at least to the beginning of the first pre-Christian millenium, although he makes that statement without taking the Scandinavian rock drawings into account whose dating, still to be discussed, must be decisive here. Neckel, on the other hand, starts from the lost Balder *song*[6] and finds for this a first *terminus ad quem* in the Husdrapa, a Skaldic song about the Jarl Olaf Pai from 985 A.D., since in the ruler's hall of that Jarl the Balder myth was pictured in full according to that Drapa. As such pictorial representation presupposes the song, Neckel arrives at a second, earlier *terminus ad quem* around 900 A.D. That is convincing—*for the song*. If Neckel goes back even further and suggests a date in the sixth century A.D. because a later transmission of oriental vegetation gods to Northern Europe was unthinkable, Much's reply is valid that this transmission had taken place at least one and one half millennium before. The fact is that between the first irruption of religions from the Near East into the North and the full unfolding of the Balder myth as a song about two millennia have passed. The Balder song, reproduced in extracts by Snorri, obviously belongs in the same group of songs as the Völuspa and Grimnismal, Vafthrudsmal, etc., with their allusions to the Balder myth in its youngest form. There is not the slightest reason to date any one of those documents earlier than the tenth century A.D., where the Völuspa, with its developed doctrine of the new Balder-aeon, was undoubtedly the youngest of those products, while the lost Balder song, which does not yet contain that doctrine, may well have been the oldest of them. But they belong in a single movement that was in essence no longer mythopoeic, but theologically speculative, hence explicable only by intense Christian influence. Presumably, that movement lasted all through the tenth century.

5. Much, "Balder," *Zeitschrift für das deutsche Altertum* 61 (1924), pp. 93ff.
6. Neckel, p. 230.

With that, the last phase would be dated with sufficient exactitude, the oldest pushed back into grey antiquity. It remains to date the middle stage of the myth, and that means the actual rise of the myth of the dead god on which everything depends in our context. Its dating has never been attempted for the simple reason that the Balder myth was never sharply distinguished from the Freyr myth and the Wanic religion. Yet Much, in searching for the date of the Balder myth, has unconsciously given a decisive hint. But with that we enter an entirely new field.

Helgi

Much has linked Balder not only with Siegfried, but also with Helgi, and has drawn conclusions regarding contents and date of the Balder myth from that link. But the Helgi saga has come down to us, in the Edda and elsewhere, in fragments only, and the older of its two principal versions, the *Helgakvida Hundingbana* I, is very remote from the Balder myth, since there the hero appears only as a radiant victor; it is the only nontragic one among the Eddic heroic songs, expression of the flowering period of the Vikings—a short phase in which the tragic sense of fate was overlaid by the feeling of strength and the jubilation of victory. *Helgakvida Hundingbana* II, on the other hand, is filled with the most profound tragic sense, but at the same time with such wild erotic paroxysms that it is impossible to date the version we know earlier than the late eleventh century. Thus the paganism dominating the foreground in the text is deceptive; still, the long song, or rather the preserved fragments, carries much authentic pagan material.

In its basic features, this younger phase is indeed very close to the Balder myth: the returning dead Helgi, who calls his surviving wife Sigrun to his side; the night of love she spends with him in his grave; his demand she should no longer cry for him, and her hope that if she obeyed, he would return every night; the deception of the subterranean spirits who have inspired Sigrun with that hope, whereas just the drying up of her tears of blood frees Helgi from the magic that forced him back to the scene of his life; finally the later death from love of Sigrun, no longer described—all those are features turning around the same theme as the Balder myth, the impossibility of a true reawakening of the dead.

But the ideas about postmortal existence are different—here the grave, there Hel; there is no trace of a ritual of cremation; and generally only the central theme and no particular feature coincides with the myth of the god. Obviously, we are dealing here with a latecomer specimen of the kind of poetry that once created the Völuspa cycle of Eddic songs of gods, among them the lost Balder song. The poet of this late version of the Helgi saga has, in composing his song, used material not used in the Balder song which is in part considerably more archaic than the latter. But all that does not yet justify an identification of Balder and Helgi, parallel to that of Balder and Siegfried, as Much has suggested it.

But Much has been more lucky with his picking from the archaic remnants in *Heldakvida Hundingbana* II. He has proved that Helgi falls victim to a clan vengeance for his slaying of Hunding, and he has shown that the avenger was originally Hunding's son Hoeðrodd—which leads directly to the name of Hoeðr, the brother and murderer of Balder. Nor is the woman missing for whom Balder and Hoeðr originally fought: it is Sigrun—only that in the Helgi saga it is not Helgi and Hoeðrodd, but Helgi and Hunding who are fighting for her. All that has little relation with the treatment of the Balder myth by Snorri, but it corresponds rather closely to the version of Saxo, where Hotherus and Balderus are mounted warriors fighting for a woman. Thus here indeed a piece from another Balder song, known to Saxo but not to Snorri, has reemerged in an old version of the Helgi song since covered by later materials. But this does not affect anything referring to Balder's fate after his death, for Saxo knew nothing of a survival of Balderus in any form whatever, and this old Balder song could have just as well ended with Balder's death as with the hope for his return in the coming year.

But Much has yet gone one step further. He has shown that *Helgakvida Hundingbana* II contains quite a number of Suebian personal names and place names from East of the Elbe, and has concluded that there exists a very archaic part of the saga referring to the Suebian people at a time when they were still settled in that area. He puts the end of that period in the third pre-Christian century; the most recent research would rather put it in the first pre-Christian century. Among the placenames unearthed by Much, one deserves the highest attention: the Fjøturlundr—grove of fetters—which he convincingly identifies with the holy grove of the Semnones mentioned by Tacitus,[7] which apart from the priestess only people in fetters could enter; there, the annual human sacrifices were brought to the Magna Mater, probably under the name of Nerthus. And this is now the place where the vengeance of Hunding's clan catches up with Helgi! It would be absurd to assume that a place so loaded with significance could have got into the saga by accident or error. No doubt—

---

7. Tacitus, *Germania*, ch. 39.

one version of the saga, surely the very oldest, reported not on a duel of heroes, let alone on a dead god, but on a human sacrifice.

That seems confusing but may easily be clarified. Evidently the Wanic religion, like all the Near Eastern cults of that period, was based on a concept of the oneness of men and gods which we can hardly duplicate any more. First there is on one side the priestess identified with the Magna Mater; on the other the priest king, where he exists at all, is often a mere "king for a year" identified with Adonis. The drama of death and awakening of the god is not only realistically represented, that representation is also identified with a corresponding drama in the divine world. In a full identification of the divine couple with a human one, first the *hieros gamos* (ἱερός γαμός) is consummated by king and high priestess, then the year's king is sacrificed. In sober reality, all this is naturally performed by mere humans, but from the religion's point of view it would be meaningless to ask whether the actors are gods or humans—they are both *in uno actu*. But if the person sacrificed is a god and a king at the same time, then it is by no means strange that he becomes the subject of a myth—rather he is that already, for just in this role consists the myth which is presented in a "real drama" and which could therefore be called a "realized myth." The mention of the grove of fetters in the saga as the place where Helgi was killed shows that the innermost core of the Helgi saga was simply the Freyr myth, from which the Balder myth later split off.

That very oldest layer, which we can now characterize clearly, is incompatible with the other version unearthed by Much, in which Helgi is killed in combat with Hoedrodd-Hoedr. True, Neckel has declared Saxo's version to be based on an arbitrary intrusion of ideas of medieval knighthood into a much older myth, but that is hardly convincing; for there exists an infinite amount of anthropological and mythological material proving that the replacement of one god-priest-king by his successor did not always take place by sacrificing the incumbent holder of that dignity, but often enough also by a duel, or even by a long series of duels in which the incumbent defended his place against pretenders by slaying them—until one arrived who was stronger than he, slew him and took his place. Such is the famous case of the god-priest-king of Nemi which Frazer made the starting point of his fundamental studies in that field; in historic times that priest was an escaped criminal, but no doubt there had once existed a real kingdom. There are plenty of analogies among the primitives. The corresponding sagas can only be understood as a direct and unchanged reproduction of such "realized myths:" if there one god slays the other, even slays him in open combat as

Hotherus slays Balderus in Saxo, in order to gain power over the great goddess, we are not faced with stories of purely symbolic significance, but with an exact account of the "real-mythical" change of throne in the priest-kingdom, which in the domain of the fertility cults was repeated from generation to generation. If it remains unclear in the account whether the actors were gods or men, that ambiguity is contained in the realized myth itself which identifies the two.

We can now attempt to review the whole in an ordered manner. Snorri's account represents the youngest phase of the saga, and the layer of the Helgi-songs linked with the grove of fetters the oldest one. Another layer also proven to exist in the Helgi songs and openly visible in Saxo's account of the Balder myth is the middle one, for the ritual underlying it stands in the middle between nature cult and heroic myth. It is still tied up with the nature cult inasmuch as it deals with the succession of one god-priest-king by another. But the position of woman is already profoundly changed: while in the Adonis myth she preserves and saves, she is here already a mere object of the struggle between the men. While as priestess in the genuine Adonis-cult she determines the human representative of the dying god either by oracle or free choice, now the sword decides between the pretenders.

With that, the ritual of the change of god-priests, which once was a real-mythical embodiment of the course of nature, has been separated from the latter. The throne no longer passess from hand to hand in regular intervals and in the main no longer in ritual form, let alone according to the calendar with the changing seasons. Rather, the substance of the principle followed is that rule belongs to the strongest—a principle only very loosely linked with the nature myth. Accordingly, what matters in the person of the victor is less and less the god, less also the priest, but more and more the ruler.

The change of throne, originally a ritual act almost without political significance—as it took place annually and each incumbent was destined to an early sacrificial death—now becomes a distinctly political act, limited only by the condition that the crown must be won in a duel and not in a tribal war or by other means. Accordingly, there evolves a type of hero who wins the crown no longer according to eternally fixed procedures, but by his own bold initiative and ruthless staking of his life. It is a purely human type. Yet one step further, and those bold fighters will refuse to submit to the ritual of the duel, in which they are bound some time to be defeated as they grow older; they will attempt to maintain their rule by all political means at their disposal. Where their own arm became too weak, their followers will offer their youthful arms to protect the ruler from the consequences of age, as appears tangibly in the conduct of king Ermanarich in the Hamir song. With that, we have finally arrived in an age of lawlessness.

Thus Saxo's account of the Balder song proves to be an intermediate link indispensable for understanding the transition from the Adonis myth to Snorri's account. But at the same time it shows that the study of that evolution cannot be kept in the framework of an analysis of the Balder myth. We had started from the Siegfried saga which in appearance at least deals with the human, not the divine. But the Siegfried archetype led us back to the Balder archetype; behind the saga about men, a myth about gods was hidden. Now a third horizon becomes visible: neither the human saga by itself nor the divine myth by itself contains the solution—the real task is to *demonstrate the transformation of the divine myth into a heroic saga*. At the beginning of that process stand the realized myths and rituals grouped around the divine couple, in which the human element, including the extreme of the human sacrifice, appears to serve no other purpose than to objectify the divine—though this actually happens only in order to ensure that the divine couple properly carries out its function of preserving the plants and beasts and thus providing for the existence of the human community. The realized myth is a magic compulsion of the gods, based on a dramatic imitation of the divine myth and serving the purpose of eliminating every element of chance by the total submission of human life under the natural cycle. At the end of the same process stands the absolute power of the hero's sword, the effectiveness of which at first and on a superficial view appears to be determined purely by absolute chance.

Now the myth of the dead god is an extremely pointed expression of the new human type's way of looking on the decaying old rituals. But the new human type, symbolized in the figure of the hero, is thoroughly formed by the decay of the old religion of nature, which thought to give absolute security to human life by absolute subordination under the lawful course of nature. The Germanic concept of fate, in particular, has been formed in its most profound content by this decay of the religion of nature and by the void it left behind.

To appreciate the full significance of this revolutionary turn from a religion of fertility to a religion of the dead god—as far as that can still be called a religion—we have to keep in mind that the fate of men is usually reflected in the fate of the gods. Not only Adonis rose anew in every spring—the return of vegetative growth, identical with the return of the youthful god, was also a pledge of the return of *all* life. For those peasants, as the vegetation dies and is reborn, so is man. Conversely, belief in the irreversible death of the god of fertility is in turn an explicit, tragic renunciation of that faith. Nothing is clearer than that the myth of Balder's death is meant to reflect the radical change from an aeon of joy to an aeon of mourning. Like every great myth, the death of Balder is not a mere piece of literature, but an image of the fate of the entire culture that produced it. The world, deprived of the resurrection of that magnificent young god, has become sad, bleak, and empty—that is the meaning of the great reversal.

In contrast to the Adonis-Freyr myth, whose gradual evolution out of peasant usage would be easy to follow, a myth like that of Balder springs from one head or a small group of heads. There exists no example for a spontaneous, systematic changeover of such natural symbols as the saving mother, the procreational force of the evergreen, the victory of spring over the ice giant into their—in themselves absurd—opposites. The myth of Balder as we know it has been thought out and reflects a conscious spiritual revolution. Some parts of it, like the burning ship ritual, Nanna's death from love, and certainly the resurrection after Ragnarök are clearly late, from early or late Viking times. But it would be impermissible for that reason to assume a date from late Viking times for the Balder myth as a whole. What, then, is the alternative?

Here we return to Much's proof that the parallel expression of faith in the finality of death in the Helgi song had already gained acceptance in wide circles at a time when the Suebians were still settled east of the Elbe, hence briefly before the beginning of the Christian era.[8] This gives us a fairly exact date for the core of the myth of the dead god. But at the same time, the immense force with which that faith in the omnipotence of death was put into the center of the Helgi song, and that in explicit, mythical "polemics" against the opposite faith in a possibility of resurrection, proves that such "faith in death" was then still new to the Germanic tribes. Much's date for this epoch in the history of religion, shifted forward by two centuries according to more recent researches on the seats of the Eastern Germanic tribes, then lies not quite a century before the appearance of Arminius—which can hardly be shoved aside as a coincidence.

Not only the essence and direction of this transformation from the old religion of nature to the young heroic saga, but also its approximate date are thus becoming clear in outline. This does not yet answer the question of which forces in the life of the Germanic tribes brought about this kind of transformation at that time. But this much is clear even now: *if* the

8. See note 5 above.

process of transformation from the religion of nature to the cult of heroes becomes once presentable concretely, we shall also possess a clear picture— not indeed of the origin of the West, but of the origin of those basic features of the Nordic spirit which entered the fundamental character of the emerging West as one of two constituent elements. The other, far better known, of those two constituent elements is late antiquity.

CHAPTER FIVE

The Gods of the Ancient Germans

The hero of the Germanic saga is, then, a one-time fertility god transformed into a mortal man exposed to an uncertain fate. The idea of the hero who inescapably lives toward his tragic end is the mythical deposit from the decay of the Wanic cults that were founded on a belief in resurrection. The question thus arises: did those heroes of the saga have to face their fate alone, or were there still gods standing by their side? So far research, notwithstanding some disagreements in detail, has been unanimous in giving an affirmative answer to that question; more exactly, it took that answer so much for granted that it has never clearly formulated, let alone argued it. In doing so, it had chiefly the Ase gods, hence above all the divine triad Wotan-Donar-Ziu, in mind, but it also assumed that the Wanic cults lived on. To the Ase Gods in turn, a very great age was ascribed, so that Ase and Wanic cults were supposed to have largely overlapped in time. True, it was theoretically admitted that the Wanic cults were the older ones; yet if some of the time estimates for the origin of the Ase cults are considered, it appears that simply no room would be left for even older Wanic cults, while conversely some of the estimates for the end of the Wanic cults coincide with the overall end of paganism, so that the insight that Wanic and Ase gods represent two successive generations in time is wholly obscured. In such a view, the profound religious crisis underlying and accompanying the end of the fertility cults disappears, leaving behind an idea of the "gradual evolution" of Germanic religion suiting the taste of the nineteenth century which in its bourgeois decorum tabooed all revolutionary shocks.

We consider that concept as totally wrong. In our opinion, a deep gulf separates the Wanic cults with their predominantly female, chthonic and calendaric emphasis from the purely male, warlike, Ase cults linked to peripeties of fate not tied to any calendar. The assumption of a "gradual" transition from one religion to the other seems absurd to us, though of course there exists an objective link between the downfall of one religion and the origin of the other. That there ever existed a period of coexistence of those two diametrically opposed religious experiences can also not be presupposed but must be proved in detail—we shall try to show that this occurred only to a very limited extent. Thus the assumption of Ase cults coinciding in time with the climax of the Wanic religion is automatically excluded, and the chronological hypotheses for the origin of the Ase cults require radical reexamination—how radical is indicated by the total absence of any impact of these gods in the oldest stratum of the heroic saga.

Our last remark already offers an answer to the question raised at the opening of this chapter. No: originally no gods stood by the side of the ancient Germanic heroes on their tragic road; not before the Viking age, not before that layer of the Edda expressed most clearly in the older Helgi song, can direct intervention of the gods, and of Odin in particular, in the fate of the heroes be proven. That has often been noted, but the question of its meaning has never been raised. The epic prelude to the great cultures, the first age when they step out from ahistoric existence into historicity, is also regularly the age of the reflection of history in the ahistoric archetypes. In that process, the still impersonal numina of the primitives normally merge with the high gods of the preceding high cultures to form new generations of gods—and a new pantheon arises side by side with a new heroic saga. Without that new pantheon, the Indo-Aryan, the Hellenic, almost any heroic saga would be unthinkable; closest integration of divine existence and human fate is the very essence of all of them—except the ancient Germanic one. The absence of gods in the ancient Germanic saga is something unique. Only he who regards saga, in accordance with contemporary fashion, as mere poetry and nothing else, can ignore the historic significance of that "godlessness." In reality, the saga is for the whole long prelude to the high cultures the central medium for their becoming aware of their own situation with all its given external and internal, political and religious conditions. Political and religious upheavals are underlying those sagas without exception, but only with the ancient Germans did they lead to a saga without gods. But what would gods mean who in an age of sagas played no role in the latter? Godless did Germanic history begin (after the collapse of the fertility cults), and that fact has determined decisively not only the character of ancient Germanic paganism, but also of Germanic Christianity and subsequently of Western Christianity—and with it of Western civilization.

The songs about gods confirm what the early layers of the heroic songs show so clearly. Here, too, research has by no means been blind to the fact itself: it is generally recognized that the Eddic songs about gods are lacking in religious significance to a striking degree. Some of them, above all the whole Skrinir song with its narrative of the wooing of (G)erd by Freyr, belong to the Wanic religion: Gerd is the goddess of the earth, the Magna Mater. Most of the rest belongs in the late, theologizing phase of paganism and deals, in one or the other form, always with the doom of the gods, not with their eternal reign: it is a kind of extended lament about the dead god. In between there lie the Viking pieces, reflecting a short phase of experienced belief in gods—and even here only in an auxiliary role for heroic strength and heroic fate.

Let nobody say that an *argumentum ex silentio* could prove nothing. For this poetry does not really keep silent about the gods; only their role is even worse when they are talked about than when they are kept silent about—and even worse where the question of their existence is treated with profound seriousness (as in the Völuspa, where just for that reason their nothingness and helplessness is recognized), than where they are mocked, as in the Lokasenna. In the heroic songs their role is almost poorer where they are mentioned (but where their intervention is more than modest, as in the older Helgi song) than where they *ought* to be but are not, as with the doom of the Nibelungen in the oldest Atli song. That they are absent where they are needed most and present where they are least required, that alone argues for a phenomenon of religious history unique in an age of saga: the godlessness of the ancient Germans. Of course, absence of gods is not the same as absence of religion—but more about that later.

The poetic Edda and a few fragments in old high German furnish one group of the primary evidence. A second is offered by the Runic inscriptions, German and Nordic, which in their variety serve magic purposes. Here if anywhere the *argumentum ex silentio* is crucial: they *must* contain appeals to gods, as do Hellenic and Near Eastern inscriptions, if a living faith in high gods existed. They do indeed contain such appeals—but only after a point in time that can be shown exactly—and it follows with compelling logic that no living faith in high gods existed *before* that point in time. Here, too, the facts—the absence of names of gods during the early period—are uncontested. To escape the logical conclusions, strange auxiliary hypotheses were resorted to, first from naive prejudice, later in the service of the Nazis' Wotanomania. Thus Magnus Olsen[1]

---

1. Magnus Olsen, *To nye fund av urnordiske runer* (Trondheim: Brun i komm, 1941).

declares the naming of Gods in the runes as a younger phenomenon
showing already Christian influence—a claim we shall meet again and again
in different forms so as to explain the total absence of evidence for the
Ase gods in the early period of the Sagas. It is a fantastic explanation,
since gods normally manifest themselves by their name: to ascribe to the
Germanic tribes a taboo against divine names of the kind established in
the Jewish decalogue is to rely on an assumption based on nothing but
the complete absence of all divine names in the early period. Just as well,
an exactly opposite assumption may be resorted to according to taste—
thus Bäsecke[2] explains the absence of divine names in the heroic songs
by a very early Christian influence on the Goths, whom he supposes to
have exerted decisive influence in their time on the entire Germanic saga
poetry: "perhaps without Gothic influence it would not have arrived that
the pagan gods no longer played a role in the Germanic heroic songs."
The "no longer" in this sentence speaks volumes: it describes the existence of high gods in the early period of the sagas as so self-evident that
it becomes impermissible to doubt it—one may only ask how those un-
discoverable gods have vanished from the sagas! In what lost works of
primeval Germanic poetry the glory of the (Ase) gods is supposed to
have shone remains the Wotanic secret of the author.

   On such fantastic assumptions the attempt is then built to prove that
the Ase gods, who turn up in the early saga period neither in songs nor
in the magic formulas of Runic inscriptions, may be found *hidden* in the
personal names of that period—both in those reported in history and above
all in those mentioned in runes. It has to be recognized that this assumption makes more sense for ancient Germanic documents than for
archaic documents from most other cultures; paraphrase in fact plays a
great role there, and is known to have been raised into a basic form of
poetry in the Skaldic Kenningar. But pointing to the Kenningar of late
Viking poetry as a model for the formation of names in the period of
the early sagas merely anticipates the chief error of that whole method
of interpretation—the projection of figures from late Viking religion into
the early period of the Germanic heroic age. Just as the earlier complete
absence of divine names amply used in the Viking age should raise
suspicion against the assumption of a cult of Ase high gods in early times,
so the absence of the Kenningar in the early layers of the heroic song
should be taken as a warning against looking uncritically for Skaldic
paraphrases in the early period. That does not imply that such paraphrases
must be *completely* absent there. Only strict criticism is required—criticism

---

2. See, e.g., Georg Baesecke, *Kleinere Schriften zur althochdeutschen Sprache und Literatur*
(Bern & Munich: Francke, 1966).

in each particular case not only of the assumption of paraphrases in principle, but also, where they do exist, of the uncritical reading of an Ase god's name where a Wanic one would obviously fit in better.

We begin our examples with the oldest of all Runic inscriptions. On a not Germanic, but Etruscan helmet found in Styria and dated back to the third pre-Christian century, we find the Runic inscription *Herigast*. At once, the Wotanomanes conclude, reading heri = lord = Wotan, that this Herigast was a "Wotan's man." Now heri is first of all a simple adjective, expressing greatness and significance. That is shown in such names as the extremely frequent Heriulf, which of course does *not* mean "Wotan's wolf" (the wolf is Wotan's enemy and doom), but "powerful wolf"—a most appropriate name for a war lord, whether among ancient Germans or American Indians! Hence it is quite uncertain whether the name Herigast is theophorous at all; if that is more plausible here than in the case of Heriulf, it is so because of the second part "gast" which describes a follower, so that one may suppose that the first part may contain the name of the lord. "Great follower" makes no good sense, seems rather a *contradictio in adjecto*, "follower of lord" has no content at all. "Follower of the exalted" sounds more convincing, and the exalted might well be a god.

But must this god be Wotan—for no other reason than that the epithet heri is found later for Wotan? How does one know to whom that epithet referred in the third century B.C., for which we lack even the slightest documentary proof? It is certain only that at the time, the Wanic religion ruled in large parts of the Germanic territory, and that the name of its highest god, Freyr, also means "lord." Supposing, then, that we are dealing with an epithet for a god, what could be more natural than the assumption that the "heri" in Herigast referred to Freyr, and that the name meant "servant of Freyr"? This would imply the further assumption that the attribute "heri" was later transferred from Freyr to Odin like much else; would it indeed have been improbable that attributes of the highest Wanic god should have been transferred to the highest Ase god? In late Viking times, hardly before, Heri became a kind of alternative to Odin's proper name. Here Christian influence presumably played a role: the New Testament epithet "the Lord" for Jesus was taken over and consciously used in an anti-Christian sense.

But it is no accident that the paradigm Herigast, six centuries older than the oldest other Runic finds, goes back to the time when the Wanic religion was alive. The names from the period of the early heroic sagas do not hide any such theophorous meaning, as shown above in the example of Heriulf. Rather, we can clearly observe in that period a return of theophorous adjectives to their sober everyday meaning. Let us next take the name of Ullther (Owulthuthewar in the archaic Germanic of the runes) that is found on one of the oldest Danish runic finds, the sword clamp of Thorberg, dated about 300 A.D. The Wanic god Ull, related to Freyr and immensely popular in Wanic times, seems intended, and the name seems to mean "servant of Ull." The interpretation would appear to be beyond doubt, since the name of the god is directly contained in the name of the owner of the clamp (or in the name of the sword itself). But Grienberger has the much more plausible interpretation "*gloriae serviens*," because Ull has also an adjectival meaning of "radiant," "shining," and a cult of Ull has been proven in Sweden and also in Norway, but not in Denmark. Perhaps it should also be pointed out that 300 A.D. would be rather late for dedicating a sword to Ull. The case is interesting because the same name would have properly to be related to Ull if the sword had been found further to the North and 300 years earlier, and because it can hardly be assumed that the existence of that god was entirely unknown in Denmark; but the knowledge was irrelevant there. Here we can touch with our hands a piece of the process in which an adjective may rise to become a divine epithet and then a god's name, only to resume its adjectival role—perhaps more than a millennium later.

The inverse development, how a noun may be turned into the name of a—this time Ase—god is shown by a runic inscription on a stone from Tune: there the name is woðuriðr, and the connection with Woðan, or more exactly with his precursor Woðr, seems indisputable. The inscription belongs to the sixth century; it is the oldest of all inscriptions containing the root woð and thus highly significant. The name is difficult to interpret—it could mean "fury rider" or "Woðr rider"; at any rate it would be related to something Wotanic. But it does not prove that we are already dealing with a personal god: the furious ride of the furious host presupposes many furious riders.

Our doubt that the process of personification had matured even by the sixth century is reinforced by an inscription from about the same time on a stone in Swedish Vanga bearing the name of Haukoðr. There, the interpretation "Odin's raven" really seems obvious. And yet Noreen[3] translates, in my view not overly cautiously, "he who hunts with the hawk." A Wotanic interpretation of the oðr would in this case be questionable because it forms the second part of the word, whereas elsewhere the God's name or the divine epithet without exception makes up the

3. Adolf Noreen, *Altislandische und altnorwegische Grammatik* (Halle/S.; Niemeyer, 1923).

first part of a name. Since oðr still conserves at the same time the impersonal meanings of fury and chase, Noreen's reading must definitely be preferred. Perhaps it should be added that Wotan-Odin is linguistically distinct from woðr-oðr by the fact that the added syllable an-in clearly lifts the god above the underlying, impersonal concepts of fury and chase, while those latter ideas always remain prominent with the shorter original root. Oðr would then never have been a fully personified god but would rather denote the god in the process of the growth of this individual person out of the indistinct plurality of the furious host. That corresponds to the fact that we find several Oðr- names that can be dated just to the sixth century, but later only names with Wotan or Odin. Names with Thor come still a little later, Ziu-names are known not to exist at all. Instead of the unsupported assumptions about Christian influence inhibiting or promoting the evolution of Germanic gods' names, we thus find by our approach distinct traces of a process of personification reaching its goal around 600 A.D.

We should keep that date of 600 A.D. in mind, because it is also the date of the first Nordic inscription definitely referring to the Ase gods. It is found on the Swedish stone of Noleby and runs: *Runo fahi raginok-undo.* "Ragino," old Norse "regin," is the usual collective name of the Ase gods. The inscription describes runic signs as a divine art. [And still even here, some doubt remains about the degree of personification. True, in later Eddic texts the expression "regin" denotes without doubt, almost as a *terminus technicus* of theology, the gods living and governing in Walhall. Could it around 600 still have had a broader meaning, not sharply separating gods from mere numina? Still, the word "ruling" would hardly fit mere demons whom the ancient Germans knew how to bend to their will by various types of magic. The concept of "high gods" probably was implied from the beginning.]

Aser, the plural of As or Ase, is very close to Regin in its meaning. In the singular, it is much older than Regin in names on runic inscriptions, as shown for instance by the Jarl Asgisl, who has perpetuated himself on the stem of a lance in Danish Kragehul around 400 A.D. *Gisl* when occurring in names means a scout or guard, in its original meaning staff or stick. To call a hero a staff or a guard of gods would be meaningless in the domain of the fully developed Ase religion: there, the gods guard the men and not vice versa. It would be different with an object with magic qualities, which itself would be a dead thing and hence in need to be guarded. With that, we have arrived straight at the original meaning of the word ase or anse, which at first simply meant a beam. But particular beams in the house of a nobleman are marked by magic qualities:

they are fetishes representing the ancestors, as it were penates without images enjoying a regular cult; this worship of the ancestors of the clan Jordanes[4] still experienced in the sixth century among the Christianized and semiromanized Ostrogoths—how much more must it have survived around 400 among the Danes! In fact, it still plays a role in late Viking times in the form of the worship of the pillars of the high seat: the Viking approaching land throws one such pillar into the sea, and where it drifts ashore, he builds his new house—for there the spirits of the ancestors have taken their seat.

Asgisl thus means "guard of the clan" or of the clan spirits, just as Asmund means "protector of the clan spirits" (from *mund*, protection), or possibly in the passive sense "protected by the clan spirits." In the period preceding the full unfolding of the Ase high religion, such expressions while carrying a clear religious meaning need not yet be interpreted as referring to high gods; they may still refer to impersonal numina such as sacred house jambs, swords, and the like, whose central importance for the religion of the early saga period we have here the first occasion to point out.

Things are no different on German soil. Here, too, authentic pointers to the Ase religion are missing in personal names before the seventh century. The seemingly older Kehrlich primer, containing the all too obvious inscription "*wotani heilag*" is today regarded as a forgery. The futhark-signs (*futhark* refers to the archaic use of runes as ideograms for words) on the Herbrechtingen primer are difficult to interpret. Arntz[5] reads "wealth-giant-Ase-horse"; by relating horse to Ase, he obtains Wotan with his horse Sleipnir, with Wotan and wealth surrounding the evil giant—a supposed appeal to Wotan against giants. But we are on safe ground only with the primer of roughly equal age from Nordendorf near Augsburg which bears the three gods' names of Lođur, Wodan, Wigithonar—the first mention of Wotan's name in a document in a Germanic language, the first evidence for Thor as a high god, the first announcement of the worship of an Ase triad of gods, at the same time evidence that the third Ase standing besides Wotan and Donar was always ill-defined. Beside those highly important proofs it is of small importance that the god's name of Lođur remains somewhat problematic. From then onwards, the god's names in the runes continue without a break. They are found often both in direct appeals to them and as part of theophorous

---

4. Jordanes, *De Getarum sive Gothorum origine et rebus gestis* (Freiburg & Tübingen: Mohn, 1882).

5. Helmut Arntz, *Handbuch der Runenkunde* (Halle/S.: Niemeyer, 1944).

personal names. Among the latter there are, for reasons still to be discussed, no Wotan-names, but Thornames in ever-growing numbers.

A special discussion of personal names handed down to us not in runes but in literature would add nothing new in principle to our result. It is unimportant whether a personal name is handed down in an inscription or in a literary source: in either case, it dates from the time in which the named person lived and preserves the ideas of that time. Now the personal names are by far the best source for the chronology of living religion, with the exception of direct appeals to the gods preserved in inscriptions. In their importance as a source, they far surpass songtexts (which have never been preserved in the original form and have lost much and acquired something else compared with the former) on one side, and the place names often used in the discussion about the Ase gods on the other. For place names often endure, apart from mere sound shifts, for millennia without any visible evidence for their time of origin, which is always available for personal names—whether the latter are chronologically attested themselves, or whether only the inscriptions on which they are found can be dated.

Magnus Olsen, to whom we owe the basic and still authoritative studies on place name research and particularly on their use for the religious history of the ancient Germans, has developed ingenious methods for overcoming that difficulty. Theophorous place names, just like theophorous personal names, regularly contain a second, nontheophorous part which usually describes the character of the locality (house, temple, field, pasture, slope, etc.) dedicated to the god. Now the expressions for those topographic characteristics have changed and therefore in turn offer an indication for dating the names, hence for dating the foundation of the settlements or shrines in question. The method yields a lot of information about the extension of the cults of particular gods (for instance, our above statement about the absence of an Ullr cult in Denmark is based on the results of place name research); it also permits a clear distinction between Christian and pre-Christian layers. Yet there exists in the whole Nordic topographic vocabulary not a single expression that occurs *only* in pre-Viking times—not even the expressions for field and pasture sometimes mentioned in that context. If it were different, it would be possible, for instance, to date Odensaker in the first half of the first Christian millennium—but that is not the case. In fact, neither Olsen nor any one of his pupils has attempted to use the dating of placenames for a differential dating of the particular Germanic gods or groups of gods. Rather the situation is reversed: while in separating the foundations of Christian and pre-Christian settlements one can use the topographical parts of the place names to good effect, any attempt to fix chronologically settlements *within* the pagan period will have to start from the theophorous parts of their names. Each step towards a clarification of the chronology of Germanic pagan beliefs will be directly usable for the chronology of the foundations of Nordic settlements.

On the other hand, place name research gives a very clear picture of the territorial spread of each particular cult, and thus supplements the chronological insights gained from the study of inscriptions, songs, and personal names. The first striking impression on that issue is how thinly spread theophorous names are on the continent compared to Scandinavia. To appreciate the significance of that fact, one must bear in mind that the conversion of the Saxons to Christianity falls into the beginning of the ninth century, at the end of which the conversion of the Danes begins already. With the end of the tenth century, the normal process of conversion has been completed all over Scandinavia. Thus the delay in the Christianization of the North compared with Germany is by no means sufficient to explain the massive difference in the spread of theophorous names in the two areas—all the less, since Germany was, of course, much more densely populated at all times. One more indication pointing to a much later development of high gods in Germany than in the North!

But that difference in turn, as to be expected, is connected with the difference between Wanic and Ase religion. A very large part of the theophorous placenames in Scandinavia are of Wanic origin (formed with Ullr, Freyr, Njördr, etc.). But on the continent, Wanic place names are found only in Northern Germany proper, and even there not in large numbers. (In Eastern Germany, as in the whole area of settlement of the Eastern Germanic tribes, Germanic theophorous place names are almost wholly absent due to the exodus of the ancient Germans and to the overlaying of their traces by Slavs and other peoples.)

The density of Wanic place names in Scandinavia, their rarity in North-western Germany, their absence in Southern Germany proves that the Wanic cults had always their origin and main seat in Scandinavia—besides also in the Eastern Germanic area, as witnessed by the account of Tacitus discussed below. This finding completely agrees with the evidence of another source, to wit that of the numerous Scandinavian rock drawings showing a cult of fertility and the sun fully corresponding to all our other knowledge of the Wanic cults. The most cautious scholars date the earliest of those rock drawings to the end of the second pre-Christian millennium, bolder spirits even to its first third. So great an age and so long a duration of the Wanic cults in the North in turn excellently fits with the frequency and wide geographic spread of Wanic theophorous names all over Scandinavia.

As shown by the place names, the Wanic cults never penetrated further South than the borderline which separated Germanic from Celtic territory *before* the beginning of the Germanic Southward drive. Further South, only Ase theophorous names exist. The two most important names of Ase gods, Wotan and Donar, have a South German colonial character, and their Nordic homologues Odin and Thor have been derived from the South German forms. Thus the Ase religion has arisen in the South of the Germanic domain, hence in a region to which the Wanic cults had never penetrated as shown by place name research. That means: even if the Ase cults overlapped with the Wanic ones or at least directly followed them in terms of dates, there could still be no question of a continuity between both religions, because they belong originally to quite different regions—regions which were thoroughly different also in language and culture, inasmuch as the Wanic cults belong to a purely Germanic background, whereas the Ase cults arose on merely Germanized colonial soil and in the zone of most intense contact with antiquity.

Overlaps have taken place but are secondary. In Lower Saxony, the Ase religion pushed out the Wanic religion which had always been weak there (no rock drawings!). In Denmark, Norway, and Iceland it obtained the upper hand over the latter; only the cult of Freyr survived there besides that of Odin and Thor—all other remnants of the Wanic religion became mere literature. The couple of divine siblings alone still enjoyed true godlike worship, because the purely masculine and warlike Ase religion lacked all erotic or fertility cults, while the ethos that had been built on those cults through millennia still imperiously demanded them. In Sweden—the Germanic land farthest from the area of origin of the Ase religion-after the end of the Voelkerwanderung, that couple maintained a live competition with Odin, so that there the Ase religion never completely subordinated the Wanic religion. There, and only there, a true merging of the two types of belief took place, which still clearly manifests itself today in the tenacious survival of age-old fertility cults in Sweden.

The misleading impression of a continuity of Wanic and Ase religion is, however, less due to the Swedish development than to the purely literary Icelandic sources of religous history. That secondary overlaying of Wanic and Ase religion took place entirely at the expense of the Wanic religion—it was the fruit of a late offensive of the Ase faith against a Wanic faith which, though still intact in Eastern Scandinavia, was already moribund in Western Scandinavia and Northern Germany. Yet the picture would be incomplete without mention of a Wanic countercurrent running from North to South, but characteristically effective *outside* the cultic area. We are referring to the "secularization" of the originally Wanic Freyr-Balder archetype through the myth of the dead god into the human Siegfried archetype, already discussed in the preceding chapter. That mythical archetype, product of the decay of the Wanic faith, has radiated much farther towards the Southwest than any piece of living Wanic religion—as proved by its penetration into the narratives of Frankish-Burgundian political saga.

We are undertaking at least an attempt to fix the geographic and chronological coordinates of that radiation (with regard to the content of that archetype, we did it in the preceding chapter). The attempt is made more difficult but not impossible by the lack of material from Eastern Germanic place names. Based on the previously discussed elements of the Helgi saga (and on Tacitus), we assume that the Northern Germanic tribes migrating to the Baltic area and further South and Southeast from there carried their intact Wanic cults along with them. In Northwest Germany that proved more difficult, because the Northalbingian advance into this region was not a simple conquest but characterized by an interpenetration and fusion with non-Scandinavian Germanic tribes from which in the end the Saxon people emerged. *That* is reflected in the scarcity of Wanic place names in that region, as also in the relative frequency of Balder names among the few place names of that kind. Any chthonic cult is threatened if its carriers move too far from its great places of worship—it is attached to the soil. If ethnic and cultural crossbreeding is added, it may easily decay. Thus while later the warlike cult of the Ase flourished all the more vigorously the farther it spread, the chthonic Wanic cult succumbed even to the limited demands of a penetration of Lower Saxony starting from Slesvig. Lower Saxony was a transitional zone between the Germanic North, which had been self-contained for millennia, and the merely Germanized colonial area. It had been Germanic since the Indogermanic irruption at the latest, but had still been penetrated anew from the North and politically reorganized like the colonial area proper further South; its religion had been influenced by the Scandinavian Wanic cults but had dissolved them instead of being thoroughly shaped by them— so it was presumably that area where the decay of the Wanic religion began. In this account, we shall meet the Lower Saxon region again and again as the middle and the mediator between the other Germanic regions.

Presumably, the Siegfried figure as an archetype is of Lower Saxon origin. That it came to Scandinavia from the South, like Odin and Thor, is undisputed. Only the story of its migration is more complicated than that of the Ase gods: the latter have travelled a straight road from Southern Germany to Iceland, while the Siegfried figure was originally received, as Balder, from the North and then handed back to the North in a transformed shape. The only question is how far to the South that transformation from the dead god to the death-doomed hero took place. The answer must be: in the most Southward area still reached by Balder— therefore in Lower Saxony. That excellently fits the assumption that the Siegfried archetype merged with the figure of Arminius into a saga among the Cheruscans, the most Southern branch of the later Saxon people. That would make it also at last really comprehensible how Arminius came to arrogate to himself the divine predicate "ermin"—it adds a new dimension to his hubris. From that, the dating follows: the collapse of the Wanic cults in Lower Germany took place around the beginning of our era, not without causal connection with the contact with the Romans. Between it and the appearance of the Ase cults in the same area, no less than six centuries have passed.

Further South there was no such trough between two religions of two kinds of gods, because there the Wanic religion was missing altogether. On the other hand, the Siegfried type moved on—with the Lower German Ripuarian Franks as middlemen and in the context of the downfall of their dynasty—to the Middle Rhine and finally to Burgundy. A new condensation of disparate and antagonistic elements! If there ever was any history subject to the law of *Tyche*, it was that of the Merovingians, and indeed, it was felt as a play of wild coincidence, as one can convince oneself by reading Gregory of Tours. Here the way of thought and life of late antiquity had prevailed; and it would have remained like that if the Germanic idea of fate, coming from the North in the shape of the Siegfried archetype, had not breathed into that series of wild and ugly coincidences a meaning which could only be a tragic one. Thus at that crack in the young Frankish realm which separated the Romanic and Germanic domains, late antiquity met the high North—both ultimately imprinted by the Near East, the North through its fertility cults, late antiquity through its belief in *Tyche*; the Nordic element transformed by Lower Saxon and Lower Frankish intercession into the belief in fate, the Southern belief in coincidence heightened in passing through the Merovingian realm to total decay of all order. From the union of those two, the first germ of the Western spirit emerged.

We have moved far ahead, but we have left an enemy standing to our rear: the sources of late antiquity regarding Germanic religion. So far, we have based our conclusions on the autochthonous, Germanic sources on Germanic religious history—no doubt the methodically correct starting point. But though the representatives of the doctrine of the great age of the Ase cults include not a few opponents of the Latin and Greek sources— among them by no means only Wotanomanes—still certain quotations from Tacitus constitute the heaviest guns available to the defenders of a very old Ase high religion. True, other ancient authors offer quite different accounts. The whole field requires a brief discussion, which will throw light on further aspects of the Ase religion.

But before Tacitus, some even earlier ancient authors have to be mentioned. In their writings, Celtic and Germanic tribes can at first not be separated—as is known, only Caesar made this distinction clear, and even he still with a somewhat unsure hand. Thus we cannot bypass the statement of Strabo about the Celts: according to some, "the Gallians were said to be without Gods, but the Celtiberians and those living farther to the North to worship some nameless god."[6] Those "living farther to the North" are clearly Germanic tribes. The testimony should not have been pushed aside—showing as it does, among other points, a by no means surprising parallel between Germanic and Celtic spiritual attitudes which is quite credible for the continental Germanic tribes. The Wanic religion of the North is not relevant here, rather Strabo's testimony confirms the sharp dividing line we drew between the religion of the continental Germanic tribes and that of the Scandinavians—a view confirmed in turn by the complete absence on the continent of anything corresponding to the Scandinavian rock drawings. Aristotle, too, notes with disapproval that the Celts are alleged to be without gods; so does Ptolemy—both without distinguishing between Germanic and Celtic tribes. Strabo's slightly more exact hint at "some nameless god" offers a key for our understanding. A nameless god cannot have been a high god—but absence of gods does not mean absence of religion; it must have been a matter of mere numina.

That, at any rate, was Caesar's[7] opinion. With him, there are Gallic high gods with their altars; instead of simply assuming that Strabo and Ptolemy had been ignorant whereas Caesar knew the Gallians, it would have been wiser to take all their accounts seriously and to see the contradictions as reflexes of differences in time and space. Elsewhere Caesar supplements his statement: the Germanic tribes, he says, were thoroughly different from the Gallians in matters of religion, they had neither Druids nor a regular worship of Gods. "Only such are gods for them which they can see and which are obviously useful to them; of other gods they

6. Strabonis *Geographica*, 3 vols. (Rome Publ. offic. polygraph., 1963).
7. C. Julius Caesar, *De Bello Gallico*.

have never heard." True, in translating this passage I have put "such" and "which" instead of "those" and "whom"—but in Latin it simply is impossible to use after *dei* the neutral relative "quae" instead of the masculine "quos." I believe that the masculine form has had a misleading effect: Caesar was talking about something "immediately useful" like housebeams and swords—otherwise no gods. But this did not fit into the picture of the dominant current of research. Tacitus fitted better; Caesar was shoved aside with a wave of the hand. Yet he documents the same state of affairs which we have inferred from the Germanic sources. With the Gallians, who were hardly touched by the fertility cults, the same state of affairs was evidently reached even earlier.

Caesar's next statement, that the Germanic tribes worshipped sun, moon, and fire, does not fit his concept of a purely practical religion. It might for the fire, which could refer to a cult of smiths who in the saga are often treated as similar to the gods. But the sun and even the moon? Here we get unmistakably into the domain of the rock drawings, in which sun images and moon symbols play an outstanding role, hence into the domain of the Wanic religion. Caesar was not sufficiently informed to distinguish the Wanic high gods of nature in the North from the nameless numina of the South by geography and content. Instead he tried to harmonize the different accounts of his sources about different phenomena so as to merge them into a unified picture. That has created confusion. But his testimony about sun- and moon-cults in his own time confirms at any rate that the religion of the rock drawings was then still very much alive.

And now to Tacitus! Among the more important sources of antiquity, this rhetorical and moralistic stoic, writing from the safety of Rome, who in writing his Germania was far more concerned with sermonizing and literary effect than with exactitude, is surely the poorest. But he, too, has made use of accounts from people who were close to Germanic reality, and is not entirely worthless. His remark about the origin of certain fertility cults from far away and his (even if only half correct) comparison of those cults with that of Isis are flashes of understanding. On the other hand, he hopelessly confuses his material: for instance, he claims that Nerthus was worshipped by all Germanic tribes, while the archaeological finds attest unmistakably that she was worshipped only East of the Elbe and close to the sea; also, the connection between the human sacrifices in the "grove of fetters" and the fertility cults escapes him. The most important evidence offered by this material is the proof of very lively Wanic cults among the East Germanic tribes, and in Tacitus' own time.

For those cults Tacitus knows of two Germanic goddesses, Alci and Nerthus, and one oriental one, Isis. We are moving into a quite different field with the Latin names given by Tacitus to certain Germanic gods: he names Mercury, Mars, and Hercules. Caeser had named—not for the Germanic but the Celtic tribes—Mercury, Apollo, Mars, Jupiter, and Minerva (in this sequence). It is difficult to reject the conjecture that our rhetor has here adorned himself with borrowed plumes, simply taking over a shortened version of Caesar's list; he has only inserted Hercules in the place of Jupiter. But plausible as that may be, it is not the whole explanation and not sufficient for ignoring the passage, for it constitutes the real *pièce de résistance* of the entire Ase research. Without it, nobody would ever have spoken with so much certainty of an early origin of the Ases. As rendered by Tacitus, the passage *may* be regarded as a typical *interpretatio Romana*, an introduction of Roman gods' names for barbaric gods. Thus one looks for the corresponding Germanic names, and finds them in the Ase triad—Wotan (Mercury), Ziu (Mars), and Donar (Hercules).

But even that would be a mirage if the Germanic names for the days of the week did not exist. Only in combination with those has Tacitus become the prime witness for the early existence of the Ases. That Latin *Mercurii dies* became Wednesday (Wotansday) is supposed finally to confirm the equation Mercury = Wotan; just so the *Martis dies* corresponds to Tuesday (Alemannic Ziestag = Ziu's day). In assuming the identity of those Roman gods with the named Germanic gods, scholars not only took note of the indisputable fact that Mercury's day had been translated into Wotan's day, Mars' day into Ziu's day, but came to regard on the basis of those equations also the altars of Mercury and Mars in the Roman Germania as shrines of Wotan and Ziu that had merely been given Latin names. With that interpretation, every altar of Mercury and Mars and even of Hercules on Rhine and Mosel, of which there are many, becomes evidence for an Ase religion under Roman rule from the first century A.D. onwards. The identification between Germanic and Roman gods thus rests on two arguments, an early Roman one and a purely Germanic one of uncertain later date, on Roman altars on one side, Germanic day names on the other.

Let us first deal with the altars. They might perhaps be really regarded as altars of Wotan and Ziu if they were simply dedicated to Mercury or Mars respectively. There are very many altars just of those gods in the Roman Germania on the left bank of the Rhine—not an astonishing fact, since its Roman population consisted quite overwhelmingly of merchants and soldiers. Since the soldiers were rarely Italics, more often Gallians, in many cases ancient Germans, it is not surprising to find the Roman high gods frequently adorned in the inscriptions on those altars with non-Latin surnames. A condensation of Roman gods with local gods, not so much of the Germanic tribes but of the ethnically mixed lower stratum of the Roman Germania, has thus taken place without doubt. That could provide a triumph for the age-old Ase cults—but for the fact that all those local surnames were completely unknown elsewhere, only a few female names excepted. The local gods that were worshipped here in the shape and under the name of Roman high gods were not unnamed— they were named but unknown; they had a strictly limited range in space and time, and no literary source has recorded those names. What is supposed to prove the existence of Wotanic cults thus proves their non-existence. For since nobody in the Roman Germania was inhibited in giving local surnames to the high gods, it is quite certain that Wotan, Ziu, and Donar would have been named if those gods had been known at that time. This also disposes of the theory that the ancient Germans had had the habit not to use the names of their real gods; they did.

But now begins the game we already have come to know. Behind those numerous surnames that differ almost from one altar to the next, the Germanic high gods are supposed to be hidden—as they are supposed to be hidden behind the early Germanic personal names. As before into every Heri and As, so now a Wotan, Ziu, and Donar are read into every Channo, Thingsus, and Magusanus. Having said so much about that method before, we no longer need to refute it again at this point: it merely deserves to be condemned outright.

Nevertheless, those altars offer some hints with regard to Tacitus' Germania. Among the gods worshipped in the Roman Germania, besides Mercury and Mars also Hercules (who does not occur in the day-name argument) is frequently represented—again in harmony with the importance of the military on the Rhine frontier. Now Tacitus could have no difficulty in gathering information on the cults prevalent in the Roman Germania. Obviously he took the accounts of Caesar as a basis, crossed out Apollo and Minerva, who found little attention in the Roman Germania, and substituted Hercules for Jupiter in accordance with reports from there—and thus composed his account, which he then arbitrarily transferred to the free Germanic tribes. That we are really dealing with such a crude and arbitrary transfer of the religious ideas of the Roman frontiersmen to the free territory beyond the frontier is shown by a blatant contradiction in Tacitus' account. There is hardly anything Tacitus has emphasized so much as that the Germanic cults had neither images nor temples. How does that rhyme with cults which were by their nature cults of images and buildings? It does not rhyme at all. Where his knowledge was insufficient, Tacitus has invented.

Now to the Germanic day names, whose history is of interest even apart from the controversy about Tacitus' Germania. A great age has been claimed for them on the ground that they had shared in the second soundshift and must therefore have been older than the latter. But while this is admitted, we must recall that our ideas of the chronology of the sound shift are today quite different from what they were when that argument was first developed. While it was then supposed to have begun in the third century A.D., we know today that even with the Langobards, where it started first, it can be proved in the seventh century at the earliest—north of the Alps not before the end of that century, in Central Germany at the earliest in the eighth century, at the time of Boniface. So the argument has no relevance at all.

But above all, one ought to have taken into account that the seven-day week is not a law of nature. Even in Rome it dates only from early imperial times. What should have moved the free Germans in pagan times to adopt it? But as far as the Germans of the Roman Germania are concerned, nothing entitles us to the assumption that they had used other than the Latin names for the days of the week—as one must altogether expect in late imperial times the beginnings of a Romanic vulgar language among the frontier Germans, just as among the Roman Britons. In the free Germania, the adoption of the seven-day week presupposed the observance of Sunday by laymen, hence a considerable degree of Christianization. That is confirmed by the taking over of the Hebrew-Christian name for the last weekday in some Germanic languages (Samstag = Sabes day) which never knew another word for that day. But the importance of those facts was ignored.

But now we are facing an apparent paradox which obviously stands in the way of an understanding of the real development. Could the adoption of pagan names for the other days of the week really be due to Christian influence? That seems absurd. But already the Latin Church adopted the astrological-pagan names for the weekdays unchanged, except for the Judaeo-Christian sabbath and the "Lord's day" for Sunday, and used them without concern. The Germanic day names are nothing but more or less successful attempts at an exact translation of those Latin names, used also by the Church, into Germanic tongues.

In detail: with two of the six astrological day names, Sunday and Mo(o)nday, the translation was self-evident. Tuesday (from Tiu's day, with Tiu = Mars) corresponds to the Tacitean account of the Germanic Mars-cults, Wednesday (Wotan's day) similarly to that of the cult of Mercury, but only in the North; for in the Germanic South we get not Wotanstag but *Mittwoch*. The name of Thursday (Thor's day, German *Donnerstag* = Donar's Tag), however, contradicts the alleged Tacitean identities according to which a Roman Hercules would correspond to the Germanic Thor/Donar, where in fact Thor/Donar has here taken Jupiter's place (*Jovis dies*), because among the planets there is a Jupiter but no Hercules. Friday (Frijja's day = *Veneris dies*) has received its name for the same astrological reason and has no relation to the Germanic triad of gods discussed in relation with Tacitus' report, as little as Sunday, Monday, and Thursday. In short, the Germanic day names do not reflect a definite list of Ase gods—or their Latin correspondence in an *interpretatio Romana*—at all, but a Romanized Babylonian astrology of the seven planets, for which somehow plausible Germanic counterparts were put in rather arbitrarily, omitting in Germany Saturn, which once described the last weekday in the Roman list and has been put unchanged into the English version.

Still it remains hardly credible that the Roman Church should have favored a tenaciously surviving faith in the German gods by the invention of pagan Germanic daynames. But how if we could find a region where paganism was no longer a danger, but a Germanic translation of the days' names a compelling necessity? There is one and only one such area: Northern English Northumbria. We are encountering here for the first time the outstanding importance of this small province, also approximately covering today's Yorkshire, for the entire prehistory of the West, not in its pagan but all the more in its Christian aspects.

The Northumbrian Church, based on monasteries and not on bishoprics, had been founded not by Rome but by Ireland, or rather by the Irish monasteries in Scotland. Since the collapse of the last Arianic Churches in the sixth century, it was the only non-Roman Church on Germanic soil; and while the Arianic Germans had never had a very lively church life, the Northumbrian Church far surpassed all other Germanic Churches in culture, seriousness, and zeal. From it came Beda, the first great Germanic teacher of the Church, from it also the early Anglo-Saxon missionaries so important for the Christianization of Germany. The Northumbrian monasteries had quickly cleared out paganism in their own area—its Christianization had been the preparatory school for the later Anglo-Saxon mission on the continent. The Northumbrian Church therefore could employ pagan gods (who never meant much in its territory and soon meant nothing any longer) for the day names with the same unconcern as the Church of late antiquity employed the "star gods" of its time.

Now while the Northumbrian and Iro-Scottish monks read Latin, they preached in Germanic tongues and not in Latin, as did the continental Churches to the time of Charlemagne. The Northumbrian Church rested on a Germanic basis like the closely related Irish Church on an Irish one, and when it introduced the observance of Sunday and the seven-day week, it *had* to be done with Germanic names.

We cannot expect to find direct sources for this thesis: there is not a single mention of a Germanic day name in inscriptions or literature. The sound history of those names contains no direct hint as to their geographic origin. The sound shift they underwent in the South may just as well be a consequence of their having been taken over from the North, which did not share in the second sound shift, or a consequence of a very early origin of those names in the South German language area where the sound shift began only in the seventh century. There remains the examination of the only day name that has changed in its *wording*. Nobody will believe that an original *Mittwoch* was changed, when transferred to much earlier and much more thoroughly Christianized England, into a Wotan's day. Thus England had the priority, to wit not the completely Latinized archbishopric of Canterbury, but the thoroughly Germanic Northumbrian monasteries of Jarrow and Lindisfarne. From there the Germanic list of day names was brought to Germany, obviously by the Anglo-Saxon missionaries. That results clearly enough from the meaning of the transition from Wotan's day to *Mittwoch*.

For no missionary in Germany had to worry about Ziu or Frijja; they no longer enjoyed a living worship (Ziu was still worshipped in Saxony, but under the name of Saxnot); still less, of course, did they worry about sun and moon, whose astrological significance had never been grasped by the Germans. If the names had been introduced early, the *Donnerstag* might have been a problem, since in the early period Donar still enjoyed a lively worship. We conclude that the transfer of the pseudo-pagan day names took place at a time when also the worship of Donar had already been relegated far into the background. Now we know quite well that phase in which Germanic paganism, particularly in Southern and Central Germany, apart from the worship of nameless numina, concentrated exclusively on the cult of Wotan: that is not the phase of activity of the first Anglo-Saxon missionaries at the beginning of the eighth century, but the time of Boniface, thus chiefly the middle of that century. We now understand why then and there just the Wotan's day had to be changed into a *Mittwoch*: in Boniface's field of activity, the cult of Wotan was a living faith and Wotan the principal enemy of Christ; a Wotan's day must have given gravest offense from a Christian point of view. Perhaps the giving of a new name was also easier for Boniface than it would have been for an older missionary, a Willibald or Willibrod; for Boniface was not a Northumbrian, he came from the somewhat more Romanized western border of the Anglo-Saxon area—indeed he was himself the strongest promotor of the Romanization of German Christianity.[8] He was also the first of the missionaries from across the sea who knew how to give his Church a firm and lasting organizational basis, an indispensable precondition for a new calendar. To him, then, we ascribe, in the context of the achievement of the obligatory observance of Sunday by laymen, the introduction of Anglo-Saxon day names with one variation inside Germany.

One detail from the history of sounds may further support our thesis of the Anglo-Saxon origin of the Germanic day names. The name of the fourth day of the week in Dutch is not derived from *Mittwoch* but from Wotan's day: it is *Woensdag*. Assuming an origin of the Germanic day-names in a pagan age and from pagan ideas, that name could have arisen on the spot. But that is excluded by the state of the sound, which is marked by the loss of the middle consonant and the subsequent merger of the two vowels o and e of two syllables into oe. The starting point of that process cannot have been the high German form Wotan with a voiceless "t," for that in Dutch would just have been turned into "d": conversely a "d" from Wodan would simply have been retained. It must have been a Wođan with the affricata "đ," which the Lower Saxon dialect used, while the Lower Frankish one eliminated it, and not before the end of the eighth century; proof on one side for the Anglo-Saxon origin of the Wotan name for Wednesday, on the other for the very late transfer of this term to the other coast of the North Sea—a very natural development if we keep in mind that this area was Christianized considerably later than the Frankish Main area and Hessen.

Thus the Germanic day names, those showpieces of the believers in Tacitus' Germania and the neopagan interpretation of early Germanic history, prove to be a key link in the proof for the late origin and the early decay of the Ase high gods, and for the crucial role of Christian Northumbria in the origin of the Western spirit.

Just how short the period of Ase worship was in Southern and Central Germany becomes visible if we now, after concluding our discussion of

8. Compare with discussion of Boniface in Part II, ch. 9 below.

Tacitus' Germania, turn to other testimonials. The facts can then be summarized very simply: between Tacitus and the seventh century, there is not a single mention of a Germanic god's name in the whole of Latin and Greek literature—not even with Gregory of Tours, nor in the correspondence between Pope Gregory I and Brunichildis on the struggle against paganism. In the long series of secular authors who talked about the faith of the Germanic tribes, and of the ecclesiastic authors concerned about their conversion, there is before the seventh century not a single one who knows a Germanic god's name! We regard that *argumentum ex silentio* as absolutely decisive—both in itself and because even Latin and Greek translations of Germanic gods' names are completely missing until the second half of the sixth century. In the second half of the sixth century, one particular god's name emerges with Prokopius, an author of outstanding importance: Ares, meaning Mars and, if we attempt an identification with a Germanic god, Tiu or Ziu. To him the "Thulites," i.e., the Scandinavians, are said to offer human sacrifices.[9] According to the same source, human sacrifices were offered also by other Germanic peoples, notably the Franks, of whom he remarks in that context that despite their Christianization they are still imbued with the deepest paganism. Strange, however, that where he reports about that sacrifice of Gothic prisoners by the Franks of which he knew from his own activity as an officer in the Gothic war, he knows nothing about a god to whom these sacrifices were made. Rather "they threw the bodies of those Gothic women and children into the river as first fruits of the war . . . because they offer human and other unholy sacrifices in order to prophesy from them." Such statements about the use of human sacrifices, not generally but in the course of war, for oracular purposes are also found repeatedly elsewhere in the literature of late antiquity about the ancient Germans. The purpose there is not to invoke the favor of a god, but to obtain from certain sacrificial auguries an indication for the expediency of a battle, as indeed among the Germanic tribes of the time of the Voelkerwanderung, those war oracles seem to have been the main content of the sacrificial cults and thus of any cult of the gods.

Thus where Prokopius had exact knowledge, there was no Ares; where there was an Ares, there was no close knowledge. Jordanes,[10] who anyhow was remote from those phenomena and chased unsurely for effects of the classic type, then transferred Prokopius' testimony to the Goths—it was now they who offered human sacrifices but of course in the distant

9. *Procopii Caesariensis opera omnia*; *History of the War*, vols. 1–5 (London: Heinemann, 1960–62).

10. See note 4 above.

past (he knew that the Christianized Goths of his time did so no longer). There exists indeed not the slightest reason to doubt that the Goths offered human sacrifices in pagan times. All pagan Germanic tribes did so, as is well attested. But that the sacrifices were offered to Mars is pure rhetoric, at least with Jordanes. By itself, it would not be strange if those human sacrifices had been concentrated on a personal god in the sixth century. But even apart from the classicistic character of those reports on distant peoples and times, there is too great a lack of any other traces which would permit the assumption that Ziu had ever, apart from remote primeval times, been the leading god of the Germanic people. The question does not matter much, for not a single one of those reports refers to a Western Germanic tribe.

Fascinating, however, is the report of Ammianus,[11] the incorruptible, that the Quades had believed that the numina to whom they made offerings were located in the points of their swords. There is in that a compelling magical logic, inasmuch as in a fight, everything really depends on the sword points. There also exists a clear analogy, a similarity of the type of thinking, between the worship of the house beams in peace and of the sword points in war. One cannot, of course, generalize such an individual report without further evidence. If only we had more authors with the sharp eyes of Ammianus! But similar ideas, if not the same, were presumably underlying the warlike human sacrifices of the Germanic tribes everywhere, where not precisely defined oracular purposes furnished the occasion.

Apart from that, all those authors know that the Germanic tribes had cults not only for war. What Agathias,[12] the continuator of Prokopius, states about the Alamanns—that they "worship certain trees, rivers, hills, and valleys . . . and offer to them horses, children, and thousands of other things as sacrifices"—is found *mutatis mutandis* in all accounts ever since the time of Tacitus. Reports about cultic buildings (*fana*) and sculptures put up in them, on the other hand, refer without exception again to a later period, the earliest falling into the eighth century. We save ourselves the repetition of an argument developed already repeatedly. But those peaceful cults could only flourish among settled peoples—for only groves, trees, sources, and hills close to the worshipers settlements could become the objects of a cult. It follows that in the age of the migrations only the war cults with their human sacrifices could keep alive; one more contribution not only to the theme of the absence of

11. Ammiani Marcellini *Res Gestae* (Bologna: Zanidlli, 1973).
12. Agathiae Myrenaei *Historiarum Libri quinqae* (Berlin: de Gruyter, 1975).

gods, but generally to the gradual impoverishment of Germanic religious life in the course of the first half of the first millennium A.D.

Now it is true that one finds with *all* authors from the second to the seventh century a teeming multitude of mentions of *dii, numina,* θεοί; we only name here a few ecclesiastic authorities such as Eunapius, Augustine, Orosius, Einodius, and among secular ones Ammianus, Prokopius, Jordanes, Gregory of Tours. But just the fact that not a single one of those authors found anything specific to state about those "divinities"—while all attest to the sacrifices and the oracular practices— proves that the rites of the Germanic tribes were dedicated, be it to nameless, be it to purely local numina, and that high gods did not exist with them.

The difference between a mere numen and a god lies precisely in the personalization of the latter; indeed, that personalization is the process that causes a numen to be turned into a god. Of course, this is not primarily an intellectual process. In a fine work of his age Bergson[13] has shown that the urge for a personal god springs from the need of the human soul to *speak* to god. That is not possible with a mere numen: it is accessible only to always repeated, impersonal formulas and sacrifices. One may tame it with such formulas, compel it to spare the tamer or even to help him—but all that creates no genuine relationship. One cannot love a numen, not serve it personally, there is between man and numen no repentance and forgiveness, no aid and consolation. For that reason also such "nature gods" as sun, moon, and stars, just like such nature numina as the "spirits" of sources, forests, and mountains, are at best demigods.

The situation changes thoroughly with the seventh century. With Fredegar,[14] the continuator of Gregory of Tours, we find a first mention of Wotan whom Gregory did not know yet. The Langobards are said to have heard his voice during their crossing of the Danube—three generations before Fredegar. It is characteristic that the name occurs for the first time in the context of a tribal myth, not of a cult.

What may have originally been ascribed to an unamed numen—the encouraging voice heard at a venture important in tribal history—now appears as the mysterious manifestation of the high god. A few years later, an account of a cult is also found: the great Irish missionary Columbanus is stated in his *vita* to have encountered such a cult. The vita is dated 642 A.D. One hesitates to decide whether the account is authentic, that is, whether Columbanus really encountered a cult of Wotan around

13. Henri Bergson, *Les deux sources de la moralité et de la réligion* (Paris: Alcan, 1932).
14. Fredegarii *Chronicum libri 4 cum continuationinibus* (Hannover: Hahn, 1956).

the turn of the century, or whether the author has reinterpreted an older account about a godless pagan cult in the sense of the Wotan cult which was fully developed by the middle of the century.

At any rate, as completely as such reports were lacking before, they become now a matter of course, and since the middle of the seventh century there are few authors reporting on Germanic paganism without mentioning the cult of Wotan. Agathias, whose work dates from the early seventh century, was probably the last historian who did *not* mention it. It is true, though, that more weighty documents, as the letters of Gregory III to Boniface, still have no names of gods even in the eighth century.

Those accounts speak in the main of holy trees and heights, of sacrifices of horses and beer ceremonials, besides of course of all kinds of magic. We must keep in mind that they originate without exception in the postmigration period, hence reflect a kind of return to a peacetime religion. One really learns from them very little about Wotan, but much about the fact that a very large part of old numinous ideas and cults was transferred to the high god now that he existed. Also as a tribal god, he is now mentioned frequently, particularly in reports about the pagan prehistory of the Langobards.

Into this all-too-idyllic chorus sounds the late but well-informed account of Adam of Bremen[15] as a disonance: "*Wotan, id est furor*" (Wotan, that means fury), a statement whose correctness nobody has doubted. Certainly, it is not fury in a psychological sense that is intended in that context. Rather, as we mentioned before in discussing the personal name Odridr, Wotan is in the first place a god of storm and thunderstorm. No doubt this role of Wotan's is older than that of a numen of holy oaks, but it is closely connected with his role as god of the heights. But a god of the thunderstorm, worshipped on heights, is a description also fitting Donar. What can originally have distinguished the two? Moreover, which god that controls lightning, thunder, and thunderstorm would not be a god of war at the same time—thus an original identity of Wotan, Donar, and Ziu?

Analogies with the Aryan Indra and the Hethitic Feshub have been pointed out in order to prove the Indogermanic origin of that god, but quite without reason! The Sumeric Enlil, the Syrian Hadad have exactly the same features. Where there is storm, there are storm gods, where there are storm and war there is a merger of the gods of storm and war, as can be shown for the Syrian Hadad just as well as for the Hethitic

---

15. Adam Bremensis, see *Gesta Hamburgensis ecclesiae pontificum*.

Feschub. True, Ziu bears an Indogermanic name, whose ultimate meaning is obviously god as a generic noun. All the more remarkable that the new development was evidently not attached to him, but to the non-Indogermanic name of Wotan.

Originally all this was of course not referring to a high god of the storm, but to thunderstorm spirits, conceived now as spirits of the thunder, now of the "fury." The question of the origin of the Wotanic belief thus amounts to the dual problem of the god's differentiation out of the nameless crowd of numina on one side, and of the causes of his separation from Donar (and also from Ziu) on the other.

That the fury (old Norse oðr) is older than the furious one (Wotan), was already noted in our analysis of personal names. In looking for the transition, one can naturally not ignore the saga of the wild chase nor its literary fixation by the account of Priskos[16] on the battle on the Catalaunian plains between Chalons-sur-Marne and Troyes. So terrible was that battle between Attila and the Roman commander Aetius (in which so many of the Germanic tribes took part), that the dead continued to fight at night in the air. There is no occasion to hold the Catalaunian battle responsible for the origin of that idea, which might fit any major battle. Only it happened to be the greatest battle of the whole period of the Voelkerwanderung, and hence particularly apt to serve as a point of crystallization for the saga.

An army of the dead is thus fighting in the air above the battlefield. The link with the belief in Wotan has often been seen, but not the completely nontraditional character of the idea. The firm conviction that the basic elements of the Wotanic faith were of primeval age has thoroughly obstructed the recognition of something entirely new. Once it is recognized that this idea does not presuppose the belief in Wotan, but conversely that the belief in Wotan presupposed an earlier idea of this kind, then the real problem comes into view.

The Germanic hero is buried like all the dead—whether in an urn with ashes or in a coffin containing the corpse; the nobles at any rate are buried in a clan grave if at all possible. But there could be no more clan grave during the migrations, and the story of the burial of Alarich in the bed of the Busento river bears witness to the worries created by that fact for his comrades. It must even have occurred in special conditions that no funeral could be performed at all; the belief in places that are haunted is clear evidence of that. But what if it became a mass phenomenon? Priskos reports just that of the Catalaunian battle: there was no time to

16. For Priskos see Constantin Porphyrogenitus (Emperor Constantin VII), *Excerpta de legationibus.*

bury the dead. The link between this report and the legend of the furious host has been ignored. The dead must continue to rage in the air because they are not buried—the most horrible thing that could be said about a battle. Instead of down into the earth, they must make their way, like all the ghosts of the unburied, up into the air, continuing what they were doing at the moment of their death: fighting. They fight on over the heads of the living as long as the latter are still fighting at the same place; once the living leave the battlefield and the ravens have eaten the corpses, so that the host of the dead can no longer expect reinforcements, the host chases away, aimless, raging, and roaring, into the distance. I believe that the raven, whose feeding on corpses was proverbial in the whole ancient Germanic literature, belonged as an escort to that host of the dead long before it had found a leader in Wotan; later the attribute passed from the host to its divine leader. Both are in need of it; for side by side with the idea of the struggle of the dead in the air there stands the other idea that the spirit is only liberated when the body is destroyed—and the raging host needs reinforcements. To the wild chase belongs also Wotan's other animal attribute, the horse.

Only this vision explains the differentiation of Wotan from Donar on one side and from Ziu on the other. Ziu is, as it were, a "normal" god of war, without the horror of the absence of burial; Donar, the (as it were) "normal" god of the thunderstorm, without relation to either mass migration or mass war, burial or nonburial. The terrible trauma of the unburied masses, the importance of which for the religion of the time of the Voelkerwanderung was never properly recognized, separated the leader of the unburied from the demons of nature on one side and the demons of war on the other.

Yet the real personalization of the god, whose preliminary stages we discussed in the context of the personal names, obviously goes back to two main causes: to the end of the Voelkerwanderung and to Christian influence. The idea of the wild hunter, still alive until recently in South German folklore, had probably attached itself very early to that of the wild chase. What could be more natural than that a wild host also has a wild leader? But the leader may originally have been hardly distinguished from the host by more than the fact that he led and at the same time embodied it. With the end of the migration period, with the return of normal opportunities for the funeral of the warriors, however, the idea of the furious host must have considerably lost in importance. Then the god might have vanished together with his following, unless the Christian influence had intervened. We must realize that the Germanic tribes, beginning with the fourth century, knew no idea of a personal godhead but the Christian one: I can think of no way in which such an idea could have once more been evolved autonomously from internal German preconditions. But we can hardly ascribe its taking over by the free Germanic tribes to the wish lovingly to appropriate something impressive. Rather, enmity against the Christianized and partly romanized Frankish realm stood godfather to the rise of the Wotan figure in the North, and enmity against Byzantium to its rise south of the Alps. We know Wotan, during his short history south of the Baltic and the North Sea as well as in England, exclusively as the standard bearer in the struggle for tribal independence.

What is most striking in our reports is nevertheless, or rather for that very reason, the rudimentary character of that religion, whose true root in the demonism of death without burial was withering without being replaced by other, equally powerful motives. Though we meet the name of the god again and again in this period after the Voelkerwanderung, the reports about his cult show a relapse into the purely numinous cults before it. Wotan was a very feeble god; he succumbed in Southern and Central Germany not to Frankish state power, but to the Anglo-Saxon missionaries with only modest participation of Frankish state power. Only in Saxony he rebelled. There, his strength corresponded to the strength and will to independence of the tribal confederation—it was a purely political strength. With the collapse of the political resistance, there also the faith in Wotan collapsed almost suddenly, leaving a void of the greatest importance for the rise of the Western spirit.

It was different in the Far North, where the god had penetrated from Saxony. For understanding the initial situation of the Wotan cult in Scandinavia, one best consults the account of Adam of Bremen, according to which at the great cult center of Upsala a triad of Odin, Thor, and Freyr was worshipped; in other words, in the part of Scandinavia not looking to the sea, Wotan never gained a preferential position over all other gods. Even there the cult might have petered out unless the seagoing Germans had inspired it with new strength. The god of the battlefields of the period of the Voelkerwanderung could have experienced a second flowering in no other environment but that of the Vikings. Thus he became in the North a specific god of the seagoing heroes, as becomes visible with particular clarity in the older Helgi song.

Again, we must visualize the relation between those seaborne warriors and the other ancient Germans. Already in the Scandinavian rock drawings, ships play an immense role, and though their significance there is clearly symbolic—in the pictures, the oars are almost always missing—the boat would hardly have become such a core symbol of this culture unless it had played a highly important role in its daily life. At that time, obviously Southern Sweden was the center of sea-faring, with Southern Norway next to it; later the center of gravity shifted much more clearly Westward. But outside Scandinavia and Frisia, the Germanic peoples were strictly landbound; even the Jutes, Saxons, and Angles dropped seagoing activities as soon as they had become settled in England. For Wotan, the shift from the land battle to seafaring was a total change of environment.

The new environment was far more favorable to the god than had been the old one, inasmuch as death without funeral is a normal fate for searfarers. Burial at sea is out of the question, only cremation is conceivable—and this not while fighting is going on. In Scandinavia, this necessity was turned into virtue: in the upper stratum, not only on the high seas but also on land that double destruction of the dead bodies, the pushing out to sea of a burning ship which might be called the "Balder ritual," is frequently adopted. That rite, an extreme contrast not only to the funeral of corpses but also of urns, explicitly denies the care for the eternal rest of the dead, and replaces it with a positive accent on nonburial alien to all previous Germanic custom; just for that reason, the usage always remained controversial. It would be totally incomprehensible if we were still dealing with the dead on a battlefield on land.

But at sea, there are many kinds of dying besides the fighting death; sea voyages are undertaken not by peoples but by free, small associations of young men who have been voluntarily formed; at sea, a struggle is more often than on land a purely personal feud, and a fighting death frequently individual death. Seafaring of the Viking type puts individual death in the place of mass death. There, in the seafaring high North, it is as if the dying fertility cults had only been waiting for the emergence of that god of the unburied dead in order to blossom forth in new shape at his touch. The rite of annihilation belonging to the Balder myth links up here with the archetype of the godlike youth, doomed to death and fulfilling himself in his doom, to a transfiguration of nonburial as the boldest culmination of heroism defying all demonic forces, which assures to the hero a further life in the retinue of Odin, the god of the unburied. Here the most terrible curse is turned into the highest splendor, but only for the chosen few who defy everything that is a horror to ordinary men. A magnificent vision, profoundly influenced by Christian ideas, from which alone the concept of a transcendent life in a heavenly citadel in god's retinue can have been taken. It is an attempt to adapt those ideas to the warrior ethos of the Viking nobles and to revive paganism by this very adaptation.

Yet fundamentally the change from the concept of the furious host is not large, despite the individualization and ennoblement of the idea of the continued fighting of the unburied by its being linked with the self-fulfillment of the hero in death. The compulsion to fight on remains the fate of the unburied. How the Vikings really felt about that, we can once more find in the younger Helgi song, where the dead Helgi implores his wife to stop crying for him so that he may at last find rest in his grave. Not that this could now be the last word; since the withering of the belief in resurrection in the myth of the dead god, rest in the grave only means absolute death, and the choice between that and the eternal, aimless fighting on in Walhalla is a poor choice indeed. If the Viking aristocracy divides itself into supporters of burial and supporters of the burning ships, into admirers of Skaldic Walhalla scenes and fascinated listeners to the song of Helgi's somber cohabitation in his own tomb, such partisan division must be seen as typical for hopeless situations.

Underlying the extreme contrast is a common element—the unhealed wound which the decay of the Wanic religion of resurrection and rebirth has left behind. From that hopeless dilemma, no saving idea of a god can arise. Rather, it is just this last and highest development of the faith in Wotan which shows that death remained the unbridgeable abyss at which all Germanic paganism failed, that this failure was felt most keenly just in the Viking religion, and that the pagan North itself, from immanent conditions of its existence created by the decay of the Wanic religion, was pressing toward a Christian religion of salvation and immortality which it would have been incapable of creating from its own resources.

Wotan remained a god who could promise nothing and grant nothing. Just in the Viking age, this became clearly evident. If people during the Voelkerwanderung felt simply a horror before the not yet human demon, if people in the following period had tried to buy him by sacrifices like other demonic powers, the Viking faith makes his unreliability and ambiguity one of his basic features. True, he helps the hero, for instance Helgi in his venture of vengeance against Hunding. But he also has need of the heroes to reinforce his host, and therefore counsels them death. The helper is at the same time the deceiver, and by his deception again the power that helps the hero to fulfill his heroism in death.

Of course, the god of fury could never have emerged from the raging host as a truly personal god if he had just remained the merely eponymous leader of that rage. From the moment of his individual emergence, then, the double meaning of the West Germanic *uot* and the Nordic *oðr* appeared—a double meaning exactly corresponding to that, similarly important for religous history, of Hebrew *ruach* and Greek *pneuma*: the original sense of all those terms at once comprises mountain storm and soul or spirit. Storm is an image of the immaterial—and out of it the soul as a lifegiving principle is formed. Corresponding to that double meaning, *uot* is an expression both of extreme destruction and of highest spiritualization. The god of wild rage is at the same time a god of spiritual power.

But the unfolding of this fruitful ambiguity was so much overshadowed by the original, demonic-destructive figure of the furious host that it never wholly matured. That there was a deep gulf between the two meanings soon became conscious. (It is altogether wrong to imagine critical religious developments as long-term: they have a long incubation period, but once they enter consciousness they happen no less abruptly than critical changes in politics and art.) Finally, in the Viking age, the gulf was bridged by the idea that the god had been transformed in character and function through terrible suffering: nine days he swings hanged from the world ash, pierced by a spear, until he sees the runes lying at his feet, welcomes them with a shout and liberates himself from his plight by runic magic. Some have wanted to see in this a nature myth, completely ignoring the true spiritual content. In fact, the principal themes—the god saved and saving by his suffering, the hanging from a pole, the spear thrust, the self-awakening—document Christian influence and characterize the whole idea as an anti-Christian theological construction.

This theologem thus raises Wotan to the role of a god of knowledge and wisdom. Yet at the same time he is blind in one eye—a prophet, but only half of one. He sees the inevitable doom of gods and men, but cannot stop it—salvation he sees not. Perfidy and fraud are the chief pillars of his strength. It is as if the terrible mutual destruction and self-destruction characteristic of the oldest layer of the saga had assumed divine shape and had come to conscious, hopeless insight.

To such a god, too, one cannot pray in confidence. He, too, embodies unchanging danger just like the impersonal numina. And if his name occurs rarely in placenames, almost never in personal names, if he has only a few places of worship, no long explanations are needed. Theophorous names as well as everyday cults are intended to assure salvation. A nature god like Freyr may do that after a fashion; Wotan can do anything but that. Having arisen directly from the horrors of the Voelkerwanderung, he carries all those horrors with him as a figure of popular faith. Yet how could a helping and saving god spring just from that graphic vision of an eternity of murder and destruction? It is characteristic for the Wotanic religion that while making a healing attempt, it carries with it the original corruption in its most somber and hopeless form. Not by accident, human sacrifices and meat and drinking orgies formed the main elements of the early Wotan cult. The later Eddic theology has merely turned the horror into despair.

The cult of Thor, originated from a numinous worship of thunder, can in its mature form only be understood as a product of a deliberate contrast to the Odin cult. Not that we are dealing here with two religions fighting each other: in paganism, contrasting attitudes can be reconciled by being allotted to different gods. Thor is the counterimage of Odin, and all hearts turn to him because he is felt as a bringer of salvation, a conqueror of the despair associated with Odin.

Thor has been correctly described as the ideal image of a Viking. Not by accident he became one of the highest gods only in the Viking's land. In contrast to Odin, he is a quite unspiritual god, but also an undemonic one. He is characterized by immense physical strength, tremendous, uncalculating courage in fighting, self-confidence, success, the enjoyment of booty—particularly in the shape of beautiful maidens. He has a positive attitude to home and the tilling of the soil, even though fighting and booty are more to his taste.

But the faith in Thor did not lead any further either. If the faith in Odin in its late form undoubtedly brought spiritualization, it brought no salvation; the faith in Thor, in its turn, erected the idol of the hero *sans peur et sans reproche* (the core of the ideal of the medieval knight!) but in a primitive form aimed at bringing salvation without suffering and spiritual effort; the dream of the early Viking age when the pirates were seeking to forge their own good fortune out of a sea of European blood and tears. In the early tenth century, their sallies already hit political barriers in the outside world, while their own rising kingdoms began to tame their wild freedom from within; in Iceland where it remained untamed it led to the hopelessness of universal murder in a narrow space. We can follow the rise of a new gloom for instance in the transformations of the Sigurd saga, can observe how the destructive themes of the saga from the Voelkerwanderung reenter the song of the radiant hero. The new gloom led to a new flowering of the Odin religion.

Any religion is ultimately measured by its capacity to change the life of men from inside. For that, the faith in Thor had contributed nothing. The first great social crisis also brought the return of the despair of the age of the Voelkerwanderung which had been veiled for a short time. In that crisis, paganism finally collapsed and was replaced by Christianity— due not to external force but to inner necessity.

That necessity may be clarified by a comparison between the histories of Germanic and Hellenic religion. It is very possible, even probable, that the Hellenes during their period of migrations also lived through a phase of despair analogous to the Germanic one. It is more than doubtful whether Oedipus, in the original version of the saga, found reconciliation on Colonos, whether Orestes was originally saved from the Furies by Apollo. Here as there, the primal crimes brought about by the decay of the clan order issued into a horrible nothingness. But for the Hellenes, the living pantheon of Minoan society was within reach; they merged it with Indogermanic nature gods, who in contact with the gods of a high culture grew into true personal high gods themselves. All this was tangibly close and required no leap in their development; it was also salvation-bringing. It led from the gloom of the original Oresteia into the bright world of Homer. Not so with the ancient Germans: when they appeared on the scene, classical paganism was in full dissolution and the Indogermanic gods—themselves not yet high gods in the full sense— were far away. But from despair alone no high gods can be formed, and there was nothing older to lean on which could have given aid and support.

Thus the road and the downfall of Germanic paganism turns out to have been the exact contrary of that for which its admirers would like to take it: not the reflection of an incomparable Germanic uniqueness, but an inevitable result of a particular stage in the evolution of mankind to true knowledge. Germanic paganism could not unfold because in Europe, at that time the living core area in the development of humanity, the day of paganism was already drawing to its close, because no new branch could grow any longer on its withering trunk. Salvation, the overcoming of primal crime and of despair, lay not in the polytheism of a pantheon that was already becoming more comic than numinous, but in the faith in one savior coming from the East.

But while it would be absurd to mourn the downfall of Germanic paganism, it would also be entirely wrong to think it had vanished without a trace. It left a legacy—not chiefly in the superstitious popular usages that cause the enthusiasm of our folkloric experts, but in that fundamental experience of hopeless despair to which only Christianity offered an answer. In itself, that experience is in any case a central point of Christian teaching, and Pauline theology is quite inconceivable without it; yet it was largely lost from sight in the Hellenization of Byzantine Christianity, as if salvation depended on the formulas of the dogma alone. In occidental Christianity, however, this never-ending dialectic of despair and salvation is immediately present as a basic personal experience—and not as a mere mood coloring all life, but also as a central dogmatic problem: as a permanent debate about the relation between the reprobation following on the fall and the salvation by grace and merit. As is known, this central problem of occidental dogma has been much more hotly debated in the North than in the South, and that is no accident. But that again is due not to mere national characteristics, but to the situation created by the course of world history: the European South has made a direct transition from fully developed paganism to fully developed Christianity, the North has experienced the nihilistic interlude of a paganism collapsing into nothingness. Because of that, the North has produced the most profound statements yet about the essence of the human condition.

CHAPTER SIX

Pelagius, the Irish and the African Church

The following are passages from a letter of religious guidance, addressed to a Christian virgin of name Demetrias, written in the beginning of the fifth century A.D. For a long time this letter was wrongly attributed to St. Jerome. Being thus submerged in his voluminous writings, its powerful originality was never fully recognized.

"It is extremely difficult," so the writer of the letter says, not without a touch of worldly flattery, already in the first chapter of this theological document,

> adequately to instruct a person so keen to learn, so passionate in her search of perfection, that even the most perfect doctrine could hardly seem satisfactory to her. . . . She is not content with the ordinary, mediocre way of life . . . she rather wants something new and unusual; she is after something outstanding and singular. She wants her conversation to be as admirable as her conversion. Of noble birth in this world, she wants to be more noble still before God. . . . What genius will suffice to quench such thirst after perfection?

The real Jerome, no doubt, would have chastised such an attitude as lacking in all Christian humility, and in doing so he would have followed the teaching of all the great documents of Christian morality from the Gospels onwards. Not so our author. He starts his second chapter with a statement of his views on moral training, views which are flatly opposed to all Christian ideas about weakness in man.

Whenever I have to speak about the foundations of morality, and about the maintenance of holiness in life, I start by making people see the strength and all the aptitudes of human nature, and how much it can achieve; so that by this very start I incite my pupils to every virtue. It is then little use to them to pretend that this or that is beyond their power. For we cannot start on the road of virtue unless we take hope as our companion. Otherwise, the effort of trying collapses under the pressure of despair. . . . The more perfect therefore the sort of life we choose as our goal, the more fully must we understand that [human] nature is good. Otherwise the soul will lack determination and be slow in her efforts, to the extent to which she distrusts her powers, and will believe that she is lacking in all those abilities of which she is not immediately conscious. A good guide will, on the contrary, constantly keep before his pupil's eyes the object at which moral effort is to be directed, and will explain how great is the power of nature for the good. For he can then demand that what is demonstrably achievable should actually be achieved. . . . The virgin must learn to know her strength. When she has done so, she will be able to use it. For the best way of urging a soul forward is for somebody to teach her that she can what she wills.

God has made the whole world very good, how much more so man, the master of creation.

Every reader of this quotation must be struck by the intensely non-Christian flavor of its pride. Yet the author no doubt regarded himself as a good, even as a model Christian, and not without an element of justification. For where, in the whole of pagan literature, with the possible exception of the latest Stoics, could such intense thirst for moral perfection be found? A scrutiny of the vocabulary of our letter shows that "perfect" and "perfection" are the terms which are most in the author's mind, and invariably in connection with morality. He appears as if lashed forward by an urge to rise higher and higher. The text is strewn with comparatives of the adjectives of perfection. There is constant talk of something better, more perfect, stronger, nobler, more admirable. Effort is the dominating note. Job is described (in chapter VIII of the letter) as "God's athlete." And when, with chapter XXVII, the letter moves towards its conclusion, this conception of boundless moral improvement is once more summed up as in the fortissimo of the final bars of a great symphony.

"A holy life glories in its process of development and is in constant growth; it becomes stale and deficient if it stands still. The mind must be trained through a daily new increase of all the virtues. . . . As long as we are in this body, we must never think that we have reached perfection; for not to think so, is the way of better achieving it in actual fact. . . . When we stand still, we already decline, where we no longer progress, we fall back."

However ambitious the author's ideas about the powers of human nature, he does not limit his high-flown hopes and demands to the few elect. On the contrary, he maintains that he is speaking of human nature in general, that everybody can fulfil the highest demands of his morality. True, "we exclaim against God's word and say: it is hard, it is painful, we cannot do it, we are only men, we are encased in the weakness of the flesh." But his only comment is: "O blind madness! O profane temerity!" (Chapter XVI). For

how many philosophers (in other words: pious pagans) have we learnt, by books, by tales, and by our own experience, to be chaste, patient, abstinent, kind-hearted, the honor and delight of mankind, lovers of justice and wisdom. . . . And as all these virtues can be found together in some, and some in many, and as human nature is one in all men, by the model men provide for one another, they prove that everybody can have all the perfections (Chapter III).

It is a fantastic doctrine, but certainly not one lacking in moral idealism. Obviously Christianity, to the author, seemed to consist precisely in this moral idealism, with its exorbitant demands upon the average man, and its high-flown trust in the goodness of human nature and its capacity of unlimited progress. A doctrine more fitting for a rationalist of the eighteenth, than for an ascetic of the fifth century! Yet this document, with its intensely modern flavor, was written a few years after the capture of Rome by Alaric the Goth, in the second decade of the fifth century A.D.

The critics of the seventeenth century already suspected, and later research has confirmed their view, that the letter to Demetrias must be attributed to Pelagius, the greatest of the heretics of the Western church in Roman times. Few of the writings of this man are preserved to us: besides the letter in question, there is a commentary on Paul's letters, in particular the letter to the Romans (also attributed for a long time to Jerome), and a number of quotations from lost works. An extraordinary amount of acumen has been displayed in restituting the authentic original text of Pelagius' commentaries on Paul. Naturally so, for theologians concentrate upon doctrine, and there is no more profound, no more basic exposition of the Christian doctrine of sin and perfection than Paul's letter to the Romans. Therefore, what a Christian teacher, whether or-

thodox or heretic, says in comment on this letter must be most characteristic of his doctrinal position on the problems of sin and grace, must
be the clearest indication of his place in the history of these Christian
dogmas.

Thus, indeed, Pelagius' commentary on Paul indicates with all desirable clarity his views on these doctrines. He believes in free will. How
could he otherwise have believed that all men can become morally perfect? He believes in the fundamental goodness of human nature and
rejects the doctrine of original sin. He believes in man's capacity to
achieve the good through his own strength. He minimizes the need for
God's grace in the achievement of holiness. More exactly, he limits it
to one single point: the fullness of the insight into good and evil can only
be gained through the Christian faith. To accept this faith is as much the
work of our free will as the achievement of any other kind of perfection.
But we must be forgiven what we have sinned before becoming Christians, and this forgiveness is extended to the sinner through baptism,
which is a free gift of God, emerging out of Christ's atonement on the
cross.

Most of this doctrine is directly stated in Pelagius' commentary on
Paul, and all of it seems to have been contained in his early writings. It
involved him in the struggle with St. Augustine in which, if not he
himself, at least his doctrine succumbed. Pelagius, as the old church in
general, knew nothing of forgiveness of sin through the sacrament of
confession. Baptism, to Pelagius, was the only supernatural, sacramental
way of forgiveness. Consequently he, in common with many of the
older doctors of the church, did not encourage early baptism; the more
so, as in many parts of the Roman Empire baptism on the death-bed,
or at any rate in mature age, was still a living practice. Also, what was
the point of the remission of sins in the baptism of infants? Human nature
was good in essence, sin only an aberration of the mature mind. Little
children, when they died, went right to heaven, sinless.

It was this point which called forth the passionate protest of Augustine.
For even before Pelagius' earliest statement of his views, Augustine had
maintained that all men were damned through original sin. Original sin,
to him, was not actual sin, actual offense against the law of God. It was
the inherent stain upon human nature, deriving from Adam, transmitted
from generation to generation through the abomination of sexual procreation. Those who had thus been put into the world went right to hell
unless redeemed by the mystical powers of baptism. Thus Pelagius, in
Augustine's view, through his deprecatory attitude towards the baptism

of infants, sent children to damnation at their death. And though Augustine bore patiently many other views of Pelagius which he disliked, he could not let pass unchallenged this one. The meaning of the notion of original sin with reference to the damnation or redemption of little children became the core of the great controversy between Augustine and Pelagius. Pelagius' concept of baptism, despite its mystical elements, was mainly rationalist, and he scorned the idea of a sacrament of faith dispensed to newborn babies who could have no faith, and could not have committed any sin. The conception of Augustine was wholly mystical, and to him baptism meant not a declaration about actual faith, but an imputation of "implicit" faith, not forgiveness of sins actually committed by the newborn, but of sins imputed to him as transmitted from his parents.

The motives of Augustine in taking up, much against his will, the fight against so highly admirable and venerated an ascetic as Pelagius, are not difficult to understand. His doctrine of the baptism of infants is a result, in the first place, of his obsession with sex, an obsession he shared with almost all Christians of his age, though Pelagius, characteristically, was less subject to it than most other ascetics. But behind that motive, there stands Augustine's psychological insight, his knowledge of the weakness of man, of his absolute need for God's help, which, for Augustine, was a direct inner experience. Where Pelagius proudly asserted that everything is possible to man, Augustine, with specific reference to sex, maintained that only supernatural grace can enable man to remain chaste.

There was no less a real personal experience behind the doctrine of Pelagius than behind that of Augustine. But in this case, Pelagius the man and his conception of life were soon obscured behind Pelagins the theologian and his heretical *dicta*. Down to the seventeenth century none of his writings had been recognized as his, as all had been transmitted, not perhaps without some fraud on the part of his adherents, as writings of Jerome. His adversaries, and Augustine among them, only dealt with his heresies. That attitude remained when, in the seventeenth century, some of the pseudo-Jerome texts were recognized as belonging to Pelagius. For in the meantime, Pelagius' doctrine, which had been almost forgotten throughout the later middle ages, had again come much to the fore in the controversy between Catholics and Protestants, the latter charging the former with the taunt of Pelagianism. The new students of Pelagius were all Protestants, and they studied him in order to prove that his doctrines were pernicious—and were the same as those of the Roman church. Hence again the man disappeared behind the theologian, the fervent idealist behind the heretic, the letter to Demetrias with its intensely human touch, its exclusive interest in the moral training of a pupil, behind the sharp, short statements of the commentary of Paul, a work of dry succinctness quite outstanding among the wordy writings of the period, and with an exclusive interest in doctrinal theology. Doctrinal theology, the doctrine of free will and the rejection of original sin, can be found in the letter to Demetrias, too, but only as side issues. This letter, though always quoted in works about Pelagius, has never been used to elucidate his attitude in its fullness. This attitude is determined throughout by a passionate belief in human goodness, human progress, and the possibility of human perfection.

But why spend so much time on a heresy of the late Roman era? What is the connection between Pelagianism and the origins of Western civilization? There exists a close connection on at least three points. First of all, it is obvious, even from the few quotations given at the beginning of this chapter, that the great heretic anticipated much which today we should regard as characteristically Western. Secondly, the Pelagian controversy, as mentioned above, has flared up again and again. It constantly occupied the church in the early middle ages. It again became the central problem of theology with the rise of protestantism. It would be saying too much that the history of Western theology is tantamount to the history of the Pelagian controversy. But it is a fact that the Pelagian controversy is the biggest and longest drawn-out controversy of Western religious thought and practice. There seems to be something in the Western attitude to life which constantly brings back to the attention of men the main problems first raised by Pelagius. Thirdly and finally, from its origin Pelagianism had had its roots in the North of Europe. This geographical fact is of great importance. We are going to discuss it before taking up the more difficult problems of Pelagius' position in the context of the religion of his own era and of later times.

Jerome (the authentic Jerome, not the pseudo-Jerome who is, in fact, Pelagius himself) describes our heretic as a "Scot." Scholars are agreed that this word, then and for many centuries onwards, denoted not a Scotsman but an Irishman. In one of the two passages where he makes this statement, Jerome adds that all Irishmen are horrible and only so horrible a nation could have produced so horrible a person. In view of this rather scurrilous argument it has been maintained that Jerome was not in earnest in "denouncing" Pelagius as an Irishman. Yet the doctors of the church, when their anger was roused, disposed of a rich gamut of anthropological invective. Had not Tertullian opened his treatise against the heretic Marcion by describing, at great length, the horrors of Northwestern Anatolia, of its climate, its people, their habits, in order to conclude that only from such a dirty country could come such a dirty man as Marcion? Yet nobody ever doubted that, however scurrilous the attack, Tertullian was in earnest when he described Marcion as a man coming from Northwestern Anatolia. Why should not the same apply to Jerome and Pelagius? Unfortunately, the problem cannot be left there. For the majority of the sources, though none of them were probably quite as closely acquainted with Pelagius as Jerome (who knew him personally), describe him not as a Scot but as a Briton, "Brito" (this is the term used by Augustine), or "Britannus," "Britannicus": one source speaks of him as a "Briton from the neighbourhood of Ireland."

Which is the authentic version? It is impossible to say with certainty. One thing, however, seems certain to me. Pelagius must have been a Celt, even if he was not an Irishman, and not a Roman from Britain. For otherwise the attack of Jerome would have fallen flat on the ground. A Briton speaking British might be denounced as a "dirty Irishman" (that *is* the precise meaning of what Jerome says), but not a Roman aristocrat from England. Britannus and Britannicus are terms which could doubtless be applied to the latter, but probably not Augustine's "Brito," which seems to denote a true Briton. Also, had Pelagius not been a stranger, the sources would not so unanimously insist upon his origin. All, apparently, were struck by the fact that a man so highly educated (he knew Greek well, hence must have been rich and noble) and so arrogantly independent was, by descent and birth, only a barbarian. It is an attractive hypothesis propounded by H. Zimmer in his fundamental work *Pelagius in Ireland*,[1] that Pelagius was not his real name, but the Greco-Latin form of some Celtic name with the root "Mor" (the sea). Possibly his name, as an Irish medieval tradition has it, was Morgan.

But the most convincing proof of his close connection with, if not actual membership in the Irish church must not be sought in these controversial data about his person, but in the fate of his doctrine in Ireland. It is the main discovery of Zimmer that Pelagianism was rampant in Ireland from the beginning, and lasted there for a long time after its complete suppression in the Roman Empire. The earliest reference to the strength of the Pelagians in Ireland can be dated with great exactitude, because it refers to a problem of chronology. The annals of Clonmacnoise state that in the year 445 A.D., the Pelagians in Ireland refused to celebrate

1. Heinrich Zimmer, *Pelagius in Irland: Texte und Untersuchungen zur patristischen Literatur* (Berlin: Weidmann, 1901).

Easter according to the Roman rite, and instead fixed it upon another
date, thus introducing that Irish calendar of the Easter festival which was
to remain a bone of contention with Rome for many centuries to come.
Zimmer has elucidated that there were then no Pelagians in South Ireland,
but that the quotation in question refers to the whole of Northern Ireland,
which was altogether Pelagian, the famous monastery of Bangor being
the center of the movement. An Irish tradition, too late to deserve much
faith but nevertheless characteristic, actually makes Pelagius abbot of
Bangor before going to Rome. Thus about twenty years after Pelagius'
death (the exact date of his death is not known), the whole of Northern
Ireland was Pelagian, and that despite the solemn condemnation of the
doctrine by Augustine, and by the ecumenical council of Ephesus. How
could such a state of things have arisen, had Pelagius not been closely
connected with the Irish church from the beginning? Obviously, the
influence of Rome had been stronger than the influence of the great
heretic in the South of Ireland, but in the North, where the influence of
Rome did not reach, the Irish monks regarded him as their own man,
and did not care what foreigners decided about his teachings.

Two hundred years later we find the state of things entirely unchanged.
This time the Pope, claiming ecumenical supremacy, writes to the
churches of Northern Ireland and Scotland, forwarding and supporting
complaints of Southern Irish monasteries about the stubbornness of their
Northern neighbors in clinging to the Irish date for Easter, and to Pelagianism. "We have learnt," the holy father says, "that the virus of the
Pelagian heresy has again come to life among you. . . . We admonish
you not to stir again the embers [of a movement] whose armor has been
burnt, and which has been destroyed elsewhere two hundred years ago."

Pelagianism thus appears not only as the heresy of an Irishman, but
as an affair of the Irish church and nation, or, more precisely, of that
part of it which was farthest removed from all Roman influence, and of
the Scotish church which had been founded in and was constantly directed
from Ireland. It appears almost as the Irish national creed. And a sudden
light is thrown upon facts of early medieval history otherwise not easily
explicable. First of all, the advent of Pelagius antedates by several decades
the work of the national saint of Ireland, St. Patrick. No student of these
matters today doubts that Patrick was not the first missionary of Ireland,
and that Christianity existed there from a very early date, possibly much
earlier not only than St. Patrick, but also Pelagius. But the fact remains
that the Northern Irish church, which soon became the most important
section of the Irish church, and whose importance grew all through the
early middle ages owing to its missionary work in Scotland, Northern

England, France, Germany, and Northern Italy, was permeated with Pelagianism from a very early date onwards.

Now this church was engaged in a struggle lasting over centuries with the Church of Rome, a struggle which centered around the date of the Easter festival. Nobody could ever say why the Irish stuck so fanatically to their own calculation of the date for Easter, a method admittedly derived from the East, but now abandoned everywhere in the West. Was it sheer local stubbornness and obstinacy? It has generally been thus interpreted. But the aspect of things changes when we come to realize that while Bangor and its disciples only spoke of Easter (a question about which they could invoke an old and venerable tradition), Rome knew and occasionally said that the real trouble with Ireland was Pelagianism, the worst heresy the West had produced for centuries. It then appears that if, through their stubborn sticking to an un-ecumenical calculation of the Easter date, the Northern Irish church held aloof from the community of Western Christendom, it was not due to simple dislike of foreign interference. Rather, the quarrel about the date of Easter was more or less a pretext, and a good one, for the Irish way of determining its date was older than the Roman way; hence it could be said that even in matters of ritual Rome had departed from the good tradition. But the real reason, in the light of Zimmer's research in Irish manuscripts, would seem to have been that the Irish church realized that it had a different spirit, a different conception of grace and redemption, and therefore did not want any Roman interference, though, in view of the condemnation of Pelagianism at the council of Ephesus, this could not be admitted openly.

Be it added that the Irish church, down to late Carlovingian times, was the strongest single force in the spiritual life of the West. This is a well-known fact. But it acquires a new significance if Irish influence on the continent is no longer regarded simply as a channel through which Latin and Greek traditions were preserved, but as an independent current with a message of its own.

Yet Zimmer has failed to grasp the import of his finds. He has convincingly demonstrated the influence of Pelagius upon the Irish church, and nobody since has even attempted to controvert his views. For Zimmer based his contention not only on Irish chronicles and Papal rescripts such as those quoted above, but on the fact that the works of Pelagius, known on the continent as works of Jerome, were known in Ireland to belong to Pelagius, and nevertheless treated as authoritative. Pelagius, in Ireland, was for centuries regarded as one of the great fathers of the church. This fact opens a new avenue to the understanding of the character of the Irish church, of the Pelagian heresy, of the relations between Ireland and Rome and their struggle for control of the churches of the continent, and finally to a new appreciation of the various strands contributing to the formation of Western civilization. But Zimmer did not use his find to elucidate any of these questions. He used his Irish manuscripts of Pelagius, and his discovery of the role of Pelagius in Ireland, for the one and only purpose of the emendation of the text of pseudo-Jerome; a laborious work which has now been completed through the labors of A. Souter. Thus this German professor did not treat the emendation of manuscripts as a means of understanding history, but treated far-reaching new insights into history as a means of emendating manuscripts of secondary importance. There are people who believe that this and only this is true scholarship.

We spoke of an independent contribution of the Irish church, of Irish theology, to the emergence of Western civilization. But in this statement is implied an assumption which is in need of proof. For is Pelagianism really original? The mere fact that it was condemned as a heresy does not settle the problem. More than one view tolerated for a long time and accepted by many has finally been declared to be heretic by the Catholic church. Was Pelagianism really so new when it arose? The seventeenth century already knew that there had existed a "Pelagianism before Pelagius," convincing proof of which could be found in the assurance with which Pelagius and his friends believed themselves to be in the right and expected the majority of the churches to support them against Augustine and the African church. In fact, the originality of Pelagius can be challenged from no less than three directions. First of all, there exist ties between the theology of Pelagius and that of the Eastern church, in particular of Origen; it was upon the support of the East that the sanguine Pelagius set his dearest hopes. Secondly, Pelagianism might be regarded as being no more than an extreme formula for tendencies prevailing all through the Latin church, and interesting arguments can be brought forward in support of this view. Finally, Pelagianism might be regarded as a fundamentally non-Christian doctrine, which indeed it is in many respects, and it is then easy to show its close similarity to certain pagan philosophies, and in particular to Stoicism. This connection has been emphasized by modern protestants, such as Loofs.[2] The investigation of these problems will lead us into a detour of considerable extension, a detour parallel to that needed to prove how

2. Friedrich Loofs, *Leitfaden zum Studium der Dogmengeschichte* (Halle: Niemeyer, 1950).

original is the North-Western use of the personal pronoun. Such a digression would be a tedious affair, were it not that in its course the whole problem of the origins and the original features of Western civilization could be stated again, as when we compared Western speech with the speech of other, neighboring civilizations.

Of the three forms of "Pelagianism before Pelagius," each of which is traceable beyond a shadow of doubt, but whose meaning and extent it is necessary to investigate, the one discoverable in the Greek church is most easily dealt with. Souter has demonstrated, in the introductory volume of his new edition of Pelagius' commentaries on Paul,[3] that Pelagius knew Origen's commentaries on Paul, or rather their Latin translation by Rufinus, and was deeply influenced by them. In terms of exact theology, it is absolutely impossible to trace even the tiniest difference between the doctrines of sin, grace, works, and redemption in Origen and Pelagius respectively. Origen, and with him the whole Eastern church, taught that the will of man is free; that he can always choose either good or evil; that everybody can be saved by his own efforts; that the essence of practical, as distinct from mystical Christianity consisted in an enlarged code of morals; that the new law Jesus had brought was essentially a pedagogic teaching of a higher morality, and that the other main contribution of God to man's redemption had consisted in the sending of the holy spirit in baptism. In other respects there exists an abyss between the theology of Origen and that of Pelagius, but not in the problems of redemption. Be it added that the study of the Greek language, and of the fathers of the Greek church, was a distinctive feature of the Irish church from the days of Pelagius onwards. When the Western half of the continent had long forgotten its Greek, the monks of Bangor knew it to perfection. This can be proved throughout the centuries, down to the days of Johannes Scotus Erigena, who, in the ninth century, evolved a Platonic philosophy at the court of the French king Charles the Bald. The influence of Greek theology upon Irish theology, and upon Pelagius in particular, is a fact beyond doubt.

But something else must be considered. Theology is often apt to be a very bad guide to living religion, as, in a later, less religious age, philosophy is apt to be a very bad guide to living morality. Two authors may agree to a point in the wording of their theological and philosophical principles, and yet have totally different conceptions of life, of man, and of religious experience. It must be noted at once, in comparing Origen and Pelagius, that they are not only different, but absolutely opposed

---

3. Alexander Souter, *The Earliest Latin Commentaries on the Epistles of St. Paul.* (Oxford: Clarendon Press, 1927).

to one another in this—that to Pelagius moral theology is everything, almost as if he were a modern nondenominational puritan, whereas to Origen moral theology is a side issue, while all his interest is concentrated upon an interpretation of the metaphysical mysteries of the faith.

Here we strike one of the most distinctly "Western" features of Pelagianism. If the Pelagian controversy loomed so large in the West, but not in the East, it was because it formulated the main problems of moral theology, which to the West meant just everything, and to the East very little indeed. This situation can be expressed in a more pointed formula. *In the West the problems of the trinity and of the two natures in Christ, which dominated the theology of the East, received an ever smaller amount of attention as the West found its own soul. In the East, conversely, the problems of a Christian life receded more and more into the background, as the East found its own soul.* Already Origen had moved so far in this direction that it is impossible to state any coherent, thought-out moral doctrine of his. (This aspect of his religious attitude has been strongly emphasized in the admirable three volumes on Origen by du Fay, in French.) In order to compare Pelagian moral doctrine and Eastern moral doctrine, we must turn farther back in the history of Eastern theology, to Origen's teacher, Clement of Alexandria, who in contrast to Origen has a complete doctrine of Christian morals.

The urge toward moral perfection is the distinctive characteristic of Pelagius' morality. What is Clement's idea of perfection? It does not appear at all in his many writings on morals. But it comes in in a different context. He is also possessed by an urge toward perfection, an urge which might be described as common to the Christian way of life in general. But he does not look for perfection in the moral sphere. Here is the passage where this Greek father of the church speaks of Perfection:

"Thus Jesus becomes perfect solely through the bath [of baptism], and is made holy through the coming down of the Holy Spirit upon him. . . . And the same happens to us, for the Lord's [life] is the figure of our own life. We are enlightened through baptism, are made God's sons through being enlightened; and, being now God's sons, we have become perfect. Having become perfect, we are made immortal. . . . . This work is often called the work of grace [charisma], or of light, or of perfection, or of cleansing. It is a bath, because our sins are washed away, a work of grace, because with the sins their penalty is taken away, a work of light, because the holy saving light becomes visible through it, so that we can now clearly see the Godhead. But we call it a work of perfection, because that brings perfection which leaves nothing to be desired. And what could be lacking to the man who has received knowledge of God? Also it is absurd to assume that God's grace could be anything but perfect and complete in all respects. For the perfect being can only make perfect gifts. . . . We alone therefore, as soon as we have passed the first stages of life, are already perfect. We are in the life, for we have been separated from death. . . . But, they say, the baptized man has not yet received a perfect gift." (*The Pedagogue*, Book I, chapter 6)

It is true that, in one sense, perfection will only be achieved in eternity. But

"as far as is possible in this life . . . it is our faith that we have been made perfect. For faith is the perfect doctrine. And through faith we have life. So what can we wish for except to have this life eternally? For nothing is lacking in faith, which is in itself perfection and complete. . . . For where there is faith, there is also promise; and the perfection of promise is peace."

The supernatural light gives us the power to see sin, and liberates us from it.

It seems to me that this doctrine, which in terms of the Eastern church is perfectly orthodox, must seem almost blasphemous to Westerners: through the mere acceptance of faith, the mystical rite of baptism and the coming of the Holy Spirit consequent upon it, man is made perfect, so that nothing remains undone but the transition from mortal life to immortality? There is, quite literally, no room in this conception for moral effort, let alone a passionate urge towards moral perfection. True, Clement covers hundreds of pages with mild advice of a moral kind. But it is only advice. The central thing is the faith in the mysteries, and their performance. This, in itself, is perfection. And if further perfection is sought, it can only be sought in ever more profound speculation about the basic mysteries of the faith.

In this short comparison between one of the greatest moralists of the Eastern church, and the greatest of the older heretics of the West, the contrast between Eastern and Western Christianity can be clearly perceived. It is a well-known fact that it is not easy to point to any decisive difference of doctrine between the two. The quarrel about the *filioque*, about the problem whether the Holy Spirit was issued from Father and Son, or from the Father only, resulted in the emergence of a definite difference of faith on one point. But it is difficult to conceive, in the Western view at least, that this should be essential enough to justify a schism. The ritual of the two churches is admittedly very different, but ritual is not faith, and Rome has recognized the orthodoxy of the Greek ritual by countenancing its continuance among the Greek Uniates, when,

in the sixteenth century, it readmitted these converts from Greek Orthodoxy into the fold of the Roman Catholic church. There remains the
fact of the schism between East and West as such, of the struggle between
the independent Pope of Rome and the Emperor of Byzantium and his
patriarch. Viewed in this light, the schism is purely political, and it is
not easily intelligible why, after the fall of the Byzantine Empire in 1453
A.D., it could still not be mended. The simple fact is that the masses
in the East would never have countenanced a reunion, not owing to any
profound doctrinal differences between the two churches, but owing to
a total incompatibility of the two ways of life. This incompatibility is
embodied in the two quotations about perfection given above. The incompatibility was so great that it is impossible to express it in terms of
opposites, of incompatible answers to the same problems. The gap was
wider than that. It did not concern answers to given problems, but the
problems themselves. The aim of Eastern orthodoxy was directed towards something in which the Western church is not even interested,
and vice versa.

It is well known that the whole theology of the East, once the chaotic
enthusiasm of the first three or four generations had passed, turned about
the duplicate problem of the relations of the three persons in God, and
of the Divine and human nature in Christ. We shall see in a moment
that the West, in the earliest stages of these contentions, made an important contribution to their solution. Yet with this one interference, in
the beginning of the third century A.D., the part played by the West in
the Christological debates is finished. All the great fathers of the Greek
church, all the ecumenical councils, dealt with problems which the West
had settled once and for all and was no longer really concerned with.
This theological labor came to an end in the East about the end of the
sixth century A.D. It is remarkable that the West should never again
have touched these fundamental and intricate problems. All Christian
churches of the West (with the exception of the modern, rationalistic
Unitarians) take for granted the Christological work of the Greek church,
with all its astonishing and, to the Western mind, irrational results.
Conversely the East has not even been touched by the later stages of the
great struggle about grace and merit, sin and atonement, which was
fought in the West. Here also, in characteristic parallel to what happened
to the West in the matter of Christology, the Eastern church made one
important, initial contribution, through the Clementine-Origenian doctrine of free will. Then the East lost all interest, and the fierce struggles
of the Reformation had as little echo in the East as the Nestorian or
Monophysite troubles had in the West. Only in very recent Russian

developments, in the works of Tolstoi, Soloviev, Dostoevski, and their contemporaries, a first approach is made to a synthesis of Eastern and Western Christianity. Here, as in so many other respects, Russia appears as the holder of the keys of the future, quite irrespective of the incident of atheistic proselytism, which is already, in the main, a thing of the past.

It is, of course, true that both the Eastern and the Western type of Christianity have a common root in the work of Paul, the first theologian of the Christian faith. For in Paul, and in particular in the letter to the Romans, both the mystical atonement through the Son of God, and the practical problems of a Christian morality are to be found in outline, or, more correctly, in all essentials. Yet nowhere was this original fullness of religious doctrine maintained intact. The mysteries of the Son of Man who is the Son of God were given no more than perfunctory recognition in the West. The moral problems of law and grace were given no more than perfunctory recognition in the East. This comes out clearly when we contrast, as we did above, the Eastern and the Western idea of perfection.

It might be asked why precisely this idea of perfection should be made the touchstone of the inner meaning of religion in the various Christian civilizations. The first answer would be that the problem occurred to us as being prominent in the writings of Pelagius. But this prominence is not the result of chance. Where perfection is sought, there real emphasis is put, and only there. The idea of perfection is connected with those subject matters which are regarded as most relevant in practice. There is, to say it again, no lack of statements about the Trinity in the West. But no Western theologian could have maintained that man became perfect by being initiated, through the *mystique* of baptism, into the mysteries of the Trinity. Conversely, the Greek fathers abound in moral advice, but no Greek father has ever envisaged it as the duty of the ordinary Christian, cleric or layman, to seek perfection in the sphere of Christian morals. It must therefore be judged that the idea of perfection is the real test of what is practically most relevant in a Christian attitude, and that all literal copying of Eastern things in the West and vice versa is in the character of superficial intellectual borrowing. This applies, with particular emphasis, to Pelagius' borrowing of Origen's doctrine of free will.

In these considerations the solution of another query is implicit. Is it really admissible to take a chief heretic such as Pelagius as the embodiment of the spirit of Western Christianity? A full reply can only be found in an exhaustive survey of Pelagius' relation to other types of Christian thought, a survey which we have not yet completed. But part of the answer at least is contained in what we said above about the one-sided development given to the theology of Paul in both East and West. I should think that a heretical attitude is implicit in such one-sidedness as such. Pascal has elaborated the idea that heresy is not simply untruth, but a one-sided insistence upon certain aspects of the faith to the detriment of others. In this sense—and I believe it is the only sense in which the historian can accept the notion of heresy—the whole of both Western and Eastern Christian civilization are heretical. They are not, as is sometimes said in demagogic exaggeration, un-Christian. They are, precisely, heretical. This is a fact which is normally carefully hidden in the formulae adopted by the churches. But time and again the inherent basic one-sidedness breaks through to the surface, and then the basic heretical assumptions of either civilization are openly voiced.

No wonder then that the "orthodox" point of view so often appears as a superficial compromise, and that the deepest impulses of the Christian civilizations come out in the voices of their heretics. The East is obsessed with salvation through the mystery of the incarnation. Therefore its most intimate voice is heard, not in the smooth formulae of its great ecumenical councils, but in the teachings of Gnostics of all sorts, who regard the great majority of mankind as hopelessly dead in the flesh, whereas a small minority of "pneumatics," of mystically enlightened supermen, are automatically saved without any personal contribution on their part. Gnosticism is the constant lure, the inherent heresy, of the East. Conversely the West is obsessed with practical moral perfection. No wonder, therefore, that in a thousand different shapes the belief should crop up that it is possible and necessary to attain moral perfection, and that this is the only real meaning of Christianity. Pelagianism is therefore the constant lure, the inherent heresy of the West. It comes to the surface, ever anew, in a thousand different shapes, not the least of them the noisy verbal anti-Pelagianism of the Calvinists. The pretended anti-Pelagianism of the seventeenth century Puritans and their nineteenth century followers is perhaps the purest form of the Pelagian heresy that ever was. But about this later.

There was a time when A. Harnack convinced the whole world of Christian theology that Gnosticism was the doctrinal form of an "acute Hellenization" of the Christian gospel, that it was the Christian gospel made acceptable to Greeks trained in the concepts of Hellenic philosophy. Few will doubt, today, that Harnack's was a total mistake, and that the factual situation was the exact opposite of what Harnack thought it was: of all trends in Christian thought, Gnosticism is admittedly, despite all its attempts to express itself in terms of Greek philosophy, the most oriental one. With this we are not mainly concerned here. We must point out that an exactly parallel problem exists as to Pelagianism. At first sight it might be interpreted as something typically Latin, as Christianity made acceptable to people reared, not in an Oriental but in a Roman moral atmosphere. But Pelagius' close ties with Ireland put a mark of interrogation behind any such statement. Must not the real roots of Pelagianism be sought as far outside the geographical center of classical antiquity as the roots of Gnosticism, only in the opposite direction? Pelagius' connection with Ireland points in that direction.

But before giving a final answer to this question we must now turn towards an analysis of the relation of Pelagianism to other ways of life in the West. The essence of the Pelagian teaching, and the thing which has roused Augustine and so many others against it, is the pretence that man can achieve perfection through his own efforts. This can quite adequately be described as a pagan point of view. It is therefore natural that the best students of Pelagianism should have pointed to its affinities with pagan moral doctrine, and in particular with the teachings of the Stoics. How far is Pelagius' doctrine a reaction away from mystical Christianity towards the moral doctrine of the Roman emperors in the period of Rome's greatness?

Such a discussion must inevitably start with a succinct statement of those main points of Stoic moral teaching which have some relation to the moral teachings of the Western church and of Pelagianism. There are two of them, the one relating to the metaphysical foundations of moral doctrine, the other to practical moral doctrine itself.

The metaphysics of Stoical morality were based upon the conception of natural law. The origin of the doctrine of natural law must be sought in the writings of Aristotle, and partly even of Plato, but the Stoics were the first systematically to develop this idea, which was to be of such importance for the political and moral doctrines of the West. The idea is simple enough. Moral commands contain nothing but the natural conditions of social life. Society and human life break down unless these commands are observed. Also, a knowledge of them makes part of the natural structure of the human mind. Moral conscience is inborn.

The doctrine is, however, very far from being unimpeachable, and most certainly it is not genuinely Christian. Christian moralists, from Paul to Pascal, have constantly pointed to the fact that it is quite impossible to know good and evil merely by instinct; proof of this is the wide diversity of moral commands from one place to another. It is also not true in the least that moral behavior is natural, if by nature is meant all that really exists. It is obvious, on the contrary, that it is natural to man to behave immorally, to sin. Pelagius would not admit this. But it is on this assumption that Christianity exists. For if it were "natural" to be good, no supernatural revelation, no atonement and redemption, would be necessary at all. Christianity stands and falls with the rejection of the idea of natural law. But the idea is also incompatible with sound social doctrine, as no state, no compulsion of any kind would be necessary if it were natural to man to be good. Anarchism, then, would be the only correct social doctrine.

These criticisms point to the need for a search into the special situation which has made the Stoics adopt so unsatisfactory a notion. The explanation is not far to seek. From the fifth pre-Christian century onwards, the Greek world was subject to a process of rapid disintegration of established traditions, which, from the fourth century onwards, was brought to a climax by the collapse of the city-state, that core of Greek life. In the midst of the disintegration of all established rules and powers, thinkers were driven to search for a new, no longer traditional but rational principle on which to base the demands of morality. Unable to appeal to society and its disintegrating traditions, they appealed to "nature," to the needs and desires of the individual. As long as the rules of behavior are unchallenged, nobody ever conceives the idea of appealing to nature for stabilizing habits which are sanctioned by tradition. The emergence of a doctrine of natural law, in Greece as later in the West, always announces the decline of traditional law and morality. Behind its overemphasis on the goodness of nature, and of the natural goodness of man, there always lurks a hidden realization of the overwhelming force of evil.

This becomes even more apparent when we turn to the mainstay of Stoic practical morality, to the idea of liberty. Man, the Stoics contend, wants to be free and this is his highest right and his highest duty. It is the Stoics who have brought the idea of individual liberty to the world—for the city-state of classical Greece knew no such thing. But the proud self-assertion of this libertarian ideal should be subject to as much scepticism as the apparent optimism of the doctrine of natural law. "Liberty" as such is an empty word. Nobody can be completely free. A society, as well as a social doctrine, are defined by the extent and by the limits of the liberty they grant. We must attempt to define the Stoic sphere of liberty. Nothing is easier. For the Stoic conception of liberty is entirely negative. We want to be free; we can only be free by attempting nothing which is not in our power. The whole outside world is not in our power. To the outside world also belongs our body. Liberty consists in not being subject to it all, in keeping one's soul in complete independence from it all. The morality of Stoicism is not one of transforming life. Its belief in liberty is not a belief in the right and duty of doing things. It is a morality of abstention from all the pleasures of life, of indifference to all its pains. It is a morality, not of a good life; for it goes so far as to advise complete abstention from doing one's duty by any social group, including the state, and to advise reserve in all human contacts, including friendship. It is a morality which has undoubtedly a great deal in common with the attitude of Eastern ascetics, but nothing at all with the activism of the West. It is a morality, not of the good life, but of a serene death.

It is natural enough, therefore, that the Greek church should have adopted that morality eagerly. The "optimistic" doctrine of natural law was in flat contradiction to the moral teaching of Paul, to all that was and is specifically Christian in Christian morality. But the facile moral optimism of Clement of Alexandria, of Origen and their followers agreed with it completely. As far as this facile optimism was copied in the West, the doctrine of natural law also penetrated into the Western church. It is, to say it in one word, the logical philosophical basis for the Origenian doctrine of free will.

As to the practical morality of the Stoics, it also agreed exceedingly well with the tendencies prevailing in the Eastern church. If the doctrine of free will and natural law fitted into the all too lenient handling of the morality of the laity, the ascetic ideals of Stoicism coincided with the ascetic ideals of the Eastern religious *elite*. And it was an additional advantage of the Stoical doctrine in the eyes of the fathers of the Eastern church that it drew a sharp distinction between the ordinary man and the select few. "That type of morality", says Cicero (*De Officiis* III .4) "which Stoics call absolute morality, can only be found in the sage. . . . Only a shadow of this type of virtue, and by no means itself, can be found among those who are not perfect sages." The Stoic moral ideal is as much a thing of the few as the pneumatic-ascetic ideal of the Gnostics; both have the same content, both the same limitations. Stoicism is here seen as one form in which the world of classical antiquity gradually orientalized itself, not, in the main, as a precursor of the Western type of life.

There are admittedly also points of contact between the teachings of the Stoics and Western morality. The doctrine of the Stoics is one of the first purely individualist doctrines we know of, and this is certainly a point of great importance, a point which connects the morality of the Stoics with the view of the new, yet unborn I-saying civilization. Yet, as said above, it would be dangerous to regard the individualism of the

Stoics as tantamount to the individualism of the modern world. Stoicism is the result of the disintegration of the Greek city-state, and from this disintegration its individualism resulted. As said above, it is an entirely negative type of individualism, and the sphere of liberty of the individual in Stoic doctrine is so narrow as to be reduced, as it were, to a nondimensional point, a wholly abstract, unreal indifference to both pleasure and pain. The individual, in late antiquity, was left stranded, with no really close and binding social ties to cling to, and tossed about by the superior forces of the Empire, apt to be crushed at any moment by superior powers. In this situation, the morality of Stoicism makes sense. But it is not by any means a morality which makes the individual the bearer of positive obligations. In fact, the morality of Stoicism is not a morality of binding obligations at all, as it is really only meant for a select group of sages.

It is here that the attitude of Pelagius is totally different. And it is again in the matter of human perfection that the difference can most clearly be perceived. Real Stoic morality is only for the perfect sage. But the core and essence of Pelagius' doctrine is the heroic, though foolish assumption that everybody can be perfect. Pelagius adopts all the tenets of Stoical moral doctrine, as he adopts the substantially identical tenets of moral doctrine of Clement and Origen. But he gives them a totally different practical meaning. The Stoical and Eastern-Christian doctrine of natural law, despite its verbal assertion of the essential goodness of man, issues into nothing more than an exceedingly perfunctory set of inefficient moral admonitions for the many. Pelagius transforms it into a moral extremism meant for everybody. The Stoical and Eastern-Christian doctrine of perfection issues into the opening of an abyss between the many and the select few, the "pneumatics," the "sages," who alone can achieve perfection. Pelagius rejects this distinction between the many and the few. Through he did not dare yet to go to the end, the protestant rejection of the Catholic and Greek-orthodox division between clergy and laity, between counsels of perfection and a minimum morality lurks behind his views. With Stoics and Eastern ascetics, the idea of free-will and personal liberty becomes tantamount to an advice to flee the world, with its pains and its temptations. There is no line in Pelagius suggesting such a negative attitude to the world. Though a fervent ascetic himself, though he spent a great part of his life in the East, he apparently never thought of joining the anachoretes in the desert. His asceticism is a rule of permanent struggle *in* the world, a struggle to conquer the world. It does not point, as Stoicism does, and as was put into practice by the *elite* of the Eastern church, towards withdrawal into the desert, but towards unceasing missionary work, and unceasing struggle towards a conquest of the world for the principles of a higher morality. In one word, it points towards that basic Protestant, or more precisely Calvinist and puritan principle which Max Weber has defined as "asceticism inside the world"—living like a monk, but without being one, for the saving of one's soul is only possible through work inside this world.

One might therefore say that the relation of Pelagius to Stoicism provides a close parallel to the relation of modern I-saying speech to the "vulgar" Latin and Greek of Pelagius' age. The disintegration of the classical synthesis is the general background in both cases. But this disintegration allows of two outcomes. In itself, it is not more than a loss of previously existing patterns of life. The new pattern, however, may be oriental, may consist in a basically hostile attitude to the world, or it may consist in the development of a new positive individualism of a kind previously unknown. The second attitude was first foreshadowed when, through Pelagius, the young peoples of the North for the first time had their say in matters of Christian civilization.

Yet a third aspect of the religious situation in the age of Pelagius remains to be considered. We have seen that, as compared with the new morality of the West, Stoicism, this alleged source of Pelagianism, is hardly less oriental than Eastern Christianity; that, in fact, it is not much more than a preliminary stage of that process of orientalization of the Greek world which culminated in the way of life of the Eastern church. But does the same apply to the Western church? It has been generally recognized that from an early date Western Christianity differed substantially from Eastern Christianity. Was Pelagius' teaching really so novel? Did he not, at least, continue the traditions of the Western church? In raising this query, we come again one step nearer to a full picture of the situation in which Western morality arose.

When and where did a specifically Western version of Christianity arise? A Christian community was founded in Rome by Paul, and literary as well as pictorial documents of its existence go back to the first century A.D. Intense church life in Gaul is traceable at least in the second century. But these communities, though Western in a geographical sense, were by no means Western in their outlook and membership. The most important documents of that early period are in Greek. The membership of the early Western communities, despite an occasional conversion of high Roman officials, seems to have been overwhelmingly oriental in descent and speech. Also Western Christianity, though growing, was infinitely less strong than Eastern Authority, and it is probably exact to say that Westerners, as distinct from orientals living in the West, joined it in considerable numbers only after it had become the religion of the Emperor. But even then the Christian beliefs of the Westerners remained, apparently, a fairly superficial affair. Not only in the countryside, but even among the urban upper classes, pagan opposition in the West remained strong till nearly the end of the Empire. Many even of the "Christian" orators and poets of the fourth and fifth century in the West remain entirely pagan in outlook and tradition, and even the work of great leaders of the Western church such as Ambrose and Jerome is mainly of an organizing, propagandizing, and popularizing character. It is not at all an exaggeration to say that the West adopted Christianity from the East when through its influence in the East it had won political power, and that, in the West, it was so much adapted to the existing mentality as to be not much more than a new prop of the tottering Roman administration. Looking at it from this angle, *one might say that there was no such thing as a distinctive Western Christianity* (unless the absence of deeper religious impulses is taken as its distinctive feature) *until Christianity reached the non-Latin peoples of the North.*

Indeed there is no such thing as a development of Western Christianity on a par with Eastern Christianity. The latter had lived through a coherent process of development. Geographically, it had originated in Palestine, and expanded from there in all directions, until it covered a vast area, filling it all with intense religious life. As to contents, the main problems of its dogma had been formulated by Paul, and all the following development down to the seventh century can and must be understood as a strictly logical, though one-sided development of basic assumptions given in Paul. This unity of a geographical area with a center, and this logical continuity in the development of ideas and their expression (what one would call the coherent, continuous, logical development of style) must be regarded as essential characteristics of a fully developed higher civilization and its history. They are lacking in the case of Western Christianity. There is no geographical center—the faith did not spread from Rome, but communities sprang up wherever there were sufficient numbers of orientals, in particular Jews, to be interested—and there was not anything like a logical development of ideas. From this angle Latin Christianity appears, not as an independent unit, but as an outlying, half-barbaric offshoot of the Eastern church. That was what it looked like in the eyes of the Easterners, and it was often treated as such in the great ecumenical councils of the Eastern church.

But all this is subject to one essential qualification. There exists one geographical area of the West where Christianity, from the beginning, was the affair of Westerners, not of orientals; where it spread out from a center over a whole area; and where its religious life, its doctrine and organization, developed in a distinctive way, in a logical evolution from certain basic original assumptions. That area was Roman Africa, or, in modern terms, Tunisia and the Eastern part of Algeria. In this small corner of the Latin world, and only in this corner, can we speak of a truly independent development of Western Christianity.

Be it said at once that what is most characteristic about this region is its fundamentally non-Latin character. "Africa"—that was the name given in Roman speech to that small area—had not been Hellenized, less so, in fact, than Rome and Southern France. But it had not been successfully Latinized either. Among the masses of the population Berber speech and habits maintained themselves with a stubbornness only paralleled by the survival of the Britons in England—but the efforts at Latinization had lasted much longer and been much more intense in Africa than in Britain. If they failed so amply, it was apparently due to the fact that the small upper layer of society, which everywhere else had been the standard-bearer of Latinization, remained stubbornly impermeable to Latin cultural propaganda in Africa, and tenaciously clung to its native Punic ways. For in the Punic Carthaginians the Romans had met the only group in the West which was not at least half barbaric, but highly civilized and steeped in a civilization much older than that of Rome. No wonder then that, even after the fall of Carthage, the land-owning upper classes of the Provinces of Africa and Numidia stuck to their native speech and way of life. Towards the end of the second century A.D., with the accession of the emperor Septimius Severus, Africa became the most important province of the Western half of the Empire. The rule of an African dynasty brought about profound changes in the Empire. With Severus, for the first time an emperor ascended the throne who was not only a provincial—that, the emperors of the previous dynasty had been also—but who spoke Latin with a heavy foreign accent. He brought with him his equally Punic staff officers, and with them, for the first time, introduced an entirely military dictatorship.

The rule of the Africans in Rome was no more than an episode; but what, in matters of state, was no more than an important incident, was much more than an incident in the history of the Western church. It was precisely in the circles of the African army that was reared the first great doctor of the African—in fact of the Western—church, Tertullian, son of an African military proconsul and later a wealthy lawyer in Carthage. It is not saying too much that as in Paul there must be sought, though in an embryonic form, all the problems which later occupied all sections and versions of Christianity, so in Tertullian there can be found all the problems which were later worked out in the African church and throughout the churches in the Western half of the Roman Empire, problems which still dominate Western Christianity.

It would be of the greatest importance to know something of the character of that African civilization which was to make such an important contribution to the yet unborn civilization of the West. Yet here we are at a loss. There is no lack of material remains, but they reveal little but the ordinary conditions of life of Roman provincial landowners. As to the spiritual life of that community before it became Christian, we know exceedingly little about it. It is not before the end of the second century that it becomes vocal in literature, and our main source of knowledge are the African fathers of the church themselves. It is from them that we must form an idea of the specific character of African life in this period. Let us therefore directly turn to Tertullian's teachings. An outline of them will give most of what is important in our context in the life of the African church, and relatively little will have to be said about the other great Africans down to Pelagius' contemporary, Augustine.

In the sphere of doctrinal development the early Africans derived their problems from the orientals. They handled them in a distinctive, African-Western fashion, but the distinctiveness is not one of a metaphysical, philosophical approach. Tertullian found himself confronted, not with any specifically Western or African theological problems, but with the Gnostic and Christological controversies which kept the whole church busy at that period. These controversies were particularly acute among the wholly oriental Roman community. Here Tertullian intervened, and, surprising as it is, he worked out the formula which, in substance, was later adopted by the whole church at the council of Nicaea: Christ, the son of God, second person of the trinity, is God and man together, different from the father and identical with him at one and the same time.

The formula much impressed the orientals through its clarity. But Tertullian himself was not primarily interested in its philosophical value. On the contrary, as to philosophy, Tertullian's formula cuts short all those controversies which were the life interest of the Greek church. And this was precisely what Tertullian aimed at. For he treated the dogmatic controversies from an angle as yet entirely foreign to the orientals, a specifically Western angle. He aimed at creating a *regula fidei*, a binding rule of faith. He assumed, in fact, that it existed, and that the only task was to formulate it correctly. The aim of the rule of faith is to determine a boundary line between those who are inside the church and those who are outside. Once that rule is laid down, controversy is at an end. And this is what, in dogmatic matters, Tertullian achieved in fact. The rule of faith he established swept away all heretical objections and put an end to Christological controversy in the West. But he could never have achieved it, had the mysteries of the faith been a life problem in the West as they were in the East. He could treat them as a mere matter of church discipline, because in the West they were no more than that. In this respect, Tertullian is simply a forerunner of all those Western—not only African—churchmen who were interested in unity and hierarchy, and not in mysteries and faith.

The extreme consequence of this idea of the rule of faith can be found in the later Catholic doctrine of *fides implicita*, of an implicit faith. The doctrine is an answer to the query what is the faith of those who have neither the knowledge nor the intelligence really to understand the teachings of the church. The answer is that for them it is sufficient to believe implicitly that all the church teaches is true. The church, in this context, is a body wielding authority, not a community of religious experience. Faith, here, is subordinated to discipline.

Tertullian's idea of a rule of faith is only a special case of his wider conception of church discipline. Discipline, in all his writings, is as prominent a term as perfection is with Pelagius. And discipline remains the dominating consideration of the African church. That does not only apply to the long line of bishops of Carthage who have decisively contributed to working out the Catholic conception of the church. It applies even to Augustine, despite his much greater interest in mysticism and his relatively less emphatic interest in church organization. For it is Augustine who, through his formula *coge entrare*, "force the heretics to enter the church," has put the final touch to the doctrine of church discipline. It is this formula which lay at the basis of the persecution of heretics all through the middle ages, and which is still living, though in a secularized, antireligious form, in the wars of our period. The whole concept is foreign to the Eastern church, as to every other civilization with the possible exception of Islam. It derives from the disciplinarian conception of church life of Tertullian and of the African church. Since then, the quest for ideological unity has remained one of the hallmarks of our civilization. It is one of those elements which must be traced not to Northern but to Southern roots.

The idea of papal supremacy is also directly derived from this disciplinarian conception of the church. The Eastern church was striving painfully to maintain unity of creed on a few essentials, but it never achieved, and in fact never aimed at worldwide unity of discipline in all matters. The independence of the various patriarchs, and even of smaller church dignitaries, in all matters of discipline was never seriously contested. That allowed a wide variety of church life. In the West, so loose a tie was not regarded as sufficient. It is, in the first place, due to the systematic exertions of the Metropolitans of Carthage that the see of Rome was recognized as the supreme authority in church affairs all over the West. The process of recognition can be studied in the letters of Cyprianus of Carthage. Since the middle of the third century the Western church rests upon the two pillars of Carthage and Rome, the first giving all the essential impulses, the second providing an organizing center of authority. Here, certainly, is a body of institutions which have deeply molded Western civilization.

We said above that the Africans reshaped the dogmatic problems of the East in the light of a specifically Western conception of discipline. That conception was not originally African, nor, what is more important, originally Christian. It was a conception borrowed from the Roman military and judiciary, and introduced into church life. It is therefore surprising enough that such a Roman adaptation of an oriental creed should have taken place not in Rome, but precisely in non-Latin Africa. Is there any specifically African element distinguishable in the whole process? We think there is.

In the first place, it remains a problem why these Roman disciplinarian conceptions, entirely worldly as they basically are, should assume a religious, and still more specifically, a Christian shape at all. What, in Christian life, did give them value? Or were they not rooted strongly enough in the army and the civil service, so that the secular Roman administration was looking for a religious prop? But if so, did not the cult of the emperors provide precisely such a basis? Again, if that cult was too conventional and devoid of really religious meaning, were not the religions adopted by the soldier emperors (the cult of Mithras, of the Invincible Sun) a more fitting expression of a faith centered on discipline than Christianity, that wholly mystical religion of love? In fact, for a long time, Rome did not adopt but fought Christianity. Again, few things are as obvious as that it was not the mystical aspects of Christianity which were foremost in the minds of the Africans. At the same time it is obvious enough that a merely disciplinarian, administrative attitude to church matters would never have been sufficient to guarantee the stability of the Western church. Something more was needed, some specific fervor.

The puzzle becomes deeper as we study the history of the African church. It has been said previously that a study of heresy is invariably a useful approach to an understanding of the main problems of an orthodox body. This applies emphatically to the African church, which was torn by schisms and heresies as few others. These schisms invariably turned about church discipline, the degree of rigor or charity which should be its basis. It is impossible to overlook the fundamental practical, social-economic, and political antagonisms which underlie the history of these rifts within the African church. It is altogether obvious, and a commonplace among students of the period, that the African schisms, and in particular the fiercest of them all, the Donatist schism, which filled the whole of the fourth and the beginning of the fifth century A.D., was not much more than an "ideological" reflection of a movement of social revolution. The formal contention of the Donatists was that sacraments of priests who under persecution had denied their faith were invalid. They maintained that the patriarch of Carthage elected immediately after the end of the Diocletian persecution had betrayed his faith; that therefore his office, and the offices of all his successors and of all priests consecrated by him and by his successors, were void. Obviously, a point of dogma was involved. Are sacraments valid *per se*, or only if dispensed by firm believers? But this point of dogma, which Augustine emphasized, and which is treated as central in some modern histories of the period, was not paramount in the minds of the contemporaries. For them it was a struggle about an incorrect episcopal election, dragging on, pointlessly, over a century. Obviously, the real meaning of the struggle lay elsewhere.

In fact, in challenging the validity of one episcopal election and all priestly consecrations which had issued from it, the Donatists simply challenged the authority of the metropolitan see of Carthage, the most Latinized institution of the African church and the outpost of Roman influence in their province. Two wings are clearly distinguishable among the Donatists, the one moderate, the other extremist. The first had its stronghold in Cirta, the capital of the province of Numidia, a sort of Punic opposite number to Latin Carthage. Here the provincial, Punic-speaking, landowning class was paramount, and determined the episcopal elections. This Punic landowning class had ruled the empire under the dynasty of the Severi; had struggled unsuccessfully to maintain that preponderance under the dynasty of the Gordians; had been defeated and been subjected to fearful massacres during the second half of the third century, without, however, being broken. Now this provincial upper class struggled against Roman preponderance under the guise of Donatism. There are parallels to this in the East, where Monophysitism became the battle cry of the bourgeoisie of Alexandria in its struggle against the supremacy of Constantinople.

But besides these moderates there were extremists, hungry serfs on the large estates and, still more important (as recent French research has brought out) landless laborers of Berber speech and half-tribal, wandering habits. In their hands, in the hands of the terror-striking bands of the *circumcelliones*, Donatism became simply a movement of social revolution. In the end, the movement split. The moderate wing was reconciled to the church, whereas the revolutionary wing received with open arms the barbaric invaders, the Vandals, who followed a policy very hostile to the landowning class and by protecting the serfs carried out part of the revolutionary program. But precisely by doing so they made Donatism pointless, and soon after the Vandal invasion all trace of it is lost. Again, the more extreme sections of the Donatist movement had their counterpart in the widespread peasant brigandage of the *Bagauda*, which, in Gaul especially, undermined the Roman administration from the third century onwards and never stopped until the Barbarian invaders came and alleviated the lot of the peasant serfs. But this parallel to Donatism only brings us back to the query: why, in Gaul, did peasant unrest express itself through simple outright peasant brigandage, whereas in Africa it took on a religious shape? Here is a heretical parallel to our previous query concerning orthodoxy: why, in Africa, did Roman disciplinarianism adopt a religious hue?

But before we attempt to give however tentative an answer, we must point to modern Western parallels. We stressed the significance for the modern Western conception of discipline and ideological unity of the orthodox African doctrine. We must now stress the significance of the African heretics for the Western type of revolution. No student of medieval heresy can fail to be struck by the close parallelism between Donatism and Hussitism, that Czech movement of the fifteenth century which stands on the boundary line of medieval religious sectarianism and modern national and social revolution. The parallel is indeed amazing. At the center of the struggle is the role of the Roman priests, and the limits of their attributions. The Hussite opposition is regionalist and anti-Roman for regional and national reasons, exactly as the Donatists, and exactly as the Donatists it falls into two groups, a moderate wing of provincial landowners who only contest the supremacy of the Roman see, and an extremist wing of peasant serfs and small town laborers with a program of outright social revolution. The German reformation takes up the same theme on a wider plane, with the Lutherans and Anabaptists playing the parts of moderates and extremists respectively. And from there on, through the great English and French revolutions, the same pattern is copied though in a secularized form. That political and social revolution should not simply be a matter of redistribution of wealth and power, but a struggle between a centralist conservative orthodoxy and its antidisciplinarian heretical opponents of various shades, is an inheritance from the struggles of the African church. So powerful is history. So little do differences of race and language matter as against unity of tradition and civilization. So little are social and economic structures the only determining factors of history.

Social structure being very much the same all over the Western Empire, local tradition, the local Punic (and, to a smaller degree, Berber) spirit is the only factor available for an explanation of the peculiarities of the African church. And we can, indeed, from all sources of the third century and down to the beginning of the Donatist struggles, discern how this factor worked. The dogmatic formulae of the African church are borrowed from the East, though developed independently under the novel aspect of laying down a *regula fidei*. The idea of discipline and church authority is borrowed from Roman secular government. But in the interpretation of this idea of discipline, there is something which does not derive either from the East or from Rome. This something is all too evident in the work of Tertullian. It has made him into a heretic.

Tertullian, in all his discussions about discipline, is haunted by one single fixed idea, the idea that discipline could be too mild. Starting from entirely reasonable and moderate ideas about church discipline, he is subject to a psychologically fascinating process of growing more and more bitter and extreme, to the point of ridicule. Already the first of his heretical writings, "About a Military Crown," contains the view that it is a deadly sin for a Christian soldier to accept a crown of flowers, the usual military decoration, because flowers are made to be scented and seen, not to be put upon a head, hence accepting a crown of flowers is a behavior against nature, on a par, as it were, with unnatural vice. Thus it starts and thus it continues. Virgins must go veiled as married women do. After the death of a first wife, no second marriage is to be concluded. Baptism is the normal way of obtaining forgiveness of past sins; after it, forgiveness should be granted for one more serious offense in the whole course of a life, but not for two. Military service is altogether a deadly sin. Every sexual sin is unforgivable, and the bishop of Rome ought to be expelled from the Christian community because he takes an opposite view. Every attempt of escaping martyrdom, even by changing abode, is a deadly sin, as martyrdom is the only normal way of salvation. This extremism in matters of discipline is the specific African contribution to the life of the church.

Superficially, it appears that all this is very near Pelagius' idea of perfection. But in fact it differs from it as much as does the Stoic's idea of perfection. Every line of Pelagius shows that despite, or perhaps rather because of his high-flown moral idealism, he conceived of no such ideas. He is not concerned in the least with extending the conception of evil to the point where it includes the most innocent, the most adequate actions, such as avoiding unnecessary martyrdom. He is not concerned with making the repentance of the sinner more difficult. Being essentially concerned with the moral progress of the individual, and deeply convinced of the infinite capacity of man for infinite progress, he could never have cherished ideas and encouraged practices which were bound to spread hopelessness among the majority of believers.

On this point, the incompatibility between Tertullian's view and Pelagianism is absolute. Tertullian, in his later years, maintained expressly that the enormous majority of men, including all the members of the orthodox church, are damned, and that by nature. For, as he said in a return to Gnostic views which he himself had strongly rejected in younger years, the majority of church members are only "psychics" (men of emotions, but without spiritual awakening) and only the few inspired ones, the "pneumatics," can be saved. It is a complete return to oriental views and the direct opposite of the basic Pelagian doctrine that everybody can be saved. The fact of the matter, however strange it may seem, is that Tertullian is not concerned with the saving of souls and the perfection of individuals at all. As he grows more rigorist, he more and more embraces the belief—later to be so congenial to Augustine— that men are predestined by their natural character as psychics or pneumatics to be damned or saved respectively. There is, in the long list of Tertullian's writings, not a single piece intended to make the path to virtue easier to the individual. He is not at all concerned with that. What matters to him is to keep the church free from the unclean. All his later moral writings are, at bottom, only one long catalogue of reasons for the expulsion of church members. The method of argument is wholly legal, its aim invariably the judicial conviction of the accused. Nobody has contributed more than Tertullian to the forging of the conception of a juridical law of the church; there is no greater precursor of canonic law in the Roman sense. But what distinguishes him from the canonists is that he fills the juridical form with a military spirit, with the spirit of an army no longer of Romans but of barbarians, where, by principle, only the most extreme and cruel means of discipline are employed. Tertullian would like to make of church life a never-ending court-martial.

The African contribution to Christianity should now be fairly clear. Borrowing from the East in matters of doctrine, from the secular Roman regime in matters of church organization, the African churchmen filled these worldly Roman notions with a fanatical fierceness all their own. It is fairly clear that this disciplinarianism was the chief attraction of Christianity to the Africans. The practical morality of the Romans of the early Empire was an easy-going affair. Christianity, through its ascetic elements, provided a creed which allowed of fierceness. It is this fierceness which runs through the orthodox as well as through the heretical doctrines and practices which sprang up in Africa. Here, alone of all provinces of the Roman Empire, there develops a type of Christian life primarily concerned with morals, a true successor to the stern moralists of the early Roman republican age. Yet, in contrast to the moral outlook which later developed in the West, it was not at all an individualist outlook upon morality. We said it already: Whereas Pelagius is wholly and exclusively concerned with individual souls, Tertullian is wholly and exclusively concerned with the body of the church as such.

Each of the two attitudes has made an important contribution to the later civilization of the West. The African attitude, once deprived of its extremism, became the basis for the later attitude of the Roman church; an attitude not individualistic at all, and concerned in the first place with the authority and unity of the church as such; a true continuation of the attitude of the Roman Empire. The South never completely departed from its classical traditions, in religion as little as in speech. The Pelagian attitude became the basis of the thoroughgoing individualism of the North. The struggle and the compromises between the two attitudes make up a great deal of Western history, not only in the sphere of religion. One has only to remember that this struggle between regimentation and individualism is an essential part of the political history of Europe.

Harnack has already pointed out that, starting with Tertullian's extremism, the controversy about church discipline continues throughout the history of the Western church *diminuendo*, insofar as the demands upon the ordinary believers are concerned. The demands of Tertullian are extreme in all directions. When, in the middle of the third century, Rome and the African church are shaken by the schism raised by Novatian, the quarrel is only about the readmission or rejection of those who have denied their faith in the Decian persecution. Half a century later again, in the Donatist struggles, the objection to readmission to the church of those who lapsed under persecution has been waived completely, and the extremists only retain an objection against their readmission to the priestly function. But while the extent of the disagreement between orthodox and extremists is narrowing, the fierceness of the struggle is increasing all the time. Tertullian's apostasy to the sect of the Montanists seems to have been more or less an individual affair. Montanism shook the churches of the West and of the East. Donatism, for more than a century, estranged the great majority of the faithful in Africa from the church, and led to fierce outbursts of social revolution.

It is in these struggles that the Catholic church has developed its typical attitude against moral extremism. That was not more than a natural, inevitable result of an authoritarian, disciplinarian, and administrative point of view. Entirely in the Roman secular tradition, the Roman and Carthaginian metropolitans did not aspire to create a church for the few, but a church accessible to everybody. In that way, the extremists were the most dangerous obstacle. The church did not waver in combating them. It is in this struggle that it became the truly "catholic," the all-embracing church. But a danger was lurking behind that practical and common-sense attitude. Though the extremists from Africa had hardly created a new religious motivation for secular Roman practices, they had given them a truly religious content through their fanatical attitude. If this extremism was rejected, then the church remained little more than a body with an organization and an authority dispensing mild moral advice not very different from that of the pagans. This was what actually happened.

This extremely easy-going and nearly oriental moral laxity did, in fact, prevail over the greater part of the Western church, until Irish and other Northern influences brought about a change from the tenth century onwards. But in Africa, such a solution was unacceptable. The metropolitans of Carthage fully concurred and even led in the movement which defeated the extremists and made the Catholic church into a church offering salvation to everybody. But they could not avoid continuing to take the problems of discipline very seriously. And in doing so, they found themselves confronted with problems of which the East had had no notion, problems which brought the Africans very near to specifically Western, even specifically protestant religious experiences.

Tertullian's idea had been to drive all sinners out of the church. In doing so, he had rejected the idea of free will, and returned to the Gnostic conception of the few elect pneumatics as the only men to be saved from damnation. This conception, in his mind, developed in stages. In an earlier book, *About the Soul*, which he apparently wrote just at the time of becoming a heretic, he still maintained that there was free will. But he combined this view with another one, with the idea that man was tainted with original sin. This was no more than taking up what had been the deepest personal experience of Paul, and putting it into the logical language of the schools. Nevertheless it was a revolutionary act. For the Eastern church had forgotten about original sin for all practical purposes, and also had every reason to forget about it. For if evil was inborn in man, then apparently the Gnostics were right in maintaining that only supernatural predestination could save a very few. The struggle against Gnosticism was always paramount in the minds of the Eastern fathers, whereas problems of morality were not paramount at all in their eyes. Tertullian, in putting them into the very center of his faith, had to come back to the original Gnostic view.

And what he had defended remained valid even after his crazy extremism was rejected by the church. Just through admitting sinners to the body of the church, the church was obliged to admit that sinfulness belonged to man. No other doctrine would have served so well, precisely for the sake of rejecting the extremists' demand to purge the church from all sinners. As soon as moral issues, through the raising of the question of discipline, became paramount in the church, the church remembered what Paul had said about sin and salvation. The doctrine of original sin soon became the mainstay of the theology of the orthodox African fathers, the distinctive feature of African theology. Thus it happened that what in the East was regarded as a heresy, became in Africa the central doctrine of orthodoxy. On the basis of this doctrine, a profound personal consciousness of sin could develop, as it did in the case of Augustine. There is no reason to assume, however, that Augustine, in this respect, was more than an exception. The outlook of the church remained impersonal for a long time, directed towards problems of church discipline. Yet it was only natural now that a Manichean such as Augustine should be converted to Christianity. For the Manicheans taught that in the soul of every man there proceeded a constant struggle between inborn good and inborn evil—and what else was the doctrine of original sin? There was substance in the Pelagian taunt of Augustine that he had never really broken with his original Manicheism.

The doctrine of original sin inevitably draws after it all the problems of personal salvation. If the African church had assumed, with Clement of Alexandria, that baptism washes away all sin and makes men perfect, then there would have been no problem. But all questions of church discipline arose precisely through the experience that even after baptism men were bad sinners. What certitude, then, did the church give of salvation? It is at this point that the Africans came nearest to a modern Western conception of religion. In the mystical Eastern interpretation of Christianity, baptism sufficed for everything. In the West it didn't. What could be put into its stead? The mere putting of the problem foreshadows all the struggles of the Reformation.

Yet at the same time, the limitations of the African church, its fundamentally un-Western outlook, become also clear. It is true that Augustine was the first man after Paul clearly to see the problem of the *certitudo salutis*, the assurance of salvation. But he had no answer. The only answer the Africans gave in practice was to enhance the importance of baptism, despite the admitted incompleteness of its effects. That process can be watched throughout the history of the African church. Tertullian still held very reserved views about baptism, advising against an early and hasty performance of the sacrament. Naturally so, for he tended to regard martyrdom as the normal road to salvation, hence could not regard baptism as all-important. But as the extremists are gradually driven from the church, and the belief in original sin takes root, the practice of late baptism is more and more regarded as dangerous. It is true that baptism is now regarded as the only safe means of receiving forgiveness of sins, and that should strengthen the view that it should, if possible, be received on the deathbed only. But against this there stands the terrible danger of failing to be baptized in time, and thus going to hell. Cyprian already, only half a century after Tertullian, advises that baptism can take place immediately after birth, and not only, as seems to have been the habit in his dioceses, eight days after birth. He rejects the latter view as a superstitious remnant of Judaism, obviously out of a desire to save the many children who do not live for a week. For Augustine, the problem, as explained above, had become decisive.

In this overemphasis on baptism, which yet remains unsatisfactory, we can discern the motives which ultimately led to the adoption of auricular confession as a sacrament. The assurance of salvation could only be found—in a primarily moral and not mystical religious community—in periodical remission of sins, based upon constant self-control and searching of conscience. But the latter presupposed an individual, psychological, moralistic religious experience, which, despite the profoundly personal religious attitude of Augustine, was totally lacking in Africa. The African church disposed of no means of salvation except those provided through the mystical significance of baptism, of oriental origin. If this was not sufficient to cope with problems entirely nonoriental in character, the African church had no means of offering any assurance of salvation to its believers. It is impossible to say whether, in the course of time, it might have developed auricular confession of the type developed later in the North; for the development of African Christianity was cut short by the Vandal conquest. But was the Vandal conquest so decisive? The barbarian conquest ultimately stimulated rather than broke religious development farther North. The more likely view seems to be that the Africans were not capable of that personalism and individualism which, in the North, found a way out. In the context of African life, the personal religious experience of Augustine remained an isolated event, strong enough to lead Augustine to pose the basic problems, but not strong enough to provide any of the solutions.

In the absence of such a solution for the problem of assurance of salvation, the doctrine of predestination, of the unfathomable council of God, remained the only way out. Baptism, to Augustine, was a means of taking away original sin, but not actual sin committed after baptism. No man is free from serious blemish. Therefore no reason can be given why some should be saved and others condemned. Also, no reason can be given why some should receive strength to avoid the gravest sins, and others not. It is a matter for predestination, for the inscrutable God.

It has been rightly maintained that, despite the great authority of Augustine in the Catholic church, the Catholic church has never really made this somber doctrine its own. It was altogether too incompatible with the task of enforcing however easy a moral and disciplinarian code. It was altogether too much of a doctrine of despair. Therefore, after the collapse of the African church, the doctrine had no real following in the West for a long time. It was bound to reappear, though, where men seriously asked the question what right their life gave them to expect eternal bliss. In the meantime, Jerome as much as Ambrose, Leo as much as Gregor the Great, in practice returned to the Eastern doctrine of free will.

We have now reached the conclusion of our long *detour*, of our comparison between Pelagianism and the other religious attitudes with which it was confronted; and its profound, specifically Northwestern originality now stands out in sharp contour. For, to say it in one sentence, it was the first approach which put the moral perfection of every individual into the center of things, and by doing so, attempted something which had never been attempted before. Its connection with the Eastern church, we saw, was based on a misunderstanding. For the Eastern doctrine of free will was based on moral facility, the Pelagian doctrine on an exacting moral idealism. Its relations to classical Pagan philosophy were somewhat more real. In fact, the disintegration of the classical city-state had led to the emergence of the individual in isolation from the community, the individual whose freedom the Stoics tried to secure. Yet that freedom, in the Stoic's conception, was entirely negative, a mere freedom of renouncing everything; its sphere of liberty was, in fact, zero. Only the new optimism coming from the North, and first embodied in Pelagianism, gave this individualism a positive expression through confidence in the possibility of moral perfection for everybody, and only this confidence gave the idea of freedom a real, meaningful content. Finally, Pelagius' relation to the Latin and in particular to the African church is clearly enough revealed in his struggle against Augustine. Here a pessimistic and disciplinarian attitude conflicted with an intensely individualistic faith and moral idealism. The clash between Rome and the Protestant North was here for the first time foreshadowed, though the dogmatic formulae of that clash were to differ considerably from those which had divided Pelagius from Augustine; so that, partly, the formulae of Augustine were adopted by the Protestants, and those of Pelagius by the Catholics.

In Stoicism as in the Roman conception of church discipline and in the African doctrine of baptism and predestination, the Latin South had only formulated problems it was unable to solve. Pelagius brought a first attempt at a solution, not because he would have had some theological device to offer (on the contrary, Augustine was an infinitely deeper thinker and more accomplished theologian) but simply because he brought with him the unbroken strength and faith of a young, just awakening civilization, daring to reach for the stars.

It is true, of course, that Pelagianism had partisans not only in Ireland. But only in Ireland did it survive for a long time, and it is a mistake to maintain, as Zimmer does, that this was only due to its persecution all through the Roman Empire. The stake had not yet been invented. Heretics were not yet physically exterminated. Thus, if Pelagianism collapsed, under pressure, everywhere outside Ireland, it was due to its inherent weakness everywhere except in that island. And had not the Christian church itself actually withstood a threat of physical extermination without succumbing?

It is interesting, however, to analyze shortly the impression Pelagianism made in the Roman Empire. It is obvious from all records that it found some support in the Eastern confines of the Empire. It was acceptable there owing to the formal identity of its doctrine of free will with that of the Eastern church. The more Eastern a Christian community, the more would it dislike both the idea of church discipline and Augustine's doctrine of predestination. But the important fact is not this formal coincidence, but the fierce fight of the Eastern communities against Byzantium, a fight carried on under the banner of the Nestorian heresy. In fact, the leading Pelagian of the East, Theodore of Mopsuestia, was, at the same time, a Nestorian, and the history of Pelagianism in the East after a few years totally merges into the history of Nestorianism.

In the West it is Southern Italy and Southern Gaul where we must look for strong Pelagian influence, in other words it was concentrated in the provinces with a very strong Greek element. No wonder: those parts of the Empire must have felt most strongly the differences between the Western and the Eastern form of Christianity, and must have been interested in a teaching providing a way out of the impasse between the accepted doctrine of free will and the Roman-African insistence on original sin and sinfulness. The radical denial of original sin was such a way out. We shall find this border zone between the East and the West constantly sensitive to new departures in all aspects of life, not least in religion. But after all, the interest was greater than the determination to stick to one's guns, and Pelagianism broke down there, to live on in Ireland.

There thus remains only one task for us, in order to conclude our discussion of Pelagianism. We must discuss its relation to the Irish civilization in general. For the decaying Latin world Pelagianism meant a new light from the North, but one which the South could not accept; a trumpet-blast announcing a new confidence, a new fierce struggle towards something not hitherto attempted. But what did it mean to Ireland?

The answer to this must be incomplete. We know as little about the Irish pre-Christian background as about the parallel problem of the pre-Latin Punic background of African Christianity. But a few things are clear. Most important of them: there is no trace of any functional role of Pelagianism in the context of Irish social life. Here we are struck by a final, decisive contrast between the Pelagian type of moral idealism and the African type of ecclesiastical discipline. We saw to what an extent Latin Christianity was an attempt to keep authority and discipline going in the decaying Roman Empire by transferring it from the state to the church. We saw to what an extent the various African heresies were a "reflex" of social, regional, racial antagonisms. Not so the role of Pelagius in Ireland. The Irish church never was a disciplinarian body. It was not called in by any king or chieftain to increase his authority, as was the case with so many barbaric kings in the following centuries, when they adopted Christianity. It was not accepted in order to provide

sanctions for an otherwise unstable structure of morals and for an otherwise tottering hierarchy. Nor was it called in in order to provide an
ideology for any rising of a suppressed group. The social structure of
Ireland was of a remarkable, of an almost petrified stability. After as
before the adoption of Christianity and Pelagianism, it rested on the clan,
aspiring towards no larger unity, while the clan was ruled by a chieftain
and by elders.

The Irish church never in any sense became an administrative body.
It did not concentrate, as the Roman and African churches did, upon
teaching the laity. It concentrated upon monastic life, a thing yet unknown in the West outside Ireland, giving itself to studies unparalleled
in the West and to feats of asceticism equally unparalleled there. Its
monasticism, its asceticism, and its intellectual standards all prove a
distinct Eastern influence, much more so than a Latin one. But no utilitarian motive has led to these borrowings from the Eastern church.

Here the difference between a young, almost embryonic, and an old
and even dying civilization is clearly revealed. Late civilizations *are* largely
utilitarian. Of all the Christian churches the Latin church was the one
tied to a very old civilization. In the East, the rise of an entirely new
way of life embodied in Christianity and the many Gnostic religions
reflected a new birth, a new primitive, naive approach to life, however
old the general background of civilization in the East. In the Northwest
the church struck wholly virgin soil. But in the Western Mediterranean
the church did not much more than continue the Latin Empire. No
wonder, then, that the practical, utilitarian, economic, social, political
aspects which dominate every civilization in its decay should be so prominent in the history of Latin Christianity. No wonder also that these same
aspects should be totally lacking in the early story of the Irish church.
If the Irish adopted Christianity, and soon also Pelagianism, it was because the heroic view of life implicit in the Pelagian version of Christianity conquered their admiration, won their free love, gave an outlet
to their enthusiasm.

Here we touch one more aspect of the process of cultural affiliation.
The "soul" of an embryonic new civilization is f..ll of new stirrings to
which it is unable to give an adequate expression; unable, at any rate,
as compared with the easiness of self-expression of mature civilizations.
Upon such an embryonic new form of life an old and decaying form of
life has overwhelming power in one sense, and no power at all in another
sense. It has no power to affect its basic impulses. No force in the world
could have made the new civilization of the I-sayers into anything not
fiercely individualistic. But the specific forms of expression, the first

lines of development of the new attitude to life, could be shaped wholly and completely by the influence of more highly civilized neighbors. In adopting Christianity, Ireland chose its Pelagian version because the ideals of individual moral perfection were the only ones adequate to its individualism, and adequate to the fierceness and boundlessness of this individualism.

At the beginning of our supremely individualist civilization stands this ideal of the perfect individual. But that this perfection should be sought in the direction of ascetic morality is a fact inexplicable in terms of any inherent features of Irish civilization. It is an attitude wholly borrowed from the Mediterranean, only molded into a different meaning in the new atmosphere. In Scandinavia, the same quest for individual perfection was expressed much as the Homeric heroes had expressed it: in competitions of prowess. Ireland, owing to its geographical position, fell completely under the spell of the Christian ascetic ideal. And this ideal could penetrate it more completely because, in contrast to Scandinavia, Ireland had not even yet reached a fully I-saying speech, was still in the process of evolving its elements. It was subjected to the impact of Christianity at this entirely embryonic stage in the development of its own civilization, embraced it completely, and filled it with its own, different soul, without caring much about, even rather enjoying, the abyss which divided its sort of Christianity from the official Christian world.

Thus Western Christianity developed out of the clash and the conjunction of the political and disciplinarian Roman church and of the idealist, perfection-minded monastical Irish church. To these developments we must now turn.

CHAPTER SEVEN

The Beginnings of Western Monasticism [fragment]

The early Western theology, we saw, was African theology. It reflected strongly some of the characteristics which were later to become basic features of the Western mind, but though morality was its central problem it was unable to work these Western trends out into a coherent system of morality. Wherever it attempted to follow its assumptions down to their logical conclusions, it fell victim to the towering strength of the Eastern trends in the life of the period. To this, Pelagianism, a relatively late intruder into early Western theology, was the only exception. But Pelagianism was defeated precisely over those points in its morality which were most specifically Western, over the belief in the natural infinite perfectibility of man. Thus the development which leads from Tertullian to Augustine put the problem of a truly Christian morality in the Western sense very thoroughly, but was unable to find a satisfactory answer to it.

In our search for the origins of the Western mind as revealed in Western religion we must therefore leave African theology aside and turn to the history of moral efforts where they revealed themselves directly in a practical way. The highest embodiment of Christian morality from the beginning of the fourth century onwards was monasticism. We may indeed hope for a better reward by turning our investigation in this direction. For there is no doubt that in the emergence of Western civilization monasticism has played an extremely important, nay a paramount part. No less a man than Adolph Harnack could say that the history of the origins of Western civilization was simply part of the history of the monastic movement. This we believe to be an exaggeration. But it gives a good idea of the importance of monasticism in our context.

In studying Western monasticism one must first get rid of the popular idea, uncritically repeated by not a few church-historians, that St. Benedict of Nursia is its "father." He died presumably in 547 A.D. But monasticism in the West rose to great achievements as early as the beginning of the fifth century A.D., at the latest, and may go back three-quarters of a century farther. How then could Benedict be its "father?" We shall have to come back to the conditions out of which so mistaken a view emerged.

In the first place the monastic movement, with all its basic ideals and with its characteristic methods, was imported into the West from the East, more particularly from Egypt; and Egyptian customs, or what Westerners believed to be Egyptian monastic customs, were copied in the West down to very small details such as the choice of garments which were natural in Egyptian but very strange in Western surroundings. Not much originality can be claimed for the West in this first period of borrowing of Eastern monastic institutions. Western monasticism, in many respects, was even a vehicle of Eastern religious trends which, under the cover of the halo monasticism had acquired in the East, attacked more specifically Western attitudes. It seems that in more than one place in the West the monastic movement was at first regarded as an undesirable Eastern importation.

It is ascertainable or at least very probable that, in the West, it was first introduced into Italy. This fact is specifically connected by tradition with the sojourn in Rome of the great Athanasius, patriarch of Alexandria, chief enemy of the heresy of Arius, and then, under an Arian emperor, an exile from his see for the sake of his faith. Spreitzenhofer,[1] the only author who has conducted any systematic research into the earliest origins of Western monasticism, has made out a case for a much earlier beginning of it in Italy than Athanasius' stay in the West, which belongs to the fifth decade of the fourth century. But Spreitzenhofer makes no attempt at a clear-cut distinction between hermits living alone or in small unorganized groups and monks living in monasteries. Yet the distinction is fundamental for all early monastic history, which largely consists precisely in the transformation of the first into the second of these types. As far as I can see, Spreitzenhofer only succeeded in proving the existence of Italian hermits several decades before the middle of the

1. Ernst Spreitzenhofer, OSB, *Historische Voraussetzungen der Regel Benedikts* (Vienna, 1895).

fourth century, hermits, incidentally, who, according to his own material, were copying the model of Egyptian hermits. His failure to discover any pre-Athanasian monasteries provides further indirect proof for
the correctness of the old tradition which traces the origins of Western
monasticism in the proper sense of the word to the inspiration of Athanasius. Admittedly, conclusive external evidence for the truth of this tradition is lacking, and one might leave the question there, were it not for
certain specific characteristics of the earliest Western monasticism in Italy,
characteristics which are of utmost importance for the whole history of
Western monasticism and which can be best explained precisely by tracing them back to the teachings of Athanasius during his stay in Rome.
In order to understand all the implications of the problem, we must
throw a glance at the origins of the monastic movement in the East, and
more particularly in Egypt.

If one thing has emerged out of endless controversies, it is that the
origins of monasticism are closely connected with the end of persecution
and the rise of Christianity to the ruling religion in the Roman Empire
early in the fourth century. As long as the Christian communities were
small, there was no reason for a group of inspired ascetics to segregate
from their brethren living in the world, for all were inspired with the
same fervent spirit. Later, especially during the third century, when
many Christian communities were already very numerous, persecution
drew closely together all those who did not betray their faith under
threats and torture. But as soon as, with Emperor Constantine, the
church became a center of worldly power, millions of easy-going converts joined its ranks. The bishops, from underground leaders of an
inspired religious movement, rapidly developed into town heads deeply
involved in the most secular tasks of town administration and of imperial
politics. It was then that the desire to segregate themselves grew among
many of the more deeply believing. During the first centuries, the church
itself had been a safe spiritual fold protecting the sheep from contamination by the heathen world. Now the church was no longer such a safe
fold. The most faithful struck out instead for the even more thoroughly
protective fold of the desert.

Clearly, the monastic movement implied a criticism, not only of the
world in general and of the large and ill-assorted Christian communities
more particularly, but also of the secular clergy who were now deeply
identified with the world and whose spiritual ministrations were no
longer felt to be sufficient. Yet the bishops could let things go during
the early stages of the movement. There was no reason from any except
a pagan point of view to mind the way of life of a St. Anthony, who

withdrew into the desert, took flight from his admirers who discovered him there by withdrawing into still more inaccessible recesses, and entirely lived for his angelic and demoniac visions and for the salvation of his soul. Such men provided a saintly model in the desert, while in town and in the church they might have been troublesome. The problem grew somewhat more serious, however, at a fairly early stage, because it is not everybody's affair to part with human company completely, and because many of the most fervent believers came from the bourgeoisie of Alexandria and, owing to their urban upbringing, would simply have perished in a life such as that led by St. Anthony.

Soon, therefore, groups of hermits congregated in places unfit for ordinary human habitation, it is true, but suitable for the building of many cells within a close perimeter, so that the hermits could extend mutual help, spiritual and material, to one another, and also sufficiently close to towns for buying the most indispensible necessities and paying for them by the selling of the products of their work, mostly mats. These semieremitical colonies, such as Nitria, Scete and Kellai—all of them in lower Egypt, within the zone of influence of Alexandria—were more easily accessible than the empty desert, and left a deep imprint upon the mind of the contemporaries who saw them. Whereas we do not have one biography of a true desert hermit where fact would not be completely buried under legend, we possess fairly accurate and in some cases very shrewd and precise accounts of the lives of these semihermits. In contrast to the full hermits they did not completely dispense with the ordinary ministrations and with the sacraments of the church. Priests, even bishops, were active among them. And, lacking any coherent organization, they did not develop into an organized opposition to the secular clergy, though there is little doubt that the mystical teachings of Origen, which were increasingly disliked by the secular clergy, had their chief adherents in these circles.

But a very real problem arose for the episcopal heads of the church through the next step of the monastic movement. In Lower Egypt, the individualism of the highly intellectualized Greeks and Jews of Alexandria and of the Egyptian Alexandrians, whose mentality had been shaped by Greek and Jewish influences, excluded the idea of disciplined organized action. But now the scene shifts to upper Egypt, where towns are small, the great majority of the population are peasant serfs, education is almost unknown as is the Greek language, and where the movement assumes an entirely different, un-Greek and anti-Greek, strongly native Egyptian, "Coptic" character. It is in these surroundings that flourished the work of St. Pachomius, a retired army sergeant from central Egypt who had however selected upper Egypt, the "Thebais," as a more suitable background for his efforts.[2] He was a completely uncultured man who knew no Greek, hence had no theology of any kind. He was a layman. All he had learned were the rules of barracks life, and nobody reading his monastic rules can fail to be reminded of the discipline of the barracks. But he was endowed, like not a few of his type, with the gift of enthusiasm and, he and his followers believed, even with the gift of prophecy. He had visions, and apparently he was a towering personality, inspiring his followers with the feeling that, as long as they were under him, they were under special guidance. He must also have been an organizer of quite unusual abilities. He created the first monasteries. And he thereby confronted the bishops with an organization independent of them and potentially hostile to them.

It is not too difficult to understand the aim St. Pachomius pursued with his new creation. The eremitical and semieremitical life worked out by Alexandrians in lower Egypt was beset with both spiritual and material difficulties. Both are clearly stated in our sources. Spiritually it was dangerous to leave any but the very best and the most advanced without control and guidance, a prey to every temptation and to every heresy. Materially, even the semieremitical type of life was unfit for many. All, except if they had means of their own which they had not given away, must work to earn a living, hence those fit only for study or for mystical prayer were ill provided for. And with growing age the hardships told more and more, so that the older hermits had not more but less time for spiritual exercises than the younger elements. Pachomius himself came from a milieu where the urge for perfection was no less strong than among the hermits, but where illiteracy and other disabilities prevented its fulfilment. His institution was very largely, though by no means exclusively, a place for the higher religious training of illiterates, as well as a place where the old, the weak, the infirm and the inspired could all concentrate on their spiritual tasks, precisely because the illiterate youngsters who were apparently the majority had strong limbs and were used to the hard life of the fields and of the workshop. On the basis of their physical strength, Pachomius made his monastery—later the group of ten monasteries of the Thebais of which he was the founder and Archiman-

---

2. On St. Pachomius, see Georg Grützmacher, *Pachomius und das älteste Klosterleben* (Berlin, 1896), from the viewpoint of the German "Higher Criticism"; and against him E. Ladeuze, *Le cénobitisme Pachomien* (Louvain, 1898), extremely conservative and visibly outraged by any criticism of the tradition. The view given above is a compromise between those two extremes. Much research has been done since on details of the literary tradition, but none, to my knowledge, on the position of Pachomius in the religious crisis of his age.

drite—into a large-scale factory, producing not only mats but all sorts of things, providing for all the needs of the monastery and yielding a large surplus produce too, which was sold in Alexandria with scrupulous avoidance both of illicit gain and of undercutting.

It was a highly successful institution, entirely reasonable in its aims and methods. We can form a clear idea of the latter from the so-called "Rule" of Pachomius, which is probably not his own work, not wholly at least, but, as has been justly said, a "house rule," a sort of collection of merely practical bylaws regulating the day-to-day life of the monasteries, without any direct reference to the higher aims of monasticism. Many of these rules must appear harsh to the modern Westerner, but cannot have seemed so to the poor Egyptian laborers who formed the majority of the inmates. Monks were not allowed to stretch out for sleep, but had to sleep in a sitting position, leaning against a sort of rough cushion. But travellers know how easily, even today, the Mediterranean peasant sleeps in any position, and the suitable prop for their backs must have appeared to them a luxury. There was only one meal, in the evening, but no restrictions as to the quantity of food and as to the hour when to take it. How many Egyptian fellahs must have regarded this lack of restrictions on quantity as the nearest possible approach to an earthly paradise! The garments had to be rough—but where is the Egyptian peasant who ever knew anything but rags? The asceticism of the monastery must have been hard and irksome for the soft-bred minority, but not for the mass of the monks. For them only two aspects of monastic life must have appeared as serious restrictions. The one was the strict enforcement of chastity—even friendships and all physical contact between monks was prohibited—the other the mild enforcement of silence at certain hours and during certain occupations, which, at all times, must have gone ill with the Egyptian national character. As to obedience, it was strict enough, too, but the life of an Egyptian peasant serf was at no time of a kind to breed personal pride and a sense of independence. No monastic discipline can have been harsher than the ordinary discipline of the rod, to which they were used in the world; the more so as the use of the rod inside the monastery seems not to have been very frequent.

Leaving aside quite exceptional institutions such as La Trappe, such moderation in asceticism always seemed natural and reasonable in the West. But if one wants to understand the singularity of Pachomius' creation in the East, and at the same time the difference between Eastern and Western monasticism, it is necessary to realize that the attitude of the East to these things was and is different. The earliest hermits and semihermits in the East used to describe themselves as "God's athletes," and athletic indeed were the prowesses of asceticism in which they indulged, in the matter of sleep, of food, and everything else. Extreme cases, such as hermits spending their lives on the top of a pillar—extremes, incidentally, which belong rather to a somewhat later period in Syria than to the period now under review in Egypt—were only exaggerations of an endeavor common to all. The original dualistic view of the Gnostics, who had regarded matter as evil in itself, was not upheld by these hermits in theological doctrine. But a good deal of their way of life revealed an attitude akin to that of certain Gnostic heretics. To kill the body by all kinds of tortures was their primary aim, because they were imbued with the conviction that only those who totally killed the flesh could see the realm of the spirit. In such a view, there could be no limit to the desirability of ascetic exercises—the more excruciating, the more destructive of physical life the better. How different was all this from the mind of the Westerner Pelagius who, despite his fervent asceticism, had peremptorily pronounced "The body must be controlled, not broken." But how different also from the worldliness of the victorious church! Only by visualizing both extremes together can one realize the abyss which threatened to divide the episcopal church of the towns from the hermits of the desert.

Amidst this movement of fervent asceticism, Pachomius' creation must have seemed a more than doubtful achievement to the more extreme. In fact, so great was the prestige of ascetic prowess that Pachomius did not dare to impose limits of fasting and of vigils on his monks. He forbade interference with those who wanted to eat, but also with those who fasted for days at a time. From his point of view, which is made sufficiently clear in the "Rule" of the Pachomian monasteries, this meant that fervent ascetics were at liberty to go as far as they liked in their exertions. From the viewpoint of the hermits, as it is reflected in such documents as the "*Lausiac History*,"[3] it meant, on the contrary—and this, for them, was the most characteristic thing about this new invention, a monastery—that monks were free there to eat as much as they liked. It is the very first thing Palladios, the author of the *Lausiac History*, mentions in his description of the monastery of Tabennisi, Pachomius' first foundation.

So strange and objectionable were these things, which to us modern Westerners seem natural and obvious, that a natural explanation seemed insufficient. Only a direct divine order could excuse so much laxity.

---

3. Cuthbert Butler, ed., *Palladius: The Lausiac History* (1898–1904). The *Lausiac History*, a collection of biographies of Egyptian ascetics and of descriptions of life in the desert, is our chief source for the history of the early ascetics.

Pachomius himself seems to have stated that an angel had appeared to him and had dictated to him every word of his rule. This angelic order expressly covered the most controversial points of Pachomius' rule, which appeared as unduly lax to many contemporary hermits. Pachomius himself had been a fervent hermit before he became the founder of an order. He objected to the angel: "But there are only a few daily prayers" (in this rule), whereupon the angel replied: "I have fixed this, because it is sufficient, and because the little ones shall also be able to fulfil it so that they need not be ashamed; the perfect ones need no rules anyway." (The juxtaposition of "the little ones" and "the perfect ones" shows clearly that the "little ones" are not the children educated in the monastery, but the "little men," those who are incapable of extraordinary efforts.)

The content of Pachomius' vision is of great interest in several directions. In the first place it reveals with the greatest possible clarity the reaction of doubt and criticism which the Pachomian conception met among hermits. As usual, what to posterity appears as a gradual development from stage to stage—in this case from an extreme type of hermit life to a disciplined community life—was, in reality, a *via dolorosa* of conflicts. But Pachomius' own problems are not the most relevant thing in this context. The real relevance of the situation consists in its lasting character. For the superascetic tendencies continued in the East, not among isolated individuals or small groups, but as a permanent undercurrent, apt to come to the surface again at any time.

Here are some instances. One of Pachomius' disciples, Shnoudi (Greek: Schenute) founded an independent monastery, also in the Thebais, at Atripe, where, however, in contrast to Pachomius' view, the most extreme types of asceticism were made compulsory. The original impulse of the hermit life had thus prevailed and broken through within a monastic organization. It is true that Shnoudi's foundation did not last. If the extreme forms of asceticism did not maintain themselves in Egypt, it was because precisely during this period the Coptic element there prevailed over all other influences and the native Coptic Egyptian is not particularly ascetic. That was doubtless already one of the reasons why Pachomius' milder version of monasticism had been such a success in Coptic Upper Egypt.

But in Syria and Palestine, the hermit "athlete of God" with his Dervish extravagancies continued to hold his own against the monk for many centuries to come, until Islam in some of its forms gave another, similar, outlet to the same tendencies. Furthermore, when monasticism, somewhat later, gained credit in Constantinople and in the regions under her influence, the conception of monastic discipline had to be permanently modified by the admission of a special class of monk-hermits, monks living in separate cells, given to prowesses of the hermit life, and only very loosely connected with the monastery. As such, they exist to this day in Athos and other places. Finally, the history of the Russian church is full of returns to the old spirit of hermit asceticism.

In one word: in the East, Pachomius' conception of a type of asceticism within reach of the "little ones" remained one among several types, and not the type regarded with the highest esteem. Its exclusive prevalence was limited to a Coptic region. In the West, however, this type prevailed everywhere, after a short period of hesitation, and the prowesses of the hermits were from the beginning looked at with misgivings. The West looked upon them with feelings which may not have been dissimilar to those of an English gentleman towards a Dervish or a Fakir, with the difference that, whereas the latter to the West are exotic oddities, the Eastern hermits at one time found followers, though not very many, in the West, and were regarded as a practical danger. Here is the first fundamental difference between East and West.[4]

One more aspect of the situation is also of some importance. If the Western mentality differed profoundly from the Eastern mentality, if the West did not share the instinctive dualism and preference for self-torturing extravagances of the East, it does not follow that, during the early stages of monasticism, the West had an original conception of its own. Early monasticism was a mere modification of hermit life, which had sprung from the most profound impulses of the East. The absence of these impulses in the West meant, in the first place, that the West had no coherent conception of monasticism at all, that its attempts were weak copies of the creations of the East. Western imitators of the East could account themselves lucky if they found a type relatively adaptable to their mentality, such as the one created by Pachomius. They invented nothing, could invent nothing. How often has not St. Benedict been praised for what some regard as the fundamental characteristics of his rule, for his treatment of his own rule as only "a little rule for beginners," while the more perfect members of the community could go over into hermit life, and were not in need of rules. Our quotation above will have proved that the above-mentioned famous passage of the rule of St. Benedict is almost textually copied from the *Lausiac History* (demonstrably well-known to St. Benedict in Rufin's Latin translation) and that in this

---

4. For the whole question of the difference between Eastern and Western monasticism, see Adolph v. Harnack, *Das Mönchstum, seine Ideale und seine Geschichte* (Giessen: Töpelmann, 1921).

respect St. Benedict did nothing but copy an Egyptian institution venerated all over Italy.

It must have been highly satisfactory for St. Benedict that Pachomius' authority was there to support his views. Pachomius himself, however, had obviously not been so well satisfied. Quite apart from the angelic vision which, one among many he experienced, sanctioned his very practical ideas, he sought for further justification of his great innovation in a direction which must seem more than strange to the Western mind. According to the *Lausiac history*, he organized his monks into sections and designed each of them by a letter of the Greek alphabet. The sections, according to the *Lausiac history*, were formed along lines of spiritual characteristics. The stupid and sincere (sic) monks would be grouped into one unit and have one letter, the clever and false ones another, and so on. St. Jerome, who has also left us a description of Tabennisi (he was there as little as Palladios, the author of the *Lausiac History*), says the units were each formed out of those possessing the same skills. He reveals his thoroughly Western mind by this misunderstanding. For authentic letters of Pachomius to his later successor are extant and confirm entirely Palladios' interpretation.

What is the significance of this odd arrangement? I cannot agree with Gruetzmacher who, a typical Westerner too, assumed that it had no significance beyond the need somehow to divide into groups a very large number of monks, and that, if we did understand the puzzling references to the groups and their letters in Pachomius' correspondence, it would teach us nothing but irrelevant details of the life at Tabennisi in his day. It is impossible to bring this view into agreement with Palladios' explicit statement that the angel ordered Pachomius to keep the significance of the letters designing the groups a secret, "so that only those filled with the spirit would understand what was meant."[5] The Greek word used for those filled with the spirit is "pneumatics," a word endowed with a very specific significance in the religious language of the period. Pneumatics are those able to understand the spiritual truth, the secret revelation which opens the keys to a real understanding of the work of salvation. The apostles, by the descent of the Spirit at Whitsun, became pneumatics, and they spoke in tongues. This interpretation is again confirmed by Pachomius' letters to his successor which turn around the magic significance of the letters more than anything else, and are therefore perfectly unintelligible to us. Clearly the aspect which is paramount in Pachomius' mind, which must remain a secret from the ordinary breth-

---

5. See the Butler edition of *The Lausiac History* (note 3 above), ch. 22.

ren, but is revealed to those filled with the spirit, must be the central aspect of the whole foundation. Obviously, Pachomius attempted to make up for the defects of his monks in matters of individual asceticism (not any objective defects, but defects in the light of the extreme hermit ideal) by attributing a mystic significance to the whole monastery, whose parts apparently were made to correspond to realms of the mystical world, an identity expressed through the magical letters.

I cannot go further in my interpretation. I only wish to point out that later on the magical significance of letters became a keystone of one of the greatest mystical conceptions evolved in the East, of the Kabbala. It is apparently in this direction that Pachomius' mind was turned. Thus, even in the Pachomian institution which, on the surface, was so much what the West wanted as a model, there was a second meaning which had nothing to do with problems of practical morality and of monastic organization in the practical sense, a meaning which was meant to make up for Pachomius' practical concessions in the sphere of organization. To the West these practical concessions appeared as the very essence of wisdom. To Pachomius they appeared as grave but inevitable defects, which were, however, counterbalanced by a mystical meaning which was totally unknown to the Western imitators. The full importance of this situation only emerges when it is realized that the Pachomian and not any other monastic rule is the one Eastern rule which has decisively influenced Western monasticism.

Now here was this Pachomian organization, developing in its founder's lifetime into a congregation of ten houses (one of them a convent), whose majority were illiterate laborers used to hardship and absolute obedience, while at the top a small stratum of spirituals was imbued with a visionary mysticism and the leader of it all had angelic visions. The organization was numerous, had considerable hitting power (in the literal sense of physical strength, as the adherents of Arius soon found out in the many street battles for the faith all over Egypt) and was at the same time completely independent of the ordinary ecclesiastical hierarchy, both in spiritual and in practical matters. The congregation was extremely self-contained, priests from outside, and even hermits and later members of other monasteries were regarded with the greatest suspicion. No wonder the bishops did not like it. I do not see how Father Ladeuze could square his view that only "one or two" bishops opposed it with the explicit statement of Pachomius' official biography to the effect that in one county where the congregation flourished it was condemned by a synod of bishops, while there were quarrels with bishops in at least one other county. A synod, I should say, never consists of one man, or even of two. On the other hand, Gruetzmacher certainly exaggerates when he speaks of a general opposition of the episcopate. For such a view, there is no foundation in the sources. There is no reason to substitute a more or less general conflict to the provincial conflicts they mention.

The situation may have been similar to that which grew out of the rise of a Catholic labor democracy in the nineteenth century. There also it would be far from true to say that only one or two bishops opposed the new trend, but it would also be wrong to speak of a general conflict. The parallel is most certainly correct and is also closest in what concerns the role of the highest church authority. As Leo XIII in the nineteenth, so Athanasius as patriarch of Egypt in the fourth century secured the victory of the sincere though turbulent mass movement over the narrow-minded section of the hierarchy. Athanasius solved the problems of the young congregation by a conference with Pachomius, and the latter's first successor, together with his monks, became one of the mainstays of Athanasius in his struggle against the Arian heresy.

The alliance between the monks and the patriarch of Egypt remained in force down to the advent of Islam. The original terms of the settlement of the monastic question are not directly known to us, but their gist is clear from the position that arose. The monks refrained from any independent interference in church affairs. Henceforth, they only acted as defenders of the Patriarch, whatever the latter's attitude. They were first fervent in the defense of orthodoxy against Arianism, then equally fervent in the defense of the monophysitic heresy (which was adopted by the see of Alexandria) in a struggle against orthodoxy. In exchange, the monasteries preserved their autonomy from the local clergy. Though some rights of inspection of the local bishops must have existed, as the bishops sent to the monasteries the priests who spent the sacraments, yet in the main the monks were under their abbots only, and above the abbots there was only the patriarch. The monasteries became part of the church organization, but an independent part, with a very large measure of autonomy. The genius of Athanasius thus found a way of combining two things so incompatible as a church almost identified with the secular power and an ascetic movement rejecting the world wholesale. The two henceforth supported one another, but without interfering with one another.

Here is the second fundamental difference between West and East. The difference must be sought, not so much in the fact that occasionally in the West the regulars did not support the secular clergy—that happened occasionally in the East too, though hardly ever in Egypt—but in the fact that in the West there was no such strict division of spheres. In the West, the monastic orders threw their weight very firmly into the balance in favor of certain policies of the church, and also of the state, and were far from simply following in these matters the orders of their metropolitans. In the East, relations between the secular and the regular clergy were molded on lines indicated by the general Eastern attitude to moral problems. There was, on the one hand, the almost limitless accommodation of the secular clergy to the weaknesses of the world, and on the other hand there was room for monastic asceticism. The two extremes coexisted without fighting and without merging. In the West, the secular clergy was on the whole less secular, the regulars were less ascetic. And the two were so closely connected that they almost invariably operated in the same direction. It took a long time, however, before the Western type of monasticism was shaped. When that had finally been achieved, one of the main foundations of Western civilization had been laid.

It will now be easy to see how Egyptian monasticism, when introduced into Italy by Athanasius, became something quite different from what it had been in its country of origin. The earliest Western monasteries might ever so faithfully copy all the external details of the Egyptian monasteries and thereby make not a few enemies in the "world" among both high and low. But this faithful copying only proved the old proverb that, if two do the same thing, it is no longer the same thing. The original Eastern hermit movement was based upon a radical hostility to all material things, a hostility which had no roots in the West. Therefore, the hermit movement in the West remained always weak, and was no more than a short passing stage. The monastic movement in the East had sprung from the hermit movement and thrived on its aims and impulses, only slightly modified so as to be more practically adaptable. The West, or at least Italy during the fourth century, experienced no such powerful breathing of the ascetic spirit. Therefore, the monastic movement in the West lacked at first the fire and inspiration so characteristic of the "going to the desert"[6] in Egypt.

In the East, the independent monastic movement had come to an agreement with the secular clergy to the satisfaction of both sides, and

---

6. I have chosen the term "going to the desert" for its parallelism with "going to the people," the self-denying movement which swept the Russian intelligentsia about 1870. In both cases penance and self-abnegation were the decisive inspiring motives. There are many more parallels to those two movements in Eastern Christian history. A mass urge to throw away everything seems to be a recurrent event there, whether expressed in religious or in secular form. It has no parallel in the West, where all self-abnegation immediately turns into works of practical usefulness.

on the basis of this agreement Athanasius became the champion of monasticism in the West, too. But against a different background his influence worked out very differently from what it had achieved in Egypt. For whereas at home he had taken under his wings a powerful and inspired movement not at all of his creation, in the West his episcopal brethren had to take the initiative in creating monasteries which would not, or at least only in exceptional cases, have come into being without such episcopal prompting.

The effects were only too clear from the result. From its beginnings in the middle of the fourth century to the days of St. Benedict in the sixth, Italian monasticism has not brought forth a single powerful, impressive, or even influential personality, with perhaps the exception of Paulinus of Nola. None of the many monasteries thus created seem to have lasted over a very long time. The movement was stillborn in Italy. Monasticism, in order to live, must have its own independent formative impulses. It cannot rise as a sideline of episcopal administration. These independent impulses carry with them their difficulties and problems. The absence of them carries with it death. The creation of an artificial monastic movement by the bishops simply reflected the lack of roots of the monastic movement in Italy. It is noteworthy that Italy tried to borrow her ascetic movement from Egypt, as she had tried to borrow her theology from Africa. In neither direction was she at first very successful.

Here is a list of outstanding cases of "episcopal monasteries" collected from Spreitzenhofer's account. Rome: a monastery "in catacumbas," founded by Pope Xystus; a monastery connected with the basilica of St. Sebastian, probably created by Innocent I; a monastery connected with St. Peter, founded by Leo I; two monasteries founded by Pope Hilarius; a monastery of St. Juvenal, founded by Pope Vigilius. None of these foundations go back beyond the second third of the fifth century, and the last-named belongs to the middle of the sixth century. Accounts of earlier foundations are uncertain; but the prevalence throughout the period of episcopal as distinct from independent monasteries is obvious enough.

Upper Italy: here the earliest foundation, that of bishop Eusebius of Vercellae, goes back to the middle of the fourth century, but is not a monastery proper, but an institution for the common life of the town clergy. (Apparently, St. Augustine later copied this institution from Northern Italy, and its origins are wrongly ascribed to him.) Other upper Italian monasteries: the monastery founded by St. Ambrose in Milan; several monasteries founded in Novara by Bishop Gaudentius; the monastery of St. Agricola in Bologna, founded by bishop Eusebius; Bishop Felix founded four more monasteries in the same town; and a sixth monastery was founded there in the sixth century by bishop Petronius (one does not get the impression that all these existed simultaneously; perhaps they all collapsed rapidly, and others took their place); several monasteries in Ravenna, founded by bishop Chrysologus; a monastery founded by bishop Victor in Turin. Though these are not all the upper Italian monasteries mentioned by Spreitzenhofer, they include all those of the early period whose founders were known. There is not a single known founder of an upper Italian monastery, therefore, who would not have been a bishop!

Southern Italy: Here the monastery of St. Paulinus in Nola stands out as a private, nonepiscopal foundation belonging to the end of the fourth century. But the exception is only apparent. For St. Paulinus was not an Italian at all, but a native of Southern France, and a monk from Lerins, with which place we shall have to deal soon. It is characteristic that this alien intrusion into Italian life formed a link between half-Greek Marseilles and half-Greek Naples, to the exclusion of the purely Latin parts of the country. We shall see these two districts closely connected more than once. Other Southern Italian foundations: two monasteries founded by bishop Severus in Naples, another monastery in the same place, founded by bishop Gaudiosus. Central Italy: all information extremely vague.

Convents: these could not so directly depend on episcopal direction, and were normally founded by noble women. It appears, however, from Spreitzenhofer's account, that many of these were the sisters or other relatives of bishops.

The living tree of Western monasticism was to spring from a very different root, in a different part of the West. It grew up in Gaul, more precisely in central Gaul, where the small ascetic groups which seem to have existed all over Gaul could shape themselves into something more definite under the powerful influence of St. Martin of Tours.[7]

Martin came from Pannonia, upper Hungary in modern terms, from the border zone of the Eastern and Western Empire. Like Pachomius, he had been a soldier. It is not surprising that many soldiers took a hand in the shaping of monasticism, down to St. Ignatius of Loyola, the founder of the Jesuits. The military and the monastic discipline have

---

7. Though it seems hardly credible, there exists no serious specialized research on Martin of Tours. The gap is partly filled by the treatment in Albert Hauck, *Kirchengeschichte Deutschlands*, Part I (Leipzig: Hinrichs, 1911).

something in common. If the hermits were often described as "athletes of the Lord"—a simile taken from the individualistic competition of the ring—monastic life is called a "militia Christi." Martin was a "military tribune," a subaltern officer, as his father had been. He was therefore of a higher military rank than Pachomius, but if we are to believe his friend and biographer Sulpicius Severus[8] he strove out of humility to make men forget his rank. He had to accept a batman, Severus explains, because regulations demanded it, but he served his batman more than his batman served him. A plebeian way of life, and a great ability for getting into close contact with the poorest peasantry, characterized him as much as Pachomius.

On the whole, though by no means exclusively, the rich, educated, and noble townsmen among the ascetics preferred the hermit life to monasticism, unless they entered the monasteries as founders and abbots. The majority of the earliest monks seem to have come from the poor in Gaul as much as in Egypt. In Gaul a certain connection between a rebellious peasant movement and Christianity had existed long before Martin. The earliest version of the legend of the Theban legion connects the martyrdom of that legion under a heathen emperor with the refusal of the soldiers to fight against the Christian peasant rebellion of the "Bagauda." How far the Bagauda was in fact Christian in character is questionable, but popular opinion tended to identify the two movements. Martin's work proceeded among a badly exploited and rebellious peasantry.

He was already a Christian in his army days. Resigning at the earliest possible moment, he submitted to the religious tuition of bishop Hilary of Poitiers, then passed through a short stage of hermit life, lived in the Danube country and in Italy, and met many disappointments in his struggle against the Arian heretical church, then supported by an Arian emperor. Finding Italy unsuitable, he went to Poitiers again, founding a small monastery nearby at Ligugé. Later he went to Tours, founding a second monastery near that town at Marmoutiers. Very unlike any Eastern hermit or monk he at once started missionary work among the half-pagan peasants—the first truly Western ascetic with a characteristic urge to make the world benefit from his spiritual achievements. Hitherto, Christianity had still largely been an affair of the towns. His is the chief merit in having it brought to the countryfolk.

It is in this missionary work among poor peasants and among the poor in general that Martin's saintliness was most transparent, leaving an

---

8. *Sulpicii Severi Libri qui supersunt* (Vienna, 1866).

indelible impression upon his contemporaries as well as upon posterity. It is a real pity that Severus' attempt to prove Martin a greater miracle-doer than any other man, living or dead, has blurred to such an extent the picture of a most impressive character, as Martin must have been. There is no question in his case of a reputation growing by legend only after the hero's death. His immense popularity, and the indelible imprint he left on all who met him as a friend are clearly evident in what we know of his life. Humility and love of the poorest were combined in his character with great sternness and an inexhaustible fighting spirit. Modern versions of his life regrettably tend to obliterate the last-named characteristic, so as to produce the picture of a sugar-sweet saint. There can be no doubt that, in reality, Martin was a great fighter, and that his boundless love for the poor and suffering was matched by a boundless hatred for the proud and worldly. It is the struggle against the latter which marks him out in the history of the Western church and which was to leave profound traces behind, making a permanent imprint upon future centuries.

Obviously, the center of life, for Martin, was the church. His hatred for pride and luxury expressed itself most strongly where he thought he saw it within the church. He, so humble in his intercourse with the humblest, took pride in slighting emperor Maximus and his pious wife. But on the whole he seems to have cared little for the pride of the children of the world. His anger was concentrated against the ruling men of the church, against the priests and, much more so even, against the bishops. His life was one long struggle against the latter. Not that he included all bishops in the same condemnation. He certainly loved and admired Hilary of Poitiers. His biographer, here and there, admits the existence of other decent bishops. But it would be wrong to say that he hated and fought only individual bishops and priests for their individual vices. He fought them as a class, as a social group, as we shall soon see in more detail. Therefore, the movement he created was the exact opposite of the monastic movement of Italy. While the latter was so well-behaved that it nearly died of inanition, the movement created by Martin was at first so rebellious that it was nearly smashed in its struggle against the official hierarchy. All the antihierarchical trends which had been implicit in the early "going to the desert" in Egypt and in the earliest stages of Pachomian monasticism, became perfectly explicit and aggressive with Martin of Tours.

A habit has grown among modern writers of speaking of the hostility of the bishops to the early monastic movement, as if there had not also existed a hostility of the early monks to the bishops. This is an odd interpretation, particularly if adopted by Protestants, whom one would not expect to show any special tenderness to monks but rather to throw all the blame of the struggle upon the secular clergy. As to the specific reasons for Martin's hostility to the bishops and to the moment when it arose, one finds it stated more than once that Martin quarreled with the bishops of Gaul because they exerted successful pressure upon emperor Maximus to commit a judicial murder by executing the Spanish heretic Priscillian and some of his followers. This event admittedly marked a crisis in Martin's relations with the clergy of Gaul, as it did in general church history, because the execution of Priscillian in 385 A.D. was the first case of the execution of a heretic for his heresy, the beginning of sanguinary religious persecution within the Christian church. Martin opposed the outrage with all his strength but in vain, and when the Gallic bishops had succeeded in their sanguinary pursuit, he refused ever again to hold any community with them. But it is quite incorrect to say that the trial of Priscillian was the origin and cause of Martin's hostility to the episcopate. This hostility, to judge from the witness of his friend and biographer, had deeper roots and was of much longer standing.

In the first place, Sulpicius Severus connects the hostility of the bishops against Martin with what to him and to his circle is the most outstanding feature of Martin's life, his amazing miracles. If we are to believe Severus, they ranged from the smallest to the greatest things, from the reading of the secret thoughts of an enemy to the awakening of no less than three dead. The evaluation of Severus' stories has nothing to do with the general problem of miracles. Everybody reading his account must see that here is a man greedy to see miracles wherever he can find them, nad not in the least endowed with any caution and critical sense. Martin's followers and disciples were apparently very indignant at any investigation of these miracles under safeguards, such as the Catholic Church uses in similar matters. In chapter 24 of his biography Severus tells how the bishops assailed Martin's position and reputation, and how Martin worked many miracles to confound them. But the bishops did not believe in these miracles. It is horrible to think—Severus says in another place[9]—that somebody dared to say that probably most of the stories told by him were inventions. "Such a voice," Severus adds, "is not a man's, it is the devil's, and it is not so much an insult against Martin but an attack upon belief in the Gospels." The fanatic, impatient with any doubt or control, reveals himself all too clearly in these blasphemous words. Doubt in Martin's miracles must have been fairly widespread, and dis-

---

9. Ibid., *Dialogi*, I, 26.

cussions about their genuineness general. For Severus starts his biography with a solemn vow asserting the authenticity of his miracle stories. Yet Martin's miracles are not of a spiritual character. They do not satisfy a sense of moral justice, they do not reveal any particular spiritual truth. In the mind of his followers, at least, their purpose seems essentially to have been to reveal Martin as a superman, far superior to his adversaries. These adversaries are the bishops.

According to Severus, Martin's fight against the bishops started together with Martin's fight against the Arian heretics during his wandering years. Here already Severus brackets the Arian cause with "the wickedness of the priests." There is an element of justification in this, though a very relative one. The Arians found no support among monks, and did find a certain amount of genuine support among the secular clergy, and much more support from turncoats changing their minds with the change of emperors and of their religious opinions. The all too close connection of church and empire was reflected in this. The charge that the secular clergy was responsible for the Arian heresy boils down to the more general one that the secular clergy was involved in worldly affairs, hence no longer truly Christian.

These early antagonisms between Martin and the bishops were, however, outdistanced by the conflict which arose when he was elected bishop of Tours. He had been living for some time as the head of Marmoutiers, and his fame in the town must have been considerable, when he was made bishop by the popular vote. I should not regard as entirely trustworthy Severus' account that he was dragged out of his monastery against his will and put on the episcopal chair against his protests. This tale is too conventional, it is told of too many hierarchs of the time, to be taken to mean what it would mean today. Yet, the situation in which he was elected is clear enough and for once permits a clear appreciation of his conflicts with that body of bishops of which he was just about to become a member.

The episcopal office had become the most important office, not only in the church, but also in the towns. It was formally conferred by popular election, but in fact the local clergy and the local secular nobles generally made the choice. Being in substance a town mayor, the bishop might be a layman to the day of his election. Such a bishop from the laity might be deeply religious, as Ambrosius of Milan, or worldly and half pagan as Sidonius Apollinaris of Vienne. The electors did normally not care much, at least in the West. They wanted a head of the town. In fact, since the bishop had become the virtual head of the town in the dying Western Empire, local self-government, which had virtually disappeared, made great strides again. No wonder then that a local notable was normally the most suitable choice. No wonder, too, that episcopal elections involved all those local and political conflicts which the election of a town mayor often involves today.

Now Martin, in the first place, was not a native and not even a resident of Tours, and he was not even a native of Gaul. He did not belong to the upper classes, and sought his company among ascetics and serfs. No wonder then that this is what happened at his election:

> An immense multitude, not only from Tours but also from the neighboring towns, had congregated for the election. They all were determined to vote for Martin as the most suitable candidate. Any church, they thought, might be happy to have such a bishop. But a few, and some bishops among them, favored another candidate, and out of impiety opposed Martin, saying that he was a contemptible person, that a man of such bad looks, with dirty clothes and deformed hair[10] was unsuitable as a bishop. Thus in their folly they brought forth accusations which were the highest praise for Martin. But in this case nothing remained for them in the end but to do what the people wanted under divine inspiration. Among the bishops however a certain Defensor [one of the highest ranks of the imperial administration in the towns] resisted most strongly.

The situation is clear enough. The description of the people flocking to the town from all sides so as to take part in the voting is reminiscent of the passage in Livy where he describes how the peasants were flocking to Rome to take part in the voting for Tiberius Gracchus' agrarian law. The dividing line between the parties is similar in the two cases. On the one hand there are the town aristocracy and the official authorities, on the other hand there are the plebeian masses. The issue at stake is not directly connected with social conflicts, as was Gracchus' agrarian law; but no political event in Gaul in the fourth century ought to be interpreted without reference to the permanently smoldering peasant revolt, the Bagauda. The same social forces which fomented the Bagauda supported "men of the people" such as Martin. Yet an entirely new element, unknown to antiquity, has entered into the contest: a religion of salvation has since arisen, and its problems now overshadow the immediate social

10. Hauck, vol. 1, p. 55, relates the objection concerning Martin's "deformed hair" to an unkempt beard. I think Hauck forgets that the monastic garb was not accepted as a matter of course when Martin worked in Gaul. Hieronymus in a well-known passage describes how the populace in Rome ridiculed the tonsure. I believe that the above-mentioned passage refers to the tonsure too. It would be an interesting symptom of how thorough and comprehensive was the objection of many Gallic bishops to the monastic way of life.

problems. The struggle between patricians and plebeians is doubled by a struggle between the secular clergy (closely allied to secular town authorities) on the one hand, and the ascetics on the other. The forces of social rebellion are to a large extent transformed into forces of revolt against a secularized church.[11] The social antagonisms are the same as those which in Africa fomented Donatism. To sum it up again in the words of Martin's biographer, Severus: (Chapter 26). "O what a miserable region is ours, which did not know how to recognize the merits of such a man, though he was close at hand! But I do not make the common people responsible for this crime. It is only the secular clergy, and the bishops first and foremost, who refuse to recognize his virtue" (Chapter 26). The merging of the religious and of the social *theme* could not be more clearly expressed. And Severus goes on to explain that the secular clergy have every reason to hate Martin. Did they admit his virtues, they would implicitly admit their own vices.

Under such conditions the struggle was found to continue without remedy. Odd indeed were the ideas which emerged out of it among the ascetics. Severus asserts that Martin repeatedly pointed out to him "that as a bishop he never experienced the divine grace to the same extent as before. . . . Thus, before his episcopate he had raised two dead from the grave, but only one afterwards" (Dial. iii, 11). And Severus adds, with an almost incredible naivety, that in his biography he had altogether forgotten to mention this third resurrection from the dead. Thus, in the view of Martin and his circle, the bishops are not only objectionable, their office carries with it a curse and has the effect of impairing magical strength. Hatred and superstition could hardly go further.

11. I find myself obliged to disagree with Hauck's standard work on this point. Hauck's whole interpretation of the struggle, which in many respects is much more impartial and comprehensive than any other work dealing with the period, is based on the assumption that the ascetics, being a small handful, felt isolated and were at war with all the world. As one of several proofs, he quotes the fact that after Martin's death, an extreme adversary of monasticism was elected bishop of Tours. I think the story of Martin's election shows the whole position in a different light. This story cannot be pious exaggeration. Without very strong mass pressure, Martin's election, despite his many disabilities, would seem incomprehensible. But if the story is true, as it doubtless is, then Martin must have been idolized by the town plebeians and by the peasant serfs of his region. When Hauck speaks of an isolation of the ascetics in Gallic society, he is right as far as the upper classes are concerned, but he entirely forgets the masses. It is the most characteristic feature of Martin's career that, with his impressive personality and his close proximity to the lower classes, he succeeded in activizing them for a time, in inspiring them with his religious message and, of course, also in organizing them for his struggle against the bishops. Once he had departed, the plebeians sank back into their ordinary apathy. No wonder, then, that the town notables, once rid of so dangerous and turbulent an adversary, elected a man of a very different type as his successor, without any traceable opposition on the part of those Martin had championed.

Fairly late in Martin's career there happened the incident of the trial of Priscillian. It is unnecessary here to deal with its details. That Martin, in his struggle against sanguinary persecution, had both moral right and the letter of the law on his side, there is no doubt. It must also seem natural that he had little esteem for that kind of orthodoxy which was defended by the bishops he so much despised. He genuinely disagreed with Priscillian's doctrine. But Priscillian and his followers were fervent ascetics, and a certain affinity between theirs and Martin's attitude to the majority of the bishops may have existed. At any rate, Martin seems to have thought that their doctrinal mistakes were less bad than the worldliness and persecutory fury of the bishops. However that may be, he defended Priscillian before the emperor, threatening the latter with divine punishment if Priscillian were burnt. He also did the exact contrary from what most of his modern biographers make him do on that occasion. For once, as an exception, he consorted with other bishops, whom he otherwise regarded as infamous. He negotiated with them to save the accused, in vain. Next day he repented bitterly of this "sin." Then, Severus said, he saw an angel, who said to him: "Now see that thou restorest thy virtue, and returnest to thy constancy. For otherwise, not only thy glory but also thy salvation will be at stake." Contact with bishops, an almost inexcusable sin! And, as Severus concludes his tale of the incident, from that day onwards Martinus never was in touch with a bishop for the remaining sixteen years of his life.

Apart from revealing once more Martin's plainly superstitious abhorrence of bishops, the Priscillian crisis is important because here Martin's circle had an opportunity clearly to state its attitude to heresy. Priscillianism was a sharply marked form of Gnosticism, a tendency eliminated from the body of the church more than two centuries before. Yet Martin's attitude to Priscillian was, in the main, this: that it was a question of errors, not of heresy, of a mistaken judgment, not of a mortal sin. This remained the attitude of his circle in all the doctrinal struggles of the age. Severus' circle, after Martin's death, was apparently somehow connected with or at least interested in the struggles round the admissibility of the theology of Origen. This struggle, to Severus, transformed itself simply into a struggle of persecuting, anti-Origenistic bishops and tolerant monks. Severus' view is valueless as far as the facts of the Egyptian situation are concerned. But it is relevant that for these Gallic ascetics the cause of monasticism was identified with the cause of tolerance.

The work of Martin in Gaul started nearly a generation after Athanasius had first introduced monasticism into Italy. The lag in time was richly compensated in Gaul by the presence of genuine, spontaneous, passionate

impulses of the monastic movement. Some of these impulses were identical with those operating in the East. The rejection of the world, the
hatred for all kinds of luxury, for all implication in secular affairs were
the same. But whereas in the East this rejection of the world led up to
a mystical conception of salvation, the same could hardly be said of
Martin and his movement. In its stead we find, on the one hand, a crude,
really primeval belief that certain kinds of asceticism confer superhuman
powers, and on the other hand a merging of these magical beliefs with
impulses such as must arise from a situation of acute class tension. Martin
had identified monasticism so closely with the struggle against the established hierarchy, and with the cause of the oppressed plebeians, that
it would have had little chance of survival in an age where the hierarchy
grew more and more important. His attitude was the exact opposite of
that of the Italian monastic movement, and he certainly avoided the
impasse of lukewarmness which undermined the latter. But his attitude
threatened to lead the movement into the opposite impasse of sterile
rebellion, and at that a rebellion which was basically not of a spiritual,
but of a very crude social character. As all the ascetics were voluntarily
poor, it was easy for them to identify their cause with that of the in-
voluntarily poor. But from such a merely economic motive, an inspired
Western monasticism could not arise—any more than a Western theology
could have grown out of Donatism. There is no evidence that any further
foundations were made from either Ligugé or Marmoutiers. The impasse
was total.

Yet the specific rural character of Martin's monasticism contained
germs of fertile future developments. Pachomius' monasticism had already had such a rural character. But in Egypt there was no region which
was entirely rural. There were towns and town bishops everywhere. It
remains remarkable, nevertheless, how close the connection between a
relatively independent country life and the growth of monasteries was
even in the East. The second great monastic movement of the East, that
of Basilios, arose in Cappadocia and Pontus, the two most rural provinces
of the Eastern Empire, where even the episcopal organization had to be
modified for the sake of ministering to the populations of large, townless
country districts. Yet everywhere in the East town life prevailed and
continued to prevail in the last resort, and monasticism could do no more
than leave the church hierarchy in the towns alone and form religious
centers in the country: that was the social aspect of the pact between the
see of Alexandria and the Pachomian monks, as later of the cooperation
between Basilios and the see of Constantinople.

But in the West the situation was different. Italy, to be sure, was emphatically a land of towns, as much as ancient Greece, and perhaps the long-lasting weakness of the monastic movement there is partly explained by this. But in the other parts of the Western Empire the towns had never sucked up country life as completely as in the zone where the ancient Polis had its roots. And now, with the decline of classical civilization and with the gradual emergence of a new feudal class of landowners resident in the country (already in the Roman Empire, long before the advent of the barbarians) the situation in the West changed radically in favor of the countryside. Martin's success had something to do with that.

Only what precisely had it to do with it? If rural areas were particularly receptive to monasticism, it was certainly not for the reason that monasteries sought solitude. That explains why they grew up in lonely spots, of which there were plenty, even near the towns, in that age of depopulation. It does not explain why they grew up in predominantly rural areas. Christianity, during the first centuries, had emphatically been a religion of the towns. Not before the fourth century did it make much headway in the countryside. Where it did make headway from that time onwards, it was generally in connection with some kind of monastic movement. But it would be quite impossible to maintain that asceticism had any special affinity to the mentality of the countryfolk—the contrary was surely the case—or that it reflected any kind of interests of the landowners or of their serfs. Monasticism is not the expression of any specific mentality of the countryside; on the contrary, the early ascetic movement had drawn its recruits mainly from very large towns such as Alexandria.

I think the success of monasticism in countrified regions must be explained in terms of ecclesiastic organization. As the church had originally catered to the needs of townspeople, there was no room in the towns for an independent ecclesiastical body besides bishops and priests. The bishops would not have allowed it. But independence was precisely what the healthy and virile branches of the monastic movement wanted most. The countryside was still an ecclesiastical void, village parishes were unknown except on the Persian border and in Persia itself. In this vacuum the monastic movement did not find any spiritual inspiration, but it did not meet any administrative obstacles either. It could develop with any available human material, and develop along any lines of spiritual aims which were present among its members. Thus in the East, it developed along lines of fervent asceticism and denial of the world. In the West, it also developed along lines of fervent asceticism but from the very beginning was mixed up in the affairs of this world, identifying itself with the needs and impulses of the countryfolk. It was also filled with other impulses, as we shall see. But everywhere country life provided favorable conditions for its development, and in turn it contributed to the shifting of the spiritual center from the towns to the countryside. In the West, where this movement back to the country was to go to much greater lengths than in the East in the sphere of church life, it started with Martin, and that is not the least of his merits, and not the least of the reasons which made Gallic monasticism grow so much more vigorously than early Italian monasticism.

Martin had identified his healthy reaction against the dying towns with an extreme and crude rebellion against the church hierarchy in the towns. That would not do. Gallic monasticism could only hope to prosper after having achieved a compromise with the secular clergy, such as had been achieved by Pachomius in Egypt. But in Gaul, where the struggle with the secular clergy had been so violent, conciliation took a longer time than in Egypt, and also demanded a new departure. Such a new departure was attempted by an ascetic group more closely connected with town life and the ecclesiastic hierarchy of Southern France, shortly after Martin's death, in the beginning of the fifth century.

What would we not give for biographies less stereotyped and more precise in their facts than those of the saints of that period! Of St. Martin we can still form an idea, because he so little corresponded to the conventional picture of a saint. But despite a long biography by a friend we know next to nothing of the life of St. Honorat, the next important figure in Gallic church history. He belonged to the nobility of Arles, then capital of Gaul and one of the biggest cities of the Western Empire. He determined upon an ascetic life at an early age. Perhaps because the wild men of Martin's movement were not to his taste, he went for his apprenticeship to Italy. But here also he was disappointed, and he returned to his native Province to found the monastery of Lerins on an island of the Mediterranean. Next to Augustine, Lerins, its abbots, monks, and writings became the strongest influence in the whole Western church throughout the fifth and down to the beginning of the sixth century. Honorat himself became bishop of Arles, and a string of bishoprics of Arles, Vienne, Lyons, and other important sees of Southeastern France were filled with monks from Lerins. The contrast with Martin's bishop-hating followers could not be greater.

From the very beginning Lerins, unlike Tabbenisi and Marmoutiers, was not a monastery of the poor but of the educated nobility of the Southern French towns. We know of many monks from Lerins, and this is invariably the class from which they came. That seems also to have been the case in the episcopal monasteries of Italy. But an Eastern parallel is more to the point. St. Basilios also, unlike Pachomius, had created a monastic movement of a rather aristocratic type. And Basilios, like St. Honorat, but unlike the Italians, had founded a monastery not dependent on local episcopal support. It is impossible, however, to prove any direct influence of the Basilians upon Lerins. The monastic movement had by then passed through its stormy youth, the life of the independent hermit had become increasingly suspect, and the quiet, well-organized monastery, relatively independent of the bishops and of the town churches but not hostile to them, was winning the day. Southern France, far from being original in this matter, only shared in a trend which was as noticeable in the East as in the West.

With this new type of monasticism also went the desire for more comprehensive regulations. Pachomius had left nothing but a house rule, Martin's monks had been without any rule. Basilios, though he did not write a "Rule" in the sense given to this word later, laid down a great many rules for the life of his monasteries, concerning not only practical matters, but much more even the spiritual training of the monks. The same need was satisfied, in the West, by the abbot of a modest monastery in Marseilles, Johannes Cassianus, who kept in closest touch with Lerins. His *Monastic Institutions* became the textbook of Western monasticism. It may be rightly doubted whether Lerins received its final shape by its founder, who, for posterity at least, is a colorless figure. It seems rather to have preserved the direction imparted to it by the great mind of Cassian. It is he, at any rate, who, as a permanent proof of his paramount influence upon the Lerins tradition, planted there his specific moral doctrine, which his adversaries described as "Semi-Pelagianism." The chief champion of this doctrine after Cassian, Faustus, bishop of Riez, had been abbot of Lerins, and it is easy to prove that other outstanding Lerinians were of the same mind in this matter long after Cassian's death.

But Cassian, the man who molded the first stable Western type of monastic life, was himself an oriental, an Assyrian. This statement is at variance with the accepted tradition which makes him a native of Marseilles. But that tradition belongs to the last centuries only and can boast neither antiquity nor the slightest justification in the sources. We hear of Cassian in Marseilles for the first time as a man over forty. The tradition grew up because his description as a Scythian in the earliest sources seemed meaningless. Yet Scythia, in the language of the period, meant the country South of the Danube, and its inhabitants were probably the ancestors of the modern Rumanians. In the sixth century the

Scythians gave leading minds to the theological movement, and Scythian monasteries dominated church life in Constantinople. Cassian lived before that period. But there is no intrinsic reason to reject the statement that he came from the Balkans.

Yet there seems to be manuscript evidence to the contrary. A French scholar, father Thibaut, in a *Note biographique sur Jean Cassien* (Paris, 1931), has revealed that three of the relevant manuscripts have "Serta" instead of "Scythia." Serta, modern Seert, is a place in Kurdistan, then called Assyria or Gordyene. Locally it must have been quite a well-known place. Father Thibaut need not have taken as much pains as he did to prove its existence; there is a well-known Nestorian chronicle of Seert. But in the greater part of the Roman Empire, and especially in the West, the place would of course be unknown to ordinary scribes. It is therefore perfectly credible that copyists should have made "Scythia" out of "Serta," but it would be inconceivable that an identical Serta should appear in three manuscripts simply by mistake. "Serta" is the better version, which ought to settle the matter.

It is, however, no small matter that the man who has the best title to having created, not the first Western monastery but the first coherent type of Western monasticism, should have come, of all places, from Mesopotamia. Therefore, additional proof is desirable. Father Thibaut has pointed to certain allusions to Cassian's life in his Dialogues, allusions which fit well into this Mesopotamian origin. But I think that much stronger proof can be provided from the known facts of Cassian's life and teaching. In the first place, among all the monastic leaders Cassian is the only one whose origin was not generally known. In the case of a Roman citizen, such uncertainty would be hardly conceivable. It is more natural in the case of a Persian subject who, owing to the persecution of the church in Persia, could not live there. Gordyene passed from Roman into Persian hands as a result of Julian's catastrophic campaign, in 363 A.D., presumably in Cassian's early childhood. Persecution of Christians began soon. It is conceivable that his Christian parents wanted to remove him from a country where he could have no proper Christian education, and sent him to Bethlehem. It is equally conceivable that he did not care to stress, though he did not conceal, his origins in a country almost constantly at war with the Roman Empire, where he lived. In this light, his later life with its many wanderings and its repeated failure to take root in various parts of the empire would appear as the natural life story of a man who had no home.

It is also noteworthy that out of many possible candidates it was Cassian who was chosen by Rome, in 430 A.D., to make the representative theological contribution of the Western church to the struggle against Nestorius. For Nestorius was closely connected with the theological school of Edessa, with the theological traditions of Cassian's home region. No ordinary Westerner would have taken so much interest in this affair, and none, except Cassian's own disciples at Lerins, ever came back to it except by way of casual reference.

Cassian's own unorthodox, semi-Pelagian doctrine of grace is not comprehensible either in terms of his long training among Egyptian theologians or in terms of his close connections with Rome. Those who imagine that the fact of belonging to this or that school tradition did not in the last resort matter in the choice men made in the various dogmatic quarrels of that period are very much mistaken. It was not an age of individualism, where people formed what they believed were "their own opinions." Every heresy in those centuries was a matter of a school-tradition carried to extremes. Now the only school to which semi-Pelagianism can be related is that of Antiochia-Edessa, and we shall soon see that Cassian's doctrine can be best understood as an attempt to reconcile specifically Syrian and Mesopotamian theological doctrines with that Augustinism which dominated the West, where he was then working.

But the strongest arguments for Cassian's Assyrian descent are the peculiarities of his teaching about monasticism. His *Institutions*, which make up a textbook of oriental monastic customs for the use of the West, are primarily based on Egyptian eremitic, semieremitic and coenobitic methods and traditions. But in more than one place Cassian avers that in the West it is necessary to mitigate the rigor of the Egyptian methods by an appeal to the traditions of other oriental monasteries. Now the most important alternative Eastern tradition in his age was the one created by Basilios. It is demonstrable that Cassian knew Basilios' monastic rules, for passages from them are directly taken over in his *Institutions*. Yet Basilios is never mentioned by name, nor are his monasteries ever described in Cassian's writings, though it is likely that, on his land-journey from Syria to Constantinople, he visited them. In his writings Cassian, in an almost stereotyped manner, only mentions Palestinian and Mesopotamian monastic customs as suitable to be merged with Egyptian traditions. The mention of Palestinian monasteries needs no explanation in the writings of a man who grew up in a monastery at Bethlehem. But Mesopotamia, which was part of the Persian empire? The constant juxtaposition of Egyptian, Palestinian, and Mesopotamian methods to the exclusion of others shows that these were the types closely known to Cassian. Mesopotamia was, from the Christian point of view, an outlying and uninteresting province of a hostile country outside the borders of the Empire and already, even before Nestorius, half schismatic. None but a native of that country could have treated Mesopotamian traditions on the same level with the venerated monastic traditions of Egypt.

I should add, however, that for the interpretation of Cassian's teachings his Assyrian origin is not an indispensable thesis. What matters is that he was an Easterner, not a Westerner. Yet many details of his teachings and his career can hardly be explained without assuming a specific connection with the doctrine and interests of Antiochia and Edessa. And it is also this assumption which is best in agreement with the sources.

CHAPTER EIGHT

Boniface and the Anglo-Irish Impact on the Frankish Churches

"His name was Winfreth and he was an Anglo-Saxon"—that is about how the story of St. Boniface starts in the schoolbooks. It is a beginning which obscures the chances of real understanding right from the start. Certainly, the English origin of the "apostle of the Germans" is a historic fact of the greatest significance—even more so than is obvious at first sight. But the word "Anglo-Saxon" by no means covers this fact: Boniface, who called himself a Saxon, and his contemporaries would not have recognized themselves in this term, and the best interpreters of today's English-speaking world equally object to its application to modern conditions. Fundamentally, "Anglo-Saxon" is hardly more than a linguistic concept, which may at most be applied also to certain political and cultural developments from the eighth to the early eleventh century. But Boniface had his roots still in the seventh century.

Until the end of the seventh century, there existed, apart from numerous regional peculiarities, *two* main Anglo-Saxon cultures, confronting one another as harshly as was at all conceivable within the West. A relict of this dualism is still to be found today in the two-headed organization of the Anglican church under the archbishops of Canterbury and York, with the formal precedence of Canterbury reflecting the victory of the Southern English church and culture over the Northern English one.

Canterbury was the most Roman among all the Roman outposts. Founded by Roman missionaries, the seat of its metropolitan soon overshadowed the significance of the princeling who was the secular ruler of Kent. Canterbury never shared in that secularization, nationalization, and feudalization which characterized the life of the Frankish church in those centuries. Its liturgy, church organization, thought, and art show during that period a more directly Roman, less national or regional character than even the provincial churches of Italy.

York rose to a significant role only much later, but the northern English church was important long before York. Northumbria, long separated from Canterbury's field of radiation by a strip of pagan country, then comprised the English North and the Scottish Lowlands, and its people lived in communion not with the Southern English, but with the schismatic Iro-Scottish church. The two principal religious centers of Northumbria, Jarrow and Lindisfarne, were not bishoprics, but monasteries in the Iro-Scottish tradition—indeed they were among the great leading monasteries of that Far Western world. They celebrated Easter and ordinated their priests not according to the Roman but the Irish ritual. Their dogmatic tradition was the Irish one with its strong Pelagian coloring. Their magnificent art was purely ornamental, whereas Canterbury took over the Roman tradition of the representation of man right from the start. But above all, they shared in the Iro-Scottish missionary tradition and played an important role in the missionary activity of the Far Western church—in its late phase a decisive one.

Now Northumbria was the only Germanic area of the otherwise Celtic Far Western church. When paganism disintegrated in central England, Northumbria became the natural gate for the invasion of the Far West by the Latin church: the Northumbrian monasteries themselves came to be split between a Roman and an Irish party. The decision fell in 664 at the Whitby synod; the Irish monks were expelled from the Northumbrian monasteries, the Anglo-Saxon ones submitted to Roman discipline and adopted the Roman liturgy. That almost forgotten Whitby synod was a landmark in the emergence of the West: for here for the first time, the organization of the worldwide Roman church merged with an independent ecclesiastic and theological creation of the Northern peoples. The spirit that was born out of that fusion, radiating from its narrow Northern English home, has made a decisive contribution to the shaping of the entire West.

During the following centuries, we can trace all over the continent an Irish influence that had undergone a Northumbrian transformation. In our context, this concerns first of all church life. And here we must clarify above all that there could neither have existed a Western monasticism without the Irish nor by Irish efforts alone: not through the Irish *alone,* because as schismatics they were separated from the other Western churches, so that the continental monasteries founded by them (even the relatively promising ones of Columbanus at Luxeuil and Bobbio) could have no lasting effect; not *without* the Irish, because the creation of St. Benedict of Nursia had been buried under the Langobard whirlwind, that of St. Martin of Tours under the decay of the late Merovingian period. Only the Iro-Scottish church had developed a living, well-organized and well-disciplined monasticism filled with the spirit of the *ecclesia militans*. But only by subordinating itself to the universal church could that monasticism with its ardent missionary zeal reach the continental churches and penetrate them with its spirit; and above all, only in the framework of the Roman episcopal order and its dioceses could these monasteries have an effect that spread geographically and socially beyond their immediate surroundings. The Northumbrian transformation of the Iro-Scottish tradition thus issued into a form of church organization balancing episcopal authority and monastic intensification of the faith. That form of ecclesiastic organization, spreading from its Northumbrian cradle, has formed the West.

It may be objected that the coexistence of diocesan organization and monasticism is nothing specifically Western, but is even more characteristic for the Eastern church, where most monasteries developed in complete independence from the episcopal church. Most probably, indeed, Irish monasticism evolved (in a church which knew no bishops, but only abbots as heads of congregations) under the influence of Eastern ecclesiastic traditions. Yet with one decisive difference! The concept of the *ecclesia militans* has in the Far Western church a meaning different from that in the Eastern church. Eastern monasticism was certainly "militant" in the sense of highly drastic and frequently even violent interventions in dogmatic disputes, and hence in the politics of the Byzantine and later the Moscow state. But Eastern monasticism was never involved in the world in the sense of regarding the Christianization of the laity as its task, and indeed the Christianization of the pagans appears as marginal in the Eastern church generally. By contrast, the Far Western church, despite its purely monastic character, was thoroughly conceived as a church of internal and external mission, so that missionary work appeared even as *the* proper work of the church. Inside their territory, this missionary spirit is shown in a tough, ruthless struggle for the moral disciplining of the laymen, finding its expression in those penitentials which emerged in the sixth century first in Ireland, Scotland, and Wales, in the Seventh century also in Northumbria in great numbers, and which have, starting from there, transformed the practice of penance in the continental churches and paved the way for the truly Western, Roman-Catholic usage of confession. Outside, the same will was expressed in a never-ending sequence of at first Iro-Scottish, then Northumbrian (but not simply "Anglo-Saxon") missionaries. The Irish ones had little success. The Northumbrian ones, translating from the start the Iro-Scottish missionary tradition into Roman forms, had significant results at once. A real dynasty of heads of missions was formed: first Wilfreth, then Willibrord, finally Winfreth—Boniface. They transferred the Northumbrian type of church unchanged into Germany.

Boniface himself was not a Northumbrian (no "Yorkshireman," as the modern English would say), but Southern English. But he learnt the craft of the missionary in Germany under Willibrord. Moreover, to group him as a "Southern Englishman" would be no less misleading than to call him an "Anglo-Saxon." He came from Devonshire, the border area against the still completely Celtic Cornwall, which at that time was itself still very strongly interspersed with Celtic elements. As a child, he had been handed as an oblate to Exeter monastery. His decisive years of education he spent under abbot Aldhelm in the monastery of Malmsbury, close to the Severn river which then formed the border against a Wales that was still completely schismatic with a church based on monasteries. The monastic organization had come to Southwest England, too, from the Celtic fringe. In the region where Boniface spent his youth, the same process which in Northumbria culminated in the Whitby synod had been completed a few years earlier, though in less dramatic forms: here, too, a monasticism of Celtic style but carried on by Germanic monks had subordinated itself to the organization of the Roman church. Abbot Aldhelm himself conducted a lifelong struggle to overcome the schism at the Welsh border. Thus Boniface could smoothly integrate himself into the Northumbrian missionary traditions, because he had grown up himself in completely analogous traditions. In both cases, what was happening in the church, and not only in the church, was an interpenetration of Celtic and Germanic elements. (Bony and Sedlmayr have pointed to the special character of the architecture of this Southwestern area of England in the eleventh and twelfth centuries, and to its importance for overall European development, and have linked it with the belated arrival of the Norman conquest in this area. The above shows that in other fields, a mixed Celto-Germanic culture in the same geographical area can be shown already for the seventh century.)

We can trace the kind of ideas among which Boniface grew up from the surviving letters of Abbot Aldhelm. A more passionate profession of faith in the unity of the universal church under Rome is inconceivable. For Aldhelm, that unity was the one and all. If Boniface will later, at the beginning of his independent missionary activity, make a pilgrimage to Rome omitting all intermediate stages, he follows the example of Willibrord, but quite certainly even more the teaching of Aldhelm. The documents clearly show the motives of Aldhelms attitude. True, he polemicizes point by point against the Irish and Welsh deviations from Latin dogma and ritual. But what moves his inmost heart are not these particular issues, but the unity of the universal church as such. The schism is damnable, not just because it prepares the ground for heresy but above all in itself. The thought of this man who became so influential in shaping missionary work on the continent shows no trace of the influence of Greek theology and mysticism; it turns entirely around questions of ecclesiastic organization and of the moral discipline of monks, priests, and laymen. (This trait will be found again in Boniface, even though with a softer tone of sentiment rooted in his personality.)

One may here recognize an early form of the English concept of the life of the church; for in the tradition of the English church, after the elimination of Franco-Norman influences, questions of church organization and church discipline, hence of church policy and individual morals, have played, increasingly over time, the decisive role as compared to dogmatic questions and mysticism. Perhaps one may even talk of an all-Germanic inheritance: we find the same sharp emphasis on the inseparable connection between the unity of the body politic and the unity of the church, which proved the most powerful argument in Northumbria and in Western England, again on that unique Icelandic Althing of the year 1000 which decreed, in the interest of the unity of the body politic, a public conformity in the Christian faith, permitting the pagans a generation's grace for private ceremonies within their own homes. The freely granted conformity of individuals in all matters of essential public interest is the basic principle of those early events in church policy with their far-reaching historic effects, as of the late modern liberal political systems of the Germanic North and West.

In itself, all that is much more political and social than religious; alone it would not have been sufficient to become the spiritual basis of the West. But added to it was the fertilizing Irish impulse. In the Irish monastic church, the moral element was not just a condition of successfully living together in a community—community discipline was never the strong suit of the Celts—what mattered here was exclusively the moral self-perfection of the individual to the highest possible state of freedom from sin, the striving for moral perfection as the true worship of God. That, too, is moralism, but of a very different kind. That, too, has entered into the English religious tradition. Just as the Anglican state church embodies the principle of social conformity, so puritanism and its sects the principle of boundless moral striving. No wonder that this ultimately Celtic inheritance finds to this day its liveliest expression in Northern England, in the domain of the church of York, as the principle of the state church does in Southern England, in the domain of Canterbury. The variety of English national life, rooted much more in the event of Whitby than in the Norman conquest, is to this day based on the coexistence of those contradictions.

The missionary work of Boniface is as if drenched in all that. To take the organizational aspect first: Boniface was not an organizer by free choice, but he was a magnificent organizer, a true precursor of the empire builders, who even with a minimum of personnel and the most inadequate means subjected vast areas to the order they represented. He himself would have wanted to be a pure missionary, engaged in weaning souls away from paganism and winning them for a holy life. Just in that activity he failed: he never got close to Saxony, and in Frisia his work was destroyed again and again. Rather, his great historical achievement is the reorganization of the churches not only of Southern and Central Germany, but also those of Gaul—which had decayed and even relapsed into outright paganism.

In this activity, there occurred a single issue of serious friction with Rome, concerning—characteristically—the applicability of the Latin diocesan organization to the German language area. Pope Zacharias wanted to erect bishoprics, according to the Mediterranean model, exclusively in "populous settlements." But Boniface successfully insisted on his view that the settlements would have to be grouped around the religious centers, not vice versa. An organizing principle of the Far Western church, conceiving the role of a bishopric as analogous to that of a great Iro-Scottish monastery! Here indeed a Roman and a Far Western type of organization were merged into a system unsuitable to the world of the Mediterranean cities, but fitting for the emerging world of Western feudalism. The monasteries were certainly not to play an exclusive and not even a dominant role in that form of organization, but a disproportionately greater one than in the Southern Europe of that time—a decisive prelude for the future flourishing of Western monasticism!

What was the activity of those bishoprics and monasteries newly created or re-formed by Boniface? On a modest scale, they continued Iro-Scottish and Anglo-Saxon traditions of scholarship. But their main work, up to the rise of Cluny, consisted in moral self-training and moral discipline for the laymen. As one follows the well-preserved correspondence of this first and decisive formative personality of the churches North of the Alps, one is struck by quite a different tone sounded in moral questions than in organizational questions proper. Foundations of bishoprics are a necessity, fulfilled carefully and conscientiously. But the discipline of clergy and laity is a passion to which Boniface abandons himself without limits. Yet there is here a characteristic difference from the attitude, say, of Columbanus; although Boniface could be inexorable in what was necessary, he clearly lacked the icy rigor of the Irish puritan moral fanatics. From many intimate letters to male and female friends in his English homeland, from his desire for literature of contemplation, from his tendency to reject excesses of discipline as much as the lack of it, one seems to perceive a humane openness, nay an infinitely amiable character, and one comes to feel that his spiritual conquests on seemingly barren ground were due to his true humanity no less than to his determination and his overwhelming gift for organization. Here, if anywhere, one touches as with one's hands the interpenetration of the Celtic and Germanic characters under the aegis of Rome.

Missionary zeal had brought Boniface to Germany, but the effect of his work on world history was due to his freedom to organize and reform according to his own choice on German soil. The decisive years of his activity, beginning in 722, still precede the final consolidation of Carlovingian power. The Frankish state was glad enough that the church organizer took from it the main burden of government in those border areas that were remote and hard to control. Next to the freedom granted by that situation, Boniface profited also from the health, comparatively intact in spite of everything, of the primitive communities among which he worked. Decaying antiquity, Germanic forms of life decaying in contact with the imperial tradition, finally and above all the brutal exploitation of the church by the state, had altogether contributed to the ruin of the Gallic church. None of those influences were present in the same strength on German soil. Thus the German church, reformed in the Northumbrian spirit, could in turn become a force of reform for the profoundly degenerated Gallic church.

Perceiving in Boniface the greatest potential for church policy in their dominions, Carloman and Pippin called on him to transfer his work from Mainz and Fulda to the banks of the Seine and Oise. He had started out in order to lay the foundations for the great assault on Saxon paganism, which he expected within a short time, and then to smash it. But from his starting point in Central Germany, his work led him not to the North and East, but to the South and West, farther away from missionary work and close to the center where alone the reform of the Western church could score a decisive victory. For Boniface, this was a road of suffering, for it led him ever farther away from the struggle for souls and ever closer to high politics. His last great act was the anointment of Pippin as king of the Franks.

But the desires of men do not always lie in the direction of their greatest capacity, and the completed work proves often enough completely different from the originally envisaged goal—yet at the same time much more significant. Making his way from the Celtic fringe via Germany, acquiring, in a German church restored from ruin and corruption to strength and power, a self-made lever for world political action, Boniface became the most important link in the creation of the Western church. With the strength of the German church, he achieved the global reform of the churches North of the Alps, the penetration of the whole transalpine region with the spirit of renewal of the Celto-Germanic tradition, and at the same time, completing the work of Whitby, the most intimate fusion of Nordic with Roman traditions.

People like to say that in that wild and lawless age the sword was everything and the spirit nothing. In fact the reverse was the case: because of the weakness of state power and its inadequate penetration, the church was the only instrument that could hold together any society transcending the most primitive tribal community. Boniface's church reform was the decisive precondition for the emerging Carlovingian imperial system—a system that founded the unity of the West, even though it proved unable to maintain the political form of that unity for long. Among the men who created the unity of the West, this man with his modest goals and his magnificent success was perhaps the greatest.

As we said, that magnificent success meant a bitter renunciation for him personally. Yet he was granted what is granted to few men—returning to the dream of his youth after completing his work. He was too powerful to be a comfortable partner for Pippin. He was too gentle, too little obsessed with power, to resist him. He left the renewed church he had created in the trusted hands of a band of pupils, and returned himself to missionary work and personal preaching. Knowing well that the political situation along the coast of the North Sea made the methods of purely religious missionary work hopeless, he still followed, at last, the voice of his heart. He must have been very happy in doing that. When he saw the drawn swords of the Frisians directed on himself and his disciples, he spoke to the latter: "Fear ye not, for the Lord is with us." It was his youthful dream of a Christian death.

CHAPTER NINE

Rome's Break with Byzantium as Shown in Christian Painting

I

The visitor to Rome may spend some time before he discovers that the church of S. Clemente, near the Lateran, contains a number of mural paintings belonging mostly to the ninth and the eleventh century, respectively; some minor pieces are believed to date from the eighth and the tenth century. They are well-known to students of Byzantine art, but their significance for the transition from Byzantine to Western civilization has not been fully appreciated, doubtless owing to the regrettable specialization of historical research which invariably breaks down at the essential points of cultural transition not classified under any conventional heading. At first sight one is tempted to query the accepted dating, especially of the earlier pieces, so violently do some of them contrast with the hieratic immutability of Byzantine sacred art. Yet few works of the period can be dated more unambiguously.

The most important of the earlier paintings, an Ascension of the Virgin, represents on its left fringe Pope Leo IV (847-55), with his name next to the figure and a green quadratic "nimbus," familiar from Byzantine iconography, round his head. This piece, therefore, belongs almost exactly to the middle of the ninth century. Now the historical significance of this painting lies, to my mind, in the depicting of violent passion in a sacred story: a revolutionary innovation of far-reaching significance. This approach does not extend yet—as indeed it will not extend until the Romanesque period—to the divinity itself. At the top of the picture we see the traditional Byzantine Christ, young and masterful, sitting immobile on his throne, surrounded by floating angels; directly underneath him, Mary is standing erect in the sky, her wide-opened arms raised in a gesture of prayer and adoration which might be taken directly from a Catacomb painting of the third or fourth century. But what movement in the representation of the Apostles! True, they still fall into two sharply divided and roughly symmetrical groups of six each (the group on the left being much better preserved than that on the right). But the symmetry is no longer geometrical or formal. It is a symmetry of inner experience only, in the sense that, in each of the two groups, three of its members gaze upwards to behold the apparition (one of them so as almost to break his neck), while one averts his face, one covers his eyes and one, in looking towards his companions, stiffly raises his right arm to point to the wonder. On both sides the Apostle who averts himself dominates the group. His position focuses the attention of the spectator. Deeply bowing, so as to cover in part the bodies of his companions, he raises his left hand to his heart, as if seized by a sudden attack; gesture and expression reveal that so much glory is intolerable to his mortal frame. The same is true of the one who shields his eyes, and also of the Apostle pointing upwards with his arm. But this arm, by reaching out like a signpost from the level of the earth to that of heaven—this arm which is, as it were, torn upwards, disrupting the zonal segmentation of the picture, resembles a trumpet blow announcing the end of secular existence, the approach of a new aeon.

The Assunta of S. Clemente thus represents the climax of a development which started in the beginning of the eighth century. Previously, Roman art had been entirely dependent upon models from Ravenna and Byzantium. The independent development starting round 700 A.D. has more than one source. Rome had for centuries been intermittently quarrelling with Byzantium concerning theological questions. The latest of these quarrels, the monotheletic dispute of the seventh century, was, however, the first which led to a prolonged ecclesiastical rupture, while at the same time the Islamic onslaught weakened Byzantium, and the Byzantine bureaucracy in Italy was virtually replaced by the rule of local feudal lords. Towards the end of the seventh century the theological rupture was mended, and in the beginning of the eighth Byzantium finally repulsed the Arabs. But the breathing space was short, for the iconoclastic movement had already started, and in 726 A.D. iconoclasm was proclaimed official policy in Byzantium. It is well known that Rome reacted violently, this time simultaneously in the relgious and in the political field: Pope Gregory II, at the head of the Italian militia, led an open revolt against the Empire. His successor, Gregory III (731-41), appealed to the Franks for help. Rome thus exchanged its Eastern for a Western allegiance. And at the same time iconoclasm, in the field of art, deprived Byzantium of all those artistic activities which might have served as a model for Rome.

These facts amply explain why Rome, during the eighth century, became independent in the artistic as well as in the political field. They do not explain the development which led up to the Assunta of S. Clemente, a work not inspired by Italian regionalism but by a spirit entirely different from that of Byzantium. It is the thesis of this paper that this new trend cannot be understood without reference to the contents of the theological debates of the age, debates which are still reputed to be absurd and unintelligible but which in fact have a meaning accessible to our modern understanding. The monotheletic dispute, which marks the real point of rupture between Rome and Byzantium—though Byzantium in the end accepted the Roman doctrine, thereby once more restoring formal relations—was originally an extension of the monophysite controversy, which in its turn was the basic issue inside the Eastern Church. Did Christ in His person unite two natures, the human and the divine? Or was He wholly divine, even in the flesh? The monophysites, the partisans of the "one person, one nature" thesis (or of some similar but diluted formula), at bottom denied the significance of the Incarnation. Their adversaries upheld it. The dispute went right down to the problem, central to Christian religious experience, whether Jesus had actually suffered, physically and morally; whether, therefore, the acceptance of suffering could have a divine, hence a paradigmatic, character. Art necessarily interprets the problem much more graphically than dogma. Where Byzantium in the end, after much wavering, accepted the "two natures" formula, thus driving Egypt, Syria, and Armenia into heresy, Byzantine art rejected any representation of the suffering Christ. Here Christ appears exclusively as the *Pantocrator*, the youthful or mature, but in any case powerful and mighty Ruler in His glory, and all those depicted with Him, be they saints, emperors or bishops, acquire something of the same stately immutability and splendid majesty. Even in this form, pictorial representation of Christ remains somewhat suspect, and there exists a tendency (deriving, of course, from Catacomb art) to replace the figure of Christ by the symbol of the Lamb or that of the Cross (with, incredible as it may seem, *no* Christ on it). Martyrs, too, appear only in their glory, bearing the instruments of torture in their hands as signs of triumph.

II

The monotheletic dispute restates the monophysite controversy in almost identical terms, with this difference, that for the general problem of the "two natures" there is now substituted the rather narrower problem of the "two wills" in Christ. Clearly, if Christ had had only a divine will, totally identical with that of the Father, He could still have suffered physical pain but not moral conflict. The Mount of Olives, the anguish of the Cross, dissolved into irrelevance. Now it is, I think, important to realize that the new formula, which to the Christian East might seem a milder version of monophysitism, was to Rome a particularly obnoxious one. For to a Roman the notion of *voluntas* was central. It was inherent in the fundamental notions of Roman law, the core of the Roman administration, the whole Roman way of life which the Church had inherited. A human nature in Christ deprived of human will appeared as something blasphemous, a kind of repulsive doll. The protagonist of the Roman viewpoint, Maximus Confessor, insisted above all on the importance of the moral conflict within Christ. How otherwise could the temptation in the desert have had a meaning? Rome, in proclaiming the full human nature of Christ, "completely God, completely Man," insisted upon the positive religious value of the human person, not only capable of being saved but also able to do something to save himself. Few incidents of the period are more characteristic than the decision of the Synod of Constantinople in 692 A.D. (the so-called first Trullanum) which enthroned the Roman viewpoint as dogma, at the same time prohibiting the symbolic representation of Christ and insisting upon his representation in the flesh. It is against this background that the iconoclastic movement, which erupted almost immediately afterwards, must be understood. The question of the icons was the question of accepting or denying the divine element in the flesh.

It would be a mistake, however, to see the human will, which was now accepted as a positive religious value, in the light in which the modern world regards it. Maximus Confessor was himself a Byzantine who had found a new abode in Rome—the not infrequent example of the man who, in breaking with his native civilization, becomes the protagonist of a rival one. Yet, again quite typically, he carried a great deal of the Byzantine heritage with him. Compare him to some authentic Roman, let us say Pope Gregory the Great, and one quickly realizes that the latter's casual use of the notions of free will and personal responsibility has no counterpart in the writings of Maximus; to say nothing of the unceasing effort of will so emphatically preached centuries later by the

Miltons and Bunyans of Puritanism. Maximus has left a *Tractatus As-ceticus* which shows that human will, to him, was entirely a matter of negation. The asceticism he preaches is summed up in the one virtue of loving one's enemies, and that virtue can indeed be achieved, but only by a total repudiation of the love of the world for the sake of the love of God. Will, then, can exert itself only in denying itself. It is charac-teristic of this attitude that in the ascetic treatise the only being which appears to be endowed with dynamic energy is the devil, whereas God is in possession of the stable, unchanging qualities of strength and power. This philosophy clearly derives from the pre-Christian doctrine, both Platonic and Aristotelian, which regards immutability as the essential quality of the divine, and derives as well from its Christian amplification identifying change and changeability with the state of sin and with actual sin. In Maximus' teaching this doctrine had been joined to the Roman concept of human *voluntas* in such a way that the will appears as an essential instrument of salvation, but only in so far as it is necessary to lead man out of the realm of mutability, where alone free will can have a meaning.

To these theological concepts the Roman art of the eighth century provides a close correspondence. Its development can best be studied in the remains of Sta Maria l'Antiqua, on the Forum, which contains mural paintings from the fifth or sixth to the eighth century, and is well known to art historians and tourists. The theological significance of its paintings, especially those of the later phase (which, incidentally, have their coun-terpart in some smaller Roman churches of the period) has not to my knowledge so far attracted attention. Yet it is there that we find, dated from Pope John VII (705–7), the first direct Occidental representation of the Crucifixion, though it is not yet a Crucifixion in the later Western sense. Christ is on the Cross, but only symbolically, surrounded by a host of angels bowing down before Him in graceful and harmonious gestures, whereas lower down an immense human throng, so thick that the movements of individuals are indistinguishable, looks up to Him. The angels are very Byzantine, but the human throng is an innovation. Christ on the Cross, even in this symbolic interpretation, is a revolu-tionary conception. Nothing of the kind had been envisaged by the Trullanum decisions fifteen years earlier.

If this symbolic representation of the Crucifixion still remains timid in its attempt to convey a new religious experience, its unrestrained representation was not long in coming. In the Quiricus chapel of Sta Maria l'Antiqua, which dates from the middle of the eighth century (probably a little earlier rather than a little later), Christ on the Cross is represented in the full Western sense, in a fresco dominating the whole room. The moment chosen is that of Christ's death, when darkness falls over the earth. Above the Cross we see sun and moon, as it were, taking flight. The expression of Christ is impassive. He is suspended on the Cross without any sign of previous suffering. John, too, stands stiffly on the right, whereas the Virgin, on the left, shows faint traces of emotion. Next to the Cross we have the two soldiers, one on each side, driving their spears into Christ's body, the blood and water gushing out. Here then we are suddenly transferred from the Eastern to the Western sphere of pictorial art; we are confronted with a subject which would still have been depicted in much the same way in the nineteenth century.

Color and design, too, call for comment. The sky is dark blue, spreading an atmosphere of intense gloom over the whole scene. In this the fresco hardly differs from the mosaics of the period, characterized as they are by the almost complete abandonment of the luscious green so predominant in the Ravenna mosaics. But the function of the gloomy coloring of the Crucifixion of St. Quirinus differs from that of the still very Byzantine mosaics of the period. In their case, the dark colors produce an effect of solemn immutability beyond both joy and grief; in the Crucifixion they reflect the terrible darkness of a tragic moment, also represented by the simultaneous "flight" of sun and moon. The gloom, in the mosaics of Sta Prassede or Sta Maria in Dominica, is ontological; in the Crucifixion of St. Quirinus it is dynamic, hence tragic. Let us remember that centuries later Western drama begins to unfold with the passion plays. Here again we can grasp, visually, the transition from Eastern to Western civilization. Byzantine mural paintings of the late sixth and of the seventh century are characterized by a gradual reduction of the color scheme. In contrast to the mosaics, which more and more approach (without ever fully reaching it) a two-color setting, dark or golden background against white or brown figures, the frescoes of the period are gradually reduced to various shades of a nondescript brown. Simultaneously the limbs of the human figures atrophy, as if embodying the nothingness of all flesh; the rich vestments of the Ravenna period are reduced to rigid, almost sacklike hues segmented by equally rigid folds. The total spiritualizing of the relevant part of existence, which is the essence of the monophysite worldview, cannot but express itself in the almost total disincarnation of the irrelevant, the material part of existence, to the point where pictorial art almost ceases to depict anything.

We shall not be surprised to find this trend violently, though still clumsily, reversed in the Crucifixion of St. Quirinus. The Cross there stands against two rocks which are depicted in violent green and purple, respectively, adding another element of grim contrast and fierce passion to the gloomy background. Mary is in blue, though John and the soldiers still wear different kinds of brown. The folds are rigid, but the vestments are wide and the lines indicating the folds are broad. The figures are still stiff, but no longer disembodied. Suffering here takes the place of glory, sharp contrasts appear instead of an ever more monotonous harmony, reality usurps the place of symbolism, dynamics the place of statics. But the new dynamics do not express themselves in physical movement. Through the color scheme, they reflect directly an inner experience: another basic element of Western thought and art has thus come into existence.

III

Historically, "nothing comes out of nothing." The most revolutionary innovator is always starting from something against which he revolts, and whose features are, albeit negatively, reflected in his work. Where the gap between the old and the new seems too wide, or where the new seems not opposed to, but disparate from, the old, we shall suspect the presence of a second, as yet undetected, influence. It is of course a mistake to treat historical development simply as a series of "influences," disregarding the autonomy of every piece of human creation. But it is equally thoughtless to make some absolute spontaneity the source of all that is new, whereas the essence of the historical process lies in the work of each new generation developing a new attitude: new not in relation to an empty world but to what has been handed down to it. The sudden emergence of the fully developed representation of the Crucifixion, in the absence of any Byzantine models, at first sight seems unintelligible— such a development should take centuries, not decades. The search for possible models, however, discloses the existence of almost exactly the same pattern of representation in Syrian art. It is no doubt surprising and at first a little puzzling, but the fact seems to be that the great transition which brought into being some of the essential elements of Western religious experience and art is due to an exchange of Syrian for Byzantine models.

These models were well-known in Rome. One of them exists in the *sacra sacrorum* of the Lateran: a representation of the Crucifixion identical, but for the colors, with that of St. Quirinus. Only in the Syrian piece we have the traditional three crosses, where the creator of St. Quirinus, presumably so as to concentrate the effect, has left out the two sinners.

The Syrian piece is painted on the inside of the cover of a wooden casket containing relics from Palestine which was in the possession of Pope Leo III—the Pope who crowned Charlemagne. The latter event of course took place half a century after St. Quirinus was covered with frescoes, but experts date the Syrian piece to the beginning of the seventh century. It was certainly not an isolated piece. We know that while Byzantine art consistently represented the divine only in its immutable glory, Syrian art never abandoned the representation of the Crucifixion, and its pictorial works quite generally represent passion, and care much less for aesthetic harmony.

In comparing the Syrian with the Roman piece one can see that Rome has made certain concessions to the Byzantine viewpoint. The soldiers in the Syrian piece drive their spears violently into Christ's body, while in the Roman piece they perform this action timidly, as it were. In the Syrian piece, too, the body hangs limply from the Cross, dragged down by its weight, revealing in the artist a knowledge of the real physical effects of crucifixion; in the Roman piece, the arms lie parallel to the wood of the Cross, so that no physical effect of the torture, and in consequence no indication of suffering, is visible. In the struggle against Byzantium the Roman artist has found an ally in the mind of the non-Hellenic East, but he seems still to shudder before its implications.

If this analysis of the situation seems far-fetched, let it be remembered that the first half of the eighth century saw a succession of Popes from the East. Gregory III, who called in the Franks as an ally against Byzantium and the Lombards, was himself a Syrian. His successor Zacharias (741–52), in whose Pontificate the paintings of St. Quirinus should probably be placed, was another Easterner, and his Pontificate proceeded under the towering influence of the tradition of Gregory III. That a Syrian Pope, in his insurgence against Byzantium, should have turned to his native country for spiritual support can hardly seem surprising. Besides, the affinity between the Syrian and the Roman approach was real, at least in what divided them from Byzantium. The Antioch theological school, regardless of the many internal divisions which finally reduced it to political impotence within the Roman Empire, was united in a realistic approach to the Christian tradition, insisting upon the underlying historical facts, stressing the human aspects of the person of Christ (Arianism had its origin in the Antioch school), rejecting an entirely symbolical interpretation of the Gospels. Closer contact between Rome and Antioch might have brought out deep differences in the interpretation of the human will (in both Christ and man), but that was not to happen. In the matter of representing religious drama, and in particular Christ's suffering, Antioch and Rome thought along parallel, if not identical, lines.

Only at a later stage, represented no longer by the paintings of Sta Maria l'Antiqua but by those of S. Clemente, were the ways of Rome and those of the non-Hellenic East to part. Before this occurred, however, there was a period of very marked Syrian influence upon Roman art, revealing Rome's still unrelieved incapacity to express fully what was forming in her womb; yet Rome was all the time drawing nearer and nearer to this goal, with the help of the Syrian tradition of depicting realistically, not so much the outward movements of the body analyzed by Hellenic and Roman sculptors, but the inner movements of the soul. More subjects are now relieved of the taboo imposed upon them by the Byzantines. Dependence on the Syrian viewpoint increases, but dependence upon immediate Syrian models is lessening, or at least it would seem to be so; too much of Syrian art is lost to allow of definite conclusions in this matter.

We find an early specimen of the new art, preceding even the St. Quirinus Crucifixion, in a fresco representing the Mount of Olives. It dates from the Pontificate of Gregory III. Since the taboo on such scenes was not remotely as strong as that upon the Crucifixion, the presentation of the event is much more uninhibited. Nothing remains of the harmony of posture and movement invariably sought by the Byzantines. Jesus, clad in a robe of glaring red, is kneeling in a position almost to be described as "crouching," His disproportionate hands outstretched in a passionate gesture of imploring the Father. It must be borne in mind that the Mount of Olives, with the "Let this chalice pass, but not my will but Thine be done," was the *locus classicus* of all those who defended the existence of a purely human will, and of moral conflict and suffering in the person of Jesus. Farther behind, in sharpest contrast, we watch the three Apostles, not simply sleeping but almost visibly snoring, in positions much more appropriate to their abject human failure than to their Apostolic dignity. Clearly the painter was aware of that characteristically Western experience, the loneliness of a tortured soul amidst the indifference of the world.

And then there are, suddenly appearing and almost immediately pullulating, the endless strips of martyr stories covering the walls of Roman churches of the period and, in the first place, of Sta Maria l'Antiqua. Here again a Byzantine taboo is broken, following, if I am not mistaken, Syrian models. The number of representations constantly augments down to the age of Charlemagne, until one seems to witness a kind of sadomasochistic orgy, not pleasing to the psychologically alert mind of modern man. That should not prevent us from analyzing the purely theological aspect. We need no longer insist upon the acceptance of actual realistic suffering as part of religious experience, a basic event in the emergence of Western religion and art. It is more relevant to point out that this acceptance is still limited. For while the torturers in these paintings are employing every kind of devilish device, there is no sign of real suffering among their victims. What they display is not so much fortitude but "patience," that virtue so much lauded by Maximus Confessor in his *Tractatus Asceticus*. Their impassivity remains untouched, and at the same time meek and passive. We are still in a phase where energy is the realm of the devil alone, hence are not yet within the realm of a fully developed Western way of life. This, incidentally, is the period of the last great Roman mosaics, the last representations of divine immutability, coincident with the age of Charlemagne and of his sons.

And then comes the Assunta of S. Clemente. The preceding study of the historical background now enables us to state precisely in what consists its great innovation. It lies again, primarily, in the field of inner experience, not outward presentation. And how could it be otherwise? The art of the Christian era is never *l'art pour l'art*, it always serves to illustrate a religious concept which cannot be fully expressed in words. What is new in the Assunta is this central fact: in it, for the first time since the emergence of the Byzantine style, a Western work of art represents action, energy, passion, as something not belonging to the realm of the devil but of the divine. True, the divinity itself remains in its old impassivity, but the Apostles, saints among the saints, are here overwhelmed by the most violent emotion. For the first time, then, emotion is sanctified, is made a key element in religious experience. It would be difficult to conceive a more fundamental change. Also, whereas in Byzantine art any sign of feeling is always tamed by the harmonious movement in which it expresses itself, here the distorted necks, the arms wildly raised, the faces torn by emotion transgress every aesthetic code. Clearly the painter conceived of this disruption of outward harmony as the test of genuine religious experience. It is true that the experience itself is still entirely passive—but that is a feature which does not disappear completely down to the beginning of the Renaissance. Regardless of this qualification, therefore, we are here confronted with the completion of a new world in which depth of inner feeling is the paradigmatic attitude, replacing Oriental impassivity; in which the aesthetic code has been shattered by the irruption of this fierce religious emotion; in which, consequently, a new key subject of art, the inner man, has emerged.

The jump, again, seems too great to be completely unprepared. And again an Oriental model is not lacking. This time it comes from Armenia. The illuminated gospel of Queen Mtle, of the ninth century, contains an Assunta which, almost point for point, resembles that of S. Clemente. The gospel, admittedly, is a few years earlier than the Assunta of S. Clemente (probably 868 A.D.); but again, as in the case of the Syrian models of the Quirinus chapel, dates matter little, since the Oriental pieces, as distinct from their Western counterparts, must be regarded as specimens of a fairly rigid type. In the Armenian gospel we have, as in S. Clemente, the position of Christ right above the head of Mary. We have the same floating angels supporting Christ (though, in the upper two corners of the Armenian miniature, two angels are standing stiffly on Christ's side). The Apostles are grouped into two sections of six each, again as in S. Clemente; and here, too, they show considerable emotion.

If Syrian influence upon Rome in the age of Gregory III and Zacharias is obvious, Armenian influence in the ninth century seems less easy to account for. The explanation presumably is that Armenia, during this period, was the only Eastern Christian country spared by the iconoclastic crisis, hence the only place in the East to which Roman painters could turn for models. But one should not trust too much to the coincidence in time of the two pieces. The date of the Armenian gospel is controversial; it may be later, and also, while our knowledge of Oriental Christian art is sufficient to guide us at once to a really major innovation, we do not know remotely enough to be positive about the limits in time and space of certain iconographic types. In other words, there is no certainty that the way in which the Assunta is here presented is peculiar to the ninth century or peculiar to Armenia. All we can be sure of is that it is an Eastern, non-Byzantine type belonging to the post-Justinian period. That it influenced the master of S. Clemente does not seem to admit of any doubt, so direct are the points of comparison.

This, however, renders the more significant the changes he has introduced into his Oriental model. Far outstripping all others in importance is the change in the relation between heaven and earth. In the Armenian miniature, Mary stands in the midst of the Apostles, dividing the two groups, In S. Clemente, she is raised high above them, into an intermediate zone between heaven and earth. The Armenian painting, though meant as an Assunta, gives no real conception of a rise. The division of the fresco of S. Clemente, by creating three superimposed sections instead of two, does give such an impression, and everything possible is done by the artist to strengthen it. In the gospel of Queen Mtle, the Virgin timidly raises her hands and arms. In S. Clemente her arms are wide open, passionately outstretched towards the sky, and towards Christ enthroned in it. The two stiff angels of the Armenian models are replaced by two more floating angels above Christ's head. But it is the group of the Apostles which, in consonance with the general religious tendency of the fresco, is most intimately affected by the change. In the Armenian gospel the two Apostles nearest to Mary kneel before her almost gracefully; four in each group look surprised, perhaps amazed. The two Apostles on the outward fringes avert their faces a little. No bowing of bodies in awed terror; no craned necks, no faces distorted by the incomprehensible, and, most important of all, no distorted arms pointing wildly to heaven. It is the mutual adjustment of the deeply stirred Apostles and of the raised arms of Mary which gives to S. Clemente a grandiose movement, only to be expressed in the term *sursum*. It is this "uplift"—to use the rather cheap modern term for something which was not cheap in the ninth century, when it was born—which separates by a whole world the Assunta of S. Clemente from the Assunta of the gospel of Queen Mtle. It separates the entirely passive *emotion* of the non-Hellenic East—reflecting itself chiefly in a readiness for martydom—from the active *dynamics* of the West. The Assunta of S. Clemente is not simply full of movement; the movement also has a clear-cut unified direction (*sursum*). What is perhaps most noteworthy is the painter's preference for the straight line—so sharply contrasting not only with Byzantine art but also with Carlovingian and Ottonian liking for the soft curve. It is as if he had understood that the straight line, being suggestive of an overcoming of gravitation, is the ideal symbol of the total victory of spiritual force over the gravitation of the body. This time indeed the Western spiritual world is present—complete and unqualified.

We seem to encounter at this point the rarest of all historical events: real independent creation; though even this artist, doubtless one of the great figures in the history of art, started from Eastern models. It would be vain, however, to attempt an interpretation of his work as a synthesis of Oriental traditions with others deriving from elsewhere, perhaps from the barbarian North. Admittedly this was also the age of a great early blossoming of French art. And there, too, not unnaturally, passion, martyrdom, drama, play a part unknown only a short time before. Yet if one compares the S. Clemente frescoes with their nearest contemporary French counterpart, the frescoes of the Crypt of St. Germain in Auxerre, where the martyrdom of St. Stephen is depicted, one realizes at once that Auxerre is much nearer to the Byzantine tradition: aesthetic harmony is nowhere broken, the attitude of the Saint is still one of meek suffering. Rome, not the Carlovingian Court, is in the vanguard during this era.

What the artist of the Assunta of S. Clemente has added to his Oriental models is entirely his own.

IV

Let us attempt to visualize the background which enabled this creation to emerge. The middle of the ninth century was one of the great ages of the Papacy. Leo IV drove the Sarazens out of central Italy and built the Leonine City. His second successor, Nicolaus I (858–67), was the first to assert Papal political supremacy over the Frankish Court, to exert in a new way Papal ecclesiastical supremacy over the French bishops, and his conflict with the Byzantine patriarch Photius marks a new stage in the rupture with Byzantium. Again it was Nicolaus who, during the two preceding Pontificates, increasingly directed the whole policy of the Holy See. This short-lived phase was in every respect an anticipation of the great Gregorian reform movement of the eleventh century. It was a flash in the dark, anticipating the civilization led by the medieval Church. No wonder that it was accompanied by the sudden eruption of a pictorial style anticipating the essentials of medieval art. When it was over, Roman painting relapsed into utter insignificance, only to reemerge in the eleventh century.

Nicolaus has no independent theological contribution to his credit, nor did Rome during that age boast any leading theologian. Yet the intimate contact existing between Nicolaus and the leading French theologians of the period leaves no doubt of the interest Rome took in the first exploits of Western theology just then proceding in the Isle-de-France and Champagne, as well as east of the Rhine. There is no space here to deal with this whole subject. This much, however, can be said: from the very beginning, moral good and evil, and man's effort in combating the latter and achieving the former, play a predominant part quite unknown to the Eastern church. The dynamic *sursum* of the Assunta of S. Clemente has its spiritual counterpart in this early French theology. Thus, while it would be a mistake to suppose any direct influence upon the artist of S. Clemente other than that of the East and to a minor extent of Byzantium, his artistic achievement could very well be described as a refraction of the new Northern theology through the prism of non-Hellenic Eastern pictorial art. The age of Nicolaus I marks a definite turning away on Rome's part from Byzantium, and a merging of Roman and Northern ecclesiastical affairs, a culminating point in a development proceeding over centuries; it is only natural that, somewhat timidly in the light of the possibilities involved, but daring by contrast with tradition, art should follow in the wake of ecclesiastical policy. With a great hallelujah the West is born, a hallelujah no longer only to heaven reaching down to man, but also to man reaching up to heaven, a hallelujah no longer to the static immutable verities but to the creative possibilities of a struggling soul.

It may be fitting in conclusion to essay some more general remarks. Professor Toynbee in his writings is no doubt right in opposing to Spengler's concept of civilizations rigidly and monadically divided from one another the concept of cultural affiliation. An attempt has here been made to investigate a clear-cut case of such affiliation, and it may be suggested that the result throws doubt on the notion of the affiliation of *one* particular younger culture to an older. Such instances do probably occur—Hindu civilization is a direct revival of the old Aryan civilization, and there are other phenomena of the same kind. But they are phenomena characterized by a certain sterility. The great creative civilizations seem to have a more complex origin. If the arts are taken as a measuring stick, our Western culture is hardly at all affiliated to classical Antiquity. Assuming that the arts are a very fair choice for measuring Hellenic influence, Spengler's dictum that classical Antiquity is, to the West, really the strangest civilization of all seems fully borne out.

The present essay deals with only one aspect of a regionally limited segment of Western civilization, the one most closely linked to Byzantium. But it may be suggested that this region, namely Central Italy, at the decisive moment when for the first time Western civilization comes within sight, played a greater part than is generally recognized. In the course of this investigation, something like a casuistry of affiliation, or to use a more old-fashioned term, of cultural influence, has emerged. Part of the solution of the problem of cultural affiliation does, in my opinion, reside in a detailed analysis of various types of such influence.

During the period here under discussion, the specifically Roman way of life was submerged, though not destroyed, by the barbarian invasions. Rome in consequence was subjected to the towering influence of Byzantium. This, the domination and permeation of a weaker by a stronger civilization, is *one* type of affiliation. The weakening of Byzantium, much more than any spontaneous revival of her own forces, later enabled Rome to reemphasize her own values. A conflict between Rome and Byzantium ensued, in which Rome, unable as yet to stand upon her own feet, looked for guiding models abroad. It was a matter entirely of choice, as distinct from the irresistible and overwhelming influence of Byzantium, that

Rome in this emergency turned to the non-Hellenic East for spiritual help. With this help she could reassert, though only in part, her own conception of *voluntas*. Further events obliged Rome to stand entirely on her own feet, a task for which her own local forces were quite insufficient. In this new emergency the distant East proved not only geographically and politically remote, but also spiritually inadequate. Syria could be helpful in repulsing the purely symbolic, inhuman Christianity of Byzantium, but she lagged far behind the potentialities of the Roman notion of *voluntas* as the core of a new religious experience.

Then Rome, in circumstances not here to be discussed in detail, turned to the young Northern nations. It was neither a completely free choice nor a case of irresistible pressure. Rather, it was a case of a voluntary alliance, necessary if Rome wanted to maintain herself as a first-rate power. Northern political protection of the Roman See was short-lived and unreliable. But the North gave Rome an instinctive, yet half-mute, conception of the dynamic human personality as a central religious factor which, integrated into Christianity, could break through the impasse in which Byzantium had involved itself. *A Byzantine inheritance critically revised in the light of the Roman notion of* voluntas, *and then fertilized by Northern indiviualism, is the formula emerging from this part of our study of the origins of the West.* Naturally it found its first fully explicit statement—not yet in words but only in pictures—in Rome and not in the North. It is an almost general rule in the emergence of new civilizations that the explicit formulation of their main tenets starts in the border regions where they rub shoulders with opposing ways of life. It is conflict, and conflict alone, which brings out the great creative forces.

More specifically, France—as witnessed by the art of the ninth century—was at that time still busy trying to prove that she had successfully overcome Merovingian barbarism and become a civilized country; and what could be a more complete proof of full civilization than the integration into the incipient French tradition of models taken from the graceful forms of Byzantium, then the only repository of "cultured refinement"? Rome cared for none of these things. Ancient and proud of her heritage, she did not bother about the barbarian elements in her own makeup, but turned resolutely towards the great twofold task: to lay the foundations of her own, un-Byzantine and now already fully anti-Byzantine civilization, and to secure for it spiritual and, in no small measure, political domination of the new world of the Northern barbarians. Thus it was that Rome in her art proclaimed the new values coming from the North with a lack of inhibition which was certainly pleasing to the great Leo and the greater Nicolaus, but would have shocked the recently civilized gentlemen of the Court of the Western Carlovingians. Before France could fully join in the new movement she must first replace the Carlovingian Court, with its self-conscious imitation of Byzantium, by something less refined and more national. Only when this task had been achieved during the tenth century could France act her true role and almost at once predominate in the rise of Western civilization.

CHAPTER TEN

Primal Crime and "Social Paranoia" in the Dark Ages

In a well-known essay on the origins of human history, Siegmund Freud maintained that the origins of all civilization must be sought in a twofold aboriginal crime: the murder of the aboriginal father by his sons who wanted to possess the mother.

I do not wish to discuss the validity of this conception insofar as it refers to the earliest origins of mankind; indeed I doubt whether to them it is applicable in the literal sense in which Freud, as he emphatically stated himself, wished it to be understood. But to trace the aboriginal crime whose central role in human conduct is stressed by Freud, we need not really delve into an unknowable past, nor be content with the findings of psychoanalysis about the unconscious of modern man. Acts very near the aboriginal crime, not as a marginal incident but as a mass phenomenon, are a historical fact easy to trace in every one of the "dark ages" which regularly intervene between the cycles of higher civilizations.

We shall limit ourselves to the dark age preceding our own civilization, to the Voelkerwanderung and the Merovingian period. For the morals of that age, the "penitential books," lists of church penances for typical crimes, constitute a first-rate source. Their rare value consists in their obvious applicability to every stratum of society, not by any means exclusively to the highest layer. The earliest of them belong to Ireland, Wales, Scotland, whence they spread first to England and then to the continent. There is every reason to assume that, during the sixth and seventh centuries (the age of the earliest penitentials), life, if anything, was less brutish in Ireland and Wales than in France and Germany. Yet in those earliest penitentials, incest in an astonishing variety of detail and murder within the family are invested with a prominence which seems to make every other crime unimportant. We might even tentatively define dark ages as such periods of history when primal crime, from the dark recesses of man's mind, wells up into a regular overt occurrence.

The tale of the penitentials is confirmed by the tales of poetry. The most archaic layers of the poetic Edda—earliest self-expressions of the Germanic mind—abound with family murder, and heroism and human tragedy appear almost exclusively in its context. Thus in *Hamdismal*, in part the most archaic of all Eddic songs, Joermunrek, king of the Goths, kills his son Randver, because the latter attempted to seduce (or did seduce) the king's young wife Svanhild, Gudrun's daughter. Gudrun sends her two sons to kill the king and thus avenge their sister. On their ride, they are joined by a half-brother of Hunnic descent, whom they dislike, murder, and despoil. But when it comes to the fight with Joermunrek, the king's magic proves superior to their prowess and they die, with a cry of regret on their lips: had they only let their half-brother alive, the three of them might have been stronger than the wicked king!

There are elements of secondary distortion in this tale, but the primal crime shines unmistakably through. The extent of distortion corresponds to the degree of repression, for even in that age patricide and mother rape were not matters of course. There is no distortion at all in the matter of fratricide, and no wonder, for the historical accounts of the period also abound in tales about the mutual extermination of brothers within every Germanic dynasty. The incest theme is slightly distorted: the woman seduced by Randver is not his mother but his stepmother—and we may conclude that (though the penitentials do actually speak of incest between mother and son) the adultery of the son with his old father's young wife was a more frequent occurrence. The patricide theme, however, is more concealed. If Joermunrek is the very embodiment of the image of the "bad" father, those who set out to kill him are not his sons but his brothers-in-law (though by age, they might easily be his sons). Yet in attempting to avenge their murdered sister, they also seek to avenge her lover, Joermunrek's son. Do they not, in killing the father, aim to carry out the son's unspoken wish and testament? Still, the fact of the concealment of the patricide theme remains.

It is the very same theme which, in the Oedipus myth, is treated quite openly. Does it follow that primal crime was more deeply repressed in emerging Western than it was in Hellenic civilization? Freud has drawn that conclusion from a comparison of Sophocles' King Oedipus with Shakespeare's Hamlet. But even granting the validity of his comparison for Western and Hellenic civilization at their respective climax, it obviously can no longer apply when we compare the age of Pericles with the age of the Voelkerwanderung; it would be nonsensical to ascribe the deeper repression of primal crime to the latter. The only extant overt treatment of patricide in ancient Germanic literature points to a different conclusion.

The *Hildebrandlied*, unfortunately, is only preserved in a truncated state, and we do not know whether, in the end, Hildebrand was actually killed by his son Hadubrand who, like king Oedipus, met his father in combat without knowing him. It seems a fairly close replica of the Greek tale, but there is one essential difference: the father in the *Hildebrandlied* recognizes his son and makes every effort to convice him of their relation, but the son treats him as a coward and swindler. Clearly Germanic saga wants to heap all moral responsibility upon the son, whereas the Greek myth insists upon Oedipus' ignorance. As the end of the Oedipus myth shows, such ignorance, in the Greek conception of things, does not constitute a plea of innocence. Yet the fact remains: King Oedipus can commit the primal crime in both aspects (patricide and mother incest) only because he is ignorant, whereas no Germanic hero ever acts in complete ignorance of the essential moral factors—obviously such ignorance would have made the tale pointless to the ancient Germans. We may conclude that what makes the primal crime avowable in the Hellenic world is that no man's will, but rather fate, is responsible (though man remains accountable), whereas what makes it unacceptable in the West is the implicit acceptance of full responsibility for the committed act. Distortion, absent in the Oedipus myth, is therefore ever-present in Germanic saga: even in the *Hildebrandlied*, the nearest Germanic approximation to the Oedipus myth, there is the extenuating circumstance of Hadubrand's disbelief in Hildebrand's paternity, and then the incest theme is completely absent.

The whole of our account of Western civilization will go to prove that the idea of complete personal accountability, which so clearly underlies the Hildebrandlied, is central for Western religious and philosophical thought, in fact for the whole of Western history. We have now spotted this idea in its nuclear form in the earliest, still pagan layers of Germanic poetry. What remains striking, however, is the extreme contrast between the strength of this feeling, demonstrable even in the oldest layers of Germanic thought, and the simultaneous frequent commission of acts approaching the primal crime. It seems to be a key point of all dynamic psychology that conscience, sense of individual responsibility, results from the repression of the impulses driving man towards primal crime,

from the creation of internal defenses against those impulses: the super-
ego, in the classic Freudian view, derives from the rejection of the Oedipal
impulses. Our historical evidence does not confirm that view. In the
oldest layer of Germanic culture directly accessible to us, we find the
frequent commission of near-Oedipal crime coexisting with a sense of
individual responsibility surpassing that of the Hellenic civilization at its
climax.

Before entering into psychological interpretation, let us cast one glance
upon the historical and sociological effects of this contradiction. The
terse greatness of Eddic poetry is universally recognized. It clearly springs
from precisely this sharp, uncompromising, and unsentimental juxtaposition of abysmal crime and of a full awareness of the criminals' responsibility for its horror. Without that contrast, no great poetry of the
Eddic type is imaginable. Were it not for the acute sense of responsibility
and of deserved, tragic retribution, we should be in the presence of men
and women exclusively ruled by the law of the jungle—in other words,
not in the presence of a human society at all. Were the primal crime
suppressed to the point where the impulse toward it no longer produces
overt conflict, we should be in the presence of a society which has
succeeded in balancing repression and satisfaction of drives, in other
words in the presence of an unchanging primitive society such as we
well know from anthropological material. It is the acuteness of the contradiction between opposite extremes, family murder and incest on the
one hand, conscious guilt and responsibility on the other, which in the
Eddic world calls forth great poetry of a type unknown in genuinely
primitive society. Let us add at once that the same conflicts, though in
a stage of greater concealment, also call forth great religion and all the
other achievements of a "higher" civilization. Actually, it is the very
definition of "higher" as against "primitive" culture that the former,
owing to its unbalance between opposite extremes, is driven forward
from change to change, whereas the latter, once it has found its groove,
is stagnating in a repetitive production of emotional equilibrium. In the
extreme contradiction between crime and responsibility we have, at any
rate, found the driving force of the whole cycle of civilization, much
more tangibly evident in its earliest origins than in its later ramifications.

Yet the psychological problem remains: how can those mutually exclusive elements coexist? This query can only be solved by reference to
the historic conditions bringing the contradiction about.

Of all the situations apt to shake the carapace of custom to its very
foundations, none perhaps is as disruptive as the meeting on a level of

equality between a high and a primitive civilization, such as happened during the period of the Germanic Voelkerwanderung (and of most similar great migrations in history). Such an event presupposes a long preceding process of disintegration within the higher civilization itself, for without a previous profound shaking of its own values it could not be seriously influenced by culture contact with primitives. In the earliest history of the modern West, that side of the situation was represented by the decay and disintegration of the civilization of classical antiquity— a process which we cannot analyze here, since it would carry us back into the history of another civilization. The situation of the primitive Germanic tribes subject to that influence is more easily defined. Primitive civilizations disintegrate invariably under the impact of a higher civilization, whatever the character and tenets of the higher civilization in question. And since their defences against primeval lust and aggression are at one and the same time more inflexible and weaker than those of higher civilizations, they succumb very easily to the impact.

Once the carapace of custom is disrupted, the process acquires the characteristics of a chain reaction. Every rift opened by the devaluation of rules widens automatically and produces new rifts in other places. From generation to generation more and more rules are rejected, conduct becomes more and more irrational, the area of moral uncertainty is constantly widening, until the typical situation of the "dark ages," a situation of total insecurity and universal crime, is reached. But in all this, while there is a growing area of uncontrolled action, the counter-pressure of guilt against crime need not abate in the least. The sense of individual responsibility may, on the contrary, grow more distinct and pathetic, precisely owing to the disappearance of that cake of custom which saves the individual so many decisions.

It is not obvious at first sight why this is so, why this self-propelling process of moral disintegration should have any inherent limits, why it should not lead to the complete disappearance of all morality. The answer to this query, however, is contained in the poetic and mythological material analyzed in this study, and it is at this point that the value of dynamic psychology for an understanding of the culture cycle appears most tangibly. The process of moral devaluation starts moving in reverse at the point when the overt appearance of primal crime as a mass phenomenon comes within sight. That primal crime cannot become an ordinary mode of conduct has nothing to do with inculcated morality; the revulsion against it does, on the contrary, precede established morality. It springs—not perhaps, as Freud would have it, from the real experiences of adult aboriginal man—but certainly from the experience of the small child, in closest connection with its most elementary biological needs. Though primal crime in its fullness—killing the father and raping the mother—is in a number of cases committed as an individual act, it can never be carried out but only be approached asymptotically as a social type of conduct. When too closely approached, it exerts a magnetic repulsion no less strong than the magnetic attraction it exerts as long as it is distant. And it is this movement in reverse, this moving away from primal crime that impels the ascending branch of the culture cycle.

But it is one thing to experience the urgent need for a new set of unambiguous rules and quite a different thing to produce them. The oldest layer of Eddic tradition exhales nothing but utter despair. It is true that it also exhales an atmosphere of heroism unequalled perhaps in all human literature, but this is, in its turn, a heroism of despair. No flowers blossom on the grave of Gunnar and Hoegni in the Atlikvida, their unshakable valor in death brings forth nothing but their sister Gudrun's cannibalistic vengeance, and Gudrun in her turn, her revenge accomplished, her husband Atli, her children, all her kin killed, has nothing left but to die. The oldest layer of the Edda tradition, it is important to note, is not Norse but Gothic—and we cannot be far wrong in relating this philosophy of total despair of any human no less than of any divine order to the rapid and total collapse of the Goths and of other Eastern Germanic tribes deprived of any intelligible frame of reference by the Voelkerwanderung.

What, however, becomes of the same conflicts among the Western Germanic tribes, not so completely uprooted by the Voelkerwanderung but gradually transforming themselves under the impact of gradual territorial expansion into Gaul? We are fortunate in possessing in the Siegfried saga a Western Germanic epos closely related in part of its subject to the Gothic tale of Gudrun and Atli; in other parts it is based, as we have seen, on a series of historic crises in Western Germanic history, ranging from the struggles of Arminius to the rise of the realm of the Salic Franks through the successive annexations of the territories of the Ripuarian Franks and the Burgundians. But while our historic analysis showed that each of those crises had in fact been linked with the crucial guilt of murder among close relatives—the murder of Arminius by his kin, of the king of the Ripuarian Franks by his son, of a Burgundian king by his brother—we found that the manifest content of the saga amounted to the ever repeated, all-round denial of the guilt of those involved in the original outrages—and most particularly of the Salic Franks, whose national myth the saga eventually became. It is as a concentrated product of such a process of denial of guilt that the Siegfried saga deserves its central place in our study of the emergent West.

Generally speaking, denial of the primal crime is inevitable in one form or another. Even the myth of Oedipus denies part of the crime, since Oedipus did not recognize his father whom he murdered and his mother whom he wedded. But if denial of the primal crime is a common feature of human nature, vast psychological differences originate from the different extent and content of what is denied, from the mechanism used in the process of repression and denial, and from the substitutes evolved to replace the forbidden recollection of primal crime. The psychological situation involved in the Frankish Nibelungen saga differs basically from that of the Gothic songs preserved in the Edda. In the most archaic stratum of the Edda primal crime is committed, yet constitutes a guilt that kills. In the Frankish tale, as shown above, the primal crime which as a historical fact underlies the saga—the murder of the king of the Ripuarian Franks by his son—is totally denied, the abject killer becomes a shining hero: it is the world around him which is charged with all kinds of crimes, and with treachery in the first place. That is a mechanism not prominent in Gothic saga, but clearly characteristic of the Western Germanic culture of the Voelkerwanderung age and tangibly connected with the latter's successful survival, as its opposite is tangibly connected with the Goths' early and tragic end.

To psychology, the basic mechanism of the Nibelungen saga is well known as "projection," and where that mechanism dominates to the exclusion of objective reality, we are in the presence of "paranoia." The individual denies its own aggressive impulses, casting them out of his consciousness and attributing them instead to those against whom his aggression is actually directed. He is no longer a killer (or a potential killer): it is the others who want to kill the paranoiac. He regards himself as a persecuted paragon of all the virtues. Actually, however, the need of the paranoiac to heap all his constitutional and his acquired aggression upon his surroundings excludes any positive contact with the outside world, which now appears as wholly hostile, wholly persecutory, as filled with irreconcilable enemies who must be warded off and deserve to be destroyed; thus the paranoiac, while denying any aggression on his part, achieves his unconscious purpose of venting unlimited aggression upon the outside world, at the price of renouncing all positive, loving contact with it.

In other words, the paranoiac escapes his internal conflicts, replacing them by external ones. In this process, he achieves a regression from what is technically called positive libidinous relations to negative sadistic relations with the outside world. "Hatred," said Freud, "is older than love," and the more recent researches in the field of dynamic psychology have substantiated few points of Freud's teaching as convincingly as this. The paranoiac escapes the conflicts produced by the lure of primal crime through renouncing its positive, libidinous aspects—the desire for the mother—and taking flight into a much more archaic psychological realm where aggression reigns supreme.

The paranoiac thus denies internal conflict by projecting it into the outside world. He is not torn, he simply has enemies. That he is in a deplorable state, he only learns from outside experience. The Gothic heroes perished, distraught by conflicting obligations, but when the world of the Merovingians cried out for reform, it was because it experienced its internal regression to limitless sadism as an external breakdown of government, as a state where everybody's hand was raised against his neighbor's.

Paranoia being a mental disturbance, it may be asked whether it makes sense to speak of a paranoiac age. No human society can consist of madmen. A word about the medical characteristics of the disorder will suffice to clear up this problem. Fully developed cases of paranoiac delirium mostly occur among schizophrenics, who in any case live outside the world of human reality. Fully developed cases of paranoia without an underlying schizophrenia are extremely rare. But the predominance of paranoid features in the character structures of individuals with only mild schizoid tendencies or none at all is extremely frequent—certainly much more frequent again in our own day than in some former ages. Whereas it may not be easy to point to any sociological context for the occurrence of madness in the proper sense of the word, the historical and sociological determination of the prevalence of certain aberrant psychological types is a truism. In that sense, it is just as permissible to speak of the Merovingian age as one of predominant paranoia as it is to speak of the late nineteenth century as an age dominated by classical psychoneurosis of the type first analyzed by Freud.

It has been demonstrated, in my opinion convincingly, that the animal phobias so characteristic of a certain phase of infantile development are not simply, as Freud originally thought, hysterical (i.e., slightly travestied symbolical reflections of the Oedipus complex) but expressions of a much more archaic psychological layer of universal sadism and retributive persecution—that they are paranoid symptoms. It is interesting in this context that the symbol of the wolf, much later used by Thomas

Hobbes to describe a political system, is—apart from its appearance as one of the most frequent components in old Germanic names—particularly prominent in the literature of the fifth and sixth centuries we are analyzing here.

Thus *Hamdismal* (29):

> In fashion of wolves
> it befits us not
> amongst ourselves to strive.

Atlikvida (8), when Gunnar and Hoegni argue about Gudrun's message inviting them to Atli's court:

What seeks she to say	that she sends us a ring
woven with a wolf's hair?	Methinks it gives warning
In the red ring a hair	of the heath-dweller found I
Wolf-like shall our road be	if we ride on this journey.

And in the same poem (11) Hoegni's curse:

The wolves then shall rule	the wealth of the Niflungs
Wolves aged and grey-haired	if Gunnar is lost.
And black-coated bears	with rending teeth bite
And make glad the dogs	if Gunnar returns not.

It is the proper function of symbols to reveal what is half-repressed. They have no place in front of the overt fact. Those quotations from Gothic poetry touchingly reflect the presentiment and the horror of the coming wolfish age. When later in the Merovingian realm the queens Brunichildis and Fredegunde exterminated their rivals' kin and their own, when boundless aggression reigned supreme without conscious guilt, the language of poetic symbolism was muted. We shall see it reemerge, the wolfsymbol at the center, however, when the age of total denial of guilt has passed and men contemplate with renewed horror the abyss of the primal crime.

It is historic reality which gives this analysis of myths and symbols its relevance. The Merovingian age, if any ever, *was* an age where man to man was a wolf, an age where love and trust seemed unthinkable, an age of murder and hostility to the exclusion of trust and love. In the face of the dismal tale of Gregory of Tours, unrelieved by any redeeming feature, even the usual escapist formula of minds incapable of bearing reality—the pretence that the author "exaggerates"—could not be used. It is true that Alfons Dopsch and Henri Pirenne have attempted to draw a picture of the Voelkerwanderung age as evolutionary as if it were a story from the nineteenth century. But they have done it by simply disregarding the whole tenor of both chronicles and poetry of that age. For our context, it is irrelevant to what extent the towns remained standing and administration operating, whether their decay and disintegration proceded somewhat more slowly than earlier students of the period had maintained. For the survival of certain material aspects of Roman civilization only added to the acuteness of the contrast between civilized modes of conduct and the total collapse of rules. And their partial survival would have contained no germ of regeneration had it not been for the unbearable moral conflicts of the time, which imperiously demanded a new moral approach. To the materialistic interpretation of history, of which the bourgeois historians of the later nineteenth century much more than Marx were the standard-bearers, we oppose another view, which puts man's spiritual conflicts back into the center of the picture. The birth of a new civilization is, as we hope to show, essentially a spiritual process.

It is from this angle that the catastrophe of the Merovingian age appears in its full extent. We are speaking of unbearable moral conflicts which were killing in themselves—as the perdition of the Eastern Germanic tribes proves—and which could only be solved by the emergence of a new set of generally recognized rules. But we also said that the need for such rules does not automatically call them forth. Indeed, the attitude of wholesale denial of guilt, of paranoiac suspicion and boundless treachery, is the very opposite of such a spiritual resurrection. It is in its own way an effective method of escape from the unbearable pressure of guilt; one may even contend that it is the only alternative to annihilation. Primal crime is the head of the Medusa which kills when seen—the alternative is only to avert one's head in time. It is only from a level of subtler indirection, from a plane of half-concealment of primal crime that cultural progress can start; at the nadir of cultural decay, in the immediate presence of primal crime, the self-destruction of the Eastern, the paranoia of the Western section of the Germanic tribes actually seem to be the only available choices. It seems to follow that this alternative, like the process of the disintegration of civilization itself, is repetitive, that it presents itself in every dark age.

The paradoxical survival value of universal paranoia in such an age is undeniable: paranoia is a destructive disease, but not as destructive as the suicidal direct wrestling with primal crime. Yet it is a survival through renunciation of all higher civilization, an escape from self-destruction by self-abandonment to mutual destruction, such as the history of the Merovingian age reveals to us. Nothing, perhaps, is more characteristic of that age than its total incapacity to make of its newly acquired Christianity anything but a set of rules of protective magic, destined to insure the paranoiac against the persecution and vengeance of all those around him. Mass paranoia of this type represents a much more thorough cultural disintegration than the self-destructive conflicts of the Gothic songs—witness again the absence of any art and religion at the center of the disturbance.

How could a new civilization arise out of such an abyss? There does remain something mysterious in the process. Just as for chemistry it is infinitely easier to elucidate the decomposition of a corpse than the emergence of life, so for history it is infinitely easier to analyze the disintegrative process of a dying civilization than to understand the creative spark which makes a new whole out of a shambles of disparate cultural debris. Yet if the creation of a new civilization is no less mysterious than perhaps all creation, its stages can still be described, and the specific meaning of each of them be made intelligible.

CHAPTER ELEVEN

Stages on the Road to Western Civilization

There is no element of hope in societies as deeply paranoiac as those of the dark ages invariably are. They do, of course, seek remedies against the sufferings entailed in universal lawlessness, but it is the very essence of the paranoiac disorder that the supposed remedies should manifest the same disastrous bias as the disease itself. The paranoiac sickness is a sickness of the soul, but the age seeks a remedy not inside but outside of its own substance. It is characteristic of every paranoiac age—including our own—to believe in the effectiveness of techniques, the knack of reducing problems of the soul to the mechanical rearrangement of social factors. This, and not simply the towering impression of an old civilization, is what made the Merovingian kings turn, as a remedy for the paranoiac disruption of the old tribal order, to the social and administrative techniques of the Latin world. This is what has so deeply impressed certain historians of the early middle ages as the "continuance of the Latin tradition."

The fact, however, is that the Latin remedy for the Germanic disease proved at first totally ineffective. In the somewhat less disrupted Anglo-Saxon world, the see of Canterbury, created from Rome, provided at least an external bond. In the Frankish world, the church could not even fulfill this task but was simply dragged in all its aspects into the Merovingian abyss. The Christian religion, as said above, degenerated into pure magic. The Roman administrative methods degenerated into violence pure and simple. The last remnants of a genuine Roman civilization in Gaul ossified. It was only centuries later, *after* a spiritual regeneration of the Germanic world had taken place, that the Latin tradition could be fruitfully revived, both with regard to the church and to secular government. And when that spiritual revival had taken place, not one but at least three cultural influences became fertile: besides the traditions of the Roman government, the thought of the early church of the East and the new Arabic civilization intruding from Spain and Sicily.

These remarks imply a critique of A. J. Toynbee's notion of the affiliation of civilizations. It is not true, as he seems to assume, that a new high civilization simply adopts and adapts the inheritance of the old one. The process is much more complex. The integration of the cultural inheritance of previous civilizations is not only a slow process, it differs structurally from what Toynbee seems to suggest. For the first physical contact between the barbarians and high civilizations leads only to abortive attempts at integrating the achievements of high civilization into barbarian life. And when, after an interlude of perhaps 500 years, those achievements are actually integrated, it is no longer owing to any living contact between the old and the new culture; it is out of manuscripts, historic traditions, and travellers' tales that the *caput mortuum* of the achievements of a higher civilization is reconstructed and integrated into the growing body of a new civilization.

This *caput mortuum* is nevertheless apt to gain tremendous importance. But where, as is the case of the secondary cultural revivals of Egypt, Babylonia, India, and China after their dark ages, that *caput mortuum* of a previous civilization is almost the only cultural inheritance, the emerging new civilization is apt to be considerably poorer than the old one. It is only where the "affiliation" of the new to the old is multiple, where more than one old cultural tradition has gone into the makeup of the new, and where—besides the pressure of the old, highly civilized traditions—new, independent, semi-barbarian forces are strongly at work, that a really great new civilization can arise out of the embers of its deceased models.

That applies eminently to our own Western civilization. That we have produced more than a pale imitation of classical antiquity is due to the luck the Merovingian and Carlovingian ages had in being able to lean upon the semi-barbarian cultures of the North, not totally disrupted by culture contact with classical antiquity. Actually, the Merovingian and Carlovingian ages were turning for help to all the more or less intact barbarian cultures, not excepting the Basques. But of greater importance was the influence from the East of unadulterated Germanic tribal cultures, and still more important, in fact quite predominant, was the influence of Ireland. These were influences more immediately useful than those of the South and the Christian East, partly because in content they were more closely related to the Frankish and Anglo-Saxon cultures and partly because they themselves possessed a simply vigorous moral order.

It is quite remarkable that A. J. Toynbee, while overrating the mechanical models of decaying antiquity, should have classified as "abortive" the Irish and Norse civilizations—precisely those civilizations providing the decisive spiritual, religious stimulus for the embryonic Western civilization. Curiously, at this point Toynbee failed to make use of his own correct view of the precedence of the spiritual and religious over the material factors in history. For if indeed "the serious business of mankind is religion," then clearly the serious procreative influence upon the West was Ireland, where the West got its decisive religious impulse. We shall try to prove that all the key elements of both Irish and Scandinavian civilization were fully integrated into the civilization of the West, leaving nothing "abortive" to account for.

The origins of Irish Christianity are shrouded in mystery. Yet the Irish sagas from pagan days, preserved by a highly literate clergy, tell a story which is important beyond any factual historical information. Compared to the earlier Eddic stratum and to the other sources of German saga, they stand out by their complete harmlessness. They are tales where, not infrequently, the robbing of cattle seems the chief human interest and the main opportunity for the display of heroism. They have no touch of the fearful tragedy revealed by German saga. Irish clan society lived a traditional life, not shaken by any deep upheaval.

This society came undramatically under Christian influence, adopted undramatically the Christian faith, and with it a high degree of erudition. Yet it is only too obvious that Christianity, in Ireland, was adopted without involving that deep feeling of guilt, that abandonment into the trusteeship of Christ the Savior, which it involved in the early stages in the East. In order to realize the specific character of Irish Christianity, it is only necessary to turn to the teachings of its greatest man: the heretic Pelagius, Augustine's great adversary. (He may have been a Briton but his paramount influence upon the Irish church is today a well-established fact.)[1]

It would be one of the great tasks of church history to elucidate and trace the role of Pelagius in the emergence of Western civilization. His imprint remains a decisive element in our cultural makeup to this day. Various factors have contributed to hide that fact: first, the transmission of his writings under various other names, such as that of St. Jerome,

1. For a fuller treatment of Pelagius, see part II, ch. 6 above.

a fake only gradually cleared up since the days of Erasmus; second, the lack of realization of his decisive role in the Irish church, rediscovered only towards the end of the nineteenth century; and last but not least the total obfuscation of the meaning of Pelagianism by its involvement in the Catholic-Protestant controversy of the sixteenth and seventeenth centuries, when Protestants charged Catholics to be morally lax and "Pelagian."

Owing to this last *quid pro quo* it has long escaped notice that Pelagius, far from being a man of lax principles, was an athlete of asceticism. Whether he was a genuine Christian is another matter. We may doubt it, since he taught the possibility of a sinless life, hence rejected the dogma of man's unqualified need for forgiving grace. His whole teaching is really concentrated in this one point, that man can achieve perfect virtue if only he wants to. In this heroic but un-Christian sentiment, we find reflected a pagan tradition which we saw operating in the overdeveloped sense of personal responsibility of the earliest Eddic heroes. It can be regarded as the basic moral attitude of the West. Pelagius' Christianity consisted of nothing but that ideal of moral perfection; he had simply transferred the heroic conception of the Northern pagans from fighting to morality.

This conception inevitably antagonized the African church, spiritually the most alive of all the branches of Latin Christianity, yet living, geographically and spiritually, on the border between East and West. Pelagius succeeded in forcing the Africans to discuss his specifically Northern conception of heroic morality, thus shifting the center of Western theology from the Christological and trinitarian problems to the moral problems of virtue, sin, and grace. (This in itself should reserve for him a place among the greatest figures of Western history.) But while he forced the Africans to discuss his problems, he also forced them to define their oriental moral attitude, their deep feeling of moral inadequacy and of trusting self-abandonment to Christ's redeeming grace, in sharpest contrast to the activist, self-confident heroism of the Northern theologian. It was one of the great formative hours of history.

There is no reason to assume that this attitude was Pelagius' personal creation. Presumably, only its clearcut formulation was his personal achievement. In any case, it infused the whole life of the Irish church, making of it a monastic church, the church of an elite of ascetic athletes. Much thought has been spent on the problem why the Irish in contrast to the Latin church had a monastic in contrast to the Latin episcopal structure. The influence of St. Martin of Tours, author of an exceedingly unstable experiment in Latin monasticism, has been unduly exaggerated.

The monastic structure of the Irish church sprang directly from its extremist ideas, exactly as the episcopal structure of the Latin church sprang from its predominantly institutional character, from its solicitude for the governance of the laity.

The life of the Irish monasteries of Pelagius' day is only preserved to us by legend. But the first man to transfer Irish monasticism to the continent, the great Columbanus of Luxeuil, has left behind several documents concerning monastic life, among them a rule which by its cruelty, by its belief in the rod as the suitable remedy for everything, stands out sharply against the whole rest of Western monasticism. This extreme reliance on outward discipline is one more proof that the Irish church lived by the law but not by contrition. (All polemics stress the arrogance of Pelagius' belief in moral perfection.) It is difficult to understand how so brutal a regime could go together with genuine enthusiasm on the part of the Columban monks; yet testimony for it is so ample that we should better not doubt the fact. We should remember that their lives, too, were neither given to contemplation nor to inward penance, but to fierce struggle with men and with nature.

It was Columbanus who attempted to impose himself on the Merovingian court at the moment of its deepest moral decay. They feared him, convinced of the magic properties of ascetic prowess, but hated him and finally expelled him. His work in France seemed completely futile. But he left behind a grim ascetic tradition which contrasted sharply with the complete dissolution of the Frankish monasteries, and thus laid the moral basis for a number of monastic foundations during the two subsequent centuries, as well as for a host of individual Irish missionary enterprises. The effect was reinforced, from the end of the seventh century onwards, by the activities of a number of Saxons, who had been deeply influenced by the impact of the Scottish branch of the Irish church in Northumbria and of its Welsh branch in Southwest England; the greatest of them was Boniface. The salient feature of all those later activities is that, invariably, they did not take place on the soil of France proper—apparently regarded as hopeless since Columbanus' failure—but in the purely Germanic territories further East, many of them hardly touched by the Voelkerwanderung at all. As the Greek seed had once found a new, fertile soil in Ireland, so the Irish seed now found a new fertile soil in Germany—in both cases for the same reasons.

Thus cultural resurrection started in a zone which had never been as deeply disrupted as France proper, among conditions much more primitive but morally much healthier than those of France during the Mer-

ovingian age. And to the moral seeds implanted by the Irish and Northumbrian monks and missionaries in Western Germany corresponded
a material revival. From the seventh century onwards, as Henri Pirenne
has forcefully demonstrated, the East of the Frankish realm takes the lead
in both economic and political affairs. The Carlovingian dynasty sprang
from the borderzone between Latin and Germanic speech, and the work
of St. Boniface had secured to it a vast Germanic hinterland.

We have said something about the character of the Irish influence
which thus started to play a decisive role in so unexpected a place as
Germany. We must now also deal with the character of the Germanic
culture on which that influence was exerted. But here we must proceed
by indirection: the German documents of the seventh century are too
sparse to allow us to form a coherent picture. Much richer is the evidence
provided by the second, still pagan but no longer Gothic layer of Eddic
poetry, generally attributed to Norway and to the ninth century. Obviously, what applies to Norway at that later period need not apply to
Germany two centuries before. Yet before raising such doubts, there
will be no harm in examining a source so rich in itself, and leaving for
later discussion the query of the applicability of our findings to Germany.

The middle Eddic period is best represented—apart from certain myths
concerning the Germanic gods—by the oldest Eddic version of the Sig-
urdsaga, counterpart of the Rhenish Sigfridsaga. There could hardly exist
a more striking contrast than that between these Sigurd songs on the one
hand, and the earliest Eddic strata as well as the Rhenish Nibelungensaga
on the other. In contrast to the hopeless tragedy prevailing among the
Goths and the mood of universal treachery reflected in the Sigfridsaga,
the Sigurd songs are filled with an eager, emphatic optimism. There is
no trace of tragedy left. The patricide underlying the whole Siegfried
theme is denied in the Norse no less than in the Frankish version, but
with a characteristic difference: in the Norse saga, in contrast to the
Frankish legend, Sigurd's father is actually killed, but by another man,
and Sigurd is his father's avenger. It is in the search for his father's
murderer that Sigurd wins both the Nibelungen treasure and the sleeping
Walkyrie Brynhild, and there is no trace in the songs—later additions
apart—of any guilt implicit in these conquests. Thus the Norse version
overcomes guilt, but by making the hero the defender of the basic moral
rules, the upholder of the tribal duty of vengence, who thus acquires the
right to the spoils of his exploits. Heroic moral activism is the Viking
answer to the challenge of primal crime.

It thus appears that in this middle Eddic stage we are dealing with an
intact moral order, and indeed the high North has never been ravaged

by the cultural cyclone raging farther South. Those early Sigurd songs prove, in particular, that the basic clan duty of revenge, root of such withering doubt and terrible conflict in Gothic saga, has remained, in the North, as unambiguous and clearcut as it must have been farther South *before* the crisis of the Voelkerwanderung. Yet it would be a mistake to regard those songs as self-expressions of an unshaken archaic culture. Nowhere has heroic poetry sprung from an unshaken primitive society. The very emphasis now laid upon the matter-of-fact duty of clan revenge, the joyful accents going with it, the promise of shining, almost supernatural rewards for his father's proud avenger, show that something threatened has been reemphasized. The conception of heroism implicit in those songs is something different from the natural bravery of warrior tribes, it verges on the divine (as the "hero" of Greek religion, in close parallelism to the Nordic songs, and for the same reasons, is a half-God). The rules have remained the same but the naivety has gone out of them; they now represent not simply tradition, but a conscious creed. We have entered the age of "heroic morality."

Primal crime, which was about to well up into the open, has been successfully suppressed again. But in the process of moral readjustment in the successful defense of the tribal order, something has had to be sacrificed. The temptation of patricide could be turned into its contrary, the revenge for the murdered father, by giving up the desire for the mother. What is most characteristic of these Middle Eddic songs in comparison to those of the Gothic period is therefore the almost total elimination of woman. This seems to be incompatible with the Brynhild myth in the shape in which it appears in those songs. Yet, in contrast to the tragic feminine figures of the archaic Eddic stage, the new Brynhild is not a real woman. In this specific version of the Sigurd saga, the Walkyrie, a superhuman being won in her sleep, is not the opposite pole of man—she is simply a dummy of his desire and enjoyment. Apparently a heightened symbol of femininity, she represents in fact femininity dehumanized, soulless, and passive—a depreciation of woman, her reduction to an object of the male. And to this exclusion of the male-female relation from the sphere of basic human conflicts corresponds the enhancement of the relation between male and male, the romanticized loving friendship of a band of warriors. This cult of male friendship constitutes the central ethos of that age.

Its most emphatic expression can be found somewhat nearer the storm center of the Voelkerwanderung—i.e., somewhat nearer the temptation of primal crime—in Anglo-Saxon poetry starting with the Beowulf. It must be remembered that the Beowulf, like so many of the more important documents of Anglo-Saxon civilization, belongs to the North of the country, the merging center of Norse and Iro-Scottish influences. And indeed, in this cult of friendship, the Irish element is no less important than the Norse, though less traceable in poetry. It permeates throughout Irish monasticism and even more so Irish missionary enterprise: it was with twelve inseparable companions that Columbanus went out to re-form the continental churches. This was a feature unknown both in Oriental and in Benedictine monasticism. It constitutes, in the religious as in the secular sphere, a specifically Northern characteristic, inseparable from the heroic morality which is a common feature of the Eddic middle stratum and of the Pelagian phase of the Irish church. The parallelism between the heroic morality and the cult of male friendship among the Christian Irish and the pagan Norse goes far to prove that we are here confronted not with two civilizations but with one and the same; that the church was right in regarding Pelagianism as anti-Christian; that the difference between Pelagian asceticism and pagan self-enjoyment is superficial. The renunciation of woman, in particular, is the same in both cases, though the outward forms differ.

The difference between this solution and regression to paranoia is not as wide as it appears. For the renunciation of woman as an object of love is the same in both cases, and to man woman is the primary object of love. The paranoiac solution, which casts out love and only keeps hatred, is the thorough and logical one. The new morality of male companionship replaces hatred by love again—but love only for man to the exclusion of woman, hence love of a secondary character to the exclusion of primal love. No wonder, therefore, that in every aspect of this new morality of heroic activism aggression and destruction lurk behind the facade of optimistic trust. It is as if a small terrain were gained for love from a sea of hatred.

Now heroic morality as well as renunciation of woman recalls at once Hellenic civilization. It was exactly at this price that the emerging Hellenic world had overcome the lure of primal crime; the existence of that lure, the feeling of an abysmal danger lurking in the relation between man and woman, can be traced in the Greek myth almost as clearly as in the earliest Eddic stratum. The two starting points had been closely akin, only the subsequent roads diverged—we shall see how. And the intermediate Iro-Norse stage represents an abortive attempt—here alone the term "abortive" applies to the Irish and Scandinavian civilizations—to solve the problem in the Greek way, by an artificial narrowing of the scope of basic human experience.

Such a contraction of the scope of living, if allowed to run its course, would have affected in the long run the conception of heroic morality itself. Indeed, such a development was underway. The deepest parallelism between Pelagianism and the Sigurd songs must be sought in their attitude to wrong-doing: they both know *sin* in the sense of an infraction of rules of conduct, but *sinfulness* as a basic element of human existence is unknown to both—an attitude very proximate to that of the Greeks. From that starting point a direct road was bound to lead to a religion of merely formal correctness—the heroic morality of the Iro-Norse civilization was bound to transform itself into precisionism. And at this point, if not earlier, the close connection between the Iro-Norse stage of civilization and the puritanism of the seventeenth century, developing roughly in the same geographical area, becomes also apparent. The close relation of two phenomena so far distant in time demonstrates to what an extent even the "abortive" elements of Iro-Norse civilization have entered into the structure of the West; it proves at the same time how abortive the whole puritan strand of Western life would have been, had it not been balanced by other elements. We can, however, identify it as one of the basic ingredients of Western civilization: moralism based upon a contraction of the field of human experience.

Having identified this trend and demonstrated its broad historic significance, it now only remains to point out its role in the restoration of an ordered society by the Carlovingians, a process starting in Western Germany and thence transferred to France. In view of all that has been said, it now needs little proof that Western Germany, also one of the marginal zones of the Voelkerwanderung cyclone, participated, though in a minor way, in the general trends prevailing in the Northwestern world during the seventh, eighth, and to some extent ninth centuries. Evidence of this is sparse, but what remains to us, such as the Latin Waltharius song, reveals an attitude already well known to us. It reflects the same optimism as the Middle Eddic stratum; it is, if possible, even further removed from the moral abysses of Gothic poetry; its greatest drama is the abduction, not even unlawful, of a captive maiden, and the grim heroes of the old songs, such as Gunther and Hagen, transform themselves into slightly funny figures. The earlier Carlovingian age was cheerfully active and shunned the depths.

It was this society, somewhat archaic and somewhat superficial, somewhat integrated and somewhat shapeless, which now imposed its domination upon Merovingian France. Charles Martel, Pippin the Short, and Charlemagne imposed what today we should call law and order by the strength of their sword. They thwarted by force the brutal aggressiveness of the disintegrated Gallic society; and if it is a law of dynamic psychology that thwarted aggressiveness is driven inward, causing depression, then their rule must have produced a great many tears, though very little searching of hearts. But it is an unalterable law of all societies without exception that a social order can only last if it is "internalized," made part of the unconscious makeup of its participants. Mere outward thwarting of aggression, though an essential precondition of that process of internalization, is not itself that process.

Of this Charlemagne was well aware, and much of his effort was directed towards the goal of "moralizing" his subjects. The "Carlovingian Renaissance" aimed at revivifying the inheritance of classical antiquity, at making the ruling stratum of the new Empire "cultured"—as in our own day the Russian state makes efforts to enforce a "cultured" conduct on the part of its subjects. But such attempts to create a culture by mechanically drawing on precedent in the service of practical utility are invariably doomed to failure. Real civilization can never be fostered or imposed merely for the purpose of good government or economic progress; and the Carlovingian Renaissance, therefore, constituted merely a second failure to use the classic inheritance as a fertilizer on arid soil.

The most significant of a long series of failures in every aspect of this civilizing effort was that of the monastic reform of Benedict of Aniane. Benedict's effort had historic relevance, insofar as it represents the connecting link between the monastic rule of St. Benedict of Nursia and the monastic developments of the later half of the tenth century. The Benedictine rule had so far remained a dead letter, since Monte Cassino, the mother of the later Benedictine order, had been destroyed, almost immediately, by the still pagan Langobards, and the movement had found no new home. Benedict of Aniane now adopted that rule, filling it, however, with the grim moral and disciplinary fervor of the Irish tradition which alone was able to prompt a real monastic movement in that age. In practice, therefore, his discipline was much harder than that envisaged by Benedict of Nursia.

Yet Benedict rejected the organizational aspect of Irish monasticism: to the extreme mutual independence of Irish monasteries and mission stations he opposed an extreme, Roman version of administrative centralism under his own direction, leaving no trace of self-government to the many monasteries he reformed or founded with the help of Charlemagne. In other words, in the Gallic world the individualist moral heroism of the Irish monks had to be transformed into a motor for a centralized government effort at moral reconstruction—which resulted in an undermining of the moralism without securing the effective centralism

Benedict of Aniane had in mind. Within little more than one generation, the monasteries of Gaul were almost back at the stage of total disintegration characteristic of the Merovingian age; and this collapse of the monastic reform reflected the overall effect of the short blossoming and the rapid collapse of the Carlovingian Renaissance.

Already during the reign of Charlemagne's son, Louis the Pious, the Empire disintegrated; and during the following decades, a return of Merovingian conditions seemed inevitable. Actually, violence was hardly less general, and the lack of strength to ward off barbarian incursions was much more marked than during the Merovingian period.

Yet something fundamentally different from the Merovingian age developed. Amidst a disintegration of the public order and of human relations very similar to the early Merovingian period, there emerged the first genuine cultural revival since the end of Roman days—a revival not artificially sponsored from above and doomed to quick collapse without leaving a trace, but deeply rooted in the individual personal experiences of a whole stratum of society and therefore capable of outlasting the worst storms. Before dealing with the content of the new concept of life thus arising, it is necessary to ask how such an unexpected turn of events was possible.

It was the product of those geographical changes in the extent of certain culture zones which we have described above and which took several centuries to evolve. At the moment of the collapse of the Roman empire, Europe had been roughly divided into three culture zones: the decaying Roman West, center of the cultural cyclone; the Western Germanic tribes, soon to be completely disrupted by contact with the dying Roman civilization; and the Iro-Norse area, haven of an intact barbaric culture of heroic moralism. The first and the third of those zones had lived in segregation, though the Christian heritage had penetrated into Ireland. Contact had been perfunctory; when Columbanus failed in his heroic attempt at reforming the Merovingian court, he had nothing to do but contemptuously to shake the dust of the accursed den of iniquity from his heels.

But later the moralist heroism of the Irish church spread from Ireland to Scotland, thence to Northumbria and thence to Germany. It intermingled with the kindred heroic attitude of the pagan or recently converted Germans; and from there a breath of life had inspired the Carlovingian Renaissance, not as a message from a distant country—as Irish Christianity had vaguely haunted the rake's progress of the Merovingian world—but as an idea advancing in the mailed armor of the Carlovingian hosts and conquering France by force. It was no longer a matter of missionaries cut off from their country as the early Irish preachers of the faith had been: it was now a matter of the dominant Germanic stratum of the Carlovingian empire itself.

Hence when, in the rapid decay of that empire, its elite was dragged into the abyss, it could no longer retire into seclusion, as the Irish missionaries of the seventh century had done. It was confronted, dramatically and tragically, with the shallowness of its own ideal, with the inadequacy of the efforts of the Carlovingian Renaissance. The Pelagian ideal of moral heroism underpinned by classical education, underlying all previous efforts at reform, was now cruelly exposed. The Carlovingian elite, a thin social layer concentrated at the court and in a few monasteries such as the Carlovingian family monastery of Corbie, was delivered without mercy to the suction of universal social disintegration, threatening to drag it into the abyss. It was filled, in consequence, with an immense awareness of, a completely new awakening to, the cruelty and sinfulness of the world in which it was living. It may justly be doubted whether even the Roman and Gallic church in the days of the Roman empire had ever been filled with such a crushing feeling of guilt.

The sad career of Charlemagne's own son on the throne, the biography of Louis the Pious, can serve as a symbol of this sudden and dramatic turn. Of Germanic Carlovingian stock, he had been educated in Aquitania, in a completely alien milieu half Latin and half Basque, under the stern guidance of Benedict of Aniane himself. For the first time since the collapse of ancient Rome men of his station now underwent a more than formal, a serious and incisive religious education. How much the regimentation of life imposed by the precisionist church reformer must have contrasted with the license and violence still predominating in the world around him! The contrast filled Louis with an ineradicable feeling of guilt for the rest of his life. He was a strong man physically, given instinctively to all the pleasures his ancestors had indulged in, but he was unable to conduct himself as a ruler. Early in his reign, he had to pass sentence of death on a rebellious nephew; unable to do it, he condemned the young man to the penalty of being blinded. That act, however, led to the death of the young man—and Louis could never get over the guilt of this act, which any of his predecessors would have laughed off. Years after, he collapsed in a public penance, and after that was never able to secure the reins of the monarchy again. Out of the age of universal hatred, after the collapse of a shallow religious reformism, there arose, among a small leading stratum, a feeling of overwhelming moral and practical inadequacy.

This feeling engendered the first serious theological debate within the

Western church (the Pelagian debate had not been an internal affair of the West, but a struggle between the Irish and the African church). Three tendencies were represented. The Irishman Johannes Scotus Erigena represented the Carlovingian Renaissance and its ideology. But characteristically, he was no longer able to maintain the Pelagian moralist position implying the possibility for man to achieve perfection. Instead, he had to shift the debate to the metaphysical level. A Platonist of profound philosophical training, translator and interpreter of the Neo-Platonist Greek mystic Dionysius Areopagita, he denied the mataphysical existence of evil, declaring it to be a μῆ ὂν, something nonbeing. Accordingly, he revived the heritical doctrine of Origen, the Alexandrian theologian of the third century, concerning the ἀποκανάστασις πάντων, the complete disappearance of all seeming evil, including the devil and hell, at the end of days. But the ideological denial of the problem of sin and guilt at the moment of an unequalled upsurge of violence on the one hand, of guilt and depression on the other, was no answer at all. Johannes Scotus left no successors.

Much nearer to the real mood of the age was that remarkable Saxon nobleman Gottschalk, monk at Corbie, who revived the Augustinian doctrine of predestination in its most extreme form. There are hints that in his youth he had been involved in criminal bloodshed himself, and in any case he reflected accurately the overwhelming guilt of the age. In his soul the patricidal tendencies—it is the first instance of such a development in Western history—had been turned into their direct contrary. So overwhelming is his guilt, so total his submission, that he does not even discuss the relation of man's merits to salvation. Concerned exclusively with God and not at all with man, he hardly cares to speak of saving grace at all; he can only repeat, in ever-recurring words, that God is master and that he alone decides on the eternal destiny of all men, regardless of their own aims and efforts. He underwent cruel torture for his views, which indeed were incompatible with any efforts of the church to improve public morality. The retort of archbishop Hincmar of Rheims, the great worldly metropolitan of the Carlovingian church, was perfectly pertinent: such a theology might give a sense of self-denying security to individuals, but it was incompatible with the notion of individual responsibility on which all morality rested.

Gottschalk had moved to the opposite extreme of Pelagius, thus forcing the official church in its turn to reemphasize the free will, to assume a half-Pelagian position and to discard the merely verbal Augustinianism which it had professed for so long. But the formal assertion of free will was certainly no remedy for the sudden irruption of overwhelming guilt

characteristic of the second generation of the ninth century. An astonishing number of leading men of the Carlovingian circle more or less
supported Gottschalk's theology.

The saving formula, however, had been pronounced two decades before the Gottschalk controversy. In 831 A.D., Paschasius Radbertus, later
abbot of Corbie, had proclaimed (though not yet with all its later logical
stringency) the dogma of Transsubstantiation, which was from then
onwards making its way through Western Christianity. That doctrine
asserts the physical presence of Jesus Christ in the Eucharist, claiming
that the bread and wine of the sacrament are the real flesh and blood of
the Savior. It is a sharply anti-Augustinian doctrine, since St. Augustine
had positively taught the merely symbolic and commemorative character
of Holy Communion. Some fathers of the Eastern Church had been
nearer Paschasius' view, but to quote them only helps to prove that the
whole matter, in the East, had been treated as a legitimate subject of
disagreement, not suitable for dogmatic fixation. Paschasius, in reviving
those older views, claimed for them obligatory acceptance as a basic
doctrine of the Christian faith.

Herein lies his crucial importance. He must be regarded as the originator of the Western doctrine of sacraments, and therefore implicitly as
the originator of the dogma of the "treasure of the church" dispensed
by the clergy, a doctrine upon which the authority of the Catholic Church
essentially rests. This immense historical role of the man has been little
recognized, even less than that of Pelagius, and his name remains unknown outside the circle of the initiated to this day. For Protestant
theology, which correctly diagnosed the relevance of the innovation,
rejected it (like everything it classified as an innovation) and therefore
gave no credit to the innovator; while Catholic theology, always intent
on attributing its current doctrine to the earliest Christian age, denied
the innovation and thereby denied the achievement of one of its greatest
men.

Actually, Paschasius' dogma represents a decisive stage in the emergence of Western civilization as a whole, a historic process which can to
a large extent be identified with the history of the Western church. That
history, up to the point here under consideration, proceeded in three
stages. At first, organizing activities primarily conducted by the African
church had resulted in the establishment of a church discipline centering
round the see of Rome. Then, the Irish church, its spirit embodied in
the theology of Pelagius, had given a more than organizational, a genuinely spiritual impulse, which however was utopian in character. Now,

as that impulse of heroic moralism came into direct conflict with the disintegrated society of Gaul, it transformed itself into something going much farther than mere utopian moralism—into a metaphysical doctrine of salvation and a sacramental ritual based upon it. Thus and only thus the Western church was enabled to survive.

But the new doctrine, however different from the Pelagian faith of an earlier age it may have been, integrated into its fundaments such elements of Pelagianism as were not utopian. The sacrament of the Eucharist is the physical integration of the Savior's body by his believers. That seems a conception worlds apart from Pelagius' moralism. But in dealing with the effects of the sacrament (not a few of them belonging to the realm of magical medicine), Paschasius nevertheless stressed that Holy Communion "washes away our crimes."[2] Pelagius had taught that it was possible for man by his own unaided effort to avoid all crimes. This, in that later age of crushing guilt, was rightly regarded as nonsense. But the sacrament now provided what man's unaided effort could not provide: the wiping out not of crime but of its effects. The methods of dealing with sin have become different, but the old Pelagian concern with sin as the central problem of Christianity remains. The approach to sin has gained in depth, but the specifically Western moralistic approach to the Christian faith has not been altered thereby. Roman (i.e., Western) Catholicism is a non-Pelagian answer to a Pelagian problem.

But was it an effective answer? The peculiar difficulty of that query appears in the treatment the dogma of the Eucharist has received by most of the secular historians. Nobody doubts that the great controversies about sin and grace, the great ecclesiastic struggles turning round properly moral problems, are part of history in every one of their aspects. The historian is aware that he cannot bypass the Gregorian reform of the Lateran council, but one would search in vain, in any of the current histories, for an appreciation of the emergence of the Eucharistic dogma. Its effects, to the average modern mind, are almost as recondite and as indistinct as those of the great Christological and trinitarian controversies of the Greek church, which to modern authors, even of a Roman Catholic persuasion, do not infrequently appear just as so much mumbo-jumbo. And yet the dogma of the Eucharist is as much concerned with the basic moral problems, hence as much part of our Western inheritance, as the patently moralistic sacrament of confession or the doctrine of predestination. It only expresses moral problems in a language which is no longer intelligible to the modern mind, because it identifies the material with

2. Paschasius Radbertus, *Liber de corpore et sanguine domini*, II, 3. (Turnholti: Brepols, 1969).

the spiritual, which later centuries have attempted to segregate most sharply from one another.

In order to understand its meaning, it will be useful to consider what had gone before and what followed. During the age of universal hatred, the spiritual had been drowned, as it were, in the material. The regression from the stage of personal love to the stage of the craving for objects—which is such an essential feature of paranoia—excludes any but material desires. Few things are more characteristic of that age than the abnormal role played by treasures—actually a treasure is at the center of things in the Gothic, the Rhenish, and the Nordic version of the Nibelungen saga. And nothing more telling can be said about the relations between persons in that age but to point out that Sigurd treats the acquisition of Brynhild on the same level as that of the dragon's treasure: as a highly desirable piece of booty. In such an age, the spiritual is bound to descend to the level of crudest materiality, religion transforming itself into the possession of things—particularly relics—valued entirely on the same level as amulets and other magical devices. The materialization of the spiritual is, incidentally, the essence of magic. And the Eucharist, in that age, is only such a piece of protective magic.

Jumping over many centuries, we witness, at the other end of the scale, a religious sentiment which cannot bear the slightest interference of the physical with the divine. Luther had already taught that the essence of the Eucharist did not consist in the miraculous transformation of the physical elements into Christ's body, but in the spiritual union of the believer with his savior in the act of Holy Communion. Calvin, going one step further, had denied any independent efficacy to the sacrament and had made it a mere function of divine predestination. It is owing to the prevalence of that spirit that today we fail to understand the incisive practical meaning of the Eucharist in the age which first conceived of it as the central sacrament of the Christian faith.

For the concept of the Eucharist as taught by Paschasius stands exactly in the middle between the magical and the symbolic interpretations of the sacrament. It takes it as entirely real, in the physical sense ("the *real* flesh—the *real* blood of Christ"), and it regards the physical miracle of transsubstantiation as absolutely essential to the effectiveness of the sacrament. The recipient of the Eucharist eats and drinks the body of his Savior. That is magical faith in the effectiveness, the exclusive effectiveness of the material. It is even a magical procedure of infinitely greater effectiveness than any known to the Merovingian age, since that age possessed only material magical objects, whereas the Eucharist is the incorporation of the divine Savior himself. In that sense, Paschasius' doctrine may be regarded as the climax of magical thought. It is also characteristic that Paschasius, at the same time, taught the physical integrity of the Virgin, not only in conception but also in delivery—another instance of the extreme preoccupation with physical reality as a pledge of spiritual reality.

But in another sense this stressing of the physical aspects of religion is deceptive. The most extreme physical miracles are no longer used in the same context as more modest miracles were used a few generations before. The physical properties of the divine no longer serve as means by which to acquire physical control over it, so as to treat it as a piece of private property. That is already implicit in the concept of the physical integration of the Lord's body itself, all too obviously serving as a symbol that henceforth God will operate on the believer no longer from without but from "within," in other words no longer by—mainly hostile—compulsion but by a transformation of the believer's heart. The extremest physical miracle, transsubstantiation, serves as a pledge that purity, hitherto an elusive ideal, can actually be achieved by way of direct divine intervention. The material is invoked to gain access to the spiritual; and to an age just emerging out of paranoia and universal hatred, none but a material pledge could serve that purpose. The doctrine of transsubstantiation stands at the exact point of transition from the age of hatred to the age of guilt. Without the doctrine of the Eucharist, the age would have relapsed into the Merovingian position; with its help, it could overcome the disintegrative effects of overwhelming guilt, without at the same time denying personal responsibility and throwing the whole blame upon the outside world. This, incidentally, is the essence of the Catholic attitude to sin and salvation.

The precise meaning of the physical integration of the Lord's body will come out more clearly by a comparison of the Eucharist with a counterpart in the early Eastern church. There, too, we meet the notion that man can be transformed by the action of supernatural forces which have taken possession of him from *within*. But no stretching of meanings could convey the idea that the earliest church was primarily concerned with such actions as deriving from *divine* forces. Much the contrary: "possession" to the earliest church means possession by evil spirits, whereas the divine forces, Christ and after his Assumption the exorcists acting on his behalf, act from outside; by contrast, to the West it is Christ who, in the Eucharist, takes "possession" of the faithful, thus helping them to ward off the evil influence exerted by devils and demons from outside. There is also this difference, that the "possessed" of the early Christian age seem to be helpless victims of the demons possessing them—how indeed could man resist the action of supernatural forces acting from within his own being? By contrast, the healing effect of the Eucharist is not irresistible at all: Paschasius strongly insists on the need to receive the sacrament in the right spirit, and this to such an extent that he shrank from evolving the doctrine of transsubstantiation to the full.

Here everything is closely interconnected, everything is rooted in the same fundamental difference of approach to man's position before the moral judgment of God. To the East, man is essentially passive in the process of salvation, a process that has taken place entirely outside him, which has relieved him of guilt without any contribution on his part; hence evil, in all its forms, is conceived as something operating within him and salvation as outside interference. Such a conception contrasted crassly with the spirit of Pelagianism, with the central belief of the West that man *himself* must work his salvation. Even the collapse of Pelagian pride in the ninth century did not make the passive Eastern approach to the moral problem more acceptable. In order to call in the help of the Savior—for the first time not in magical but in spiritual terms—the Eastern relation between salvation and evil had to be reversed, salvation had to be made an instrument of the moral effort, hence a force working from within, and also a force no longer compelling but strictly subsidiary to the individual's own will. The basic Pelagian conception had not been abandoned—it had only been transformed and strengthened by the introduction of a new mystery of the faith.

For a full understanding of the meaning of incorporation, the psychology of the unconscious is indispensable. Research in this field has of late tended to stress with growing insistence the importance of early phases of ego development, at an age when the dividing line between the individual and the outside world is not yet clearly drawn. The infant, up to the age of about 18 months, tends both to experience internal events as action upon it from outside, and conversely to "introject" the impact of other persons, i.e., to treat them as if they were part of the ego and operating from within; hence the tendency violently to eject the former influences, as far as their impact is felt to be hostile—a process known as "projection," which we recognized as the basic mechanism of paranoia. Introjection and projection actually form an insoluble complex of closely correlated reactions to the outside world. With those psychological factors in view, it should be clear without much comment that a doctrine emphatically stressing, as the central religious experience, a process of introjection to the exclusion of projection must be of overwhelming importance for the personality structure of those concerned.

Projection—the assumption that all hostile influences come from outside without any aggressive intention of the individual itself—we saw as the basic paranoiac attitude; it aims at creating a sharp dividing line between the individual and an entirely hostile world. It is obvious that the stressing of the opposite process of introjection aims directly at overcoming the paranoiac attitude, at furthering close identification between the individual and the outside world. From whichever angle we look at the new sacrament, we are always led to the same conclusion that it corresponded exactly to the needs of the moment when profound guilt replaced universal paranoia.

But the dogma of the Eucharist has its contradictions which have so far remained in the background of our investigation, simply because we spoke of the introjection of the Savior in terms too general to bring out its pitfalls. Projection is entirely hostile in character, and introjection is the contrary of projection; but it does not follow that introjection is entirely an act of love. Its primeval origin is an act of devouring the desired object—an act satisfying both an intense desire to identify oneself with it and a destructive desire directed against it. It corresponds to a stage even more archaic than projection, to a stage of development where love and hatred are not yet separated, where desire merges both into one. The psychological representative of that stage is the later sucking phase, that phase when sucking gradually transforms itself into biting, hence into the desire to devour—a psychological counterpart to the physiological transition from liquid to compact food. The historical and sociological counterpart of this physiopsychological stage is cannibalism, which has been unjustly regarded as an act of pure hostility—the victims of cannibalism are highly esteemed for their unusual qualities—but which certainly is not an act of pure love. The religious counterpart to it all is, of course, the totem feast, the tearing to pieces and the collective devouring of an animal representing both the tribal ancestor and the tribal god.

Catholics have expressed their horror at the comparison between totemism and the Eucharist, but since at the center of both is the physical incorporation of a godhead, expressions of horror are not an answer to an inescapable problem. The affinities of the two rites are undeniable. The differences are at first less obvious. They do, however, reach into the deepest psychological layers. The totemic animal is torn to pieces, in the extreme case by the teeth of all the tribesmen. But the strictest prohibition is directed against touching the Eucharist by the teeth. The prohibition would be pointless, were it not directed against an underlying instinct. The fact, however, remains that what makes the essence of the totemic orgy—the tearing to pieces of the god—is what is most strictly prohibited in the Eucharist. The latter has to be swallowed, not eaten, has to be consumed like a liquid, not like a compact body. In other words, the psychological attitude requested from the faithful is that of the suckling *before* the biting stage, of the infant at the mother's breast, receiving satisfaction without the interference of any aggression. The infant at mother's breast is the embodiment, the quintessence of love without aggression, in other words of the stage of primal purity. It is this stage the Eucharist aims at restoring.

In doing so, the dogma proclaims a religious ideal of no less unattainable elevation than the Pelagian morality. That statement does not, however, involve a final judgment. All civilization is, on the contrary, built on such unattainable ideals of one kind or another, upon a set of choices between incompatible desires, where the fulfillment of some requires the rejection of others. That is the greatness of all higher civilization, but also its tragedy. It is the force driving it from achievement to achievement. It is also, however, the worm gnawing at its core. In studying the self-contradictions implicit in the dogma of the Eucharist, we are touching upon the basic self-contradictions of our civilization, which in their turn determine its cyclical development from cradle to death.

In the first place, to the extent that man could achieve a suckling's love, pure of all traces of aggression, he would by the same token become incapable of any kind of personal love. For the suckling's satisfaction at mother's breast is satisfied desire for an object, not love of a person. It belongs to the essential insights of dynamic psychology into the human condition to understand that love of persons is a secondary emotion, conditioned by the devouring impulse, by processes of hostile projection and by outright hatred, as well as by the interference of guilt. The secondary feelings of love to the exclusion of all hatred which we all try to achieve in the relation with our nearest are not the same as the primary impersonal satisfaction of the suckling, which may appear to us as an unachievable ideal but which actually contains only a first nucleus of the feelings constituting adult love. Love without aggression, personal relations without "ambivalence" belong to the world of daydreaming. Hence the sacrament based upon a search for such feelings can never completely achieve the sought-for effect and can never completely assuage the feeling of guilt.

But the difficulties are actually of a much more specific kind. Sucking is a process connecting infant and mother, and its religious counterpart should therefore refer to a mother and not to a father god. This remark could of course serve as an opening statement for the discussion of one of the most salient features of Catholicism, the cult of the Virgin, acquiring a new fervor from the end of the tenth century onwards—thus testifying to the incompleteness of the solace provided by what we might well call the sacrament of incorporation.

In this tangible return of religion from a purely male to an at least partly female interpretation of the divine we have to consider two wide evolutionary cycles, the one concerning the respective role of maternal and paternal deities, the other the actual position of women in society—two sets of facts not as closely connected as is sometimes assumed. In one sense the new importance of the Eucharist, paralleled even in Paschasius' own doctrine by a new emphasis upon the cult of the Virgin and soon to be followed by a much greater veneration for the "mother of God," represents a return from a completely patriarchal religion to a less exclusively patriarchal one. This, of course, implies as little a return to the cult of the *Magna Mater* as the Eucharist involves a return to totemism. In both cases certain affinities undoubtedly exist, but they do not justify crude and ignorant identifications of strictly separate phenomena. For the fact is that the *Magna Mater* was as little an embodiment of motherly love as the totem-feast was entirely a love feast. The great cults of feminine goddesses are all shot through with rituals of rape on the one hand, of castration on the other. All that can be said is that, despite the primeval conflicts between man and woman embodied in the rites of the *Magna Mater*, they presumably protected men somewhat better against the feeling of boundless isolation, of helpless exposure to divine vindictiveness, than cults such as that of Yahve. In this sense, the Eucharist rite and the Virgin cult following in its step served the alleviation of unbearable tension by reintroducing a maternal element into religion. If our Western civilization has a broader sweep and a greater daring than either the Hellenic, the Hebrew, or the Eastern Christian civilization, this no doubt is partly due to the balance it succeeds in keeping with regard to the two sexes.

But the opposite also applies: the Eucharist doctrine is not only a prelude to a new acceptance of femininity into religion, it is also the product of a reduction of the status of femininity in social reality. There cannot be any doubt that the Eddic poems reflect a state where woman is a strong, independent agent, and the Icelandic sagas of a later age make us see that role of woman in old Germanic society in all the explicitness characteristic of a realistic literature. But there is also no doubt that since the Germanic conquests the position of women, especially in the higher strata, had been constantly declining, and that by the tenth century it had reached a nadir not very far from its nullity in ancient Greece. In any case a paranoiac age, as we already had occasion to say, is a (male) homosexual age, where women can have no honor of their own. The reintroduction of woman into the context of personal sentiment—as distinct from merely sexual and material desires—thus becomes an integral part of the struggle against universal hatred. The psychological attitudes springing from the relation between mother and son are used to break the evil self-perpetuation of homosexual aggression. The psychological attitude underlying the Eucharist paves the way for the restoration to woman of the role she had played in old Germanic society.

But—and this is the salient point—all this happens only in a limited sphere, in a limited sense. The Savior is a male divinity. The crucial psychological fact about the Eucharist remains that attitudes congenitally directed towards the mother are here transferred to a male God. And here, for once, the parallelism between totemism and the Eucharist dogma is not superficial and misleading, but recondite yet essential. For the rite of tearing a godhead to pieces must also, originally, have formed part of the worship of a maternal goddess and/or a maternal ancestor—cannibalism as a whole has to be related to the biting stage and totemism is essentially a substitute for cannibalism—and was later reinterpreted in patriarchal terms. Freud, at a time when he was still completely engrossed with the Oedipus complex, and almost unaware of the pre-Oedipal connotations of the mother-son relation, completely overlooked that aspect of totemism—as he did most other factors concerning the role of women in society. Actually, so classical an oral rite as is totemism could never at the same time be an entirely Oedipal rite, based exclusively upon the conflict between the aboriginal father and his sons. Totemism corresponds exactly to the transition from a matricentric to a patricentric society—and so does the dogma of the Eucharist. And in this position, torn between allegiance to the male and to the female principle, Western civilization will remain throughout its history, in sharpest contrast to the unambiguously patriarchal Hellenic and Hebrew and to the more or less unambiguously matricentric Minoan civilization.

Yet even this statement should serve only as a preface to the feature at one and the same time most obvious and most essential of the Eucharist, its connection not just with any "male godhead" but with Jesus Christ, the suffering son of God. It is with him that the believer is identified in the sacrament, and it could not be otherwise. For is not the historical and psychological root of the new mystery universal guilt? And how could guilt of such depth go together with identification with a father god, with a claim to his superhuman strength and power? The totemic rite—like any cannibalistic rite on an Oedipal basis—involved such an identification: the eating of the father to acquire his strength and his prerogatives. The Eucharist, by contrast, implies identification with the voluntary humility of God's son, with his absolute, self-effacing obedience on the Mount of Olives. Its whole meaning consists in a physical identification with Christ's self-denial as a means of purification and as a protection against guilt. In the sign of Gethsemane to overcome universal hatred—that is the moral meaning of the sacrament. Incorporation of the suffering God—the totemic rite applied to a *suffering son* god, not to a triumphant father god—is the natural instrument of personal salvation in an age standing at the dividing line between a paranoiac craving for objects and a normal longing for love.

At this point the close connection between Paschasius' doctrine of the Eucharist and his doctrine of the Holy Virgin comes again to view. Other religions, too, it is hardly necessary to say, have their virgin goddesses; but they are never at the same time mother goddesses. The Holy Virgin, with a rank practically divine, is a most specifically Roman Catholic creation. The Eucharist, as we saw, is based upon the willing renunciation of aggression, the willing acceptance of suffering obedience. So, we may now add, is the cult of the Holy Virgin. For it draws an incisive line of division between the tender and the aggressive feelings which, combined, constitute the normal approach of the male to the female, the normal attitude of sexual desire combined with personal attachment. The Holy Virgin is the embodiment of the mother loved but not desired; it is, as much as the Eucharist, the direct denial and/or rejection of the Oedipus complex. The two doctrines together constitute an attitude of guiltlessness and loving attachment, based upon basic renunciation.

We can thus amplify the formula used above. We said Western civilization, throughout its course, was wavering between allegiance to male and to female supremacy. We may now add that in both respects, it attempts to renounce aggression and to put submission into its stead. That also, in both respects, it challenges the most powerful human instincts is another story.

The terrific burden thus incurred needs hardly any elaboration. It is, however, important to weigh the advantages gained by the acceptance of such a burden. One of them, without any doubt, is a much greater measure of authenticity and frankness of thought than any civilization has ever achieved. So much has been said, and often so ineptly, about the "inhibition of thought" that goes with unquestioning acceptance of religious beliefs. Against this view, it should be stressed that all civilizations have their pre-natal Merovingian age of universal hatred, and that they all are shaken out of it by the impact upon them of primitive societies; in other words, that they all pass through the shock of universal guilt. What distinguishes our own civilization from others is the acceptance of guilt as the pivotal point of our conception of life. To see the importance of that act, we must appeal to the basic insight of the more modern—in contrast to the more primitive—version of psychoanalysis: that guilt can be, and very frequently is, unconscious. Whole civilizations, and preeminently the Hellenic civilization, acquired the knack of cushioning the full impact of guilt; but they could only achieve that by a highly artificial restriction of their world, by the elimination of the concept of personality. To us their civilization conveys a nostalgic feeling of the "innocence of nature"; we tend to forget the price that was paid for it. Our civilization differs from theirs not by greater hypocrisy, but by a fuller confrontation of the basic facts of human existence. If we have produced what is doubtless the most vigorous civilization hitherto created, it is essentially due to this plucky facing of an almost unbearable issue.

But to admitted guilt belongs penance, and such penance may indeed constitute an unbearable burden—a burden we share with the only other civilization that has fully admitted guilt, that of the Hindus. The burden we bear is heavier, however, owing to the intrusion of elements absolutely opposed to the self-punishment which is the only antidote to admitted guilt.

In the meantime, however, we have once more to return to the problem of cultural affiliation. We have attempted to show to what an extent the supposed affiliation of the West to classical antiquity was fictitious and how, during the whole incubatory half millenium of Western civilization, affiliation to Eastern Christianity, in its turn, must be reduced to the one simple fact that the Irish adopted Christianity from the East, and reinterpreted it in terms of their own heroic ideals. But as we now touch upon the real birth of Western civilization in the late Carlovingian period, things appear in an entirely different light. The sacrament of the Eucharist, basic embodiment of Western faith in the matter of sin and salvation, is unthinkable without the full development of "Greek," i.e., Syrian and Alexandrian theology. It is true that the West then showed, and will continue to show throughout its history, very little interest in the complex Christological theology of the East: of that whole body of doctrine, which was brought forth in the East during centuries of thought and struggle, the West adopted not much more than the simple notions of Christ, son of God and himself God, God and man in one person, Savior of mankind through his obedient suffering, which took away the sins of the world. But those notions, in their apparent simplicity, could not have been evolved without the whole body of Eastern Christian doctrine on which they rested. In adopting them, the West adopted the quintessence of the work of a different civilization.

It is true that the meaning of that inheritance was at once deeply transformed. What, in the East, had been a *gnosis* and *pistis* destined to lift man from the abyss of his guilt, was made in the West, in apparent crudity, the object of a physical incorporation destined not to eliminate guilt but to enable man to struggle with it. Yet it remains a fact that here much more than mere words were borrowed from the East, that the Eastern tradition was accepted in its real sense and transformed without destroying it. At this moment—and not one moment earlier—the West actually comprehended the meaning of the dogma of the lamb of God that is at the same time the Savior of mankind; this moment and no earlier moment witnessed the actual conversion of the West to Christianity, and at the same time—as is the case with every genuine process of civilization—the birth of an original, independent Western Christianity. Only after this basic act of cultural affiliation could further cultural inheritances—that of Rome, of the Arabs and of the Hellenes—be integrated into Western life.

But this process of cultural affiliation is something very different from the process generally understood by that term. It is not a process continuous in time and contiguous in space. What classical antiquity left behind were ruins disintegrating despite all efforts; and the organizational achievements of the Roman church could not have stopped the disintegration without the new spark. That spark itself, however, was not tied to the cultural inheritance in time or space. It was the free and conscious adoption, at a decisive moment, of an alien cultural inheritance containing a word capable of resolving an impasse. That impasse, in its turn, had arisen, not out of the contact of barbarians with a living past, but out of their contact with a rotting corpse, a contact which, at a certain degree of intensity, had driven those undisrupted primitive civilizations into despair, hence into the search for a way out. Such, strange as it may seem in our mechanical age, are the creative ways of a young and living civilization not in need of accepting its food passively from "superior" neighbors, but perfectly able to find it where it grows most rewardingly. *The Pelagian notion of total personal responsibility, combined with the total acceptance of saving self-punishment symbolized in the Eucharist—that is the kernel of Western civilization.*

CHAPTER TWELVE

Postscriptum:
The *Chanson de Roland*

I

Of all the old French epics, the *Chanson de Roland* is by far the most vigorous, and therefore the one whose magic has endured into the modern age. It is also, as we shall attempt to prove, the earliest Western epic no longer confined to archaic tribal Germanic concepts. Much is therefore to be learned from it about the roots of Western civilization.

But before entering upon an analysis of its content, the question of its date must first be resolved, since we have to know the historical context of its appearance so as to understand its meaning. Part of that question is fairly easily settled by reference to the various locations attributed in the text to the residence of Charlemagne. It is today generally acknowledged by students of the *Chanson* that the bulk of the text, as it has come down to us in the Oxford manuscript, falls roughly into two sections, one of which makes Charles reside in "Ais" (Aix-la-Chapelle), whereas the other locates his residence in "Louën" (Laon). The last-named section must roughly belong to the period when Laon actually was the capital of the French Carlovingians, the years 936–997 A.D. Mireaux, the latest student of the Chanson, has traced, in this section, allusions to the end of the Carlovingian dynasty, brought about by the betrayal of the bishop of Laon. That conjecture seems entirely acceptable. It brings the Laon section of the Chanson down to the years immediately following the downfall of the last Carlovingians, and therefore roughly to the year 1000 A.D.

But textual criticism, in these matters, is far in advance of interpretation of poetical meaning. The latter, in the case of the *Chanson de Roland*, has received scant attention, but deserves study. The "Laon" sections of the *Chanson* are primarily those sections dealing with the mourning for the dead Roland. They are suffused with a somber gloom not paralleled in any later medieval poetry. No wonder, if Mireaux is right and if that section of the Chanson primarily reflects the gloom of the defeated Carlovingian party! But the date itself is also noteworthy. Modern research has added many qualifications to the statement of the chronicler Raoul Glaber, who reported that the West expected the end of the world in 1000 A.D. But Glaber's statement, even if historically incorrect, must yet reflect the mood of his age; an inference confirmed by other contemporary documents ranging over a wide geographical area, from the Norse Völuspa through the last despairing Anglo-Saxon battle-songs and through the Laon section of the *Chanson de Roland* to the Cluniac theological writings. The end of the tenth and the beginning of the eleventh century was a period of unparalleled gloom and mourning, and we should beware of simple explanations, such as references to the barbarian invasions of the age; when the height of gloom was reached, the worst of the invasions were already a thing of the past, the power of the Magyars had been broken, the Normans had adopted Christianity, the Sarazens were in retreat. The reasons for that gloom must lie deeper, and it is precisely an analysis of the *Chanson de Roland* which can throw some light upon them.

But let us first turn to the other, the "Aix" section of the *Chanson*. One of its parts, the "Baligant episode," can be left aside. Though it constitutes no less than a third of the whole poem, it is a later addition, full of allusions to the first crusade, and therefore presumably written a little after 1100 A.D. To this section we shall not return. What about the rest of the Aix section? It is not as obvious as it appears to most students that this part is altogether later than the Laon section, and that the correct location of Charles's capital was due to better historical knowledge. We should have to accept a very late date for this section to make such an argument acceptable, which, as we shall attempt to show, is incompatible with other data. We regard it as likely that the main outlines of the Aix document go back to a period relatively close to Charlemagne's own reign, though at that time, the disaster of Roland in the valley of Roncevalles was probably not treated in an epic, but in short songs such as we know from contemporaneous Scandinavian literature. To determine the content of this oldest shape of the Roland tale is a matter of mere speculation. We may perhaps assume that, in a form similar to that of the Norse songs commemorating succinctly the death of a hero, it related how Count Roland, betrayed by a personal enemy, fell into a trap at Roncevalles and killed thousands of pagans before coming to an heroic end. Upon that brief nucleus the Laon section seems to have elaborated, turning Roland's end, in the style of its own period, into a symbol of the inevitable downfall of all that is great, admirable, and lovable.

But we are only on the brink of our real problem. For most certainly the Laon section and presumably the Aix section have been reshaped at the hands of a great poet who introduces himself to his readers in the last line of the text as it has come down to us:

Ci falt la geste que Turoldus declinet

"Decliner," in the Norman dialect of the Oxford version, means "transform," "reshape." The term thus attests expressly the existence of an older text (presumably indicated by the term "la geste") which Turoldus transformed. The transformation, presumably, concerned both the original parts of the Aix and the whole of the Laon section. But who was this Turoldus? About him a great deal more can be discovered.

His name, to begin with, is a Viking name, Thorold, derived from the Norse god Thor. I do not think that the whole of Norse literature has a single Thor name which does not belong to a member of the aristocracy. Thorold or Turold, then, was a member of the Norman aristocracy. That disposes of the theory that the text, as it lies before us, got its last trimming in the Isle-de-France. The poem, as it lies under our eyes, is of Norman origin. But the query remains: is it of Anglo-Norman or of Franco-Norman origin? To this, too, there is an unambiguous answer.

It is truly astonishing that some of the best scholars have described Turoldus as "unknown". Three times already students of the *Chanson* discovered that a man called "Turold" appears in the famous Bayeux tapestry, generally dated 1077 A.D., depicting the Battle of Hastings and the events leading up to it. Three times, therefore, a connection was established between the Tapestry and the *Chanson*, but three times that find was forgotten by students of French medieval epic literature; in part, perhaps, because the whole significance of the find was not brought out by those who made it. It is necessary, at this point, to go into some detail.

It is not, unfortunately, entirely clear to which figure on the Tapestry the name Turoldus belongs. It might belong either to a person on the left of the inscription, a nobleman taking part in an embassy sent by William the Conqueror to Brittany in 1064; or it could refer to another member of the embassy, a dwarf holding two horses. The inscription stands over the dwarf's head. Since he is a dwarf, he can hardly be a stable servant. But who is he then? The choice between the two figures must remain unsolved. Personally, I prefer the dwarf, on the assumption that a noble warrior, at that early date, would hardly have taken pride in poetry; the age of troubadours and trouvères was not yet. I find it attractive to think of Turoldus as a member of a noble Norman family, cowed and despised owing to a grave physical deformity, and seeking consolation in poetry describing feats of superhuman prowess and at the same time the downfall of even the proudest warriors. But that must remain conjectural.

That one of the two persons in question actually *is* the Turoldus of the *Chanson* is not so conjectural. It is indicated, in the first place, by the astonishing fact that in the whole Tapestry Turoldus is the only figure appearing without an indication of who he was. He must, in consequence, have been a person extremely well-known, so well-known that the designer of the Tapestry assumed that every member of the Norman courts at Caen and at Westminster would at once know who he was. May he not have been known as the poet of the *Chanson*?

That might seem to attribute too much interest in literature to the warriors of the Conqueror. But at this point we can quote another indication, the validity of which has been unduly questioned. Two Anglo-Norman chroniclers, one and two generations after the Battle of Hastings, tell us that on the eve of that decisive battle the *Chanson de Roland* was "sung." "Singing" does not seem a very adequate term, due perhaps to the fact that in the course of time the underlying event was obscured. The Chanson is not fit for community singing and it is too long to be recited in full in one evening. Probably somebody recited sections from it. That somebody is not difficult to detect. Does not the Tapestry indicate clearly enough that Turoldus was directly connected with the battle? Since he was at the Norman court in 1064, since he appears in a work of art devoted to the Hastings battle, since his poem was recited there, what is more natural than to assume that he himself recited it?

In any case, we are now much closer to defining the historical context of the *Chanson* as we know it through the Oxford version. It is Franco-Norman in origin, its author belonged to the Norman aristocracy, it was written not very long before the year 1066 A.D. How long before? That cannot be said with the same assurance. I think, however, that the mention of the recital at Hastings provides a clue. Even two generations after the event, that recital was still remembered as something worthy to be reported. Why? Was it extraordinary to recite poetry on the eve of battle?

Certainly not. Was it due to the fact that the author himself recited his poem? Certainly not, since that was then the normal procedure. Was it due to special interest in the personality of the author? Hardly, since apparently the new version of the *Chanson* was his only major achievement, and interest in personal artistic performance was quite alien to the age. What was it then? I think, and I shall try to show in what follows, that the *Chanson* was at Hastings recited for the first time, that it must have been written quite shortly before the battle, and that its contents were so staggering as to remain unforgotten for ages. So let us now turn to those contents.

The reciting of the Chanson on the eve of that great battle which determined so much of Western history, and was known by the participants in advance to decide many key issues, is not such a matter of course as those who accept the report of it seem to think. The *Chanson* is primarily a gloomy story of defeat, of the hopeless fight of a handful of men against treason and superior strength. Their physical force and their heroism are of no avail, nor is the call for help Roland sends out at the last moment. Charlemagne, it is true, takes his vengeance, the pagan king and all his host are killed, the traitor comes to an ignominious death. But Roland's betrothed dies of sorrow when she learns the news, Charlemagne finds himself bereft of his foremost paladin and in all his mourning finds no consolation. Was this a song fit to be recited to William's hosts, blessed by the Pope, led by a harsh realistic ruler not given to sentiment, with most of the odds in his favor? Was no better choice available? And if, owing to the chance presence of Turoldus in William's camp, it was the *Chanson* and not something more suitable to the moment that was recited, would that have been worth remembering and recording? Or is there a hidden meaning in the *Chanson*, something obvious to the host at Hastings but not so obvious to moderns? That is what I think, and what, I believe, a closer analysis of the *Chanson* reveals. It is noteworthy that what constitutes the central moral issue of the *Chanson* in its Oxford version has been little stressed by most of its students.

II

The battle is about to start. In the dim light of the somber pass of Roncevalles, Roland and his friends become aware of the innumerable host of the pagans surrounding them on all sides. They have been betrayed (it is this betrayal that most commentators stress). There is no hope of victory. What are they going to do? At this moment Roland is approached by Oliver, his closest friend.

> Dist Olliviers: "Paiens unt grant esforz,
> De noz Français m'i semblet aver mult poi.
> Cumpainz Rollanz, kar sunez votre corn:
> Si l'orrat Carles, si returnerat l'oz."
> Respunt Rollanz: "Je fereie que fols;
> En dulce France en pudereie mon los,
> Sempres ferrai de Durendal granz colps. . . ."

> Says Oliver: "Pagans in force abound,
> While of us Franks but very few I count,
> Comrade Rollanz, your horn I pray you sound!
> If Charlès hear, he'll turn his armies round."
> Answers Rollanz: "A fool I should be found;
> In France the Douce would perish my renown.
> With Durendal I'll lay on thick and stout."[1]

With the brevity characteristic of Nordic poetry—and the Chanson de Roland with all its problems remains unintelligible without reference to Viking morality and values—the moral problem is put, exactly as a moral dilemma is at the bottom of every Norse saga. Faced with overwhelming odds, Oliver advises they should call for help. Roland regards it as a dishonorable proposition; he will only trust his good sword Durendal. And the debate, the utterly characteristic Viking debate, continues.

> "Cumpainz Rollanz, l'olifant cor sunez
> Si l'orrat Carles, fera l'ost returner.
> Sucurrat nus li reis od sun barnet."
> Respunt Rollanz: "Ne placet Damne Deu
> Que mi parent pur mei sient blamet,
> Ne dulce France cheit en viltet,
> Ains i ferrai de Durendal asez. . . ."

> "Comrade Rollanz sound the olifant, I pray;
> If Charlès hear, the host he'll turn again;
> Will succour us our King and baronage."
> Answers Rollanz: "Never, by God, I say,
> For my misdeed shall kinsmen hear the blame.
> Nor France the Douce fall into evil fame!
> Rather stout blows with Durendal I'll lay. . . ."

1. This translation, and those given subsequently, are taken, by kind permission of Chapman and Hall, from *The Song of Roland*, trans. by Charles Scott Moncrieff.

The honor of the clan (mi parent) and of the tribe (dulce France) would be tainted by a call for help. A proud man must stand by himself alone. The "olifant," the horn, may apparently be used for gathering the host under its commander, but not for a call to the king for succor. And the debate goes on.

> "Cumpainz Rollanz, sunez votre olifant:
> Si l'orrat Carles ki est a porz passant
> Je vous plevis, ja returnerunt Franc."
> "Ne placet Deu," co li respunt Rollanz,
> "Que co seit dit de nul hume vivant
> Ne pur paien que ja seie cornant.
> Ja n'en avrunt reproece mi parent. . . ."

> "Comrade Rollanz, once sound your olifant!
> If Charlès hear, where in the pass he stands,
> I pledge you now, they'll turn again, the Franks."
> "Never, by God," then answers him Rollanz,
> "Shall it be said by any living man,
> That for pagans I took my horn in hand.
> Never by me shall men reproach my clan."

The repetitive statement is a particularly impressive poetic device. Roland, indeed, has no more to say but that it is against his honor. Oliver, therefore, is compelled to contest the absolute validity of the *point d'honneur* and to oppose to it practical considerations.

> Dist Ollivier: 'D'ico ne sai ja blasme
> Jo aie veut les Sarrazins d'Espaigne:
> Cuvert en sunt li val i les muntainges,
> E li lariz et trestutes les plaignes.
> Granz sunt les oz de cele gent estrange;
> Nus i avum mult petite campaigne.'
> Respunt Rollanz: 'Mis talenz en est graindre.
> Ne placet Deu ne ses seintimes angles
> Que ja pur mei perdet sa valur France!'
> Mielz voeill murir que huntage m'atteignet
> Pur bein ferir l'Emperere nus aimet.'

> Says Oliver: "In this I see no blame;
> I have beheld the Sarrazins of Spain;
> Covered with them, the mountains and the vales,
> The wastes I saw, and all the farthest plains.
> A muster great they've made, these people strange;

> We have of men a very little tale."
> Answers Rollanz: "My anger is inflamed.
> Never, please God His Angels and His Saints,
> Never by me shall Frankish valour fail!
> Rather I'll die than shame shall me attain.
> Therefore strike on, the Emperour's love to gain."

The emperor, Roland says, has no use for an army of cowards. And at this point, with admirable laconic precision, the poet steps in with his own balanced judgment.

> Rollanz est pruz et Olliviers est sages.
> Ambedui unt merveillus vasselage.
>
> Pride hath Rollanz, wisdom Oliver hath;
> And both of them show marvellous courage.

Thorold takes pains to make us understand that, while Roland, as the course of the battle will show, has somewhat greater physical strength than Oliver, the latter is not one whit less valiant than his friend. But whereas Roland's only quality is "prowess," the typical conduct of the savage, lone-fighting Viking hero, Oliver disposes of a new quality which has no place in the original Viking code: *Sagesse*, judgment.

The debate continues, in unchanged terms, down to the point where the battle starts, a battle where, by his deeds, Oliver proves that in the matter of valiance he is fully Roland's equal. But the poet, speaking through the terms of his description, and using with marvellous skill elements of the first gloomy version for a new and different purpose, does not hide his own view, based not upon subjective but upon objective factors.

> "Tant bons Français perdent leur juvente!
> Ne reverront lur meres ne lur femmes,
> Ne cels de France qui as porz les atendent.
> Carles li Magnes en plurat, ni se dementet.
> De ço ki colt? N'en avunt succurance."
>
> "So many Franks lose their young lustihead,
> Who'll see no more their mothers nor their friends,
> Nor hosts of France that in the pass attend.
> Charlès the Great weeps therefore with regret.
> What profits that? No succour shall they get."

The Emperor, as Roland says, has certainly no use for cowards. Yet is he not right in shedding tears over the loss of all those proud warriors who might have been saved so easily? But the battle goes on, and it takes the poet another thirty-six stanzas before Roland, convinced by disaster, changes his mind:

> Co dist Rollanz: "Cornerai l'olifant.
> Si l'orrat Carles, ki est a porz passant:
> Je vus plevis, ja returnerunt Franc."
> Dist Oliviers: "Verguigne serait grant
> Et reprover a trestuz vos parents.
> Iceste hunte durreit l'ur vivant.
> Quant je l'vus dist, n'en feistes nient.
> Mais ne l'ferez par le mien loement.
> Si vous cornez, n'iert mie hardiment."

> Then says Rollanz: "I'll wind this olifant,
> If Charles hear, where in the pass he stands,
> I pledge you now they will return the Franks."
> Says Oliver: "Great shame would come of that;
> And a reproach on every one, your clan,
> That shall endure while each lives on the land.
> When I implored, you would not do this act,
> Doing it now, no praise from me you'll have."

And in the next stanza Oliver threatens to shame Roland before his betrothed Alde, Oliver's sister, so that she will never lie with him. The denouement now arrives:

> Co dist Rollanz: "Pur que me portez ire?"
> E cil [Oliver] respunt: "Cumpainz, vus le feistes;
> *Kar vasselage par sens n'en est folie;*
> *Mielz valt mesure que ne fait estultie.*
> *Francais sunt mort par votre legerie*
> Carles jamais de nus n'aurat service.
> Si m'creissez, venuz i fut mis sire,
> Ceste bataille oussum faite et prise,
> O pris o morz i fust li reis Marsilies.
> Vostre proesse, Rollant, mar la veismes.
> Carles li magnes de nus n'aurat aie:
> N'ient mais tels hums desques a l'Deu juise.
> *Vus i murrez, et France, en nert hunie.*
> Hai nus defait la leial cumpaignie:
> Einz le vespre ierst mult grief la departie."

Then says Rollanz: "Wherefore so wroth with me?"
He answers him: "Comrade, it was your deed:
Vassalage comes by sense, and not folly;
Prudence more worth is than stupidity.
Here are Franks dead for all your trickery;
No more service to Carlun may we yield.
My lord was here now, had you trusted me,
And fought and won this battle then had we,
Taken or slain were the king Marsilie.
In your prowess, Rollanz, no good we've seen!
Charlès the Great in vain your aid will seek—
None such as he till God his Judgment speak—
Here must you die, and France in shame be steeped;
Here perishes our loyal company,
Before this night great severance and grief."

Then Roland, in rage and shame, sounds the horn until his temples burst, and thus he dies.

III

There are in the finest kind of poetry key passages entirely self-explanatory, where mere quotation is tantamount to interpretation. This is here the case. No shadow of doubt remains about the poet's meaning, about his conclusion. Knightly conduct does not imply folly, measure is better than proud stupidity, Roland has destroyed the army by his irresponsibility, thus bringing upon his head much greater shame than by the sounding of the horn. And it only adds to his shame—a fact Oliver brings out by threatening Roland that he will dishonor him in the eyes of his bride—that now, when it is patently too late, the violent fool, unable to accept frankly the consequences of his folly, sounds the horn—to no purpose.

The poetic beauty of Turoldus's epic, however, resides in the balance he establishes between this severe censure of Roland's actions and a deep understanding of his motives. The obvious didactic purpose of the poet does not blind him in the least to human tragedy. Not only does he take over and perhaps enhance all those stories of the unparalleled prowess of his hero which must, in part at least, go back to the earliest version of the Roland saga. Not only does he show full understanding of the need for such "valiance" in knightly combat. Beyond all this, he also understands that a fire-eater such as Roland must act exactly as he does, that it is inconceivable for him to subordinate the impulse to fight alone to a thoughtful weighing of chances. As Roland is, thus he must be, thus he is adorable, much as the poet, in a wider wisdom ("sagesse") disapproves of his conduct as a principle of military action. By this profound human understanding he raises his poem to the level of stark tragedy.

This tragedy, like all great tragedy in world literature, immediately assumes a meaning far wider than the personal conflict which specifically embodies it. The tragedy is by no means Roland's own tragedy alone; it is the tragedy of the lone wolf enhanced by Scandinavian poetry. That poetry had expressed its deepest meaning in the figure of the great outlaw who, dragged into crime by the demands of a warrior's honor, stands up alone against the whole community for years, finally to perish in tragic heroism. Roland's action, his refusal to rely on the community to which he belongs, tends essentially to this type of personal fulfilment. But the day of the lone wolf is gone. To the tragedy of final defeat in the struggle against society, which is the essence of the early Scandinavian sagas and was also implicit in the Laon version of the Roland saga, there is now added the more profound tragedy of quixotic action out of social and historical context. In Turoldus' version, the *Chanson de Roland* is a precursor of Cervantes' great satire. As Cervantes proclaims the end of the age of the knights-errant, so Turoldus proclaims the end of the age of the lone Nordic warrior, who is the more admirable the more he stands alone.

The intimate merging of didactic purpose and sense of tragedy not only confers poetical beauty upon Turoldus' epic, it also enabled it to fulfil a definite sociopsychological function. For a century before Hastings, the Dukes of Normandy had striven successfully to bend the Viking warriors under their iron hand. The Norman knights must have been acutely aware of the length of the road they had travelled since their ancestors had roughly taken possession of the rich coastlands at the mouth of the Seine, and the process cannot have been much to their liking. The *Chanson*, therefore, must be reckoned among those literary products which are helpful in bringing about adaptation to bitter but inevitable realities. The poet is out to show that the ideal of a warrior's prowess is not diminished by subordination to the collective purposes of the community at war. He helps his audience to integrate into their personalities the harsh demands of personal service to a master and of submission to his ends. He teaches them a sense of responsibility, he proclaims that prowess without such responsibility is shameful. Not all his listeners on that portentous eve-of-battle meeting will have agreed with him. But none of them, we may be sure, missed the point, so entirely missed by most modern commentators.

But the poet rendered his subtlest service not to his great master, the Conqueror, whose aims no doubt he profoundly understood and shared, but to his more humble listeners whom he led out of a psychological impasse. The new discipline was not simply an outside force breaking destructively into a well-integrated sociopsychological structure. For at least a century, the Nordic world had sunk into deeper and deeper gloom precisely owing to the incompatibility of the lone-wolf ideal with the higher level of social integration reached in the Western world from the middle of the tenth century onwards. By making his audience see all that is quixotic, irresponsible, and simply stupid in that lone-wolf ideal he diminishes its prestige, and helps his listeners to discard what is antiquated and to transform what is still adaptable in that ideal. The new notion of knightly service to which, for the first time, he gives poetic beauty and thereby esthetic and ultimately moral sanction, represents not only a social necessity, but also a way out of the absolute despondency characteristic of the poetry and thought of the preceding age, and helps to open the way to that broad cultural movement known as the "renaissance of the twelfth century," distinguished by its assertive optimism. A look at that glory, the *Abbaye des Hommes* in Caen, that structure shining in clarity, grandeur, and light, whose construction followed the *Chanson* and the Battle of Hastings by only a decade, due to the joint efforts of the Conqueror, of his archbishop Lanfranc and of a great anonymous architect, shows that in the world from which the *Chanson* issued a new spirit was born.

Here a word is perhaps in order concerning the specific circumstances which gave birth to Turoldus' version of the *Chanson*. It is somewhat surprising that of all the many heroic tales at their disposal, the Conqueror and his entourage chose precisely the chronologically and geographically distant Roncevalles epic as a medium to express their thoughts. Before Turoldus, allusions to the Roland saga appear here and there in the sources, but few and far between; it is only after Hastings that the prestige of this saga suddenly reveals itself in numerous traces. Why then precisely Roncevalles?

An obvious explanation offers itself. No more than two years before Hastings the Western world had witnessed the first proto-crusade, the attack of a Western host, largely consisting of Norman knights, upon the town of Barbastro in Aragon, then one of the richest towns of Europe. The Sarazens were driven from the town, which was sacked and subjected to every kind of outrage. Then, a few months' life with the refinements of Oriental civilization were enough to disintegrate the Western host completely. The Sarazens counterattacked, retook the town, and destroyed the Christian army. Turoldus, since he shows a total ignorance of Spanish geography, cannot have taken part in the campaign. But it is inconceivable that a man living at William's court should not have known the Barbastro story in all its human detail. In the passage describing how the traitor Ganelon succumbs to the seduction of Moorish refinement he reveals an understanding of what had happened at Barbastro. But most of all it was probably Barbastro which attracted the attention of the Norman court to Spain and to the Roncevalles saga.

That dates the birth of the Turoldus version roughly to the year 1065 A.D., and also gives it an even more precise meaning. At Barbastro, the Norman knights had behaved without purpose and without discipline. The Conqueror and his entourage must have been well aware of the need to provide against a repetition of such events. The *Chanson de Roland* served to bring home the moral. The lesson was well learned; witness again the Bayeux tapestry, where we watch the Norman cavalry, riding behind their banners and attacking in serried ranks the valiant but disorderly host of Harold's *Huskarlar*. Turoldus's epic and the Bayeux tapestry convey the same lesson, the lesson which was the essence of the Conqueror's system, and more important to him in his victories than the use of cavalry against infantry and other technical devices.

IV

I hope thus to have shown that the *Chanson de Roland* corresponds to one of the most incisive moments in the history of Western civilization, to the final break with the aboriginal Germanic tradition of lonely prowess. It would be easy to define this break in terms of the victory of "sagesse," in other words, of rational conduct, over the berserk furor of the typical Nordic warrior. But that, while not incorrect in itself, represents an inadmissible simplification. The full meaning of the great innovation which took place in Normandy at that epoch can only be brought out by comparison with parallel moments in the development of other civilizations, and, in the first place, with that of classical antiquity.

If we accept, as most modern scholars do, a fairly late date for the shaping of the *Iliad* and an even later one for the *Odyssey*, then an arguable parallel emerges between the role of the *Iliad* in Hellenic and of the

Chanson de Roland in Western history. It need not unduly disturb us that the *Chanson*, regardless of its enormous prestige, never acquired quite that unchallenged authority which Homer enjoyed among the Hellenes; that was mainly due to the competition between knightly and ecclesiastical views, traditions, and writings, for which there was no parallel in ancient Greece.

But even apart from this, what a profound contrast between the one and the other! This contrast resides, in the first place, in the hidden dramatic character of the *Chanson*, so sharply opposed to the genuinely epic character of the *Iliad*. In Homer a broad tale of interesting events, enjoyed in all their details; in Turoldus a crisp drama, mounting to its tragic climax through a conflict within the soul of the two protagonists, Roland and Oliver, expressing itself in a tragic clash between them; corresponding to this, in Homer, an expansive *prolixe* type of speech, full of similes and thus sharply contrasting with the brevity which characterizes the debates of the *Chanson* no less than those of its Norse precursors. In contrast to the harmonious ideals of classical antiquity, an essential characteristic of Western civilization is here foreshadowed: the compulsion to choose between mutually exclusive principles of conduct.

Investigation of points of detail reveals some of the roots of this contrast. In what it regards as generally accepted values, the *Iliad* is presumably nearest to that oldest version of the Roland saga which is wholly lost to us. In both cases prowess seems to be the most esteemed virtue. But already in this earliest version, the Roland story must have stressed struggle against overwhelming odds and a lonely end in a way totally unknown to Homer; already, loneliness seems to be a chief attribute of the Western hero, whereas the Hellenic warrior finds himself embedded in a texture of social contacts from which he never emerges into true solitude.

But the really decisive fact is that the Greek conception, at bottom, never transcends this starting point. Those Homeric heroes remained the poetical models of conduct down to the end of Greek civilization. It is as if the present models of our own civilization were still the Beowulf, the Edda, the early Icelandic sagas and the Laon version of the *Chanson*. In political life and in military techniques, the Hellenic and even more so the Roman world far outpaced the Homeric beginnings, but not in poetry, which is the ultimate sanction of values and reflects the integration of ideals into the typical personality structure of a given age. Here we directly touch upon the reasons for the collapse of classical civilization.

Where the Hellenes stopped, the West at once went forward to say it again. The late Edda, the early saga, the Laon version poetry embodies a lone-wolf ideal where mere personal prowess transforms itself into the starkest imaginable tragedy. The hero *must* perish, that is almost part of his definition, and therefore all life is infinitely sad. It is as if the fate of Achilles were proclaimed the common fate of all noble beings. But the lone-wolf ideal is not simply veneration of the man who (like Ibsen's "enemy of the people" a thousand years later) "stands all by himself." The saga heroes, as well as the Roland of the Laon version, are dragged to their fate, not by a coarse desire to fight it out on every suitable or unsuitable occasion, but by their unwilling involvement in inescapable obligations dictated by society and embodied in the notion of honor.

To this central Western notion there is no counterpart in classical antiquity, the Greek term *timé* and the Latin term *honos* carrying entirely different connotations. A proof of the difference is that a sulking Achilles, a wily Odysseus, while they may have their counterpart in early Nordic and Western fiction, cannot even be conceived as the model heroes they are in Homer. There exists, in the Edda, the sagas and the early French epics, an inescapable punctilio of faultless conduct, inescapable because this punctilio is seen as being identical with the core of the nobleman's person itself, so that an infringement of the rules of conduct is tantamount to spiritual death. This is no more than a definition of the very notion of honor. The Greeks knew nothing of it. It is based on that very un-Hellenic notion, the value of a solitary soul—a notion which, as every study of early Western poetry reveals, anteceded Christianity and gave Western Christianity its specific moralistic tinge.

The most characteristic feature of this aboriginal Western concept of Man is its "holism," its refusal to admit that man is a pluralistic being, its unquestioning assumption that in its every act a soul reveals itself as a whole. It is this "holism," again preceding all higher developments of Western civilization, which from the beginning turned the Western mind towards a systematic approach in all matters, and in particular towards long-winded debates about ultimate moral principles which, beginning with the Edda, issue finally into the poetry of Shakespeare and Racine. It was this "holism" which was incompatible with a merely practical adaptation to new necessities, such as Greek civilization achieved in its later stages. To Hellenes, military discipline and rational conduct in the service of the community were acceptable; but their submission to them was superficial—as that of Southern Europeans is even today. To the Germanic warrior, the Viking in particular, such submission was at first incompatible with his personal integrity, and, to become acceptable, had to be integrated into the very depths of his personality structure.

Actually, of course, the two notions of personal honor and social discipline remained at war throughout the long feudal age. But it is also noteworthy that, where originally rejection of all subordination and practical rationality had been most complete—in the Viking world—submission to rigid discipline and to the purposes of the state was later also the most complete. It is from the Norman kingdoms that centralized administration and rational government permeated the rest of the Western world. We have hinted at the role which Turoldus played in creating the ideology of that transformation. But more important than his immediate services is the fact that in doing so he anticipated history by centuries. The centralism of the Conqueror was a short-lived experiment, and the four rulers who followed him on the English throne wasted his inheritance. The morality defended by Turoldus, in the final analysis, seems better suited to the Spanish infantry, the Swiss and Swabian *Landsknechte* of the fifteenth and sixteenth, and to the Spanish and French monarchy of the sixteenth and seventeenth, than to the Norman monarchy of the eleventh century. Yet it must not be forgotten that Henry II of England, Philipp Augustus of France, Frederick II, German Emperor and Norman King of Sicily, and last but not least the great Popes from Gregory VII onwards had striven after exactly such an ideal. At the very beginnings of civilized Western poetry Turoldus implicitly proclaims the ideas which have guided the modern state in its history.

In all this, one essential question still remains unanswered: which force was it that proved strong enough to carry the load of this incredible transformation of lone-wolf prowess into disciplined subordination? To this, the *Chanson* affords only a partial reply. At every point it invokes the duty towards the Emperor. And there actually is no doubt that this appeal, far from being merely reminiscent and poetic, carries a practical political meaning. The Norman dukes *did* attempt to appropriate for themselves the traditions of the Carlovingian empire. At this point the basic meaning of the Laon and of the Turoldus versions intertwine. The author of the Laon version had shed tears over the downfall of the Carlovingian dynasty and over the disappearance of the idea of centralized discipline which Charlemagne's heirs had, however ineffectually, defended. It is a mistake to imagine that the transition from Carlovingian to Capetian rule meant nothing. It meant precisely the frank abandonment of the crown to the egoistic claims of feudalism. If Turoldus takes up Carlovingian ideals in the name of his master, we perceive how the Conqueror himself wished to achieve Carlovingian aims by more efficient methods, in the more propitious Norman milieu.

Yet, however much Norman tradition may have furthered his plans, the decisive impulse, no doubt, did not come out of this milieu, but from an outside force. It was not the Norman knighthood, but the French Church, then shining in the glorious climax of the Cluniac monastic movement, which had transformed the self-assertive prowess of the warring nobleman into the self-denying prowess of the ascetic nobleman. The *Militia Domini*, which the Conqueror attempted to enforce, would have been meaningless to his knights, had it not been preceded by the stark heroic reality of the *Militia Dei* as practiced by the Cluniacs; a practice and a scale of values rooted, unlike the prowess of William's warriors, not in early Norse, but in early Irish traditions. But that is a different story.

PART THREE

Reflections on Present and Future

CHAPTER ONE

After the Atom:
Life out of Death or Life in Death?
[1947]

Suppose there should be another world war, what will be the destiny of Western civilization? I am not predicting that there will be another world war. It is too early for positive assertions in this matter. But few people will deny that it is a real possibility. In view of the uncertainty of coming events speculations based upon the worst may seem a piece of irresponsible scare-mongering. But *if* the worst happens, there may be scant opportunity for contemplation after the event. With wide-open eyes and knowing the stakes, we are facing the possibility of ultimate disaster coming to us in perhaps less than a score of years. Is it not our duty to do our best to think out the implications while there is still time to think, to try now to envisage the worst case? In smaller matters it may be wise to let an emergency come, and to trust nature to find a remedy. In supreme issues such as these, indifference, not foresight, is the final capitulation.

Trying to visualize the shape of the world after a supposed atomic war, we must first register the foreseeable elements in such a clash. Assuming that the Western democracies are at present still sole possessors of the secret of the atomic bomb, these Western powers would find their military advantage in striking now, in making preventive war. No eighteenth-century cabinet and few nineteenth-century cabinets would have shrunk from such a decision (they had no atomic bombs at their disposal, of course, and the stakes were infinitely smaller). But it is certain that neither America nor Britain will go to preventive war now. The struggle against Hitler has amply proved that no Anglo-Saxon democracy of our age ever fights a war except under direct threat of extinction; and the present trend towards military retrenchment in both countries, in the midst of growing international tension, confirms this forecast. There will never be war unless a totalitarian power goes to war. As the twentieth century proceeds, the story about capitalist imperialism inevitably going to war has become complete nonsense and vicious demagogy. The only problem is whether totalitarian dictatorships can be prevented from going to war in the long run. I am not going to try to answer this query at present.

But if Russia, the one big remaining totalitarian power, should at some time go to war, we should not imagine that she will follow in Hitler's footsteps. Germany was quite unsuited for the task of world domination, and only a maniac with an hysterical following could make the attempt—apart from the invitation to try proferred by Chamberlain, Daladier, and the rest. Next time, if there is to be another time, there will presumably be no such attempt at abject surrender on the part of the democracies, but also the aggressor will not go to war with such hectic and fundamentally inadequate preparation as Hitler did. It is, among other things, quite unlikely that Stalin himself wants war or will make war. No man of his age would hanker after such ordeals. If, at some later time, Russia goes to war, she will have tested the ground well in advance, and thoroughly, and will feel sure of success. The *present* high state of international tension is largely, though not exclusively, bluff.

Now, it is one thing for the Russians to feel sure of victory and quite another thing for them to win. I am convinced that for the most deep-seated reasons no totalitarian power is capable of correctly assessing the balance of strength between its own power and that of its democratic adversaries. Dictatorships cannot understand the intrinsic strength which lurks behind the surface weaknesses of democracy. And a totalitarian dictatorship cannot even correctly assess the various technical factors affecting the overall balance of strength, because no country, in an atmosphere of propaganda and terrorism, can properly assess its own defects and its adversary's advantages. Not for a moment do I doubt that the democracies will win in the end, though a dictatorship always feels sure of victory in the beginning. All dictatorships overrate themselves; also all democracies tend to underrate their own strength. The West is immensely ahead of Russia in industrial potential, and that means in the power of its weapons. Russia, despite all the blustering arrogance of the Communists, takes a very low place on the list of those countries which might catch up with America. If a Russian leader should cross the boundary line between peace and war, he would doubtless destroy a great empire, but it would be his own.

Unfortunately, that optimistic forecast does not exhaust the problem. Should Russia go to war, she would first make good all damage done by the last war, she would certainly have carried political permeation of her enemies to the highest obtainable degree, and she would also certainly have the atomic bomb and far-distance missiles to hit directly across the ocean. In the meantime, undoubtedly, the Western world would not have lost its present advantages in the race of scientific warfare, and would have developed weapons still more terrible. That would give it victory. But Russia would not go to war without possessing weapons capable of working terrific destruction in the heart of the territory of her enemies. That is the position from which to start any argument about future civilization after an atomic war.

It is exceptional for civilizations to disappear in one crash. It has happened, in the case of the Aztecs, of the Incas, of the Assyrians, though in the last case only after a preliminary period of decline. It is not likely to happen with a structure as big as Western civilization. But at the same time, it would be a gross mistake to expect our civilization to issue from every disaster with renewed vigor. The continent of Europe, the heart of Western civilization, is already in a process of decline so obvious, so penetrating and so rapid, that the most serious doubts about the possibility of full recovery are justified. If the English-speaking countries receive a similar blow in a future world war, the chances are that they will go the same way, though perhaps not so fast. The disproportion between tasks and means would probably become too large to be overcome. After victory, the English-speaking countries would find themselves in virtual control of our planet, but their resources, reduced by terrific destruction, would hardly be adequate for shouldering the task. Yet peace could only be preserved by maintaining English-speaking world supremacy. Every great war increases the dependence of the ruling classes, whatever their structure, upon the masses. Yet, amidst general destruction, the demands of the masses for a higher standard of living could not be fulfilled, and it is not likely that the normal mechanism of production could be made to work again while these demands remain unfulfilled. The great conflicts in the political field would be resolved, the road to an Augustan age would be open, but, as after the end of the Roman civil wars, there would be few people to enjoy it, the recovery would be largely fictitious, promise and meaning would have gone out of life. The new world empire would rest on universal exhaustion rather than on strength, and, in view of the terrific destruction preceding its creation, it would presumably be more short-lived than were other world empires.

The flaw in this whole argument is that it is too mechanical, or, if you will, too pragmatic, meaning by "pragmatic" too much tied to the chain of cause and effect, neglecting the vast basic general trend, which will find its way whatever the details of future history. It might be argued with considerable justification that a healthy civilization always overcomes the worst disasters, as Western civilization overcame the death, within two years, of a third of Europe's population during the "black death" epidemic in the fourteenth century. Conversely, a declining civilization might fade out even without a major catastrophe, or, more exactly, would find any normal conflict developing into a major catastrophe because it is no longer able to cope with normal problems. It is also possible to point up the links between the evolutionary and the pragmatic point of view. If our Western civilization were still healthy, would it show our present high social tensions? Would it have tolerated, and still tolerate, the repeated challenge by alien totalitarian forces, refusing to strike at them up to the moment of supreme necessity? Is the totalitarian menace really so strong intrinsically? Is it really the case that Germany, under a madman's rule, and Russia with half her population still living in straw-covered huts, were bound to become serious threats to the West? Is it not rather fatigue and inertia in the Western world, reluctance to make sacrifices in time, which has made the challenge so serious? No doubt Churchill was right in calling the war against Hitler the most unnecessary of all wars.

Only against this wider background is there an answer to the query about the future. We may ask ourselves whether it is worthwhile defending a civilization showing so much intrinsic weakness. But once already in our generation, when the ultimate challenge came, the West proved itself less weak than it appeared to be. Only, in the event of a third world war, the alternative will be different. The real alternative will not, as in the case of the anti-Nazi war, be surrender without a fight or survival through a terrific fight. It will be submission to totalitarian slavery or a war which *must*, inevitably, mark the beginning of a sharp decline of the Western world, even *after* victory has been won. The nature of this specific challenge is not yet clearly realized. As usual, we are thinking in terms of last time's danger, while, by our good will and our retrenchment policy, we busily prepare an entirely different challenge to ourselves. We think in terms of a possible hard struggle to preserve freedom. We should think in terms of a struggle where, indeed, we may preserve freedom, but at the price of remaining maimed for the rest of our existence as a civilization. Only when this true character of the challenge will become apparent will the real temptation to give in arise. Yet, in view of what has happened since 1914, and of what is happening now, I am convinced that the West, if challenged, will take up the challenge and win. This, I do not doubt, will be the decision of the West if the worst happens, whatever the consequences.

But *why is a relapse into barbarism, with all the dreadful things it means for the individual and for the community, preferable to enslavement to a totalitarian power?* The answer can be found in a comparative analysis of various types of decaying civilization.

As far as I can see, the decay of civilization invariably takes place along one of two alternative lines of development, two alternative trends which lead to either slavery or barbarism. To some extent, these two types are mutually exclusive.

I can think of no better illustration of my thought than the story of the Struldbrugs in the third book of Gulliver's Travels. Swift, as my readers may remember, speaks of a race of men enjoying eternal life on this earth, men who are blessed with the exemption from life's most bitter ingredient, from death; men who cannot die, the most happy, nay, the most unhappy of all men. For it would be asking too much of the Creator, so Swift says, to endow them not only with immortality but at the same time with eternal youth. All they achieve is the unbearable dotage of an eternal old age, of bottomless melancholy, of boundless hatred of all life. It is a vision, intended successfully to cure men of the desire to avoid death. It is only a vision—where individuals are concerned. In the case of civilizations it is a reality. We are surrounded by Struldbrug civilizations, and a very unpleasant sight they are.

Amidst the nations of the West, the Jews present the clearest case of such a Struldbrug civilization, and the whole Jewish tragedy really comes down to this fact. The individual members of the Jewish community can perhaps individually, with great difficulty, escape the curse of cultural Struldbrugism, by intermarriage with Gentiles, by total assimilation, by cutting their ties with their community and blending into their surroundings. But a Jewish community, as long as any exists, will be a Struldbrug community.

Swift speaks of the moment when individuals, so far normal, though singled out by a mark on their heads as future Struldbrugs, become aware of their Struldbrug existence, and cease to be normal men. In the emergence of Struldbrug civilizations, there are such moments, too, moments when a civilization stops both growing *and* declining, becomes impermeable to any transformation from within, so as to remain identical to itself, unchanging for all times in its inner structure, changing only as the result of favorable or destructive interference from without. In the Jewish case, which is perhaps slightly more marked and paradigmatic than other similar cases to be mentioned soon, this moment of turning from normal growth and aging to Struldbrugism can be named and dated. It is the year 69 A.D., when the destruction of the Temple appeared inevitable to all except a few maniacs, and when, in view of the inevitable fall, Rabbi Jokhanaan ben Sakkai made his own private peace with the Romans, and in exchange got leave to found the university of Yabne. On the day of the fall of the Holy City, Rabbi Jokhanaan gave his disciples the watchword that, now that the center of the cult was destroyed, the "law" must be the only binding tie of Judaism, and that hence a final, unambiguous fixing of the contents of the law was a life-and-death question for the survival of Jewry.

I have experienced few things more tragic than watching young Jews (in internment as "enemy aliens" during the war) hotly discussing the rights and wrongs of that decision, and of the political lines of the various Jewish parties involved in the rising of 66–70 A.D. as if they discussed the rights and wrongs of Churchill vs. Chamberlain in 1939–40. The time-lessness of that debate, the irrelevance of nearly two thousand years of history intervening between the founding of Yabne University in 69 A.D. and the internment of young Jews as enemy aliens in Britain in 1940 A.D., made a ghastly impression upon me. Yet their attitude was perfectly apposite. For though there have been significant developments in the field of theology, metaphysics, and law in the Jewish community since, these developments only led to the expulsion of their standard bearers from the Jewish community. The community as a whole has since struck to Yabne lines, and in the sense of real historical time—as distinct from abstract chronological time—the problem of Yabne vs. Jerusalem—rab-binic religion vs. Jewish State—was more immediate to these Jews than the fight of Churchill vs. Chamberlain, already well outdated by events, could be to any reasonable Englishman during the blitz winter of 1940–41. Admittedly Zionism, as A. J. Toynbee has pointed out, is an attempt to organize Jews as a Western nation and to break with the tradition of a purely rabbinic community. As far as this attempt succeeds, it will inevitably lead away one section of Jewry from their own culture, and, by a more or less clean break with the past, will make them part of the Western world. But this is not inner development, as little as the parliamentary representation of West Indian Negroes is an outcrop of African culture. Any part of Jewry which remains fixed upon its own foundations, rather than going over wholesale to an alien civilization, will remain tied to the Yabne tradition, without change or alteration. As likely as not, in the end, the Zionist movement will split into one section completely adopting Western ways and another one returning to Yabne. At any rate, even if this should not be so, Jewry, for eighteen hundred years, has remained timeless, unchanged, and unmovable. That is the exact meaning of cultural Struldbrugism.

We have chosen the Jewish case merely because it is obvious to everybody's eyes and can be understood without much reference to historical and anthropological material. But once the basic facts of this case have been pointed out, other similar cases come to mind. There are, in the first place, a number of small cases structurally parallel to the Jewish case to such an extent as to be practically identical. What about those Parsees who, in the beginning of the seventh century A.D., fled before the Arab onslaught and have lived on in India ever since? Their vernacular, but not their sacred idiom has been transformed—as is the case with the Jews—yet without becoming identical with the idiom of the population surrounding them—also as with unassimilated Jews; the parallel could be carried much further. What about those so-called "Assyrians"; in fact, the last remnant of the once great and mighty Nestorian civilization? What about the Copts, the Armenians, the endless variety of religious and cultural residues complicating the structure of modern Syria, and making it so thoroughly archaic in type?

Our planet is strewn with Struldbrug civilizations, with cultures neither growing nor decaying, cultures no longer changing in time, cultures which can only remain what they are or disintegrate and perish under outside pressure—civilizations timeless, invertebrate, ossified.

I do not intend to go into too much detail, important though a discussion of details might be in a different context, for I do not want to go beyond what is necessary to illustrate our present problem. It needs stating, though, that, in contrast to Swift's poetical vision, Struldbrug cultures are in reality not absolutes, that, in contrast to Swift's Struldbrugs, they can die, if only by outside interference, and also that there are transitional cases. I do not think it is quite impossible, even for civilizations which seem totally ossified, to undergo a transformation and, instead of falling to ashes, to come alive again under the life-giving impact of other, younger civilizations. I believe it is even possible to evolve a casuistry of such possibilities—but here is not the place to do it. Before studying shades, main types must be clearly defined.

There exists an opposite type of decline, which is typified by the decline of Rome. To an amazing extent, Roman civilization did not ossify, and never stopped developing, though this statement is only partly true. The Greek provinces of the Roman Empire did partly ossify into Byzantine civilization. Byzantine civilization is one of those border cases where it is as impossible to speak of complete ossification as of full and complete natural growth. That part of the Empire became finally ossified only in an alien shell, as part of the Turkish Empire. The case is relevant to our own problem, for obviously the ossification of our modern Western civilization within the shell of Russian rule would provide a close parallel. But the Western part of the Roman Empire "relapsed into barbarism," and, after the "dark ages," evolved into another more powerful civilization, pregnant with immensely bigger achievements. It would be easy, again, to point to other historical parallels, which we shall leave aside. One element of the situation working, in this case, for relapse into barbarism rather than Struldbrugism was the belatedness of Roman civilization, the fact that Rome only half belonged to the higher civilization of classical antiquity, that its more important growth belonged to the latest phase of that civilization, that, originally at least, it was on the fringe of that civilization geographically. The parallel with the position of modern America is striking, and I should not shrink from drawing the obvious inferences about the future.

For the Roman citizen of the fifth century it was no doubt greatly preferable to inhabit Byzantium rather than Rome. The life of Byzantium may have been oppressive in many directions, but its citizens enjoyed the benefits of law and order, of learning and manners, of cults and arts proper to a higher civilization. The inhabitants of Rome were helplessly exposed to the murdering, looting, and raping of the hosts of Alaric and Genseric, and watched the city falling into ruins and the countryside becoming deserted. But, looking backwards, we can see that the devastated provinces of the Western Empire became the cradle of the most creative civilization mankind has so far produced, whereas Byzantium, which never experienced a catastrophe of this kind, not even through Turkish conquest, produced no more than a second-rate aftermath of the grander civilization which had preceded it. The argument may seem abstract, too abstract. But for this one time I wish to argue the case on the broadest background available, and I see no other background as broad as this one.

Clearly, the case is closely related to the survival of freedom, of independence, and of the West. It is related to freedom, though not in the sense that during the five centuries of the Roman Empire the West would have been less autocratically ruled than the East. As autocracy developed, it took its symbols and methods more and more from the East until, from the time of Diocletian onwards, no difference was left between an oriental kingdom and the Roman Empire. At the same time the West, by way of disintegration, broke loose from autocracy. The Germanic states arising in the West were not autocracies. Though the political rights of the Germanic freeholders declined, feudalism checked the power of the ruler and of the state, and out of feudalism grew the representation of the subject and all modern political liberty. *While the West, after a terrific and long-lasting crisis, moved towards liberty, Byzantium, maintaining order and civilization, moved deeper and deeper into autocracy.*

The moment came when it was no longer important whether this autocracy was exerted by a national dynasty or by foreign conquerors—a moment which must come in the history of every autocracy. By its own choice Byzantium preferred the Turk to the Latin. The loss of freedom within had led to subjection from without. The West, starting from the same roots but developing in the opposite direction, had by that time evolved into a welter of free and independent national units.

And it should not be forgotten, in this context, that the geographical layout then presented an exact parallel to our present geographical situation. As between Hellenes and Persians, as between Western feudalism and Byzantium, so today between the Anglo-Saxon powers and Russia it is a question of West vs. East. This is not incidental. The history starting in Ionia in Homeric times, and leading to modern London and Washington, is a history of growing freedom. The history starting, much earlier, in Sumer and Egypt, and leading through Assyria, Persia, Byzantium to Moscow, is a history of lasting and basically unchanging autocracy. The clash remains the same, the controversy over thousands of years remains the same basic, decisive controversy, the red thread of the history of higher civilization. Only the border between West and East has moved to and fro.

Under Alexander the Great the West, which had started so late, moved deep into Asia. Under Diocletian the East had reached Britain. In the later Middle Ages the West extended up to Kiev. Today, Germany, not only politically but also spiritually, is largely a prey to the ways of the East. Also, the geographical center of the controversy has constantly shifted northwards, both in West and East. But there is no difficulty in recognizing in the antagonists of today the same forces that fought at Salamis in 480 B.C.

We Westerners may well take deep comfort in our troubles, with perhaps much worse in store for us, in the thought that while the East has not progressed much since the days of the Assyrian Empire, the West has progressed immensely. It was, in all its phases, a creation of Northern

barbarians who had been touched by Eastern influences without submitting to them. At every stage of their development, the Western nations and civilizations were threatened not so much with conquest by
the East, but with assimilation to its civilization. The Asiatic wave which
nearly engulfed Hellas in the seventh century B.C. was much more dangerous than the ten years between Marathon and Salamis. But it was
precisely the reaction against the Eastern permeation which led to the
final self-assertion of Hellenic civilization towards the end of the sixth
century and which, apart from all its intrinsic glory, enabled the Hellenes
to withstand the onslaught of the hosts of Xerxes. The East reasserted
itself against Alexander's conquests. But the East itself could exist only
within the shell of the Roman Empire and, when within its borders the
civilization of the East became paramount, that involved the escape of
the West from the bondage of the East. There is no need to carry the
account down into modern times.

The East cannot understand the intrinsic strength of the West. Eastern
autocracies always thought it an easy task to conquer the West, and
always failed. Today we are confronted with a new onslaught whose
peculiarity it is that Russia has borrowed so much of Western technique.
But Western technique cannot adequately function in an Eastern context.
Clearly, looking at our present woes in so large an historical context,
we have every reason to be cheerful—not cheerful for our personal destiny,
which is not likely to be pleasant, but cheerful for the destiny of the
values on which we live.

But how does all this relate to the respective effects of Struldbrugism
and barbarism upon the future of civilizations? There exists an obvious
affinity between ossification and autocracy. Effective autocracy excludes
genuine development. Yet it would be a great mistake to think in terms
of crude, simple alternatives. Eastern civilization, autocracy, ossification,
are not one and the same thing. It may be argued that the oldest civilizations of the East had the germs of both autocracy and liberty in them,
and that not before Assyrian times had the decision fallen in favor of
absolute autocracy. More important, there are many Struldbrug civilizations without political autocracy. The Jews are a classical case.

But there seems to be good reason, nevertheless, to relate these apparent exceptions to autocracy. For they have all happened within the
geographic region of the autocracies. Is it not that groups deprived of
their secular rulers have instead submitted to the absolute rule of an
absolute law? It certainly applies in the case of the Parsees. And in India
we can see the political autocracy of Rajas and later of Sultans exist side

by side with the absolute tyranny of the caste Dharma. The relation between Sultanism and Moslem law is also a case in point. Political autocracy and unchanging custom really seem to belong together, and to part company only in case of inescapable necessity. The West never knew either.

Again, admittedly, our Western constant change is nearer to chaos, and that is the objection of the East against us. It is true that there exists as little stringent connection between chaos and the West as there exists between autocracy and ossification. Absolutes are always wrong in the interpretation of history. But affinity between the West and chaos is not smaller than between the East and rigidity. The East, too, has known chaos, a very great deal of chaos. It happens where autocracy and unchanging custom are sapped from within to the point of collapse. Then, after a longer or shorter transition, there occurs a return to the older forms. In the West, we have so far had only one big transition, that from classical to Western civilization. That one transition seems to prove that the West is incapable of real rigidity without leaning upon Eastern models and forces. The law of the West, so far, has been to develop, to grow, and to disintegrate when growth is no longer possible. In the East, the periods of chaos are short-lived; rigidity predominates. In the West, autocracies are short-lived, and mainly borrowed from the East. Prediction is, of course, dangerously difficult. But, so far, everything seems to point to the conclusion that we have again, for the second time in Western history, reached one of the great turning-points. The tendencies towards autocracy, rigidity, and Struldbrugism are flowing strong again, but the forces of resistance will again be stronger.

It is a sad and tragic thought that the victory of these forces of resistance may involve, not, as we all wish, further growth, but simply disintegration. As I have tried to show, disintegration is the only possible prelude to further growth. The interlude may well last for centuries and be gruesome. But it is the only road leading further on towards the intrinsic goals of human development.

The lure of submitting to a world autocracy with its prospects of order, security, and avoidance of disaster, is only the temptation to sell the right of the first-born for a mess of pottage. It is more than doubtful whether Western civilization can continue in its present shape. In all probability we are at the beginning of a transition, long, painful, and uncertain, to another civilization. This is not a matter for our choice. But it would be our choice to submit to a world autocracy and, thereby, to cast away the possibility of further human development. Whether the challenge will materialize we cannot know now, but we shall know within a decade or two. If the challenge materializes, we shall be able to fight it and to ward it off—if we have the right spirit.

Whole nations cannot be sustained in such a struggle by far-flung hypotheses about history past and future. But those inclined to ask for ultimate justification of their actions should know that they cannot undertake that struggle in an optimistic belief in linear progress. The course of the struggle itself would belie their optimism; they would collapse under disillusion. If the struggle comes, the hardest, most bitter, most pessimistic assumptions about the future in store for us are in order. And yet, not since Salamis, and not since the days when Charles Martel defeated the Arabs at Tours, was there a struggle so full of meaning. For such is the paradox of human affairs that men, by walking with open eyes towards the disintegration of their own civilization, may yet serve and experience the fullness of life, whereas those shrinking from the catastrophe may work for ultimate death, and experience it in their own souls. In times such as these there is only one upright attitude: *Amor fati.*

CHAPTER TWO

Will Technology Destroy Civilization?
[1951]

A common and increasing disillusionment with technology today marks contemporary thinkers of the most divergent tendencies. A classic expression of this feeling was Aldous Huxley's *Brave New World*, a utopian novel portraying a world whose every problem and every difficulty has been solved by technology, but which for this very reason has become emptied of all meaning. Arnold J. Toynbee, though not envisaging any utopian ultimate in technology, also seems to lean to the view that modern technology is at bottom worthless—for "mankind's serious business is religion"; all that we need in the way of secular culture was already produced by the Greeks—in our technological efforts we are only the bad imitators of a past civilization.

The same tendency of thought has had such important representatives in Latin countries as Ortega y Gasset and Paul Valéry. But it has met with its strongest response in Germany. I mention here in particular only the Jünger brothers. Ernst Jünger, in his book *The Worker*, unlike Huxley, does not "reject" technology on aesthetic grounds or any other; but his positive conception of a perfect *"Arbeitertum"* (workers' civilization) came very close to Huxley's utopia and yielded nothing to it in point of horror. Friedrich Georg Jünger, for his part, has launched an all-out campaign against technology—to what effect, we can see in Otto Veit's *Die Flucht vor der Freiheit* ("Flight from Freedom," Frankfurt, 1948), which by a startling simplification would hold technology responsible for all that endangers our culture today.

Let me say at once that I do not deny the dangers of technology, which are tremendous. But what strikes one constantly about these lamentations over the evils of technology is their minimization of its unique achievements in modern times, achievements by no means limited to the sphere of the "practical." On the contrary, spiritual values of the highest order are inseparable from technology. Nor can you draw a line between technology and science—if only because without modern instruments there would be no modern science, as without science there would be no technology.

No one will deny that our science, in the course of its development from Galileo to Einstein and from Boyle to Planck and Rutherford, has penetrated the "interior of nature" as never before. Even supposing that technology is in fact as destructive in its consequences as many now claim it to be—is that all there is to it? For my part, I believe that as surely as the human spirit exists to illumine the cosmos with its knowledge, so surely does the modern conquest of nature represent this spirit's sublimest, most heroic achievement. However great the emotional price we have paid for the "disenchantment of the world" that inevitably followed on this conquest of nature, however dreadful our psychic distress—still, what does this matter against the fulfillment of an eternal task of the human race?

In dismissing as an incidental matter the knowledge we have finally won of the basic structure of the material world, the critics of technology for the most part overlook the fact that these very insights have given us a glimpse into the basic structure of all existence, spiritual as well as material. Are these insights tragic in their refutation of cherished illusions?—well, all culture is tragic, all culture is paid for by the surrender of primitive consolations of the human soul. And may one not ask whether the real threat to culture does not perhaps come from those who have not the fortitude to face up to the consequences of this greatest of human triumphs, and must therefore take flight from reason?

But is the flight from reason and technology at all possible? We ought to put this question to ourselves, not in any aesthetic and utopian fashion, but in complete and deadly earnest. Let us say, conditionally, "yes," a flight is possible. The condition is: the reduction of the "white" population to a fraction of its present size; for the present European and American population levels, unlike the Asiatic, are dependent entirely upon technology. A sharp fall in our population is, of course, not out of the question. It is unfortunately more than merely conceivable that an atomic war might utterly destroy tens of millions of lives as well as our technological resources and abilities. In the absence of such an event, technology will certainly endure, so that we can only discuss the possibility of its disappearance by assuming an atomic catastrophe.

Bertrand Russell recently suggested that such a disappearance might be effected by a destructive outbreak of mass hatred against technology following an atomic holocaust. This vision of an outraged humanity turning upon science is an ever recurring one. Spengler, it might be remembered, held that technology was something specifically "Western": peoples of alien cultures mastered technology only in order to use it in their struggle against the West; with the downfall of the West, they would cast it aside as "a monkey would a walking stick." Toynbee, too, would seem to expect much the same thing.

But is not Spengler's dark estimate of the future of technology intimately connected with his gross underestimation of what was really taking place in science? It was around 1914 that Spengler, himself originally a mathematician, disputed the possibility of any further significant advance in scientific theory, conceding a future only to purely practical technology. Obviously he mistook the actual depth of the current of science—mistook it grossly. Recent scientific developments, flatly contradicting him, have completely revolutionized our conception of the world. Hence a discussion of the problem cannot start out from any notion of a decline or "end" of science, but must begin by answering the question: *Is it conceivable that, as a result of enormous material and spiritual catastrophes, all the knowledge and skills we have acquired in the last three hundred years could be lost?*

Pointing to earlier cases of cultural decline does not in itself mean very much. To draw a parallel between our own situation and the decline into barbarism and the "dark ages" that marked the end of antiquity is certainly misleading. As Spengler pointed out, there is always more than one parallelism to choose from. You have to have what Spengler calls a "physiognomic pulse" to understand which parallels are valid and which are not. The parallel with the decline of antiquity is not. Although it is true that there was a sharp falling-off of urban life at that time, no real deterioration took place in technology. One of the most important arguments against a too simple notion of progress is contained in the fact that from the end of the Old Kingdom in Egypt (third millennium B.C.) until the eleventh century of our era, actually no real change occurred in technology—a state of affairs that speaks stronger than anything else for the Spenglerian thesis of the distinctively Western character of technology.

But there are two sides to this coin of "Western science." Not only

modern machine technology, but also something so seemingly insignificant as the European method of harnessing draught-cattle, profoundly
affects population growth, the rise of cities, etc![1] Will other, "colored"
civilizations cast this achievement aside as a monkey would a walking
stick? If not, where is the point beyond which they will refuse to borrow
from Western culture? Or, as in Samuel Butler's *Erewhon*, will some one
year finally be fixed, and all technological innovations made prior to it
accepted, and all those made afterwards rejected?

At this point Alfred Weber, the contemporary German sociologist,
has attempted to offer us a way out of our difficulty. For the most part
he accepts, if not Spengler's, at any rate Toynbee's theory of culture
cycles. But he limits the cyclical theory to that sphere which Spengler,
in contrast to *civilization* (the technical arts), calls *culture*—the sphere of the
spiritual. According to Alfred Weber, history shows that *civilization*, if
spared from purely external disruptions, develops according to a law of
linear progress. Progress in the technical arts of civilization, once made,
is handed on and learned, and so can never be lost.

This is a plausible theory, but it is difficult to verify: it is hardly
possible to compare the course of technological progress in various recorded civilizations for the reason that only the earliest river cultures of
the Orient on the one hand, and our own civilization on the other, ever
made any decisive technological advances. Moreover, the technological
achievements of Ancient Egypt and Sumeria, unlike our own, did not
spring directly from the soil of these two cultures, but were end products
of a technological revolution begun several millennia before these cultures
arose, a revolution that consisted chiefly in the passage from the hunting
economy of the Old Stone Age to the agricultural, pastoral, and hand-
icraft economy of the New.

And here we have stumbled on the key! This revolution leading from
the Old Stone Age to the New, paving the way for all the high cultures
of antiquity—this is the only event in the history of man's conquest of
nature that can compare in significance with that technological revolution
which began in Western Europe in the eleventh century, died out about
the thirteenth, and sprang to life again in the sixteenth. Any opinion on

1. Not long ago an extraordinary French cavalry officer, Count Lefèbvre de Noëttes,
a man gifted with the keenest historical intuition, showed that at the beginning of modern
Western culture, about the end of the eleventh century, a new method of harnessing
draught-oxen came into use that quadrupled their pulling power and led to a social revolution of the first order. Comte Lefèbvre de Noëttes, *L'attelage: Le cheval de selle à travers
les âges.* (Paris: Picard, 1931).

the fate of modern technology has to reckon chiefly with this great parallel case from our prehistory.

It is no good to say that we know the revolution of our own day well enough by observation from its very midst, without resorting to such doubtful parallels. We don't know it. We know indeed whence it came, but in all likelihood its curve is still only at its beginning and we haven't the faintest idea where it is headed, or how steadily or how fast. For the prehistoric Neolithic side of the parallel, we have a complete curve.

When one compares the Neolithic (New Stone Age) and Western technological revolutions, the first thing one notices is an extraordinary similarity in the wealth of negative and positive consequences following from both. On the positive side, the Neolithic technological revolution created incomparably more favorable conditions for the life of the human species. Cultivation of the land made possible a tenfold increase in population, led to a lengthening of the average life span, and brought about a substantial increase in comfort (huts instead of caves). But against this must be set an unmistakably sharp decline in culture. It is of course very difficult, because of the absence of written documents, to compare the spiritual life of late Paleolithic (Old Stone Age) times with that of the early Neolithic period. Yet such art works as we possess supply definite hints. The scanty geometrical ornamentation of Neolithic pottery cannot even remotely compare with the splendid cave paintings of the Magdalenians. In these two kinds of art one confronts the expressive forms of two entirely different kinds of "humanity": in the cave paintings an art of restless boldness and the deepest inner freedom, in the pottery a narrow, timid botching of materials and forms. The wide-ranging hunt freed the spirit, the sod fettered it. As in its cultural, so evidently in its social results too, the triumph of husbandry was extremely disadvantageous. The hunter was "free and equal," the husbandman became a slave and his master a despot.

The first result of the Neolithic technological revolution, then, was the almost complete disappearance of the Paleolithic cultural inheritance. But only apparently and for a time. Much of it was preserved, especially among pastoral tribes, out of which developed the equestrian peoples. And these same bearers of a few musty and cramped traditions became the ruling classes of the high cultures that now arose, and which could have hardly come into existence without them. Thus on the new foundation of Neolithic economy the ancient, temporarily obscured spiritual traditions of Paleolithic times prevailed again. And this fusion of old cultural and new civilized values created the very high cultures of antiquity whose achievements in every respect far surpassed those of Paleolithic times.

As can be seen, the parallels with our own epoch are in many respects extremely close. On the other hand, it is vitally important that we should not view the gigantic crisis of our day crudely or narrowly, and it is narrow to regard it as simply one of many cyclical crisis in human culture. The crisis of our age is much more than that: it is the second great phase in the development of civilization. Our crises is not a duplication of an earlier crisis. It is, even when compared with that of the Neolithic Age, unique.

The Neolithic technological revolution came to a standstill early in the course of the Ancient Egyptian and Sumerian cultures, and it seems clear that no cultural motive in the narrower sense was at work, but rather a new environmental problem. It was a revolution that grew out of the battle with hunger. Empirical investigation confirms this inference. Late Magdalenian man had brought the technique of hunting to such a pitch of perfection that his life acquired enough room for him to experience higher cultural needs. But with the end of the Ice Age, the earth's last great geological revolution, game decreased and the amount of arable land increased. The hunting economy collapsed, and man was forced with ever greater rigor to devote all his energies once again to the simple struggle for survival, and to the building up of a village economy. The Neolithic revolution was a revolution from "without," one compelled by nature; and the very rise of the civilizations born of that revolution made its continuation unnecessary, for the new large states possessed organizations that more than assured the physical existence of man.

With the Western technological revolution, the case is reversed. Western science is a profound expression of Western man's orientation toward life, death, and reality. It is not merely a response to an external physical stimulus. Western society in its early stages did not have to face any new and fundamental problems. There was the problem of overpopulation; but earlier societies, too, had been obliged to reduce their excess populations, and this they did by colonization and conquest. Western society is probably the first in whose early stages expansion did not play the decisive role. In place of colonization outward, there was followed a course of colonization directed within—the progressive clearing of woodland for the plough—facilitated after a few years by the first perceptible increase in the productivity of human labor through an increase in animal tractive power. This unique course, a revolution from "within," was the result of the unique nature of Western culture, and is closely bound up with the West's distinctive urge to freedom.

The assertion of one's individuality in society is intimately related to the assertion of one's individuality against nature. And just because the Western technological revolution proceeded from "within," from a cultural spiritual drive to know the universe and master it, and was not prompted solely by necessity, for that very reason it became, not peripheral, but central to the whole history of the West, and now stands as its greatest achievement. Precisely because of the deeply spiritual character of this technological revolution, precisely because of the intimate connection between technology and freedom, because of the inseparability of Western (and *only* Western) technological, economic, and political development, all aiming at freeing the life and spirit of the individual, it is an offense against our most precious values to exalt other aspects of our culture, such as literature, art, and religion, *at the expense* of science, technology, and the advancement of knowledge generally.

Granting all this, is it still possible for something specifically Western in its development to continue to flourish outside the West should the example of the West cease to exist? The Neolithic revolution, we now can see, just because it came *only* from without, consisted of easily acquired skills and devices that could be and were handed on indefinitely. The Western technological revolution, on the other hand, is so completely defined from within, is so specifically—even in its underlying moral ideals—Western, that it is easy to doubt the possibility of its being transmitted. There is, for example, the enormous yet still hardly adequate violence—hardly adequate in so far as it does not achieve the ends for which it is intended—with which Russia is carrying out its policy of industrialization. Can something so patently artificial—that imitates the external and material sides of technology completely divorced from its deep cultural roots and impulses—endure, once its immediate stimulus—competition with the West—is removed?

I need scarcely remark on the falsity of Spengler's belief in the complete destruction, with a culture's downfall, of every distinctive value of that culture, the falsity of his doctrine of cultures as windowless monads. There is an enormous body of evidence to contradict Spengler on this point, evidence he never once tried to refute, but simply ignored. Not only the extrinsic values of civilization, but the most intrinsic cultural values too, have been handed on from society to society and epoch to epoch, and the fact that modern technology is intrinsic to the Western spirit, and not—as Spengler, Aldous Huxley, F. G. Jünger, Otto Veit, and countless others declare—a purely external body of knowledge and skills, is no argument at all against its transmissibility. It is only that the transmission of specific spiritual attitudes from one culture to another takes place according to different and more complicated laws than govern the simple learning of a quantity of knowledge and a number of skills.

Anglo-American ethnology has collected a huge amount of material bearing on the transmission of cultural values, but, so far as I know, the only one to attempt to draw any general inferences from it as to the relation of high cultures to each other is Arnold J. Toynbee. His notion of "affiliated civilizations," however, seems too narrow to me; he does no more than point to the fact that cultures follow one another in time and are the heirs of their predecessors. With Toynbee every later culture would seem to be the heir of some single earlier one. But the historical reality is much more complicated than that. True, there are cases—the "second" Chinese culture, for example, beginning with the older Han Dynasty—where a new culture is built almost exclusively upon a single ancient model (one is tempted to say that these "second" cultures fell considerably behind the "first" in creative strength). But what is much more frequently the case is that a new culture is first an amalgam and then a fusion of the basic elements of several older cultures. The Old and the New Testament cultures are classic examples of this. One arose in the borderland between Egypt and Babylon, and the other on the boundaries of Hellenism and the Orient. The further analysis of such cases as these is bound to throw some light on our own problem as to the future of technology.

Here we must first note that what distinguishes the rise of a new culture is the conscious opposition it puts up to the introduction of certain foreign values. Early Judaism leaned to a limited extent on Babylonian cultural tradition, but toward Egypt it felt only the bitterest hostility. Early Christianity had some affinities with the religious traditions of Near Eastern syncretism, but it strictly enjoined any traffic with Greek paganism. Naturally, it was inevitable that the Jews should borrow certain elements of higher political organization, and the Christians various formal elements of culture, from hated neighbors, but the borrowing was strictly limited to "external" things. With time, however, there came a mingling and assimilation.

In the very same way, one might say, Russia today cannot avoid adopting our technological methods, while at the same time she tries to isolate herself as much as possible, spiritually and politically, from the West. And it is this resistance to a foreign culture that makes her adoption of certain of the external values (external from the Russian but not from the Western point of view) of our civilization so artificial and forced. However, the upshot of this will in all likelihood be not at all as Spengler

thought—Russia and Asia ultimately casting aside these temporary borrowings from Western technology "like a walking stick." It is far more
likely that, as in every analogous earlier case, the external borrowing of
a foreign civilization will be succeeded by a centuries-long process of
inner assimilation.

But does this analogy hold up against the possibility that all of our
higher culture will be swept away by a few hundred atomic bombs?
Toynbee, with his particularly strong antipathy to modern technology,
goes so far as to consider the possibility of our technological development
leading to the complete destruction of all civilized peoples and the elevation of the Central African Pygmies to the position of the chief bearers
of human culture. Against such a view of things there is little one can
say in the way of conclusive argument. But an examination of historical
precedents will disclose another perspective.

When one surveys all of human history, it can be seen that the periods
in which cultures decline are indispensable intervals of cultural renewal.
In the "dark ages" the modern Western spirit was gestative. The historical
process just referred to, whereby a new culture results from the assimilation of elements from different older cultures, takes place without
exception amid the catastrophic collapse of all the older cultures figuring
in the process—takes place, that is, amid the upsurge of barbarism.

Vigorous and independent cultures resist to the death the challenge of
a different culture. In their late stages they do not undergo a process of
change, but tend rather to harden and grow rigid. Only when this period
of rigidity is followed by collapse does the creative process of fusion
begin. The mechanism of cultural renewal, the decisive connecting link
in the chain of human history, can be unhesitatingly called history's most
universal law, admitting of not one exception. A *chaos precedes every
cultural cosmos*. Chaos is not downfall, not ruin. It is the necessary connecting link between the end of one creative process and the beginning
of another.

We hear it said that, regardless of the outcome of the present struggle
between East and West, the world is "entering an era of barbarism."
What in actual fact is "barbarism"? It is not the same thing as cultural
primitivism, a turning-back of the clock. It is rather a phenomenon that
manifests itself within the temporal and spiritual boundaries of high
cultures. It is a condition in which many of the values of high culture
are present, but without that social and moral coherence which is the
precondition for a culture's rational functioning. But for this very reason
"barbarism" is also a creative process: once the overall coherence of a

culture is shattered, the way lies open to a renewal of creativity. To be sure, however, this way may be through a collapse of political and economic life, and centuries of spiritual and material impoverishment and terrible suffering. Our own particular brand of civilization and culture may not survive unimpaired, but the fruits of civilization and culture, we may be sure, will in some form survive. There is no historical warrant for believing that the slate will be wiped clean.

Let us try for a more balanced perspective of this whole popular question of "the threatened disappearance of civilization." It is hardly to be doubted that we are now living at the beginning of a period of "barbarism." It cannot logically be proven that, like every earlier crisis of its kind, it will be a creative transition and not the end, although an inner consciousness should tell us that the highest stage reached in the development of the human spirit could hardly be the immediate prologue to its final downfall. The legend of the Tower of Babel has indeed a point for us, insofar as it is true that, build we ever so high, an end is reached to all our building. Yet the truth of the legend is temporally circumscribed: for *the end was no end at all, but a new beginning*—over and over again we build our Tower, and right now higher than ever. And here, if I may, I should like to take leave of history.

I have already expressed my repugnance to an attitude that, in dealing with the problem of technology, would ignore the *truth* of modern science. Spengler vainly sought to demonstrate that Euclidean geometry was true only for antiquity. The fact is of course that it is true for all ages, only we have come to understand that it is a partial truth, that it is true when certain postulates are given. The same thing holds for modern technology and science. Once discovered, these truths are a universal possession of humanity, because they are not only human truths, but in accord with cosmic reality. Very possibly such truths can be lost sight of in chaotic transitional periods, but is it conceivable that they should vanish as if they had never been discovered? Or isn't it far more likely that, after having been purged in the fires of a great cultural change, they should first really begin to shine forth?

And now the cat is indeed out of the bag. I have gone and blabbed my faith in progress, that unpardonable sin. Yet I do not mean that automatically, steadily accelerating progress in which Condorcet, Hegel, and Buckle believed, not a progress that can dispense with cycles and relapses, not a progress on an ever rising historical escalator that one can commit oneself to with smugness and equanimity. Still, much has happened in the course of our evolution from primordial atom to amoeba, from amoeba to man, and from Peking Man to Planck and Rutherford; and it seems absurd to me to imagine that in all this there is little more that is worthy of philosophical and religious notice than is involved in lamenting the sins and sufferings of existence.

We all know that the chief concern of the opponents of this qualified belief in progress is with the "timeless," and it is to the "timeless" that I too am led. The kernel of the faith in progress, it turns out, is a faith in the effective significance of objective truth in human life. Is it an accident that all those who deny progress, from Spengler to Barth, are the very ones who deny the efficacy of all the truths that man perceives by his unaided intellect? And is not truth one of the chief aspects of the divine? And in this respect, on the same level with morality? To deny the truths perceived by man, is it not to deny the stamp of divinity upon creation? Is not faith in progress perhaps in the end only a faith in God's positive working in history—and not outside of history?

But in Germany especially, this faith in the positive significance of truths perceived by man's unaided intellect is zealously combated. Is not this zeal perhaps only a disguised version of the old Lutheran belief in the devil's rule over the world? And this belief in the devil as "Prince of this world," reaching as it does by hidden ways from the Albigensians to Luther and ultimately uniting Lutheranism with Gnostic demonology— isn't this belief ultimately the root of all German evil? *Sapienti sat.*

CHAPTER THREE

Toynbee and the Future of the Jews
[1955]

Under the title of "The Modern West and the Jews," A. J. Toynbee devotes a subsection of Volume 8 of his *Study of History* to the fate of Jewry under the Nazis and to subsequent developments in Israel. His remarks therein about Zionism and Israel have, quite rightly, outraged Jews and other people. Mr. Toynbee equates the monstrous crimes perpetrated upon the Jews of Europe by the Germans with what the Israelis did to the Arabs of Palestine, and seems to find the Israelis as much at fault as the Nazis were! One might attribute this slanderous indictment of Zionism to Mr. Toynbee's weakness for symmetry and parallels, for likenesses and correspondences in general. But from the tenor of his other remarks about the Jews and things Jewish, it seems plausible to conclude that something more fundamental is at work than a historical or literary device. Toynbee is swayed by certain misconceptions as to the nature and history of Jewry as a people and as a spiritual tradition. These misconceptions have the force of an animus—one symptom of which is the surprisingly small part he assigns to Judaism in the origins of Christianity, and his tendency to overstress the originality of the latter's universal and redemptive aspects to the neglect of everything Prophetic in the Old Testament.

But Toynbee is a professional historian and only an amateur theologian. It is his historical assumptions, definitions, and verdicts that require examination first and demand to be taken most seriously.

Mr. Toynbee does not regard the history of the Jews as *altogether* unique, and in this he is, of course, right. The transformation of a tribal kingdom into a nonterritorial *millet* community whose religious and national identity coincided, was a frequent phenomenon in the Middle East after the fall of the Assyrian empire in the seventh century B.C. From then till the disintegration of the Ottoman Turkish empire, the Middle East was largely made up of such *millets* (the term itself is of Ottoman origin): that is, groups separated by religion rather than language, living side by side in the same countryside and the same towns. In this situation the religious community filled many of the social and political functions—though by no means all—that the linguistically unified nation does in modern Europe. The Armenians and Parsees, like the Jews, are classical examples of such "religion-nations," and to them could be added the Copts as well as the many other *millet* groups Toynbee mentions as existing at large in the Arab world, and particularly in Lebanon and Syria.

Toynbee defined the *millet*, and described the Jews as constituting one, in the first volume of his *Study of History*. What he saw as the basic sociological reason for the "Jewish tragedy" in Europe was the collision between the *millet* type of community and the territorially, linguistically, and politically unified national structures into which Western civilization is organized. The conflict was inevitable because the two types of structure were incompatible. In this reviewer's opinion, Toynbee is again right. Where he goes astray, however, is in assuming, implicitly and without evidence, that the Jews must remain a *millet* in order to survive as Jews. This error vitiates almost everything else he has to say about the Diaspora. Yet he seems to be aware that the history of Jewry since the eighteenth century is that of an abandonment of the *millet*—or ghetto—and an increasing integration in modern Western civilization, and that this has been done without appreciable loss of ethnic identity. The contradiction stems from the fact that, though the Jews have refused to fit themselves into Toynbee's scheme, he insists on retaining it nevertheless. This, as well as his bias against Judaism as such, may help explain the acrimony of his remarks about them.

In Toynbee's scheme, modern life is faced with a choice between "archaism" (or ossification) and "futurism" (or nihilism). How could the Jews, an archaic community to begin with, and remaining one until very recently, have so resolutely chosen the alternative of "futurism"— that is, to establish a Jewish territorial state in Palestine and at the same time to modernize themselves in the Diaspora? Not only should they, in Toynbee's view, have remained a *millet* in order to stay devout and ward off modern "secularism," but also because in his view the *millet* will be more viable than the nation-state as a basic institution in the next, "religious" phase of world history.

The first thing to ask in following the train of thought that has led Toynbee into error about the contemporary Jews is whether the *millet* they formed in the past can be defined in the same terms as the communities formed by the modern Assyrians, the Copts, the Armenians, and the other *millets* that, unlike the Jews, have remained largely tied to the Middle East. The answer touches on the very essence of the Jews as a people.

As I have said, *millets* are nations that are defined by religion, not by territory, political forms, or language. Hence the content of its religion plays the chief role in determining the history of a *millet* people. Toynbee, for all his professed solicitude for religion, overlooks this factor of content and judges from form alone: accordingly, the history of the Jews in the Diaspora should be more or less like that of the Armenians and Copts in their Diasporas. But it is not. The reason, though it may be concealed from Toynbee, is not hard to find. Like the Jews, the Armenians, Assyrians, Copts, etc. all have had pre-*millet* pasts as territorially and politically unified nations. Unlike the Jews, however, none of these other *millet* peoples is connected by religion with its pre-*millet* past, and none acquired its status as a *millet* in quite the same way. Neo-Babylonian, Hellenistic, Roman, and Moslem conquerors imposed that status on these peoples by force of arms, and in most cases before they had adopted their present religion or even a precursor of it. As they were deprived of political independence by an outside "universal state," so they were converted to the Christianity to which they all adhere as *millets* by what was, more often than not, an outside "universal church."

With the Jews it was quite otherwise, the relation between their *millet* and pre-*millet* phases being directly inverted. Israel's religious transformation, culminating in Judaism, was already implicit in Mosaic law, and proceeded rapidly after the beginning of the Prophetic age, which came before there was any serious foreign threat to either Israel's or Judah's political integrity. The Prophets emphasized righteousness and devotion to the sole and unique Jehovah at the expense, if necessary, of state power. When Israel and then Judah collapsed under foreign invasion, the latter at least was so penetrated by Prophetic teaching, and the teaching itself so advanced, that Judah was able to preserve her national identity despite the loss of both homeland and political independence. Thus, with the First Exile, Jewry became the first people able to safeguard its identity solely by means of religion and ritual: hence the prototype of all the other *millet* peoples. It was because they more or less created, and *chose*, their conception of themselves as a religious community that the Jews remained a peculiar people, even after one section of them returned to their homeland under Persian rule and reassumed a more conventional outward aspect as a nation. And it was by triumphantly reviving the *millet* conception later on, after the fall of the Second Temple and their final dispersion, that, to the amazement of the Gentiles, the Jewish nation survived an even more catastrophic political defeat than the Babylonian conquest.

But the point here is not so much the success of the *millet* form as a means of national survival, as the fact that the Jews were the only people to *choose* the *millet* as their own creation, rather than have it imposed upon them by others. They were able to do this because their own, native religion, with its "premature" belief in a single almighty God, had under the duress of exile sloughed off almost every trace of tribalism and almost every attachment to a political end, and shifted its center of gravity to the spiritual plane. All the other *millet* peoples, with the sole exception of the Parsees, have no memory, cultural or religious, of their pre-*millet* histories. The Jews, on the other hand, emerging from a disintegrating *millet* world today, still retain a continuity with their pre-*millet* past. That past holds something tremendous—the revelation of a faith and an outlook which mothered the two universal faiths of Christianity and Islam. This Jewish past is not a contrived or reconstructed historical memory, as the "primordial" Teutonic past of Wotan and Walhalla was for the crackpot ideologues of Nazi Germany, but was always, and remains, a living, active, natural force.

One's past largely determines one's future. The living past of a *millet* people who remember nothing before their *millet* is likely to bring in the future either the continuation of their *millet* existence or their disintegration as a group. The Jews, despite Mr. Toynbee, are not faced with these exclusive alternatives because their memories leap back over two thousand years of ghetto life to the Prophets and the Exodus. The Jewish identity has not quickly disintegrated under the impact of modern life as the ethnic identities of other *millets* have. Religious or irreligious, the Jews have maintained their character and continuity as Jews almost everywhere.

Einstein, opposing the antirationalism inherent in the empirical outlook of a Planck or a Heisenberg, insists upon the need, the possibility, and the obligation to render the universe intelligible in terms of a single rational principle—just as the Deutero-Isaiah insisted on the intelligible unity of God's governance of the world. If the Jewish contribution to every activity, good and bad, on behalf of social justice and liberalism is so disproportionately large, it is not simply because Jews themselves hope to gain by this, but also because Isaiah and Micah are still part of the Jewish consciousness. And the latter-day return to Zion evokes, and invokes, the memory of a similar return after the First Exile.

Obviously, the preghetto past of Jewry is not the "ghost" Toynbee says it is. Nor is the Jewish invocation of such a remote past "archaistic": it is at one and the same time a reaching back and a reaching forward in which the past reinforces the advance into the future. Little in modern Jewish existence reminds one of the arduous, half-frustrated efforts by which the Arabs and the Persians—let alone the smaller *millet* peoples— now try to modernize themselves. Jews play a leading role, as a type as well as individuals, in many fields of modern life, and are able to contribute their share without undue effort in those where they do not lead. Jews themselves often ascribe this to their superior intelligence, but they are wrong. While ghetto existence did put a premium on intellectual at the expense of physical and certain practical capacities, religious tradition had a much greater and stronger hand in shaping Jewish character in the long run, and the Prophetic impulse spurs Jews to eminence much more than their supposed intellectual superiority does. Without that impulse, Jewish intellectuality (which is more a matter of training than of innate endowment) might find no better task for itself than money-making.

Toynbee attacks Jewish secularism in its assimilationist as well as its Zionist form. Theodor Mommsen, the German historian whose account of the fall of the Second Temple certainly reveals that he was aware of Jewish failings, showed a profounder understanding of the characteristic Jewish relation to past and future. The Jew, he said, is as ready to adapt his outward conduct to whatever milieu he finds himself in, as he is unwilling to surrender one parcel of his inmost being to it. The Jewish character can be described as a synthesis of well-nigh complete stability with well-nigh complete variability. This makes Jewish participation in non-Jewish culture something unique and special—and since the demise of their original pre-Hellenistic civilization, the Jews have always had to live with, or participate in, one non-Jewish culture or another. If the Jewish combination of outer assimilation with inner aloofness or detachment has proved disturbing to Gentiles, for the same reason it has been most fertile and creative, whether for the Jews themselves or for the "host" culture.

The Nazis, alas, paid the Jews the inadvertent compliment of resenting their inner aloofness and the contributions it enabled them to make: it was the one grain of reality at the center of the horrible myths they wove out of their hatred for the Jews, which was also an inverted fascination with an unreachable essence. Whereas Toynbee's objurgations of Zionism and his animus against Judaism in general relate to some of the most superficial aspects of contemporary Jewish life, the Nazis distorted and diabolized an aspect infinitely more profound, namely, the stiff-necked Jewish insistence on remaining Jewish under all circumstances.

Toynbee makes too easy an identification between modern Western secularism and the contemporary Jewish variety. The two may have converged until recently (with the happy result of releasing the Jews from the ghetto) but now they seem to be diverging. Gentile secularism appears to be heading towards a pure empiricism and relativism, whereas the Jewish kind still clings to the notion of human existence as something rationally and metaphysically intelligible and purposeful. Witness the extent to which Jewish secularism produces people *religiously* and disinterestedly dedictated to universal causes. Secularized Puritanism, which used to produce similar fruits, no longer does so to the same extent as secularized Judaism because it lacks the same inherent continuity with Prophetic tradition.

If the modern world, both Western and Communist, continues to adhere, as seems likely, to its present course of ruthless practical "realism," with its growing contempt for reason and humanism, then it may well fall to the Jews (amid the laughter of an incredulous world) to play a major part in the preservation of our cultural heritage. It may be they who will do most to enable high culture to survive until the advent of more propitious times—as the Greek and Latin Church Fathers performed a similar function during the last stages of the decay of classical civilization.

Secularism passes easily over into nationalism, however, and it is for its nationalism, as incorporated in Zionism, that Toynbee inveighs most bitterly against modern Jewry. Since the present writer is neither a Jewish nationalist nor a religious Jew—though very much a Jew according to the Nuremberg laws—he will not, he hopes, be accused of partisanship in his refutation of Toynbee's slanders. For slanders they are.

In Toynbee's view, the Israeli has become an entirely "new man" because he has divested himself of his Jewish past; and it is the Israeli in general, not this or that individual Israeli with fascist leanings, that Toynbee describes as "half American farmer-technician, half Nazi sicarius." This is an elegant way of calling the Israelis "half Nazi gangsters," since *sicarius*, as Horace and Cicero used the word, means "assassin." This is no slip of the pen; on one page Toynbee states that "on the Day of Judgment the gravest crime standing against the German National Socialists' account might be, not that they exterminated a majority of the

Western Jews, but that they had caused the surviving remnant of Jewry to stumble. . . ." In other words, the *worst* thing the Nazis did was to push Zionism into militant and decisive action.

Toynbee diagnoses Israeli behavior as motivated by the "impulse to become a party to the guilt of a stronger neighbor [the Nazis!] by inflicting upon an innocent weaker neighbor the very sufferings that the original victim had experienced." He adds that the impulse behind the deeds of Palestinian Jewry since 1948 reflects what is "perhaps the most perverse of all the base propensities of Human Nature." That is: the Israelis have, in effect, treated the Arabs in the same spirit as that in which the Nazis exterminated five and a half million Jews!

He is able to draw up this calumnious indictment of Zionism only by ignoring all the really relevant factors. Zionism acquired more than a tincture of aggressive modern nationalism from its surroundings, just as traditional Judaism acquired more than a tincture of rigid ritualism from its premodern environment; but the fundamental fact in both cases is not the excessiveness but the incompleteness of the coloring received from tendencies prevalent in the surrounding milieu. Antiritualistic as well as mystic trends ran through *millet* Jewry (which could not be said to anywhere near the same degree of the Armenians or Copts), and these foreshadowed the day when ritualism would cease to be the hallmark of Jewry.

In our time Zionism, though derived from Western nationalism and in its birthplace exposed to contamination from the resentful nationalism of Central Europe, did not aspire to manhandle others as others had manhandled Jews; Zionism was born in the first place out of the desire for refuge from the renewed anti-Semitic persecution in Russia and all the German-speaking countries in the latter part of the nineteenth century. The militancy of Zionism at any moment has always been proportional to the degree of anti-Semitism in the environment; it has been militant out of the plain necessities of defense, not out of its inner logic. In this way, again, Jewry, while adapting itself externally to non-Jewish forms—nationalism in this case—keeps its inner autonomy.

Jewish nationalism, unlike the French variety, did not come to fulfill democratic aspirations; such aspirations the Jews could pursue outside Zion. Nor did it spring from the Romantic movement, as German nationalism had; or from a new identification, like that of Russian nationalism, of state with religion. The midwife of Jewish nationalism was the Dreyfus Case at the end of the nineteenth century. It first became an effective force in answer to Jewish misfortunes during the 1914–18 war, and reached a stage of extreme militancy only after the recent world war and the Nazi murder camps, when the Jewish remnant in Palestine had to choose between independence and self-defense on the one hand, and massacre at the hands of the Arabs on the other. If Zionism continues to be militant in Israel, it is largely because the threat it had to ward off with arms in 1948 is still present.

But persecution was not the only parent of Zionism. There was also the dream of social justice, a direct heir of the Prophetic tradition. Israel's socialist institutions are somewhat out of proportion to her present state of economic development, but certain socialist ideals have been realized by the Israelis as nowhere else in the world. At the same time socialism has contributed enormously to making Zionism a fundamentally pacifist movement and to mitigating what tendencies it has towards aggressive nationalism.

Another major motive of Zionism has been the desire to return the Jews to the land and to a rural way of life. This desire may not be Prophetic in origin, but there is no question but that the idealization of rural life is a strong Prophetic theme. The most immediate reason for this Zionist tendency, however, was a growing reaction against the terrible vocational specialization and narrowness imposed on the Jews by *millet* life and the ghetto. Nor could Jews have a land of their own unless they worked it themselves and spread over its countryside. Cooperative socialism and the return to the land became almost one and the same thing in Jewish Palestine. This is one of the facts that Toynbee conspicuously omits when he characterizes the youth of the *kibbutzim* as "half American farmer–technician" and "half Nazi sicarius."

The double impulse towards social justice and the rural way of life explains that feat which Toynbee—with the grudgingness that accompanies everything he has to say in favor of Jews—calls a "left-handed tour-de-force," and at which he expresses amazement: the self-transformation of ghetto-dwellers into efficient farmers within the space of a single generation. But in view of the Jew's average level of culture, the Jewish tradition of flexible and infinite external adaptability, and the equally Jewish and older Prophetic tradition with its power to inspire self-dedication and self-sacrifice, the Jewish return to the land becomes less surprising than might appear at first glance. What it did reveal was the true character of the modern Jew, refuting the slanderously distorted image he had received in the Diaspora. If Toynbee regards this as a "tour de force"—which has the connotation of being unnatural—it is because he accepts the distorted version of the Jewish character which holds that

Jews can never make good farmers or good soldiers. Unable to account for the facts that contradict this version, he vents his puzzlement in angry denunciation of the facts.

Concluding his "essay" on modern Jewry, Toynbee speculates with a good deal of relish on the possibility of conflict between the Jews remaining in the Diaspora and those who now become Israelis in Palestine. There is indeed a real problem here. To a Western urban sector given over to intellectuality and business, Jewry has now added a rural Middle Eastern one given over to practical tasks and agriculture. Though it would be vain to deny the possibilities of tension between the two sectors, it nonetheless takes Toynbee's spite, and superficiality, to overlook the astounding success with which Jewry has maintained its solidarity over the past two thousand years, though scattered among such different countries and civilizations. This capacity for unity in diversity—a capacity that belongs uniquely to the Jews—is as alive today as it ever was and, actually, the obstacles it has to cope with seem less formidable at the present moment than for a long time in the past.

Half the test has already been passed insofar as the *Galut* no longer objects as it used to, before Hitler, to the very project of Zionism and the *Yishuv*. Now non-Zionist as well as Zionist accepts the Yishuv. What remains of the test is for the Yishuv to pass. To urge all Jews, especially those in the West, to migrate to Israel is not only visionary; it is false. It is right and proper that Tel Aviv should concern itself with concrete, practical matters, but Jewry's spiritual concerns cannot be attended to there on the same level as in New York or London. The Yishuv and the Galut *together* constitute and realize the fullness of Jewish experience and potentiality. Alone, the Galut cannot divest itself sufficiently of the handicaps of the ghetto past; alone, the Yishuv cannot become full heir and continuator of Jewish spiritual tradition. The Yishuv-plus-Galut is something entirely different from a Western nation-state: it is the fulfillment of Jewish diversity-in-identity. Without the Galut, the Yishuv would be the dwarfed parody of a Western nation-state and prey to all sorts of pathological distortions in its isolation—aberrations of the kind we have seen recently in Eastern and Central Europe. Without the Galut, the Yishuv might prove Toynbee half right.

It further characterizes Toynbee's attitude towards Israel that, while stressing the possible tensions between New York and Tel Aviv, he should neglect entirely another major aspect of Jewish diversity-in-unity. The future of Jewry as a whole probably depends to a greater extent on eventual relations between European (including American) and Oriental

Jews than on those between Israeli and American Jewry. The deepest cleavage existing within Jewry is between Europeanized and Orientalized Jews. It is a problem to which Zionists gave little thought in the past. If the two groups cannot merge or work out a common type in Israel, then—and only then—the Israeli experiment will have failed on the spiritual plane.

The chief importance of Jewish secular "assimilationism" does not lie in its effect on Jewish survival, but in the part it may play in the survival of spiritual and intellectual tradition should the world lapse into totalitarian neobarbarism. Similarly, the success of the ethnic merger toward which Israel is now challenged to move, though decisive for her own future, is even more decisive for the future of mankind. Even Mr. Toynbee will agree, I feel, that relations between East and West will be the dominant concern in the next phase of world history. In this perspective, the open or concealed racism of all the countries of Anglo-Saxon culture, together with the growing impotence of the nonracist French, leaves Israel as the only place within the orbit of genuinely Western civilization where East and West can meet inside the same national community with the possibility of physical and cultural interpenetration. Is this too much of a load to put on Israel? Does it exaggerate her importance to the rest of the world? I think not.

While Jewish history has never had a great material impact upon other peoples, its spiritual impact has been of a depth and extent that are unparalleled. Here again, the Nazis in their mixture of animal and metaphysical hatred saw truer than Toynbee does with his malicious and contrived formulations. The Nazis at least grasped the enormous importance for the world of Jewry as a *spiritual* entity—though, or precisely because, it was a spirit in whose light they saw themselves condemned. They appreciated the attractive power of Jewry and its eminent role as a conductor of spiritual currents, which was all the more reason why they wanted to destroy it. Today this role is perhaps more crucial for the rest of mankind than ever before. Should a merger of East and West inside Israel be achieved, Diaspora Jewry will feel the effects immediately, and we may be sure that through that Jewry they will be rapidly conveyed to the rest of the world.

Appendix I:
The Sources and Their Handling

As indicated before, part of the texts printed in this book are based on previously published essays, another part on hitherto unpublished manuscripts. In a few cases, several essays or manuscripts have been condensed into a single chapter of this book as indicated below. Here is the list:

Part I

Chapter 1: "Thinking beyond Spengler," first appeared in *Der Monat*, Berlin, October 1955 as "Spengler Weitergedacht."

Chapter 2: "Toynbee and the Culture Cycle," first appeared in *Commentary*, New York, March 1956 under the same title.

Chapter 3: "The Antinomy of Death and the Culture Generations" is a condensation of two published essays: "The Concept of Death," published in *Twentieth Century*, London, April 1955, and "Todeskontradiktion and Geschichte," posthumously published in *Der Monat*, Berlin, December 1959.

Chapter 4: "From Minoan to Greek Mythology," first appeared in *Psyche*, Heidelberg, April 1957 as "Zwei Abhandlungen zur griechischen Mythologie."

Chapter 5: "The Philosophical Background: Beyond Space and Time" first appeared in *Twentieth Century*, London, November 1954 as "Beyond Space and Time."

Part II

Chapter 1: "The Rise of the I-Form of Speech," is the text of an unpublished manuscript in English. Instead of a passage overtaken by the author's later work, a long quotation from an essay on the same subject in his German book *Drei Abhandlungen zur deutschen Geschichte* (Frankfurt: Klostermann, 1947) has been inserted in translation.

Chapter 2: "The Mythical Starting-Point" is the translation of an unpublished and incomplete German manuscript.

Chapter 3: "Historic Layers in the Siegfried Saga," is the translation of an unpublished German manuscript, with sections from another unpublished German manuscript inserted.

Chapter 4: "The Archetypes in the Siegfried Myth" is the translation of a German manuscript, again with sections from another manuscript inserted.

Chapter 5: "The Gods of the ancient Germans," is based on the condensation of one long and one short unpublished German manuscript. Part of the same ground is also covered in an essay published in *Neues Abendland*, August 1955, entitled "Die germanischen Götter-Legende und Wirklichkeit."

Chapter 6: "Pelagius, the Irish and the African Church," is the text of an unpublished manuscript in English, without the annexed Latin extracts from Pelagius' writings.

Chapter 7: "The Beginnings of Western Monasticism," is the text of an unpublished and incomplete manuscript in English.

Chapter 8: "Boniface and the Anglo-Irish Impact on the Frankish Churches," is a translation of an essay published in German in *Neues Abendland*, entitled "Bonifacius-Stifter des Abendlandes."

Chapter 9: "Rome's Break with Byzantium as shown in Christian Painting," appeared first in *Twentieth Century*, London, December 1953, under the title "Some Sources of Modern Europe."

Chapter 10 and 11: "Primal Crime and 'Social Paranoia' in the Dark Ages" and "Stages on the Road to Western Civilization," contain the text of two connected, hitherto unpublished English manuscripts.

Chapter 12: "Postscript: The *Chanson de Roland*" appeared first in *Twentieth Century*, London, July 1953, as "On the *Chanson de Roland*."

Part III

Chapter 1: "After the Atom: Life out of Death or Life in Death?" appeared first in *Horizon*, London, November 1946 as "After the Atom."

Chapter 2: "Will Technology Destroy Civilization?", appeared first in *Commentary*, New York, January 1951, under the same title.

Chapter 3: "Toynbee and the Future of the Jews" appeared first in *Commentary*, New York, May 1955, under the title "Toynbee's Judgment of the Jews."

Three of the magazines used—*Horizon, Twentieth Century* and *Neues Abendland*—no longer exist. I express my thanks to the editors and publishers of *Commentary, Der Monat* and *Psyche* for kind permission to reproduce the essays first printed by them. My thanks go also to the Vittorio Klostermann Verlag for permitting the use of the long quotation from one of Borkenau's books included in Part II, chapter 1.

The general arrangement of this book is justified in the Introduction. The same applies for the sequences of chapters in the central part presenting Borkenau's manuscripts and scattered essays on the origin of the West. Borkenau had indicated that he wanted his book on that subject to begin with the linguistic chapter, and there is internal evidence that the manuscripts now forming chapters 2–5, 6 and 7, and 10 and 11 belong together respectively. The sequence among those three groups and the place of insertion for the essays now forming chapters 8, 9, and 12 the editor had to decide.

The editor, who has also translated the German texts, has tried to present Borkenau's thought on the problems of the comparative theory of civilization and on the origin of Western civilization as fully and fairly as possible. He believes that he has kept cuts to the inevitable minimum. In particular, he has *not* cut out repetitions of the same basic ideas in different contexts. Cuts were inevitable, however, where the same detailed material was treated in different, overlapping drafts on the same subject, as in the English and German essays on the antinomy of death, and in overlapping manuscripts on Germanic mythology and religion. In those cases, a careful condensation of the different texts was attempted with the aim of including all relevant points from each of them. The editor's additions at the seams have not been specially marked, because they are confined to insignificant connecting sentences and the briefest summaries of the cut pieces whose content has been presented more fully elsewhere.

As mentioned in the Preface, not all Borkenau's manuscripts had been fully prepared for publication, hence they did not always contain footnotes with references to the literature mentioned in the text. The editor has filled this gap where he found it possible, but did not succeed in all cases; the footnotes have therefore had to remain incomplete. The editor's added footnotes consist of source references only, and have not been specially marked: all footnotes commenting on the text or supplementing it in any way are the author's own.

Finally, in consciously refraining from inserting any ideas of his own, the editor has also not tried to eliminate contradictions which show the author's trying out different explanations for the same phenomenon at different times; instead he has indicated one or two of them in the Introduction. While all the unpublished manuscripts were written roughly in the postwar years, after 1945, the dates of writing of individual manuscripts were unfortunately not indicated, nor are they otherwise known. Editor's corrections have been confined to obvious slips or typing errors.

Appendix II:
Books by Franz Borkenau

Der Übergang vom feudalen zum bürgerlichen Weltbild: Studien zur Geschichte der Manufakturperiode. Paris: Alcan, 1934. Reprinted Darmstadt: Wissenschaftliche Buchgemeinschaft, 1971.

Pareto. London: Chapman & Hall, 1936.

The Spanish Cockpit: An Eye-Witness Account of the Political and Social Conflicts of the Spanish Civil War. London: Faber & Faber, 1937. Reprinted Ann Arbor: University of Michigan Press, 1963.

The Communist International. London: Faber & Faber, 1938. Reprinted with an introduction by Raymond Aron, *World Communism: A History of the Communist International.* Ann Arbor: University of Michigan Press, 1962.

Austria and After. London: Faber & Faber, 1939.

The New German Empire. Harmondsworth: Penguin Books, 1939.

The Totalitarian Enemy. London: Faber & Faber, 1940.

Drei Abhandlungen zur deutschen Geschichte. Frankfurt/Main: Klostermann, 1947.

Der europäische Kommunismus: Seine Geschichte von 1917 bis zur Gegenwart. München: Lehnen, 1952. English trans.: *European Communism.* London: Faber & Faber, 1953.

Karl Marx: Auswahl und Einleitung von Franz Borkenau. Frankfurt: S. Fischer, 1956.

Index

477